Orel
R.
S.
F.
S.
R.
Voronezh
Kursk
River
Snov
Seym
River
Don
River
Kharkiv
Myrhorod
N
E
Poltava
Andriivka
Starobil's'k
Donets
River
Kremenchuk
Lozova
II
Pavlohrad
rovohrad
Katerynoslav
(Dnipropetrovs'ke)
Synel'nikove
II
V. Mykhailivka
(Dibrivka)
Kryvyi Rih
Oleksandrivs'k
(Zaporizhia)
I
Volnovakha
Matviiv Kurhan
River
Huliai-Pole
Nikopil'
Orikhiv
Polohy
Rostov
Don
Taganrog
Mariupil'
(Zhdanov)
Tokmak
River
aiv
Melitopil'
Berdians'k
Dnieper
Kakhivka
Kherson
Perekop
SEA OF AZOV
Krasnoperekopske
CRIMEA
Symferopil'
Sevastopil'

PUBLICATIONS ON RUSSIA AND EASTERN EUROPE
OF THE INSTITUTE FOR
COMPARATIVE AND FOREIGN AREA STUDIES

Number 7

This book is sponsored by the Russian and East European Program of the Institute for Comparative and Foreign Area Studies (formerly Far Eastern and Russian Institute), University of Washington, Seattle.

The Anarchism of Nestor Makhno, 1918–1921

AN ASPECT OF THE UKRAINIAN REVOLUTION

Michael Palij

UNIVERSITY OF WASHINGTON PRESS
SEATTLE AND LONDON

Printed in the United States of America

Library of Congress Cataloging in Publication Data
Palij, Michael
The anarchism of Nestor Makhno, 1918–1921.
(Publications on Russia and Eastern Europe of the Institute for Comparative and Foreign Area Studies; no. 7)
Bibliography: p.
Includes index.
1. Ukraine—History—Revolution, 1917–1921.
2. Makhno, Nestor Ivanovich, 1884–1934. I. Title.
II. Series: Washington (State). University.
Institute for Comparative and Foreign Area Studies.
Publications on Russia and Eastern Europe; no. 7.
DK265.8.U4P23 947'.71'08410924 [B] 76–7796
ISBN 0–295–95511–2

Publications on Russia and Eastern Europe of the Institute for Comparative and Foreign Area Studies is a continuation of the series formerly entitled Far Eastern and Russian Institute Publications on Russia and Eastern Europe.

To My

Mother and Father

Contents

Illustrations

Preface

This study deals with the history of the Ukrainian peasant partisan movement in southeastern Ukraine. The movement was organized and led by Nestor Makhno, an anarchist of Ukrainian peasant origin who had been imprisoned in 1908 for his terrorist activities. Although Makhno began his activities shortly after his release from prison in Moscow in March 1917, the partisan campaign did not reach major proportions until the summer of 1918. In that year Makhno's efforts were directed mainly against the regime of Hetman Pavlo Skoropads'kyi and its German and Austrian supporters, while during 1919–21 his struggle was against the Bolshevik and anti-Bolshevik Russian forces. The development of the Makhno phenomenon, which played a prominent role in the Ukrainian Revolution and the Russian Civil War, was possible only because of the instability in Ukraine resulting from foreign invasions, the failure of the Ukrainian government to establish firm local authority, and the weakness of the political and national consciousness of the populace.

The history of the Makhno movement, despite its significance to the history of the Ukrainian Revolution and the Russian Civil War, has generally been neglected. Most of the works, monographic and periodical, that do deal with the subject were deliberate distortions by Soviet Russian writers. Obviously the Communist party promoted writing about Makhno because it was interested in discrediting him, not only in the eyes of the people of Ukraine and the Soviet Union, but also abroad. Also, most of the sources on Makhno are located in the archives of the Soviet Union. Anti-Bolshevik Russian writers have produced very little indeed on the Makhno movement. Treatment of the subject is mostly incidental in works dealing with anarchism and other problems. Ukrainian historical literature about Makhno is also very scarce and includes not one monographic study, but only articles and incidental references in works dealing with other problems. Ukrainian historians have been generally silent, because Makhno is viewed as a Russian or an international anarchist of Ukrainian origin, and his movement as a spontaneous force not tempered by national interests. Makhno himself and his associates, being very sensitive to the opinions of historians, wrote only a little about their movement. Western scholars have often studied Makhno's partisan army in the course of other research, but few have concentrated on it as a topic of a separate historical study. No real effort has been made by scholars to locate and use the sources hitherto available, which have been augmented in recent years by the publication of new archival materials. Western historiography has thus far failed to produce a comprehensive objective study of the Makhno peasant partisans. Our study will attempt to supply this scholarly lacuna.

Acknowledgments

To my former teachers—Professor Herbert J. Ellison of the University of Washington and Professors Anna Cienciala, Charles F. Sidmand, Ambrose Saricks, and the late Oswald P. Backus III of the University of Kansas—profound gratitude for their invaluable advice and encouragement in the preparation of the doctoral dissertation from which this study emerged. The nature of the topic involves an exceedingly complex historical period, and the evaluation of a variety of political and socioeconomic currents inevitably presented the author with difficult questions of interpretation. The accumulated knowledge of these five professors of East European history, and their considerable interest in the complex structure of the revolution and civil war in the former territories of the Russian Empire, provided me with an invaluable pool of information and advice in my enterprise. In accordance with custom, I alone take full responsibility for any errors of fact or interpretation that may have occurred.

For the financial assistance that made it possible for me to undertake the travel necessary to complete the research and to devote an uninterrupted period to the project, I am indebted to the University of Kansas General Research Fund. The monies made available to me from this source were essential for the completion of my task.

Many persons helped to make this study possible. I am grateful to the staff members of the Reference Department of Watson Library at the University of Kansas and the University of Colorado Library for source material obtained through interlibrary loan service, and also to the staff members of the Hoover Library at Stanford University; the

Library of Congress; the New York Public Library; the Ukrainian Academy of Arts and Sciences in the United States in New York; the Bibliothèque Ukranienne Simon Petlura in Paris; and the Bibliothèque de Documentation Internationale Contemporaine, Université de Paris, for services rendered in connection with my research for this study.

I am also grateful to Professor André de Saint-Ratt for making his excellent private collection of civil war material available to me, to Professor Evhen Onats'kyi, Dr. Zynovii Knysh, Dr. Liubomyr Wynar, Dr. Eugene E. Petriwsky, Petro Postoliuk, Dmytro Mykytiuk, and A. Skirda for assistance in obtaining some useful research material. Further, I wish to thank the late General Mykhailo Sadovs'kyi and the late Professor Vasyl' Dubrovs'kyi for valuable written information; and Dr. Cyrille Radeff, Lev Bykovs'kyi, the late Dr. Fotii Meleshko, and the late Professor Stepan Ryndyk for providing me with valuable reminiscences. I am deeply indebted to Stephen H. Klemp for a careful job of reading and editing the prepared chapters. I also wish to thank Professor Sergej V. Utechin of the Pensylvania State University for reading several chapters and Professor Sidman for reading the entire manuscript. Finally, I am particularly grateful to Margery Lang, editor for the Institute for Comparative and Foreign Area Studies, and to Professor John S. Reshetar, Jr., for their intelligent, understanding, and meticulous attention in the preparation of the manuscript for publication. In concluding these ackhnowledgments, I want to express my deep gratitude to my wife, Maria, who helped me in all phases of my study, and was an unfailing source of encouragement throughout.

"We do not wish to accuse, but to comprehend the whole truth, the real truth from the beginning to end."

—Borys Krupnyts'kyi
in *Do metodolohichnykh problem ukrains'koi istorii*

THE ANARCHISM OF NESTOR MAKHNO, 1918–1921

Prelude to Revolution

The Destruction of National Autonomy

The Ukrainian Revolution of 1917–20 was a crucial period in Ukrainian history, but it occurred at an especially unfavorable time for national aspirations. National development was not complete when the Revolution broke out in 1917, for the Russian administration in Ukraine had greatly hindered its development. The stunted state of the Ukrainian political, cultural, and socioeconomic heritage had a profound impact upon the course of the Revolution, the formation of the Ukrainian state, and its subsequent failure.

That impact began with individuals, of course, and Nestor Makhno, whose partisan activities affected both the Revolution and its failure, was more an anarchist than a nationalist. Although wishing to free Ukraine from the oppression of government, he fought against fellow Ukrainians with whom he disagreed as he fought with them when they shared a common enemy, the Russian Volunteer Army or the Bolsheviks. His story is one of a man concerned with freedom from government; his prerevolutionary activity, not strongly identified with the cause of Ukrainism, and his imprisonment gave him no basis for constructive principles to attain freedom, no vision of unity. His curious history can be understood only in the light of the history of Ukraine, where this account must begin.

Political autonomy in Ukraine had been extinguished late in the eighteenth century by Empress Catherine II. In an instruction in 1764, she advocated complete "administrative unification and 'Russification' " of Ukraine and the Baltic provinces. In the fall of the same year, the hetmanate was abolished in Ukraine and the Little Russian College, headed by Count Peter Rumiantsev, was created in its place.[1]

Between 1764 and 1775 Russian power in Ukraine steadily increased. The independent Zaporozhian Sich,[2] the original center of Ukrainian Cossacks, had a sociopolitical order of its own that constituted a continuous threat to the successful imposition of Russian serfdom, but both the Sich and the hetman state lay in the path of Russia's access to the Black Sea. Therefore in 1775, at the close of the Turkish War, the victorious Russian Army suddenly besieged the unsuspecting Cossacks and destroyed the Sich. Higher ranking officers who surrendered to the Russians were sentenced to hard labor in Siberia, their property confiscated, and the rank and file were dismissed. The majority of the Cossacks, however, escaped from the Sich and settled at the mouth of the Danube in Turkey. From the "free lands" of the Cossacks, who had for three centuries defended Ukraine against the invasions of Tatars and Turks, Catherine carved out large estates mostly as grants for her favorites.[3]

In 1784 Prince Potemkin, to prevent the flight of still more Cossacks from Russian control, persuaded Catherine to reactivate the Cossack organization. Known as the Black Sea Cossacks, they were settled between the Boh and Dniester rivers. In 1792 they were resettled near Azov and Black seas in the Kuban River Basin, and formed the nucleus of the Kuban Cossacks. In the early nineteenth century, they were joined by a considerable number of those who had previously escaped to Turkey. As early as 1751, Russia had established within the Sich large colonies of Serbs under direct Russian administration and control.[4] After 1775, increasing numbers of Russians, Bulgarians, Moldavians, Armenians, Greeks, Jews, and especially Prussian Mennonites, as well as more Ukrainians, were settled in the free lands of the Cossacks.

After the destruction of the Sich, Catherine issued a decree in 1783 that abolished all Ukrainian political institutions and privileges. The hetman state was divided into provinces (*gubernii*) like Russia itself, and the Cossack organization was abolished and converted into regiments of the Russian regular army. The officers were permitted either to join Russian units or to retire from military service; those in the highest grades, however, were eventually granted the same rights and privileges as the Russian nobility.[5] The rank and file were made into a separate, free, social class of Cossack peasants. At the same time, the Ukrainian peasantry of the former hetman state was reduced to the status of the Russian serf, and remained in unrelieved social and cultural darkness for several generations.

Many of the higher ranking officers, eventually convinced of the futility of struggling against Russian rule, endeavored to preserve their land and their status as noblemen, and sought careers in the Russian government, where a number held high posts. Prince Oleksander Bezborod'ko was the main adviser and secretary to Catherine II, and imperial chancellor under Paul II; Prince Viktor Kochubei, Count Petro V. Zavadovs'kyi, Count Oleksander Rozumovs'kyi, and Dmytro Troshchyns'kyi were among the ministers of Alexander I. An even greater number of Ukrainians served in various Russian civil institutions and in the army, eventually finding the institution of serfdom to their personal advantage.[6] Their acquiescence, however, not only widened the gulf between them and the rest of the people, but tied them to Russian interests, with little sense of kinship with the Ukrainian populace.

After the partition of Poland in 1772, 1793, and 1795, the lot of the people worsened in the annexed Ukrainian provinces. Prior to the partition, popular revolts had limited the growth of the landlords' power, but now the Russian Army and police system sanctioned the rule of the Polish landlords over the Ukrainian peasants.

Galicia and Bukovina were annexed by the Hapsburg Monarchy, the former from Poland in 1772, the latter from the Ottoman Empire in 1775. Carpatho-Ukraine remained under Hungarian control. Thus, by the end of the century, Ukraine was divided between Russia and Austria-Hungary.

The elimination of Ukrainian self-government was accompanied by the destruction of the autonomy of the Ukrainian Orthodox church. Undermining began in 1686 when the Russian government forced the metropolitan of Kyiv (Kiev) to accept the jurisdiction of the patriarch of Moscow. Prior to this time the Ukrainian church, though nominally under the control of the patriarch of Constantinople, had actually operated independently.[7] During the seventeenth and the first half of the eighteenth centuries, the church had been under the patronage of the hetman and was respected by the entire population for its spiritual and cultural work.

The complete subordination of the Ukrainian church to Moscow dealt a severe blow to its further development, because the government worked through the Russian church to implement unification and centralization of the empire. The authority of the metropolitan of Kyiv as head of the Ukrainian church greatly declined, election of the church hierarchy eventually was abolished, and church publications and school programs were subjected to suspicious and hostile Russian censorship.[8]

The Ukrainian church, as well as national life in general, suffered from the exodus of intellectuals to Russia. They had been faced with two alternatives—to work for the glory of the Russian Empire, or to defend the rights of Ukraine and risk perishing in Siberian exile. Like the ancient Greeks who, having been conquered by the Roman Empire, helped to create Roman classical culture, Ukrainian intellectuals built Russian culture. During the reign of Peter I, for example, almost all high ecclesiastical offices in Russia were occupied by Ukrainian graduates of the Kyiv Academy. From 1721 to 1762 almost all rectors and prefects, as well as about fifty teachers, of the Moscow Academy were Ukrainians, a state of affairs that prevailed until the reign of Catherine II.[9]

In 1786 episcopal and monastic estates were confiscated and each monastery was allotted a fixed number of monks who received salaries from the Russian government.[10] In the nineteenth century the Ukrainian church lost its national character and became an agency of Russification; ecclesiastical schools served to denationalize the theological students.

Institutions of higher learning and secondary schools, though established and funded by the church and monasteries, had been open to all classes, and the majority of the students were laymen. The schools were originally national in character, and Catherine considered them centers of opposition: during her reign she aimed at the complete destruction and Russification of the Ukrainian educational system. The schools, their financial support undermined by the Russian seizure of church property in 1786,[11] gradually decayed, for state appropriations for schools in Ukraine were inadequate. Consequently the schools were reorganized with Russian as the language of instruction and with an entirely different character and purpose. Enrollment was restricted to a limited number from the privileged aristocratic and ecclesiastical classes, while the purpose was mainly to train administrative functionaries. These schools gradually became the primary instruments of Russification in Ukraine.

It was the lower levels of the school system, however, that suffered the most from Russian policies. With the introduction of serfdom, the peasants lost their personal freedom, initiative, and economic independence, and were unable to support the local schools. Because of the absence of compulsory general education, the alien language and spirit, and the poor quality of the schooling, the majority of the population was condemned to illiteracy and backwardness. According to the census of 1897, 13.6 percent of Ukrainians, representing 23.3 percent of the men and only 3.9 percent of the women, were literate. In comparison, the literacy rate in the Russian Empire as a whole was 29.3 percent for males and 13 percent for females.[12]

The Ukrainian press and printing houses suffered an even worse fate. In 1720, even before the destruction of national autonomy, Peter I issued a ukase that banned the printing of any book not in Russian, and during the entire eighteenth century Ukrainian printers struggled under this decree—a fatal blow to cultural life in the country. In 1769 not only was the Pecherska Lavra monastery in Kyiv denied permission to reprint a primer, but all previous editions of the work were removed as well.[13] In 1800 the earlier decree was reconfirmed and its application became increasingly strict. As a result, all works of Ukrainian literature, including those of the most prominent authors, were disseminated in manuscript form. This was the case with the well-known anonymous work *Istoriia Rusov*, the chronicles of Samovydets, Velychko, Hrabianka, the works of the philosopher Hryhorii Skovoroda, and even the first work of modern Ukrainian literature, the *Aeneid* of Ivan Kotliarevs'kyi.

Thus very few Ukrainian books were published in the nineteenth century. From 1848 to 1870, for example, fewer than 200 were published, in marked contrast to the three years of Ukrainian independence, when, in spite of technical difficulties, lack of funds, and the chaos of war, 2,496 books were published.[14]

The elimination of political autonomy and national institutions was only the means for the larger goal, the complete Russification of Ukraine. Throughout the tsarist period, the regime spared no effort to eradicate every vestige of national culture and consciousness. The name Ukraine was forbidden and even the substitute, "Little Russia," although used as a generic term for the area, did not appear on the political map of the Russian Empire as a distinct entity. Written records were pre-empted by the Russians and the official Russian history, representing Moscow as the legitimate successor to the heritage of Kyiv, went unchallenged.

The ruin of national life was nearly complete. Some of the wealthy sent their children either to the newer and more fashionable schools of St. Petersburg and Moscow, or to schools in Western Europe. Ukrainians who served in the government were usually given posts outside Ukraine, while the administrative personnel in Ukraine itself were largely Russian or other nationalities. The large estates were mostly in the hands of Russians, Poles, or Russified Ukrainians, as were commercial and financial institutions. Ukrainians were denied even the minimum of rights guaranteed under the law. The people, nonetheless, retained their language and a vast store of rich folklore and song used on various special occasions and preserved especially by the Kobzars (Minstrels).

The final elimination of Ukrainian autonomy in 1783 coincided with the successful conclusion of the American Revolution, which was followed by the French Revolution and the Napoleonic wars. These crises created a new Europe in which various subject nations began successful struggles for statehood. Ukraine, however, was denied the opportunity to be included in the new order.

The Political Awakening

Toward the end of the eighteenth century, when the disappearance of Ukrainian national existence seemed imminent, the political aspirations of the Ukrainian nobility were reawakened, especially among the educated classes and nobility of Left Bank Ukraine, where the political and cultural traditions of the hetman state survived. Despite their submission to the Russian regime, these classes retained a love of the native history and language, defending the old order and culture, and resisting Russian innovations. They also maintained the tradition of participation in public affairs, and struggled to retain their positions in the country's administrative system.

The regime's attempt to deny the Ukrainian nobility the same rights as their Russian counterparts prompted a group of political leaders to seek foreign assistance. In 1791, at a low point of Russo-Prussian relations, Vasyl' Kapnist, former marshal of the Kyiv nobility, secretly discussed with the Prussian Minister E. F. Hertzberg the possibility of impending war and of Prussian aid for the incipient Ukrainian independence movement. He failed, for Hertzberg did not believe the deterioration of relations with Russia was sufficiently serious to result in war. The effort to take advantage of Russian political crises to further the national cause continued into the nineteenth century. Some hopes were aroused by the revival of the Cossack army in 1812, the year of Napoleon's invasion of Russia, but the Cossacks were used only for Russian ends and after the war they were either absorbed into the Russian Army or demobilized.[15]

Failure to achieve political concessions for Ukraine did not deter the political leaders. The poor social and political conditions created a favorable atmosphere for revolutionary activities and for acceptance of western European radical ideas, which entered Ukraine by way of soldiers returning from the Napoleonic wars, literature supplied from abroad, and foreign intellectuals working in Ukraine. These influences paved the way for the Masonic movement.

The best known lodges were those in Poltava, Odessa, and Kyiv. Among the members of the Poltava lodge were such prominent figures in Ukrainian history as Ivan Kotliarevskyi, Vasyl Lukashevych, and

Kapnist. Some were nevertheless dedicated to the formation of the Slavic federation, or to the cause of Polish independence, and, although the Masons were not especially interested in the Ukrainian question, their organizations later formed the groundwork for the national movement.

The influence of the Masonic lodges and the exposure of many officers to Western thought during the Napoleonic wars stimulated the development of secret political societies in the Russian Army, known after the abortive coup d'état on December 14, 1825, as Decembrists. They, too, neglected the Ukrainian problem in their programs and activities, but some of their writers expressed sympathy for Ukraine and her past in their works, and the movement in general awakened the spirit of nationalism among the more enlightened Ukrainians. The Decembrists also influenced the later development of Ukrainian political and cultural movements, especially the program of the Brotherhood of Saints Cyril and Methodius.

After the Decembrist revolt new oppressive measures were introduced by Nicholas I. In November 1830, Poland broke its union with the Romanov dynasty and began a war of liberation. The governor-general of Ukraine, Prince Nikolai G. Repnin, was ordered to organize eight Cossack cavalry regiments of one thousand volunteers each, to be supported largely by the Ukrainian nobility. A measure of social relief was promised to encourage enlistments. Before the Polish war ended, however, the Russian government, fearing Ukrainian separatism, recalled the Cossack regiments. Six of them were incorporated into the Russian Army; the other two were sent to colonize the Caucasus. The disappointed Cossacks protested in vain, and some of their leaders were executed.[16] Moreover, when Repnin tried to improve the socioeconomic conditions of the Cossacks and lower classes, an attempt that gained him the lasting esteem of the people, he was accused of Ukrainian separatism and relieved of his post in 1834.

After the suppression of the Polish uprising, a de-Polonization campaign was launched to weaken the Polish landlords in the Right Bank Ukraine. Although there was no question of emancipation of peasants, the government did introduce "Inventory Regulations" determining the mutual rights and obligations of landlords and peasants, including the number of days the peasants had to work for the landlords, and defining the character of work for men and women. Working during holidays was prohibited, and the arbitrariness of landlords, such as in sending the peasants to the army or exiling them to Siberia, was limited. The Regulations, sponsored by General

D. G. Bibikov, governor-general of Kyiv in 1838, were implemented on the Right Bank and temporarily improved conditions. However, the introduction of the Regulations created great uncertainty among both landlords and peasants, and when in 1852 a new governor largely nullified the Regulations, the lot of the peasants worsened. Peasant revolts became more frequent. In the spring of 1855, during the Crimean War, eight districts of the Kyiv province were involved in revolts that were suppressed by military force, with many people imprisoned or exiled to Siberia.[17] Russia's defeat in the Crimean War brought about a period of far-reaching reforms, including the end of serfdom, which offered new opportunities for the Ukrainian national movement.

The Cultural Awakening

The setbacks in the struggle for political freedom compelled Ukrainian leaders to devote their attention to cultural problems in the struggle against Russification. A number of the more nationally conscious nobility, including some who held high offices in the empire, devoted themselves to the study of national history, folklore, and especially the Ukrainian language, the living symbol of nationality.

Class interest, however, was the primary impetus to historical research, for many nobles turned to the collection of documents—chronicles, deeds of kings, tsars, and hetmans, court decisions, and petitions—that would serve to substantiate their claims to noble status. This activity was also considered patriotic, as it not only aroused national consciousness, but also defended the rights, privileges, and freedom of Ukraine.

Among the most important contributors of Ukrainian historiography, who either collected and preserved documentary materials or published them in their writings, were Prince Oleksander Bezborod'ko, Vasyl' H. Ruban, Oleksander I. Rigelman, IAkiv A. Markovych, Hryhorii A. and Vasyl H. Poletyka, and Oleksii I. Martos. The most significant work of the period was the anonymous *Istoriia Rusov* (History of the Rus'). Probably written at the end of the eighteenth or the beginning of the nineteenth century by Hryhorii A. Poletyka, it was widely circulated in manuscript before being published in 1846. The work is historiopolitical, covering Ukrainian history from its origins to the end of the hetman state. Its importance lay not in its substance but in its effect as a catalyst of national consciousness and its impact on modern Ukrainian historiography.[18]

Although these works had a considerable influence upon national development, the book that marked the beginning of modern Ukrainian literature, and of the national renaissance, was Ivan Kotliarevs'kyi's poem *Aeneid* (1798), a travesty on Virgil's classic. In it, the Trojan soldiers are used allegorically to represent the Ukrainian Cossacks who escaped from the Sich in 1775 and their heroic past and traditions are expertly portrayed. The work also brought to the attention of the upper classes the deplorable conditions of the peasants, whose lives were depicted with an intimacy and affection that evoked sympathy for everything Ukrainian. The primary importance of *Aeneid*, however, was that it was the first book written in the Ukrainian vernacular, which gained a stronger position as the sole national language, especially since the literary language, a mixture of Ukrainian and Old Slavic, was prohibited by the Russian censorship. The *Aeneid*, widely read by educated Ukrainians, appeared in three editions in ten years.

Kotliarevs'kyi gave Ukraine a modern language (though it was not used with full effectiveness until the middle of the nineteenth century) and tied the historical traditions of hetman Ukraine to contemporary conditions. Other writers, among them the novelist Hryhorii Kvitka-Osnov'ianenko and the poet Petro Hulak-Artemovs'kyi, wrote in Ukrainian about national customs and traditions. Ethnography proved to be another source of national revival. Under the influences of West European Romanticism and the teaching of Johann von Herder, young and enthusiastic scholars turned to the study of the peasants, their folksongs, historical poems, legends, proverbs, manners, and customs.

From the turn of the century until the emancipation of the serfs in 1861, Ukrainian cultural life centered in the universities. The University of Kharkiv (Kharkov), established in 1805 through the efforts of the Ukrainian nobility and merchant class, was the first modern institution of higher learning in Ukraine,[19] and in the first half of the nineteenth century, an important center of Ukrainian revival. A large number of outstanding Ukrainian scholars and littérateurs formed a literary circle, with such members as the rector of the University, the poet Petro Hulak-Artemovs'kyi, the ethnographer Izmail Sreznevs'kyi, and prose writer Kvitka-Osnov'ianenko.[20] It was also at Kharkiv that the first Ukrainian periodicals appeared: *The Ukrainian Herald*, 1816–19; *Kharkov Demokrit*, 1816; and *Ukrainian Journal*, 1824–26.

A second modern university was founded in Kyiv in 1834. Although established primarily to instill in its students a Russian spirit, it played as prominent a role in the Ukrainian renaissance as the Kyiv Academy had in the past, due to the activities of distinguished Ukrainians like the first rectors, Mykhailo Maksymovych, Mykola Kostomarov, and Panteleimon Kulish, who converted the nominally Russian university into a Ukrainian scientific and cultural center. A new journal, *Kiev Information*, was published there from 1835 to 1838 and from 1850 to 1857. Other centers of Ukrainian culture were the college in Nizhyn, established by Besborod'ko, and the Richelieu Lycée in Odessa, which was raised to university status in 1864. The first newspaper in Ukraine was the *Odessa Herald*, published from 1825 to 1892.[21] Many young Ukrainians attended universities in Russia or Western Europe as well.

Among the institutions playing an important role in the national revival was the Provisional Commission for the Study of Ancient Documents, established in Kyiv in 1843. Its mission was to collect and control all the archives and collections of historical documents to demonstrate that Ukraine was "Russian since time immemorial," and that the policy of Russification was justified by history.[22] This work, however, was entrusted to Ukrainians who were primarily concerned with scholarship. The Commission was most active in the 1860s when Russia increased its opposition to Polish influence in Right Bank Ukraine. Its main publication, in which a high level of scholarship was maintained, was *Archives of South-West Russia*.

During the 1840s and 1850s, the Ukrainian renaissance found its most vibrant expression in the works of Taras H. Shevchenko, the nation's greatest poet. Shevchenko, a serf of Cossack lineage, was born in Kyiv province in 1814. Because he showed talent for painting, he was eventually freed through the efforts of such prominent men as the poet Vasilii A. Zhukovskii, the actor Mykhailo S. Shchepkin, and the painters Karl P. Briullov and Aleksei G. Venetsianov, who wished to enter him in the Academy of Arts in St. Petersburg.[23] His true genius, however, lay in his poetry.

Ukrainian history, Ukraine's wealth and scenic beauty, all placed in cruel contrast to the actualities of national life, deeply affected Shevchenko's thought and permeated his work. In 1840 he published his first collection of verse, *Kobzar* (The Minstrel) to which other more important poems were soon added. This work later became a national gospel of the Ukrainian movement. Using at first typical romantic motifs from Ukrainian life and legends, he later turned to themes of the Cossack period, describing and idealizing the Cossack campaigns against the nation's enemies. When he returned to Ukraine, however, his more matured realization of the unbearable sufferings of the people wrought a change in his themes. Later poems made a passionate appeal for national independence, human equality, and social justice, attacking Russian serfdom, despotism, and suppression of other nationalities.

Thus by the mid-nineteenth century, Ukrainian national leadership passed from the nobility to the intelligentsia, and was distinguished by its tendency toward democratic political and social reforms. At the University of Kyiv, a literary group, united by a common view of the nation and its past, carefully studied the latest political and cultural movements among the Slavs. Out of this group, late in 1845 or early in 1846, on the initiative of Mykola Kostomarov, Mykola Hulak, Vasyl' Bilozers'kyi, Shevchenko, and Panteleimon Kulish grew the first Ukrainian secret society, called the Brotherhood of Saints Cyril and Methodius after the famous "Apostles of the Slavs."[24]

Their political program was expressed in Kostomarov's *Books of Genesis of the Ukrainian People*, and also in letters, documents, Shevchenko's poems, and *Istoriia Rusov*. It called for a federation of autonomous Slavic republics, headed by a generally elected assembly that would meet in a free city, Kyiv.[25] The program also included guarantees of freedom of conscience, thought, speech, religion, and press; the abolition of serfdom and corporal punishment; and elimination of illiteracy. The Brotherhood was based on the principles of Christianity and democracy. It was in no sense a Ukrainian nationalist organization—the name was common to all Slavic peoples. Moreover, although some members did advocate revolutionary action, none had connections with any military organization that might carry out their plans.[26]

In April 1847 the society's existence was revealed to the authorities and its members were arrested. Some of the leaders were punished by short terms of imprisonment or exile, but Shevchenko was sentenced to ten years as a private in a Central Asian disciplinary garrison and specifically forbidden by Nicholas I to write or draw.[27]

Although the Brotherhood's activity was of short duration, its basic ideas left a deep impression upon its members as well as other educated Ukrainians. Its suppression marked the beginning of a new period of systematic persecution of the Ukrainian movement that lasted, except for brief interludes, until 1917.

After the Crimean War, however, Alexander II introduced a number of reforms that made cultural activities possible. Former members of the Brotherhood were released and some of them, including Shevchenko, Kostomarov, Kulish, and Bilozers'kyi, settled in St. Petersburg, where conditions were more favorable for literary activities than in Ukraine. They established a printing house, which in 1861 began to issue a scholarly periodical, *Osnova* (Foundation).[28] However, after the death of Shevchenko in 1861 the group's activity declined, *Osnova* ceased publication in 1862, and other publications were suppressed.

The group centered around *Osnova* moved then to Kyiv, where they faced new problems.

The Emancipation of 1861 revolutionized social relations; Ukrainian leaders sought to improve the wretched conditions of the peasants through education, organizing Sunday schools to teach illiterates, and publishing textbooks and periodicals. In larger cities, societies (*hromady*) were founded for cultural purposes, such as the organization of theatricals, choirs, libraries, and public lectures. The *hromady* also encouraged the educated people to wear national costumes and speak the national language.[29]

At the same time the so-called *Khlopomany* (peasant-lovers) movement developed out of the "Ukrainian school" in Polish literature. The *Khlopomany* joined with Ukrainian students at Kyiv University to form the "Ukrainian Community" (Ukrains'ka Hromada).[30] Neither group, however, formulated definite political goals or programs and their activities were limited to educational and cultural work. Though the movement never achieved a wide following, it nevertheless contributed to the development of Ukrainian culture. One member in particular, Volodymyr Antonovych, became the most prominent figure in the national movement between 1860 and 1890.

The national movement met with opposition during the reign of Alexander II (1865–81), although this was generally considered a period of limited liberal social and administrative reforms. In 1862 the government accused Ukrainians of conspiracy with the Poles and the creation of propaganda aiming to separate Ukraine from Russia. The tsar was particularly alarmed by the Polish insurrection of 1863, and subsequently the Russian publicist Mikhail Katkov originated a campaign in the press against the Ukrainian movement, which he described as a "Polish intrigue." In the summer of 1863 Peter Valuev, minister of the interior, issued an edict declaring that "there never was any separate Ukrainian language, there is none now, and there cannot be any." He decreed that henceforth only belles-lettres could be published in Ukrainian; religious works (including the Bible), textbooks, and popular literature were forbidden.

Russian progressives, including Alexander Herzen, Nikolai Dobroliubov, and Nikolai Chernyshevskii, protested the persecution of Ukraine. Even the minister of education, A. V. Golovnin, defended the Ukrainian language, stating "that the government should not censor books in such a manner merely because of the language, without examining the contents."[31]

As a result of the suppression of national life within the Russian

Empire, literary and political activities were transferred to East Galicia where, under the more liberal government of Austria, it was possible to publish books and establish literary and scientific societies. In 1873, the Shevchenko Society was founded in L'viv, and later it became the center of Ukrainian studies for both parts of Ukraine.

While Russian policy continued unchanged until the 1905 Revolution, its application was neither uniform nor consistent. After a decade, a short relaxation once more made literary and educational activities possible. Kyiv again became the center of national life and a newspaper, *Kiev Telegraph*, was published in Russian. A southwestern branch of the Russian Geographical Society was established in Kyiv in 1873. The impressive achievements of Ukrainians at the Archaeological Congress Kyiv in 1874 provoked Russian reactionaries, who saw separatist tendencies in both the society and the congress.[32] Thus, although the effect of concentration on cultural and scientific activities was to divert attention from political movements, the government renewed its attack on the Ukrainian revival.

Early in 1875 a commission composed of the minister of the interior, the minister of education, and the chief of police reported that the literary activity of the Ukrainophiles was dangerous to the unity of the empire. Consequently on May 18, 1876, Alexander II issued a secret decree from Ems, Germany, that forbade the printing or importation of books, pamphlets, and musical lyrics in Ukrainian, and proscribed public lectures, drama, and concerts. The language was permitted only in historical documents and belles-lettres, the latter in Russian orthography only. Moreover, Ukrainian manuscripts were subject to a double censorship, both locally and in St. Petersburg, a restriction not applied to other national languages. At the same time the *Kiev Telegraph* and the southwestern branch of the Geographical Society were abolished. Many Ukrainians were dismissed from their posts in the universities or civil service, and some were banished to remote provinces.[33]

The Ems decree was technically illegal for it had been formulated in a secret meeting of two ministers and the chief of police, and it had not been approved by the Council of Ministers. Nor was it ever announced publicly. The target of the decree was not the content of the works involved, but the language itself. Thus when the British and Foreign Bible Society asked to distribute Ukrainian-language Bibles among the troops in the Russo-Japanese War (1904–5), permission was refused, although Russian Bibles were freely distributed. By making reading matter more scarce, the edict also caused an increase in illiteracy to 80 percent.[34]

The Ems decree guided Russian policy until 1905. In that year the Russian Academy of Sciences adopted a report, written by two Russian philologists of the government, which recognized Ukrainian as a separate language.[35]

The Valuev edict and the Ems decree had two distinct consequences for the Ukrainian movement—the depoliticization of national life and a split in the intelligentsia over the question of methods. The willingness of the older generation to persevere in the struggle for nationhood was considerably undermined. Its principal representatives, Kostomarov and to a lesser extent Antonovych, advocated concentration primarily on cultural problems in order to placate the Russian regime. In 1882 the Old Society (Stara Hromada) of Kyiv established a scholarly periodical, *Kievskaia Starina* (Kyivan Antiquity), which was a forum for Ukrainian studies until its cessation in 1907. Only after 1890 did some articles in Ukrainian begin to appear; however, from the beginning the editors attracted many prominent scholars who gave the periodical a distinct national character.[36]

A unique figure, in both his influence on, and position in, the national movement of the late nineteenth century, was Mykhailo Drahomanov (1841–95), a scholar, folklorist, historian, and political leader of Cossack origin. After Drahomanov received his degree, the University of Kyiv sent him to Western Europe (1870–73) to study ancient history. On his return he was appointed professor, but two years later, because of his activity in the national movement, the tsar ordered him to resign.[37] Subsequently he left the country and settled in Geneva, where he published the Ukrainian-language periodical, *Hromada*, as a free national forum, and also wrote a series of pamphlets and articles in European languages about Ukrainian national aspirations and Russian policy in Ukraine.

Subsequently, Drahomanov turned his attention to Ukrainian problems in Austria, where the national movement was less restricted. In his prolific writings, especially his correspondence with Ukrainians in East Galicia, he advocated a more active political life and concentration on the education and organization of the masses. For these purposes he formed the nucleus of a new progressive movement, which in 1890 became the Radical party, directing its appeals primarily to the peasants.[38]

Drahomanov was also influential among Russian revolutionary émigrés, as the editor of a Russian periodical, *Vol'noe Slovo* (Free Voice) from 1881 to 1883. He opposed not only tsarist policies in general but also Russian revolutionary terrorism and centralism.

In the history of the Ukrainian national movement, Drahomanov stood halfway between the Brotherhood of Saints Cyril and Methodius and the generation that formed an independent democratic republic in 1917. Politically, he favored wide decentralization of the Russian Empire on the basis of national autonomy, a liberal constitution, and a parliamentary system. Against the prevailing currents of his time, he transformed the heretofore literary and ethnographical national movement into a political and social one.

An important advancement of the Ukrainian cause was the establishment of a Chair of Ukrainian and East European history at the Polish-dominated University of L'viv in 1894, and the appointment to it of a prominent historian, Mykhailo Hrushevs'kyi (1866–1934). Hrushevs'kyi, like Drahomanov, for twenty years symbolized the unity of both parts of Ukraine; however, his political thinking tended to promote national independence. Although he was a prolific writer in several fields, his most meritorious work was in historiography, where he devised a unified and well-founded scheme demonstrating the continuity and geographical integrity of Ukrainian development, thus providing a sound historical basis for the movement toward independence. He followed this scheme in his monumental *History of Ukraine-Rus*.[39] Another important accomplishment was the reorganization, under his leadership (1897–1913), of the Shevchenko Society, which subsequently became a center of Ukrainian studies and gained wide scholarly recognition.

In 1897 a clandestine congress in Kyiv of the representatives of all Ukrainian *hromady* formed the General Ukrainian Democratic party. Largely literary at first, it assumed a more political character; in 1904 it became the Ukrainian Democratic party, and later the Democratic Radical party (UDRP).

Also in 1897, a student group was founded in Kharkiv that in 1900 was reorganized into the Revolutionary Ukrainian party (RUP) with branches in other cities. Until 1904, it was composed primarily of students, but later it became a party of intelligentsia.[40] Its first platform called for "one indivisible, free, and independent Ukraine from Carpathians to the Caucasus," and declared that "as long as the one enemy is left in our territory we cannot lay down our arms."[41] Mykola Mikhnovs'kyi, who wrote the platform, believed that social emancipation would occur once independence was attained. Other members, however, thought that socialism and revolution should be the primary goals. In 1902, Mikhnovs'kyi and his followers formed the Ukrainian People's party. In 1904 the revolutionary group seceded to form the Ukrainian Social Democratic Union (Spilka), which in 1908 affiliated itself with the Russian Social-Democratic Labor party. It represented the agricultural proletariat. Although a strictly Ukrainian party, it paid little attention to the national question. In 1905 RUP was reorganized into the Ukrainian Social Democratic Labor party and subsequently adopted a Marxist point of view.[42] Though their spheres of activity were limited, these illegal organizations increased the national consciousness of the population by distributing free literature, and gave the movement a political and economic character.

Changes in economic and social structure, brought about by industrialization and railway construction in the second half of the nineteenth century, also contributed to the upsurge of political activity toward the end of the century. Ukraine was one of the world's most important exporters of grain, and the introduction of the sugar beet intensified the growth of agriculture. Prior to the First World War, Ukrainian wheat exports accounted for 90 percent of the total for the Russian economy.[43] Russian policy was to maintain Ukraine in a colonial state, as a supplier of agricultural products and raw materials and a market for manufactured goods. It was permitted to develop only such industries as had no natural base in Russia or industries that provided raw materials or partially processed goods for Russian industry. The regime built railway lines that connected Ukraine with Russia or served the strategic plans of the empire.[44]

Nevertheless, in the last quarter of the century heavy industry began to develop near the rich coal and ore deposits of the Donets Basin, Kharkiv, and Kryvyi Rih, spurred principally by foreign capital. On the eve of the First World War the Donets Basin supplied 55 percent of Russia's coal and 83.5 percent of its coke.[45]

Along with industrial expansion, the composition of the population changed radically. Old towns grew and many new ones were founded. In addition to an extensive Russian immigration, the number of other nationalities in Ukraine increased and gradually the Ukrainian population in the major cities and industrial centers became a minority. Most of the nationalities, conservative or radical, tended to support Russian policy in Ukraine. Moreover, much of the urban population was infected by the Russian revolutionary movement, providing a natural milieu for Russification. All these changes in the social, national, and economic structure of Ukraine strengthened the ties to the Russian Empire and severely handicapped the national revival, though their full impact was not evident until the Revolution.

Although the Ukrainian movement was intensified at the turn of the century, it was the unsuccessful Russo-Japanese War and the Revolution of 1905 that brought to the surface the hitherto clandestine social and national forces. The peasant uprisings in Ukraine in 1905–6 were among the most violent in the Empire,[46] and the strikes and demonstrations in the larger cities led to armed clashes.

The tsar's October Manifesto in 1905 helped considerably in calming the Revolution by promising favorable reforms, and spurred Ukrainian leaders to increase their activities. Never officially repealed, the Ems decree was no longer enforced. Within a few months there were thirty-four new publications in Ukrainian. Simultaneously societies of enlightenment (*Prosvita*) were founded throughout the country. Great hopes were held for the First Duma, and national leaders established a center in St. Petersburg to give assistance to the forty-four Ukrainian noble and peasant members. They also published a journal in Russian, *Ukrainian Herald*,[47] and prepared a declaration demanding autonomy for Ukraine, but on the eve of its presentation the Duma was dissolved.

The Second Duma, with forty-seven Ukrainian deputies, was weakened because the most experienced politicians from the First Duma who had signed the Viborg appeal were disfranchised.[48] The new parliamentary club demanded more rights for Ukraine, including self-government within the framework of the empire. The delegates published their own organ in Ukrainian, *Native Cause*. However, the Second Duma was also dissolved and a change in the electoral law resulted in an almost complete lack of Ukrainian representation in the Third and Fourth Dumas.[49]

The brief respite of the 1905 Revolution quickly changed to reaction, and political freedom again disappeared. Ukrainian was not allowed in the schools and universities, although this privilege was granted to other languages. The Ukrainian press was abolished and most branches of *Prosvita* were closed. Political groups were suppressed. Consequently, many politicians who escaped arrest left Ukraine and settled either abroad or in the centers of greater freedom such as Moscow and St. Petersburg.[50]

In 1908, on the initiative of the Democratic Radical party, Ukrainian political groups that stood for autonomy and a democratic system formed the secret Society of Ukrainian Progressives (TUP), which, until the Revolution of 1917, dominated national political life. Its aim was to gain piecemeal political and cultural concessions from the regime.

In spite of restrictions and persecution after 1905, the Ukrainian movement did gain ground in all aspects of public life. Ukrainian representation in the Duma manifested to the world the existence of the

Ukrainian problem in the Russian Empire, and the outbreak of the First World War aroused hopes for far-reaching changes.

The war, however, brought a new wave of repression, and there was a strong agitation in Russian circles to eliminate the Ukrainian movement completely. In 1914 the government suppressed all Ukrainian cultural and educational activities and the entire press was closed. Many prominent politicians and scholars, including Hrushevs'kyi, were exiled despite declarations of loyalty, and others went abroad. In August 1914, Ukrainain political émigrés in Lviv formed the League for the Liberation of Ukraine. Later moving to Vienna,[51] the League planned to create a Ukrainian state from the Ukrainian territory seized by the German armies, and to give courses in citizenship to all Ukrainian prisoners of war.

Russia's desire to annex East Galicia, Bukovina, and Carpatho-Ukraine and consequently to Russify the population was related to its entry into the war. When Russian forces occupied East Galicia in the first months of the war, the newly appointed governor-general, Georgii Bobrinskii, declared East Galicia to be "the real cradle of Great Russia," and referred to an "indivisible Russia," which would extend as far as the Carpathians. The Bobrinskii administration began a systematic suppression of Ukrainian schools, organizations, press, and bookshops as a prelude to exile of numerous leaders, including the Ukrainian Catholic (Uniate) metropolitan, Count Andrii Sheptyts'kyi.[52] Steps were taken to abolish the Ukrainian Catholic church and to force the acceptance of Russian Orthodoxy.

As the western part of Russian Ukraine became devastated by the war, the disruption of the economy, the shortage of farmhands, and the continuing persecution of the Ukrainian movement made conditions unbearable. Opposition to the regime and its social order steadily increased and contributed to the outbreak of the Revolution.

Although Ukrainian political thought and aspirations were not completely extinguished by the destruction of the hetman state, the modern national revival, confined as it was primarily to the cultural sphere, could offer little in the way of practical administrative and political experience. Prior to 1905 under Russian rule there was no legal means of forming political parties and the administration of the country was largely in the hands of non-Ukrainians. The intelligentsia was divided over the conflicting currents of national independence and socialist internationalism. Thus the Revolution proved a difficult testing ground for national leaders in their efforts to build an independent state.

1. The Ukrainian Revolution

The Central Rada

After the outbreak of the March Revolution and the collapse of the Russian monarchy, the leaders of Ukraine declared the nation's right to self-determination. On March 20, 1917,[1] on the initiative of the Society of Ukrainian Progressives (TUP), the Ukrainian Central Rada (Council) was formed, composed of the municipal and cultural organizations of Kyiv and representatives of political parties and professional organizations. It served originally not as a parliament, but as a center of instruction and mutual information. There followed formation of local radas, committees, or other organizations that spontaneously recognized the Central Rada's authority.[2]

The spirit of the Rada and the nation in general was greatly stimulated by the first purely Ukrainian political demonstration in Kyiv on April 1, 1917, in which tens of thousands participated. The prevailing slogans of the day were "A free Ukraine in a free Russia!" and "Independent Ukraine with its own hetman!" The demonstrators swore before the portrait of Taras Shevchenko not to rest until Ukraine became a free autonomous state. From April 19 to 21, the Rada convoked a Ukrainian National Convention in Kyiv to gain wider support and popular approval for its actions. The convention, attended by about nine hundred representatives of soldiers, peasants, laborers, cultural and professional organizations, and political parties, sanctioned a larger Central Rada of similar composition under the presidency of Hrushevs'kyi.[3] By manifesting national unity and laying the foundation for a government, the convention opened a new period of the national revolution—a political struggle to shape the destiny of the nation.

Cultural and political life was also revived. The press and publishing houses were reopened to meet the demands for printed works, especially textbooks for renascent Ukrainian schools, and organizations for the retraining of teachers were set up. *Prosvita* societies, libraries, and bookstores were reestablished throughout the country. The old parties were reorganized and new ones were established: the three major ones were the old Democratic Radical party (which in June 1917, became the Ukrainian party of Socialists and Federalists), the Ukrainian Social Democratic Labor party, and the newly organized Ukrainian party of Socialist Revolutionaries; a number of minor parties also existed.

There was an especially impressive resurgence of national activity in the Russian Army, and four million soldiers affirmed their Ukrainian nationality and a desire to form their own units. Alongside the soldiers' committees that were organized under the authority of the Executive Committee of the Soviet's Order No. 1 of March 14, 1917,[4] Ukrainian military councils, clubs and other organizations supporting the Rada began to emerge.

It was demanded that the units quartered in Ukraine be composed only of Ukrainians. The initiative for creating separate Ukrainian units came from the Hetman P. Polubotok Military Club, which was founded on March 29, 1917, in Kyiv, by officers Mykola Mikhnovs'kyi, and two brothers, Oleksander and Pavlo Makarenko,[5] and from the Ukrainian Military Organizational Committee. Although these demands were resisted by Russian authorities, on April 1 the First Ukrainian B. Kheml'nyts'kyi Regiment was organized from soldiers temporarily stationed in Kyiv.[6]

The First Ukrainian Military Congress in Kyiv on May 18–25, 1917, consisted of over seven hundred delegates representing nearly one million men from the fronts, the rear, and the fleets. The Second Military Congress of June 18–23 was even more impressive. Despite a ban by Alexander F. Kerensky, minister of war, it was attended by 2,500 delegates representing 1,736,000 men, mostly front-line soldiers.[7] Shortly thereafter the First Ukrainian Peasants' Congress in Kyiv on June 10–15 had 2,500 delegates, including many village teachers, from about one thousand rural districts. The First Ukrainian Workers' Congress, which met in Kyiv on July 24–27, consisted of nearly three hundred delegates. The congresses sought to unify and direct the military, peasant, and labor movements and to show support for the

Rada. They adopted resolutions urging the Rada to be firm in its demand for territorial autonomy from the Provisional Government, and to issue a proclamation of an independent Ukrainian republic.[8]

The Rada's cautious demand for autonomy of Ukrainian-inhabited territory was rejected by the Provisional Government on the ground that the problem of autonomy should be decided by the Russian Constituent Assembly. Consequently on June 24, 1917, the Rada, without separating from Russia, proclaimed its First Universal:

> Let the Ukrainian people on their own territory have the right to manage their own life. Let a National Ukrainian Assembly (Sejm), elected by universal, equal, direct, and secret suffrage, establish order and a regime in the Ukraine. Only our Ukrainian assembly is to have the right to issue all laws which are to establish this regime. . . . No one knows better than we what we need and which laws are best for us.[9]

Four days later the General Secretariat, a Ukrainian government, was established, headed by Volodymyr Vynnychenko, a Social Democrat.

Subsequently, the Provisional Government delegated three ministers, Kerensky, Mikhail I. Tereshchenko, and Irakly G. Tsereteli, to Kyiv for negotiations with the Rada and on July 16 the Provisional Government recognized the autonomy of Ukraine and the formation of separate Ukrainian military units, although the Kadet ministers resigned on the ground that "it put an end to the authority of the Provisional Government in Ukraine." It was, they said, for the "Constituent Assembly to determine the form of government for the Ukraine and not for the Ukraine itself."[10] At the same time, the Rada proclaimed its Second Universal, recognizing the All-Russian Constituent Assembly and declaring that it had no intention of separating from Russia. Also under the agreement, the national minorities in Ukraine (Russians, Poles, and Jews) sent their representatives to the Central Rada, which now became a territorial parliament.

All these changes were to be formulated in a Statute of the Higher Government of Ukraine, which the Provisional Government did not confirm, but issued instead on August 17, a "Temporary Instruction" that greatly reduced the scope of the proposed statute. The General Secretariat was to be an organ, not of the Central Rada, but of the Provisional Government, "the membership of which shall be determined by the Government" in agreement with the Central Rada, augmented on an equitable basis with democratic organizations representing other nationalities inhabiting the Ukraine." The number of secretaries was reduced from fourteen to seven, and the legislative power of the Rada was also denied. Moreover, the territory under its jurisdiction was reduced from twelve to five provinces, Kyiv, Volyn', Podillia, Poltava, and Chernyhiv.[11]

The Rada, asserting that the original agreement had been violated, accepted these terms as a basis for further struggle against Russian centralism. As a first step to strengthen Ukraine's position, the Rada consulted with other nations of the former Russian Empire having similar interests. On September 21–28 a congress of ninety-two Ukrainian, Belorussian, Georgian, Jewish, Estonian, Latvian, Don Cossack, Polish, Moldavian, Tatar, and Turkestanian delegates gathered in Kyiv to discuss the transformation of the centralized Russian state into a federation of free states. The congress did form a Rada of Nations headquartered in Kyiv, but the subsequent crisis in Russia reduced it to small importance.

The Provisional Government, in ratifying Ukrainian autonomy, had no intention of honoring the agreement. In Vynnychenko's terms, the Instruction was a truce rather than a peace settlement. The Kerensky government blocked administrative reorganization and Ukrainization of the army, ignored the Secretariat, and tried to administer Ukraine directly.[12] The position of the Secretariat was extremely difficult, for it was responsible not only to the Rada but also to the Provisional Government, and the latter sought to impede its actions.

The weakening of Kerensky's government strengthened the Secretariat. It presented to the nation constructive programs for maintenance of the political rights of the Ukrainian people within a federated Russian republic of equals; termination of the division of the Ukrainian nation caused by the Instruction; the extension of the Secretariat's competence as a fully authorized autonomous government; and finally, the early convocation of the Ukrainian Constituent Assembly to bring the Ukrainian people's struggle for liberation to culmination.[13] However, in dealing with such issues as the agrarian and labor questions, and state control over banking, commerce, and industry, the Secretariat was very circumspect.

The Kerensky government used the coming Ukrainian Constituent Assembly as a pretext to begin legal prosecution of the Rada and the Secretariat and called its members to Petrograd to explain the purpose of "convoking a sovereign Constituent Assembly." This action aroused protest in Ukraine and Vynnychenko, addressing the Third Ukrainian Military Congress, declared that the Secretariat would not enter into relations with Kerensky's government and would only discuss the question of a final delineation of its functions. Moreover:

The secretaries-general must declare categorically that they are not officials of the Provisional Government, that the General Secretariat was not established by it, but is the organ of Ukrainian democracy. Because of this the General Secretariat is in no way responsible for its acts before the Provisional Government.[14]

This chapter of Ukrainian-Russian relations was closed by the Bolshevik seizure of power in Russia on November 7, 1917. Although a potential threat to the Rada arose from Russian rightist elements in Kyiv, it was thwarted by the Rada and the socialist groups of the national minorities, who organized a Committee for the Defense of the Revolution. At the same time, the Rada expressed its readiness to fight any attempt to introduce Bolshevik rule in Ukraine. Nevertheless, the Bolsheviks began to agitate against the Rada and, whenever possible, tried to seize local governments by force, though without success.

On November 20 the Rada issued the Third Universal, declaring de facto national independence: "We, the Ukrainian Central Rada, carrying out the will of our people, announce that henceforth the Ukraine is the Ukrainian People's Republic."[15] Nevertheless, relations with Russia were not broken off:

Without separating the Russian Republic and destroying its unity, we shall firmly establish ourselves on our own land in order that with our strength we may help the rest of Russia . . . to become a federation of free and equal peoples.[16]

At that time, however, the statement had no real meaning, for the Rada did not recognize the Bolshevik regime.

The Third Universal proclaimed the democratic principles of freedom of speech, press, religion, and assembly; the right of unions to organize and strike; the security of the individual and his property; the abolition of capital punishment and amnesty for all political prisoners; it established an eight-hour work day; acknowledged the right of the government and the workers to control industry; abolished the right of private ownership of land and recognized the land as belonging to all of the people, without compensation to the former owners; and proclaimed the principle of national autonomy for all national minorities in Ukraine.[17]

One of the greatest obstacles to establishing effective Ukrainian authority was the potential threat represented by the concentration of Russian forces in Ukraine. Early in 1918 there were close to one hundred thousand Russian officers in the main Ukrainian cities, and the movement through Ukraine of active and demobilized soldiers, especially deserters, made it difficult to maintain order. Even prior to the Revolution there were over 195,000 deserters from the front, and on August 1, 1917, there were 365,000; together with those hiding to avoid conscription, the "greens," they totalled approximately two million by October 1, 1917.[18] Worse hit were the provinces adjoining the front, Volyn' and Podillia.

Some of the urban proletariat, lacking a fully developed national consciousness, were more attracted by radical Bolshevik programs than by the Rada's hesitant approach to social problems. In the cities there were large Russian, Jewish, or Polish populations that were either hostile or indifferent to Ukrainian statehood, and officials, industrialists, and the landed aristocracy, largely non-Ukrainians, feared the confiscation of their properties by a Ukrainian government, and so preferred a Russian one.

At the beginning of the Revolution the peasants and soldiers were the strongest supporters of the Rada, but the peasants were only potentially active nationalists; a vast majority of them were far more concerned with the solution of the agrarian question. Some, especially the rural proletariat, because of the Rada's irresoluteness on agrarian reform, were won over by the Bolsheviks.

As for the formation of a national army, there were two feasible alternatives: Ukrainization of the Ukrainian soldiers in the Russian Army or creation of a volunteer force. Both the Provisional Government and the Russian command were opposed to any Ukrainian army. However, many units were spontaneously nationalized by the Ukrainian councils and committees, eventually encompassing nearly a million and a half of the four million Ukrainians in the army, while the creation of volunteer units was not directly within the control of Petrograd. The idea of a regular army was not popular among the major parties in the Rada because they saw in it a threat to the Revolution. Most importantly, the weariness of four years of war and Bolshevik propaganda contributed to the disintegration of the Ukrainized military units.[19] Consequently the concept of an army composed of Free Cossacks and other volunteer units finally prevailed. When Soviet Russian forces invaded Ukraine in January 1918, the nation's armed forces were not so well prepared as they had been some months earlier.

Although the collapse of Kerensky's government favored the course of Ukrainian independence, the establishment of a strong and stable government proved very difficult in an atmosphere of social and economic chaos, the administrative inexperience of the leaders, and the Bolshevik threat. The Bolshevik seizure of power in Russia radically changed the course of the Ukrainian national revolution. Prior to and during 1917, the Bolsheviks had opposed any Russian suppression of non-Russian nationalist movements within the empire and under the

Provisional Government were willing to support the Rada in its demand for a separate Ukrainian Constituent Assembly. On June 17, 1917, Lenin, for example, declared:

> The Russian Republic does not want to oppress any nation, either in the new or in the old way, and does not want to force any nation, either Finland or Ukraine, with both of whom the War Minister is trying so hard to find fault and with whom impermissible and intolerable conflicts are being created.[20]

Recognition and encouragement of the nationalities was, however, primarily a political tactic aimed at weakening the monarchy and the Provisional Government and gaining the support of their enemies. Lenin saw nationalism as an ephemeral phenomenon that would yield to the internationalism of the proletariat and the formation of a new state. When this vision did not materialize, and they were faced instead with a myriad of independence movements and the disintegration of the old state structure, the Bolsheviks hastily revised their policy of self-determination. The change was bound to be felt first and most strongly in Ukraine, for that nation, more than any other, by its size, population, geographical location, and natural resources, was considered important to Russian interests. Georgii L. Piatakov, a Russian Jew born in Ukraine, stated bluntly in 1917: "On the whole we must not support the Ukrainians, because their movement is not convenient for the proletariat. Russia cannot exist without the Ukrainian sugar industry, and the same can be said in regard to coal (Donbas); cereals (the black-earth belt), etc."[21]

At first the Bolsheviks tried to prevent stabilization of the Ukrainian government by spreading incendiary appeals, fomenting class hatred, and sending Bolshevik bands into Ukraine. These actions were to be followed by armed uprisings of Russian soldiers and workers. On December 12, the government discovered a revolt planned for Kyiv on the next day. Its leaders were arrested, and the Russian units involved were disarmed and deported to Russia.[22] Subsequently the First Ukrainian Corps, under General Skoropads'kyi (later hetman) and some Free Cossacks, disarmed the Russian Second Guard Corps led by the Bolshevik Evgeniia B. Bosh, which was moving from the front to aid the uprising in Kyiv. They too were returned to Russia.

The tension between Ukraine and Soviet Russia mounted when the Secretariat ordered troops in Ukraine not to obey the order of the Bolshevik government and denied the right of the latter to negotiate peace for Ukraine. On December 17, the Bolsheviks sent the Rada an ultimatum that "recognized the complete independence of the Ukrainian Republic" but at the same time accused the Rada of disorganizing the front by recalling Ukrainian troops, disarming Bolshevik troops in Ukraine, and supporting General Aleksei M. Kalendin's counterrevolutionary rebellion in the Don Basin. These practices were to be abandoned within forty-eight hours or the Bolshevik government would consider the Rada "in a state of open warfare against the Soviet Government in Russia and in Ukraine."[23]

Simultaneously the Council of People's Commissars induced the Kyiv Soviet to call an All-Ukrainian Congress of Workers, Soldiers, and Peasants on December 17 in opposition to the Rada. However, the Bolsheviks controlled only 60 of the 2,500 delegates, and the Congress expressed confidence in the Rada, protesting the ultimatum. On December 18 the Secretariat rejected the ultimatum arguing that it was impossible "simultaneously to recognize the right of a people to self-determination, including separation, and at the same time to infringe roughly on that right by imposing on the people in question a certain type of government."[24]

The Bolshevik delegates, enraged by the unexpected turn of events, walked out of the Congress. Later they and their sympathizers in the Kyiv Soviet, numbering altogether nearly 125, went to Kharkiv, where they joined the Bolshevik-controlled Congress of Soviets of the Donets and Kryvyi Rih basins. This rump group appointed a Central Executive Committee that announced it was henceforth to be considered the sole legal government of all Ukraine. In the name of this puppet regime Lenin's Soviet Russian government waged war against Ukraine.

In early December the Bolsheviks had concentrated troops, mainly workers and sailors from Petrograd and Moscow, near the Ukrainian border under the command of Vladimir A. Antonov.[25] They were later joined by various local elements. The Bolshevik invasion of Ukraine, which began on January 7, 1918, in four separate attacks, was greatly facilitated by insurrections of mostly non-Ukrainian groups in the cities and at railroad stations along their route. The Rada's forces were outnumbered, inadequately equipped, and disorganized by the impact of the Revolution. The Bolsheviks occupied one city after another: Katerynoslav (Ekaterinoslav) on January 10; Poltava, January 20; Odessa, January 30; Mykolaiv (Nikolaev), February 4; and on February 8, after eleven days of heavy bombardment and street fighting, Kyiv was captured and the Rada was forced to evacuate to Zhytomyr.[26]

In this critical situation the only recourse was to make a separate peace with the Central Powers to obtain their support in defending the country. Consequently, on January 22, 1918, in its Fourth Universal, the Rada announced: "On this day the Ukrainian People's Republic becomes independent, self-sufficient, a free sovereign state of the Ukrainian People."[27] This document only confirmed that the political bond between Ukraine and Russia was severed by the Bolshevik invasion.

Aid from the Central Powers, however, was conditional upon cessation of the war against them. France and Britain had granted Ukraine de facto recognition at the end of December 1917[28] and had tried to persuade the Rada to continue the war against the Central Powers. The Allies, however, were not in a position to give military assistance, for the only access was via Bolshevik-controlled Murmansk and Archangel or Vladivostok.

The Rada feared that the peace negotiations between the Bolsheviks and the Central Powers, begun at the end of December at Brest-Litovsk, might result in Germany's ceding Ukraine to the Bolsheviks. Moreover, the desire for peace was so strong among the Ukrainian population that the Rada would have been "unable to withstand this current, especially if the Bolsheviks managed to conclude peace with the Austro-Germans."[29]

Under these circumstances, the Rada sent a separate delegation to Brest-Litovsk to make peace with the Central Powers. Although the Russian delegation agreed to the participation of the Ukrainian delegation, its head, Leon Trotsky, tried to discredit it; he even invited a delegation from the Ukrainian Soviet Government,[30] and tried to prove that the Rada no longer existed. The Germans favored Ukrainian participation in the conference because they wanted to secure their supplies and put pressure on the Bolsheviks.

By the peace treaty between the four Central Powers and Ukraine, concluded on February 9, 1918, Ukraine, including Kholm, was recognized as an independent republic. Austria promised to unite Bukovina with East Galicia and set up a new Ukrainian Crown Land with political and cultural rights within the monarchy. In return, Ukraine agreed to provide the Central Powers with at least one million tons of surplus foodstuffs.[31]

Subsequently, the Rada sought Austrian and German aid in expelling the Russian forces, believing that an adequate force could be composed of the existing Ukrainian units in the Austrian Army and the Ukrainian prisoners held by the Germans. They asked that these troops, estimated at thirty thousand men, be employed in Ukraine. The Central Powers refused, arguing that the time required to bring the troops from other areas was too great, though they undoubtedly were also anxious

Pavlo P. Skoropads'kyi

Volodymyr K. Vynnychenko

Symon Petliura

Mykhailo Hrushevs'kyi

to assure their own control of Ukraine. Through the ensuing deployment of the Austrian and German armies, Ukraine became in effect an occupied nation.[32]

The Austro-German forces, including some Ukrainian troops, followed the railways, meeting little Bolshevik resistance; by the end of April Ukrainian territory was cleared of Soviet Russian troops. On March 29, 1918, at Baden, an agreement was made on the partitioning of spheres of interest. Germany received northern Ukraine, the Crimea, Taganrog, and Novorossiisk; Austria, the provinces of Podillia, Kherson, and parts of Katerynoslav and Volyn'.[33] Authority was vested primarily in the Commander of *Heeresgruppe* Kyiv, Field Marshal von Eichhorn, while General Wilhelm Groener, German chief of staff in Ukraine, was charged with securing the supplies. The German and Austro-Hungarian diplomatic representative played a secondary role. Austro-German Ukrainian policy in 1918 went through three major phases: cooperation with the Rada; support of the hetman government; and a belated attempt to support the Ukrainian independence movement once the war was lost.

After its return to Kyiv, the Rada government of Vsevolod Holubovych, a Socialist Revolutionary who succeeded Vynnychenko on January 30, 1918, faced overwhelming obstacles to the establishment of internal order. The retreating Bolsheviks had looted the banks, damaged the railroads, and flooded the mines. The country swarmed with anarchist, foreign, and reactionary military bands that opposed the Republic. The presence of German and Austrian troops led to strong criticism of the Rada, even though it publicly declared that Ukrainian sovereignty would not be limited, and Hrushevs'kyi assured the people that the troops would remain only so long as they were needed for the liberation of Ukraine.[34]

The main crisis, however, stemmed from the Rada's socialist policy, especially the land reform law of January 31, 1918. The Rada announced its continuation of the economic reforms outlined in the Third and Fourth Universals, including nationalization of agriculture, industry, and banks; all were intended to weaken Bolshevik propaganda against the "Ukrainian bourgeois government." Given the economic state of the Central Powers, they could hardly be in sympathy with the agrarian reform the Rada was sponsoring. They were concerned solely with having a government that could guarantee the delivery of supplies.

In 1917, rural disorders occurred; the peasants appropriated the lands, and the harvest was not gathered in the normal way. The peasants, in the face of the landowners' intensive reaction, were uncertain as to the future disposal of the harvest and hesitated to cultivate the land.[35] The cattle had been either slaughtered or driven off during the Bolshevik occupation. The sugar factories were standing idle.

As spring approached, apprehension mounted among the German and Austrian authorities. Moreover, the conservative wealthy classes, largely non-Ukrainians who were hostile to the Republic, attempted to discredit the Rada and suggested deposing it. The Germans, with supplies scarce and the Ukrainian economy in chaos, were receptive to such approaches. They found it much easier to get supplies from the landlords than from the peasants, who could hide their grain and cattle and were unwilling to relinquish them, especially for paper money.[36]

The Central Powers also doubted the Ukrainian government's capability "either of settling the unrest in the country or of delivering grain to us."[37] The most serious act of intervention occurred on April 6 when von Eichhorn issued an order that caused critical conflicts both in Ukraine and in the Reichstag. The order notified the peasants that (1) cultivators of the soil would keep the crop and get current prices; (2) anyone holding land beyond his capacity to cultivate would be punished; (3) where peasants were unable to cultivate all the land and where landowners do exist, the peasants must provide for planting, without prejudicing the rights of the land committees to divide the land. Peasants were not to interfere with the cultivation and land committees were to provide the landowners with horses, machinery, and seed.[38]

The Rada bitterly resented the Eichhorn order, proclaiming that the German troops had been invited to assist the reestablishment of order, but within the limits indicated by the government of the Ukrainian People's Republic. Arbitrary interference in the social, political, and economic life of Ukraine, it continued, was completely unwarranted. Eichhorn contended that he was merely reinforcing the previous appeals of the Ministry of Agriculture.[39]

Increasing German interference in Ukrainian affairs placed an added strain upon German-Ukrainian relations. The Rada sought popular support by rescheduling the meeting of a Ukrainian Constituent Assembly, earlier postponed by the Bolshevik invasion, for June 12, but on April 28, the German military authorities dissolved the Central Rada. The next day a congress called by the Union of Landowners in Ukraine proclaimed General Pavlo Skoropads'kyi hetman of Ukraine. Ukrainian conservative elements welcomed the election of the hetman, hoping he would protect Ukraine against the invasion of the Bolsheviks and the Germans' interference in the country's internal affairs.

The Rada fell through a combination of its own inadequacies and unfavorable circumstances. The free general elections in 1917 proved that the Rada reflected the mood and aspirations of the Ukrainian people, but it had failed to translate this mood into a concrete program of administrative, social, and military reform not only because of lack of qualified personnel, both civil and military, but also because it lacked a clear plan and the determination to carry it out. The Rada's irresolution about agrarian reform gave the Bolsheviks a strong propaganda weapon in their promise of land for the peasants. It failed to establish close contact with the cities and its authority in the provinces was scarcely felt. The Rada failed to organize a defensive force capable of defending the independence of the country, thinking in terms of a militia rather than a regular army. It was too often involved in negotiations with the Provisional Government and in trivial ideological disputes among the parties and groups. Because of its broad interpretation of democracy, it did little to prevent the hostile activities of the Bolsheviks and of non-Ukrainian conservatives. Though the Bolsheviks fomented class war, the struggle remained basically a national one—Ukraine versus Russia—and it was not by chance that the Bolshevik occupiers of Kyiv were greeted by a Russian.[40]

The Hetman State

The ouster of the Rada and the establishment of the hetman state opened the second period of the national Revolution, a restoration of the old order. The head of the new government, Pavlo Skoropads'kyi (1873–1945), was a general in the Russian Army and a descendant of the brother of Ivan Skoropads'kyi (hetman from 1709 to 1722). He was trained in the tsar's Page Corps and began his military career as commander of a Cossack company during the Russo-Japanese War. In 1914 Skoropads'kyi went to war as a colonel of the Cavalry Guard and rose rapidly to the rank of major general, serving on most major fronts with Baron Peter N. Wrangel, who was his chief of staff. His sister-in-law was married to Field Marshal von Eichhorn.[41] Although Skoropads'kyi was raised in Ukraine on his parents' large estate[42] and was conscious of his nationality, his participation in the Ukrainian national movement dated only from July 18, 1917, with his Ukrainization of the 34th Army Corps (the First Ukrainian Army corps). This unit was to save the Rada from pro-Bolshevik troops at the end of October.[43] A month later, on the eve of the Bolshevik invasion, when the nation most needed him and his troops, Skoropads'kyi resigned under pressure from Rada circles, who suspected him of desiring to become military dictator. Their distrust was intensified by his election on October 1917 as honorary head (otaman) of the Free Cossacks, a spontaneous paramilitary movement organized in the summer of 1917 to suppress banditry.

On the day of the Rada's deposition, Skoropads'kyi, as hetman of all Ukraine, issued a manifesto (*Hramota*) that ordered the dissolution of the Rada and the land committees, and the dismissal of all ministers and their deputies. All other public servants were to remain at their posts. The right of private ownership was restored; all acts of the Rada and the Provisional Government regarding property rights were abrogated. The hetman promised to transfer land from the large estates to the needy peasants at its fair value, to safeguard the rights of the working class (railroad employees in particular), and to provide for election of a parliament.[44]

The proclamation of April 29 was widely resented, but brought no open resistance, mainly because of the presence of German and Austro-Hungarian troops. Some people accepted the new government, hoping it would maintain order and provide security from Austro-German interference and from the Bolsheviks. Among this group were hundreds of thousands of Russians, "the elite of the Russian bourgeoisie and intelligentsia, who had fled to Ukraine from Soviet Russia."[45] The refugees regarded Ukraine as a temporary haven and as a base for their struggle against the Bolsheviks to restore the empire. This idea was vividly expressed by a Russified duke, G. N. Leikhtenbergskii:

> I accepted "Ukraine" independent and sovereign, as a step, a point in which organizational and creative forces would be concentrated, from which at a certain moment the resurrection of Indivisible, Great Russia could begin.[46]

The Rada leaders decided to lead a resistance movement, with the principal arm of the struggle transferred to the All-Ukrainian Peasant Union and its partisan units. During the first two weeks of the hetman administration a number of congresses of oppositionists took place in Kyiv. On May 8–10, about twelve thousand delegates of the Second All-Ukrainian Peasants' Congress met illegally in the Holosiiv Forest near the city. On May 13–14, the Second All-Ukrainian Workers' Congress, which included Russian and Jewish delegates in addition to Ukrainians, convened, also illegally. Delegates of both congresses, as well as the UPSR and USDRP, whose congresses met at about the same time, adopted a series of similar resolutions advocating restoration of the Ukrainian People's Republic; convocation of the Ukrainian Constituent Assembly; transfer of land to the peasants without compensation to owners; guarantee of all liberties proclaimed by the Third and Fourth Universals; and formation of local armed groups for an uprising.[47]

At the outset, the hetman's policy was not radically different from the Rada's, although more moderate. He tried to draw his support from among the middle and smaller property owners, but was dependent on the German and Austrian authorities, who were increasingly influenced by the reactionary upper class.[48] Skoropads'kyi wanted a government composed of moderate liberals, and the first prime minister, Mykola Sakhno-Ustymovych, tried to form a Socialist-Federalist cabinet. These overtures to the party were refused more on psychological than ideological grounds. Ustymovych resigned and was temporarily replaced by Mykola Vasylenko, then by Fedir A. Lyzohub, whose cabinet included only one active Ukrainian leader, Dmytro Doroshenko, minister of foreign affairs; other cabinet members were involved in Ukrainian cultural life, but some were hostile to Ukrainian independence. The ministers were not without experience, though some lacked understanding of the social and national spirit of the time.

Similarly, the provincial and local administration was largely staffed by conservatives recruited from the various minorities and the Russian refugees, partly because some Ukrainians refused to join the hetman government and partly because there was a tragic shortage of Ukrainian professional people.[49] Thus the hetman government included a large number of former tsarist officals, from ministers to village police.

The ubiquitous Russian reactionary organizations, which were closely associated with the Volunteer Army and other Russian centers outside Ukraine, enjoyed complete freedom, including publishing newspapers in which they conducted an anti-Ukrainian campaign for restoration of the Russian Empire. There were three major Russian organizations operating in Ukraine, all with headquarters in Kyiv: the Council of State Unification, the Union for Resurrection of Russia, and the Kyiv National Center. The National Center was a sociopolitical organization of all non-Socialist political parties, including the group of Vasilii V. Shulgin, and were the most hostile to the hetman state.[50] Their program called for "struggle against Ukrainian independence, support of the Volunteer Army, informing the Entente 'about real conditions in Ukraine.'" Furthermore, the Center ceaselessly told the Entente that "there never was a Ukrainian state; the 'Ukrainians' are not a nation, merely a political party fostered by Austro-Germany."[51]

Although in these conditions a normal national development was difficult, the hetman made sincere efforts to promote Ukrainian culture. The new Ukrainian National University in Kyiv was converted into a state institution, while a new Ukrainian university in Kamianets-Podils'kyi, a historical and philological college in Poltava, and an academy of sciences in Kyiv were established. Chairs of Ukrainian history, law, language, and literature were founded in the various universities, and new secondary schools were founded or Ukrainized. A system of adult education was organized. A national gallery, a national museum, state archives, a central library, a Ukrainian state theater, and a dramatic school were established in Kyiv. A large fund was allotted for the publication of textbooks, and scholarships created for gifted students. The Ukrainian church was granted some autonomy, though limited by the opposition of the Russified hierarchy. Furthermore, owing to the cooperation of the upper class, the early stages of the hetman period were marked by financial stability and a balanced budget.[52]

The hetman government strove to pursue an independent foreign policy. It sought termination of the guardianship of the Central Powers, with a pledge of their assistance in joining to Ukraine her borderlands, Kholm, Bessarabia, the Crimea, and the Kuban; recognition from neutral states and possibly from the Entente; and a peace settlement that would delimit the border with Soviet Russia.

Austria-Hungary postponed indefinitely ratification of the Treaty of Brest-Litovsk because of the secret clause that provided for unification of Eastern Galicia and Northern Bukovina into a separate Ukrainian Crown Land. Additional strain was created when Austrian authorities refused to allow the Ukrainian commissioner to function in the Austrian sections of Kholm and Pidliashshia, which by the treaty were recognized as Ukrainian lands. Although Germany ratified the treaty, German officials made little attempt to understand Ukrainian problems. The Romanian occupation of Bessarabia in March after a secret agreement with Germany was protested by the hetman government and went unrecognized. The question of Crimea was complicated by the Germans, who sponsored a Russian Crimean territorial government, eventually to be reunified with Russia. The hetman considered this a potential threat to Ukrainian independence, and in June he addressed a note to the German representative in Kyiv urging inclusion of Crimea in Ukraine and placed an embargo on all goods entering Crimea except war material and supplies for the Central Powers. As a result, the Crimean government agreed to unite with Ukraine and was granted autonomy.[53]

The hetman sought a union of the Kuban with Ukraine and on May 28 a Kuban delegation came to Kyiv to discuss the union and liberation of the territory from the Bolsheviks. A plan to send a division

(15,000 men) under General Natiiv to drive out the Bolsheviks failed because the Germans hampered its implementation, and a ranking Russian official in the hetman War Ministry obstructed Natiiv's movements until Russian troops under General Mikhail V. Alekseev could capture Ekaterinodar in August. Although the Kuban was controlled by Denikin's Volunteer Army, consular representatives were exchanged and a treaty signed in mid-November. In view of the Soviet Russian threat to Ukraine, the hetman was interested in having friendly relations with the government of the Don region, but the achievement of this goal was complicated by territorial conflicts, and by the Russophile policy of the head of the Don government, General Peter N. Krasnov. Though it meant the loss of part of Ukrainian territory and population, the hetman came to terms with the Don government on August 8 in order to secure an ally and reduce the length of the Russian frontier.[54]

The hetman sought a modus vivendi with the Volunteer Army, and asked General Krasnov to mediate between him and Denikin. The hetman agreed to supply the army of the Don, the Volunteer Army, and the Kuban with arms, ammunition, and funds for use against the common enemy. However, Denikin, a proponent of "one, indivisible, Russia," desired the destruction of both bolshevism and Ukrainian independence and demanded a unified government and military command under his own leadership. The hetman complained:

> I don't understand Denikin. He is suppressing everything—it is impossible. . . . Return to the Empire and the establishment of Imperial authority is impossible now. Here in Ukraine, I had to choose—either independence, or Bolshevism, and I chose independence.[55]

Vital to the hetman's foreign policy were the peace negotiations with Soviet Russia and Lenin's government representatives signed an armistice in Kyiv on June 12 that included recognition of the Ukrainian state and an agreement to exchange consuls. However, the Bolsheviks, anticipating Germany's defeat in the west, did not sign the formal treaty, and at the beginning of November, negotiations were suspended. The abortive negotiations provided the Bolshevik delegates with a fruitful opportunity for propagandizing.[56]

The organization of Ukrainian armed forces was a most difficult problem. An earlier Rada plan for a regular volunteer army, to consist of eight corps of infantry and four and one-half divisions of cavalry, was ordered into effect by the hetman. The infrastructure for a sizable army, including a General Staff, was prepared; general conscription was decreed, but the army remained in embryo to the end of the hetman period. The German authorities and Russian military commanders assigned by the hetman government opposed a strong Ukrainian army as a threat to their positions. Also, most of the Rada's military units had been demobilized by the Germans, and the remaining units had most of the Ukrainian officers replaced largely by Russians. Though Ludendorff complained as early as June that "Ukraine has not yet been successful in building up its own army," only slight changes in Germany's attitude occurred when the hetman visited Emperor Wilhelm II on September 4.[57]

In July the Serdiuk Division, which performed for the hetman a role analogous to that of the Russian guard regiments, was formed from well-to-do peasant volunteers. In August a unit of Sich Riflemen was reinstated in Bila Tserkva.[58] The hetman also allowed the formation of a special corps of Russian officers in Ukraine and, later, Russian volunteer groups in the large cities, both as parts of the Ukrainian Army. Russian leaders, with government support, established bureaus to recruit Russian refugee officers for the Volunteer Army, the South Army, the Astrakhan Army, the Saratov Corps, and others.[59] The existence of these Russian formations substantially restricted national life.

The hetman, whose power was erected on a weak foundation, was buffeted by the currents of the Austro-German forces inherited from the Rada, the reactionaries in his government, who were merely tolerating the hetman state as long as circumstances made it necessary, and the revitalized nation with its social and political aspirations. Favoritism toward the upper class had disastrous consequences and governmental policy was marked by a number of reactionary decrees that turned the population, especially the peasants, against the regime. The press was subjected to strict censorship or altogether suppressed; congresses and meeting of parties and organizations were restricted or prohibited; zemstvo institutions and *Prosvita* associations were severely limited; many national leaders, peasants, and workers were arrested; strikes were banned, and the eight-hour day was abolished.

The regime's reactionary character was most clear in its appointment of local non-Ukrainian landowners as elders of the provincial and district administrations. In May, in an effort to restore agricultural normality, the government ordered restoration to the landowners of all property expropriated during the early stages of the Revolution. The landlords were authorized to use military force to defend or retake their property, to collect compensation for damages, and to introduce compulsory work programs for urgent agricultural projects at wages established by a governmental commission.[60]

As a result, many landowners undertook punitive expeditions, seizing the expropriated property, including livestock and implements, as well as demanding excessive damages. These expeditions were accompanied by looting, destruction of peasant property, and severe punishments, even executions. The punitive detachments, consisting of former Russian officers, adventurers, and criminals, operated in the name of the hetman government, to its discredit.[61]

Such activities, together with the stepped-up requisitioning of grain and other foodstuffs by the Germans and Austro-Hungarians, led first to passive resistance and sabotage, and then to local revolts. The landlords, appealing to the government and occupation authorities for help, had ready compliance.

Thus the punitive expeditions and peasant uprisings spread and intensified and in some districts neither the state police nor the German detachments were able to control the situation. Partisans attacked isolated military units and guard detachments at railway stations, bridges, and depots. The Germans introduced field courts to deal summarily with the population by issuing collective fines and shooting hostages, at times at the rate of ten Ukrainians for one German. German civil authorities in Ukraine protested to Berlin against the military command's brutality, urging that the interests and moods of the population be taken into consideration, but with little effect.[62]

The strongest and best organized peasants were in Zvenyhorodka district and the adjacent areas of Kaniv, Uman', and Tarashcha districts in Kyiv province, headed by Mykola Shynkar, former commander of the Kyiv Military District during the Rada period. According to one peasant leader, at the beginning of May there were eighteen separate battalions of peasants numbering about twenty thousand men. Although the government and the German authority in Kyiv were informed of the existence of the peasant organizations, they could not uncover them, and in retaliation punitive detachments brought terror in the villages. This, in turn, provoked major insurrections throughout Zvenyhorodka and Tarashcha districts that spread to other places.[63] On June 10, the German ambassador, Baron Mumm, informed the Foreign Office in Berlin:

> Conditions in Zvenyhorodka are more serious than has been officially stated. The peasants . . . have driven back German military units, and are temporarily holding them in check. Reinforcements have been sent to this region tonight and it is expected that they will reestablish order.[64]

According to the hetman's intelligence agent, A. Shkol'nyi, during the June insurrections the peasant battalions had grown to about thirty thousand, with two batteries of field artillery and two hundred machine guns, and new groups were joining each day.[65]

Although the peasants had initial success in seizing territory, they could not stand against regular troops, for they were unorganized, undisciplined, and inadequately armed. Some withdrew or dispersed, while the main body of the Tarashcha peasants, under Hrebenko, crossed into Russian territory. Following the suppression of the uprising, over ten thousand people, both peasants and those from the educated class, which had not participated, were arrested and sent to camps in Germany.[66]

Besides the Ukrainian resistance activities, Russian Communists, Socialist Revolutionaries, and other groups terrorized and sabotaged the occupation forces, the hetman regime, and the population. In midmorning on June 6, ten large munitions depots exploded in Zvirynets', a suburb of Kyiv, killing or wounding about seventeen hundred persons. The whole suburb was destroyed, and about ten thousand people lost their homes.[67] Eight days later, a big fire of undetermined origin swept over the Podol in Kyiv and on July 31, munitions stores on Dar'nytsia Street in Odessa erupted in a series of explosions that killed several hundred people.[68]

The terror culminated in the assassination of von Eichhorn and his adjutant, von Dressler, on July 30. The assassin, a twenty-four-year-old Russian Left Socialist Revolutionary sailor and two accomplices came into Ukraine at the end of May on orders from the party's Central Committee in Moscow. There was also an abortive attempt to murder the hetman at Eichhorn's funeral. The Eichhorn assassination paralleled the assassination by the same party of Count Wilhelm von Mirbach-Harff, the German ambassador to Moscow, on July 6.[69]

The anger of the population against the terror and pillage by the Soviet Russian troops during their brief occupation in February 1918 was so great that the population had welcomed not only Ukrainian, but German and Austrian troops, as liberators.[70] However, the Ukrainian policy of Eichhorn and Ludendorff aligned the people against the Germans and Austrians and, consequently, drove the peasants and workers into the arms of the Bolsheviks. The repressive policies of the hetman and his largely foreign entourage brought into existence self-defense forces—the partisan movement, which acted not only against his regime and its German-Austrian supporters, but subsequently, against the Bolshevik "Red" and anti-Bolshevik "White" Russian forces in Ukraine well into the 1920s.

2. The Partisan Movement

The formation and effective operation of partisan groups was possible because of the residue of military experience and weapons from the war. During the chaotic self-demobilization of the Russian Army,[1] soldiers often carried weapons home with them. The peasants expropriated weapons from the Germans at the end of 1918, and from the retreating Bolshevik and Denikin troops. The rapid changes of government and continual disorder prevented many people, especially returnees from the front, from settling down to peaceful work and almost every village became an arsenal of arms and experienced manpower for the partisan movement.[2] This situation was noted by a contemporary Western observer:

> The entire population is armed to the teeth with rifles, revolvers, and even armoured cars. There is no lack of ammunitions or of fortifications with trenches and barbed wire. As every male has served in the army, the quality of the armed force at the disposal of the villages is by no means despicable.[3]

The hetman government, by discharging from the army a large number of young and patriotic Ukrainian officers with combat experience, added to the opposition and created ready cadres of partisan leaders.[4]

The partisan movement had its roots as far back as spring 1917, during the Central Rada, when groups appeared to keep order in the areas through which the Russian troops from the front were crossing, but it did not develop fully until the hetman period. Local revolts occurred as early as May 1918 and subsequently the entire country became the scene of growing insurrections. The partisans enjoyed the sympathies of the local population, which helped them and provided a well-organized intelligence service that enabled them to strike their adversaries' most vulnerable spots: staff headquarters, ammunition stores, military stables, and lines of communication and transportation. They demoralized the enemy by ambushing smaller military units, committing individual acts of terror, and spreading false rumors. When confronting larger enemy forces, the partisans would call peasants from several villages, who came, both on foot and mounted, carrying sticks and scythes, their number having a frightening impact upon the enemy. The partisans used surprise and hit-and-run tactics. Usually they attacked either at times of poor visibility, in bad weather, in difficult terrain, or in villages. Their main weapons were machine guns and hand grenades.[5]

From the ideological, organizational, and strategic points of view, the partisan movement can be divided into three distinct chronological periods: the first, up to the summer of 1918, though its ideological characteristics carried over through spring 1919; the second, through the end of 1920; and the last, after 1920. During the first period nearly every village and district had an armed group organized by political or military adventurers. As a spontaneous movement, many of its leaders lacked both adequate education and national or ideological consciousness. Each local partisan leader acted independently, recognizing no authority and having no connection with the Ukrainian regular army. The rank and file consisted of a mixture of patriots and adventurers and both they and their leaders were easily misled by the enemy's propaganda.[6]

The second period was marked by a radical change, brought about by the exploitation and terrorism of the police and landlords, the Austro-German punitive expeditions, and by the invading "White" and "Red" Russian forces. In contrast to their previous invasions of 1918 and 1919, when they hardly touched the countryside, the Bolsheviks in 1920 organized special detachments to expropriate food, clothing, and arms from the peasants. In this period the number of partisans substantially increased and movement was better organized, with better leaders, many of whom were regular army officers. Consequently, the struggle was greatly intensified—from April to June 1919 there were 328 uprisings.[7] Thus instead of a "march on Europe," the Bolsheviks had to fight the people for Ukrainian grain.

Although at the end of 1920 the Ukrainian regular army was compelled to retreat, reorganize, and employ guerrilla warfare, the partisans, who now numbered 40,000, intensified their resistance to the Bolshevik occupation.[8]

It was during this third period that the first organized resistance with the ideological platform of the liberation movements was established. According to Soviet sources the peasants hated the Bolsheviks: "Killing Soviet agents, militia men, Red Army soldiers, making attacks upon the Soviet district authorities, railroad depots, destroying food requisition detachments . . . such was the everyday practice of the bandits."[9] The intensified partisan movement was largely in response to the Bolshevik terror and requisition policy in Ukraine. In 1920 the Bolshevik authorities requisitioned from the peasants 160 million poods of grain, over 6 million poods of meat, 30,000 poods of potatoes, 225 million poods of eggs, about 300,000 poods of fruit, and a large quantity of sugar. Moreover, the Red Army requisitioned separately from the civil authorities, collecting, for example, 25 million poods of grain at the end of 1920.[10]

The Ukrainian partisan movement suffered from deficiencies of leadership, logistics, and organization. Although the partisans, driven by the enemy's oppressive measures, improved their organization and consolidated local groups into districts, they remained isolated from one another and were never organized into a nationwide force under unified leadership. The Directory made no serious effort either to help the partisan leaders unite the entire movement under one leadership, or to coordinate actions between the army and the partisan groups. It underestimated the importance of the partisans' role in the struggle.[11] General Iurko Tiutiunyk observed: "Nobody, except the Red Russians, paid proper attention to the activities of Hryhor'iv, Zelenyi, Anhel, Sokolovs'kyi, and other partisan leaders."[12] Although the Directory appointed I. Malolitko (pseudonym, Satana) in July 1919 to coordinate the partisan groups, he was not known to the partisans nor did he come into contact with them. In September, the Directory appointed Omelian Volokh, one of the military leaders, to head the partisan movement, but after his appointment he played only a negative role. It also established at Kamianets' a Central Ukrainian Partisan Committee consisting of representatives of Socialist parties and organizations, but this body, designed to coordinate and unify partisan organizations, never undertook any serious activities.[13]

Although almost all the partisans strongly supported the principle of Ukraine's sovereignty and defended it against both the Whites and Reds, their political tactics too often diverged. They could have played a much more positive role in the struggle against the nation's enemies if the Directory had paid more attention to them and given them proper assistance.

The Bolsheviks, on the other hand, appreciated the power of the partisan movement and skillfully maneuvered it to their side, declaring that they were coming into Ukraine to fight a common enemy, the White Russians. Trotsky issued orders to the Red troops: "Ukraine is a country of Ukrainian workers and working peasants. Be aware that our aim is liberation, and not enslavement, of Ukraine."[14] At the same time, however, the Bolsheviks mercilessly combated the partisans behind their lines. On February 28, 1920, Trotsky issued a secret order concerning military policy in Ukraine:

> The liquidation of the professional Ukrainian partisan movement is not only a necessary precondition to the formation of effective [soviet] Ukrainian units, but a question of life and death for the Soviet Ukraine. Military units operating on Ukrainian territory are strictly forbidden to include partisan groups either within their ranks or as separate 'volunteers.' . . . All partisan units should be immediately disarmed, disbanded, and those resisting should be destroyed.[15]

Thus the Bolsheviks, after the liquidation of other fronts, were able to overpower the partisan groups.

Although Bolshevik influence in Ukraine had been greatly weakened by their brutality during the occupation in early 1918, they took advantage of popular resentment against both the hetman and the Austro-Germans to renew their propaganda among the population. Following withdrawal from Ukraine in March–April 1918, many Bolsheviks remained in the country, hiding in the forests, villages, and cities. This fifth-column movement carried on propaganda and later became the nucleus of the Bolshevik partisans, as indicated in the memoirs of one Communist:

> Following the instruction of the Central Revolutionary Committee, we created a military organization. In Kyiv itself two headquarters—one for the town and one for the guberniia [province]—were established. The town headquarters directed about a score of military groups formed from the workers. Instructors were sent from Moscow. These were well trained military men who had recently undergone a special course of instruction. . . . Later we gave up forming detachments of workers and decided to form mainly detachments of peasants.[16]

These activities were aided by the "peace delegation" of Khristian G. Rakovskii and its military expert, Colonel A. Egorov, in the Soviet consulate in Kyiv. The hetman government took preventive measures, but was held back by German authorities in Kyiv.[17]

The main base for the formation of the partisan groups was the "Neutral Zone"[18] used by the Bolsheviks as a staging area for partisan action in Ukraine. Numerous refugees, driven from Ukraine by German repression, gathered in the buffer strip, especially during the second half of 1918. These partisans and later arrivals were enlisted into the Bolshevik ranks. The largest group, of about three hundred to four hundred men, was the Tarashcha partisans who participated in major insurrections in the districts of Tarashcha, Zvenyhorodka, and Uman', Kyiv province, in June 1918. From these partisan refugees the Bolsheviks formed the so-called "Tarashcha Division" consisting of four infantry regiments and one artillery brigade. After the fall of the hetman government, about eight hundred of the partisans returned to Ukraine; however, the Bolsheviks retained the name Tarashcha Division to increase their appeal to the Ukrainian population.[19] The Neutral Zone also provided agitators and cadres for partisan groups and played a significant role in the Bolshevik war against Ukraine.

Besides the Ukrainian and Bolshevik partisans, there were partisans who, because of chaotic conditions and the power vacuum created by the Revolution and civil war, gained a degree of control over isolated areas and declared themselves independent. They fought everybody, foreign and native, who tried to invade their territory and interfere in their affairs. One such peasant partisan movement in southeastern Ukraine, under the leadership of the anarchist Nestor Makhno, played a significant role in the unification of the Huliai-Pole (Gul'aipole) region. Makhno understood the revolutionary spirit of the masses and was able to put it to effective use against his enemies. His effective struggle against various enemies would not have been possible without substantial support from the local peasants. The phenomenon can be understood only in terms of the socioeconomic problems in the region of the Makhno movement.

3. The Socioeconomic Background of Peasant Unrest in Makhno's Region

Partisan activity covered a wide area, bounded by the Don Basin in the east; a line running from Starobilsk to Kharkiv and Myrhorod in the north; a Myrhorod-Odessa line in the west; and the Black and Azov seas in the south. However, the Makhno movement was limited to Katerynoslav, Tavriia, and parts of Kherson, Kharkiv, and Poltava provinces. Katerynoslav province, the center of the movement, comprised a land area larger than the Netherlands. After its establishment in 1783, it formed, together with three districts of Kherson, and border strips of Tavriia and Kharkiv provinces, the Free Lands of the Zaporozhian Cossacks, whose republic, the Zaporozhian Sich, had been destroyed by Catherine II in 1775.[1] Although class differences existed during the last years of the Zaporozhian Sich, the officers among the Cossacks having accumulated considerable wealth, socioeconomic conditions were far more tolerable than in the rest of Ukraine. The Zaporozhian Cossacks opposed the reduction of the peasantry to serfdom and the farther a landlord's estate lay from Zaporozhia, the heavier were the burdens of the peasants working it. The heritage of the Sich's socioeconomic order remained strong in the thinking of subsequent generations, especially as serfdom in Ukraine did not develop as a result of social conditions, as it did in Russia, but was imposed. Retaining the memory of freedom, the population preserved the tradition of struggle to achieve it. Thus serfdom in southern Ukraine was not as widespread nor as exploitative as it was in the other parts of Ukraine. For example, in Katerynoslav province during the 1780s and 1790s, there were only about six thousand male serfs out of a total population that fluctuated between five hundred thousand and one million.[2] Even on the eve of emancipation the proportion of serfs in steppe Ukraine was lower than in most other Ukrainian provinces.

After 1775 the Cossacks who did not escape to Turkey or were not exiled by the Russian government remained as free peasants. However, after the Russo-Turkish Wars of 1769–91, Russia began to distribute Zaporozhian land, along with the new territories acquired in the war, to Russian and Ukrainian high officials, army officers, civil servants, and gentry. Fearing serfdom, many peasants fled, for the most part to the Don and Kuban basins. On May 3, 1783, the Russian government introduced serfdom. As the process of land distribution continued and serfdom penetrated deeper, the uprisings and flights of peasants in protest assumed large proportions. As early as 1799, the peasants of Katerynoslav province staged an armed uprising against the distribution of lands and subsequently escaped to the Don Basin. In 1811, a group of three hundred armed peasants from Katerynoslav district fled to Moldavia.[7] In 1815, the peasants of the village Voskresens'ke, in Pavlohrad district, refused to work for the landlord Ozerov.[3] In 1817, a group of six hundred peasants at Huliai-Pole rebelled against the landlords, refusing to work on their estates on the ground that "they were state peasants" (*Kazennogo vedomstva*) during the period of the governorship of General Khorvat and in 1795 had been unjustly transformed into serfs. Furthermore, they "began to argue that they were Cossacks."[4] Antipathy toward serfdom was constantly alive among the peasants.

After the Crimean War in 1856, thousands of peasants from Katerynoslav and Kherson provinces fled with their belongings to Crimea in search of freedom. They were encouraged by "ill-intentioned hatemongers of Russia" spreading rumors that the tsar was granting land and freedom in Crimea. There were serious clashes between the peasants and troops and many people were killed or wounded.[5]

As a result of the peasant emigration, the Cossacks' lands became more and more sparsely populated. The new landowners were able to induce many peasants, especially from Left Bank Ukraine, to settle on their lands by promising them freedom from all obligations for twenty or more years. Also the transfer of peasants by landlords who moved from northern Ukraine to the south played an important role in the process of colonization. In 1843, for example, 145,000 peasants were transferred from Poltava province to the south. Another large group of settlers consisted of foreigners who came, spontaneously at first, and later under the influence of a system of special grants and privileges, including complete religious tolerance, offered by the Russian government. Two manifestoes issued by the government on December 4, 1762, and on June 22, 1763, which were widely circulated in Europe by Russian agents, promised all foreigners most liberal terms and "the Monarchical favor." Consequently, large numbers of Armenians, Bulgarians, Georgians, Germans, Greeks, Italians, Jews, Moldavians, Russians, Serbs, and Wallachians settled in southern Ukraine. During the first phase of settlement the largest ethnic group, the Serbs, came from Austria as early as 1751 and later settled within the borders of the Sich directly under Russian administration. Old Believers of Russian origin, who came mainly from Right Bank Ukraine, Moldavia, Bessarabia, and Poland, were granted wide privileges, including exemption from military service.[6] They, the Armenians, and the Greeks were the only groups that settled and lived in close-knit communities. Although the colonists were their own masters, in the course of time many of them mixed with the local population. On the other hand, the colonists' freedom, religion, ideas, and traditions of previous struggle for national liberation had greatly affected the local Ukrainian population.

The largest and most successful groups of settlers were the German religious sects, the Hutterites and Mennonites. The Hutterites came from Austria via Transylvania (1755) and Wallachia (1767) and settled in Chernyhiv province in 1772. In 1842, they moved south where they established several villages. The Hutterites received extensive privileges, including religious toleration, exemption from military service, and financial aid. As they began to lose their privileges they decided to move to the United States and settled in the Dakotas in 1874.[7]

The settlement of the Mennonites on the Cossacks' land was more successful and lasting. In 1789, 228 families came from East Prussia and settled on the Khortytsia, a tributary of the Dnieper. In 1797, 118 more families in the colony grouped into eighteen villages. The continuing immigration was so successful that by 1845 there were 100,000 Mennonites settled in Katerynoslav, Kherson, and Tavriia provinces.[8] By that time, the government had practically ceased to offer its earlier generous inducements to prospective colonists, but immigration continued throughout the nineteenth century.

The early Mennonites received most generous grants and privileges. Transportation and construction of their villages were financed by the government; each family was granted sixty-five dessiatines (or little more than 175 acres) of the best black soil land and a loan of five hundred rubles ($250.00), and other necessary economic support. Also each village was granted a large free pasture and forest for its use. Moreover, each family was granted, like the nobility, monopoly of distilleries and breweries. As conscientious objectors, Mennonites were exempted from military duties; they were also exempt from taxation for thirty years.[9] Finally, the colony was granted self-government, including the rights to establish its own churches, schools, and other cultural, economic, and political organizations in which only the German language was used. These privileges and grants to the German colonists were all the more extraordinary in that they were given simultaneously with the destruction of Ukrainian political autonomy and the introduction of serfdom in Left Bank Ukraine by the Russian government.

The settlement of southern Ukraine changed the agricultural patterns and economic conditions of the peasants. In the middle of the nineteenth century, the raising of sheep for wool was supplanted by the cultivation of grain; by the end of the century metallurgical and coal industries augmented the economy.[10] Transportation expanded, facilitating grain export and the development of heavy industry. The growing labor force, coupled with the turn toward industry, further heightened Ukrainian rejection of serfdom. Tsar Alexander II's Manifesto of February 19, 1861, abolishing serfdom, was not successful in its goal of providing land of their own to peasants, for little land left the landlord's hands, and that turned over to peasants in Katerynoslav province, for example, was given for community landholding, often at an inflated price.[11]

Nor did all peasants receive land—household servants and serfs of small landowners were emancipated without it. Further, liberation was incomplete: ex-serfs were under state supervision, could not leave their villages without permission, and could not send their children to secondary schools.[12]

The peasants hardly understood the allotment and compensation provisions and found it difficult to believe that they had received freedom without free use of the land, pasture, and forest resources. During the first decade of the postreform period there were eighty-eight uprisings involving 188 villages in Katerynoslav.[13] Since the income of many peasants from their allotments was not enough to make the payments, desertion was frequent, although those who remained were then additionally burdened by the requirement for collective redemption.

Gradually, the situation of the peasants deteriorated as per capita land allotments diminished with the increase of population. Thus, between 1880 and 1900, the average allotment decreased from 3.6 to 2.3 dessiatines. In addition, the peasantry began to be differentiated into the rich, the middle, and the village proletariat. New holdings gained either from landlords or other peasants went largely to those who were already relatively better off. As the size of land allotments decreased, the peasants tried to solve the problem by renting land and pastures from the landlords. The owners, however, were often reluctant, judging that the poorer the peasants were, the cheaper would be the labor force. From 1881 to 1900 there were uprisings in more than forty villages in Katerynoslav, frightening both the regime and the landowners.[14]

The Marshal of the Nobility of Katerynoslav province, on September 20, 1883, reported to Minister of Interior D. A. Tolstoi that panic existed among the nobility of the province, because of the peasant disturbances in Novomoskovs'k district.

> The peasants firmly declared that they would take the land they considered theirs away from the landlords. They reasoned that even if the land was appropriated to the landlords in the past, this was unjust because it [the land] was acquired by the blood of their parents and their peasant ancestors.[15]

The marshal tried to convince the minister that the peasant uprisings might spread to other provinces or even to the entire empire.

Toward the end of the century the peasant mass movement against the landlords intensified and several radical groups were drawn together to form the Socialist Revolutionary party, which subsequently tried to divert the peasants' revolutionary energy from economics to politics. The peasants' dissatisfaction with the emancipation land settlement erupted in the spring of 1902, mainly in the provinces of Kharkiv and Poltava. More than 160 villages were involved in the disturbances and some eighty estates were attacked within a few days. Only military force was able to put down these uprisings.[16]

The peasant uprisings of 1902 recurred in 1905 in the aftermath of the unsuccessful Russo-Japanese War. During the spring, disturbances took place in two districts of Katerynoslav province; in the summer, in four; and in the fall, in all eight districts. There were strikes and demonstrations in the city of Katerynoslav that led to clashes with the police. Although the Revolution of 1905 was a failure, it did induce the government to make some concessions, the most important of which, in its effect on the peasants, was a series of land reforms introduced by Prime Minister Peter A. Stolypin with the decree of November 9, 1906; the law of June 14, 1910; and the Land Settlement Act of May 29, 1911. The aim was to abolish communal tenure, enclose scattered strips into compact holdings, and establish the peasants as individual farmers, owners of their allotments. Stolypin's measures were dictated by far-reaching political aims and economic reasons; they were designed to favor a landed middle class that by its nature would be conservative, and on which the regime could rely. Because these reforms coincided to a considerable extent with traditional Ukrainian peasant land usage, the wealthier peasants gladly accepted them and began to consolidate their lands into single units, providing for a more rational farm economy. In Katerynoslav province in 1905, there were 270,000 peasant landholdings, and during the period from 1907 to 1914 over 142,000 peasants left the village communes.[17] The Stolypin reforms, however, gave no relief to the poorer peasants because their lack of farm implements compelled them to sell their land. Judging from Stolypin's statement in the Third Duma that "the government had placed its wager not on the needy but on the strong—the sturdy individual proprietor," he had no intention of doing otherwise. This statement was interpreted by his critics as evidence of the determination to sacrifice the interests of the poorer peasants to those of a well-to-do minority. Stolypin's land reform, however, cannot be evaluated because it would have required a score of years to produce lasting results. In Ukraine the acuteness of the agrarian problem had not subsided by 1917, but had grown even worse, becoming a major issue during the Revolution.

4. The Peasants and the Ukrainian Government

Under the tsarist regime in the prerevolutionary period, Ukrainian leaders lacked governmental sanction, nor did subsequent circumstances enable them to face the problems of the peasantry to attempt land reform. Consequently, it was difficult to find the wise, determined leadership that the critical conditions during the Revolution demanded. Of the the three major political parties, the Ukrainian Social Democratic Labor party had the most intellectual and experienced leaders; however, it was unprepared to face the agrarian problems that the Revolution had exacerbated and had no ready program for land reform. The smaller Ukrainian party of Socialists-Federalists, although it had well-qualified cadres of intellectuals, had no clearly defined land program either, until the beginning of the hetman period, in the late spring of 1918. The third and largest party, the Ukrainian party of Socialist Revolutionaries, whose members were brought under the influence of Russian Socialist Revolutionary ideology, was more influential among the peasants than the others because it called for more radical reform.[1] However, even this party had no clearly defined land program. One of its leaders wrote:

> On the agricultural question the Congress, [which met on April 17–18, 1917] . . . stood, in its majority, on the point of view that under the conditions of Ukrainian economic reality it is difficult to carry out desired land reform, namely socialization of the land, and that the party . . . will insist on transferring all state, crown, and private land in Ukraine into a Ukrainian Land Fund, from which the land should be redistributed (for utilization) through public organizations

among peasants. The question of compensation for the owners . . . was blurred by a vague phrase that the "expenses of carrying out the land reform must be debited to the account of the state."[2]

On the peasant question, the Central Rada reflected, in general, the attitude of its parties. In the spring and summer of 1917, the Rada had to devote most of its attention to political problems. In the fall, the Rada, under the combined pressure of the peasants' national and local congresses and the propaganda of the Bolsheviks, who were trying to undermine the Rada's position by alienating the peasants from it, turned its attention to socioeconomic problems. The Third Universal of November 20, 1917, abolished the right of private ownership of land:

> . . . within the territories of the Ukrainian People's Republic all existing rights of ownership in land belonging to [landowners] . . . as well as udal, monastery, cabinet, and church lands, are abolished. . . . the land is the property of the whole working people. . . . the Ukrainian Central Rada . . . instructs the General Secretariat of Agriculture to work out immediately a law for the administration of these lands by land committees. . . .[3]

The delayed land law was finally passed hurriedly at the end of January 1918,[4] under the threat of chaotic and arbitrary distribution of landlords' land and tools, as had occurred in some areas, and, above all, in the face of the Bolshevik invasion. On January 22, 1918, the Rada proclaimed in its Fourth Universal:

> The commission for the settlement of the land question . . . has already worked out a law for the transfer of lands . . . without compensation; this law is based on the principle of the abolition of the right of ownership and of socialization of land. . . . every effort will be made to enable the committees to transfer the land to the toiling peasants before spring work begins.[5]

The belated socioeconomic reforms merely added fuel to the Bolshevik propaganda fire and weakened the ties between the Rada and the active revolutionary elements of the peasants, workers, and soldiers, turning some to indifference and even hostility toward the Rada.

The Bolshevik invasion, interference in Ukrainian affairs, and the fall of the Rada prevented the plan from being carried out. On the day of the establishment of the hetman state, the hetman dissolved all the land committees and annulled the land law:

> The right of private property, which is the basis of civilization and culture, is hereby fully restored. All [previous] ordinances . . . insofar as they infringed upon the right of private property, are declared null and void. Complete freedom to buy and sell land is also reestablished. Measures will be taken toward the alienation

of lands of large landowners at their actual cost and toward their distribution among needy peasants.[6]

On June 14, a provisional law was issued, permitting free sale and purchase of land to a maximum of twenty-five dessiatines per person. On August 23, a State Land Bank was opened to help finance the distribution of parts of the large landed estates. These laws reestablished the right of the landowners to their land and made it possible to receive payment for the property from the state treasury. The hetman's agricultural policy, like Stolypin's, was designed to create a large number of small and relatively prosperous landholding peasants who would provide a stable social basis for the political order. Although it promised a new and just land reform, the commission selected to draft the land law sabotaged it by not appearing until November, on the eve of the fall of the government.[7] The land reform, if carried out, might have satisfied a large portion of the peasants, but instead the hetman's government faced violent peasant insurrections, which played an important role in bringing about its downfall.

The new government, the Directory of the Ukrainian People's Republic, prepared a land reform based, with certain changes, upon the law of the Rada. On January 8, 1919, the land law was approved by the Directory and subsequently by the Congress of Toilers. It provided for nationalization of the land with all small-scale landholdings up to fifteen dessiatines remaining the property of their former owners. The larger estates, including church, monastery, and state lands, were transferred to the land fund to be distributed largely among the poor and landless peasants, at not less than five and no more than fifteen dessiatines each, for permanent use. A subsequent law of January 18, 1919, provided two additional dessiatines for those who would enlist in the Republican Army. In general, the land law was received favorably by the parties and the peasants, but its implementation was possible only in a limited area because of the Bolshevik invasion in December 1918. The main objective, the occupation of the Left Bank, was accomplished by means of revolts in the Ukrainian rear combined with frontal attacks.[8]

The Central Rada and the Directory failed to solve the agricultural problem; the hetman government did worse. It was constantly a step behind the revolutionary spirit of the peasants. Its policy was to carry out the land reform legally for approval by a future Constituent Assembly. For this reason it was not able to compete with the Bolsheviks, who were promising the land to the peasants immediately, or even with

Makhno, who was giving the land to the peasants as soon as it was captured. For the peasants, the land was a primary question and those forces that would not interfere in the division of land would get their support. In Left Bank Ukraine, in particular, where the Bolshevik invasions occurred and the subsequent Russian Civil War raged, the Ukrainian government did not have sufficient time for a normal agrarian reform. In a revolutionary period, radical peasant attitudes demanded swift and decisive action. Moreover, in Katerynoslav and Kherson provinces the Cossack traditions of independent military communities and freedom both from landlords and governmental bureaucracy survived more than in any other part of Ukraine.[9]

Although Huliai-Pole was established at the end of the eighteenth century, after the destruction of the Zaporozhian Sich, the Cossack traditions there were strong. During the Revolution Huliai-Pole was still divided into seven territorial areas, called *sotnia*[10] (hundred), which in Cossack times meant a military unit, a company, including a territorial administration. The spirit of the Cossack tradition[11] is evident in the reaction of the people in Huliai-Pole, as described by Makhno, against the temporary Bolshevik authority at Oleksandrivs'k (Alexandrovsk), who seized the textiles they had exchanged for flour with the workers in Moscow:

> This was a gathering of a real Zaporozhian Sich, this, of which we are reading only now. . . . They met to decide a problem, not of "religion" and "the church"—no, they met to decide a question of abuse of their rights by a bunch of hired governmental agents; they met quite impressively.[12]

The attitude of the peasants toward the Makhno movement might be described as ambivalent. It reflected the circumstances in which they lived and the degree and nature of their contact with him. To illustrate, the railroads were the main means of transportation for Austro-German troops in Ukraine. Hence the trains were the main target of the Makhno partisans who were seeking arms. Along the Synelnikove-Oleksandrivs'k (Sinel'nikovo-Alexandrovsk) railroad line, Makhno encountered troop trains, attacked, and forced the Germans to abandon large amounts of arms, goods, and food expropriated from the people in Ukraine. Makhno took the arms and munitions and distributed all other materials among the peasants, especially the poor.[13] It would not be difficult to guess the feelings of these peasants about Makhno. In the village of Volodymyrivka, near Huliai-Pole, a group of partisans attacked a sleeping Hungarian unit and killed eighty men. Subsequently an Austrian punitive expedition executed forty-nine innocent peasants and set the whole village on fire. A few days later a Galician Ukrainian officer of the Austrian Army, who participated in the punitive expedition, came to Huliai-Pole to obtain fodder for horses. While discussing the incident with some of the peasants, one of them stated: "Oh, he should die, this Makhno, so much trouble and misfortune he has brought us, but he also is defending us from plunderers, Bolsheviks and all the other rascals!"[14]

The Cossack tradition of social and political freedom survived in the memory of the people in the region of the Makhno movement more than in other parts of the country and helped to shape their thinking. For the peasants the questions of landownership and human rights were a predominant concern and no regime had solved them satisfactorily. Years of struggle for land and freedom had left a strong mark on popular consciousness. Although the region was rich in military potential, with strong historic traditions that could have served the national cause, it was nationally and politically undeveloped,[15] with not enough military and political leaders who could inspire, organize, and lead the peasants against the country's enemies. The leadership therefore devolved on partisan leaders such as Makhno, Hryhor'iv, and others who fought only for their own limited purposes and thus contributed to the fall of the independent Ukrainian state.

5. The Anarchism of the Peasants and Makhno

In spite of peasant following and the existence of anarchist groups in Ukraine, especially in the south, it would be a mistake to assume that the peasants in the region of the Makhno movement were anarchists; in reality, they knew and cared very little about anarchism or Marxism. They instinctively maintained their deep love of liberty and of land, for serfdom came later than in Russia or in Poland and the old ideals of individual freedom and human pride had not been eradicated.[1] Although some of the anarchist principles were quite compatible with traditional peasant aspirations, the basic desire of the Ukrainian peasants was not the creation of an anarchist utopia but the expulsion of all the foreign invaders who exploited them and disrupted their way of life. Emma Goldman and Alexander Berkman, the Russian-American anarchists, were told while in Kyiv during the summer of 1920 by American anarchists living there:

> In Ukraine . . . the situation differed from that of Russia, because the peasants lived in comparatively better material conditions. They had also retained greater independence and more of a rebellious spirit. For these reasons the Bolsheviks had failed to subdue the south.[2]

Goldman was also told that "the Ukrainian peasants, a more independent and spirited race than their northern brothers, had come to hate all governments and every measure which threatened their land and freedom." Goldman's friends considered that the Ukrainian peasant partisan movement was "a spontaneous, elemental movement, the peasants' opposition to all governments being the result not of theories but of bitter experience and of instinctive love of liberty. [However] they were fertile ground for Anarchist ideas."[3] Based on their experiences, the Ukrainian peasants, who had little acquaintance with political theorists, would have agreed with Bakunin's idea that every form of the state is an evil that must be combated.

Ukrainian peasants had little reason to expect any good from the state. For decades the Russian regime gave the peasants only national and sociopolitical oppression, including conscription for military service, taxation, and ruthless enforcement of order. Experiences with the "Reds," "Whites," Germans, and Austro-Hungarians had taught them that all governments were essentially alike—taking everything and giving nothing. Therefore, the peasants were more apt to revolt than to create or support a national government. They felt the Revolution gave them the right to secure the land and to live peacefully on it. Unable to see any necessity to substitute another regime for the fallen tsarist one, they wanted to be left alone to arrange their lives and affairs. Moreover, the political and national consciousness of the peasants was weak and the Ukrainian government, as has been shown, had neither time nor opportunity to strengthen it.

What was true of the peasants holds also for the partisan groups, composed as they were primarily of peasants. The third anarchist conference of "Nabat" in Kharkiv at the beginning of September, 1920, concluded:

> As regards the "Revolutionary Partisan Army of Ukraine (Makhnovites)" . . . it is a mistake to call it anarchist. . . . Mostly they are Red soldiers who fell into captivity, and middle peasant partisan volunteers. . . . Through two years of struggle against different regimes . . . there was created in the center of the army a nucleus that assimilated the slogans of nongovernment and free Soviet order.[4]

According to Goldman's American anarchist friends in Kyiv:

> There was considerable difference of opinion, however, among the anarchists concerning the significance of the Makhno movement. Some regarded it as expression of anarchism and believed that the anarchists should devote all their energies to it. Others held that the *povstantsi* represented the native rebellious spirit of the southern peasants, but that their movement was not anarchism, though anarchistically tinged. . . . Several of our friends took an entirely different position, denying to the Makhno movement any anarchistic meaning whatever.[5]

Makhno tried to strengthen his movement ideologically by inviting anarchists to his camp. Goldman was told that "Makhno had repeatedly called upon the Anarchists of the Ukraina and of Russia to aid him. He offered them the widest opportunity for propagandistic and educational work, supplied them with printing outfits and meeting places, and gave them the fullest liberty of action." Makhno wanted to enlist more anarchists for educational purposes among the partisans and peasants since he and his associates were insufficiently trained in propaganda. Goldman was informed that Makhno often said: "I am a military man and I have no time for educational work. But you who are writers and speakers, you can do that work. Join me and together we shall be able to prepare the field for a real Anarchist experiment."[6] However, there were not many who wanted to join Makhno because the anarchists in Ukraine

> . . . did not idealize the Makhno movement. They knew that the *povstantsi* were not conscious Anarchists. Their paper *Nabat* had repeatedly emphasized this fact. [However] the Anarchists could not overlook the importance of popular movement which was instinctively rebellious, anarchistically inclined, and successful in driving back the enemies of the Revolution, which the better organized and equipped Bolshevik army could not accomplish. For this reason many Anarchists considered it their duty to work with Makhno. But the bulk remained away.[7]

Also, according to Volin, one of the reasons the anarchists were reluctant to join Makhno was their "distrust for an 'unorganized' and impure anarchism."[8]

Makhno was aware of the social nature of the revolution whose instrument he felt he was and his close familiarity with the needs of the peasants enabled him to exploit the affinities between their goals and his own. Makhno's attitude concerning the state was in close harmony with the mood of his partisans, who from personal experience were inclined to regard the state as an unmitigated evil. Profound hatred and distrust of political parties and of the state as an organ of power characterize all Makhno's actions and public proclamations. For example, as soon as the Makhno forces entered a city or town they immediately posted on the walls notices to the population such as:

> This army does not serve any political party, any power, any dictatorship. On the contrary, it seeks to free the region of all political power, of all dictatorship. It strives to protect the freedom of action, the free life of the workers against all exploitation and domination. The Makhno Army does not therefore represent any authority. It will not subject anyone to any obligation whatsoever. Its role is confined to defending the freedom of the workers. The freedom of the peasants and the workers belongs to themselves, and should not suffer any restriction.[9]

This philosophy appealed to peasants who had acquired their land from big proprietors and wanted to retain possession. They believed as strongly that land was intended by God for their use as the tsar believed in divine right. According to the resolution on the land question adopted by the congress of the Huliai-Pole area of the Makhno movement on February 12, 1919, "The land belongs to nobody and it can be used only by those who cared about it, who cultivated it. The land should be transferred to the working peasantry of Ukraine for their use without compensation."[10]

Makhno was not only against landlords, but he contested the power of all invaders into the territory of his movement and thereby offered the peasants freedom from both landlords and bureaucrats. He vividly expressed this attitude after his return from Russia in the summer of 1918:

> I returned again to you [comrades] so we might work together to expel the Austro-German counterrevolutionary armies from Ukraine, to overthrow the government of Hetman Skoropads'kyi and to prevent any other regime from replacing him. We will work in common to organize this great thing. We will work in common to destroy slavery so we may set ourselves and our brothers and sisters on the road of the new order.[11]

Makhno's attitude stemmed primarily from his anarchist convictions. On another occasion, he said:

> During its long history under the yoke, the Ukrainian peasantry, not exploiting other's work, unyielding to outside pressure, preserved in itself the spirit of freedom. Everywhere, this spirit of practical revolution of workers and peasants broke through the walls of reaction and found space in the spontaneous impulses of revolution to gain as much freedom as possible for its development. Therein is openly revealed the peasantry's kinship with the ideas of anarchism.[12]

Although Makhno was adequately trained to understand the basic ideology of anarchism, he made no real attempt to put the anarchist ideal of a free, nongovernmental society into practice. His partisans and the peasants understood the slogan "free anarcho-communes" to mean free individual farms, and decentralized democratic self-government. This was a spontaneous manifestation of the Ukrainian peasants' anarchism.[13] Makhno saw anarchism in the context of the peasants' struggle for freedom, for to him anarchism and freedom from social oppression were one and the same.

The group to which Makhno adhered, the Anarchist-Communists, was established in Huliai-Pole in 1905,[14] and it was in contact with the anarchists of Katerynoslav via Valdemar Antoni,[15] who was responsible for establishing the Huliai-Pole group. It was supported primarily by local peasants, and employed both expropriation and terror against the local bourgeoisie, government institutions, and police. In such an environment Makhno had no opportunity to acquire much theoretical knowledge of anarchism. He recalled:

> Our group had in its ranks not a single educated theoretician of anarchism. We all were peasants and workers. We came from school with incomplete education. Anarchist schools did not exist. The bulk of our knowledge of revolutionary anarchism came from long years of reading anarchist literature and the exchange of opinions among us and the peasants with whom we exchanged all we read and understood in the works of Kropotkin [and] Bakunin. For all these we are obliged to com[rade] Valdemar Antoni (he was Zarathustra).[16]

Although Makhno later improved on his knowledge of anarchism through his reading in prison and talking with anarchist prisoners, especially Peter Arshinov,[17] the situation in Huliai-Pole worsened in comparison with the prerevolutionary years, because many anarchists were arrested or executed. In this respect Katerynoslav, even after the Revolution, was not much better. According to Makhno:

> C[omrade] Mironov and I came to the Federation of Anarchists to get from its ranks a few brave propagandists and call them from the city into the village; however, although the Federation had improved in comparison with the month of August, when I . . . visited its organization—club and so on—still its manpower was small. It barely served the city and its satellites Amur, Nyshn'odniprovs'k, and Kodak.[18]

Although some anarchists and nonanarchists credited Makhno with being a theoretician, he was not of much account as an anarchist theorist, though he was imbued with anarchist ideas.[19] To him anarchism was not a doctrine, but a way of life; he strove toward anarchism "not from idea to life, but from life to idea."[20] I. Teper, one of Makhno's former followers, quoted Makhno: "I am a revolutionary first and an anarchist second."[21]

Before the Revolution there were various anarchist groups in Ukraine, such as Anarchist-Communists, Anarcho-Syndicalists, and Anarchist-Individualists, whose ideological differences were not clearly defined. They all retained the elements of Proudhon's theory—particularly his federalism and emphasis on workers' associations. While all three groups drew their adherents mainly from the intelligentsia and the working class, the Anarchist-Communists made efforts to enlist soldiers and peasants into their ranks. Although they might appear as an offshoot of international anarchism imported via Russia, these groups were in reality a typical Ukrainian phenomenon.[22]

The Anarchist-Communists drew their inspiration from Bakunin and Kropotkin. The term *anarchism-communism* was coined by the latter who advocated its use at an international anarchist congress in Switzerland in October 1880. Kropotkin believed that it conveyed the idea of harmony between individual freedom and a "well-ordered" social life. Anarchism-communism viewed the individual as a social being who could achieve full development only in society, while society could profit only when its members were free. Individual and social interests were not contradictory but complementary and would attain natural harmony if the state did not interfere. The Anarchist-Communists envisioned a free federation of communities in which each member would be rewarded according to his needs.[23]

The Anarcho-Syndicalist doctrine was a blend of anarchism, Marxism, and trade unionism. The Anarcho-Syndicalists believed that trade unions or syndicates could serve both as an organ of struggle to ameliorate the conditions of the workers and as a foundation on which the future free society might be constructed. In their opinion social change could be achieved through economic or industrial action. The Anarcho-Syndicalists were strongly against a centralized state; indeed, they intended to abolish the state and to run society through syndicates associated with industries and localities. The state might be overthrown by acts of sabotage, boycotts, and local strikes, but the supreme instrument for overthrowing the state was the general strike. The Anarcho-Syndicalists' economic principles were sometimes accepted by Anarchist-Communists. Hence small-town anarchists often made no clear-cut distinction between the postulates of anarchism-communism and anarcho-syndicalism.[24]

The Anarchist-Individualists believed in absolute freedom of the individual, who had the right to do whatever he wanted. Everything that would curtail his freedom was opposed. The Anarchist-Individualists were against the state and sought its abolition; they were against all of the values of bourgeois society—political, moral, and cultural. They wanted the total liberation of the human personality from the fetters of organized society. Moreover, they rejected both the territorial communes of the Anarchist-Communists and the workers' trade unions of the Anarcho-Syndicalists because they believed that only unorganized individuals were safe from coercion and domination and thus capable of remaining true to the ideals of anarchism.[25]

These anarchist groups in Ukraine were weak and without prominent leaders, but Bolshevik persecution of anarchists in Soviet Russia served to strengthen anarchist groups in Ukraine. The reason for their persecution was, according to the statement of Feliks E. Dzierzynski, supreme head of the Russian Cheka, to a correspondent of *Izvestiia*:

> Among them were distinctly counterrevolutionary characters. We had definite evidence that the leaders of counterrevolution wanted to use criminal elements centered around the Federation groups to rise against the Soviet authority. . . . [However] the blow inflicted by the Soviet authority against the anarchists on April 12, 1918, in Moscow was of great importance in strengthening the achievements of the October and the Soviet authority. In the heart of the young Soviet republic were liquidated rotten centers of treason and counterrevolution. "Simultaneously with disarmament of the anarchists, crime in Moscow decreased 80 percent," while counterrevolution lost a number of strongholds upon which it reckoned.[26]

In Moscow on April 12, 1918, according to Dzierzynski, "during four hours all anarchists disappeared, everything was expropriated."[27] In Petrograd, on April 23, the Cheka disarmed anarchists in all clubs and apartments. In other cities the anarchists either resisted the Cheka, or simply capitulated. According to *Izvestiia*, on April 26, 1918: "Under the flag of 'ideological' anarchism in the [metropolitan] centers and in the provinces different dark characters and robbers continued to rise, creating panic and terrorizing the population."[28] By May all anarchist groups in Soviet Russia were disarmed or destroyed. According to the Bolshevik authorities, "The experience in Moscow, Petrograd and other cities proved that under the flag of the anarchist organizations were hooligans, thieves, robbers, and counterrevolutionaries, secretly preparing to overthrow the Soviet Government."[29]

In the light of this situation in Soviet Russia, the Russian and Jewish anarchists began to escape to Ukraine where they enjoyed more freedom than in Russia. Among prominent anarchists who participated in anarchist activities and joined the Makhno movement were Volin (Boris M. Eichenbaum), Peter A. Arshinov (Marin), Aaron Baron and his wife Fania, IAkov Sukhovolskii (called Alyi), and Aronchik. Besides them, a number of lesser known anarchists from Soviet Russia came to Ukraine either individually or in groups. For example, in May 1919, a group of thirty-six anarchists from Ivanovo-Voznesenske, near Moscow, arrived at Huliai-Pole and joined either village communes, combat detachments, or propaganda sections. A few of them became prominent in the Makhno movement.[30] Among them were Makeev, Aleksandr Cherniakov, Petr Rybin (called Zonov), Viktor Popov, Mikhalev-

Pavlenko, and IAkovlev (Kohan, called IAsha). Subsequently refugees from Russia linked up with the anarchists in Ukraine to unite the various anarchist groups, including Anarchist-Communists, Anarchist-Individualists, and Anarcho-Syndicalists, into one movement.

From November 12 to 16, 1918, at the First Conference in Kursk, all of those groups organized a Confederation of Anarchist Organizations of Ukraine named Nabat (Alarm), with a six-man Secretariat. Kharkiv was chosen as the headquarters, but there were branches in other major Ukrainian cities, including Kyiv, Odessa, and Katerynoslav. The conference dealt with world-wide, Russian, and Ukrainian conditions, participation in the partisan movement, and above all, the unity of all anarchist groups.[31] It considered the Russian Revolution as the first stage of a world-wide revolution that would be followed by revolution in Central Europe, including German, Austro-Hungary, and Bulgaria. The future revolution in West Europe, including France, Great Britain, and Spain, would be the third and last stage of the European revolution and would presage a world-wide revolution that would then develop along social and anarchist lines.

The conference recognized that because of "totally exceptional circumstances" a new, second revolution was developing with the Ukrainian partisans that was a favorable base for the social and anarchist revolution, and hence the necessity for wide, active participation on all levels by anarchists in the partisan and the general revolutionary movement in Ukraine.

The final organization of the Nabat was accomplished at its First Congress, at IElysavethrad on April 2–7, 1919. In the light of the positive anarchist role in the development of the Revolution, the congress called upon anarchists of Ukraine, Russia, and abroad to form a "united anarchism" while guaranteeing a substantial measure of autonomy for every participating group and individual. As the Kursk conference had done before, the congress resolved that the anarchists should ignore the Bolshevik regime and, if necessary, carry armed struggle against it, while disavowing those anarchists who supported the regime. They decided to boycott the Red Army, denouncing it as an authoritarian organization and called on the anarchists to carry on a propaganda campaign among its soldiers. But the most pressing task of the anarchists was to shape the Revolution into a social and anarchist revolution and to defend it. The congress pinned its hope for such a change on a partisan army organized spontaneously by the revolutionary masses themselves, undoubtedly considering the army of Makhno to be such a "partisan army."[32] In late spring of 1919, after the IElysavethrad congress, a few of the members of the Nabat's Secretariat, including Volin and Baron, came to Makhno proposing an organizational scheme. The Secretariat would join the Revolutionary Military Council and head the cultural section of the partisan army to conduct political and ideological propaganda. The partisan army, instead of moving from one area to another, should try to establish a territorial base, and Makhno was to make efforts to unify all partisan groups in the region, making his army a formidable force that would be able to defend its territorial base. Thus would begin the anarchist third revolution that would lead to the establishment of a classless society. Some of the anarchists from the Nabat organization joined the Revolutionary Military Council and directed the cultural section of the army. Some joined fighting detachments, though not many remained in them for long.[33] The establishment of a territorial base, however, was impossible to realize because of the overwhelming forces Makhno faced, demanding the tactic of constant movement.

Meanwhile, as the organization Nabat established its headquarters and branches in some major Ukrainian cities, it began to publish leaflets, pamphlets, and newspapers.[34] Circumstances favored such activities since a number of educated and experienced anarchists had already come from Soviet Russia, including Volin, Arshinov, and Baron. Moreover, Makhno "had repeatedly urged the anarchists through the country to take advantage of the propaganda possibilities the south offered. [He promised] he would put everything necessary at our disposal, including funds, a printing-press, paper, and couriers."[35] A number of newspapers, mostly entitled *Nabat*, appeared in Ukrainian cities and towns, including Kharkiv, IElysavethrad, Oleksandrivs'k, Odessa, and Huliai-Pole, in either Russian or Ukrainian. Among the most important were three. *Put' k Svobode* (Road to Freedom) appeared daily and sometimes weekly and was devoted primarily to libertarian ideas and everyday problems including information on partisan activities, military proclamations, and orders. This paper was also published in Ukrainian under the title *Shliakh do Voli; Holos Makhnovtsia* (The Makhnovist Voice) and dealt primarily with the interests, problems, and tasks of the Makhno movement and its army.[36] The third, *Nabat*, the main anarchist weekly newspaper, was concerned largely with anarchist theory and doctrine. The Nabat organization also published a pamphlet dealing with the Makhno movement's problems, the economic organization of the region, the free soviets, the social basis of the society that was to be built, and the problem of defense.[37]

Nabat shared the vicissitudes of the Makhno movement. It carried on its activities freely as long as the region was controlled by Makhno, but whenever the Bolshevik and anti-Bolshevik Russian forces prevailed, the anarchists were forced underground. Finally, when the Soviet Russian forces overwhelmed the Makhno army in 1921, the anarchist movement ceased to exist as a vital force in Ukraine and in Russia. Many anarchists were either executed, arrested, banished, or silenced.[38] When Goldman and Berkman visited Lenin in 1920 to plead on behalf of the anarchists in the Russian prisons, Goldman reported that Lenin responded indignantly: "Anarchists? Nonsense! Who told you such yarns, and how could you believe them? We do have bandits in prison, and Makhnovtsy, but no *ideiny* anarchists."[39] For those anarchists who survived both at home and in exile there remained the bitterness of having seen the Revolution develop into the antithesis of all hopes and expectations.

6. Nestor Makhno

Nestor Ivanovych Makhno was undoubtedly the most bold, capable leader and the most striking personality in the partisan movement during the period of the Revolution. In curious contrast to this striking personality, his physical appearance was rather unimpressive. Although strongly built, he was rather short, and his right shoulder was slightly higher than the left. He had long, blackish-brown hair, a pockmarked face of pale gray. His nose was round, slightly hooked, and the cheek bones were rather high. However, his eyes, small, dark, and penetrating, made a deep and lasting impression. One observer reported that his wife still, after years, had his face, especially his eyes, burned in her memory, while another perceived "an indomitable, an almost superhuman, will" in their expression.[1] Appearance and character aside, the key to an understanding of Makhno's activities and his movement lies in his background and early life.

Makhno was born on October 27, 1889,[2] in Huliai-Pole, a town of about thirty thousand inhabitants, including adjoining small villages, in the Oleksandrivs'k (Zaporizhia) district, Katerynoslav (Dnipropetrovs'ki) province.[3] He was the youngest son of a poor peasant from Shahariv, a few miles north of Huliai-Pole, where his father worked as a stablekeeper on the Shabels'kyi estate. The original family name, Mikhnenko, later had become Mikhnenko-Makhno.[4] By the time of Makhno's birth his parents had moved to Huliai-Pole, where his father was hired as a coachman by a Jewish industrialist and merchant, B. Kerner.[5] When Makhno was eleven months old his father died, leaving him and three brothers, Sava, Omelian, and Hryhorii, in the care of their mother.[6]

Because of the family's poverty, Makhno went to work at the age of seven minding cattle and sheep for the peasants of his town. From age eight to twelve, he attended the local school, then worked full time on the estates of landowners and on the farms of rich German Mennonite colonists.[7] Subsequently, Makhno worked as a painter in a local factory. As a result of the injustice he experienced at work and the terror of the Russian regime during the Revolution of 1905, Makhno, like many other people, became interested in politics. In the next year, under the influence of the local anarchists, especially of Oleksander Semeniuta, he joined the ranks of the local peasant Anarchist-Communist group. During the Revolution, there was no serious disorder, arson, or assassination of governmental officials in Huliai-Pole, yet the regime dispatched a detachment of mounted police to suppress gatherings and meetings in the town and terrorize the population. Whoever was caught on the streets was brutally whipped. Those who were arrested in their homes were led through the streets and beaten with the butts of muskets to instill fear among the people. These brutal measures left an indelible mark in the town and sowed the seeds of covert unrest that infected the people, especially the young, in Huliai-Pole.[8]

In 1905, under the influence of Valdemar Antoni, a peasant Anarchist-Communist group was organized in Huliai-Pole. It was associated with an anarchist group in Katerynoslav and Antoni became liaison agent between them and a leader of the local group,[9] which consisted of about ten young men, mostly sons of poorer peasants. Antoni and Semeniuta (who had deserted from the army and was living under the assumed name of Korobka) smuggled arms and illegal literature for the group.

Soon the anarchists began to print proclamations and to expropriate money and jewelry from rich individuals and government institutions with a motivation, according to one of the anarchists, Ivan Levadnyi, that was "strictly political, in that all its actions were dictated by the idea of 'people's freedom.' "[10] For about one year nobody knew that these activities, which now included murder, were conducted by the local anarchists. However, as the group intensified its activities, the police, through spies, learned on July 28, 1908, that Semeniuta had come to Huliai-Pole to meet with the anarchists in the house of Levadnyi. The chief police officer Karachentsev sent an official, Lepetchenko, with about ten policemen to arrest the group. During the action Lepetchenko was killed and one policeman and Semeniuta's younger brother Prokip were wounded. Although his brother carried the latter away, the next morning the mounted police spotted Prokip and he shot himself. The others escaped in the night to Katerynoslav. Soon after, Karachentsev followed the group and after two weeks of searching, he arrested several of them, including Naum Al'thauzen, Khshyva, Ivan Levadnyi, and Nazar Zuichenko, at Amur, a suburb of Katerynoslav.[11]

At the end of 1906, Makhno was arrested and accused of killing officials but was released for lack of evidence. A year later he was again arrested and, along with others, accused of a "number of political assassinations and expropriations."[12] During the judicial inquiry no evidence was found and after a few months he was released on bail. However, in August 1908, on the basis of the denunciation of a member of the group, Al'thauzen, who was, according to Makhno, a police informer, Makhno was arrested and put in jail in Oleksandrivs'k.[13] In March 1910, Makhno and thirteen others were tried by the Odessa district military court in Katerynoslav and sentenced to death by hanging.[14] After fifty-two days, because of his youth and through the efforts of his mother, the death penalty was commuted to life imprisonment at hard labor. He served his sentence in the Butyrki central prison in Moscow.[15]

The Butyrki prison was one of the worst penitentiaries in Russia. Known for its unusually severe regulations because major revolutionaries or criminals were confined there, these regulations were made even more severe after the Revolution of 1905. Butyrki served not only as a prison, but also as a place where prisoners were gathered prior to transportation to Siberia. It was within the walls of Butyrki that Makhno served more than eight years.

Makhno was a restless and turbulent prisoner, stubborn and unable to accept the complete denial of freedom. Always in conflict with the prison authorities, he spent much of his time in chains or in damp and freezing confinement, which probably contributed to his contraction of pulmonary tuberculosis. Although prison life was very difficult, Makhno, thanks to the rich library at the prison and the companionship of political prisoners, especially the anarchist Peter Arshinov, acquired a general and political education, learning Russian grammar and literature, history, geography, mathematics, and political economy.[16] Makhno's prison experience shaped his later life and activities. It was there that he became a confirmed anarchist, hardened by years of suffering, learning, and introspection. He also developed an intense hatred of prisons and all authority. Later, during the Revolution, whenever he seized towns and cities, one of his first acts was to release all prisoners and burn the prison. On March 2, 1917, after eight years and eight months in prison, Makhno was released, along with all the other political prisoners, under the Provisional Government amnesty. After spending three weeks in Moscow to meet the leading Moscow anarchists, Makhno returned to Huliai-Pole, "the place of my birth and life."[17]

In Huliai-Pole Makhno, as the only ex-prisoner repatriate, became a most respected personage. The remaining members of the anarchist group, as well as many peasants, came to visit him the day he returned home. After an exchange of information, Makhno proposed to begin organizational work immediately. He sought to organize peasants in Huliai-Pole and its region and associate them with an anarchist group. He wished to forestall other political groups, such as Socialist Revolutionary and Social Democrats, from dominating the peasants. Although the other members demurred, pointing out that their aim was to spread anarchist propaganda, Makhno had his way, and on March 28–29 a Peasant Union was established with Makhno as chairman. Subsequently, he organized such unions in other villages and towns of the area. Makhno had no faith in the local authority because it was headed by foreign elements who, in his opinion, would not be responsible to the people for their actions,[18] and appealed for reorganization of the administrative body, urging the local intelligentsia, peasants, and workers to take the local government into their own hands. Consequently Makhno succeeded in bringing six representatives of the Peasant Union into the Public Committee, with himself as its vice-chairman. In the meantime, he also became chairman of the Agricultural Committee, chairman of the Union of Metal and Carpentry Workers, and chairman of the Medical Union.[19] Thus, from the outset Makhno, the ex-prisoner, by force of his personality assumed a leading role in Huliai-Pole with a determination to carry on the work of the Revolution among the masses.

The problem that concerned Makhno most was that of organizing and uniting the peasants into an alliance in his territory to make them a formidable force capable of driving out the landowners and the political authorities. His ultimate objective was the transfer of all lands owned by the gentry, monasteries, and the state into the hands of the peasants or to organize, if they wished, peasant communes. This would be accompanied by the disappearance of the state as a form of organized society. Makhno and his associates devoted time and energy to intensive propaganda activities among the peasants within and outside the province by means of calling regional peasant assemblies both at Huliai-Pole and elsewhere. The Peasant Union and the peasant-dominated Public Committee at Huliai-Pole were recommended as examples to the delegates of the meetings. Thus Makhno and his associates brought sociopolitical issues into the daily life of the people, who in turn supported his efforts, hoping to expedite the expropriation of large estates because they feared that "the revolution would be destroyed, and we would again remain without land." On August 5–7, the provincial congress at Katerynoslav decided to reorganize the Peasant Unions into Soviets of Peasants' and Workers' Deputies. This change was duly carried out at Huliai-Pole and Makhno remained the chairman.[20]

The political crisis that developed in Russia in the second half of August and culminated on September 8–9 in a conflict between the commander in chief of the Russian army, General Lavr G. Kornilov, and the prime minister of the Provisional Government, Kerensky, had strong repercussions in Huliai-Pole and its area.[21] On the eve of open conflict, Makhno assembled all the landowners and rich peasants (kulaks) of the area and took from them all official documents relating to their land, livestock, and equipment. Subsequently an inventory of this property was taken and reported to the people at the session of the local soviet, and then at the regional meeting. It was decided to allow the landowners to share the land, livestock, and tools equally with the peasants. The soviet also organized a Committee of the Poor to control the landed gentry. Simultaneously, Makhno had the local police neutralized by depriving them of their authority to arrest.[22] However, the realization of these decisions was delayed because dissatisfied elements organized and began to protest and denounce Makhno to the provisional authorities.

When the conflict broke out Makhno received two telegrams from Petrograd recommending that he organize local defense. In response, the soviet organized a Committee for the Defense of the Revolution headed by Makhno. Subsequently, the committee decided to disarm all the bourgeoisie, the landowners, rich peasants, and the wealthy German colonists in the area of Huliai-Pole as well as "to expropriate its rights to the people's wealth: the land, factories, plants, printing shops, theaters, coliseums, movies, and other forms of enterprises in its possession."[23] Some of the idealists among the anarchists formed a number of free agricultural communes consisting of volunteer peasants and workers where an elected committee of elders would allot the work alongside their fellow farmers. Makhno became a member of Commune No. 1.[24]

In order to strengthen the anti-bourgeois position of the Makhno group the committee and the soviet decided to call a regional gathering in collaboration with the Anarchist-Communists and jointly with the

Makhno and partisans. *Left*, Semen Karetnyk; *center*, Makhno; *right*, Fedir Shchus'.

Union of Metal and Carpentry Workers at Huliai-Pole. The aim of the meeting was to deprive the Huliai-Pole Public Committee of its authority to decide any problem of importance without the approval of the people.[25] In reality this decision transformed these institutions into advisory bodies while the group of anarchists became a major power in the area. Moreover, it accustomed people to the ideas of a stateless society.

As Makhno's power increased, his activities among the peasants in the Huliai-Pole region gradually extended beyond propaganda to armed raids on estates of landlords and rich peasants, including German colonists. These expeditions to "expropriate the expropriators" were often excessively violent. Those who resisted the seizure of their properties, or tried to hide valuables or money, were intimidated, terrorized, or even shot, although usually the owners did not resist. Gradually Makhno extended his raids to railways and depots, holding up freight and passenger trains. The raiders expropriated everything they needed, especially arms, ammunition, and military equipment, while other goods were distributed among the peasants of the surrounding villages.[26] Personal property of train passengers was confiscated and those who did not cooperate were executed, especially if they were landlords or officers, whom Makhno saw as standard-bearers of an old, foreign servitude. Although Makhno's methods as an agent of vengeance were violent, his men rarely molested poor peasants or workers. Hence Makhno's popularity grew among a considerable part of the peasantry and his following increased. Some, including a criminal element, joined Makhno for the sake of adventure, others to get rich. Most of Makhno's followers, however, were young men from both the rich and the poor peasantry.

Makhno's activities were, to a great extent, influenced by socially radical forces. Although Makhno had no serious competition from patriotic Ukrainians, who stood for law and order, he was under strong pressure from the fast spreading propaganda of the Bolsheviks, who used such slogans as "take everything, everything is yours" and "expropriate the expropriators." Makhno tried to be more extreme than the Bolsheviks—his appeals to the peasants were simple and effective: "Divide the land among yourself, justly and like brothers, and work for the good of everyone."[27]

The chaotic conditions in the region nurtured another anarchist leader, Maria Nikiforova, who exercised a substantial influence upon Makhno from the very beginning of their acquaintance. A member of a local anarchist group, she was engaged in terrorist activities in the years

1905–6, which led to a sentence of death, later commuted to life imprisonment. She served part of her sentence in the Petropavlovsk prison in Petrograd, and in 1910 was then exiled to Siberia, whence she escaped, first to Japan, and then to the United States. In the summer of 1917, she returned to Oleksandrivs'k, where she soon organized a combat detachment and began to terrorize people in the city. She especially hunted army officers and landlords, killing them. Later she moved to IElysavethrad, organizing and commanding a combat regiment "Black Guard," which fought each succeeding regime, including the Germans and Denikin. Her main goal was the destruction of all state institutions. In August 1917, she seized and robbed a military storehouse at the station of Orikhiv. Subsequently, she attacked the regiment in the town, disarmed and dispersed it, executing all captured officers. Part of the confiscated spoils she delivered to Makhno.[28]

The division of the lands of the gentry, the church, and the state, as well as the neutralization of the local police and Public Committee, proceeded largely unopposed and without bloodshed. The peasants and workers felt they had, for the time being, consolidated their revolutionary achievements; they took little further interest in outside affairs. The Central Rada exercised little effective control there because the province was separated from Ukraine, while the Provisional Government was powerless to interfere. Although the conflict between the peasants and the wealthy class did not develop into an open war, it planted the seeds of a sociopolitical conflict that would ripen the following summer, when the troops of the Central Powers were invited into Ukraine.

7. Makhno's National Consciousness

Although Makhno was not a Ukrainian nationalist patriot, he was an anarchist and a conscious Ukrainian in his own way. The question of his national consciousness cannot be separated from contemporary conditions. Besides his inadequate education, poverty, and the oppressive policy of the tsarist regime in Ukraine, Makhno's association with anarchist groups and his long years of imprisonment in Moscow directed him away from Ukrainian cultural and political organizations. His knowledge of Ukraine's history and her current national problems was very limited. Anarchism tied Makhno to the Russian revolutionaries and their ideas, directly and indirectly. He called Bakunin "great," "a tireless revolutionary." He not only admired Kropotkin, but visited him in Moscow and gave him material help. Although he mistrusted Lenin, he visited him and respected him as a revolutionary leader. However, he knew very little about Ukrainian national leaders. He referred to Hrushevs'kyi as an "old man" though he was only fifty-one. He knew that Vynnychenko was a "socialist" who "participated in the life and struggle of the toilers" but he disliked him and Petliura because they helped conclude the Brest-Litovsk treaty with the Central Powers and subsequently brought Austro-German troops into Ukraine.[1] However, he did not take into consideration the Bolshevik invasion that had forced the Rada to invite the Germans. As a result of Makhno's long years of imprisonment, he had almost forgotten his native language. The question of Ukrainian language did not seem to bother him for some time, but in the course of the Revolution his view changed markedly. On his train trip from Moscow to Ukraine in the summer of 1918, Makhno found that the conductors, when addressed in Russian, would not answer, but demanded that the inquiries be made in Ukrainian. "I was struck by the request, but there was nothing I could do. And, not knowing my own native Ukrainian language, I was forced to use it in such a [manner], in addressing those around me, that I was ashamed. I thought quite a bit about this incident."[2] After he and his companions escaped to Romania and then to Poland, they were interned in a camp, Strzałków, with the troops of the Ukrainian People's Republic. There Makhno very often complained that: "In that damned prison [in Butyrki, Moscow, I] completely forgot my native language." Another time he would say: "Finally I must learn my native language."[3] In the preface to his memoirs that he published in Russian Makhno regretted that they appeared"not in Ukraine and not in Ukrainian." He felt, however, that "the fault is not mine, but that of the conditions in which I find myself."[4]

Makhno was nevertheless aware of his nationality. In certain circumstances he would avoid mentioning his political affiliation, but he never failed to admit or, if necessary, to defend, his nationality, even in complicated questions and situations. He never referred to his native land as "South Russia." When Makhno visited the Kremlin in July and an official, looking at Makhno's document, asked: "Then you, comrade, are from South Russia?", Makhno replied: "Yes, I am from Ukraine." From there he went to the office of IAkov M. Sverdlov, who asked: "But tell me what are you, Communist or Left S[ocialist] R[evolutionary]? That you are Ukrainian I see from your discussion, but to which of these two parties you belong is difficult to understand."[5] When later he met both Sverdlov and Lenin, during their discussion about anarchism in Ukraine, Makhno not only employed the proper name of his native land, but he even reproached the Bolsheviks for calling Ukraine South Russia:

> The Anarchist-Communists in Ukraine—or as you, Communist-Bolsheviks, are trying to avoid the word Ukraine and are calling it "South Russia" . . . have already given too much proof that they are entirely associated with the "present."[6]

In his writings Makhno always made a clear distinction between Ukraine and Russia: "The echoes of the October coup in Petrograd and in Moscow, and then in all Russia—came to us in Ukraine at the end of November and at the beginning of December 1917."[7] Makhno also had his opinion about the cause of the failure of the Ukrainian Revolution. Although the idea of self-determination had strongly manifested itself in Ukraine, at this time it had not adequately developed. Among the Ukrainian people there appeared a number of different political groups, each of which interpreted the idea of self-determination in its own way, according to its own interests. The Ukrainian working masses neither sympathized with, nor followed, them.[8]

Apart from Makhno's sentiment for his native land, "the wide Ukrainian steppes and the plentiful green grain,"[9] and the national tradition, the most significant influences that increased Makhno's national consciousness and the success of his movement were certain elements among his partisans and his wife. In the summer of 1919 Makhno married Halyna Kuz'menko, the daughter of a police official. She was born about 1895[10] in Pishchanyi Brid, in the IElysavethrad (Kirovohrad) district, Kherson province. She studied at a teacher's college for women at nearby Dobrovelychkivka and in 1918 was employed by the Ministry of Labor in Kyiv and later the same year she was assigned to a new state gymnasium at Huliai-Pole to teach Ukrainian and history. There she became acquainted with Makhno. She impressed people as being courageous, literate, and beautiful.[11] According to an eyewitness, she was: "very handsome, a brunette, tall, slender with beautiful dark eyes and fresh though dark complexion. [She] gave the impression of being a good woman. . . . [She] participated in attacks fighting and shooting a machine gun."[12] These traits were also noted by Goldman and Berkman when Makhno's wife visited them in Kyiv in peasant dress to hide her identity from the Bolsheviks.[13]

Makhno's wife was also a good conversationalist; she liked to debate and she held strongly to a position she considered right.[14] According to Goldman:

She possessed considerable information and was intensely interested in all cultural problems. She plied me with questions about American women, whether they had really become emancipated and enjoyed equal rights. . . . Did the American woman believe in free motherhood and was she familiar with the subject of birth control? . . . I mentioned some of the literature dealing with these subjects. She listened eagerly. "I must get hold of something to help our peasant women."[15]

She had strong political convictions and a definite concept of the role of the partisans in the struggle against the Bolsheviks and Denikin:

"I regard the *povstantsi* movement," she said, "as the only true proletarian revolution. Bolshevism is the mastery of the Communist Party, falsely called the dictatorship of the proletariat. It is very far from our conception of revolution. . . . Their aim is State Communism, with the workers and farmers of the whole country serving as employees of the one powerful government master. Its result is the most abject slavery, suppression, and revolt, as we see on every hand. . . . Our aim is the class organization of the revolutionary toiling masses. That is the sense of the great Ukrainian movement and its best expression is to be found in the Makhnovshchina."[16]

Makhno's wife continued to be interested in national problems after she left the country. When she, together with Makhno and his associates, was brought into the Ukrainian troops' internment camp in Poland, she became an active member of an Association of Ukrainian Women Teachers in the camp.[17]

During most of 1919 and after, the Left Bank, where the Makhno partisans operated, was the main arena of the Russian Civil War. Hence it was largely in the hands of either the Bolshevik or anti-Bolshevik Russian forces. The warring of the two occupying forces and their suppressive policy aroused the people's national-political consciousness and resistance. As an eyewitness observed:

The announced mobilization by the Volunteer Army failed. Peasants liable for conscription went into the forests with arms in their hands and hid from the punitive detachments of the state police. . . . On the surface of life in the village began to appear the Petliura movement, which soon inclined to the anarchist slogans of Makhno, who was accepting into his ranks all who were ready for an open struggle against the Volunteer Army as an authority that was hanging peasants.[18]

Patriotic Ukrainians on the Right Bank joined the Ukrainian regular army but on the Left Bank, in the later stage of the Revolution, many patriotic Ukrainians, prevented by the presence of the Russian forces from joining the Ukrainian Army, joined either Makhno or other partisan groups. According to a Ukrainian officer, when some Makhno men who were captured by the Ukrainian troops were asked why they had joined Makhno, they replied: "There is nobody else [to join]."[19] According to another partisan, the main motive for joining Makhno was the unbearable conditions in the villages and towns: "I joined the Makhno army . . . because the Denikin men came and looted the village, taking horses and ruining homesteads. So I took arms and went to fight; if perish, then perish."[20] The increasing number of nationally conscious Ukrainians among the Makhno partisans gradually gave the group's ideology a more national character, which was marked by a change in the name of the partisan army from "Revolutionary Partisan Detachments of Bat'ko Makhno" to "The Revolutionary Partisan Army of Ukraine (Makhnovites)" in the summer of 1919.[21]

From the fall of 1919 onward, Makhno widened the scope of his activities and increased his resistance to both the Bolshevik and anti-Bolshevik Russian forces. Under the influence of patriotic partisans, he not only entered into negotiations with the Ukrainian Army command, but also occasionally coordinated his activities with the Ukrainian troops. In addition, during the winter campaign of 1919–20, many of Makhno's partisans joined the Directory's troops and the Ukrainian Galician Army, with which Makhno maintained liaison.[22] He also began to render assistance to partisan groups that recognized the Directory, including partisan leaders Petro Petrenko, Hladchenko, Diakivs'kyi, and others. He made peace with all of them, entered into agreements of nonaggression, and cooperated in coordinated actions against the Bolsheviks. A number of other partisan detachments joined Makhno.[23] The partisan leader Khrystovyi headed a delegation that visited Makhno in August of 1920 at Zinkiv, in Poltava province. His group consisted of about six hundred partisans with a regular army organization. At Khrystovyi's headquarters were official liaison personnel, distinguished senior officers, from the Ukrainian Army. Khrystovyi proposed unification with Makhno under the condition that Makhno would transfer his activities to the Khrystovyi territory. Although Makhno declined Khrystovyi's offer, he aided Khrystovyi by supplying him with machine guns and ammunition, and also sent him a machine-gun detachment consisting of 170 men to fight against a brigade of internal security troups (VOKhR).[24]

Moreover, Makhno's slogans assumed a more pro-Ukrainian, patriotic, and, at the same time, a more anti-Russian tone. Makhno began to brand the Bolsehviks not only as social, but also as national enemies; at the same time, his newspapers blamed the Bolsheviks for preventing the Ukrainian people from "creating their own life by themselves" and urged them to "take the authority into their own hands."[25] Also, the newspapers and Makhno himself appealed to the people to fight against the "Moscovite oppressors" and to "liberate our native Ukraine from the Russian yoke." According to information given to the Bolsheviks by Makhno's associate Viktor Bilash, Makhno was preparing a proclamation (a "Universal") announcing his intention of joining the Ukrainian Army to liberate "mother Ukraine."[26] Teper, another Bolshevik author and a former anarchist, confirmed Makhno's intentions. According to him, Makhno decided to put aside

> . . . all earlier declarations and began to work out a new declaration in a completely different spirit. Basically he outlined a project for national liberation of Ukraine. Subsequently, Makhno intended to draw into the ranks of the Makhno movement the nationally minded Ukrainian intelligentsia and through them the Petliura bands operating on the Right Bank. However, part of the commanding staff strongly protested this declaration and he had to put it aside.[27]

According to the representative of the Directory, Panas Fedenko, "Makhno's minister," Shpota, who in September 1919 visited the Directory at Kamianets', admitted that the mass of the Makhno partisans wished to join the Ukrainian Army. However, the Russian anarchists working with Makhno, such as Arshinov, Volin, and Zinkovskii (Zadov), who were influential at Makhno headquarters, obstructed such a unification.[28]

Although at the beginning of his movement Makhno cooperated with the Bolsheviks twice for brief periods on a local level against the Ukrainian troops, he resisted all attempts by them to establish their authority in Ukraine. At the end of December 1918, Lenin wired the Bolsheviks in Katerynoslav, appointing Makhno commander in chief of Soviet troops in the Katerynoslav province. Makhno rejected this emphatically:

> There are no Soviet troops here. The main forces here are the revolutionary partisan Makhno men whose aims are known and clear to all. They are fighting against the authority of all political governments and for liberty and independence of the working people.[29]

Moreover, Makhno's socioeconomic programs attracted not only the upper economic stratum of the young peasants, but also poorer peasants and workers, as well as many non-Ukrainian elements, including the Russians, Jews, Greeks, Bulgarians, and Poles of the region and outside. Many of these men, especially the non-Ukrainians, would otherwise have been drafted by one or the other of the Russian armies and would have been fighting against Ukraine. Trotsky voiced his concern over this circumstance, declaring that the Makhno partisans were a greater threat than Denikin because "the Makhno movement developed in the depths of the masses and aroused the masses themselves against us."[30]

The presence of Makhno's educated, patriotic, and active wife in the partisan army, as well as a large number of patriotic Ukrainians, made Makhno and his associates more aware of Ukrainian national problems and later compelled them not only to assume neutrality toward the Ukrainian Army, but, to some extent, to cooperate with it against the common enemies, the Bolshevik and anti-Bolshevik Russian forces in Ukraine.

8. Makhno, the Bolsheviks, and the Central Rada

News of the Bolshevik coup in October, which reached Huliai-Pole in early November, created relatively little stir among the local peasants. The Bolshevik slogan "land to the peasants and factories to the workers" were acceptable to them, though it seemed that the Bolsheviks were promoting a cause that had already been achieved around Huliai-Pole in August and September. According to Makhno:

When Ukrainian peasants in a number of provinces refused to pay the second part of their annual rent to the gentry and the rich peasants, and were seizing their lands and tools as public property; when they were sending their delegates from the villages to the workers in the cities, to arrange with the latter for seizure of the plants, factories, and other branches of enterprises for their own management and, weapons in hand, [were] defending their free society of toilers—at that time there was no October. . . . Thus the Great October in its strict chronological sense, appeared to the Ukrainian revolutionary village automatically as a period of the past.[1]

Hence, it was not so much the October coup as the subsequent Bolshevik invasion of Ukraine that turned Makhno and his followers from meetings and agitation toward partisan warfare.

For Makhno this change was an important problem because as an anarchist he did not wish to serve any one regime. He advocated destruction of any government be it native or foreign, rightist or Communist. In his opinion all forms of government represented the violence of a minority over the majority. Makhno was guided by a strong belief in freedom and in the ability of men to govern themselves. Therefore, he appealed to the peasants:

. . . we will destroy the servile regime . . . and lead our brothers upon the path toward a new order. We will establish it upon the foundation of a free society; its construction would permit all those who do not exploit the work of others to live, free and independent of the state and its bureaucracy, even of the Reds, and to build our whole sociopolitical life complete, independently at home, among ourselves.[2]

The Bolshevik invasion of Ukraine also determined Makhno's relationships with both the Bolsheviks and the Central Rada. Although he and his followers welcomed the overthrow of the Provisional Government, its replacement by the Bolshevik regime displeased them because "the peasants and workers saw it as a new period of governmental interference in the revolutionary work of the toilers at home and, consequently, a new war of the authorities against the people."[3]

Although Makhno considered the Bolsheviks an alien dictatorship, he often served as their ally because they were, as he said, for the revolutionary cause. His association with the Bolsheviks was also directed against the national authority, the Central Rada, because in his opinion, native governments were no different from foreign governments, and "the toilers have no interest in either."[4]

When the Provisional Government first established its authority in the area of Huliai-Pole, Makhno's anarchists collaborated with the rest of the population, including the educated Ukrainians, to exclude the foreign element from the local administration. Makhno pointed out to the public the inadmissibility "of a 'Public Committee' in revolutionary Huliai-Pole that is headed by people unknown to the population, from whom the people cannot demand any responsibility for their actions."[5] Simultaneously, he proposed an extra meeting of elected representatives to decide this problem. The teachers present at the meeting joined him and the superintendent of the school, who had placed his school at the disposition of the meeting. Subsequently, when the supporters of the Rada began to extend their influence in Katerynoslav province, the anarchist group at Huliai-Pole assumed a negative attitude toward the Rada, considering it a government of bourgeois nationalists. In the summer at a meeting in Huliai-Pole a Ukrainian Socialist Revolutionary exhorted the public to:

Think that in contrast to the "mean Provisional Government in Petrograd," our Ukrainian government, the Central Rada, was organized in Kyiv. It is really revolutionary, in Ukrainian territory, only it is able and authorized to establish freedom and a happy life for the Ukrainian people! . . . But the toilers of Huliai-Pole were deaf to the appeal. . . . They . . . overwhelmed him by shouting: Down from the podium! We do not need your government![6]

In September the Anarchist-Communists, the Soviet of Peasants' and Workers' Deputies, the Union of Metal and Carpentry Workers, and the Land Committee issued a joint resolution stating:

> The congress of the toilers in the area of Huliai-Pole decisively condemns the claims of the governments—the Provisional Government in Petrograd and the Ukrainian Central Rada in Kyiv—to rule the lives of the toilers and calls upon the local Soviets and all the toiling population organized around them to ignore all decrees issued by these governments.[7]

One group of patriotic Ukrainians, the supporters of the Rada, attempted to destroy the influence of the anarchists in Huliai-Pole. On December 25, 1917, a delegation visited IUrii Mahalevs'kyi, the commander of a Ukrainian military unit at Oleksandrivs'k, seeking assistance against Makhno. Being preoccupied with other problems, he only supplied the group with arms and ammunition. However, the subsequent Soviet Russian invasion prevented the realization of the plan.[8]

The hostility of Makhno and his followers toward national government was put into action at the beginning of January 1918. At a meeting of the soviet in the area of Huliai-Pole it was decided to join the invading Bolshevik troops because the Rada,

> though headed by Socialist Revolutionaries and Social Democrats in its struggle against the Bolshevik-Left Socialist Revolutionary bloc, aimed not only at driving the *katsaps* out of their native land, mother Ukraine, but also at suppressing the signs of social revolution in general.[9]

In response to the appeals of the anarchist group several hundred men, mostly anarchists, joined Makhno. This combat unit, headed by Makhno and his brother Sava, joined the Bolshevik forces in Oleksandrivs'k.[10] On January 15, 1918, the weak Ukrainian forces in Oleksandrivs'k withdrew and the Bolshevik troops, supported by the local anarchists and led by Maria Nikiforova, occupied the city.[11] However, it was the passage of eighteen troop trains of Don Cossacks coming from the front through Katerynoslav province, by way of Kryvyi Rih, Apostolove, and Oleksandrivs'k that provided the catalyst for Makhno's call to arms. Reiterating an accusation made earlier by the Bolsheviks, Makhno denounced the Rada for shielding the Don counterrevolution of General Kaledin by allowing the Cossacks to cross Ukraine.[12] The Bolsheviks, Makhno, and Nikiforova decided to disarm the Cossacks to prevent a strengthening of Kaledin's forces, and Makhno seized the Kichkas railroad station where there was a famous suspension bridge across the Dnieper. At first the Don Cossacks tried to force their way, but when this failed, they agreed to lay down their arms on the condition that they would be allowed to proceed to the Don. The Bolsheviks, however, broke this agreement, sent them to Kharkiv, and took their horses. Although Makhno stated that the Bolsheviks "behaved, not like revolutionaries, but like Jesuits, promising them one thing, and doing another,"[13] he and his men apparently committed crimes of their own by throwing some of the Cossack officers from the Kichkas bridge into Dnieper.[14]

During the short period of Makhno's collaboration with the Bolsheviks, he came to the conclusion that cooperation with them "even on the front of the defense of the revolution," was impossible. He was disturbed when he arrived in Oleksandrivs'k and found that not only were prisoners arrested by the Provisional Government not released by the Bolsheviks because they supposedly would not respect the Bolshevik authorities, but even more arrests had been made since the Bolsheviks' arrival. Makhno became convinced that the Revolution was in danger from all sides, including the Bolsheviks. He observed that the freedom achieved by the Revolution was not for the people but for the parties, and that "the parties would not serve the people, but people, the parties."[15] Thus, it was necessary to prepare the people against their enemies. To Makhno, "the real spirit of revolution" existed in the village, while in the city there was "a counterrevolution." After deliberation, Makhno and his closest friends decided to break with the Bolsheviks under the pretext that the supporters of the Rada were trying to reassert authority in the area of Huliai-Pole. Makhno resigned from the Revolutionary Committee in Oleksandrivs'k and departed with his detachment to Huliai-Pole.

Although the anarchist group began to influence and lead the peasants from the end of spring 1917, it was more as underground than legal action. The Huliai-Pole soviet, which, in reality, performed administrative functions, formed a Revolutionary Committee headed by Makhno, with the aim of organizing standing revolutionary detachments. Such a formation was stimulated by an application of anarchist economy. The peasants in Huliai-Pole had more grain than they needed, but lacked manufactured goods, so they decided to send a representative on a tour to Moscow and other cities in Russia to arrange an exchange of commodities. In Moscow they met with success; two trade union representatives came to Huliai-Pole to work out details and subsequently grain was sent off under an armed guard. The Moscow workers held to their part of the bargain and a consignment of textiles and other manufactured goods was dispatched to Huliai-Pole. However, it

Anarchist group from Huliai-Pole. *Front row, from left:* Nestor Makhno, Waldemar Antoni, Petro Onyshchenko, Nazar Zuichenko, Luka Korostyliv; *back row:* Oleksander Semeniuta?, Luka Kravchenko, Ivan Shevchenko, Prokip Semeniuta, Ihor Bondarenko, Ivan Levadnyi.

was held up by the Bolshevik authority in Oleksandrivs'k. This action brought about intense indignation among the peasants and they threatened

> to march on the city to disperse the useless authorities harmful to the work of the toilers, who sat there. The demand of the peasants was not an empty phrase: the toilers at this time had . . . cadres of revolutionary youth, completely sufficient to militarily occupy the city of Oleksandrivs'k and to disperse, if not to shoot, all the governmental officials.[16]

The Bolsheviks, however, gave way and the consignment was duly released and distributed among its rightful recipients. This incident made the peasants more aware of the necessity of their own armed detachments. They also found a source of arms (rifles, machine guns, and hand grenades) at the Oleksandrivs'k Anarchist Federation, and to augment their arsenal Makhno and Nikiforova jointly disarmed a battalion of Ukrainian troops stationed in Orikhiv near Huliai-Pole.[17]

The Brest-Litovsk peace treaty between the Central Powers and Ukraine concluded on February 9, 1918, and the Rada's subsequent request for Austro-German aid in expelling the Russian forces from the country had repercussions in Huliai-Pole and its area. The supporters of the Ukrainian government there were encouraged by the news and consequently increased their activities. The anarchists, who vehemently opposed the Rada's invitation of Austro-German troops into Ukraine, and feared that they might lose ground in Huliai-Pole, turned to "terror against all who dare now or are preparing in the future, following a victory of the counterrevolution over the revolution, to persecute the anarchist idea and its nameless bearers." Makhno's first victim was one of the Ukrainian leaders in Huliai-Pole, a Socialist Revolutionary and former military officer, Pavlo Semeniuta (Riabko), who publicly supported the Rada's policy. He was assassinated by the anarchists, and later their secretary, Kalashnikov, stated that "it [the anarchist group] killed him and [is] ready to kill in the future such an unworthy."[18]

In the meantime the Austro-German and Ukrainian troops were moving deeper into Ukraine and Makhno began to urge the Revolutionary Committee to organize all its existing detachments in Huliai-Pole and its area into free battalions and to supplement them, especially with anarchists. This action was carried out under the slogan:

> Revolutionary toilers, form free battalions for the defense of the revolution! The Socialist State supporters betrayed the revolution in Ukraine and are bringing against it forces of a black reaction from foreign countries.[19]

Makhno succeeded in forming several military units under his command, consisting of over seventeen hundred men, and a medical service unit. Toward the end of March the Ukrainian troops supported by the German and Austrian forces approached the Dnieper and on April 14 they took Oleksandrivs'k.[20] The Bolshevik troops gave no effective resistance and their retreat became a general flight. However, they did try to arm the pro-Bolshevik elements in Ukraine,[21] and handed over to Makhno six artillery pieces and three thousand rifles with eleven cars of ammunition.[22] Makhno dispatched several detachments, including cavalry, to the Oleksandrivs'k front to assist the Bolshevik troops. Although more units were soon ready for the front, they failed to get expected arms from the Bolsheviks because a wire connection with their headquarters was broken.[23]

Meanwhile, when the commander of the Bolshevik southern front, Aleksander T. Egorov, was informed of Makhno's military activities, he summoned him to his headquarters at Fedorivka for consultation. When Makhno reached Egorov's headquarters, however, he found that he had moved eastward and while searching for Egorov Makhno learned that Huliai-Pole had been taken by the Ukrainian and German troops. The military authorities burned his mother's house and shot his elder brother Omelian, who was an invalid war veteran. Some of the anarchist leaders who did not escape were arrested by the local supporters of the Ukrainian government with the assistance of the Jewish detachment organized earlier. Also an active member of the anarchist group, Lev Shneider, joined the supporters of the Rada.[24] Makhno made an effort to rally some retreating military units, including Nikiforova's detachment, but failed.

About that time he met a number of his anarchist friends and his brother Sava, who advised him not to return to Huliai-Pole because the military authority had put a price on his head. They decided to join Petrenko's troop train and move eastward toward Taganrog, the rallying center of the Bolshevik troops and their administrative agents.[25] While approaching Taganrog the Huliai-Pole anarchists, learning that the Bolshevik authorities had begun to disarm all independent combat detachments, decided to disperse into small groups and to infiltrate the city. Some of them, including Sava Makhno, returned to the front zone to locate other friends and direct them to the others.

In Taganrog Makhno and his friends had to face another disappointment. The Bolshevik authorities arrested Nikiforova and disarmed her detachment, accusing her of committing robberies in IElesavethrad. The men of the detachment not only refused to join the Bolshevik units but demanded the release of Nikiforova. Other detachments and the Taganrog anarchists supported their demands while Makhno and Nikiforova promptly sent a telegram to Vladimir A. Antonov-Ovseenko protesting the action and demanding her release. His prompt reply gave them some satisfaction but did not provide her release: "Both the detachment of the anarchist Maria Nikiforova and comrade Nikiforova herself are well known to me. Instead of being engaged in disarming such revolutionary combat units I would advise that they be created."[26] In spite of protests, Nikiforova's trial was held at Taganrog on April 20.

At the trial, Garin, the commander of the Katerynoslav-Briansk anarchist armed train, declared that

> . . . he was convinced that comrade Nikiforova, if she indeed has been called to the witness stand, then it is only because she sees in most of the jurors real revolutionaries, and believes that once she is released, she will be given back her own and her detachment's arms and will go to battle against the counterrevolution. If she had not believed in this and had foreseen that the revolutionary court would follow in the footsteps of the government and its provocateurs, then I would have known also about this and liberated her by force.[27]

Under such a threat the court released Nikiforova and the arms were returned to her unit.

The persecution of the anarchists launched in Taganrog and its area by the Bolsheviks was not an isolated case. During April–May 1918, the Bolshevik regime staged an antianarchist drive, disarming and destroying all anarchist groups in Soviet Russia. With these events in mind, Makhno realized the anarchists could not depend upon the Bolsheviks whose apparent aim was "to exploit the Anarchists-Revolutionaries in the struggle against counterrevolution so that those bearers of an unreconciled spirit of revolution remained at the war front until death."[28]

Taking into account these persecutions, the Huliai-Pole group at Taganrog recommended that Makhno and Borys Veretelnyk organize a conference to decide on future policy. At the end of April, they met at the Taganrog Anarchist Federation and after discussion of the recent mistakes, failures, and the existing situation, decided that late June and early July, the harvest season, was the best time for meeting the peasants in the fields and learning about their feelings concerning their enemies. It was agreed that the participants in the conference should infiltrate back to their area a few at a time. On reaching their destinations the first arrivals would send information to the others left behind.

After learning about conditions in Huliai-Pole and the surrounding area, they were to organize small combat units of five to ten men each chosen from the peasants and workers. By drawing others into these units, they would create potential fighting units in Huliai-Pole and eventually in the whole area with the aims of committing acts of individual terror against the military commanders and organizing collective peasant attacks against returning landlords who had left their estates in the previous year. A secondary mission was to collect arms from the enemies and prepare the group for a general peasant uprising against the Austro-German troops, reestablishing the order that was brought by the Revolution. Finally they agreed that Makhno, Borys Veretelnyk, and a few others would make a two-month trip to Soviet Russia to see at first hand what had happened to the anarchists under the Bolshevik regime and what their plans were for the future. Makhno also wanted to find out what help and what obstruction he might expect for his revolutionary action at home.[29]

The negative attitude of the Makhno group toward the national government cannot be explained by anarchist ideology alone. Although the population of Katerynoslav province was about 80 percent Ukrainian, the commercial, political, and cultural organizations, administration, press, and schools, especially in the cities, were largely in non-Ukrainian hands. There was a relatively small percentage of educated patriotic Ukrainians to provide leadership in all spheres of national life. Most of the workers' leaders were either non-Ukrainian or denationalized ones, while many workers and some peasants were under the influence of Bolshevik ideologies. Consequently, political education and national consciousness among the population were low.

While, despite the challenge of intensive Bolshevik propaganda, the local Ukrainian leaders carried on successful enlightening work among the officers and soldiers in the cities of the province, the so-called Kerensky July offensive against the Central Powers removed the best and most nationally conscious men from the barracks to the front; those who remained were badly demoralized by the Bolshevik and anarchist propaganda and the local national leaders could not find needed support.[30] Moreover, the separation of Katerynoslav province from Ukraine and the obstacles posed to the Rada's work by the Provisional Government and its supporters created adverse conditions. Thus, after the fall of the Provisional Government, it was difficult for the Rada either to establish strong authority in the province that would prevent harmful elements from influencing the course of the Revolution, or to introduce a healthy policy to gain public confidence and support.

9. Makhno's Visits with Kropotkin and Lenin

Of the Russian centers that Makhno wanted to visit, Moscow, Petrograd, and Kronstadt, the first was of special interest because "he had a vision of meeting many and diverse revolutionaries in the center of the paper revolution" to gain ideological inspiration and advice from them that he would subsequently turn into practice.[1] He wanted to find out the fate and future plans of the anarchists; he also wanted to ascertain what Bolshevik supremacy meant in practice and the attitude of the workers toward the regime. Moreover, Makhno needed to know at first hand what assistance and what opposition he might expect from Moscow in his future struggle in Ukraine. Makhno's odyssey through Soviet Russia was a long list of depressing features: anarchy, persecution, and disappointment. When the Bolshevik troops moved north into the Don territory and Russia under German pressure, Makhno, like many others, joined them. On his way he observed the military weakness of the Red Guards and their plunder of the local population.

In Tikhoretskaia, north of Rostov, Makhno and one of his companions were arrested and sentenced to death by the local authority for participating in a requisition of food for the troop train. Only Makhno's violent protest and a document identifying him as chairman of the Huliai-Pole Committee for the Defense of the Revolution saved them from execution.[2]

In Tsaritsyn (Volgograd) most of the pro-Bolshevik armed detachments coming from Ukraine were disarmed and integrated into the Red Guards. Some of them, especially those consisting of Ukrainian elements, were dealt with very roughly. For example, the detachment headed by Petrenko refused to be disarmed. After a few skirmishes the Bolsheviks arrested Petrenko and executed him while his men were put into Bolshevik units. This and other acts of the Bolshevik authorities deeply depressed Makhno; he felt that "the government is persecuting revolutionary goals altogether." Because of his close association with the Petrenko men, Makhno feared he would be arrested. He traveled down the Volga to Saratov, where he encountered new trouble connected with the arrival of a well-armed anarchist detachment of two hundred and fifty men, known as "the Odessa Terrorists," who had forced their way to Saratov, but refused to be disarmed. Armed clashes ensued between the unit and the Cheka. The intention of the Odessa Terrorists, like the Petrenko detachment, was to go back into Ukraine via Voronezh-Kursk to fight the Austro-German troops. Again in close contact with the terrorists, Makhno hastily escaped to Astrakhan where he entered the propaganda department of the local soviet, but the Bolshevik authorities soon became suspicious of his activities among the troops. Makhno gave up his job and went to Moscow via Tsaritsyn, Saratov, and Tambov.[3]

Arriving in Moscow at the beginning of June, he visited a number of Russian anarchists, among them Aleksander A. Borovoi, Lev Cherny, T. Grosman-Roshchin, A. Shapiro, and his old friend Peter Arshinov. He had, as well, lengthy discussions with people of other political affiliations. He also attended a number of anarchist, socialist, and Bolshevik lecture meetings and conferences, including the All-Russian Congress of Textile Unions. Although Makhno found some of his contacts and meetings impressive for their cultural and theoretical range, he felt that, though it was a critical time, the majority of anarchists were idling without purpose. In contrast to the revolutionary work of the Ukrainian peasants, in Moscow there was much talk, writing, and advice to the crowds at the meetings but neither the will nor the courage to face the task of reorienting the course of the Revolution. As a result of this disappointment he decided to go back to Ukraine sooner than planned and to instigate an uprising of the peasants against the Austro-German troops and the hetman regime. He felt that his activity in Ukraine would "manifest to all friends of the paper revolution where to seek vital and healthy strength for our anarchist movement."[4]

While thinking about the discouraging state of affairs of the Russian anarchists, Makhno decided to visit their nominal leader Peter A. Kropotkin, from whom he expected answers on all vital questions. Makhno visited Kropotkin on the eve of his departure. Kropotkin received him politely and they spoke at length concerning the tangled situation in Ukraine, including the Austro-German occupation, the hetman government, and the anarchist method of struggle against all forms of counterrevolution. Makhno felt that he received satisfactory answers to all the questions he posed; however, "when I asked him to give me advice concerning my intention to go back into Ukraine for revolutionary work among the peasants, he categorically refused to advise me, saying: 'This question involves great risk to your life, comrade, and only you yourself can solve it correctly.'" As Makhno was leaving, Kropotkin said: "One must remember, dear comrade, that our struggle knows no sentimentality. Selflessness and strength of heart and will on the way toward one's chosen goal will conquer all."[5] Years later Makhno wrote:

> I have always remembered these words of Peter Aleksandrovich. And when our comrades come to know all that I did in the Russian Revolution in Ukraine and then in the independent Ukrainian Revolution, in the vanguard of which the revolution-Makhno movement played so outstanding a role, they will recognize in my activities that selflessness and that strength of heart and will about which Peter Aleksandrovich spoke to me.[6]

Makhno's other significant meetings in Moscow were with IAkov M. Sverdlov, chairman of the All-Russian Central Executive Committee of the Soviets, and with V. I. Lenin, in mid-June. The problem of living quarters brought Makhno to the Kremlin and to the office of Sverdlov, who became interested in Ukrainian problems. It is hard to believe that it was only housing that brought him to the Kremlin. It is more likely that Makhno tried to meet some of the Bolshevik leaders and to find out for himself what assistance or opposition he might expect from the Bolsheviks in his future struggle at home.[7]

Sverdlov and Makhno had a brief discussion concerning the recent Bolshevik invasion of Ukraine. According to Sverdlov, the Red Guard's chaotic withdrawal from Ukraine was owing to the hostility of the peasants. He maintained that the "majority of the peasants in the South are 'kulaks' and supporters of the Central Rada." Makhno denied this charge, using the Huliai-Pole anarchists' activities as proof. Sverdlov, however, was not convinced: "Then why did they not support our Red Army units? We have testimonies that the southern peasants are poisoned by extreme Ukrainian chauvinism and everywhere they were welcoming German expeditionary forces and the units of the Central Rada with a special joy as their liberators."[8] Subsequently, Sverdlov offered to arrange a meeting for Makhno with Lenin, who he felt would like to hear about "the real feelings of peasants" in Ukraine.

The next day at one o'clock Makhno along with Sverdlov was received by Lenin with paternal simplicity. Lenin, shaking hands and clasping Makhno's shoulder with the other, seated his two visitors and told his secretary they were not to be disturbed for one hour. Lenin sounded out Makhno on the attitude of the peasantry toward the Soviets, the Austro-German forces, and the differences between the Bolshevik and anarchist conceptions of revolution. He tried to discuss the problems in great detail. Lenin wanted to know what the Ukrainian peasants in Makhno's area made of the slogan "All power to the local Soviets." Makhno replied that they took it literally, assuming they were to have complete control of all affairs affecting them, to which he added that he felt this was the correct interpretation. In response, Lenin said: "In this case, the peasants from your area are infected with anarchism." Makhno responded: "Do you think that is bad?" Lenin replied: "I did not say that. On the contrary, it may be to the good, for it would speed up the victory of communism over capital and its authority."[9]

He went on to observe that mere peasant enthusiasm would burn itself out and could not survive serious blows from the counterrevolution. Makhno pointed out "that a leader should not be a pessimist or a sceptic." Subsequently Lenin observed that the anarchists had no serious organization, they were unable to organize either the proletariat or the poor peasants, and thus were unable to defend them.

Lenin was particularly interested in the performance of the Red Guards. He asked about the Bolshevik propaganda in the village, to which Makhno replied that there were few propagandists in the villages and that they were helpless. Then Lenin turned to Sverdlov, saying: "[By] reorganization of the Red Guard into the Red Army, we are following the true path to victory of the proletariat over the bourgeoisie."[10] He asked Makhno about his plans in Moscow, and when Makhno told him that he was going home illegally, Lenin commented to Sverdlov that the anarchists had plenty of fanaticism and self-sacrifice but they were shortsighted; they neglected the present for the far distant future. Then he told Makhno he must not take this too personally: "You comrade, I think, have a realistic attitude toward the burning evils of the day. If only one third of the Anarchist-Communists in Russia were such, we, the Communists, would be prepared to make a certain compromise and cooperate with them for the sake of the free organization of producers."[11]

Makhno protested that the Revolution and its achievements were dear to all anarchists. Lenin retorted: "We know the anarchists as well as you. . . . Most of the anarchists think and write about the future, without understanding the present: that is what divides us, the Communists, from them."[12] Makhno stated that as a simple, ill-educated peasant, he could not properly argue about such complicated questions. However, he added:

> I would say, comrade Lenin, that your assertion that the anarchists do not understand "the present" realistically, have no connection with it, and so forth, is basically wrong. The Anarchist-Communists in Ukraine—or as you Communist-Bolsheviks are trying to avoid the word "Ukraine" and are calling it "South Russia"—at this point, "South Russia" has already given too many proofs that they are entirely associated with "the present." The entire struggle of the revolutionary Ukrainian village against the Ukrainian Central Rada proceeded under the ideological leadership of the Anarchist-Communists and, partly, the Russian Socialist-Revolutionaries —who, of course, had entirely different aims in their struggle against the Rada, than we Anarchist-Communists. You Bolsheviks did not exist in the villages, or when you did, you had absolutely no influence.[13]

Finally Lenin asked if Makhno would like help for his illegal journey to Ukraine, and receiving an affirmative answer, instructed Sverdlov to call upon Mr. Karpenko or Volodymyr P. Zatons'kyi[14] to make arrangements. Then he told Makhno to go, the next day or the day after, to Karpenko, who would help him across the frontier. Makhno asked: "What frontier?" Lenin replied: "Don't you know that a frontier has been established between Ukraine and Russia?" "But you consider Ukraine as 'South Russia,' " noted Makhno. Lenin responded: "To consider is one thing, comrade, and to see in reality is another."[15]

Makhno left Lenin with mixed feelings of reverence and resentment. Although Lenin made a strong impact upon Makhno by his personality, his interest in details, and political devices, Makhno knew that it was Lenin who was most reponsible for the drive against the anarchists in Moscow and other cities. During their discussion, however, Lenin told Makhno that the "Soviet government launched a campaign in the centers of revolution not against anarchism but merely against the banditism that had penetrated its ranks." Makhno felt that "it would be difficult to find in any other political masters a greater insincerity and hypocrisy than that displayed by Lenin in this case, especially with reference to anarchism."[16]

Makhno's experience in Russia, especially in Moscow, was also depressing. He was not only disgusted at the Bolshevik mistreatment of the anarchists, but also disappointed at seeing a general eclipse of the movement. In some centers the anarchist groups had either disintegrated or were disorganized and ineffective. He felt that those groups that remained active were spending their time in theoretical discussions, infatuated with their own words and resolutions, but lacking the will to fight for their ideals. Makhno's anarchist friends were vague and left him ideologically in the air and even Kropotkin gave him encouragement and sympathy, but no practical guidance.

Makhno decided to rely on his own intuition. In contrast to the Russian anarchists, who were divided into a number of groups, Makhno stood for the unity of all anarchists, which he felt was a mark of strength. This feeling only confirmed his conviction that he should return to Ukraine and his followers as soon as possible. He felt that the toiling peasants and workers should depend upon their own strength and devices to liberate themselves from the Austro-German forces.

A few days after Makhno visited Lenin, Zatons'kyi provided Makhno with a false passport in the name of Ivan IAkovlevich Shepel, a schoolteacher and a reserve officer from Matviiv-Kurhan county, Taganrog district, Katerynoslav province. On June 29, Arshinov accompanied Makhno to the Kursk station in Moscow and saw him off. Although the train was crowded and hot, Makhno felt better than in Moscow, which was alien to his spirit and temperament.[17] Makhno's trip was slow and difficult, but he reached Kursk and then Belenkino, the terminal, and crossed the frontier without incident. The final stage of his train trip was dangerous because the authorities apparently were informed of his return, and at one place he had to jump from the train to avoid arrest. From there he made his way on foot for twenty-five versts[18] to the village of Rozhdestvenka, about twenty versts from Huliai-Pole, where he hid at the home of a peasant, Zakhar Kleshnia.[19] There he established his conspiratorial headquarters and made contact with his friends at home. Subsequently Huliai-Pole and its area became the center of the Makhno partisan movement against the Austro-German troops and the landlords' punitive detachments.

10. The Origin of Makhno's Partisan Movement

Most of Katerynoslav and Kherson provinces had been assigned to the Austro-Hungarian sphere of influence by the Baden agreement concluded between Austria and Germany on March 2, 1918. Hence in addition to the hetman authority, there was an Austro-Hungarian garrison in Huliai-Pole. At the same time, many of Makhno's supporters (the anarchists and members of the Committee for the Defense of the Revolution and of the local soviet) were either executed, imprisoned, or suppressed.[1] Under these circumstances, it was risky for Makhno even to reside in his home town, not to mention the danger of resuming revolutionary activity. However, he was impatient and eager to organize an independent peasant revolutionary force in the Zaporizhia–Sea of Azov region.

His first action was to issue, on July 4, a secret circular exhorting the peasants to expel the Austro-German troops from Ukraine, overthrow the hetman government, and establish a new order "on the basis of a free society, a structure that would allow those who did not exploit the work of others to live independent of the state and its agencies, including the Reds."[2] The message was circulated in several handwritten copies among the more trusted peasants. Three days later, a second circular outlined a program of action:

> Our primary task . . . should be to achieve a distribution of our people in Huliai-Pole such that there will be adequate numbers in each part of the village. They will be responsible for grouping around themselves a large number of energetic, daring peasants willing to make sacrifices. From these groups they should select daring

men to conduct an action against the Austro-German troops in isolated areas and, if possible, against the landowners at the same time.[3]

Should this action succeed, the enemy's garrison was to be attacked.

Makhno, tired of inactivity in Rozhdestvenka, felt he should be in Huliai-Pole to carry on his work. Consequently, in spite of his friends' warnings of the danger to himself as well as the possibility of reprisals against his followers, one night he arrived on the outskirts of Huliai-Pole, accompanied by two armed men. He remained in hiding in a cottage for several days visiting his old friends at night to discuss the previous spring's events and organizing three-to-five man "initiatory groups" in the area. This laid the groundwork for the later development of the movement.

Makhno's activity was abruptly interrupted by an uprising in the neighboring village of Voskresenka. A group of peasants who had received his earlier circulars and taken them to heart, organized a "Makhno detachment" and attacked a German punitive unit, killing the commander and several soldiers. The uprising not only prompted local authorities to launch house-to-house searches and make arrests, but revealed Makhno's presence in the area. He was hastily smuggled to Rozhdestvenka, then to Ternivka, some fifty miles away, where he hid in the house of his uncle, Izydor Peredyrii.[4] Since he was using the document issued by Zatons'kyi in Moscow, his relatives accordingly spread the word that he was a schoolteacher who had left his town because it was near a war zone.[5]

The situation in the village, however, was still precarious. Makhno hid in the countryside by day, entering the village only at night. This behavior appeared suspicious to the people, especially to the young revolutionaries, who became convinced that he was a government agent and developed a plan to assassinate him. However, Makhno unwittingly saved his own life when he made a propaganda speech against the actions of the Austro-Germans and the hetman regime that removed the doubts about his role in the village.[6]

Observing a fighting spirit among people in Ternivka, Makhno began to organize a paramilitary unit. At first, because premature action would only bring disaster, he intended to establish contact with Huliai-Pole and other towns. However, while he was en route to his home town the people informed him of strict repressive measures undertaken by the punitive expedition. He decided to return to Ternivka to instigate uprisings against the landowners and disperse them from their "counterrevolutionary nests."

Conflict between the peasants and landowners was growing steadily more serious. The peasants particularly resented those owners who had abandoned their holdings at the beginning of the Revolution, only to return with the Austro-Hungarian and German troops, demanding that the crops grown by the peasants in their absence be turned over to them. The landlords used their power uncompromisingly, not only taking back their estates, but robbing the peasants of their crops, and all too often beating, imprisoning, or even executing them. The peasants' bitterness was reflected in one of Makhno's slogans: "Death to all who, with the help of the German-Austrian-Hetmanite bayonets, took from the peasants and workers the fruits of the Revolution."[7]

Although the Ternivka detachment's stock of arms was small, consisting of weapons left by the retreating Bolsheviks, Makhno made a series of successful raids against the estates and punitive detachments. While investigating these actions, the police learned of the presence of a "strange teacher" in the village, so that Makhno had to move again, first to Slavohorod, then to Novo-Hupalivka, where he organized a partisan "initiatory group" but was discovered by the police before he could initiate any action. He then moved to the islands on the Dnieper, where he joined a group of about three hundred men from the First Cossack Volunteer Division (Blue Coats). This unit, originally formed from Ukrainian prisoners of war in Germany, had been demobilized by the Germans after dissolution of the Rada, but some had escaped, with arms, into hiding. Makhno attempted to instigate a rebellion against the "enemies of the Revolution" but the men remained loyal to their commander, who supported the hetman government, and only a few were persuaded to return with Makhno to Ternivka and Huliai-Pole.[8]

Makhno returned to Huliai-Pole at about the same time as his anarchist friends from Russia. In discussing future courses of action, Makhno advocated an immediate armed uprising, while others believed it more practical to await the anticipated arming of the Russian anarchists by the Bolsheviks. Makhno had substantial objections to the latter alternative. First, from his own experience in Russia he knew that the Russian urban anarchists came mostly from the commercial class, who did not understand the peasantry. Moreover, they, "like the Marxists, had fallen into a stupid mistake in regard to the peasantry, considering it as a reactionary-bourgeoisie class incapable of offering active creative forces to the revolution." Thus he expected that they would not come into the countryside, but entrench themselves in the cities, as they had in 1917, contacting the peasants only through messengers, propaganda, and pamphlets.

Second, while independent anarchist forces might be welcomed, a force dependent on the Bolsheviks would be controlled by the Bolsheviks.[9] Finally, he feared that to delay the uprising would be to relinquish the initiative to other political groups, especially those who expected to draw support from Moscow, whereas he was convinced that the peasants should rely only on their own strength and devices.

Makhno's view eventually prevailed, and the group began to organize combat detachments of peasants from Huliai-Pole, Marfopil, and Stepanivka. They attacked and destroyed a number of estates before the state police and Austro-German troops were able to suppress them. Again Makhno and his associates hid in the neighboring villages, where they continued to propagandize and organize small units with small arms and police uniforms. Toward the end of September they moved toward Huliai-Pole, destroying a detachment of state police en route.[10]

A few days later, Makhno's boldness and military skill were manifested in an encounter with a combined Austro-German and state police detachment that, while patrolling, came to Marfopil, where Makhno and his men were staying. The anarchists retreated, leaving their horses but taking the rifles and one machine gun on a cart. When some twenty-five troops took up the pursuit, Makhno turned around, drove directly toward the pursuers, and identified his group as militia. This ruse enabled them to reach almost point-blank range before the deceit was discovered and to inflict several casualties. Among the prisoners were two Galician Ukrainians, who were sent back to their Austrian units with a propaganda letter advising the rank and file to:

> Disobey their officers; to cease to be the assassins of the Ukrainian revolutionaries, peasants, and workers, to cease to be the hangmen of their revolutionary liberation work; but instead to shoot the officers who had brought them into Ukraine and made them the assassins of the better sons of the toiling people; and to return to their fatherland to start a revolution there and liberate their oppressed brothers and sisters.[11]

As retribution, the owner of the house where Makhno stayed was executed by the Austrian military authorities, many peasants were arrested, and the village had to pay a fine of 60,000 rubles.

After the victory the Makhno group held a meeting and decided that the men from distant areas should return to their homes to start uprisings, while Makhno's group moved to the Huliai-Pole area. Once in Huliai-Pole, Makhno called a meeting of about four hundred men in the fields to plan an attack on the garrison there. Although there were two companies of Austro-German troops and about eighty state police, the attack was successful and only the garrison headquarters' staff managed to escape to safety. The insurgents seized the post office, the press, and the railroad station. Soon after they issued two propaganda leaflets explaining the aims of the revolution and calling upon the peasants in the area to support it.

Makhno, however, realized that there was no prospect of a successful defense of the town against the regular troops; therefore, he prevented mass participation in the action to avoid subsequent reprisal by the authorities. When Makhno received intelligence from the stationmaster about the arrival of two Austro-German troop trains he staged a harassing attack to force their deployment, then retreated through the town destroying a number of landlords' estates and capturing horses, rifles, and machine guns. The detachment stopped in the village Dibrivka (Velyka Mykhailivka) about thirty-five versts from Huliai-Pole.[12]

Dibrivka proved to be a milestone for Makhno's partisan movement. From the children in the village, Makhno learned that a partisan detachment was stationed in the famous forests near the town. Its leader, Fedir Shchus', a former sailor on the mine layer *Ioann Zlatoust* and the son of a Dibrivka peasant, had taken the place of the original leader, Nykyfor Brova, who was killed in the second half of July 1918, by the hetman police and the Austrian troops at a *mechetna* (farm).[13] Under Shchus's command the unit grew to about sixty effectives, plus some wounded, by the time of Makhno's arrival. It was well organized and armed with rifles, machine guns, and hand grenades, but clothed somewhat less well, in Austrian, German, or Ukrainian military uniforms, or even civilian dress.[14] Although Makhno had met Shchus' during the fighting against the Austro-German troops the previous spring, and again at the Taganrog congress, he hardly remembered him. However, he immediately contacted Shchus', appealing to him to leave the forests, unite both detachments and fight "against all those who, on behalf of the authorities and the privileged bourgeoisie, were raising their swords against the toilers, against their freedom and rights."[15] After a brief reflection, Shchus', with the approval of his men, agreed to join Makhno. This union at the end of September resulted in a combined force of over one hundred men.

Subsequently, the partisans moved into the village, where they remained for several days conducting propaganda meetings and sending instructions to other places concerning future actions. In these propaganda speeches Makhno spoke for the first time of a new adversary,

Nestor Makhno

"the restorational forces," that is, the Volunteer Army under General Denikin. He was at pains to emphasize that the new enemy was more menacing than the present ones.[16]

Before the reorganization of the two detachments was accomplished, a combined force of Austrians, police, and landlords attacked them at Dibrivka. Under cover of night and with the use of machine guns, the partisans managed to retreat into the forests. Makhno proposed a counterattack to ascertain the strength of the enemy, but Shchus', fearing reprisals against his village, refused. When the punitive force entered the village the next day, according to peasant informers and Makhno's agents, it consisted of one battalion (about five hundred men) of Austrian troops, about one hundred state police, and some eighty landlords and German colonists. Moreover Makhno learned that the enemies were expecting further reinforcement, apparently intending to annihilate the partisans.[17]

To thwart these plans, Makhno again proposed an attack before the reinforcements arrived. Shchus' was opposed to this idea also, so Makhno addressed both groups and rallied the peasants directly, stating:

> In this complicated situation it is better to die in an unequal, but decisive fight against the hangmen before the eyes of the toiling people they have persecuted . . . than to sit in the forests and wait until the bourgeois sons come, assisted by hired hangmen, to destroy us.[18]

Consequently, the partisans, the peasants, and finally the cautious Shchus', accepted his proposition, a major victory for Makhno and his leadership in both partisan groups. Both the partisans and the peasants in the forests of Dibrivka proclaimed "We are with you, comrade Makhno." And from now on you are our "Ukrainian Bat'ko, lead us into the village against the enemy."[19]

Subsequently, an attack was planned that took into consideration the small size and inadequate arms of the partisan group. Makhno sent Shchus' with a small unit to attack from the opposite side while he, with the main body of the partisans, moved in surreptitiously in small groups toward the main square where the punitive force was encamped. By climbing over the back walls and fences, they occupied the shops and houses overlooking the square without being detected. The troops were resting, with their arms stacked. When Makhno's men opened fire at eighty to one hundred yards' range, the panic and confusion among the troops was so great that Makhno succeeded in routing the enemy and capturing most of his arms and horses. The captured Austrian soldiers, including some Galician Ukrainians, were released; the police were executed. Makhno's victory was complete and from this time on his partisan group was known as the "Bat'ko Makhno detachment."[20]

A few days later, a new punitive expedition, consisting of several Austrian infantry and cavalry battalions with a number of field guns, augmented by several detachments of police, together with landlords and German colonists, arrived. Part of this unit shelled the village and then set a fire that destroyed all but a few of the 608 homes. Those who did not escape had their homes burned or were whipped, arrested, or executed.[21] Simultaneously the main force attacked the partisans in the forests under artillery support and wounded both Makhno and Shchus'. To avoid encirclement and annihilation, Makhno had no alternative but to retreat from the forests and move into other areas. They withdrew across the river Kaminka unnoticed.

For a while in the area of Dibrivka Makhno conducted partisan-style harassment operations that were very effective because the partisans were disguised in police uniforms. During this period they attacked several small groups of landlords and German colonists returning from the Dibrivka expedition. Their confessions led the partisans to their estates or settlements, which were subsequently disarmed and burned. A similar fate befell some rich peasants.[22] The partisans also destroyed a number of local police headquarters and Austro-German garrisons as well as stopping in villages and calling peasant meetings at which Makhno would deliver propaganda speeches.

The dramatic events of Dibrivka closed the formative period in the development of Makhno's partisan movement and opened a new permanent stage in the region of Huliai-Pole. The partisans became a unified combat force that steadily grew stronger in numbers and in weapons. It assumed a definite name, "The Revolutionary Partisan Detachments of Bat'ko Makhno," and a unified leadership. The river Kaminka was Makhno's Rubicon.

11. Organization and Tactics of Makhno's Partisan Army

The Dibrivka incident raised doubts in Makhno's mind as to the wisdom of his policy of vengeance and destruction. After a thorough discussion with his closest friends Makhno decided that thenceforward the real aim of partisans should be:

> To expropriate as much arms and money as possible from our enemies, and to raise the peasant masses as soon as possible; to unite them, to arm them to the teeth, and to lead them on a wide front against the existing system and its supporters.[1]

This opinion was motivated by his desire to free the region from all authorities and to establish a permanent operative headquarters of the partisan movement at Huliai-Pole. According to Makhno's wife: "His ultimate plan is to take possession of a small territory in Ukraine and there establish a free commune. Meanwhile, he is determined to fight every reactionary force."[2]

With the approval of the partisans, Makhno and his associates formulated a requisition system for arms, light carts and carriages (later known as *tachanky*), essential supplies, horses, and money. Subsequently the partisans moved from estate to estate and from one area to another, avoiding villages and propaganda speeches, but continuing to attack and disarm Austro-German and police detachments. In the course of a few weeks Makhno collected a large number of carts, horses, supplies, and a substantial amount of money, and the number of partisans increased day by day.

Thus the Makhno detachments not only grew but changed their entire structure, being converted into light, mobile, and rapid combat detachments on carts and horses. This action showed to the population their determination in fighting "the enemies of the revolution." The increasing threat of Makhno's units caused many landlords, especially those who had returned to their estates the previous spring, to abandon their estates and settle in the population centers where they could be protected by the Austro-German troops. This shift facilitated Makhno's work and served to increase his control in the countryside.

The growing strength and increasing activities of the partisans evoked further counteractions by their enemies. On the way through the districts of Berdians'k, Mariupil', and Pavlohrad, Makhno encountered and defeated an Austrian battalion and a police detachment at Staryi Kremenchuk. However, the next day at Temerivka, where the partisans stayed overnight, they were suddenly attacked by a strong Hungarian unit that forced its way into the village. The partisans, confused and disorganized, were pushed out of the village into the fields where they became easy targets. Many were killed or wounded—among the wounded were Shchus', Karetnyk, and Makhno. This defeat, however, did not change Makhno's resolve to move to Huliai-Pole.

The partisans were involved in numerous skirmishes in the area before they could enter the town.[3] Subsequently, Makhno called a meeting of partisans and some peasants to give them a report on his activities. It was decided to disarm all the "bourgeois" in the area. Makhno also sent a telegram to the authorities at Oleksandrivs'k prison, mainly for propaganda purposes, demanding the release of the Huliai-Pole anarchists. Although the authorities did not comply, they responded favorably, assuring him that they would come to no harm.

The most important decision Makhno made at the meeting was to transform the initial local underground groups into revolutionary combat formations drafted from the villages of the Huliai-Pole area. These units were to consist of cavalry and infantry on light carts with machine guns mounted on them, able to move with great speed, one hundred versts in twenty-four hours.[4] The decision was motivated by Makhno's plan to establish fronts in the areas of Chaplino-Hryshyne and Tsarekostiantynivka-Polohy-Orikhiv against the Austro-German troops, the Don Cossacks, the police and landlord detachments, and against Mikhail G. Drozdovskii, who in the spring of 1918, with a unit of about two thousand men, advanced through South Ukraine from the Romanian front to the Don Basin.

Some of Makhno's friends considered his plan impossible, pointing out they had no professional officers to lead large front operations. Makhno, however, felt that commissioned officers with "revolutionary passion" could manage responsible military operations. Eventually certain of his friends were persuaded of their military competence and made front commanders: Petro Petrenko was entrusted with the Chaplino-Hryshyne front and Tykhenko, Jr., and Krasovk'kyi jointly with the Tsarekostiantynivka-Polohy front. The Orikhiv front remained temporarily unoccupied. Although the commanders had local initiative, in over-all operations they were subordinated to the main staff of the partisan detachments of Bat'ko Makhno and to Makhno directly.[5]

As the plan of the partisans' reorganization was agreed upon, each of the new commanders with his staff moved to the area of his assignment. Meanwhile, Makhno and his partisans of the Huliai-Pole area toured Oleksandrivs'k and Pavlohrad districts for three weeks, while Makhno reorganized local partisan groups into larger combat detachments subordinate to his main staff, in order to make possible larger military operations in the region. At this time Makhno's group fought a number of Austro-German and police units and detachments of landlords and of the German colonists. Although suffering heavy losses, the partisans expelled their adversaries from the region and were then free to carry on their activities thereafter. As the number of partisans and skirmishes grew, Makhno became aware that a tighter military organization was essential if his partisans were to withstand the constant assaults of the enemy.

The organization of the Makhno Army was a process of several stages. Its troop strength changed frequently depending upon political and military conditions and the threat to the region of the Makhno movement. Its main organizer was Makhno, who had neither military training nor previous military experience, but was an able organizer and a born tactician, especially resourceful in the arts of guerrilla warfare. The character of the army was a projection of Makhno's own character. According to his chief adversary, General Slashchov:

> There is one thing for which he must be given credit, that is, skill in forming quickly and in controlling his detachments, instilling, in fact, a very strict discipline. Therefore, an engagement with him always had a serious aspect, and his feats of arms, energy, and ability to direct operations gave him a great number of victories over opposing armies.[6]

Slashchov recognized that Makhno's military skill in directing operations was not attributable to his previous education.

Other military men also credited Makhno with innate military talent. General Mykola Kapustians'kyi sketched him as:

Characteristic group of Makhno men

A man of strong will, sound wisdom, determination, personal courage, with desire for power and good judgment of human psychology. Moreover, Makhno had organizational abilities and, finally, he had the sense, in time of danger, to ally himself with one of his adversaries who at the moment showed more power and strength.[7]

General Mykhailo Omelianovych-Pavlenko confirmed that "Makhno personified the obscure rebellious demands of the masses [but] knew how to organize them into a fighting force, to work out a discipline specific for the Makhno men and even his own tactical methods. This externally unimpressive man became a dictator and leader of the masses."[8]

Because of Makhno's brilliant military successes, it was sometimes assumed that the army's operational tactics must be in the hands of professional officers. Hence a rumor sprang up that Colonel Kleist of the German General Staff was with Makhno and directed his operations, guided perhaps by Makhno's firm will and familiarity with the local population.[9] Omelianovych-Pavlenko maintained that "An able military organizer Vasil'ev, assisted by sergeant Dovzhenko, seaman Liashchenko, and others, gave the Makhno bands the appearance of partisan detachments."[10] General Kapustians'kyi even insisted that in organizing his staff, Makhno: "Under threat of execution, forced military specialists to work in it. [And] as a chief of staff, Makhno, it seems, appointed an officer with a military academy education."[11] A Russian general supposed that Makhno "had a regularly organized staff, with general officers, divisions, and regiments, mainly cavalry and machine gunners, their own supply bases, and regularly functioning hospitals with doctors and nurses and other staff," taken over from his enemies.[12]

There was, however, no evidence that Makhno had any such officers on his staff. One of the Don Cossack officers who fought Makhno reported: "Once there was a feeling that the operative work and the formation of the units of his army had been in the hands of a well-trained officer of the General Staff; in reality such an assumption was simply baseless."[13] Although Makhno had undoubtedly had opportunities to attract professional officers to the partisan army, he had not done so, apparently for fear of competition. For example, at the end of 1918, when Makhno attacked the Ukrainian garrison in Katerynoslav, the artillery brigade commander, Colonel Martynenko, defected and turned over sixteen field guns to Makhno. Although Makhno welcomed him into the partisan ranks, he later shot him for fear of rivalry.[14]

As the Makhno army gradually grew, it assumed a more regular army organization. Each tactical unit was composed of three subordinate units: a division consisted of three brigades; a brigade, of three regiments; a regiment, of three battalions, and so on. Theoretically commanders were elected; in practice, however, the top commanders were usually carefully selected by Makhno from among his close friends. As a rule, they were all equal and if several units fought together the top commanders commanded jointly. The army was nominally headed by a Revolutionary Military Council of about ten to twenty members chaired at times by Makhno, Volin, and Liashchenko, among others. Like the commanders, council members were elected, but some were appointed by Makhno. However, the council had no decisive voice in the army's actions; Makhno and his top commanders made decisions without taking account of the council's opinion, while other problems were decided by the top commanders themselves. There also was an elected cultural section in the army. Its aim was to conduct political and ideological propaganda among the partisans and peasants.[15]

The army was made up of infantry, cavalry, artillery, machine-gun units, and special branches, including an intelligence service. Because the success of partisan warfare depends upon mobility, the army, at first composed largely of infantry, gradually was mounted in light carts and armed with machine guns during 1918–19, and during the years 1920–21 became primarily a cavalry formation. The artillery was comparatively small because it was less applicable to partisan warfare.

Over half the troops were volunteers, including adventurers, who were the bravest men from villages and towns. The rest were conscripts, men who generally were less privileged. The troops wore whatever they pleased; some had military uniforms of different armies while others were dressed in civilian clothes or simple peasant dress, all of similarly heterodox color.[16]

The army had no reserves and, because of its great speed and constant movement, there were neither troop trains nor central supply bases. Makhno depended upon the peasants and his enemies. He used to say: "My supplies are the Soviet trains,"[17] though he did attempt to organize his supply base in the summer of 1919, when he reorganized his army. Similarly there were no field hospitals, but only a few doctors, physicians' assistants, and nurses, some of whom had been trained in a military hospital in Katerynoslav. The army depended upon peasant houses and occasionally town hospitals.[18] According to an eyewitness: "When the local peasants found that a Makhno detachment had arrived [in the village they] were very glad and immediately allocated the wounded among the houses, fed them and dried their clothing."[19]

When on the move, Makhno's column was several versts long. The supply train moved at the head; the infantry, on carts and other vehicles, moved behind it, followed by the cavalry, which guarded the rear and provided flank security by using adjacent roads. Makhno rode a cart or a horse either behind or alongside, and sometimes rode up and down the column to maintain order. The marching troops were occupied with singing or playing small instruments, such as mouth organs. Although many of the Makhno partisans had an inclination for drinking, during troop movements and in action the consumption of alcohol was prohibited under threat of execution on the spot; this was strikingly similar to the Zaporozhian Cossacks' policy. A teacher in whose house Makhno had once stayed later told one of Denikin's generals that "Makhno made upon him an impression of a modest, reserved, and decidedly not bloodthirsty man; he was always busy with his chief of staff of military operations and did not participate in drinking with his bands." During the stops the troops made camp in a circle with the staff in its center, forming a defense against attacks from any quarter.[20]

Even Makhno was uncertain of the number of men he led, for the conditions of partisan warfare constantly changed the army's size and no personnel records were kept. The army's strength fluctuated with the extent of the threats and terror waged in the country by the different enemies. Makhno often counted the potential partisans in the countryside who in case of need would join his army. In his words: "The army consisted of over thirty thousand armed men and over seventy thousand organized in the villages and towns . . . who because of lack of arms remained at home."[21] Moreover, there were a number of independent partisan groups that called themselves Makhno partisans to increase their prestige.

In the spring of 1918 Makhno formed several military units, consisting of about seventeen hundred men, and a medical service unit to fight the Austrian and German troops, supporting the Central Rada against the Bolsheviks. Soon, however, the units joined the Ukrainian troops. Although during the summer of 1918 Makhno organized partisan detachments to fight the Austro-Germans' and landlords' punitive expeditions, they were underground militia rather than regular combat detachments, for Makhno lacked a territory under his own control in which to erect a standing army. Toward the end of September 1918, Makhno's combat unit consisted of about fifty to sixty partisans, united in the Dibrivka forests with Shchus's well-organized and armed partisan detachment of over sixty men.[22] The defeat of the Austro-German punitive expedition at Dibrivka sealed this union of a combined force of over one hundred partisans that was named "The Bat'ko Makhno Detachment" after its recognized commander.

As the activities and popularity of Makhno grew, a number of independent partisan groups joined Makhno.[23] The Makhno partisan group steadily grew stronger in number and in weapons and eventually assumed a new name, "The Revolutionary Partisan Detachments of Bat'ko Makhno," and a unified leadership. Gradually the units changed their entire structure, being converted into light, mobile, combat detachments on carts and horses. The punitive expeditions against the peasants substantially swelled the ranks of Makhno's group. Although toward the end of 1918, he had over six hundred men, including cavalry, the lack of arms and equipment prevented Makhno from organizing an army.[24] Makhno recalled that when he left the Dibrivka forest many peasants begged: " 'Give us arms, we will go now with you. . . .' We had no arms . . . and, almost with tears in our eyes, we were compelled to leave these peasants in the forests."[25]

This situation changed when the defeat of the Central Powers in the west demoralized their troops in Ukraine and the partisans were able to disarm the troops or to buy their weapons. Before they retreated from Ukraine, however, two new enemies began to threaten the country: the Volunteer troops from the south, and the Bolsheviks from the north. In the winter of 1919, when the Denikin troops began to oppress the population and many of the peasants mobilized by Denikin went over with their arms to Makhno, the number of Makhno troops grew to over sixteen thousand. As the Denikin threat increased, Makhno joined the Bolsheviks, who agreed to supply arms to fight the common enemy. By mid-May the Makhno Army had 20,000 infantry and 2,000 cavalry with two heavy artillery pieces, five guns, and a large number of machine guns.[26]

The subsequent break with the Bolsheviks temporarily disorganized the army and decreased its size, but the terror used by both Denikin and the Bolsheviks gave Makhno new recruits and new support from the peasants. Moreover, the large partisan groups of the assassinated Hryhor'iv joined Makhno. Thus by the end of July, his army had increased again to 15,000 men. After the defeat of the Bolsheviks in Ukraine and their retreat, Makhno units that had remained in the Red Army since June rejoined him, bringing arms and a number of other Red units. At the beginning of August the Makhno Army numbered 20,000.[27] Toward the end of September when Makhno defeated Slashchov and stalled his advance into Denikin's rear, more independent partisan groups joined him; thus at the beginning of October the army had 25,000 men. At the end of the month, the army's growth, including separate partisan units in the countryside, peaked at about forty thousand.[28]

During the winter of 1919–20 Makhno suffered serious setbacks. After Denikin had been defeated and had withdrawn from Ukraine, Makhno was still confronted with the Bolsheviks, who were now free to turn their attention to the partisans. At that time, 50 percent of the partisan army, including Makhno and some of his staff, contracted typhus and went to villages for cure, while many others hid in villages waiting for further developments.[29] However, although the partisan army was badly disorganized and substantially weakened, it remained at over ten thousand. In contrast to 1919, at the beginning of spring 1920 it was divided into small local defense detachments acting independently as an underground force. Only the core of the army—cavalry and cart-mounted machine-gun regiments—continued its previous operations under Makhno's command. As the political situation changed, the local detachments could be quickly augmented by volunteers.[30]

At the beginning of fall, the army consisted of 12,000 men. In mid-October, when Makhno concluded an agreement with the Bolsheviks, he dispatched against Wrangel an army of about ten thousand, including fifteen hundred cavalry, while about three thousand, including one thousand cavalry, remained with him in Huliai-Pole. However, as soon as Wrangel was defeated, the Bolsheviks turned against their ally Makhno, as they had after Denikin's defeat the year before. His Crimean Army almost completely annihilated, Makhno was left with a detachment of about three thousand. During the winter of 1920–21, the army again increased, for a while, to over ten thousand men.[31] As the Bolsheviks ended their hostilities on all other fronts they overwhelmed Makhno by dispatching a large number of troops and armor against his detachments. Under such conditions he could not organize a large unified army. According to Makhno, in the spring of 1921 his army consisted of 2,000 cavalry and several regiments of infantry. For the rest of the campaign, which ended in August, the size of the partisan army fluctuated from 1,000 to 5,000. Moreover, for tactical reasons, it was divided into small units of 200 to 500 men each, operating separately.[32]

Makhno's successes in the field depended not so much on the strength of his army as on military tactics, which he tailored to the conditions he faced. The secret of Makhno's triumphs was mainly in the mobility, maneuverability, bravery, and fire power of his troops. His cavalry could cover from eighty to one hundred versts a day, while a regular cavalry unit moved only forty to sixty versts. This speed was maintained by exchanging horses with peasants. The slogan was: "Each village is a horse depot." As a rule, Makhno avoided major battles with powerful adversaries. According to an eyewitness: "We tried to surround the enemy and draw him into a major battle, but Makhno was clearly avoiding a general confrontation even though he was aided by an excellent knowledge of the terrain and a widespread network of informers."[33] When, however, he encountered superior enemy forces he would draw up a wide front line of infantry supported by heavy machine-gun fire and then the cavalry reserves would attack the enemy's flanks and rear to break their formation.

On other occasions, forced to confrontation, he would strengthen his lines by summoning peasants from the villages, on foot and mounted, carrying sticks and scythes to create panic among the enemy by their number. According to the same eyewitness:

> Ruses that Makhno used bore witness to his unusual cunning. Once during a battle we observed on the skyline numerous troops of cavalry that, it seemed, aimed at attacking our rear. Panic spread among our ranks, but soon our reconnaissance unit explained this matter; Makhno mounted on horseback the peasants from the villages and simulated an encircling maneuver. It must be admitted that he was not without imagination.[34]

When this tactic failed, Makhno would contain the enemy with machine-gun and artillery fire, then skillfully retreat in a loose formation at great speed, disappearing from view and leaving behind an extra detachment to mislead the enemy. Later he would reappear with his main force in the rear to attack enemy staff and headquarters, creating panic and demoralization.[35]

There were, of course, other factors contributing to Makhno's success. He often took the enemy unaware by conducting operations at night, in bad weather, in difficult terrain, or in villages and towns. Moreover, Makhno had a well-organized and efficient intelligence service that was particularly effective because of the active support of the rural population. When cornered by superior forces, the partisans would disband, bury their weapons, and mingle in the villages as peaceful peasants, only to reassemble again when the enemy had passed, uncover their arms, and attack again from the least expected quarter.[36] An eyewitness admits:

> Makhno gave us a bad time by attacking suddenly and forcing us to be in a constant state of readiness, which prevented us from unsaddling our horses and laying our arms aside even for a minute. We pursued Makhno with a cold fury engendered of

hatred of the bloody leader who gave us no respite. . . . [Therefore] the only effective way to fight Makhno was, in an encounter, to strike down his units, not allowing them their usual practice of disappearing into the woods or dispersing in the villages, hiding sabres and rifles under the straw, acting as peaceful peasants who would attack us suddenly at the least expected moment.[37]

A Bolshevik officer describes an incident illustrating cooperation between partisans and peasants. As a Bolshevik unit was pursuing several partisans who vanished in a village "as if the earth had swallowed them,"

in one of the yards an old man is winnowing rye while a young man is threshing corn, urging on the horses. "Oh, old man, did you see which way the carts went?" "Of course, I saw them; they went there, to the steppe, there is the cloud of dust." "And who is threshing corn for you?" "That is my son Opanas, so stupid and mad that he doesn't utter a word." The Reds rushed in the direction indicated to overtake the carts. Meanwhile the "mad boy" pulled out a rifle from the cornstack and unhitched the horses from belt-drive; three other "mad boys" came out to help him harness the horses to the cart hidden under the straw and together they moved out from the village in the opposite direction.[38]

Makhno usually tried to destroy the enemy from inside, although such activity was very risky and demanded skill and personal bravery. According to an eyewitness:

The calmness of Makhno's men while preparing for the battle was amazing. At that time when the shrapnel was exploding about forty paces away, Makhno's men were washing, combing their hair, and waiting for orders. And how much military skill was manifested among the leaders and partisans. . . . Makhno's first action was to explore the area where he was staying.[39]

Makhno was a good example for his men, always at the head of his troops in attack and last to retreat, fighting and showing a reckless bravery. Often his men had to stop him from going too far ahead. Makhno was wounded about twelve times, twice seriously.[40] One eyewitness reported that when Makhno was forced by General Slashchov from Katerynoslav at the end of November 1919: "Makhno left last, and ten minutes later, on Sadova Street, the same along which Makhno had just quietly ridden, restraining his hot horse with difficulty, appeared riders with officers' epaulets upon their shoulders."[41]

One of Makhno's first uses of his unorthodox tactics was in the summer of 1918, when he organized a group of twenty partisans armed with rifles, hand grenades, and a few machine guns that were loaded on carriages and covered with rugs. This unit, disguised as a wedding party with music, and with the men dressed in festive women's garb, traveled to a village near Huliai-Pole where a German unit was garrisoned. As the curious Germans watched the "wedding party," the partisans, when they reached point-blank range, pulled out their weapons and began to shoot. At the end of October 1919, after several days of unsuccessful fighting against Slashchov to take Katerynoslav, Makhno sent a group of partisans into the city dressed as peasants on their way to buy provisions. When they reached the marketplace, they produced weapons and, in coordination with the troops outside the city, drove the enemy out.[42]

In the summer of 1921, when Makhno was surrounded by Red Army troops, there seemed to be no way out. While waiting for Makhno to break through the line, one of the Red brigades noted the approach of a detachment with red banners, singing the *Internationale*. Believing it to be a Red unit that had just defeated Makhno, the Red troops were unprepared when Makhno attacked, disarmed them, and slipped out of the circle.[43] Throughout the campaign on many occasions, Makhno displayed similar skill and boldness.

From the beginning of his military activities, Makhno's desire was to free his region from the enemy. In contrast, therefore, to his anarchist friends who considered their main goal to be the spread of anarchist propaganda among the population, Makhno believed in organizing military force. The terror and exploitation in the wake of the foreign invasions of the region drove the people to the support of the Makhno movement; this was essential to its success. They provided Makhno with recruits, informers, horses, provisions, shelter for the wounded, and hiding places for partisans.

Although Makhno had neither military training nor previous military experience, he organized partisan units and united them with other partisan groups in his region to form a most effective, mobile partisan army. He introduced the practice of burying arms and dispersing men in small groups in the villages, to reassemble them when the enemy had passed and attack again in the least expected quarter. This operation was possible because Makhno had a well-organized intelligence service and the cooperation of the people, a host of wise and brave collaborators who turned the partisan army into a fighting force to be reckoned with.

According to a Soviet eyewitness:

> From the military viewpoint, the Makhno movement represented a rather formidable and large force. In the pages of civil war history, the amazing tricks that Makhno's cavalry and machine gun units played should undoubtedly be noted. Makhno's raid during the advance from Kyiv province to Katerynoslav province,

his own region, was really amazing. There were moments when Denikin units outnumbered the Makhno army many times, surrounded it so strongly that not the slightest possibility of escape could be foreseen—and here Makhno's men were saved by their bravery, boldness, and resourcefulness, which together composed a great military talent that not only Makhno, but also many other commanders, [had].[44]

12. The Overthrow of the Hetman and the Establishment of the Directory

Over-all popular dissatisfaction with the national, social, and agricultural policies of the hetman government brought about not only peasant uprisings but sharp opposition from the political parties. Although in the early days of the coup the hetman "had a clear intention to give the government a national Ukrainian character,"[1] by inviting the leaders of parties to enter the government and administration, they chose to form an opposition rather than to accept the hetman's invitation. In mid-May they organized the Ukrainian National Political Union (Ukrains'kyi Natsional'no Derzhavnyi Soiuz) in Kyiv "to save threatened Ukrainian statehood and to consolidate all forces for the purpose of creating an independent Ukrainian state." It was composed of the Independist-Socialists, the Socialist-Federalists, the Labor party, the Democratic Farmers party, the Council of the Railroad Trade Unions of Ukraine, and the Council of the All-Ukrainian Post and Telegraph Association. The Social Democrats and Socialist Revolutionaries participated only on a consultative basis.

On May 24 a delegation of the Union presented a memorandum to the hetman charging that the cabinet was Ukrainian neither in its composition nor in political orientation. Largely Russian Kadets, Octobrists, and other non-Ukrainian groups inimical to Ukrainian statehood, such a cabinet could not possibly enjoy the confidence of the broad masses of population. Further, the memorandum pointed out, under the hetman government many Russians of different views had joined forces in working against Ukrainian statehood and for "one and indivisible Russia." It also criticized the bans on congresses of zemstvos, cities, workers, and peasants, which had brought strong protests and denounced the new administration's policy of restoring the old regime with its national and social injustices, and the ministers of education and justice for failing to Ukrainize the schools and courts. The situation in the other ministries, the church, and the army, was still worse. It appeared, the memorandum continued, that the government was ignorant of the occurrence of the Revolution. The growth of anarchy and disorder in the villages and the spread of bolshevism have been attributed to the hetman government. The solution of these problems supposedly lay in the establishment of a Ukrainian national government that would enjoy the confidence of the Ukrainian people.[2]

On May 30 the Union issued appeals to the German people, calling upon them to abide by the Treaty of Brest-Litovsk by ceasing to intervene in the internal affairs of Ukraine and ceasing to support the non-Ukrainian element against the Ukrainian statehood.[3] The memoranda remained unanswered.

The Congress of the All-Ukrainian Union of Zemstvos, which had developed into a center of opposition to the government, met in mid-June and sent a protest to the hetman criticizing the government for such oppression as widespread arrests, punitive expeditions, denial of civil liberties, and suppression of zemstvo and *Prosvita* societies. When this protest failed to change the hetman's policy, Symon Petliura, who under the Central Rada was secretary of military affairs, sent, as head of the Kyiv provincial zemstvo and All-Ukrainian Union of Zemstvos, a memorandum to the German Ambassador Mumm, with copies to the ambassadors of Austria-Hungary and Bulgaria, informing them of arrests, which included national leaders, by both the government and the Germans. He pointed out that such action would not promote Ukrainian-German friendship. Petliura's activities and popularity worried both the hetman regime and the Germans. He was, therefore, arrested on July 12. Although there were strong protests against his arrest and petitions for his release, Petliura was kept in jail until the beginning of November. In the meantime, a strike of civil service employees in the Ministry of Agriculture was precipitated by the dismissal of a number of employees who had stayed on from the period of the Central Rada. The strikers demanded the reinstatement of these employees, dismissal of the "Russifiers" hired in their place, and the use of the Ukrainian language. Employees from some of the other ministries joined the strike, demanding the use of Ukrainian in the offices.[4]

In July the leaders of the opposition, in order to strengthen their position vis-à-vis the government, transformed the National Political Union into the Ukrainian National Union (Ukrains'kyi National'nyi Soiuz), which was composed not only of political parties, including the Social Democrats and Socialist Revolutionaries, but also of cultural, professional, peasant, and labor organizations. Its first president was the editor of the newspaper *Nova Rada* Andrii V. Nikovs'kyi, a Socialist Federalist, who on September 18 was succeeded by Volodymyr Vynnychenko. The principal aims of the new organization were: establishment of a strong and independent Ukrainian state; a legal government responsible to a parliament; democratic suffrage on a direct, general, equal, secret, and proportional basis; and the defense of the rights of the Ukrainian people and their state in the international sphere.[5]

For some time the hetman had planned to strengthen his cabinet and to bring into the government representatives of the national democratic group. He accepted the new National Union as the embodiment of this group, and on October 5 invited its leaders to negotiate reorganization of the government. After a short period of cabinet crisis, on October 24 a new cabinet, headed by Fedir Lyzohub, was formed. Although Dmytro Doroshenko remained as foreign minister, he was not a candidate of the National Union. On October 29 the hetman proclaimed that he would strengthen the independence of Ukraine, introduce land reform, and call a diet. Although the new cabinet carried through various measures that previously had been delayed, including land reform, it had neither genuine support among the more radical circles nor enough time to complete its planned work. The National Union participated in the formation of the new government, but Vynnychenko soon publicly announced that the National Union could not accept responsibility for the actions of the new cabinet and would stand in opposition to it.[6] The hetman not only distrusted the National Union but he suspected that it was plotting against his government.

The tense and confused situation was brought to an end by the defeat of Germany on the Western front and the signing of the Armistice on November 11. The hetman and Ukraine in general were confronted with a dangerous situation because "the Armistice had prescribed the immediate evacuation by the Germans of the Ukraine," hence the possibility of a new Soviet Russian invasion.[7]

To prevent this, it was imperative for the hetman to come to an understanding with the Entente. Although the leaders of the Entente welcomed a union of all anti-Bolshevik forces for a struggle against Soviet Russia, they did not favor Ukrainian independence, demanding instead federation with non-Bolshevik Russia. The hetman decided upon federation, hoping this policy would convince the Entente of his good faith and loyalty. The new orientation was expressed on November 14 by a declaration of a federative union with a future non-Bolshevik Russia. Simultaneously, almost all Ukrainian ministers left the government, and a new cabinet was formed under Sergei N. Gerbel.[8]

The declaration of a federation only accelerated the long-planned mass insurrection against the hetman government. On November 13 the leaders of the National Union met in secret in Kyiv and elected the "Directory," an executive organ of the National Union consisting of five members, to lead the insurrection: Vynnychenko, president; Petliura, commander in chief, both Social Democrats; Fedir Shvets, Socialist Revolutionary; Panas Andriievs'kyi, Independent Socialist; and Andrii Makarenko, Railroad Trade Union.[9]

One of the first acts of the Directory was a proclamation to the people issued on the night of November 14 that stated:

> On behalf of organized Ukrainian democracy, from the whole active national population, who elected us, we, the Directory of the Ukrainian National Republic, proclaim: General Pavlo Skoropads'kyi is a coercionist and usurper of the people's authority. His whole government is proclaimed to be annulled because it is antipeople, antinational.[10]

The government was accused of oppression and destruction of the people's rights. The hetman and his ministers were advised to resign immediately to preserve peace and prevent bloodshed. All Russian officers were told to surrender their arms and leave Ukraine or be deported. The hope was expressed that the soldiers of the democratic German Republic would not intervene in the internal struggle. An appeal was made to all honest Ukrainians and non-Ukrainians to stand together with the Directory as a friendly armed force against the enemies; subsequently, all the social and political achievements of the revolutionary democracy were to be restored. "And the Ukrainian Constituent Assembly shall firmly strengthen them in the free Ukrainian land."[11]

Bila Tserkva, where the Sich Riflemen had recently reassembled with the consent of the hetman after being disarmed at the end of the previous April, was chosen as the center of insurrection and the headquarters of the Directory. On November 16, the Riflemen took the city; the next day, they captured Fastiv and began to move toward Kyiv. Although other Ukrainian units and thousands of peasants joined the Sich Riflemen, they encountered a serious obstacle in the German troops. After some armed clashes an agreement was concluded with the Germans in the Bila Tserkva area by which the Directory promised not to attack the Germans if they did not intervene in the internal Ukrainian struggle. This was, however, only a local success. At that time the hetman sent the Russian volunteer units and some Ukrainian troops, altogether about three thousand men, against the Directory's advancing forces. On November 18 between Motovylivka and Vasyl'kiv the hetman forces were routed, the best Ukrainian unit, the Serdiuks, defected to the Directory, and the remnant retreated to Kyiv. In the meantime the whole of Ukraine was aflame with partisan uprisings and gradually the partisans began to join the regular Ukrainian troops. In the countryside German troops proclaimed neutrality while the Russian volunteers and the punitive units ran away or joined the Directory. Within a few weeks the Right Bank was under the control of the Directory.[12]

On November 21 the Directory's troops began the siege of Kyiv and could have taken the city if the Germans had not reversed the Bila Tserkva agreement and decided to hold Kyiv. Subsequently a line of demarcation was established between the Ukrainian and German troops.[13] The Germans, however, recognized the futility of their position: their troops in Ukraine were demoralized by the defeat in the West, the revolutions in Ukraine and at home, and the hostility of the Ukrainian population, and now their only desire was to go home. In the German garrison in Kyiv, the German higher command sent its representative to Koziatyn to meet with the representatives of the Directory, Dr. Osyp Nazaruk and General Mykhailo Hrekiv. On December 12 they signed an agreement guaranteeing the Germans safe passage home in return for German neutrality. Simultaneously the Ukrainian troops attacked the hetman's units, consisting of Russian officers, and in two days of fighting defeated them. About two thousand were interned but most of the units withdrew to the Left Bank or hid in the city. There was sporadic resistance by the hetman's units in the Chernihiv area and Volyn' province. On December 14 the Ukrainian troops entered Kyiv.[14]

The hetman, having cast his lot with the Germans, was now compelled to share their fate. The same day, one month after the declaration of a federative union with a future non-Bolshevik Russia, the hetman abdicated:

> I, hetman of all Ukraine, have employed all my energies during the past seven and one-half months in an effort to extricate Ukraine from the difficult situation in which she finds herself. God has not given me the strength to deal with this problem and now, in the light of conditions that have arisen and acting solely for the good of Ukraine, I abdicate all authority.[15]

Simultaneously the government also resigned; a few days later, the hetman, disguised as a wounded German soldier, along with his wife dressed as a nurse, left Kyiv for Germany by way of Holoby, Volyn', in a German troop train.[16]

The hetman worked throughout the period of his administration under highly unfavorable conditions inherited from the Central Rada. Moreover, he had not assumed office by the will of the people and thus he lacked popular support. Although the title "hetman" was appealing to the population, the very conservatism it reflected was incompatible with the radical period. The hetman's government and administrative apparatus were weakened by being erected in part on a foundation of non-Ukrainian elements that either had no understanding of the social and national problems or were opposed to Ukrainian statehood. Moreover, Russian organizations and military formations in Ukraine made attempts to discredit the hetman regime in the eyes of the population, tolerating the hetman state only as long as the circumstances of international politics made it necessary. The hetman's government was also weakened by the refusal of many Ukrainians to join it for political and psychological reasons and by the systematic Austro-German interference in Ukrainian internal affairs. In effect, there were two governments side by side. Government policy was characterized by a number of reactionary decrees and by punitive expeditions that turned the population, especially the peasants, against it.

Finally, the international situation was unfavorable to Ukrainian statehood. The hetman's association with the Germans prevented him from establishing cordial relations with the Entente, which supported the non-Bolshevik Russian forces, with whom it induced the hetman to federate. Federation was considered by the people to be foreign rule and a return to the hated old political system, and moreover, it implied that Ukraine would continue to be the main base of the struggle for a non-Bolshevik Russia. These sociopolitical and national factors explain the spontaneity and success of the uprising.

On December 19 the Directory entered Kyiv. As the government of the reestablished Ukrainian People's Republic, the Directory issued a declaration[17] on December 26 proclaiming Ukraine free from punitive expeditions, gendarmes, and other repressive institutions of the ruling classes. It restored individual autonomy, and reinstated the eight-hour workday, collective bargaining agreements, and the right to strike. It declared that the right to govern the country should belong only to those classes that created material and spiritual values; the nonworking classes should have no voice in the government. The sociopolitical objectives stated in the declaration satisfied neither those on the Left nor those on the Right, and its appeal to the populace was blunted because news of the declaration did not reach the provinces for some time.

Simultaneously the three parties that were represented in the Directory, the Social Democrats, Socialist Revolutionaries, and the Independist Socialists, formed a cabinet headed by Volodymyr M. Chekhivs'kyi, a Social Democrat, who also held the portfolio of foreign affairs. No effort was made to reconvene the Central Rada because it had been discredited by its cooperation with the Germans prior to the hetman coup. The new government had to face difficult foreign problems and such domestic problems as the organization of administration and defense. Most of the administrative personnel of the hetman regime either escaped or went into hiding, leaving the new government without enough trained administrators to fill the positions. The inability of the government to establish a firm and effective administration brought about anarchy. Some local partisan leaders were cut off from the center by Russian military operations and thus were unable to work with the government. Others were unwilling to subordinate themselves to the government and even followed independent courses in opposition to it because the objectives of the masses were far more radical than those of the government.[18]

Defense, however, soon became the main issue of the time. During the uprisings against the hetman regime the Directory's call to arms was obeyed by hundreds of thousands of peasants and workers. When the Directory entered the capital, it had some one hundred thousand troops, thirty thousand near Kyiv alone. Moreover, "the troops that entered Kyiv were admired by all for their discipline, training, and their lusty and strong bearing." However, the enthusiasm of the volunteers soon began to evaporate and the forces rapidly dwindled. To prevent their disintegration and to reorganize many of the partisan units that were dedicated to the national cause, vigorous measures were needed to organize them into a disciplined force. The creation of a reliable regular army to meet the threat of an imminent Soviet Russian invasion was beyond the Directory's power because it had an inadequate number of officers, arms, and uniforms.[19] It would have been impossible, even under the most favorable conditions, to organize a strong army in two or three weeks.

The most positive development during the critical period of the Directory was in the relations between the National Republic and the western part of Ukraine. The breakup of the Hapsburg monarchy in October 1918 created the opportunity for former Austro-Hungarian subjects to establish their own independence. In the Ukrainian region of the monarchy the population had organized a National Rada in L'viv, which subsequently proclaimed an independent state, the Western Ukrainian People's Republic, on November 1, 1918. The National Rada decided to seek unification with the Ukrainian National Republic.

As early as December 1, the representatives of the Western Ukrainian Republic, Lonhyn Tsehel's'kyi and Dmytro Levyts'kyi, signed a preliminary agreement with the Directory at Fastiv in which both sides agreed to unite. They also agreed that West Ukraine because of its cultural, social, and legal particularism was to enjoy autonomy. On January 3, 1919, the National Rada unanimously ratified the Fastiv Agreement, and on January 22 the act of union was finally approved by the Directory.[20]

By this agreement, sovereignty was to reside in the Directory. The National Rada, however, was to exercise authority in West Ukraine until the convocation of the Constituent Assembly. Although the union was a significant historic act, it was more nominal than actual since both parties were soon at war against different enemies: the Western Province (Oblast) of the Ukrainian People's Republic, as it was named after the act of union, against Poland, and the People's Republic against the second Bolshevik invasion.

The problems of union, consolidation, and defense were to be dealt with by the Congress of Toilers, a parliamentary assembly consisting of 528 indirectly elected delegates from the Ukrainian People's Republic and 65 from the West Ukrainian Republic, which was convened in Kyiv on January 22, 1919. However, the Congress was interrupted on January 28 by the Bolshevik frontal advance on Kyiv. The Congress sanctioned the principle of general democratic elections to parliament and organs of local government and adopted a resolution expressing "full confidence in and gratitude to the Directory for its great work in liberating the Ukrainian people from the landlord-hetman government." The most important achievements of the Congress, however, were the formal proclamation of the union of the two Ukrainian republics and the legal confirmation of the Directory, which it invested with supreme authority, including the right to enact laws and the defense of the state, until the next session of the Congress.[21]

After the triumph of the Directory, the most serious threats to Ukrainian political independence were the French intervention in the south and the new Soviet Russian invasion. The intervention stemmed from the Anglo-French Convention of December 23, 1917, which was rooted in the Entente's resentment of the Bolshevik negotiations with the Central Powers, the disclosure and rejection of the secret treaties, and the repudiation of tsarist debts. France, in particular, had special interest in Ukraine, where it had large investments before the war.[22] Consequently, the Entente decided to support the Russian anti-Bolshevik movement to overthrow the Soviet Russian regime.

To achieve this goal, France and Great Britain divided Eastern Europe into spheres of influence:

> Under the agreement of the 23rd December, 1917, between ourselves and France, we assume responsibility for the Cossack territories, Armenia, the Caucasus, Georgia, and Kurdistan, while the French control is extended to Bessarabia, the Ukraine and Crimea. Northern Russia is recognized by the French Government as under our control. Poland falls to France. . . .[23]

Hence both powers not only decided to intervene in the former Russian empire, but to aid the tsarist generals by supplying them with arms, ammunition, equipment, money, and instructors. From November 17 to 23, 1918, representatives of various Russian political groups and the Entente held a conference at Jassy, Romania, requesting help against the Bolsheviks. They also worked out a plan of political action for the Entente in "South Russia."[24] Although the groups were sharply divided over the type of government, the conference accelerated the intervention.

On December 17, the French 156th Division, consisting of 1,800 men under the command of General Borius reached Odessa from Salonika.[25] Subsequently Borius went ashore to discuss the military situation with the French consul, Denikin's representative in Odessa, the commander of the Polish troops, and the commander of the Volunteer Army forces. He proclaimed the purpose of the intervention to the local population:

> France and the Allies have not forgotten the efforts made by Russia at the beginning of the war and now they are coming into Russia to provide the opportunity for healthy elements and Russian patriots to establish in the country the order that was disturbed during the long period of the terrible civil war.[26]

Simultaneously he announced his assumption of authority and command of all military units in the Odessa region, including the Volunteers, and appointed General Aleksei Grishin-Almazov, commander of the Volunteers, military governor. By it Borius created a problem for the French because Grishin-Almazov was Denikin's officer, but Denikin operated in the British Zone and had no authority over Odessa, which was French Zone. Moreover, the authority in Odessa was in the hands of the Directory. Thus an open conflict between the French and General Denikin ensued. According to Denikin, to deny the French "the honor of 'taking' Odessa and thereby providing a pretext for its occupation," Grishin-Almazov offered to clear the city of Ukrainian troops, using his unit from the steamer *Saratov*, which was anchored in the harbor, to secure the French disembarkation.[27] Borius accepted the offer and the Volunteers, under the cover of the guns of the Allied warships, landed and attacked the Ukrainian troops.

The French troops who disembarked on December 18 did not participate in the actual fighting, but two battalions of the 176th Regiment seized control of the public buildings and protected the Volunteers' rear from a Ukrainian counterattack. The Ukrainian troops, consisting of about four thousand men, hesitated to employ their full fire power lest they precipitate a clash with the French, which the Directory had proscribed, assuming that French troops would be used only against the Bolsheviks. After hours of prolonged fighting the Ukrainian troops withdrew from the city to throw up a defensive perimeter around its outskirts.[28]

By the evening of December 18, the Ukainians sought a truce; their sole condition was the removal of Grishin-Almazov from the military governorship. Borius rejected their demand and laid down his own conditions: an immediate cease-fire, the surrender of their arms, and the evacuation of the city, warning that if his demands were not met the Ukrainian troops would be regarded not as belligerents, but as bandits, and shot on sight.[29] Consequently the Ukrainian troops capitulated, although many refused to surrender their arms, and by December 22, Odessa was under the control of the Allies.

Although this was a humiliating experience, the Directory was not in a position to enter into a war with France; rather, it was seeking understanding and technical aid from her. On January 14, 1919, General Philippe d'Anselme arrived in Odessa to take personal command of operations in Ukraine. The following week the combat strength of the Allies was augmented by the arrival of the first contingent of Greek troops, the remainder of whom reached Odessa in February. In March, French units were moved from Romania into Ukraine. Their arrival brought the total Allied strength in Odessa to 12,000 men: 6,000 French, 4,000 Poles, and 2,000 Greeks.[30]

It is evident that the French military had no intention of doing serious fighting, fearing that "their troops were not reliable and combat orders would not be carried out."[31] However, the separation of Odessa from its supplies of food, water, petroleum, and other necessities, and the threat of open rebellion among the poorly fed, unemployed, and Bolshevik-agitated workers, impelled the Allied forces to expand the occupation along the Black Sea coast to include the major cities in Tyraspil, Birzula, Voznesenske, Mykolaiv, and Kherson.[32]

The state of war between the Ukrainian troops and the Volunteers in South Ukraine thwarted d'Anselme's mission, which depended upon the concerted action of all anti-Bolshevik forces and neither the Directory nor Denikin could hope to defeat the Bolsheviks while fighting each other. General d'Anselme tried to avoid favoring any one anti-Bolshevik force to the exclusion of the others, but in his opinion, it was Denikin who was primarily responsible for preventing reconciliation of differences between the various anti-Bolshevik forces, thus undermining the success of the Allied mission in Ukraine. General d'Anselme was interested mainly in the military aspects of the situation in Ukraine, and left political matters to his chief of staff, Colonel Freidenberg.

Although the French Command favored the restoration of a united Russia, it preferred to negotiate with the Directory rather than to fight it. This was not a new policy, but a temporary change stipulated by circumstances, according to Freidenberg:

> France remained faithful to the principle of a United Russia. But now it is not a matter of decision of this or that political question, but exclusively a matter of making use of all anti-Bolshevik forces, including Ukrainian, in the struggle against the Bolsheviks.[33]

General Henri Berthelot, commander in chief of Allied troops in southern Russia and Romania, spoke in the same vein: "I can assure you most firmly that I am supporting a United Russia and I do not recognize independent Ukraine. But under the circumstances, for a time I must negotiate with the independists."[34]

As early as January 1919, the Directory dispatched Generals Mykhailo Hrekiv and Matveiev to Odessa with the intention of establishing contact with the French military and obtaining technical aid. Although the mission of General Hrekiv failed to achieve any immediate results, the Directory sent Dr. Osyp Nazaruk, press chief of the government, and Serhii Ostapenko, minister of trade and industry, with full authority to conclude political, trade, and military agreements with the French.[35]

Colonel Freidenberg gave them an arrogant reception, presenting a long list of demands and conditions: Vynnychenko and Chekhivs'kyi were to resign because of their alleged bolshevism, and Petliura, known for his pro-Entente sympathies, had to be ousted because the French army could not cooperate with a "bandit chieftain"; the Directory's members should be acceptable to France; the sovereignty of Ukraine would be decided only at the Paris Peace Conference; during the struggle against the Bolsheviks France was to control the railways and finances of Ukraine; the Directory was to organize an army of 300,000 men in three months, in which Russian officers from the Volunteer Army must be given commissions; and the Directory must request France to accept Ukraine as a protectorate.[36]

The Directory responded to the French conditions on March 6, 1919, at the Birzula railroad station, insisting, in turn, upon recognition of the independence of Ukraine and the sovereignty of the Directory; permission for the Directory's delegation to participate in the Paris Peace Conference; return of the Black Sea Fleet to Ukraine; recognition of the autonomy of the Ukrainian Army with a position for its representative in the supreme Allied command; and prohibition of service in the Ukrainian Army by Russian officers.[37]

Although the negotiations in Odessa were becoming more and more disappointing, the Directory persevered in its efforts because Ukraine was under attack from all sides: the Bolsheviks were advancing from the north and the east, the Poles were pressing in the west, and the Allied and Volunteer units were threatening to move from the south. In the light of these circumstances the Directory sent another delegation headed by Justice Arnold Margolin to Odessa, on January 26, 1919.

This delegation attempted a new approach by presenting on February 5 a joint memorandum of the representatives of Ukraine, Belorussia, the Don, and the Kuban concerning their countries' political aspirations, the methods of fighting the Bolsheviks, and the aid they expected from the Entente. The delegations expressed their opposition to federalism imposed from above, requesting instead support for their national aspirations and their governments, arguing that bolshevism could be combated most effectively by appealing to national patriotism. Therefore, they asked the Allied Command for technical aid: firearms, ammunition, heavy artillery, tanks, armored cars, shoes, boots, clothing, and medical supplies. In return, they agreed on the principle of a general staff that would direct military operations on the basis of mutual agreement, without intervening in the internal political life of the new states.[38]

After several weeks of conferences between Ukrainian and French representatives, the French military, with d'Anselme representing the

Entente, presented a draft of a French-Ukrainian agreement that recognized the Directory as a sovereign government of the Ukrainian Democratic Republic, and the Ukrainian Army as an internally independent unit of the anti-Bolshevik army in the Ukrainian Zone, with representatives on the supreme command of the Entente. The French further agreed to take steps to admit the Directory's representatives to the peace conference, promised agrarian reforms, and consented to convoke a parliament based on universal, equal, secret, and proportional suffrage. France assured the Directory that during the war no units of the Volunteer Army should be present, or participate, in military operations on the territory of Ukraine, and that the Odessa, Mykolaiv, and Kherson districts would be part of the Ukrainian zone under the authority of the Directory. On the other hand, the proposal also stipulated that changes in the Directory's membership during the war against the Bolsheviks could be made only with the approval of the Entente, and the supreme staff of the Entente would control Ukrainian railroads and the transportation of all armed forces, as well as Ukrainian financial affairs. However, in late March the French in Odessa received orders from Paris not to sign the agreement, apparently because of conflicting interests of France, Britain, and Italy in regard to the future economic possibilities in Ukraine.[39]

The intervention of the Allies in southern Ukraine and the Directory's negotiations with the French in Odessa greatly complicated the situation in Ukraine by creating two conflicting points of view in the Directory and the parties. One group, represented by Vynnychenko, wished to seek an understanding with the Bolsheviks against the Entente. The other, led by Petliura, desired coalition with the Entente against the Bolsheviks. Petliura's viewpoint finally prevailed, and although the representatives of the Entente had no understanding of the Ukrainian cause, the Directory continued to try to negotiate an agreement to the very end of the intervention.[40] At the end of September 1919, Petliura expressed his feelings concerning the Entente's attitude toward Ukraine:

> We might have been the best means in the hands of the Entente for driving the Bolsheviks back into Russia. But, for reasons of their own, the Great Powers back[ed] Denikin against us and so split our joint strength. It almost seems as if the Entente does not want to beat the Bolsheviks.[41]

The Bolsheviks exploited these negotiations with the Entente, spreading propaganda that the Directory had made a secret agreement against the interests of the people. The Bolsheviks:

> . . . unmasked to the people the Directory's betrayal. To prove it the Bolshevik committee in Kyiv printed and spread, even among the delegates of the [Labor] Congress, the agreement signed by the Directory with the French command according to which the Directory handed Ukraine over to the disposition of French imperialism. Thus, the "toiling" mask was ripped off the Directory and it was shown to the masses that it is the enemy of freedom and national independence of the Ukrainian people.[42]

They suggested that the Directory was planning for a new form of intervention in Ukraine and intervention was not popular after the experience with the Austro-German troops. The peasants, in particular, distrusted the forces of the Entente because they associated them with the Volunteer Army and believed they would renew the rule of big landowners. Thus the French intervention strengthened pro-Bolshevik sympathies among the population.[43]

Moreover, political developments in Germany and Hungary greatly assisted the Bolsheviks, who convinced some Ukrainian leaders that the world-wide social revolution was taking place and that Ukrainian national questions would be solved automatically by the revolution. The Bolsheviks were adroit in the use of untruth, knowing from experience all the ways to use propaganda. The Ukrainian government, not able to match the Bolshevik propaganda skills, found that its orientation toward the Entente undermined its prestige and aroused opposition from both the Right and the Left.

As well as propagandizing Soviet Russia was preparing for a new invasion. For this purpose a Ukrainian Revolutionary Council, consisting of Stalin, Piatakov, Zatons'kyi, and Antonov-Ovseenko, was established on November 17 and masked by the name "Group of the Kursk Direction."[44] There were disagreements among the Bolshevik leaders concerning the intervention in Ukraine. The assumption of the rightist group was that the potential for revolutionary action in Ukraine was too small and they would not gain a following among the workers and peasants. The leftist group, however, thought that in the event of Austro-German withdrawal from Ukraine they could succeed in seizing power before the Ukrainian national leaders could take the initiative. Their opinion was shared by Stalin.[45]

Subsequently on November 20 a Provisional Workers' and Peasants' Government of Ukraine was secretly formed in Kursk, a Russian city near the Ukrainian border. On November 28 the new government formally held its first assembly at Kursk, attended by Antonov-Ovseenko, Sergeev (Artem), Zatons'kyi, Emanuil I. Kviring, and Chairman Piatakov. The aim of Moscow's appointed government was to shield Soviet

Russia's invasion of Ukraine. On December 6, 1918, the troops of the "Kursk Direction" launched military operations against Ukraine on two axes toward Gomel-Chernihiv-Kyiv and toward Vorozhba-Sumy-Kharkiv.[46] According to Antonov-Ovseenko, the commander in chief of the Bolshevik Army, there were three main objectives: to take Kharkiv, with its railway junction, as a base for further expansion; to occupy the Donets Basin with its industries and coal mines, breaking military and economic ties between central Ukraine, the Donets Basin, and the Don; and to advance southward to Crimea to forestall the Entente's intervention.[47]

The Bolsheviks took the Allied intervention as a serious threat. Leon Trotsky identified Bolshevik policy with regard to the intervention as derived from:

> . . . the need to forestall the possibility of an advance by the Anglo-French forces from the South. The more swiftly and resolutely we push our possible Ukrainian-Entente Front to the south, away from Moscow, the more advantageous it will be for us. In the event of a real attack of large forces the greatest advantage for us would be in establishing our line along the left bank of the Dnieper and destroying all lines of communication and bridges on the right bank. For this we need to advance to the Dnieper as soon as possible.[48]

To accomplish these objectives Antonov-Ovseenko dispatched orders to all who might be useful to the Bolsheviks, including the rebel units and local Bolshevik organizations, to foment insurrections along the lines of their advance, to organize intelligence systems, and to seize ammunition factories and even certain towns. At the same time they were "to prevent by every means possible the advance of counterrevolutionary forces from Kyiv toward Kursk and Briansk."[49] The combination of strong conventional attacks with fifth-column activities and rebellions enabled the Bolshevik forces to advance successfully into Ukraine. The advance was also facilitated by the seizure of large stores of German and Ukrainian military material, left by the hetman government.[50]

Consequently the Ukrainian minister of foreign affairs, Volodymyr Chekhivs'kyi, on December 31, 1918, and on January 3 and 4, 1919, sent a series of notes of protest to the Soviet Russian government concerning its military operations in Ukraine, demanding an explanation and seeking an agreement to avoid war. On January 5, the Soviet Russian commissar of foreign affairs, Georgii V. Chicherin, denied all Chekhivs'kyi's allegations, entirely misrepresenting the situation as a Ukrainian civil war: "Military action on Ukrainian territory at this time is proceeding between the troops of the Directory and the troops of the Ukrainian Soviet Government, which is completely independent."[51]

On January 9, 1919, the Ukrainian government's reply called the denial "either a willful distortion of the truth or a complete lack of information."[52] However, the Directory expressed its willingness to enter into peace negotiations and commercial relations if Soviet Russia would withdraw the troops from Ukraine in forty-eight hours. Chicherin reiterated his previous denial, but nevertheless proposed Moscow as a meeting place for peace negotiations. The Directory, under pressure from Chekhivs'kyi and his supporters, accepted this proposal and sent a small delegation headed by Semen Mazurenko to Moscow. It was instructed to seek a settlement with Soviet Russia even at the price of introducing a soviet form of government in Ukraine. It was also authorized to conclude an economic agreement and a military alliance for defensive purposes only, if Soviet Russia would end the invasion and recognize Ukrainian independence.[53]

This attempt to find a modus vivendi with Soviet Russia can be understood only in the light of the weakness of the Directory and of the growth of a revolutionary radicalism in the working classes and in both of the main Ukrainian parties—the Social Democratic and the Socialist Revolutionary. Although the Ukrainian delegation was engaged in negotiation in Moscow, the Bolshevik troops continued the invasion. Consequently, on January 16, 1919, the Directory declared that a state of war existed between Soviet Russia and Ukraine.[54]

While the Bolshevik troops were advancing from the north and southeast, the anti-Bolshevik Russian forces were moving into Ukraine from the Don, the Romanians occupied Bessarabia and Bukovina, the Poles were fighting the Ukrainians in Galicia, and the Entente was moving troops north from Odessa and the Crimea. At that time the Ukrainian Army, except for a few regular formations left from the hetman period, was just in the process of organization. The best military units, those on which the Directory relied, were the Sich Riflemen Corps and the Zaporozhian Corps. The Directory's forces consisted largely of partisan detachments, some of which were undisciplined and commanded by politically and nationally immature leaders.[55] In the course of time, a few of the detachments were swayed by Bolshevik propaganda and chose some critical period to proclaim their neutrality or even to defect to the Bolsheviks. Given this deteriorating military situation, the Directory could offer no effective resistance to the advancing Bolshevik troops.

In early January 1919, the Bolshevik troops occupied Kharkiv and Chernihiv. As the enemy approached the Dnieper near Kyiv, the Directory evacuated on the evening of February 2 to Vinnytsia, which then became its temporary capital. On February 5, after heavy fighting, the Ukrainian forces retreated from Kyiv to the west. The next day Bolshevik troops occupied Kyiv.[56]

Chekhivs'kyi's and Vynnychenko's abortive efforts to find an agreement with Soviet Russia brought about a cabinet crisis. The decision to send a peace delegation to Moscow and the prospect of a Soviet form of government was not approved by Petliura and the military commanders. Moreover, with the success of the Bolshevik invasion, the leading circles increased their efforts to gain the Entente's support of their resistance. To facilitate the Directory's negotiations with the French representatives in Odessa, the Social Democrats and Socialist Revolutionaries on February 9 withdrew their members from the government. Petliura, however, resigned from his party while Vynnychenko, president of the Directory, on February 11 handed over his authority to Petliura and left the country. On February 13, Serhii Ostapenko, the former minister of trade and industry, set up a new cabinet that consisted mainly of Socialist-Federalists. However, because it based its plan on the support of the Entente, ignoring Ukrainian national interests, the Ostapenko cabinet not only failed to achieve support from the Entente against the Bolsheviks, but it antagonized a large segment of the Ukrainian population. Moreover, the absence of such prominent leaders as Hrushevs'kyi and Vynnychenko, and the Socialist parties, which had substantial popular support, gave the Ostapenko cabinet the appearance of a "bourgeois" government, which the Bolsheviks used in their anti-Directory propaganda. At the end of March 1919, Red troops forced the Ukrainian Army to retreat to the former Austrian border and isolated its left flank, in the area of Uman'.[57] Some military leaders, attempting to counteract the influence of the Bolshevik propaganda among the population and the troops, adopted some of their slogans and opened independent negotiations with the Bolsheviks or even joined them.

In the light of the deteriorating military situation and the lack of support for the Ostapenko cabinet, the Directory called upon Borys Martos to form still another cabinet on April 9, in Rivne. By including Social Democrats and Socialist Revolutionaries, as well as representatives of western Ukraine, the Directory hoped to gain popular support.[58] The new cabinet issued a declaration on April 12, 1919, directed "to all Ukrainian Socialists, peasants and workers who, unable to stand the foreign yoke, rose behind the front against the Russian Communists to fight for a free and independent Ukraine."

The Bolshevik occupation authorities had no intention of granting political or cultural concessions. On March 19, 1919, at the Eighth Congress of the Russian Communist Party (Bolsheviks), Lenin remarked: "Ukraine was separate from Russia by exceptional circumstances, and the national movement has not taken deep roots there. Insofar as it did exist, the Germans stamped it out."[59] The policy of Russification and exploitation of Ukraine went on at full speed. The Ukrainian language was completely proscribed in state institutions and printing houses. As early as February 13, 1919, the head of the Provisional Soviet Government of Ukraine, Christian Rakovskii, at a meeting of the Kyiv City Council of Workers' Deputies, declared that the attempt "to institute Ukrainian as a state language is a reactionary measure, and entirely unnecessary to anyone."[60] The administration requisitioned buildings of Ukrainian cultural institutions for state purposes. Former tsarist gendarmes, police, and secret agents who had entered the Cheka persecuted the Ukrainian intelligentsia. The Bolsheviks regarded Ukraine as a colony, primarily as a source of food. Lenin admitted receiving reports that "stocks of food are immense, but it is impossible to transport everything at once because of lack of apparatus."[61]

Therefore, the Ukrainian villages were invaded by the Russian foodstuff requisitioning units:

> The Workers' and Peasants' Government was tirelessly exporting from Ukraine to Muscovy everything it could lay its hands on: bread, sugar, meat, factory machine tools and equipment, farm implements, furniture from buildings, and even musical instruments—all these were taken and requisitioned without any kind of compensation. . . . With this brutal requisition policy in the villages, a policy that did not differentiate between poorer peasants and the richer or "kurkuls," the Committees of the Poor were disregarded and by a simplified system of requisitioning, the Red Army men seized from Ukrainian peasants everything that could be removed—grain, cattle, poultry, plows, even women's clothes.[62]

This policy was passed off by Lenin on March 13, 1919, as voluntary assistance from a friendly Soviet Republic:

> In Ukraine, we have a fraternal Soviet Republic, with which we have the best of relations. This republic resolves the question of help, not in terms of petty trading, not in profiteering, but is guided by an exceptionally warm desire to help the hungry north. The first special obligation of each citizen of Ukraine is to help the north.[63]

However, as Alexander G. Schlichter, then commissar of food supplies of Ukraine, wrote in 1928:

> Every pood was soaked in blood: By July 1 the government had acquired not fifty, but only eight and a half million poods. However, three-quarters of this was in

Ukraine and was rationed to proletarian centers (primarily to workers of the Donets Basin) and to the Red Army. Only about two million poods were sent to Moscow and Peter[sburg].[64]

This policy of requisition and persecution of everything Ukrainian brought about mass uprisings, even among some Ukrainian Communists who were attempting to establish an independent Soviet Ukraine. From April to June 1919, there were 328 uprisings of the people against the Bolsheviks.[65] The Directory established contact with the partisans acting in the Bolsheviks' rear and gained more response among the population for the national struggle.

During the first half of March 1919, Ukrainian troops made a coordinated attack from the north and south on the Bolshevik forces in the region of Berdychiv-Koziatyn-Zhytomyr. The Bolsheviks were forced to retreat, and at the end of March the Ukrainian troops approached Kyiv from the north.[66] On March 25, 1919, Jukums J. Vācietis (Vatsetis), the commander in chief of Bolshevik forces, wired Antonov-Ovseenko:

It was necessary to pursue with full intensity the complete destruction of any sort of organization among the troops of Petliura. . . . At the present, when Petliura has again appeared near Kyiv, we must undertake all measure for final destruction of Petliura. I recommend that you . . . stop the development of actions in the direction of the Romanian border as well as toward the Black Sea coast; transfer from there all unneeded troops against the troops of Petliura . . . your westward advance is necessary to lead to the borders of southeastern Galicia and Bukovina.[67]

Although Ukrainian troops were victorious in the central sector, their southern flank became seriously exposed after the allied troops left the Black Sea coast and Odessa under the pressure of Hryhor'iv's thrusts. After strengthening their forces, the Bolsheviks counterattacked in the Ukrainian central sector, also making heavy use of propaganda among the troops and population, and cut off the southern group from the main force. To save the situation, the southern group was ordered to drive back the Bolsheviks by a counterattack from the southeast; but the commander of the Zaporozhian Corps, Omelian Volokh, independently opened negotiations with the Bolsheviks. Subsequently, the Bolsheviks attacked again, forcing a large part of the group to retreat on April 16, 1919, to Romania, where they were disarmed. Only two weeks later the Ukrainians succeeded in making their way through East Galicia and Volyn', to rejoin the main force, but none of the equipment surrendered was ever returned, in spite of an agreement to do so.[68]

While the Bolsheviks were concentrating large forces against the northern group of the Ukrainian Army, its commander, Volodymyr Oskilko, attempted a coup against the government. Although his adventure failed, it demoralized and confused the Ukrainian troops and helped the Bolsheviks to defeat them.[69] The Ukrainian forces did manage to undermine Bolshevik initiative and were, along with Hryhor'iv, responsible for preventing their advance into Romania and Hungary, yet they failed to achieve a decisive victory. Consequently, they retreated to the border of Galicia where they defended a small territory.

At the time when the Directory was struggling against the Bolshevik and anti-Bolshevik Russian forces, the Western Ukrainian People's Republic was defending its territory from an invasion by Poland. The government believed that the Entente and the peace conference would, in accordance with the principle of national self-determination, compel the Poles to evacuate eastern Galicia. However, France was committed to the idea of a "strong Poland" as a future counterpoise to Germany in Eastern Europe and looked with disfavor on Ukrainian independence. Great Britain was supporting the Russian anti-Bolshevik leaders, while at the same time seeking an agreement with the Bolsheviks; neither of these policies was favorable to the Ukrainian national aspirations. The United States, on the other hand, was little interested in Eastern Europe; its attitude was that nothing should be done to prejudice the future claims of the Russia that might emerge after the victory of the anti-Bolshevik generals over the Bolsheviks. Thus Ukraine was isolated from the Western powers.

In January 1919 a peace conference commission arrived in Poland for mediation in the Ukrainian-Polish war and demanded suspension of hostilities as a condition for negotiations. The Ukrainian government acceded to this demand and on February 28, the commission presented a plan by which Ukraine was to leave to the Poles half of the ethnically Ukrainian territory, including the Drohobych-Boryslav oil fields. This decision, which was to remain in force until the peace conference settled the Polish-Ukrainian frontier, was unacceptable to the Ukrainians.[70]

On April 18, as the campaign continued, the Supreme Council created a commission with representatives of the Allied and Associated Powers, headed by General Louis Botha of South Africa, to deal with the Ukrainian-Polish problem. After several weeks of hearings, on May 12 the Botha commission proposed a conditional armistice, leaving to the Ukrainians the Drohobych-Boryslav oil fields and limiting Polish and Ukrainian forces in eastern Galicia to twenty thousand men each. This proposal was, however, rejected by the Poles.

While the Botha Commission was attempting to settle the conflict, the Poles were preparing for renewed aggression and on May 15, reinforced by six divisions (100,000 men) formed, trained, and equipped in France, began a general offensive. The poorly equipped Ukrainian troops could not stand for long against a large and fresh Polish army. On May 21, the Ukrainian delegation in Paris sent a note to the president of the peace conference asking for a halt to the Polish offensive, but no action was taken.[71]

As the Poles advanced eastward, the Romanian command of the Bukovina-Khotyn front demanded that the Ukrainians evacuate the southern part of eastern Galicia.[72] This change represented a serious setback to the Galician Army through the loss of its only supplies of ammunition and its isolation from the outside world. On May 26, the Ukrainians abandoned Stanyslaviv (Ivano-Frankivske), the temporary capital of western Ukraine, and retreated to Chortkiv. During this critical period, the Galician Army launched on June 7 the "Chortkiv offensive," driving the Polish forces back to the west about eighty miles. After three weeks of successful fighting, the Ukrainian advance halted, having expended the available ammunition and supplies. The Poles had concentrated a large force and launched a new offensive along the entire front. At the end of June the Galician Army began a general withdrawal, conducting only rearguard actions to assure an orderly retreat.[73]

On June 25, the Supreme Council decided the fate of eastern Galicia by authorizing Poland to occupy it:

> To protect the persons and property of the peaceful population of eastern Galicia against the danger to which they are exposed by the Bolshevik bands, the Supreme Council of the Allied and Associated Powers has decided to authorize the forces of the Polish Republic to pursue their operations as far as the river Zbruch. This authorization does not in any way affect the decisions to be taken later by the Supreme Council for the settlement of the political status of Galicia.[74]

On July 2, the Ukrainian delegation in Paris protested this act, declaring: "The decision of the Supreme Council does not embody the triumph of right and justice."[75] The protest, however, was ignored.

Under these circumstances the Galician Army had no recourse but to abandon its territory and retreat across the river Zbruch, where the Directory troops held a narrow but gradually expanding strip of territory. The West Ukrainian government faced two alternatives: to join the Directory against the Bolsheviks, or to accept the Bolsheviks' offer of an alliance and supplies of arms and ammunition against Poland. The government decided on the former course, and on July 16, the army of about one hundred thousand men and a majority of the civil administration began to cross the Zbruch.[76]

The trauma of the move was described by an eyewitness:

> Grief gripped my heart in my breast as I watched the Ukrainian people of Galicia being forced to abandon their own land. And before whom? Before Polish invaders who for an entire century had been filling Europe and America with their weeping and prayers to God and the people that they were unfortunate, enslaved. And now —they themselves were coming to enslave our land by fire and sword; they were coming not even on their own strength, but by the aid of the French.[77]

Almost immediately after the completion of the crossing, the two armies began their offensive because the size of their small territory, only thirty-five kilometers in breadth and fifty-five kilometers in width, did not permit a defense in depth against the repeated Bolshevik attacks. After consideration of other directions for an advance, Petliura decided to push the operation toward Kyiv, with precautionary thrusts both to the north, on Shepetivka, and to the south, on Odessa. In spite of strong Bolshevik resistance, the Ukrainian troops advanced rapidly, aided in part by the advance of Denikin and by the uprisings of the partisans in the Bolsheviks' rear.[78] Although the Ukrainian command secured its rear in the west through the mediation of the Entente and by signing an armistice with the Poles on September 1, it neglected to coordinate its advance with Denikin's simultaneous offensive in the Left Bank or to issue a timely and precise order governing the actions of its troops in case they encountered the Denikin troops.[79] Petliura hoped that the preemption of Kyiv might force Denikin to recognize a communality of interest against the Bolsheviks, and to advance north rather than open another front.

In spite of the Bolsheviks' staunch defense in the Kyiv area, after several days of fighting the Ukrainian troops entered the capital on August 30. The next day, Denikin's superior force made its way into the city and the Ukrainian troops withdrew from Kyiv to avoid opening a third front. Thus Denikin's attack not only prevented a Ukrainian advance against the Bolsheviks, but saved the latter's position in Ukraine by enabling three divisions of the Fourteenth Army, which had been cut off by the Ukrainian and Denikin troops, to pass from the region of Odessa-Voznesenske north to Zhytomyr, where they joined the main Bolshevik forces. Although the Directory tried to avert conflict with Denikin, both through negotiations with him and appeals to the Allies, it failed, and on September 24 it declared war and turned its main forces against Denikin.[80]

The retreat from the liberated capital was a great psychological and strategic blow to the Ukrainian Army. Exhausted by constant fighting, lacking ammunition and equipment, it could not withstand for long the attacks of Denikin's well-nourished and well-armed forces. Moreover, the cold and rainy autumn followed by an early heavy winter, coupled with the lack of clothing and medical supplies, brought about a disastrous typhus epidemic that spread among soldiers and civilians. In the area of operations, all residences and public buildings were filled with sick soldiers; hospitals intended for 100 accommodated more than 1,000 patients. Thousands of soldiers were dying from disease while others, nearly barefoot and badly clothed, froze in the open fields. The peasants were decimated by disease while giving aid to the soldiers.[81] The blockade by the Entente prevented the Ukrainian government from obtaining medical supplies and ultimately the fighting strength of the Ukrainian Army was reduced by 70 percent by the spread of typhus.

This tragic situation was described by an American correspondent:

> It is not too much to say that about every third person in Kamenets has typhus. In other cities the situation is the same. In the army it is even worse. At Vapniarka I was with Petliura at a review of a frontier garrison where out of a thousand troops at least two hundred had had typhus. Against this epidemic Petliura's government is quite powerless to make headway. The Ukrainians are condemned to death by the fact that the Entente is backing Denikin. In an interview I had with Petliura he begged that, if only for humanity's sake, the Red Cross would send over a mission to fight typhus. Let me add here that right across the river in Romania are all the medical supplies necessary. . . . We do not ask for any gratuitous help from the Allies. We only want our frontiers opened so that we can trade our products for manufactured articles and equipment. Let them open Odessa. We do not ask them to pour in supplies free of charge to us, as they do to Denikin.[82]

The Galician Army, however, suffered the most. As General IUrko Tiutiunyk observed, its situation "was indeed desperate: there were neither ammunition, medicine, food, clothing, no reinforcement of men and horses. . . . [Moreover] there was no hope that the situation could soon change in our favor."[83] Gradually the Ukrainian troops retreated northwest, where they found themselves surrounded by hostile forces: the Poles on the west, the Bolsheviks on the northeast, and Denikin on the south and southeast.

Therefore the commander of the Galician Army, General Myron Tarnasv'kyi, who felt the military pressure at the front, decided to negotiate with Denikin. He knew the Volunteer Army was a "living corpse," but could still crush the disease-weakened Ukrainian Army.[84] Although the president of the Western Ukrainian government, Dr. Evhen

Petrushevych, opposed such a venture, the general unilaterally sent a mission to negotiate for the exchange of prisoners of war and to find out on what terms Denikin would conclude an armistice with both Ukrainian armies. On November 1 the delegation contacted General Slashchov who told them Denikin was willing to negotiate with the Galician Army as an extraterritorial army, but not with the Directory's army, which, in his opinion, belonged to the Russian state and must be demobilized.[85]

On November 6, 1919, the Galician delegation and representatives of the Volunteer Army signed a preliminary treaty at Ziatkivstsi, a railroad junction west of Uman'. The treaty provided for full internal autonomy of the Galician Army under control of the government of the Western Province of the Ukrainian National Republic. The army itself was guaranteed a rest period before being redeployed, during which it would be transferred to a region free of typhus, given medical support, and reinforced with Ukrainian Galician prisoners from foreign countries and Russian territories. The Sich Riflemen were not considered a Galician unit. Liaison officers would be assigned from the Denikin command. Finally, it was agreed that the Galician Army would not be employed against the Directory.[86]

General Tarnavs'kyi and his chief of staff, Colonel Shamanek, were removed from their commands by the Western Ukrainian government and, together with others who negotiated with Denikin, were put under court-martial, but the final Galician-Russian treaty was signed in Odessa on November 17, 1919, and ratified within forty-eight hours. Although the Galician-Russian agreement was only a tactical expediency "to save the Army," the Directory considered it an act of betrayal.[87] Facing a highly unfavorable military situation, Petliura decided to continue the fighting in the form of guerrilla warfare and seek support from the Entente via alliance with Poland.

The Directory had had to face more serious domestic and foreign problems than its predecessor, the hetman government. Although initially it had received overwhelming support from the population, it was ill prepared to guide the state in such a revolutionary period. The Directory itself was not internally united, in action or idea, concerning state problems. Such leading figures as Hrushevs'kyi and Vynnychenko found themselves outside the government and eventually left the country at the time when they were most needed. Moreover, the constant changes of the cabinet from socialist to nonsocialist to please foreign powers undermined the confidence of the radically minded population in its government. The Directory's social policy satisfied neither the upper classes, especially not the landlords, nor the revolutionary peasants and workers. It also failed to win the understanding and cooperation of the national minorities in Ukraine.

The activities of the hetman and his supporters, the Germans and Austrians, had strengthened the Bolshevik sympathies among the lower classes; the Directory's hesitant social policy only served to reinforce these sympathies. This was possible because the first Bolshevik invasion of 1918 had given the population little insight into their methods and aims in Ukraine. The Bolsheviks exploited the government's weakness through the skillful use of propaganda of untruth. In contrast to the anti-Bolshevik Russian forces, the Bolsheviks waged imperialistic war against Ukraine under the slogans of national and social liberation.

Compounding these problems of political support were several failures of leadership and administration on the part of the Directory. It failed to establish a viable regime in the country largely because of the chaos created by the Bolshevik and anti-Bolshevik invasions and the Russian Civil War, which was fought largely on Ukrainian soil. Consequently some of the distant regions were controlled by politically and nationally immature partisan leaders who were unwilling to subordinate their actions to the Directory and at times followed an independent course in opposition to the government. Moreover, the existence of a group of left Socialist Revolutionaries known as Borot'bists, who were attempting to establish a Soviet Ukrainian government independent of Russia, weakened the Directory's position. The administrative apparatus was disorganized; although some personnel left the country or went into hiding, leaving the government with a great shortage of trained personnel, the Directory failed to enlist and train the new constructive elements, including non-Ukrainians, whose participation would have increased the commitment of the various national groups to the government.

Militarily, the Directory thought more in terms of a militia than a regular army, and took no steps to remedy the shortage of well-trained, patriotic officers, and to organize a strong army. It also failed to exercise leadership in uniting the partisan groups and coördinating their activities with those of the army. Because of the lack of munitions and armament plants in Ukraine, the Directory badly needed arms and ammunition, but it could not obtain them from abroad. After January 22, 1919, when there was one Ukrainian Republic, the Directory and the West Ukrainian government did not merge and, more importantly, they neglected to unite the military commands of their two separate armies.

In its foreign policy, the Directory's diplomacy did not wield sufficient influence to gain the material aid and diplomatic support it needed from the Entente and the neutral states. The Directory had to fight simultaneously two or even three enemies, which was beyond its power, yet it failed to neutralize at least one front. Instead of doing its utmost to organize the people's support and confidence, the Directory relied too much on efforts to get aid from the Entente. Its fruitless negotiations not only undermined its own unity and aroused opposition from the parties, but gave the Bolsheviks a basis for accusing the Directory of inviting a new foreign invasion.

Thus the Directory struggled against overwhelming odds, without adequate arms, military equipment, or medical supplies. In the midst of all this, a typhus epidemic decimated the army and civilian population. Consequently the superior invasion forces of the Bolsheviks and of Denikin compelled the ill-equipped and exhausted Ukrainian Army to retreat to the western limits of the Right Bank, seeking the support of the Entente through alliance with Poland. The Directory concluded the treaty of Warsaw with the Poles; the political agreement was signed on April 21, 1920, and the military on April 24. In spite of the alliance, the sacrifice to the Poles of Ukrainian territory, and the military campaigns with the Poles against the Bolsheviks, the Directory failed to gain the support of the Entente. Moreover, after the defeat of the Bolsheviks, the Polish government, ignoring the Directory, made its own separate peace settlement.

13. Makhno and the Directory

The rapid political change, the fall of the hetman regime, the establishment of the Directory, and the second Bolshevik invasion had their repercussions in the Makhno movement. Makhno was taken by surprise when the news came that the hetman regime, which he was then fighting, had been overthrown and the Directory was assuming power:

> All this happened on about the 20th of November, 1918. At one village, Alievo, . . . I considered it necessary to call a rally of the peasants at the village. I . . . began to speak to them about their servile conditions under the oppression of the hetman and his friends, the Austro-German Junkers, who were brought here and put on their necks by the Central Rada.[1]

However, for these peasants the hetman regime was already a thing of the past, because "on this day the village had received a telegram . . . relating . . . that a coup had occurred in Kyiv: Hetman Skoropads'kyi was overthrown, the Ukrainian Directory headed by V. Vynnychenko was organized."

After a local teacher had read the telegram to the peasants and given a speech, he asked: "What position will you, Bat'ko Makhno, and your revolutionary-partisan forces, assume toward the Ukrainian Directory[?]" This question confused Makhno and made him nervous because "in this village I did not expect it, and therefore, it made me somewhat sad—all the more because at this rally there was a mass of partisans, and the question about political confidence in Vynnychenko was unusually grave; the answer demanded not only truth but also serious, responsible substantiation." After a while he overcame his nervousness and began to argue that although Vynnychenko was a "Socialist, and a Socialist who participated and is participating in the life and struggle of the toilers," now he had joined with Petliura, who brought the Austro-German troops into Ukraine. Therefore, "I do not think that the revolutionary-partisan movement under my leadership can find a common language with this Ukrainian Directory; especially as the program of the Ukrainian Directory and how and by whom it was elected, is still unknown to us." In conclusion he declared: "We will not recognize the Ukrainian Directory . . . we will not carry on an armed struggle against the Directory, but we will . . . make preparations for this struggle against it."[2]

After the rally Makhno's close associates, especially Oleksander Marchenko, judged that he had spoken correctly. Semen Karetnyk, in addition, took the position that the Directory would not be able to maintain its authority over all Ukraine, because the "Revolution in the village is assuming an openly antigovernmental character . . . which we should support with all our power." Most of Makhno's associates agreed with Karetnyk and decided that as soon as they arrived at Huliai-Pole they would issue a declaration against the Directory as a government and as antirevolutionary. In and around Huliai-Pole, according to Makhno, the majority of the people shared their point of view concerning the Directory. To assure that the people in the freed areas "correctly understood the revolutionary position of Huliai-Pole . . . toward the Directory" the partisans launched a campaign with this purpose.[3] Thus from the very outset Makhno tried to prevent the Directory from establishing its authority in the area where his partisans operated.

Before the fall of the hetman regime Ukrainian leaders in Katerynoslav, headed by the brothers Mykola and Havrylo Horobets,[4] organized a Katerynoslav Republican Regiment (Kish) to prevent a local Bolshevik uprising, because the hetman Russian force was ineffective. When the Directory began a general uprising, the Ukrainian troops disarmed the state police (Varta) and assisted in establishing the local authority of the Directory. However, this action was threatened by the local Bolsheviks and by the Eighth Corps, which was organized during the hetman periods, under the command of General Vasylchenko and General I. G. Konovalov, his chief of staff. It was composed of two infantry regiments, originally about three to four hundred men, largely Russian officers; by mid-November the Corps had over one thousand men. At the end of November, when the Ukrainians left, it became strictly a Russian formation and began to use Russian as the official language. There also was a Russian volunteer detachment of officers, about one hundred and fifty men, which served the City Council and then joined the Corps. In the midst of the struggle, the commander of Ukrainian forces established contact with Makhno who subsequently sent two representatives, Oleksander Chubenko and Myrhorods'kyi, both left Socialist Revolutionaries.[5]

The Ukrainian commander proposed to join forces against the common enemies and reestablish a Ukrainian authority; Makhno, however, had instructed his delegates "to sound out the ground among the soldiers of the Katerynoslav garrison and the young staff officers . . . and to establish secret contact with them."[6] Makhno had no intention of joining forces with the Directory, because he regarded it as a worse phenomenon than the Ukrainian Central Rada, but he felt the partisans were not in a position at that time to launch an open campaign against it.[7] Makhno found himself caught between the forces of Denikin and those of the Directory.

Also there were still the Austro-German troops. Thus:

> The slightest decision by the Ukrainian Directory directed against us could force us to withdraw a number of combat units from the front lines against the volunteer units of the Denikin army and in this way, so to speak, 'to liquidate ourselves' in the fight against the Denikin forces without a prospect for successful victory in the struggle against the troops of the Directory.[8]

Makhno felt that to dare such a fight he would need at his disposal "at least a 70- to 100,000-strong well-armed partisan army" and so decided to maintain a cautious neutrality, allowing, among other things, the passage of enlisted men mobilized by the Directory through his territory. However, he ordered all the trains carrying them stopped for propaganda meetings directed against the government in general, and the Directory in particular.[9]

In the meantime, the Ukrainian forces in Katerynoslav grew stronger. At the beginning of December the Russian Eighth Corps was driven out of the city by Ukrainian troops after one day of fighting. Subsequently the Eighth Corps moved to the Crimea and at the beginning of January 1919, it joined the Russian troops there. Soon afterward Ukrainian troops disarmed the Austro-German troops stationed in Katerynoslav, obtaining large quantities of arms. On December 22, 1918, the Ukrainian troops dispersed the Katerynoslav Soviets and on December 26, they disarmed the Bolshevik military revolutionary headquarters and attacked the Bolshevik detachments located at Nyzhniedniprovs'k, a suburb of Katerynoslav, on the left bank of the Dnieper.[10]

In response, the local Bolsheviks offered Makhno command of their detachments with the aim of seizing the city. The offer was accepted and, on December 27, the united forces' several thousand men began to attack. To increase his chance of victory, Makhno used deception, sending an empty train into the city on a foggy morning followed by another armored train loaded with troops, which was then able to occupy the station and its surroundings. Simultaneously, he opened heavy artillery bombardment from the left bank of the Dnieper. During the fighting a Ukrainian artillery officer, Colonel Martynenko, changed sides and joined Makhno with sixteen guns and their teams, greatly facilitating Makhno's victory. After three days of heavy fighting Makhno occupied a larger area and late on December 30 the Ukrainian troops retreated. The city, particularly the center, was badly damaged by the shelling, which had killed about two hundred people and wounded fifteen hundred. As soon as Makhno seized part of the city, he released the prisoners, who began to plunder, despite Makhno's orders to the contrary and the shooting of several looters.[11]

Makhno's triumph, however, was short lived. The next day the Ukrainian troops, reinforced by the Sich Riflemen under Colonel Roman Samokysh, counterattacked. Makhno and his Bolshevik allies were badly beaten and suffered heavy losses. About two thousand Bolsheviks drowned in the Dnieper while attempting to escape across the frozen river. Makhno lost about six hundred men and with the remaining four hundred he retreated to Synel'nikove on the Left Bank. There he and his detachment rejoined the one commanded by Petrenko. Although his partisan group was substantially weakened, a number of independent partisan detachments soon joined him, swelling the force to over six thousand men who were, however, badly armed and clothed. Later, more partisan groups joined, among them a detachment from the area of Starokostiantynivka and others from the areas of Berdians'k, Mariupil', and Melitopil'.[12]

Meanwhile Makhno's detachments had resumed fighting the Ukrainian troops retreating from northeastern Ukraine before Antonov-Ovseenko's advancing Red Army. Their aim, however, was not primarily to fight, but to capture certain supplies. On January 6, 1919, Makhno's units attacked the city of Lozova but were beaten back with some losses. Those taken prisoner confessed that "they wanted to capture spirits, sugar, and manufactured goods." As the Ukrainian troops were crossing Katerynoslav province a more serious struggle occurred near Hubymikha on January 17, and Makhno was defeated.[13]

The situation changed as the Bolshevik forces advanced deeper into the Left Bank. On January 20, after a sixteen-day battle, Antonov-

Ovseenko captured Poltava while the Second Division of Pavel E. Dybenko occupied Synel'nikove. Meanwhile Dybenko established contact with Makhno and they agreed to attack Katerynoslav. Bitter fighting and heavy bombardment of the city continued for five days and it was only when the sixth Soviet Regiment crossed the Dnieper and attacked the city from another side that the Ukrainian troops were forced to retreat. On January 27, 1919, the Bolshevik forces occupied Katerynoslav.[14]

After the withdrawal of the Ukrainian troops to the Right Bank, Makhno found himself caught between the Bolshevik and anti-Bolshevik Russian forces. Makhno's previous inimical attitude toward the Directory and its troops, marked by both combat and propaganda, now entered a new phase, which might be described as an unwritten agreement of neutrality.

14. Makhno and the Bolsheviks

After the occupation of Katerynoslav and Kyiv, the Bolshevik armies advanced against the Ukrainian troops of the Directory, intending to cut them off from the ports of the Black Sea and subsequently to destroy them. Then they intended to attack the Allied forces in southern Ukraine and advance to Hungary through Romania to assist the Hungarian Communists.[1] Besides the Ukrainian and Allied forces, the Bolsheviks were facing the Denikin troops; for this they sought explicit support from leftist partisan leaders, including Makhno.

The Red Army representative Dybenko and Makhno's representative Chubenko met at Nyzhniedniprovs'k on January 26, 1919, where they agreed to unite their forces against the "counterrevolution" on the following terms: (a) all the Makhno detachments would be incorporated into the Red Army as the "Third Trans-Dnieper Brigade"; (b) this unit would receive military supplies, food, and financing from the Red Army and be responsible to it; (c) it would retain its internal organization intact with an elective commanding body and regulate the interrelation of the regiments by the staff; (d) Makhno would remain commander of the Brigade, but it would receive political commissars down to the regimental level appointed by the Bolshevik authorities, whose duties would be political indoctrination for the units and overseeing the execution of orders from the center; (e) detachments would be transformed into regular regiments; (f) it would be subordinate to the commanders of the Division and of the front in operational and administrative matters; (g) it could not be removed from the front against Denikin; and (h) it would retain its name of Revolutionary Partisan Army and its black flags.[2]

There was no mention of civil administration of the territory of the Makhno movement. The agreement with Makhno and other partisan leaders marked the beginning of a number of Bolshevik successes in South Ukraine. Makhno partisans operated against the Volunteers in two directions, south from Oleksandrivs'k and southeast toward Mariupil', where they encountered formidable Denikin forces.

As early as December 19, 1918, Denikin transferred General Vladimir I. Mai-Maevskii's Third Division, with armored trains, cars, and airplane units, from the Kuban to the region of IUzivka-Mariupil'-Berdians'k-Synel'nikove, aiming to cover the Donets Basin, and secure the left flank of the Don Army. However, according to Denikin:

> Mai-Maevskii got into a very complicated military and political situation in the region where the partisan groups of Makhno, Zubkiv, Ivan'ko, and other Petliura otamans, Bolshevik troops of Kozhevnikov's group, and the German soldiers from the troop trains mixed together. The Kuban separatists raised strong protests against "invading Ukrainian territory"; the Don Otaman persistently demanded an advance to Kharkiv, which was occupied by the Bolsheviks on January 3, and deployment along the northern borders of Ukraine. For two months Mai-Maevskii and his 2,500 men (later 4,500) strenuously and persistently defended themselves against Makhno, Petliura, and two Bolshevik divisions.[3]

At the end of January 1919, Denikin dispatched reinforcements, two cadres of officers and volunteers from the Ninth Cavalry Division. They formed a Composite Regiment against Makhno, who was opposing Mai-Maevskii's advance to the Donets Basin. According to reports of February 16 and 18, the partisans took Orikhiv, Novoukrainka, Novoselytsia, Velykyi Tokmak, Tsarekostiantynivka, and Polohy, capturing armored trains, field guns, machine guns, rifles, and other materials.[4] When in mid-March Makhno threatened Mariupil', General Elchaninov, the commander of the city garrison, dispatched the Composite Regiment, consisting of over four hundred men, plus detachments of the Second Cavalry of General Drozdovskii's regiment, the Smolensk Ulan Regiment, mobilized officers living in the city, and a battery of two guns.

Toward the end of March Makhno defeated the Denikin troops at Manhush whence they retreated eighteen versts east to Mariupil'. With most of the troop commanders wounded, all available forces gathered to defend the city. However, after ten days of fighting Makhno occupied it, driving the enemy into the sea. Subsequently Makhno seized a number of railway stations along the Sea of Azov, including Berdians'k, and was threatening to take Matviiv-Kurhan, to cut the Denikin forces off from their large military stores at Taganrog to the south.[5]

In mid-April the Third Cavalry Corps, under General Andrei

Grigor'evich Shkuro, jointly with the Composite Regiment drove Makhno from Mariupil' and the area including Huliai-Pole, with the aim of isolating Makhno from his allies, the Bolsheviks, and destroying him. During the spring and summer bitter fighting between them developed in the south of Left Bank Ukraine. According to Arshinov: "During this period Makhno's men advanced at least five or six times almost to the walls of Taganrog."[6] Both sides suffered heavy losses, but the civilian population suffered more, not only from military activities, but from reprisals and robberies by the Denikin troops. Thus from the beginning of 1919, an anti-Denikin front was firmly established, extending along the Sea of Azov west of Taganrog via Mariupil'-Berdians'k to Melitopil', and north to Oleksandrivs'k-Synel'nikove and Novomoskovs'ke.[7]

As an anti-Denikin front was established and the region was secured from Denikin's troops, Makhno faced the problem of organizing the region. The Makhno movement, however, was a military one, not political in nature. Fighting took up most of its time; that preoccupation and the tumultuous conditions caused by the civil war in the region were most unfavorable for domestic policies. With many enemies and forced to move constantly, Makhno could not control a large populated territory long enough to introduce a sound civil administration. Moreover, he had no adequate administrative apparatus for this purpose, for even anarchists from the Nabat group were ideologically opposed to serving in administrative units.[8] From the summer of 1918 to the beginning of 1919, the Makhno movement was essentially a peripatetic one, lacking territorial control. This situation changed when the Ukrainian troops withdrew from the Left Bank in the winter of 1919, and Makhno found himself in the region south and east of Katerynoslav between the Bolshevik and anti-Bolshevik Russian forces.

Thus when the Bolsheviks and Makhno had reached an agreement on January 26, 1919, one important question remained unsettled, the political status of the territory under Makhno's control. The Bolsheviks apparently thought either of recognizing autonomy for the region of the Makhno movement,[9] or they considered making agreements with Makhno concerning military matters, while the civil question would be their prerogative after the occupation of the region. As they advanced into the region, the Bolsheviks preceeded cautiously in order not to offend their allies to the point of precipitating an anti-Bolshevik reaction. According to an eyewitness, a commander of a Bolshevik regiment that was dispatched to the southern front warned his soldiers in a speech that "in the territory occupied by Makhno we have to be especially vigilant and flexible; not for a single moment should we forget either the peculiarities of the condition confronting us or the hopes entrusted to us by the command of the Soviet army."[10]

Makhno, on the other hand, took it for granted that the political autonomy of his region would not be touched and that the population would be allowed to live without Bolshevik interference. Hence, Makhno and his staff continued the military and sociopolitical organization of the territory that the partisans dominated from the end of January to June of 1919, and then from October to the end of the year. During 1920 and 1921, Makhno's territorial control was substantially limited in duration and space.

When Makhno detachments entered a certain city or town, they immediately announced to the population that the army did not intend to exercise political authority. In the army's judgment, "it is up to the workers and peasants themselves to act, to organize themselves, to reach mutual understanding in all fields of their lives, insofar as they desire it, and in whatever way they may think right."[11] Simultaneously, Makhno's command issued a proclamation to the people dealing with basic questions. All orders of the Denikin and the Bolshevik authorities were abolished.

The most important question to the peasants was that of land. Therefore, according to the proclamation, the holdings of the landlords, the monasteries, and the state, including all livestock and goods, were to be transferred to the peasants. This transfer, however, was to be implemented in an orderly way and dictated through decisions made in general meetings where the interests of all peasants would be considered. The same situation applied to the workers, since all factories, plants, mines, and other means of production were to become property of all of the workers under the control of their professional unions. The free exchange of manufactured and agrarian commodities was allowed until workers and peasants formed professional organizations to control such exchange.

According to the proclamation, workers and peasants were to establish free non-Bolshevik soviets that would carry out the will and orders of their constituents. Only working people, and not representatives of political parties, might join the soviets. The existence of compulsory and authoritative institutions was prohibited; the state guard and police force were also abolished. Instead, the workers and peasants were to organize their own self-defense force against counterrevolution and banditry.[12]

In contrast to the Bolshevik regime, freedom of speech, press, assembly, and association were proclaimed as an inseparable right of each working man. Several newspapers of various political orientations including Bolshevik, left Socialist Revolutionaries, and right Socialist Revolutionaries, appeared in the territory under Makhno's control. However, it was prohibited for them to propagate armed uprisings against the Makhno movement.[13]

Also, in contrast to the Bolshevik and anti-Bolshevik Russian forces that annulled each other's currencies whenever they occupied the same territory, Makhno annulled none. He recognized currencies of all forces occupying the region, including Ukrainian, Denikin, Don, and Bolshevik. Moreover, Makhno allowed money from the tsarist and Provisional Government regimes. Makhno's financial policy was determined by his knowledge that the working people had accumulated currencies from different sources and feared their discontinuation. The businessmen and bankers accepted Makhno's program. Makhno, however, never issued currency of his own.[14]

Although war conditions made the organization of schools difficult, plans were made, especially in Huliai-Pole. A school commission of peasants, workers, and teachers was assigned the task of devising an educational plan, including the establishment of schools and their economic support. The commission's plan was to employ the educational ideas of the Spanish anarchist, Francisco Ferrer. Schools were to belong to the working people themselves and to be entirely independent of the state and the church. Religion, however, was to be taught in the schools. Teachers were to receive their livelihood from the communities they served.[15] Courses were organized for illiterate and partly literate partisans. Some courses in political matters were offered for partisans, including history, political economy, theory and practice of anarchism and socialism, history of the French Revolution (according to Kropotkin), and history of the revolutionary partisan movement. Special attention was given to the organization of a theater that performed for the partisans and civilian population, and which would serve both as entertainment and propaganda.[16]

As the sociopolitical organization of his region developed, Makhno and his staff had to devote special attention to the organization of a partisan army to meet the threatening military situation. As early as January 3, 1919, Makhno called a partisan conference of forty delegates at Polohy station, the primary concern of which was the unification of all partisan groups of the region under one command, their reorganization, the obtaining of arms and ammunition, and the organization of a defensive front. The delegates resolved to form an operational staff that would be the highest military organ of the partisan army. Its tasks were the reorganization of the partisan groups into regiments, provision of supply bases, distribution of arms, planning combat operations, organization of new detachments, and disarming of all nonsubordinate units. Although the conference dealt primarily with military organization and defense of the territory, it devoted some attention to the civil problems and resolved to support the local soviets and prevent military control of them. All the estates in the region controlled by Makhno were to be transferred to the disposition of the workers and to be defended by organized local armed detachments until the meeting of a general peasant congress. Those armed detachments should be at the disposition of the local soviets, supporting their authority and assisting them in combating banditry.[17]

Subsequently, on January 4, Viktor Bilash, head of the operational staff, presented a reorganizational plan that he had formulated for the front. To make the partisans' operations more effective, some of the less cooperative commanders of the formerly independent groups were summoned to operational staff headquarters where they were kept occupied with operational matters. The southern front against Denikin, which extended 225 versts, was defended by five regiments.

At the beginning of 1919, two congresses were held that dealt with military and sociopolitical organization. Those two congresses formed the beginning of what might be called the political government of the Makhno movement; they were composed of delegates of peasants, workers, and partisans and were considered as the supreme authority of the region. The first congress, held on January 23, 1919, at Dibrivka, was limited in size and scope. It was composed of one hundred delegates under the chairmanship of K. Holovko. Its main object was to strengthen defense, especially against the growing threat of the Volunteer Army. To regulate the manpower problem the delegates resolved to mobilize men who were willing and able to carry arms (especially those who served in the army during the war) to defend the Revolution. The second congress, which was held on February 12, 1919, at Huliai-Pole, had 245 delegates representing 350 districts. Its chairman was Veretel'nyk and Makhno was chosen to be honorary chairman.[18]

The consensus of the congress was strongly anti-Bolshevik and favored a democratic sociopolitical way of life. Most of the delegates were against the Bolsheviks and their commissars. One delegate complained:

Who elected the Provisional Ukrainian Bolshevik Government: the people or the Bolshevik party? We see Bolshevik dictatorship over the left Socialist Revolutionaries and anarchists. Why do they send us commissars? We can live without them. If we needed commissars we would elect them from among ourselves.[19]

The delegate from Novopavlivka *volost*, complained:

A new government has appeared somewhere in Ukraine that is composed of Bolshevik-Communists; this government is already attempting to introduce its Bolshevik monopoly over the soviets.

He pointed out that at the time when

you peasants, workers, [and] partisans were enduring the pressure of all the counterrevolutionary forces the Prov[isional] Govern[ment] of Ukraine was sitting . . . in Moscow, in Kursk, waiting until the workers and peasants of Ukraine liberated the territory from the enemies. Now . . . the enemy is defeated . . . a Bolshevik government is coming to us and is imposing upon us its party dictatorship. Is this admissible? . . . We nonparty partisans who rose against all our oppressors will not permit new enslavement no matter from which party it comes.[20]

The delegate from Kherson province, Cherniak, spoke in the same vein: "No party has a right to usurp governmental power into its hands. . . . We want life, all problems, to be decided locally, not by order from any authority above; and all peasants and workers should decide their own fate, while those elected should only carry out the toilers' wish."[21]

Makhno concluded his speech with:

If our Bolshevik friends are coming from Great Russia into Ukraine to help us in the hard struggle against the counterrevolution, we will say to them: "Thank you, dear brothers." If, however, they are coming with the aim of monopolizing Ukraine, we will say to them: "Hands off." Without their help we will raise ourselves to the point of liberating the working peasantry; without their help [we] will organize a new life in which there will be neither landlords nor slaves, neither oppressed nor oppressors.[22]

Thus the congress warned the peasants and workers that

the political commissars are watching each step of the local soviets and dealing ruthlessly with those friends of peasants and workers who act in defense of peoples' freedom from the agency of the central government. . . . The Bolshevik regime arrested left Socialist Revolutionaries and anarchists, closing their newspapers, stifling any manifestation of revolutionary expression.

Therefore, the congress "urges the peasants and workers to watch vigilantly the actions of the Bolshevik regime that cause a real danger to the worker-peasant revolution." This anti-Bolshevik attitude was also shared by the anarchist Nikiforova who came from her visit in Moscow to attend the congress. She delivered a speech condemning the Bolsheviks for their use of terror against the anarchists in Russia.[23]

The congress also devoted its attention to the problem of mobilization. Although the Makhno partisan army at this time numbered some thirty thousand men,[24] the Bolshevik policy of violence to the peoples' freedom and the Denikin threat demanded greater strength. After a long and passionate debate, the "Congress rejected 'compulsory' mobilization, opting for an 'obligatory' one; that is, each peasant who is able to carry arms, should recognize his obligation to enlist in the ranks of the partisans and to defend the interests of the entire toiling people of Ukraine."[25]

The main contribution to civil administration was the establishment of a Regional Revolutionary Military Council of Peasants, Workers, and Partisans, a permanent body consisting of representatives of thirty-two *volosti* of Katerynoslav and Tavriia provinces and partisan units. The council's task was to ensure the execution of the resolutions of the congresses, which were to be held at regular intervals: however, it had no authority to take any political or military initiative.[26]

The congress accepted a resolution

> . . . against plunder, violence, and anti-Jewish pogroms committed by various obscure individuals disguising themselves under the name of honest partisans. . . . In some places national antagonism assumed the form of Jewish pogroms—a result of the old outlived dictatorial regime. The tsarist government was poisoning the irresponsible masses against the Jews, hoping to hurl down all its own evils and crimes upon the poor Jews and thus turn the attention of all toiling people away from the real reason for their poverty—the tsarist dictatorship's oppression and its freebooters.[27]

On the land question the congress resolved that:

> The land question should be decided on a Ukraine-wide scale at an all-Ukrainian congress of peasants on the following bases: in the interests of socialism and the struggle against the bourgeoisie, all land should be transferred to the hands of the toiling peasants. According to the principle that "the land belongs to nobody" and can be used only by those who care about it, who cultivate it, the land should be transferred to the toiling peasantry of Ukraine for their use without pay according to the norm of equal distribution.[28]

The resolution of the congress, which was written by the anarchists, left Socialist Revolutionaries, and the chairmanship, was accepted 150 to 29, with 20 abstentions. It was also approved by Makhno.[29]

The conflict of the Bolshevik authorities with the population also included the Makhno partisans. Makhno's aim was to fight the more dangerous enemy, the Volunteer Army, but he misjudged the Bolsheviks' strength and aims. He assumed that the coming conflict with the Bolsheviks could be confined to the realm of ideas, feeling that the strong revolutionary ideas of the peasants together with their distrust of the foreign invaders were the best guarantees of the territory of the Makhno movement. But, by making an agreement with Makhno, the Bolsheviks hoped not only to use the partisans to their own ends but to absorb them into the ranks of the Red Army and subsequently to neutralize them. This would free the hands of the Bolshevik authorities to pacify the populace and to reduce it to obedience.

The Bolsheviks, however, soon found that their hope was in vain. Although they had success on the front, their attempts to establish control in the newly occupied territories only antagonized the population. In Katerynoslav, five days after the occupation of the city the Extraordinary Commission (Cheka) began to arrest "counterrevolutionaries," who were imprisoned or shot without trial. At the same time the city was surrounded by military guards who mercilessly seized the produce that peasants attempted to bring to the market. The city's stores of food were monopolized and forwarded as supplies to Moscow, subjecting the people of the city to terror and famine.[30] It was the agricultural policy, however, that set the peasants against the Bolsheviks. The Provisional Workers' and Peasants' Government of Ukraine decreed that all lands formerly belonging to the landlords should be expropriated and transformed into state farms. Sugar refineries and distilleries, with all properties belonging to them since 1913, would also be expropriated by the state.

The Bolshevik expropriation policy was countervailed by the peasants' resistance based upon their assumption that "the land belongs to nobody . . . it can be used only by those who care about it, who cultivate it." Thus the peasants maintained that all the property of the former landlords was now by right their own. This attitude was shared not only by the rich and middle peasants but also by the poor and landless, for they all wished to be independent farmers. The poorer the areas, the more dissatisfied were the peasants with the Bolshevik decrees.[31]

Thus Communist agricultural policy and terrorism brought about a strong reaction against the new Bolshevik regime. By the middle of 1919, all peasants, rich and poor, distrusted the Bolsheviks. On March 27, in the area of Orikhiv, Tavriia province, a former Makhno detachment, consisting of some two thousand men, two guns, and eight machine guns, arose against the Communists.[32] Three hundred Bolshevik cavalrymen were promptly sent from Oleksandrivs'k to fight the partisans, but instead they joined them and began to move toward Oleksandrivs'k.

Because of apprehension that the uprisings might spread to the entire area occupied by Makhno troops, it was decided "to take extraordinary measures . . . to suppress the uprisings [however] it was necessary to dispatch only Russian or international units; local troops were unsuitable for this purpose." Accordingly a regiment of internationalists[33] was dispatched from the front against the partisans. Subsequently more uprisings took place in other areas. According to a report on April 4, partisan bands had destroyed railway and a reparation train in Ol'shanytsia, Poltava province, while another detachment of 150 men from Lubni district moved against the Communists at Zolotonosha, Poltava province.[34]

The anti-Communist attitude of the rural population was shared by some of the troops. Strong propaganda was conducted in the army against the "Moscovites" and the "present authority." Anti-Communist feeling was particularly evident in the First and Second Divisions that were organized in the Neutral Zone in 1918, and consisted partially of Ukrainian refugees. At one regimental meeting, some soldiers called for an uprising against the Communists and at the same time glorified Makhno.[35] One of the Communists, IAkovlev, in a speech in 1920, complained that at that time (1919):

> [Makhno] was a real peasant idol, an expression of all peasant spontaneity struggling against . . . Communists in the cities and simultaneously against city capitalists and landowners. In the Makhno movement it is difficult to distinguish where the poor peasant begins [and] the "kulak" ends.[36] It was a spontaneous peasant movement. . . . In the village we had no foothold, there was not one element with which we could join that would be our ally in the struggle against the bandits.[37]

The more oppressive the Bolshevik policy, the more the peasants supported Makhno. Consequently, the Bolsheviks began to organize more systematically against the Makhno movement, both as an ideology and as a social movement. The campaign was waged in the press, speeches, and orders of the central authorities. Makhno and his movement were described as "kulak . . . counterrevolutionary," and his activities were condemned as harmful to the revolution. Meanwhile the flow of arms, ammunition, and other supplies for the Makhno partisans was substantially reduced.[38]

At this point, the Revolutionary Military Council called a Third

Regional Congress of Peasants, Workers, and Partisans at Huliai-Pole on April 10, 1919. It was composed of delegates from seventy-two districts representing over two million people. Its aim was to clarify the situation and to consider the prospects for the future of the region. The congress decided to conduct a voluntary mobilization of men born in the ten years from 1889 to 1898, beginning on April 27, and rejected, with the approval of both rich and poor peasants, the Bolshevik expropriations.[39]

The activity of the congress irked the Bolshevik authorities. Dybenko dispatched a telegram to the congress declaring it "counterrevolutionary" and branding its organizers as "outlaws," in response to which the delegates voted an indignant protest. Later the council sent Dybenko a lengthy sarcastic reply: "'Comrade' Dybenko, you are still, it seems, rather new in the revolutionary movement of Ukraine, and we shall have to tell you about its very beginnings." It denounced the Bolsheviks who, it said, came to "establish laws of violence to subjugate a people who have just overthrown all lawmakers and all laws . . . if one day the Bolshevik idea succeeds among the workers, the Revolutionary Military Council . . . will be necessarily replaced by another organization 'more revolutionary' and Bolshevik. But meanwhile, do not interfere with us."[40]

Although the conflict did not break Makhno's military cooperation, it embittered the Bolshevik authorities because they lost their hope for easy integration of the region of the Makhno movement with its difficulties created by the partisans. The Bolshevik agents in the area reported that "in the Makhno region there is presently no possibility for the activities of the Communists, who are secretly killed."[41]

Apart from the Bolsheviks' objections to the congresses, which Makhno encouraged and protected, direct difficulties between Makhno and the Bolsheviks also developed. When Makhno's troops occupied the city of Mariupil' on March 27, large stacks of coal and grain were found that the Bolshevik leaders wanted to send to Russia. Makhno, however, refused to deliver the commodities save in exchange for manufactured goods. These conflicts convinced the Bolsheviks that they had to overcome the Makhno movement by force. The anti-Makhno campaign, especially in the press, was intensified, denouncing the partisans as "anarcho-bandits" and "kulaks."

Meanwhile Trotsky, who had arrived in Ukraine to lead the forthcoming offensive, advised Lenin:

To obtain bread and coal from the Mariupil' area and discipline Makhno's anarchist bands, we must organize a large detachment, consisting of a reliable Cheka battalion, several hundred Baltic Fleet sailors who have an interest in obtaining coal and bread, a supply detachment of Moscow or Ivano-Voznesenske workers, and some thirty serious Party workers. Only on these conditions will an advance in the Mariupil'-Taganrog direction become possible.[42]

Other Bolshevik leaders, however, undertook a number of investigative visits to Makhno, attempting to improve the situation by criticism and friendly persuasion. On April 29, Antonov-Ovseenko paid a visit to Makhno at Huliai-Pole to inspect his front and to find out the mood of the partisans.[43] On May 4–5 Lev B. Kamenev (Rozenfeld), deputy chairman of the Politburo, visited Makhno at Huliai-Pole, on the authorization of the All-Russian Council of Defense, to assure Makhno's cooperation. Although during his visit Kamenev tried to display a friendly attitude toward the partisans and peasants, calling them heroes for fighting bravely against their enemies, when he spoke about the Bolsheviks' policy of supporting poor peasants, they protested, maintaining that "we are all poor." In his official meeting with Makhno and his staff, Kamenev became less friendly, complaining about transportation difficulties, persecution of the Communists in the area of Makhno's operations, and about the independent mobilization by the Revolutionary Military Council, which he suggested should be dissolved. Makhno's answer was that the council was elected by the people and could be dissolved only by them.[44] He also spoke of the population's resentment of the Communist commissars sent from Russia and of the Cheka's activities.

The visit had no material effect on relations between the Bolsheviks and Makhno, nor did it change the opinions of either party. However, later Kamenev assured Dybenko that "all rumors of separatist or anti-Soviet plans on the part of the brigade and its commander, Makhno, are baseless. I saw in Makhno an honest and brave fighter who is fighting the Whites and foreign conquerors under difficult conditions."[45]

Soon, however, the whole military situation changed when Otaman Hryhor'iv, the main commander on the southwestern front, staged an uprising against the Bolsheviks that soon spread across three provinces and collapsed the southwestern front. This uprising subsequently affected Makhno's relationships with the Bolsheviks, who feared a similar occurrence on the southeastern front, and with Hryhor'iv himself.

15. Nykyfor Hryhor'iv

Next to Makhno, Nykyfor Oleksandrovych Hryhor'iv was the most prominent and colorful partisan leader of the Revolution. He succeeded in uniting over twenty partisan groups under his command, organizing them into a strong army in the lower Right Bank. A gifted and remarkable organizer, a brilliant and fearless commander who knew and enjoyed fighting, he was also the personification of the desires and ideas of the peasantry. Physically he was a medium-sized, stocky, strongly built brunet with a nasal voice and a pockmarked face that gave him a rather stern appearance. He acted self-confidently, with the composed bearing of the military profession.[1]

Hryhor'iv was born about 1885,[2] in Zastavia, a suburb of Dunaivtsi, in Ushytsia district, Podillia province. He was the eldest of four children; his father, Oleksander Servetnyk, was a state alcoholic beverage manager, and his three uncles were all literate, respectable, rich peasants. Nykyfor changed Servetnyk to Hryhor'iv, probably because he found the two side by side in the local or family records. Hryhor'iv first attended school at Dunaivtsi and later completed a two-class state school in Nova Ushytsia that was known as the best school in the district.[3]

During his school years, in his room shared with seven schoolmates, he would talk at night with great enthusiasm about the Zaporozhian Sich and the Cossacks, assuring them that when he was grown up he would join the Don Cossacks. However, neither he nor his schoolmates knew what happened to the Sich and the Cossacks, or that the Kuban Cossacks were the descendants of the Zaporozhian Cossacks. In fact, several years later he did try to join the Don Cossacks but was rejected. However, when the Russo-Japanese War broke out, Hryhor'iv joined the Cossack cavalry and fought in Manchuria. After a distinguished war service, he joined the police force at Proskuriv (Khmel'nyts'kyi). In 1914 he volunteered for the army and eventually rose to the rank of staff captain, serving in the Fifty-Eighth Infantry Regiment. He was wounded several times and decorated for his distinguished service.[4]

In the Revolution of 1917, Hryhor'iv was commander of a troop-train station at Berdychiv. He was very active in the Ukrainian military movement and was popular among the soldiers of the Berdychiv garrison. Hryhor'iv and a senior commissioned officer, Servetnyk, very often defended the Ukrainian movement in the meetings of the Executive Committee of the Southwestern Front (Iskomitiuz).[5] He also played an active role in the soldiers' revolutionary committee and in the Ukrainian Military Congresses. It was then that he became associated with Symon Petliura. During the Central Rada he was otaman of the Ukrainian troops and supported the Ukrainian government. After the fall of the Central Rada he supported the hetman government, but after several months he became disillusioned and joined the opposition. As early as August 1918 Petliura commissioned him to prepare an uprising against government and Austro-German forces in Kherson province. When the uprising began, Hryhor'iv led a popular revolt in the Oleksandriia district. After establishing the Directory's authority in the area of operation, Hryhor'iv annulled all the hetman's decrees and reinstated the "Universals" of the Central Rada, establishing local democratic self-government, and organized self-defense forces in the towns and villages.[6]

Hryhor'iv's real career began during his struggle against the Germans and Allied intervention. For this purpose he tried to unite all the partisan groups that had come into existence during the uprising under his control. In his "boastful telegrams" to Petliura at the beginning of December, he claimed that he had brought 117 small partisan groups under his command, which, by December 10, consisted of 4,000 cavalrymen, 200 grenadiers, and an undisclosed number of infantry as well as 2 secret units in the city of Mykolaiv. After organizing a strong force Hryhor'iv advanced against the Germans at Mykolaiv. Nine versts from Mykolaiv he defeated a Volunteer unit at Vodopii. Subsequently, Hryhor'iv came to a modus vivendi with the Germans and on December 13 the partisans entered the city. However, the German command, under pressure from the commander of the British fleet near the city, forced Hryhor'iv out.[7]

At the end of December Hryhor'iv sent a terse ultimatum to the Germans at Mykolaiv demanding their withdrawal from Ukraine:

I, Otaman Hryhor'iv, in the name of the partisans whom I command, rising against the yoke of the bourgeoisie, with a clear conscience, declare to you that you appeared here in Ukraine as a blind instrument in the hands of our bourgeoisie, that you are not democrats, but traitors to all the European democracies. If in four days you do not abandon Mykolaiv, Dolyns'ka, and Znamenka, by foot, beginning at twelve o'clock on the thirty-first, none of you will ever see his fatherland. You will be destroyed, like flies, at the first wave of my hand. We will not provide transportation for you. You had adequate time to leave without saying goodbye. We consider you as accursed enemies, but for humanity's sake we are giving you four days for withdrawal.[8]

As long as the Germans supported the hetman government, they were the enemy of the Directory; however, after the fall of the hetman and the Soviet Russian invasion, the presence of the German troops was not a threat to the Directory. Moreover, although the Germans were Hryhor'iv's target, the real power behind them was the Allies and Denikin. At that time the Germans were not at war with the Directory, but were charged by the agreement with the Entente to maintain peace in Mykolaiv. Thus Hryhor'iv's military activity was in conflict with Directory policy. Although the Entente's representatives in Odessa ignored Ukrainian national interests and were tactless in their dealing with the Ukrainian government, the Directory tried to reach an understanding with the Entente at any cost and gain its support in the struggle against the Red Army. Because of its acquiescence to the Entente and its supporters, the Russian Volunteers, the Directory not only lost the support of some parties and of the population, but "aroused opposition from both the right and left." In early January Hryhor'iv revolted against the Directory because it had forbidden him to move against the forces of the Entente.[9]

In cooperation with the Bolsheviks, Hryhor'iv tried to achieve what he could not with the Directory, to "drive the Entente into the sea." At the end of January 1919, Hryhor'iv initiated negotiations with the Red Army command by sending a telegram to the Bolshevik revolutionary committee in Oleksandrivs'k:

I, the otaman of the partisans of Kherson and Tavriia provinces, wish to speak with the representatives of the authority in Oleksandrivs'k and to transmit very important information. Will a representative of this authority speak with me? I shall at once inform you of our platform, if the authority in Oleksandrivs'k is democratic, not Cadet. Therefore, listen: with the capitulation [probably-declaration] on January 25 [1919] Soviet rule has been established in Ukraine. The Directory has fallen.

To replace the Directory a new government has been formed of left SRs [Borot'-bists] and Ukrainian Bolsheviks. . . .[10] All twenty of my partisan detachments are fighting against the independents and the supporters of the world bourgeoisie; we are against the Directory, the Cadets, the English, the Germans, and the French, whom the bourgeoisie have brought to Ukraine.[11]

The Oleksandrivs'k Committee forwarded reports of their negotiations to the commander of the Kharkiv group of the Soviet Army, Vladimir K. Aussem, and received the following reply:

Having heard the report of the representatives of your committee on the negotiations between your delegation and Otaman Hryhor'iv, I have to inform you that the High Command of the Ukrainian Soviet Red Army can enter into negotiations or agreements only upon these conditions: unconditional recognition of Soviet authority in Ukraine as represented by the Provisional Workers' and Peasants' Government, which at the present is in Kharkiv, . . . and subordination to the high military command of the Soviet Red Army of Ukraine.[12]

Although the Bolsheviks recognized the importance of Hryhor'iv's twenty detachments of 23,000 men, with some artillery and a considerable number of machine guns,[13] they correctly estimated that the success of their advance on Kyiv would weaken Hryhor'iv's bargaining power and cause him to submit. In a telephone conversation with a Bolshevik representative on February 1, 1919, he recognized the supremacy of the Kharkiv government and the Soviet military command, albeit conditionally:

I wish to regard our agreement, or more precisely my agreement, with you as tactical. I agree to your conditions and recognize your supreme command, provided that in the future the decision of unification of the higher command rests with your center and ours. I think that your command and ours will reach an agreement, since we shall not argue over authority. Power should belong to the people through their elected representatives; our supreme authority and yours are temporary and revolutionary. The permanent government will be formed not by us or by you, but by the people.[14]

Khristian Rakovskii, the head of the Kharkiv government, reported to Chicherin that:

Hryhor'iv recognized the supremacy of the authority of the Provisional Workers' and Peasants' Government of Ukraine and the Command of the Revolutionary Military Council, leaving it to the Ukrainian SR government, established on the right bank of the Dnieper, to negotiate a political agreement with us.[15]

Although circumstances brought about the merging of Hryhor'iv's partisan army with the Red Army, he did not share Bolshevik political goals. His alignment with them reflected the confidence of the peasants in Bolshevik promises. Like Makhno, he retained command of his forces and continued to be as active as before, but completely avoided political issues. His immediate aim was to free South Ukraine of the foreign armies of the Entente, Denikin, and Germany and to prevent them from capturing equipment and supplies, especially several vessels anchored near Mykolaiv. However, he did not clarify the object of his cooperation with the Bolsheviks.

Because the Bolshevik "reserves were exhausted . . . the main task of the offensive on Odessa fell upon Hryhor'iv's detachments." He advanced in the direction of Kherson, Mykolaiv, and Odessa along the railroad lines, taking station after station.[16] On March 9, he attacked Kherson, which was defended by a Greek infantry battalion and a French company, supported by a pair of mountain guns and the artillery of French vessels on the Dnieper. After several days of fierce battle the Allied troops were driven out of the city, losing more than four hundred men, as well as two armored trains, and considerable armament.[17] Hryhor'iv claimed that only nine partisans were killed and thirty-seven wounded. This military reversal produced a very painful impression upon the French Command and greatly demoralized the Allied soldiers and sailors in Mykolaiv and Odessa. However, it was the population that suffered most, partly from artillery and small arms fire, but especially from an Allied atrocity that took at least five hundred lives.[18]

Hryhor'iv's next target was Mykolaiv, thirty miles northwest, where the Fifteenth Landwehr Division, consisting of 15,000 German troops, was garrisoned. Although the Germans wished to avoid confrontation with Hryhor'iv, they were under Allied military control. The Allied command knew that with morale in their units at a mutinous level, it would be impossible to hold Hryhor'iv's forces. Thus they evacuated by ship to Odessa[19] leaving the Germans to do their fighting. Subsequently Hryhor'iv sent an ultimatum to the Germans, saying that in a few days he would take the city Mykolaiv by storm:

> We know you want to go home. Then go! The conditions of your departure have been outlined by the Provisional Workers' and Peasants' Government. Do not expect other conditions and, if you do not go home, you will die.

Given the circumstances, Hryhor'iv's threat was sufficient to bring about the German capitulation on March 12.[20] The partisans were engaged only in minor skirmishes. Now the road was open to Odessa, the last Entente stronghold.

Hryhor'iv's victories in Kherson and Mykolaiv had important effects on both sides. The partisans' spirit was greatly improved by their victory over the supposedly invincible Entente forces, and in both cities they captured large amounts of war material that was needed for the rapidly growing army. Hryhor'iv's fame, and the confidence of the population in him, increased. It seemed that he had absorbed the Bolsheviks rather than being absorbed by them. At the same time, the propaganda of pro-Hryhor'iv and pro-Bolshevik elements found receptive ears among the Allied troops, especially sailors. Demoralized to the point of mutiny, they either refused to fight the partisans or fled from them. They showed no interest in a foreign war that they neither wanted nor understood. Part of the civilian population also contributed to the demoralization in the city. "Refugees from Bolshevik Russia [had] increased the population to nearly 800,000, or 30 per cent above normal,"[21] and they had no other occupation than spreading rumors about a workers' armed uprising in the city and evacuation of the Entente's forces.

Meanwhile, Vladimir Antonov-Ovseenko, Commander of the Red Army in the south, was displeased with the uncontrollable Hryhor'iv and tried to assign the attack against Odessa to other units. However, heavy fighting broke out with the Directory's Ukrainian troops around Kyiv and some Bolshevik units from the Odessa front had to be sent there. Thus Hryhor'iv advanced against Odessa, taking enemy strongholds either by threats or in battle. On March 19, Hryhor'iv inflicted about five hundred casualties on Entente and Denikin troops at Berezivka, capturing five tanks, four guns, and one hundred machine guns. Although the Allied command announced on March 20 that Allied forces would defend the city and provide supplies,[22] they failed to do so, in spite of numerical superiority. According to Denikin's staff sources on March 22 there were two French and two Greek divisions, a portion of one Romanian division, and a Volunteer Army Brigade of General Timanovskii in the Odessa area. These thirty-five to forty thousand troops were provided with superior weapons and equipment, including artillery and tanks, by the Entente, had naval support, and were led by experienced professional officers. Opposing were about fifteen thousand partisans.[23] The French command tried unsuccessfully to stifle news of Hryhor'iv's approach. It created panic among the refugees from the bourgeois and the nobility in the city, stirred up the workers, and encouraged the underground Bolshevik organization to surface. There were attempts to negotiate with Hryhor'iv but he refused.

The situation changed on April 2 when General Franchet d'Esperey, commander in chief of Allied forces in the Near East, told General D'Anselme, commander in chief of Allied forces in South Russia, that the cabinet of Georges Clemenceau had fallen as a result of displeasure with his Ukrainian policy. (Actually Clemenceau's cabinet fell only on January 20, 1920.) D'Anselme issued an order to evacuate Odessa, which was published by the local newspapers with the explanation that "the Allies . . . found themselves unable to supply provisions for Odessa in the near future. Therefore, with the intent of lessening the number of consumers [it had been] decided to begin a partial evacuation of Odessa." It was, however, Hryhor'iv's advance, which began on April 2, and fear that their troops would not take orders, that compelled the French to evacuate. As early as April 3, some Greek troops, several thousand Volunteer Army men, and thirty thousand Russian civilians departed overland toward Akerman, Romania.[24] On April 5, the last French ship left the port of Odessa.

After a victorious entry into Odessa Hryhor'iv declared on April 7:

> After incredible exertions, sacrifices, and tactical maneuvers, the French, Greeks, Romanians, Turks, Volunteers, and our other enemies have been cut to pieces at Odessa. They have fled in a terrible panic, leaving colossal trophies that have not yet been counted. The flight of the adversary was so swift and panicky that even d'Anselme begged for at least three hours for the withdrawal, but this was refused him, and departing, he forgot his trunk.[25]

His first general command was to keep order and peace and to prevent disturbances. He prohibited bearing arms, sale of alcohol, and the purchase, sale, or hoarding of war material. He also proscribed search, arrest, and requisition of property without warrant. He appealed to the officers of the Volunteer Army to leave their units and join the toiling people. Such orders made Hryhor'iv appear to be a revolutionary acting against the reaction of the landlords and the foreign intervention, yet the only political element in his order was a prohibition against opposing Bolshevik authorities.[26]

After the victory over the Allied and Denikin forces Hryhor'iv accomplished his main goal and became the otaman of the partisans of Kherson and Tavriia provinces. The Bolsheviks, however, reversed their "old" slogan "without annexations and reparations" and decided to carry the proletarian revolution into the heart of Europe. On April 9, 1919, a representative of the Council of People's Commissars of Ukraine sent a message to Antonov:

> Before the victors of Odessa new perspectives are opening: the rebelling workers and peasants of Bessarabia, Bukovina, and Galicia are calling to us for assistance. The hands of the Red Army of the Hungarian Socialist Soviet Republic stretch out to them through the Carpathians. The workers and peasants of Ukraine are convinced that their revolutionary advance guard—the Ukrainian Red Army—will carry out its slogan: "Forward, forward, always forward."[27]

As Hryhor'iv was consolidating his victory in South Ukraine, two new problems were developing for Soviet Russia; hostilities with Romania, and provision for assistance to the Hungarian Soviet Republic. After the outbreak of the Revolution Bessarabia had declared itself the Autonomous Republic of Moldavia but remained within the Russian state. In November 1918, supported by the Entente, Bessarabia renounced its autonomy and joined Romania. As the Red Army invaded Ukraine, the Soviet Russian government began organizing a rebellion in Romania and prepared a plan for its invasion. This action was designed not only to recapture Bessarabia, but "as a means to untangle the European revolutionary forces, a means to break into Europe."[28]

The invasion was intensified by the Hungarian revolution. As the democratic government of the new Hungary, headed by Michael Karolyi, failed to win the sympathy of the Entente and had to accept the latter's demands for territorial concessions, including Transylvania, to its neighbors, it decided to form a coalition government with the Communists. Consequently, on March 21, the new government proclaimed Hungary a Republic of Workers,' Peasants,' and Soldiers' Soviets under Bela Kun. The new government opposed the Entente's further demands and war against Romania became inevitable, but it realized that its future existence depended upon direct contact with Soviet Russia. The Directory's envoy in Budapest, Mykola Halahan, felt that he could use the Hungarian situation to end the Russo-Ukrainian war. He advised Bela Kun to convince the Soviet Russian government that its assistance could not reach Hungary in time unless a peace agreement with Ukraine was concluded. Welcoming the proposition, Bela Kun on March 31 invited Vynnychenko, the former president of the Directory, to Budapest. The Hungarian government

> . . . expressed a desire to mediate between the left Ukrainian Socialist factions and the Soviet Russian government concerning the establishment in Ukraine of a real Ukrainian national Soviet government. This government would set aside the Directory and the Galician State Secretariat, to bring under its aegis all Ukrainian Socialist groups and above all the Galician Army. Thus Hungary, Galicia, Ukraine, and Russia would become a united Soviet front.

Vynnychenko, however, laid down a number of conditions:

> Recognition of an independent and sovereign Ukrainian Soviet Republic; Ukrainian national Soviet government; a defensive-offensive military alliance of the Soviet republics; a close economic alliance; and advance into Galicia.[29]

Although these conditions were relayed by the Hungarian government to Moscow, and Bela Kun was "deeply convinced" that success was assured, the negotiations came to naught, for Soviet Russia was interested in its own expansion rather than in independent, albeit Soviet, republics. However, Soviet Russia welcomed the emergence of a Soviet Hungarian government as a sign of an imminent world proletarian revolution that should be used for its own ends. Meantime, at the Entente's instigation, Romanian troops were enlarging their occupation of Transylvania, threatening Bela Kun's regime. The Hungarian government asked Russia to make a diverting attack on Romania: "If you can make even a little conquest, a little demonstration on the Romanian front, if you can cross the Dniester for even three days, and then return, the panic would be tremendous."[30] Soviet Russian strategy in Ukraine was definitely shaped by the desire to establish contact with Soviet Hungary and give military aid but on their own terms. On March 26, I. I. Vācietis, the commander in chief of Bolshevik forces, wired Antonov-Ovseenko to limit his activities on the Romanian front, to destroy the Ukrainian forces, and move toward East Galicia and Bukovina to establish a "direct, intimate contact with the Soviet armies of Hungary."[31]

Antonov-Ovseenko had already been working on a plan to aid Soviet Hungary through Bessarabia and Moldavia, but at that time his attention was focused on the campaign against the Directory and Hryhor'iv's race toward Odessa. In connection with this situation Antonov-Ovseenko wrote to Rakovskii:

> Presently campaigns are being conducted in Kyiv and Odessa on whose results will depend the future fate of Soviet power not only in Right Bank Ukraine and the entire western front, but also on the front of social revolution in Hungary [and] Germany.[32]

The main force the Bolshevik leaders planned to use against Romania was Hryhor'iv's partisan army of 15,000, and Antonov-Ovseenko tried to persuade Hryhor'iv to prepare for the invasion. On April 23 he described bright prospects for the coming campaign:

> Look, all Europe is in ferment. Uprisings of workers in Austria. Soviet governments in Hungary, Bulgaria, Turkey are ready to throw themselves against Romania. The Bessarabian peasants are waiting for us to arise as one. . . . Look at the map. You will advance along the road of Suvorov.[33]

Subsequently he renewed the persuasion with a veiled threat:

> We know which way you are pushed. But I reply to your accusers that Hryhor'iv cannot break with the affairs of toilers; and Hryhor'iv is too wise; he knows the powers of the Soviet government. It sweeps away all who betray it.[34]

Antonov-Ovseenko was well aware of the partisans' dissatisfaction with the Communist regime. At the end of March Antonov-Ovseenko, Hryhor'iv, and the Communist Shums'kyi visited a large village, Verbliuzhka, Hryhor'iv's capital, where each of them delivered a speech. Antonov-Ovseenko's and Hryhor'iv's speeches dealing with their victories were applauded; however, when Shums'kyi, talking about the land policy of the Soviet Russian government, uttered the word, "commune" the entire crowd roared wildly. "If Hryhor'iv had not protected Shums'kyi. . . ." Antonov left the statement unfinished. The population was provoked by activities of the Russian foodstuff requisitioning units that invaded the Ukrainian villages and which Lenin admits to sending for the "pumping out" of Ukrainian bread.[35]

The Bolshevik Ukrainian policy was also shocking to Hryhor'iv, and in a telegram to Rakovskii he threatened: "If in my footsteps there will grow as shabby a government as I see now, I, Otaman Hryhor'iv, will not fight. Take the boys and send them to school, and give the people a reasonable government that they would respect."[36] Because of the strong resistance of the Ukrainian population and the extreme indignation of Hryhor'iv's troops Antonov-Ovseenko advised the government: "You must recall the Muscovite food requisitions units. First organize a local authority and only then, with its assistance, pump out the foodstuffs."[37]

In the meantime the situation in Soviet Hungary worsened. On May 1, the Bolsheviks dispatched an ultimatum to Romania demanding withdrawal from Bessarabia, and on May 3, a second, demanding withdrawal from Bukovina. On May 6 a Provisional Workers' and Peasants' Government of Bessarabia formed in Odessa and issued a manifesto proclaiming the establishment of a Bessarabian Soviet Republic as a part of the RSFSR.[38] On May 7 a representative of the Hungarian government appeared in Kyiv to inform the Bolsheviks that only the Red Army could save Soviet Hungary. Antonov-Ovseenko at once ordered his new commander on the Odessa front to send troops, including Hryhor'iv, against Romania. Hryhor'iv feigned loyalty to the Bolsheviks as long as possible. However, when he received definite orders to advance on Romania, he staged an open revolt that became generally known only on May 9, when he issued a "Universal" (manifesto) to the Ukrainian people, skillfully appealing to their grievances and exhorting them to advance on Kyiv and Kharkiv:

The political speculators have cheated you and exploited your confidence by a clever move; instead of land and liberty they violently impose upon you the commune, the Cheka and Moscow Commissars. . . . You work day and night; you have a torch for light; you go about in bark shoes and sack cloth trousers. Instead of tea you drink hot water without sugar, but those who promise you a bright future exploit you, fight with you, take away your grain at gunpoint, requisition your cattle, and impudently tell you that this is for the good of the people.[39]

He called for the organization of councils on all levels, from village to province. Each council should consist of representatives of each party and nonparty that supported the Soviet platform. It should include all nationalities in proportion to their number. Hryhor'iv believed it would be a real democratic people's authority: "Long live freedom of speech, press, assembly, unions, strikes, labor, and professions, security of person, thought, residence, conviction, and religion."[40] The manifesto was written in Ukrainian and Russian and widely distributed in the area under Hryhor'iv's control. It was also sent by wire to other areas.

Both the manifesto and the plan for the uprising were developed by Hryhor'iv in conjunction with his chief of staff, IUrii Tiutiunyk. Tiutiunyk had proposed to free the territory between the Boh and Dnieper, then join the Ukrainian Army, simultaneously sending a number of small partisan units and separate organizers to the Left Bank to terrorize the Bolsheviks. Hryhor'iv, however, pursued his own plan to advance toward Kharkiv and free the Left Bank. He wished to be the leader of an independent force between the Ukrainian and Volunteer armies, hoping that all would fight the same enemy, the Bolsheviks. At that time his force consisted of close to twenty thousand men, forty guns, ten armored train platforms with mounted guns, and large amounts of small arms and ammunition.[41] Hryhor'iv divided his force into three groups: he himself led the main force toward Katerynoslav-Kharkiv, Tiutiunyk moved toward Kyiv, and Pavlov was fighting toward Cherkasy. The Bolsheviks mobilized all available forces, including those from the Romanian, Ukrainian, and Crimean fronts. They were organized in three groups under the command of Voroshilov, their aim being to encircle Hryhor'iv's troops. They also carried on an extensive propaganda campaign against Hryhor'iv among their troops and the population. During the initial phase Hryhor'iv was fighting the Bolsheviks along railroad lines and in urban centers. By dint of hard fighting and successful propaganda the uprising spread through three provinces. Hryhor'iv's initial success stirred great concern in Moscow, which increased when the Directory's troops began to pin down the Bolsheviks by attacking from the north and south near Kyiv.[42]

Moscow panicked when in mid-May the anti-Bolshevik Russian

army of General Nikolai N. IUdenich advanced across the Estonian border toward Petrograd. On May 19 Lenin sent an urgent telegram to the southern front: "The attack on Petrograd increases tenfold the danger and the supreme necessity of suppressing the [Hryhor'iv] revolt immediately at all costs." On May 26 Lenin again stressed in his telegram to Rakovskii the necessity of fighting Hryhor'iv:

> Do not miss any opportunity for victory over Hryhor'iv. Do not permit a single soldier who is fighting against Hryhor'iv to leave. Issue and implement an order for the complete disarming of the population. Shoot mercilessly on the spot for every concealed rifle. The whole issue at the moment is a speedy victory in the Donets Basin, the collection of all rifles from the villages, the creation of a firm army. Concentrate all your strength on this effort, mobilize every single worker.[43]

Although Hryhor'iv successfully fought the Bolshevik forces, he could not match their growing power for a longer period and at the end of May his main forces were defeated. Some partisan groups left Hryhor'iv, including Tiutiunyk, who moved westward with a group of 3,500 men to join the Ukrainian Army. Hryhor'iv was forced to abandon the railroad lines and move his troops to forests and villages where he mobilized new recruits and continued partisan warfare.[44] On June 28 Hryhor'iv, in a letter to the Ukrainian government, depicted the damage he had done and admitted defeat:

> Now our situation is critical; our division is facing five Communist divisions. We completely destroyed three Communist divisions while two others were only ripped. . . . Completely demolished [Bolshevik] transport, telegraph, and telephone connections in Ukraine . . . disorganized communications, mobilization, and supply to the front. However, we had to leave the railroad lines, lost many troops, guns, almost all our supplies, and now have changed to the partisan warfare.[45]

In mid-May the Volunteer Army, which was struggling against the Makhno and Bolshevik troops in southeastern Ukraine, began its major advance in the direction of Moscow. The main weight of the offensive was transferred to Ukraine, and under pressure from Denikin, Makhno retreated westward to the area of Hryhor'iv's operations. There was a certain common ground for cooperation between Hryhor'iv and Makhno because both were hostile to the Bolshevik regime and its dictatorial methods and both drew much of their strength from the population's hostility to the Bolsheviks. In his letter to the Ukrainian government, Hryhor'iv expressed this attitude: "We broke away from the Communists and we fight them because 90 percent of the people do not want communism and do not recognize the dictatorship of a party or the dictatorship as an individual." Hryhor'iv and Makhno were in contact for some time and carried on negotiations about joining forces against the Bolsheviks.[46] Hryhor'iv notified Makhno, it seems, after each of his victories over the Entente's troops, and hoped that after the uprising started, Makhno would join him.

On April 10, 1919, the Katerynoslav Communist party committee reported that

Makhno's men are conducting negotiations with Hryhor'iv about a simultaneous action against the Soviets. Today we caught Makhno's delegate to Hryhor'iv. We command the taking of urgent measures to liquidate Makhno men, as of now in Makhno area there is no chance for the Communists to work because they are secretly killed.[47]

The Bolsheviks feared the possibility of a Makhno-Hryhor'iv union. On May 12, after Hryhor'iv issued his universals, Politburo deputy Lev B. Kamenev, who had met with Makhno the week before, wired Makhno:

The decisive moment has come—either you stand with the workers and peasants of all Russia, or you open the front to the enemy. There is no place for hesitation. Report to me immediately the location of your troops, and issue an appeal against Hryhor'iv, [and] send me a copy in Kharkiv. I would consider an unanswered letter as a declaration of war. I rely on revolutionary honor—yours, Arshinov and Veretel'nyk.[48]

Although Makhno was against the Bolsheviks, he assumed a neutral position. His response to Kamenev was to issue an order to his troops:

Use the most energetic measures to save the front; do not allow the revolution and its external front to be betrayed in any way . . . the quarrel between Hryhor'iv and the Bolsheviks for the sake of power cannot force us to weaken the front where the White guards tried to break through and suppress the people. As long as we do not overcome our common enemy, the White Don; as long as we do not surely and securely feel the freedom we conquered with our hand and rifles, we will remain at the front, fighting for people's freedom, but not for the government, not for the meanness of political charlatans.[49]

At the same time, Kamenev reported that Makhno said:

I and my front will remain unchangeably true to the revolution of the workers and peasants, but not to institutions of violence like your Commissars and Chekas. . . . Now I do not have accurate information about Hryhor'iv and his movement. I do not know what he is doing and what his intentions are; therefore, I cannot issue an appeal against him until I receive more evidence.[50]

In the light of Hryhor'iv's uprising and Denikin's advance, Makhno was a source of worry to Moscow. On May 7, two days after Kamenev had met Makhno at Huliai-Pole, Lenin had sent a telegram to Kamenev: "Temporarily, as long as Rostov had not been taken, it is necessary to deal diplomatically with Makhno's troops; send Antonov there and make Antonov responsible for Makhno's army." Subsequently Kamenev wired Lenin: "[I] think that Makhno at present will not decide to support Hryhor'iv; however, the ground is ripe for the breaking."[51]

The Bolsheviks were trying not only to prevent Makhno from following Hryhor'iv, but to use his assistance against him. However, the Bolsheviks were not the only factor. Makhno had much personal antagonism against Hryhor'iv, who was his rival for power and fame. Hryhor'iv was a professional officer of lifelong experience, who manifested great personal bravery and military ability. Also he was his own man, one who intended to command and not to be commanded. If his uprising were successful, he would probably try to extend his domination to Makhno's territory and try to absorb the Makhno movement. Both leaders operated in, and recruited from, the same general region. Makhno realized this, and he did not wish to be guided by Hryhor'iv. Makhno had his own plan, and his devious mind worked toward the destruction of Hryhor'iv's power and the absorption of his troops.[52]

On July 27, 1919, Hryhor'iv was assassinated. According to the most widely known version, related by Arshinov and Makhno himself, although it was undoubtedly composed after the fact to serve Makhno's ends, a congress of partisans from Katerynoslav, Tavriia, and Kherson provinces was called at Sentove, near Oleksandriia in Kherson province. About twenty thousand partisans and peasants attended. Hyrhor'iv, speaking first, identified the Bolsheviks as the main enemy and stated that it was necessary to seek any ally, even Denikin, against them. Makhno then criticized him, saying that an alliance with "generals" would mean "counterrevolution," and thus Hryhor'iv was an "enemy of the people." He also accused him of conducting a pogram in IElesavethrad in May 1919. Sensing something amiss, Hryhor'iv belatedly drew his side arm, but Makhno's associate, Semen Karetnyk, had already begun to shoot at him. Then Makhno cried "Death to the otaman!" and killed him. Several members of Hryhor'iv's staff were also shot. Later, Hryhor'iv's partisans joined Makhno. The assassination was recorded in the minutes: "The perpetrator of pogroms Hryhor'iv was assassinated by responsible Makhnovites: Bat'ko Makhno, Semen Karetnyk, and Oleksander Chubenko. The Makhno movement accepts complete responsibility for this act before history."[53]

There was, however, a very different version related soon after the event by Makhno himself to Fotii M. Meleshko, who was doing educational work among the partisans. Makhno supported his story with documents. He said he had met Hryhor'iv on July 27 at Lozova, Oleksandriia district, to discuss unification of their forces. Hryhor'iv had a much larger group of supporters present, but was not expecting anything, while Makhno had his plan well thought out. At the outset Makhno and Chubenko accused Hryhor'iv of betraying the Revolution by planning to join Denikin. Makhno said he had caught two of Hryhor'iv's officers, who confessed they had been sent to Denikin to negotiate. By this move he hoped to undermine the partisans' confidence in Hyrhor'iv. Hryhor'iv then tried to defend himself by reasoning that all the strength should be concentrated against the main enemy, the Bolsheviks, even if this required an alliance with Denikin.[54] When Karetnyk began to shoot him, Hyrhor'iv, showing characteristic strength and bravery, broke through the circle and took refuge behind a tree, where he defended himself until he finally fell dead with eight bullets in him. His chief of staff, Kaluzhnyi, was also killed. Makhno's men then disarmed Hryhor'iv's partisans. Makhno explained why he had killed Hryhor'iv and offered them a choice of joining him or returning home.[55] Because of his bravery, Hryhor'iv was buried with honors, as a military hero. Subsequently, Makhno wired the news to Lenin.[56]

Although the Hryhor'iv movement lasted less than one year, it greatly affected the course of the Ukrainian Revolution and the development of the international situation. By abandoning the Directory and joining the Red Army, Hryhor'iv accelerated the Bolshevik advance in Ukraine. Although Hryhor'iv reflected the mood and social aspirations of the Ukrainian peasants in his particular region, he failed to lead the people toward a national goal—to join with the Directory in defending the independence of Ukraine. Hryhor'iv not only defeated the Entente's intervention in South Ukraine, but he thwarted Bolshevik plans for spreading Communist revolution in Europe. Instead of advancing with the Red Army into Romania and Hungary to rescue the Bela Kun Communist regime, the Bolsheviks had to withdraw their troops from the Denikin front to quell Hryhor'iv. Thus his uprising against the Bolsheviks helped to accelerate Denikin's advance into Ukraine against the Bolsheviks and subsequently against the Ukrainian Army.

16. The Bolsheviks Break with Makhno

Although the Bolsheviks appreciated Makhno's struggle against Denikin, they also recognized his movement as an organized force opposing Bolshevik dictatorship in Ukraine. Even before Makhno destroyed Hryhor'iv, the Bolsheviks renewed their anti-Makhno propaganda. Trotsky, in particular, led a violent campaign against the Makhno movement. He published a series of defensive articles in his paper *V puti* [On the road] in which he charged that all the Makhnovites' talk of "down with the party, down with the Communists, long live the nonparty Soviets!" was only a cunning device to conceal the anarchists' ambition to establish a government of the "kulaks."[1] At the same time, the supplies of arms and other war material to Makhno were stopped, thus weakening the Makhno forces vis-à-vis the Denikin troops. Trotsky, an advocate of extreme centralized discipline, concluded that Makhno's army was more of a menace than the Denikin army and declared in June of 1919, according to Emma Goldman, that

> . . . it were better to permit the Whites to remain in the Ukraina than to suffer Makhno. The presence of the Whites . . . would influence the Ukrainian peasantry in favor of the Soviet Government, whereas Makhno and his *povstantsi* would never make peace with the Bolsheviki; they would attempt to possess themselves of some territory and to practice their ideas, which would be a constant menace to the Communist Government.[2]

In his speech delivered at the Tenth Congress of the Russian Communist Party in March 1921, Lenin, though not referring specifically to Makhno, obviously had him in mind when he said: "This petty bourgeois counterrevevolution is, no doubt, more dangerous than Denikin, IUdenich, and Kolchak put together because we have to deal with a country where proletarians constitute a minority."[3] In view of Bolshevik hostility and the Denikin offensive, the partisans' Revolutionary Military Council decided to call a fourth congress of peasants, workers, and partisans of Katerynoslav and Tavriia provinces and the adjacent districts in Kherson and Kharkiv provinces. The Council sent telegrams to these places informing them of the calling of an extraordinary congress on June 15, 1919, at Huliai-Pole.[4]

Trotsky's response was an order issued on June 4:

> To all Military Commissars and the Executive Committees of the districts of Oleksandrivs'k, Mariupil', Berdians'k, Bakhmut, Pavlohrad, and Kherson. . . . This Congress is directed squarely against the Soviet government in Ukraine and against the organization of the southern front, which includes Makhno's Brigade. The result of this congress can be only a new disgraceful revolt in the spirit of Hryhor'iv, and the opening of the front to the Whites, before whom Makhno's Brigade incessantly retreats because of the incompetence, criminal designs, and treason of its leaders.
>
> 1. This Congress is forbidden and in no case shall it be allowed.
>
> 2. All the worker-peasant population shall be warned orally and in writing that participation in the Congress shall be considered an act of state treason against the Soviet Republic and the front.
>
> 3. All the delegates to this Congress shall be arrested immediately and brought before the Revolutionary Military Tribunal of the Fourteenth, formerly Second, Army.
>
> 4. Those who would spread the call of Makhno and the Executive Committee on Huliai-Pole shall be arrested.
>
> 5. The present order shall take effect as soon as it is telegraphed and shall be widely distributed locally, displayed in all public places, and sent to the representatives of district and village authorities, in general to all Soviet authorities, and also to the commanders and commissars of the military units.[5]

The Fourth Regional Congress, called for June 15, could not take place. Neither Makhno nor his staff received any communication about this order, and found out about it only three days after its publication. On June 9 Makhno sent a telegram from the Haichur station to the Fourteenth Army, to Voroshilov, Trotsky, Lenin, and Kamenev:

> The whole official press, and also the Communist-Bolshevik party press, has spread rumors about me that are unworthy of a revolutionist. They wish to make me seem a bandit, and accomplice of Hryhor'iv, a conspirator against the Soviet Republic for the purpose of reestablishing capitalism. . . . This hostile attitude of the central authorities toward the partisan movement, which is now becoming aggressive, leads unavoidably to the creation of a special internal front. . . . The most effective means of preventing the central authorities from committing this crime is, in my opinion, evident. I must leave the post I occupy.[6]

Subsequently Makhno handed over his command and left the front with a few of his close associates and a cavalry detachment. However, he called upon the partisans to remain at the front to hold off Denikin's forces. At the same time his regimental commanders promised to await the proper moment to return under his command.[7] Meanwhile, Trotsky, instead of sending a replacement for Makhno, ordered Voroshilov and Commissar Valerii Mezhlauk to arrest him, but Makhno was warned in advance and escaped. However, on June 15–16, members of Makhno's staff, Mykhalev-Pavlenko, Burbyha, and several members of the Revolutionary Military Council, including Oliinyk, Korobka, Kostyn, Polunyna, and Dobroliubov, were captured and executed the next day.[8]

As soon as Makhno left the front he and his associates began to organize new partisan detachments in the Bolsheviks' rear, which subsequently attacked strongholds, troops, police, trains, and food collectors. At about the same time, the Makhno movement was seriously threatened by the major offensive of the Volunteer Army. This was the main enemy that Makhno fought, stubbornly and uncompromisingly, from the end of 1918 to the end of 1919. Its social and anti-Ukrainian policies greatly antagonized all segments of Ukrainian society. The result of this was an increased resistance to the Volunteer Army and its regime and a substantial strengthening of the Makhno movement.

17. The Volunteer Army and Makhno

During the winter of 1917–18, a Volunteer Army had been formed in the Don Basin by General Mikhail V. Alekseev, the former commander in chief of the Russian Army, with the permission of General Aleksei M. Kaledin, ataman of the Don Cossacks. To aid the recruiting, Alekseev organized secret societies in Russia and Ukraine, helping officers to make their way to the Don. These societies were in close contact with public organizations that aided them financially. Initially the organization grew slowly, but the escape of generals Lavr G. Kornilov, Denikin, Ivan P. Romanovskii, Aleksandr S. Lukomskii, Sergei L. Markov, and others from Bykhov on December 2, 1917, had a felicitous effect on the movement's growth.[1] Kornilov intended to proceed to Siberia and organize a strong army, but the representatives of the National Center in Moscow who came to Novocherkassk insisted that Kornilov remain in the Don and work with Alekseev and Kaledin. Kornilov finally consented and on January 7, 1918, the supreme authority of the Russian anti-Bolshevik movement was vested in a triumvirate composed of Alekseev, who assumed authority over political and financial affairs; Kornilov, who was entrusted with the organization and command of the army; and Kaledin, who was responsible for organization of the Don Army.[2] Thus Alekseev's volunteer organization became a Volunteer Army.

Officers, military and naval cadets, students, and high school boys began to arrive and enlist, but there were very few soldiers among the volunteers. An officer of the German command in Kyiv acknowledged that the Volunteer Army was steadily growing, but that it was "All officers; there were, however, no soldiers in it."[3] Hence the Volunteer Army took on a class rather than a national character, was strongly sympathetic to the old order, and had no appeal to the lower classes of society.

As the threat of the Bolsheviks increased, Kornilov decided to launch an expedition against them in Tsaritsyn; however, the Don Cossacks, especially those regiments returning from the front, were unwilling to fight; they too were imbued with bolshevism. Moreover, Bolshevik pressure on Novocherkassk compelled Kornilov toward the end of January 1918 to transfer the headquarters of the army to Rostov, but by February 22, Bolshevik advances forced him to retreat toward the Kuban Basin, where the Cossacks were less affected by Bolshevik propaganda than were those of the Don.[4] Kornilov also hoped to get in touch with the British at Baku. In the meantime, Ataman Kaledin, having failed to gain support from his Cossacks in defending the Don against the Bolshevik invasion, committed suicide on February 24, 1918.[5]

The nucleus of the Volunteer Army retreated into the steppe, surrounded and assailed by Bolsheviks, more numerous and better armed than the Volunteers. In Ekaterinodar, Kornilov had expected to find a large quantity of war materials, reinforcements, and an opportunity to rest; but before he reached it, it was surrendered to the Bolsheviks, and the government of the Kuban fled into the villages in the foothills of the Caucasus. Kornilov established contact with the forces of the Kuban government and with difficulty persuaded them to agree on unification of both armies.[6] On April 8, 1918, this army of about seven thousand men attacked the Bolsheviks in Ekaterinodar. Although the army had experienced commanders and military training, it was severely beaten because of the Bolshevik superiority in numbers and artillery. On April 13, in spite of great losses, Kornilov was preparing a second attack when he was mortally wounded. Although the command immediately passed to General Denikin, the death of Kornilov and heavy losses broke the spirit of the troops and the planned attack was given up. Denikin decided, with the Kuban government and the Rada, which gave the Volunteer Army substantial material and moral support and new recruits, to retreat northward together toward the Don. The fighting continued during the movement, and after almost two weeks, on May 4, 1918, Denikin brought the five-thousand-man army to the frontier of the Don and Kuban Basins. Over four hundred of his men were killed and more than fifteen hundred were wounded.[7]

After receiving information about the uprisings in the Don, Denikin decided to assist the Don Cossacks, hoping to gain new recruits and arms, and also to enhance his own political standing in the Don. The Kuban government and the Rada, however, decided to return to the Kuban to fight the enemy at home.

The Volunteer Army, despite the high quality of its leaders, its military training, and the courage of its men, failed to free the Kuban Basin from the Bolsheviks, just as it had failed before to defend the Don Basin. The population of those regions had not yet decided which side it would support. As General I. A. Poliakov observed: "according to a rough estimate about six thousand officers were idle in Novocherkassk." Similarly, General Kornilov complained about the attitude of young men in Rostov: "how many young men loaf in crowds at Sadova. If only a fifth of them would enlist in the army, the Bolsheviks would cease to exist."[8]

On the other hand, the anti-Bolshevik forces had not accepted the new order that was brought to life by the Revolution. After the death of Kornilov, the leaders of the movement strove to reestablish the old order. According to General Shkuro:

> Kornilov's program was clear and understandable; with the gradual success of the Volunteer Army, its program became more and more unclear and blurred. The idea of democracy was not carried out decisively in anything. Even we, the senior commanders, now could not answer the question of what exactly is the program of the Volunteer Army at least in its basic features.[9]

The founder of the Volunteer Army, General Alekseev, in a letter to Vasilii Shulgin on June 5, 1918, wrote:

> Concerning our slogan—Constituent Assembly—it is necessary to keep in mind that we brought it up only because of necessity. It will not be mentioned at all in our first proclamation, now being prepared. Our sympathies ought to be clear to you, but to reveal them here openly would be a mistake because the population would give it a hostile reception. We disassociate ourselves from the former slogan. To declare a new one we need appropriate conditions, especially territory under our control. This will come about as soon as we switch over to our active program.[10]

After Ataman Kaledin's suicide, the Cossacks began to act on the appeals he had made and stand up against the Bolsheviks,[11] but lack of good organization kept them from concerted action, and soon they went back to their settlements. The Bolsheviks gradually extended their regime to almost all the main centers of the Don, but the wholesale requisitions and plundering by the Red troops created a great deal of hostility. According to a former Bolshevik official:

> In the towns were dozens of different Red detachments. Most of them were disinte-

grating and addicted to banditism. They demanded much for their maintenance and refused under various pretexts to go to the front. Looting, theft, assaults, robberies increased.[12]

These activities brought about widespread uprisings against the Bolsheviks at the end of March 1918. The Cossacks received support from the troops of Colonel Drozdovskii, who came from the Romanian front, and unsuccessfully attacked the Bolsheviks in Rostov on April 21–22, 1918. On April 25 he advanced to Novocherkassk and, with the Cossacks, drove the enemy from the capital of the Don. Meanwhile, German troops were advancing to the Don from Ukraine, driving the Bolsheviks from Taganrog on May 1, and from Rostov on May 8. On May 11, after General Anatolii M. Nazarov, the successor of Ataman Kaledin, and six other officers were arrested and executed by the Bolsheviks, the Assembly of Don Cossacks elected General Peter N. Krasnov Ataman of the Don. Krasnov entered into negotiations with the Germans and succeeded in obtaining arms and ammunition for the newly formed Don Army.[13] He then proposed that Denikin join him to fight the Bolsheviks at the Tsaritsyn (Volgograd) front:

Tsaritsyn would give General Denikin a good, strictly Russian base, gun and munitions factories, and a great amount of different military supplies, not to mention money. [Thus] the Volunteer Army would cease to depend upon the Cossacks.[14]

Denikin, however, replied that under no circumstances would he go to Tsaritsyn, arguing that the Kuban Cossacks would not follow him and without them the Volunteer Army would be too weak. The real reason, however, was Denikin's desire to acquire a large quantity of supplies, especially military ones, in the Don and to enlist the Cossacks in the Volunteer Army because he did not wish to be accompanied by a separate, though associated, army. Moreover, at the end of May 1918, Hetman Skoropads'kyi was negotiating with the Kuban delegation in Kyiv concerning a union of Kuban with Ukraine and the liberation of the Kuban from the Bolsheviks. Plans were made to transport 15,000 Ukrainian troops across the Sea of Azov, in order to prevent Denikin from obtaining control of the Kuban. Denikin wished to forestall this expedition to the Kuban.[15] Thus, the roads of Denikin and Krasnov parted; the Cossacks advanced northward, driving the Bolsheviks from the Don during May, while Denikin was preparing for the second march southward toward the Kuban.

By the end of May, the Volunteer Army consisted of five infantry and eight cavalry regiments and five batteries, in all nine thousand men and twenty-one guns. Soon the Army had been strengthened by

Colonel Drozdovskii's unit consisting of about twenty-five thousand well-armed and equipped men, including artillery, armored cars, and even airplanes.[16] On June 10, the army began to advance south along the railroad lines, its ranks being gradually swelled en route by anti-Bolshevik Cossack partisans and by defecting Red soldiers, especially those who had been conscripted from the local Cossacks. By the middle of July the army consisted of about thirty thousand men. With this strength Denikin attacked an eighty-thousand-man Bolshevik force with one hundred guns and large reserve supplies, which was, however, poorly organized, led, and disciplined. Denikin captured substantial quantities of stores, locomotives, and rolling stock, and gained control of several vital railroad junctions, undermining Bolshevik military initiative. Although he had lost 25 to 30 percent of his men, Denikin attacked large Bolshevik forces in Ekaterinodar and on August 16, after three days, captured the city.[17]

Denikin's immediate aims after capturing Ekaterinodar were to drive the Bolshevik forces out of the Kuban and North Caucasus, to strengthen the Volunteer Army, and to establish relations with the Allies. By capturing Ekaterinodar and Novorossisk, Denikin consolidated his control over the west Kuban. In the fall serious fighting developed around Armavir and Stavropol between Denikin's forces of more than thirty-five thousand men, and the hundred-and-fifty-thousand-man North Caucasian Red Army over control of the rest of Kuban and North Caucasus. Although the Volunteer Army and the Kuban Cossacks were weaker, they successfuly resisted the Red Army's offensives. Concurrently, a bitter disagreement developed among the Bolshevik leaders concerning the strategy to defeat Denikin that substantially weakened the Bolshevik effort. Moreover, the Bolsheviks' military situation was unfavorable, as they had lost the main towns, the more fertile crop lands, and many supplies to Denikin and by the beginning of 1919, they finally were routed. Denikin captured more than fifty thousand prisoners and large military stores.[18]

On January 24, Sergei Ordzhonokidze, the commissar on the Caucasus front, cabled Lenin:

> The Eleventh Army has ceased to exist. It has finally gone to pieces. The enemy occupies cities and *stanitsas* almost without resistance. . . . There are no shells or bullets. . . . We are all perishing in the unequal struggle, but we will not disgrace our honor by fleeing.[19]

Denikin secured his rear by defeating the North Caucasian Red Army and proceeded north in pursuit of the Bolshevik forces. In spite of a lack of cooperation between the Volunteer, Kuban, and Don armies, they succeeded in driving the Bolsheviks from the Don and Kuban basins and the North Caucasus.

While the fighting was still going on, General Alekseev, the supreme leader of the Volunteer Army, died on October 8, 1918. After his death the command of the army passed to General Denikin while nonmilitary affairs were referred to a "Special Council" (*Osoboe Sovieshchanie*) attached to the commander in chief in Ekaterinodar. Toward the end of the year, with the Bolsheviks in the northern Don threatening Novocherkassk, and under pressure from the British military representatives, the Don government concluded an agreement with Denikin that guaranteed the Don's autonomous status while Krasnov "reluctantly and half-heartedly" recognized Denikin as commander in chief of the "Armed Forces of South Russia," including the Don Army, in operational matters.[20]

In the meantime the strength of the Volunteer Army substantially increased following a forced mobilization in the occupied region outside the Kuban, and the use of the Red prisoners. Moreover, in November of 1918, about five thousand Terek Cossacks, who opposed the Bolsheviks, joined Denikin. Subsequently Denikin reorganized all his forces into three armies: the Volunteer Corps, under General Vladimir Z. Mai-Maevskii, including the original Volunteer Army, which then lost its "volunteer" character; the Caucasian Volunteer Army, including the Kuban and Terek Cossacks, under General Wrangel; and the Don Cossack Army, under General Krasnov.[21]

Next to the liberation of the Kuban and North Caucasus, the most crucial need of Denikin was Allied aid. Prior to February 1919, the main source of war supplies was that captured from the Bolsheviks. The Allies' assistance materialized only when Denikin established contact with them by capturing Novorossisk on August 26,[22] Bulgaria capitulated in September, and Romania reentered the war on the Allied side in November. At first the British government was reluctant to support the Russian anti-Bolshevik movement because, as Winston S. Churchill stated:

> The Armistice and the collapse of Germany had altered all Russian values and relations. The Allies had only entered Russia with reluctance and as an operation of war. . . . Therefore every argument which had led to intervention had disappeared.[23]

Lloyd George later echoed this point, noting that with the end of war, "every practical reason for continuing our costly military efforts in Russia disappeared."[24]

However, the British government sent a military commission to

Novorossisk and upon its recommendation the War Cabinet decided on November 11, 1918, "to give General Denikin at Novorossisk all possible help in the way of military material."[25] By February of 1919, the aid promised had begun to arrive in substantial quantities. According to General Wrangel: "Boats laden with war materials and drugs, things of which the Army was in great need, had arrived at Novorossisk. [Also] they promised us tanks and aeroplanes." Between February and the winter of 1919, Britain supplied Denikin with 558 guns, 250,000 rifles, 12 tanks, 1,685,522 shells, 160 million rounds of ammunition, 250,000 uniforms, and a substantial amount of medical supplies, plus about 100 airplanes.[26]

This aid was accompanied by a team of military advisors and technical experts whose duties were to receive and distribute British munitions to the Russian troops, and to teach them how to operate the tanks, airplanes, and other weapons. There was also a British medical staff that served many Russian officials attached to the mission at Taganrog. The amount of British military aid to Denikin could be judged from Denikin's confession to a British war correspondent on December 23, 1919: "To announce to the world that British help will cease on a certain date is almost tantamount to telling the common enemy the exact extent of our resources."[27]

As a result of the defeat of the Reds in the Kuban and North Caucasus, Denikin became overconfident. Prior to his advance into Ukraine, he called a war council to outline his campaign. Instead of throwing the main force released from the North Caucasian war against Tsaritsyn, the Bolshevik stronghold on the Lower Volga, to join Admiral Aleksandr V. Kolchak and advance toward Moscow, Denikin decided to concentrate most of the troops in the Left Bank, mainly in the Donets Basin. The troops in the Crimea were to strike toward Kyiv, while the rest of the forces were assigned to the Tsaritsyn front. Wrangel, however, objected to this plan and proposed:

> The available troops should not be moved towards the Donets coalfield area, but into the Manych lake district, there to undertake a joint operation with Admiral Kolchak's Army, which was coming up from the Volga . . . but it was of no avail. General Denikin stuck to his point of view.[28]

Undoubtedly Denikin's principal objective was not only Moscow, but occupation of Ukraine. The united advance of the Ukrainian Galician and the Directory's armies from the west toward Kyiv worried Denikin, as he wished to prevent the Directory from reestablishing authority in the entire Ukrainian territory. A Soviet author admits:

Denikin's July plan foresaw the achievement of an ultimate goal: the seizure of Moscow [by units] converging on the city from several directions, none of them being definitely emphasized. A second feature of this plan, however, was the avid desire to occupy as much territory as possible, as . . . virtually no operation had been conducted in either of the mentioned directions for two months because the most attention had been given to the occupation of Ukraine. . . . when the Denikin movement had at its disposal its only chance of furthering its success along the Kharkiv-Moscow path, the most critical direction for the RSFSR. While at the time [July 1919] conditions had appeared more favorable for Denikin to make such a bold decision, to say the least, the situation in September was not at all predisposed toward him, and after September a "march on Moscow" became a senseless adventure.[29]

At the beginning of May 1919, the reorganized and strengthened army of 64,000 men occupied an area northwest of Rostov that gave Denikin control of the Sea of Azov, the estuary of the Don, and the hubs of important railways.[30] In mid-May Denikin began a major offensive against the Bolsheviks. As his forces advanced in Ukraine, the Directory's forces were fighting the Bolsheviks in the west and the partisans were destroying the Bolsheviks' rear and demoralizing them, thus helping Denikin. To the partisans the main enemy was the Bolsheviks, because Denikin's attitude toward Ukraine was either unknown or clouded by his planting of public notices and rumors that there was an agreement between him and the Directory.[31] Under these pressures the Bolsheviks were unable to organize an effective defense. The seriousness of the situation is admitted by the Soviet source:

The conditions at the Denikin front coincided with a radical deterioration of our front against Petliura. There our army is in a still worse situation, the partisan movement reigns to the utmost extent, the composition of commanders [and] political commissars are lacking. Moreover, the ultimate effect of the wave of "kulak" uprisings directed [against us] was to support Petliura and Denikin. Thus a most critical and complicated situation is arising for us.[32]

Also Denikin admits the situation in Ukraine was against the Bolsheviks:

A conflict between the Soviet government and Makhno was growing. . . . Ukraine was swarming with partisan detachments . . . not recognizing any authority, fighting in the rear, spreading propaganda, even occupying Kyiv a few times. Moscow's *Izvestiia* ascertained on the entire frontline area many "counterrevolutionary uprisings" in which not only kulaks and Black Hunreds counterrevolutionaries, but also some of the cheated groups, the middle and poor peasants, participated in armed actions. The reasons for this phenomenon the official organ saw in the misbehavior of the Soviet troops, in heavy recruitments, requisitions, and in "the stupid wilfulness of pompadours intoxicated with power."[33]

The resistance of the Bolsheviks was decisively broken and they retreated in panic toward Russia, terrorizing the population on their way. Their main concern was the evacuation of Ukraine with as many men and as much rolling stock as possible. Denikin advanced rather rapidly along four axes, all of which ultimately would lead to Moscow: toward Tsaritsyn, hoping to unite with Kolchak; toward Kharkiv, to occupy the Left Bank; toward Crimea, Odessa, and Kryvyi Rih, to occupy the Right Bank; and toward Voronezh. His strategy was to control large areas by holding the main railroad junctions.[34] As Denikin advanced, gradually extending the area of his occupation, he recovered a great amount of loot from the retreating Bolshevik troops.

Wrangel meanwhile became increasingly critical of Denikin's plan and after capturing Tsaritsyn on June 30, "proposed that we should entrench ourselves on the Tsaritsyn-Katerynoslav front for the time being, so that the Volga and Dnieper would be covering our flanks." On the next day, however, Denikin issued an order to advance toward Moscow, according to which Wrangel was to move on Moscow via Saratov and Nizhnii-Novogorod; Sidorin's Don Cossacks via Voronezh-Riazan; and the Volunteer Army, under General Mai-Maevskii, via the shortest route to Moscow, from Kharkiv-Kursk-Orel-Tula. Apparently Denikin planned for himself what he had accused Wrangel of on reading his report: "I see! you want to be the first man to set foot in Moscow!"[35]

Wrangel condemned Denikin's order as a "death-sentence for the armies of South Russia." He pointed out:

> All the principles of strategy were ignored; there was no choice of a principal direction, no concentration of the bulk of the troops in this direction, and no maneuvering. It merely prescribed a different route to Moscow for each of the armies.[36]

Gradually the differences of opinion between Wrangel and Denikin had a demoralizing effect on the troops, as it became known in the spring and summer that Wrangel insisted on an advance to the east to unite with Kolchak; that he sharply criticized the extension of the front in the west toward Kyiv, and that he had forewarned of the dangers of forcing the march to Moscow.[37]

As the Denikin forces occupied more Ukrainian territory, he introduced measures to suppress national and social currents and to deny all accomplishments of the Revolution. On the eve of the occupation of Kyiv, Denikin issued a declaration to the people of "Little Russia":

> Regiments are approaching old Kyiv, "mother of Russian cities," in an unabated stream, to recover for the Russian people their lost unity, the unity without which

the great Russian people, powerless and divided, losing its young generations in civil war, would be unable to uphold its independence; the unity, without which a complete and proper economic life is unthinkable. . . . Long before 1914, the Germans, wishing to weaken the Russian state before declaring war, strove to destroy the unity of the Russian race which was carved in a difficult struggle. With this aim, they supported and encouraged in South Russia a movement aiming at the separation from Russia of its nine southern provinces in the name of a "Ukrainian State." . . . Former German supporters, Petliura and his companion-in-arms, are set on the division of Russia, they are continuing now to advance their evil effort to establish an independent "Ukrainian State" and struggle against the rebirth of a United Russia.[38]

In the same vein at a dinner given by Katerynoslav authorities in his honor, when the representatives of Ukrainian organizations spoke about the right of Ukraine to independence: "Denikin rose from his seat, angrily struck the table and brusquely declared: 'Your bet on an independent Ukraine is lost. Long Live One and Undivided Russia! Hoorah!'" According to General Shkuro, Denikin also referred to Petliura: "Your bet on Petliura is lost. . . . Petliura will be hanged as a traitor, if he falls into the hands of the Volunteer Army."[39] The regime carried on an anti-Ukrainian campaign, which it called a struggle against Bolshevism, closing cooperatives, libraries, bookstores, newpapers, Prosvita associations, and other cultural institutions. Ukrainian signs were replaced by Russian; the elected city authorities and the Zemstvos personnel were replaced largely by Russians. Even the name *Ukraine* was prohibited and replaced by the pejorative *Little Russia*. Ukrainian teachers, workers in cultural and cooperative institutions, and others were often executed, as for example, in the summer of 1919, when Denikin men killed eighteen Ukrainian cultural workers at IElysavethrad, Kherson province, including T. Bilenko, the chairman of the Union of Cooperatives and a member of the Labor Congress.[40]

The commander of the Volunteer Army, General Mai-Maevskii, issued a decree that bound Ukrainian schools to return to teaching in Russian. No funds from the treasury were to be appropriated for the 'Little Russian" schools. Moreover, the city authorities and the zemstvos were forbidden to open schools that would teach in Ukrainian and Ukrainian studies were abolished. General Shilling, governor-general of Tavriia province, issued an order demanding that all soldiers and officers of the Ukrainian Army return to the ranks of the Volunteer Army not later than October 26; otherwise they would be treated "as traitors to their own state." This order, however, did not apply to the higher ranking officers who, no matter when they returned to the Russian troops, would be hanged as traitors to Russia.[41]

According to a Ukrainian officer of the Galician Army who visited General Slashchov in his headquarters, the general handed him an official leaflet, issued by the staff of General Shilling and directed to the command of the Ukrainian Army as an "order":

In view of the victories of the Russian arms, the army should assemble in places indicated by the command of the Denikin army in order to surrender all weapons and property to the units of the Denikin army! The "soldiers" then should demobilize and wait for a mobilization order; the officers would be transferred to the Denikin army on the basis of the mobilization, except officers of the general staff, against whom an investigation would be conducted by the court for rehabilitation. In case of not obeying this order, the army would be considered rebels and would be punished according to the paragraph on war conditions.[42]

In a discussion with different Russian officers in headquarters, the same officer got the impression that the generals of the Ukrainian Army would be shot outright.[43] A prominent Don Cossack statesman, A. Ageev, in a letter that received wide dissemination, wrote about Denikin's policy toward Ukraine in a similar vein:

In the struggle against the Bolsheviks, we had an ally which drew itself against a portion of the Soviet troops. And horrors! Instead of [gaining] an ally, we opened a new front, which we did not need at all to the delight of the Bolsheviks, but to our misery. Military units were sent to this front beyond the Dnieper at a time when the Don Cossacks were straining all their forces to the utmost in the struggles against the Red hordes. And when we Cossacks said: "Come to an agreement with Georgia and Ukraine, establish a federation to fight with common forces against a common enemy, the Bolsheviks," we were again accused of "separatism." . . .[44]

Wrangel also denounced Denikin's policy as "narrow and uncompromising," pointing out that he persecuted all whose ideas differed from his own and everyone who had any kind of connections with organizations hostile to the Volunteer cause. Hence:

He had hunted down not only those who had been in touch with the Bolsheviks in some way or another, perhaps against their will, but also anyone who had been connected with Ukraine, the Georgian Republic, and so on. This insane and cruel policy provoked a reaction, alienated those who had been ready to become our allies, and turned into enemies those who had sought our friendship. . . . [Moreover] the same relationship had been established with the civil population in the recently occupied territories.[45]

The anti-Ukrainian campaign of the higher echelons was practiced as well by the bureaucracy and troops. There was no difference of opinion among different representatives or supporters of the regime concerning Denikin's policy in the occupied territory. It was, in reality, a restoration of the old regime. Denikin admitted that:

The head of internal affairs, [N. N.] Chebyshev, was appointing governors almost exclusively from people who occupied those positions prior to the revolution, wishing to "use their administrative experience." . . . Behind them followed lower agents of the previous regime—some were afraid of the revolution, others embittered and revengeful.[46]

Although these bureaucrats had experience, they were psychologically so alien to the accomplished revolution that they could not understand it. Thus they tended to live in the past, which they tried to restore in form and in spirit. According to a member of Denikin's Special Council, N. I. Astrov, the main feature of the Denikin regime was:

Violence, torture, robberies, drunkenness, odious behavior of the representatives of the regime on the local level, impunity of known criminals and traitors, poor, inept people, cowards, and debauchers on the local level, people who brought with them to the villages their former vices, incapability, idleness, and self-confidence, [which] discredited the new regime.[47]

Pavel Miliukov pointed to the causes of the vices and the behavior of the bureaucracy:

The possibility of profit and class interest attracted to the administrative positions either criminal elements, former policemen, or former landlords. To these and others the meaning of "strong" authority was entirely pre-reform. [However] in view of the complete impossibility of real control, it manifested itself with a chaos and impunity which was unknown even during the old regime.[48]

Miliukov felt that instead of putting the state authority between the landlords and the peasants: "The circumstances of the White movement, to the contrary, dumped the peasantry into the hands of the landlords and [thus] revived the old hatred of the weak who had become strong, for the socially strong [who were] ruined by the revolution [but had] temporarily regained power."[49]

The behavior of the Volunteer troops in the occupied territory was even worse than that of the bureaucracy, if only because they had greater power.[50] A Russian war correspondent observed:

Robbery was institutionalized. Nobody paid any attention to it up to the very end. The soldiers robbed, the officers robbed, and many generals robbed; owing to a servile press, they acquired reputations as national leaders and heroes.[51]

The population suffered especially from the counterintelligence service, which carried its activities to an unlimited wild arbitrariness. According to Denikin himself the counterintelligence service that was established in units and organizations at all political and military levels, created a sort of atmosphere, a painful mania, all over the country, spreading through mutual distrust and suspicion. . . . It is necessary to say that these organs, covering the territory of the South with dense nets, were sometimes hotbeds of provocation and organized robbery. In these respects the counterintelligence services in Kyiv, Kharkiv, Odessa, and Rostov on the Don were especially notorious.[52]

The behavior of the Volunteer Army in the occupied territory was unequivocally justified by its commander, General Mai-Maevskii, in a conversation with General Wrangel:

"You see, in wartime you must leave no stone unturned and neglect no means by which you may achieve your ends. If you insist on the officers and men living like ascetics, they will not fight much longer." I was highly indignant. "Well, then, General, "he said, "what is the whole difference between the Bolsheviks and ourselves?" He answered his own question without pausing, and he thought his answer irrefutable. "Is not the whole difference simply that the Bolsheviks have not scrupled about their means, and therefore have gained the upper hand?"[53]

Although the Kolchak government recommended a more flexible policy in Ukraine and the use of Ukrainian troops in fighting the Bolsheviks, Denikin refused, because this was contrary to his idea of "One and Indivisible Russia." Denikin's diplomatic expert, A. A. Neratov, confirmed Denikin's attitude toward Ukraine: "To recognize Petliura and work together with him would be to recognize the dismemberment of Russia."[54] The oppressive policy of the Denikin regime in Ukraine convinced the population that it was as bad as the Bolshevik regime, and brought a strong reaction that led able young men, especially after the announcement of the Denikin mobilization, to leave their homes and join Makhno or other partisan groups. Nevertheless, Denikin believed that the Ukrainian peasants and partisans were fighting the Bolsheviks as their class enemy. According to a Soviet author: "Denikin has not considered that the revolt of the peasant elements against the proletarian dictatorship still does not indicate readiness to go with the Whites."[55]

In the light of this development, Nestor Makhno decided to take stronger action against both the Bolsheviks and Denikin. In his words: "When the Red Army in south Ukraine began to retreat . . . as if to straighten the front line, but in reality to evacuate Ukraine . . . only then did my staff and I decide to act without losing a single day."[56] For a while Makhno fought Denikin's troops near Oleksandrivs'k, but Denikin's superior power forced him to retreat toward IElysavethrad, on the Right Bank.[57] There he encountered the Bolshevik Fourteenth Army. Although it was isolated in the region of Odessa-Kherson-Mykolaiv-Kryvyi Rih, it tried to force its way northward.[58] Makhno recalled that he ordered Kalashnykiv, Budaniv, Holyk, and Dermenzhi, the partisan commanders who remained with the partisans in the Red Army at the anti-Denikin revolutionary front, to seize the front line staff and its commander, Kochergin; [and to] "arrest all political commissars and unreliable commanders for disposition by the deputy commander of the front line, Kalashnykiv."[59]

Moreover, he sent agents among the Red troops, who with the Makhno men carried on a "devilish" propaganda along the theme: "The Bolsheviks sold Ukraine to the generals. Those who want to fight for the blood of their brothers and the country join Makhno." With such propaganda as this combined with sabotage, they demoralized the Red troops. The slogan: "Troop trains are yours!" was effective. Troop trains, garages, and military magazines were looted; railroad depots were set on fire and blown up. Moreover, there were mutinies in some Bolshevik units.[60] An uprising instigated by Makhno men broke out in one brigade of the Fifty-Eighth Division. Mutineers destroyed the headquarters and arrested the whole staff, including the commander, G. A. Kochergin, his wife, and the commissars. When Division staff called Kochergin's headquarters the reply was: "There is no Kochergin Brigade—it was transferred to the disposition of the commander in chief of the Revolution, comrade Father Makhno. Soon we will reach you." Although later the wounded Kochergin and some members of his staff escaped, others were shot and the brigade was lost. In addition, a few armored trains joined Makhno. The uprisings spread to other units and Makhno men seized the commander of the Fifty-Eighth Division, Ivan Fedorovich Fed'ko (originally Fedotov), and the commissar, Mikhelovich. Fed'ko was accused of having: "sold all of us to Denikin. . . . Bat'ko Makhno, the commander of all armed forces of southern Russia, accepts us in his army." They labeled Fed'ko and the commissar as traitors who should be executed,[61] although later they escaped, but another brigade stationed at Bobrynets' went over to Makhno. According to an intercepted Bolshevik radio telegram of August 17: "The units of the Third Brigade joined Makhno. Kochergin and the Political Commissar were executed. The entire area north of Mykolaiv is in the hands of partisans and Makhno's bands."[62]

Meanwhile, Makhno's detachments from the Red Army, including Red units, began to arrive, carrying with them all the arms and ammunition they could acquire. The Bolshevik command, fearing mutiny among its troops, was unable to oppose them. Also, a number of independent partisan groups joined Makhno.[63]

At that time Makhno's troops reached the size of a normal army, estimated at about twenty thousand. At the town of Dobrovelychkivka, Kherson province, where he stayed from the beginning of August to

September 10, Makhno decided to reorganize the army into three infantry brigades, one cavalry brigade, an artillery detachment, and a machine-gun regiment. An elite squadron of fewer than two hundred of the most highly experienced and dedicated cavalrymen, led by Petro Havriushenko, called Havriusha, was formed as Makhno's bodyguard. Simultaneously, the army's staff was reorganized and substantially enlarged, including skilled personnel.[64] The army also included an intelligence service.[65]

The reorganized army was renamed "Revolutionary Partisan Army of Ukraine" (Makhnovites). This army was now mobile, either on horseback or "wheels," light carriages with springs called *tachanky* that were drawn by two or three horses, with another in reserve behind the cart, and with the driver and usually two soldiers behind him. A machine gun was installed on the back seat between the two soldiers. This infantry on carts moved at a speed of eighty kilometers a day, and even, if necessary, over one hundred. A black flag was flown on the first carriage with the slogans: "Liberty or Death" and "The Land to Peasants, the Factories to the Workers" embroidered in silver on both sides.[66]

As Makhno regrouped his army, he had to face not only the Bolshevik Fourteenth Army in retreat from the Crimea and Odessa forcing its way north to Russia, but also a strong Denikin force. Hoping to destroy one of the forces that opposed his occupation of Ukraine, Denikin threw his best regiments under General Slashchov into the battle against Makhno. The Fifth Division operated in the IElysavethrad area; there was a Don Cossack cavalry brigade in the Voznesenske area; to their south was the Fourth Division, while the Fourteenth Infantry Division and the Crimean Cavalry Regiment operated around Odessa. After the retreat from the railroad lines IElysavethrad and Voznesenske, Makhno operated from Novoukrainka in the area of IElysavethrad and Voznesenske. Other Makhno detachments swarmed throughout the IElysavethrad, Katerynoslav, Mykolaiv, and Uman' districts. Toward the end of August the Fifth Division and the Don Cossack cavalry brigade were ordered to drive Makhno's partisan army out of Novoukrainka. Makhno, however, launched a vigorous counteroffensive, taking a number of towns and putting Denikin troops in a critical situation, though his main concern had been to capture ammunition, which his troops badly needed. To forestall Makhno's offensive, an additional military unit was formed from the Fourth Division, consisting of its escort staff, brigades of the Thirteenth and Thirty-Fourth Infantry Divisions, the First Symferopil' Officers' Regiment, and a separate cavalry brigade consisting of the Forty-Second Don, the Labinsk, and the Tamansk regiments. Thus Makhno was confronted with an additional formation consisting of 4,700 cavalry and infantry and fifty guns. According to Makhno, Denikin concentrated a strong force against him, some twelve to fifteen regiments, including the First Symferopil' Officers' Regiment.[67]

Although Denikin's troops made great effort to take the initiative from Makhno, he conducted quick and demoralizing raids against them, especially on their rear. The situation, however, grew worse for Makhno when on September 10 at Pomichna, Denikin launched a major attack, capturing 400 of Makhno's men and three guns. Abandoning the railroad line, Makhno blew up two armored trains, and as his forces decreased and he ran short of ammunition, he retreated toward the Mykolaivka-Khmilove line to the Myrhorod-Uman' area, where a new phase of the fighting developed. During this fighting Makhno stubbornly resisted the enemy when he was surrounded at Novoukrainka and later at Uman'. He was retreating, fighting back stubbornly, and counterattacking, often with considerable tactical success. While his main force fought major battles, numerous separate detachments assisted him by attacking the enemy's rear. Makhno retreated until his whole army was cut off on the south and east by Denikin, and on the west and north by the Ukrainian forces.[68]

Although the immensity of his goal was out of keeping with his military strength, Denikin continued to fight both Makhno and the Ukrainian Army. Following Makhno's footsteps, General Slashchov felt the time was ripe to surround Makhno in the Uman' area and liquidate him before he joined "His half-ally, half-enemy Petliura." At Uman' Makhno made contact with a brigade of Ukrainian Sich Riflemen who were also at war against Denikin. Realizing that an understanding between them was the only sensible solution, Makhno proposed "military neutrality." The Ukrainian troops needed to secure their eastern front, and Makhno agreed to help fight Denikin. Subsequently Makhno paid a visit to Ukrainian headquarters in the city and obtained an agreement with the Ukrainian command to take care of his 4,000 wounded and ill partisans in the city hospitals.[69]

Makhno, however, had no intention of keeping his agreement because his retreat was a forced strategy that brought only a temporary solution. Makhno considered that the more Denikin's troops advanced to the north and northwest, the more vulnerable they became in their rear because of the great extension of the front. Through good intelligence and close contact with the peasants he was well informed about the movement and strength of the Denikin troops and the difficult situation in the region Denikin had occupied.

Throughout the summer and early fall of 1919, Denikin enjoyed substantial success, occupying a large part of Ukraine and southern Russia. On June 24 he occupied Kharkiv; six days later, Wrangel was in Tsaritsyn; and on July 31, Poltava fell into Denikin's hands. A month later Kyiv was liberated from the Bolsheviks by the united Galician and Directory armies but soon abandoned to Denikin. In the south, Denikin occupied Kherson and Mykolaiv on August 18, and Odessa five days later. He was also successfully advancing into Russia, taking Kursk on September 21 and Orel on October 13. The path to Tula, the capital of the province and the center of the armament industry, was open. The Bolsheviks became alarmed. According to Trotsky "Denikin set himself the goal of penetrating deep into the rear of our army to appear suddenly in Tula and wreck its factories, thus destroying the great arsenal of the Red Army."[70]

By mid-October Denikin had reached the line of Voronezh-Orel-Chernihiv-Kyiv-Odessa and was very optimistic:

> In his opinion everything was going splendidly. The possibility of a sudden change in our luck seemed to him to be out of the question. He thought the taking of Moscow was only a question of time, and that the demoralized and weakened enemy could not make a stand against us.[71]

Denikin expected to reach Moscow by winter and overthrow the Bolshevik regime. To his friend N. I. Astrov, he said: "Do not worry, everything will be all right, and I will drink tea in your house in Moscow." The "Osvag" had already prepared proclamations and posters with portraits of the Volunteer Army's leaders to post in the streets of liberated Moscow.[72] However, in Denikin's success lay his weakness. The line of his positions showed a considerable bulge with the concomitant danger of an open flank and rear. Wrangel warned:

> We were building on sand; we had bitten off far more than we could chew. Our front was too long in comparison with the number of our forces; we had no organized bases and strongholds in our rear. . . . I drew his attention to the movements of the brigand Makhno and his rebels, for they were threatening our rear. "Oh, that is not serious! We will finish him off in the twinkling of the eye." As I listened to him talking, my mind filled with doubt and apprehension.[73]

Makhno's main adversary, General Slashchov, confirms Denikin's disregard of Makhno's partisans in his rear:

> The "Whites," in spite of the advice of the commanders combating Makhno, looked on his liquidation as a question of secondary importance and all their attention at first was directed against Petliura. This blindness of the "Stavka" and the staff of the forces of New Russia was frequently and severely punished.[74]

While caught between the armies of the Directory and of Denikin, Makhno rapidly and in complete secrecy prepared an offensive against Denikin in which he displayed the greatest skill and bravery of his entire military career. He left all the wounded, sick, and unreliable men in the care of the Ukrainian troops, and cut his support to a minimum. This flexible, completely mounted army could attack without preparation by artillery fire. There was no question of failure or retreat; the decision was to attack the Denikin forces, destroy them, and penetrate behind their lines.[75]

On the evening of September 25, Makhno's First Brigade launched an attack against Denikin's forward troops near the village of Kruten'ke. The enemy soon retreated to take up better positions and to draw Makhno's unit into a trap. Makhno, however, purposely did not pursue, and misled them into thinking he had moved back westward. Several hours later, after 3 A.M., Makhno made an unexpected frontal attack on the main force near Perehonivka. In the course of the ensuing intense fighting, which continued for several hours, Makhno and his cavalry escort moved in the darkness to outflank the enemy. Just as the outnumbered and exhausted major troops of Makhno began to lose ground, Makhno attacked the enemy's flank. This maneuver decided the battle. First Makhno destroyed a battalion of the Lithuanian Regiment, and a battery of the Fourth Artillery Division,[76] and then he attacked the First Symferopil' Officers' Regiment, forcing it into an orderly defensive retreat that ended in a rout. The men retreated in panic, abandoning their arms in an attempt to reach the river Syniukha, some fifteen kilometers distant. Makhno, however, sent his troops at full speed in pursuit, while he moved with his cavalry escort to overtake them on the other side of the river. Makhno's main force caught the enemy near the river and decimated it. Most of those who managed to cross the river were taken prisoner or killed by Makhno. Only a small number escaped.

Although Makhno exaggerated when he spoke of "complete annihilation," the regiment did suffer heavy losses; according to Denikin's sources, 637 men were killed or wounded, including 270 officers. After its defeat at the Syniukha the regiment ceased its operations against Makhno. While Makhno was fighting Denikin southeast of Uman', General Skliarov attacked Uman' from the southwest, forcing the Ukrainian troops to retreat.[77] Makhno's sick and wounded, who were unable to retreat with the Ukrainian troops or to hide, were killed when the enemy entered the city.

Although Denikin used a large force against Makhno, he failed to destroy him in the Novoukrainka and Uman' operations because he divided his attention between Makhno and the Ukrainian Army. Moreover, there was no coordination of Denikin's various units, and communication with the armed forces command of New Russia in Odessa was poor. Makhno, energetic and well informed, took advantage of Denikin's mistakes and inflicted heavy losses on the enemy. The developments resulting from his defeat decided Denikin's fate. According to a Denikin officer fighting against Makhno:

> People interested in the history of the civil war, 1917—1920, came to the conclusion a long time ago that the breakthrough of "Father Makhno" in the fall of 1919 disorganized the rear of the Armed Forces of South Russia and thus tipped the scale in favor of the Reds.[78]

After the victory at Perehonivka the road to Denikin's important centers was open. Three parallel columns of Makhno's troops advanced eastward at the great speed of one hundred versts per day, avoiding battles with large enemy forces and joined by many independent partisan groups en route. Denikin's garrisons and the civil authorities, ignorant of the defeat at Perehonivka or Makhno's whereabouts, took no defensive measures and Makhno very often took Denikin's posts by complete surprise. In several days Makhno took Dolyns'ka, Kryvyi Rih, and Nikopil', where he destroyed three regiments.[79] Subsequently he captured the Kichkas bridge on the Dnieper and on October 5, the city of Oleksandrivs'k, where he established his base.

Apart from the military problems, Makhno was confronted with the organization of the local authorities. First he called a meeting of workers from different branches of industry, informing them about the previous victorious fighting and the war situation in the region, and then asked the workers to organize the management of factories, plants, railroads, and other branches of industry by their own means and under their own control. On the question of salaries, Makhno advised the workers to set their own wages, organize their own pay office, and carry on commercial exchange directly with consumers. The railroad workers consented to go along with Makhno's policy, organizing the train system and setting fees for transportation.[80] At the meeting in Oleksandrivs'k, in his main speech, Makhno appealed to the populace to organize a civil self-government so as to secure the territory and guarantee its people's freedom. His organizational plans did not develop sufficiently, mainly because of the proximity of this territory to the front and a lack of initiative and experience of its people.

Meanwhile, the Revolutionary Military Council convoked the Fifth Congress in Oleksandrivs'k from October 20 to 26, 1919, with about

270 delegates, including 180 peasants in attendance, It was chaired by Volin. The congress resolved to strengthen, organize, and prepare supplies for the army. It formed committees, consisting of peasants, workers, and partisans, to convene future congresses that would deal with the organization of social and economic life in the region. However, the main concerns of the congress were the current problems, the primary one being the organization of the army. In principle the congress rejected a regular army based upon compulsory mobilization, but the critical situation at the front and the need to defend the territory made it necessary to resort to voluntary mobilization of men between nineteen and forty-eight. Each new regiment was to include a staff and an economic-judicial organ, for the congress intended to make the partisan army a people's army.[81]

One of Makhno's proclamations illustrated what voluntary mobilization entailed:

> Why do you sit at home, friend? Why are you not in our ranks? Are you waiting for a Commissar to come with a punitive detachment to take you by compulsory mobilization? Do not deceive yourself that he will not find you, that you could hide, escape. The Bolshevik regime already proved it would stop at nothing: it would arrest your family and relatives, it would take hostages and, if necessary, it would shell the entire village by artillery fire, and . . . you and your friends . . . would sooner or later be taken by the regime into the army. And then, it would send you with arms in hand to kill your brother peasants and workers—revolutionary partisan—Makhno men.[82]

To assure the growth of the army, the congress resolved to organize local free social-economic organizations and commissions composed of working people, to obtain "contributions" from the bourgeoisie, and to gather uniforms for the partisans. These organizations were to cooperate closely with Makhno's army supply commission. They were responsible for providing support for the partisans' families and for the poorer population. Finally, the congress had chosen a commission to convene the next congress to deal with the social and economic organization of the region controlled by the Makhno army. Appealing to the population to support the recruitment of volunteers for the army, the congress also established a committee to provide food distribution at stations and hospitals and to take care of the wounded and the sick. The primary source of the food would be free gifts from the peasants, the spoils of victory, and requisitions from privileged groups. The congress recommended that the Revolutionary Military Council take strong measures against drinking, including the execution of offenders, to prevent a demoralization of the army.[83]

The basis of justice was also laid down by the congress:

On the question of the need to organize a judicial administrative apparatus, we suggest as a basic principle that any rigid court, police machinery and any fixed "codification of laws" constitute a gross violation of the population's rights of self-defense. True justice should not be administratively organized, but must come as a living, free, creative act of the community. . . . Law and order must be upheld by the living force of the local community, and must not be left to police specialists.[84]

As the Revolutionary Military Council organized sociopolitical life in the region, Makhno and his staff continued to fight Denikin, occupying a number of cities and towns, including Polohy, Melitopil', Huliai-Pole, Synel'nikove, and Lozova. At that time Makhno's army increased to about twenty-five thousand men. In late October, the height of the army's growth, it consisted of about forty thousand men, including the separate partisan detachments operating in the countryside.[85] When the commander of one such detachment bearing Makhno's name contacted Makhno, he replied: "All the detachments bearing my name may act independently. You are not alone; many units bearing my name are scattered throughout Ukraine. The time will come when we will all unite into one great anarchist army and will defeat the enemy."[86]

Makhno, however, was primarily interested in the Azov Sea ports and on October 6 he decided to take Berdians'k where, according to the British war correspondent,

a huge quantity of our small-arms ammunition and 60,000 shells were stacked for months. . . . The British Mission, who considered the town to be vulnerable, warned the Russian staff repeatedly. Just as the battles were opening which should have given Denikin permanent possession of Kyiv and Orel, Makhno the brigand sprang into activity near Katerynoslav, and within ten days he had blown the Berdians'k dump sky-high."[87]

Attacking from the coast to prevent the enemy's escape by sea, Makhno captured large stores of war material, including sixteen British and Russian guns, thirty trucks, five cars, one airplane, and a large amount of ammunition. On October 23 Makhno captured the other main port, Mariupil', cutting Denikin off from the Sea of Azov and consequently threatening his main supply base, Volnovakha. Makhno decided to attack the city, in spite of the concentration of Denikin forces there, and although after five days of fighting he failed to capture Volnovakha, he effectively eliminated it as a supply base because all railroad junctions were in Makhno's hands.[88] In the meantime, when Makhno appeared without warning in the area of Taganrog, Denikin's headquarters:

Panic reigned everywhere—panicked foreign missions, panicked staff ladies; some even succeeded in evacuating. Officers were called hastily. [People were] saying that the Makhno detachments were seizing Mariupil', and that Makhno partisans were eighty versts from Taganrog. There was almost no force that could oppose them. The Kuban Cossacks recalled from the front could not arrive in time because of the damage to transportation and "bandits" who were destroying trucks. A regiment of officers coming from the Caucasian coast was stopped at sea by the storm.[89]

In discussion with K. N. Sokolov, Denikin admitted the situation was very serious with Makhno within two days' ride of Taganrog. Some advised the chief commander to leave.[90] According to another eyewitness the situation was "absolutely critical":

All Denikin could muster up were the two hundred-odd officers of headquarters, a company of war-wounded veterans and a few tanks. . . . I was having tea at the British Military Mission when the news of the coming of Makhno spread. A list for volunteers to go out to fight him was passed around the tea table. I signed this list and thus for three days found myself in a force of British cavalry. We were drilled by General Thompson, commanding the British Mission. Several British naval officers also signed the list, and the sight of a long-legged naval commander on a horse was something never to be forgotten. Just as suddenly and just as mysteriously as he had appeared, Makhno vanished. Evidently he overestimated the forces defending Taganrog. If he had only dared to attack the city he would have had us, General Denikin and all.[91]

Hodgson confirms this situation in Taganrog:

The British Military Mission at Taganrog, although only a staff nucleus engaged in getting supplies up and teaching Denikin's soldiers, at once put itself in a state of defence. A mounted mobile column of thirty-two officers was formed, and although it has been claimed that the effort had a calming effect on the local population, I am inclined to think that it only accentuated the panic. . . . The whole incident was nerve wracking, and should have given Denikin both a foretaste and warning of what was to come.[92]

Makhno continued to drive Denikin's forces out of his region. One of Denikin's important strongholds was Katerynoslav, which Makhno tried to capture. After twelve days of fighting Makhno applied his earlier military ruse, sending his partisans dressed in peasant clothes

. . . into the town, ostensibly to buy provisions; having arrived at the marketplace, they pulled out their weapons and joined with their fellows who had surrounded the town. A panic seized the inhabitants; the Governor [Shchetinin] hurried away in a special train; and, after the militiamen had put up the best fight they could against superior numbers, darkness came on, and the bandits were masters of the town.[93]

Toward the end of October, Makhno took the city, which he controlled for six weeks. He issued a manifesto as soon as the partisans entered the city, appealing to the populace to preserve peace, to surrender their weapons, and to turn over to him Denikin's officers hiding in the city. He demanded contributions from the richer segment of the population and expropriated whatever money had been left in the banks by Denikin, subsequently turning to the poor with a large amount of money and material support. Also he opened the gates of the prisons and burned them.[94] Despite a prohibition by Makhno, the partisans, especially the released prisoners, were guilty of some looting. However, according to an eyewitness: "Under Makhno there was not such widespread looting as under the Volunteers. A great impression was made on the population by Makhno's personal on-the-spot execution of several looters who were caught in the market place."[95]

An episode occurring there sheds some light on the behavior of the partisans. An elderly gentleman taking a walk was stopped at a corner by a partisan who ordered the gentleman to remove his pants and give them to him. The gentleman protested, but promised to take the partisan to his nearby apartment and surrender his trousers. When the gentleman complied, the partisan exclaimed:

> Well, that is the way it should have been a long time ago! I requested trousers from six passersby, "please give me some trousers because mine are completely worn out." All responded that they had no spares. And now I have found some. Father Makhno prohibited us from robbing. "If you do need something," he said, "take it, but nothing more." Now, I need nothing more![96]

According to another eyewitness, as Slashchov drove Makhno out of the city, his troops repeated earlier practices of General Shkuro's troops:

> I blushed from pain and shame when people with officers' epaulettes on their shoulders entered apartments and looted them as suddenly, openly, and shamelessly as did wild Ingushes and Chechens. . . . In addition, Slashchov's men began to pull out the partisans who were left in the hospitals with typhus, and hang them from the bare trees.[97]

In the late fall of 1919 Makhno's military success peaked. At that time he controlled the larger part of the Left Bank from Katerynoslav to the Crimea and was threatening even Taganrog, Denikin's headquarters.[98] Makhno's success against Denikin was facilitated by the population, especially the peasants, who were antagonized not only by the repressive policy of the troops, the police, and bureaucrats, but especially by the returning landlords. According to an eyewitness, the wide peasant masses of Ukraine were indignant at the returning of the landlords to their estates, the restoration of large latifundia, and the arbitrariness and violence that had been a characteristic peculiarity of the local agents' policy. Exhausted by constant conscriptions, requisitions, and robberies by the military units, and disappointed in the land measures of the "Stavka," they readily joined Makhno-like bands and began to carry on a most relentless struggle against the Volunteer Army. . . . We hate the commune whole heartedly, the peasants were saying, but still more, we hate the landlords who are tearing our skin off us. We do not need Communists, either red or black.[99]

General Wrangel confirms this situation and the spontaneous reaction of the population against the Denikin regime:

Risings were breaking out in the interior; rebels under the command of the brigand Makhno were sacking the towns and looting the trains and commissariat depots. Disorder was at its height in the country. The local authorities had no idea how to make themselves respected; abuse of authority was the order of the day; the agrarian question was more bitter than ever.[100]

When General Mai-Maevskii encountered strong resistance from the peasants in Ukraine, he asked Denikin to speed up land reform because the peasants "are interested in and waiting for land reform. Promises have lost their meaning; fodder is commandeered under threat of execution." Denikin replied: "I do not attach great importance to this matter. It is unnecessary to pay attention to the peasants. Take warning measures against lawlessness [and] do not show weakness of authority. . . . With regard to the peasants—this question will be settled in Moscow."[101] A foreign eyewitness observed:

Conditions behind the lines were more chaotic than ever. Makhno was looting trains and depots with impunity, and White officialdom was losing what little control over the civilian population it had. . . . The peasants were crying for land and getting a stone in answer.[102]

Although the strength of the Volunteer Army on the fronts against the Bolsheviks and the Ukrainian Army was hardly adequate, at the end of September Denikin found that

the situation was becoming dangerous and demanded radical measures. In spite of the seriousness of the situation on the front, it was necessary to withdraw some units from it and to use all the reserves to suppress the uprising.[103]

Two combat groups were formed to fight Makhno. A corps under General Slashchov, with Colonel Dubiago as his chief of staff, was dispatched to the Right Bank, mainly in the region of Kherson, Mykolaiv, and Katerynoslav. It consisted of the Thirteenth and Thirty-Fourth

Infantry divisions and was later joined by the Don Cossack Brigade. The other group, under General Revishin, was formed on the Left Bank with its headquarters at Volnovakha railroad station. It consisted of the Chechen Cavalry Division, the Terek Cossack Cavalry Division, a separate Don Cossack Cavalry Brigade, the Composite Regiment of the Ninth Cavalry Division, and the Composite Infantry Regiment.[104]

In mid-October Denikin began operations against Makhno, aiming to bottle him up between the Sea of Azov and the Dnieper. Since Denikin's supply base and immense stores of munitions were located in the towns between Volnovakha and Mariupil', Denikin threw a large force supported by armored trains and cars against Makhno. Fierce fighting developed in the area of Mariupil', Berdians'k, and Velykyi Tokmak and both sides suffered heavy losses.[105] Gradually Makhno was forced to retreat north to Huliai-Pole where his army of about ten thousand men fought large Denikin forces, including the Terek Cossack Cavalry Division and the Don Cossack Cavalry Brigade. Makhno, fearing encirclement, retreated west to Oleksandrivs'k. After heavy fighting in the city he crossed the Dnieper to the Right Bank and advanced to Katerynoslav. The Chechen Cavalry Division also had crossed the Dnieper and occupied the city, trying to establish contact with General Slashchov, but Makhno attacked and drove them out. While General Slashchov was struggling against Makhno on the Right Bank, General Revishin established a defensive line along the left bank of the Dnieper to prevent Makhno from crossing the river.

After several months of hard fighting the Denikin troops came to regard Makhno's army as their most formidable enemy. According to Mai-Maevskii's aide, Pavel Vasil'evich Makarov: "The commander feared Makhno more than the Reds [because] Makhno was always appearing unexpectedly, and therefore, was impeding Mai-Maevskii's deployment for an attack." Nevertheless, Mai-Maevskii also admired Makhno, and told Makarov: "I am watching his activities and [I am] not against having such an experienced commander on my side."[106]

Also other commanders of Denikin troops expressed

> . . . highest admiration and respect for Makhno. His military achievements are being called heroic. In their opinion Makhno also commands a good and brave soldiery. They are talking about his activities on the Left Bank, about the capture of Katerynoslav in the rear of the Denikin Army and about his attack on Taganrog (the Denikin headquarters) . . . with visible fear.[107]

The conditions in Denikin's rear echoed on the Bolshevik front, and the Bolsheviks fully exploited this situation. A Soviet author admits:

A rapid growth of peasant uprisings in Denikin's rear threatened even his headquarters, Taganrog, forcing him not only to bring up all his reserves to fight them, but also to recall a number of units from the front for this purpose. . . . This, of course, greatly influenced the outcome of the battle: the Eighth Army was saved from defeat because the enemy's Voronezh group was weakened and subsequently was not only unable to develop an active operation on its own, but could not even offer a more or less firm resistance to Budenny's cavalry, soon to advance in the area of Voronezh. Already during this period of general fighting Denikin showed signs of a complete lack of strategic reserves at the front and in the rear.[108]

The author's conclusion is that as a result of the partisan uprisings: "the rear of the counterrevolution [Denikin] disintegrated, and the disintegration of the rear brought with it also disintegration of the front."[109]

While Denikin was preparing for a final drive on Moscow via Orel-Tula, the Bolsheviks concentrated newly organized cavalry units, reinforced by infantry and machine-gun companies, for a bidirectional counterattack against the Orel-Kursk railroad line and against Voronezh. Moreover, the Bolshevik success on the Kolchak front and Wrangel's retreat to Tsaritsyn enabled them to bring additional forces to the Denikin front. When the Red Army began its successful advance on the central front, Wrangel proposed that Denikin recall from the Tsaritsyn front two cavalry corps, and unite them with Mai-Maevskii's cavalry units and a few Don Cossack cavalry divisions for a major attack in the direction of Moscow. Denikin turned it down. Later, he was forced gradually to recall the cavalry corps from the Tsaritsyn front to support the retreating Volunteer troops, but they had no decisive effect upon the situation.[110]

Hard fighting continued for several weeks, with the advantage inclining to the Bolshevik side. In this fighting the Bolsheviks defeated the Volunteer troops at Kursk and Kastornaia, an important junction on the Kursk-Voronezh railroad. The capture of these cities and the railroad enabled the Bolsheviks to drive a deep wedge between the Volunteer and the Don armies, forcing them to retreat.[111] According to Wrangel,

The enemy's cavalry had penetrated our front line at the junction of the Army of the Don and Volunteer Army, and was now threatening the rear of the latter. Orel and Kursk had been abandoned, and the front was rapidly drawing in on Kharkiv. Further back, the province of Katerynoslav was a prey to risings. The people's discontent grew with our reverses.[112]

The victory commenced a new stage in the campaign and the initiative definitely passed to the Bolsheviks. Their forces advanced rapidly southward, encountering only minor resistance. Kharkiv was surrendered to the Bolsheviks on December 12 in utter confusion. Institutions were evacuated without direction or destination. A British merchant coming from Kharkiv witnessed:

> Towns and stores had fallen into the Bolshevists' hands like a ripe fruit. The Volunteer General, Mai-Maevskii, had published a flamboyant circular denying the possibility of the town's falling, and ordering every one to remain quietly at his work; but, meanwhile, his staff and everybody else . . . disappeared in their trains down the line to safety, and the bibulous old man himself went away.[113]

Another eyewitness confirms these circumstances: "Still on December 7, 1919, the Kharkiv City Council was assured of the complete safety and strength of the city of Kharkiv, but on December 11 there were no authorities of the Denikin organizations."[114]

Although Denikin replaced General Mai-Maevskii with General Wrangel on December 9, he could not save the Denikin army.[115] According to Churchill: "During November Denikin's armies melted away, and his whole front disappeared with the swiftness of pantomime."[116] The Donets Basin was surrendered almost without a struggle. Kyiv was abandoned on December 16 and the Volunteer troops under General Bredov retreated west to Poland where they were interned. General Slashchov's Corps, which was engaged, according to Denikin, in an "exhaustive battle against Makhno in Katerynoslav province until mid-December" retreated to the Isthmus of Perekop where it made a stand.[117] In addition, the Caucasian and Don armies were forced to retreat south.

Denikin's entire military organization was collapsing; his defeat and rapid retreat were largely determined by conditions in the rear. He admitted that his reserves and part of the line troops recalled to the rear were engaged in

> putting down uprisings instigated by Makhno and other "otamans" which spread over most of the territory of Ukraine and New Russia. . . . Part of the forces of Kyiv province waged a struggle against the Petliura men and the partisans.[118]

Two courses of retreat were open to Denikin: to the Crimea or to Rostov. The Crimea afforded good protection and the probability of saving most of the equipment, whereas Rostov meant exposure to Bolshevik flank attacks. However, the Don, Kuban, and Terek Cossacks, who formed a majority of the army, preferred to retreat homeward, that is, to Rostov.[119] Therefore, Denikin, against Wrangel's advice, decided to move to Rostov, hoping to rest his troops and to introduce some reforms. Only a small number of troops sought refuge in the Crimea. In the interim, however, the Bolsheviks captured Novocherkassk and on January 8, 1920, the Volunteer forces, after three days fighting, abandoned Rostov, fearing encirclement. In the opinion of a British war correspondent: "After the fall of Rostov, the Volunteer administration practically ceased to exist." Denikin's regime in Rostov was characterized by ever increasing speculation, disorder, and general economic chaos. In a dispatch to Denikin dated December 9, 1919, Wrangel describes the conditions of the army: "A considerable number of troops have retreated to the interior, and many officers are away on prolonged missions, busy selling and exchanging loot, etc. The army is absolutely demoralized and is fast becoming a collection of tradesmen and profiteers."[120]

Although Denikin, with his front protected by the Don and Manych rivers and the rich Kuban Basin with its railway network to the rear, could have continued fighting the advancing Bolsheviks, the spirit of the Kuban Cossacks and the people had completely changed since the previous year because they had lost confidence in the Volunteer Army. Moreover, Denikin's prestige as a leader was destroyed by the overwhelming defeats he suffered. Therefore, Denikin tried to gain favor by making political concessions and introducing a number of civil reforms to liberalize his regime; the moment, however, had long since passed when any change could forestall the inevitable consequences of his previous policy. After Denikin lost the battle near Rostov, his forces retreated, fighting delaying actions to cover their retreat to the port of Novorossisk, the last foothold in the Kuban, which became "a hellhole of disease, insurrection, chaos, and confusion." Amid these conditions, on March 27, 1920, the Volunteer Army and a portion of the Don Army were evacuated into the Crimea. The Kuban Cossacks, numbering, with refugees, the Rada, and the government, over forty thousand men, plus about twenty thousand Don Cossacks, moved along the Black Sea coast toward Georgia, constantly harassed by Red troops on the way. As the Bolsheviks advanced, they greatly improved their military situation by capturing large stores of military supplies from depots and supply trains. Tens of thousands of horses, hundreds of trucks, countless tons of munitions, and invaluable modern equipment such as tanks, airplanes, locomotives, and guns supplied by the Allies, fell into Bolshevik hands.[121]

Denikin's radical reverse came to a great extent as a result of his defeat in Ukraine. As General Tiutiunyk rightly remarked: "Without realizing the strength of the partisan movement, it is difficult to comprehend what happened to cause the Red Army, which had retreated toward Moscow in panic, suddenly to appear in the role of a victor."[122]

A Soviet author admitted the weakness of the Bolsheviks:

This shock group [Kutepov's corps] from Kursk rapidly advanced toward Orel pursuing small units of the Thirteenth Army, tired by long retreat. . . . The officers' shock units encountered the [Red] shock group and the result of the battle decided the fate not only of Orel, but of Tula, because deep behind the [Red] shock group there were no reserves; [although they were] called reserves, the Siberian troops and regiments freed from the fighting against the English at the Arkhangelsk front still had not arrived.[123]

Denikin admits:

The activities of the partisan groups brought very serious complications into the strategy of all the contending sides, decisively weakening in turn one or the other, bringing chaos to the rear and forcing the recall of troops from the front. Objectively, the partisans were a decisive factor for us in the territory occupied by the enemy, but, at the same time, a glaringly negative one when the territory fell into our hands.[124]

Trotsky, like Denikin, came to the same conclusion: "Makhno's volunteers, of course, present danger to Denikin so long as Denikin rules Ukraine, but, on the other hand, they betrayed Ukraine [i.e., the Bolsheviks] to Denikin. And tomorrow, after the liberation of Ukraine, Makhno men will become a mortal danger to the workers'-peasants' state."[125]

Also, General Turbin, governor of the Podillia province during Denikin's occupation, admitted to a Ukrainian: "You see, it was your peasants, no one else, who drove us out of Poltava province." Therefore, the Denikin troops retreated from the Left Bank in a great hurry, leaving a large area between themselves and the Bolsheviks. The Ukrainian partisans not only speeded up Denikin's retreat, but simultaneously fought the Bolsheviks, slowing their advance. However, the Denikin staff publicly reported it was the Denikin troops who fought the Bolsheviks there. Thus the Bolsheviks crossed the entire Left Bank almost without serious opposition from the Denikin forces, because the partisans had destroyed the latter's rear, forcing them to retreat.[126]

As an eyewitness observed:

At the end of 1919 the defeat and disintegration of the Volunteer Army was clearly marked. Without stopping, it rolled south toward the Black Sea, almost without any pressure from its adversary. The high command was constantly losing the strings of control of the armies. The ties between the higher staffs and separate military units were getting weaker with each day until they completely disappeared. Each unit began to act on its own risk and fear, retreating where and when convenient, disregarding the general situation and ignoring combat orders.[127]

The war correspondent with the Denikin troops vividly described the kaleidoscopic changes of Denikin's military fortune:

At the time when in the summer of 1919, the army, headed by Denikin, was victoriously advancing northward; when each day was bringing us always new and newer reports of victories; when the echo of the bells of Moscow, it seems, became distinctly heard in the Don, and in the Kuban, and in the Terek, and in the Crimea, and in the south of Ukraine—already at this time were heard warning voices that were indicating that the faster we advanced toward Moscow, the faster we would come to theBlack Sea.[128]

There were a number of causes for the defeat of the Volunteer Army, but the main one was the overextension of the front line to a length of two thousand kilometers, from Tsaritsin on the Volga, through Orel to Odessa. As General Vinogradov remarked: "At the end of 1919, it was not the troops of the armed forces of South Russia that controlled the huge space, but the space swallowed up the troops." No reserves were available at critical points and times. Denikin appeared to be, after the death of Kornilov and Alekseev, the ablest of all the anti-Bolshevik Russian leaders, and his forces contained the best of the elements that had fled from Soviet Russia, as well as the Don and Kuban Cossacks who, in contrast to the Russian population, were violently anti-Bolshevik; yet he disregarded the very essentials of permanent conquest, failing to consolidate his position in the conquered territory by establishing sound local governments and land reform. Denikin was lulled by his rapid success into looking upon the occupation of the large territory as a pleasant, accomplished fact.

Denikin's weakness was that he was a soldier and not a statesman. To one of his political advisors, he admitted: "I am a soldier and have never taken any interest in your politics." Denikin's nationality policy was epitomized by his motto: "A United and Indivisible Russia," a slogan that denied the newly established states formerly belonging to the Russian Empire the right to independence. Such a policy satisfied neither his allies, the Don and the Kuban Cossacks, nor his Ukrainian enemies who fought him to the very end. His socioeconomic policy, manifested by the return of the estates to the landlords, likewise antagonized the peasants and brought about uprisings.

The anti-Bolshevik movement consisted mainly of two groups: the representatives of the old, reactionary Russia, to whom the achievements of the Revolution were unacceptable; and the representatives of the democratic and liberal Russia, to whom the Revolution was the foundation on which a new Russia should be constructed. Those two hostile groups were brought together only by their fear of bolshevism. The leading role in the movement fell to the first group, which brought military dictatorship and a reactionary system, whereas the other group was politically unorganized and became aware of its political power only during the Civil War. This alliance of ideological opposites paralyzed the anti-Bolshevik movement on all levels.

To strengthen his weary armies, Denikin was compelled to conscript the non-Russian population and the Red Army prisoners, neither of whom was either loyal or willing to fight for Denikin's Russia. Exhaustion, disease, and corruption on all levels of the anti-Bolshevik movement had destroyed the discipline and morale of Denikin's forces. The final and most comprehensive contribution to the deterioration of Denikin's position were the Ukrainian partisans, especially Makhno's army, which inflicted heavy losses, disorganized communications, and destroyed supply bases, thus breaking the backbone of the offensive on Moscow. Denikin admitted: "This uprising, which took on such broad dimensions, destroyed our rear and the front at the most critical period."[129] As Pierre Berland, the correspondent of *Le Temps* in Moscow, observed:

> There is no doubt that Denikin's defeat is explained more by the uprisings of the peasants who brandished Makhno's black flag, than by the success of Trotskii's regular army. The partisan bands of "Bat'ko" tipped the scales in favor of the Reds and if Moscow wants to forget it today, impartial history will not.[130]

18. Makhno's Army Outlawed by the Bolsheviks

The rapidly changing military situation soon caused a change in the Bolsheviks' attitude toward Makhno. The advance of the Red Army southward in pursuit of Denikin, like the Denikin offensive earlier, was facilitated by Makhno's harassment of the retreating Denikin troops and by peasant uprisings. On December 8 the retreat of the Denikin army forced Makhno out of Katerynoslav, whence he retreated to the region of Melitopil', Nikopil', and Oleksandrivs'k to regroup. On December 24 Makhno's troops met the Bolshevik Fourteenth Army in Oleksandrivs'k and its commander, Ieronim Petrovich Uborevich, admitted Makhno's service in defeating Denikin. Although the Bolsheviks fraternized with the Makhno troops and the commander even offered cooperation, they distrusted Makhno, fearing the popularity he had gained as a result of his successful fighting against Denikin. A member of the Revolutionary Military Council of the Fourteenth Army, Sergei Ordzhonokidze, wired the Central Committee of the Russian Communist party, and the editorial staff of the newspapers *Pravda*, *Bednota*, and *Izvestiia*:

> In the central publications, especially in *Bednota*, they emphasized Makhno's role in the uprisings of the masses in Ukraine against Denikin. I consider it necessary to point out that such a popularization of Makhno's name, whose attitude toward the Soviet government is inimical as before, brings about in the rank and file of the army undesired sympathy toward Makhno. Such a popularization is particularly dangerous at [the time of] our advance into the region of partisans. In reality, Makhno was not leading the uprisings. The mass of people in general are rising against Denikin for the Soviet government.[1]

The Bolsheviks had no intention of tolerating Makhno's independent policy, but hoped at first to destroy his army by removing it from its own base. With this idea in mind, on January 8, 1920, the Revolutionary Military Council of the Fourteenth Army ordered Makhno to move to the Polish front via Oleksandria-Cherkasy-Boryspil'-Chernihiv-Kovel'.[2] The author of the order realized there was no real war between the Poles and the Bolsheviks at that time and he also knew that Makhno would not abandon his region. In a conversation with Iona E. IAkir, the commander of the Forty-Fifth Division of the Fourteenth Army, Uborevich explained that "an appropriate reaction by Makhno to this order would give us the chance to have accurate grounds for our next steps." IAkir answered that he knew Makhno personally, and was sure that he would certainly not comply. Uborevich agreed but concluded: "The order is a certain political maneuver and, at the very least, we expect positive results from Makhno's realization of this."[3]

As expected, Makhno and the Revolutionary Military Committee flatly refused to leave the territory. In their opinion the commander of the Fourteenth Army had no authority over the Makhno army; a large number of the partisans, including Makhno, who was in a near coma most of the time, were sick with typhus; the fighting qualities and effectiveness of the troops were greater on their own territory; and Makhno realized that an expedition against Poland would mean losing his base of power and exposing his territory to a Bolshevik invasion. Consequently the Bolsheviks declared Makhno's army outlawed. On January 14, 1920, Makhno gave up his camp and set out for Huliai-Pole without serious opposition. Some detachments that remained in the rear were seized by the Bolsheviks.[4]

After the defeat of the Denikin forces and their retreat to the Black Sea, Makhno had to face the Red troops. The winter of 1920 was a very critical period. His partisan army was disorganized and under strength. About 50 percent of the troops contracted typhus and went to the villages for cure, while others simply hid in the villages, or went home.[5] Thus the strength of Makhno's forces was substantially lower than in late 1919. The Bolsheviks, however, were in a far stronger position than the previous year; they had more, better equipped, and better supplied troops at their disposal.

When the Bolsheviks' attempts to transfer Makhno to the Polish front failed, they made a great effort to destroy him. In mid-January this task was assigned to the Forty-Second Division of the Thirteenth Army, stationed between Mariupil' and Taganrog. The division was ordered to advance toward Perekop across the Makhno region. It was transferred to the area of Volnovakha-Kurakhivka, whence the Third Brigade was dispatched to the area of Andriivka–Oleeksiivka–Velyka Mykhailivka–Huliai-Pole; while the Second Brigade was concentrated in the area of Staryi Kermenchyk–Turkenivka–Huliai-Pole. The strength of these two brigades was 4,000, plus a number of support units. The First Brigade was held as reserves between the others in the area of Maiorske–Sanzhanivka–Huliai-Pole. The task of the Red troops was to surround Huliai-Pole and destroy Makhno.

However, before they could effect this plan, Makhno retreated from Huliai-Pole, leaving a large amount of supplies and eight guns to the Bolsheviks. Toward the end of February the Red Army command transferred the Forty-Second Division as reserve to the Taganrog area because the situation in the North Caucasus became critical. Its place was taken by the Estonian Division, which was concentrated in the area of Huliai-Pole–Polohy–Kinski Rozdory–Tsarekonstiantynivka. In the meantime, Makhno harried the Red troops, destroying their staff and agents, supply base, smaller separate units, blowing up railroad lines, bridges, and means of communication, and conducting intensive propaganda among the troops. Late in February, Makhno in five days slipped his detachment secretly into Huliai-Pole and disarmed one brigade, destroying its headquarters. Some men joined Makhno while others were dispersed. Although the Red Army command dispatched a cavalry regiment that seized large supplies and killed some partisans, including Makhno's oldest brother, Sava, who was living with his family, Makhno managed to retreat safely.[6]

After these setbacks, the Bolsheviks decided early in March to organize a special task force of rear-area commanders to fight Makhno. This force, under the direction of the commander of the Thirteenth Army rear area, consisted of a cavalry division under Blinov, the 126th Brigade of the Forty-Second Infantry Division, several battalions of the Internal Security Troops of the Republic, one Cheka battalion from Kharkiv and garrisons of Hryshyne, Pavlohrad, Synel'nikove, Lozova, and Oleksandrivs'k. The plan was to surround the region of Makhno's activities and divide it into three areas (Chaplino, Hryshyne, and Volnovakha) in order to prevent Makhno's escape. The 126th Brigade and an armored train remained in reserve while the cavalry division was to hunt and liquidate Makhno.[7] Although Makhno knew about this plan, he paid little attention to the surrounding forces except for the cavalry division and during the spring and summer avoided major frontal battles against superior Bolshevik forces.

Although Makhno's struggle was a war of small engagements, it was marked by extremely violent fighting.[8] On encountering larger enemy forces, including armored trains, Makhno would skillfully retreat in a loose formation at great speed. With the same speed, he would reappear in the rear of the enemy, attacking military staffs and base areas. An eyewitness recalled:

> As our units were advancing on the left flank, suddenly machine guns began firing at our base. Shouts: "band!" caused a panic. Even though our artillery men opened fire against Makhno's men, the Makhno cutthroats spread out, slashing and shooting everyone who came within their grasp. This attack cost very dearly.[9]

Such operations were usually successful because Makhno used cavalry units and troops on carts with machine guns. His campaign was largely confined to surprise attacks on isolated Red Army units, small garrisons, requisition agents, Bolshevik militiamen, political commissars, bridges, railroads, and Bolshevik supply bases.[10] In the course of the campaign, especially during the raids, which sometimes covered distances up to 1,200 to 1,500 versts, the partisans carried on intensive anti-Bolshevik propaganda among the population. Although Makhno was merciless with the captured Red Army officers, ordinary soldiers were either incorporated into his army or released as soon as they were taken.[11] During one encounter when Makhno captured eighty Bolshevik prisoners, an eyewitness said Makhno "showed a human heart toward those prisoners." He delivered a speech to them saying: "I am freeing you, and your duty must be to tell everywhere who Makhno is, for what he is fighting and how he is fighting." After those joyful prisoners had been freed, Makhno went on:

> Those eighty souls will be the best agitators in my behalf. To some they will tell what I am fighting for, to others, how I am fighting. There will be more benefit for me from that than if I had them shot.[12]

The objectives of the Bolsheviks were to capture Makhno, to destroy his partisans and his influence in the countryside. To prevent fraternization between the Red Army troops and Makhno's partisans, the Bolsheviks extensively employed against the latter divisions of Latvian and Estonian sharpshooters and Chinese detachments.[13] Employing other new tactics, the Bolsheviks attacked not only Makhno's partisans, but also villages and towns in which the population was sympathetic toward Makhno. They shot ordinary soldiers as well as their commanders, destroying their houses, confiscating their properties, and persecuting their families. Moreover the Bolsheviks conducted mass arrests of innocent peasants who were suspected of collaborating in some way with the partisans. It is impossible to determine the casualties involved: according to moderate estimates, more than two hundred thousand people were executed or injured by the Bolsheviks in Ukraine during that period. Nearly as many were imprisoned or deported to Russia and Siberia.[14]

In spite of their merciless methods and intense propaganda, the Bolsheviks were not able to destroy Makhno in this period. Contrary to their expectations, his army was growing stronger and was reactivating and the Bolsheviks began to realize that military means alone were not enough to destroy the Makhno movement. To obtain a firm foothold in the villages in Ukraine, the Bolsheviks conceived the idea of neutralizing or placating the peasants. The Bolshevik authorities admitted having made a mistake in 1919 by introducing the Soviet farm system to occupied Ukraine, for "the peasants looked upon the attempts to socialize farming as a new form of Communist state enslavement." Although they modified their agricultural policy by introducing on February 5, 1920, a new land law, distributing the former landlords', state, and church lands among the peasants, they did not succeed in placating them because the requisitions, which the peasants considered outright robbery, continued. During the first nine months of 1920, about one thousand Bolshevik grain requisition agents were killed.[15]

Subsequently the Bolsheviks decided to introduce class warfare into the villages. A decree was issued on May 19, 1920, establishing "Committees of the Poor." This practice was transplanted from Soviet Russia where the Bolsheviks had introduced similar committees (*kombedy*) as early as spring 1918.[16] The aim was to create an auxiliary force in the villages to assist the Bolsheviks in requisitioning food and let the collectors have a share in the grain seized from the other peasants. Authority in the villages was delegated to the committees, which assisted the Bolsheviks in seizing the surplus grain and watched the well-to-do peasants to prevent their hiding food. Soviet policy was to liberate "Ukrainian poor and middle [peasants] from the ideological and material yoke of the 'kulaks' and thus to split the united front of the Ukrainian village and, subsequently, the Makhno movement as well."[17]

The establishment of Committees of the Poor was painful to Makhno because they became not only part of the Bolsehvik administrative apparatus the peasants opposed, but also informers helping the Bolshevik secret police in its persecution of the partisans, their families and supporters, even to the extent of hunting down and executing wounded partisans. Makhno and the Revolutionary Military Council viewed these committees as a typical Bolshevik organization, to be dealt with the same way as any other punitive organ. Consequently, Makhno's "heart became hardened and he sometimes ordered executions where some generosity would have bestowed more credit upon him and his movement. That the Bolsheviks preceded him with the bad example was no excuse. For he claimed to be fighting for a better cause."[18] Although the committees in time gave the Bolsheviks a hold on every village, their abuse of power disorganized and slowed down agricultural life.

Peasants' economic conditions in the region of the Makhno movement were greatly improved at the expense of the estates of the landlords, the church, monasteries, and the richest peasants, but Makhno had not put an end to the agricultural inequalities. His aim was to avoid conflicts within the villages and to maintian a sort of unified front of the entire peasantry in his region. These agricultural conditions and the actions of the Makhno partisans against the Bolsheviks' attempt to entrench themselves in the villages were reflected in the relative paucity of committees in the Makhno region. On September 10, 1920, there were only 200 committees in Katerynoslav province but 1,000 in Kherson, 442 in Odessa, 945 in Kharkiv, 1280 in Poltava, and 687 in Kyiv.[19]

This policy of terror and exploitation turned almost all segments of Ukrainian society against the Bolsheviks, substantially strengthened the Makhno movement, and consequently facilitated the advance of the reorganized anti-Bolshevik force of General Wrangel from the Crimea into South Ukraine, the Makhno region. According to a report of Colonel Noga, the representative of Denikin's staff at the Crimean group, dated March 25, 1920, the Red Army units retreated from the Perekop Isthmus so fast that the Volunteers lost contact with them. This rapid retreat was explained thus:

> In Ukraine in the rear of the Reds peasant uprising under Makhno and many other partisan detachments were staged, giving the Reds no rest. This is clear to me from the Red newspapers, letters of the prisoners, etc. And Generals Shilling [and] Slashchov view this phenomenon very favorably, but not knowing the view of the "Stavka" on this, certainly no measures had been taken to establish contact with Makhno and others. I consider this question of paramount importance because I see in it an escape from the general strategic situation. This needs full elucidation, and the sooner the better. In my opinion now the time is so critical that our motto should be: "Anyone against the Reds is with us."[20]

A Soviet author confirms this situation: "Makhno men, successfully maneuvered between the units of the Forty-Second Division, continued to roam in 'their' region. Meanwhile, the advance of Wrangel's units continued. Red Army units were retreating. . . . This was a very critical moment on the southern front."[21]

19. Makhno between Wrangel and the Bolsheviks

After evacuation of the remnants of the Volunteer Army into the Crimea, General Slashchov's Crimean Corps held the Thirteenth Red Army in check from January to March at the Perekop and Syvash isthmuses.[1] Denikin, physically and morally defeated, resigned his position as commander in chief and on April 4 at the Conference of Superior Officers, originally the Military Council (Army corps commanders or their equivalents) elected General Baron Peter Nikolaevich Wrangel commander in chief. Wrangel accepted the election by signing a statement:

> I have shared the honour of its victories with the Army, and cannot refuse to drink the cup of humiliation with it now. Drawing strength from the trust which my comrades-in-arms place in me, I consent to accept the post of Commander-in-Chief.[2]

Whereupon Denikin issued an edict stating:

> Lieutenant-General Baron Wrangel is hereby appointed Commander-in-Chief of the Armed Forces of South Russia. Sincere greetings to all those who have followed me loyally in the terrible struggle. God save Russia and grant victory to the Army.[3]

Wrangel realized that his army of 70,000, reorganized in the course of April and May, could not hope to defeat the Red forces alone. Although Wrangel was a thorough conservative, he tried to correct the mistakes made by his predecessor by introducing a new agrarian law on June 7, 1920, vesting ownership of the land in the peasants, represented by the soviets of counties and districts, whose members were elected, mainly from among the peasant owners.[4] This reform was to be carried out by Aleksandr Vasil'evich Krivoshein, the former minister of agriculture, who had carried out Stolypin's agrarian reforms. Wrangel believed his agrarian policy would secure for him the support of the peasants and would at the same time undermine the discipline of the Red troops. However, the peasants were not satisfied with the new law. Moreover, in many places news of Wrangel's agricultural reforms never reached them. In contrast to Denikin, Wrangel was willing to seek allies where Denikin had seen enemies. He tried to enlist officers and soldiers from belligerent armies. On April 29, 1920, he freed

> . . . all the officers and soldiers who had given themselves up and come over to our side before or during the struggle, from every kind of proceeding and service restriction, as well as all those who had served previously in the Soviet Army, and who had, therefore, already undergone punishment and service restrictions after the territory had been occupied by the armed forces of South Russia of their own free will; they were all reinstated in the ranks and privileges they had held on December 1, 1917. At the same time, all the officers and soldiers who had served the new States, Ukraine and Georgia, and who had undergone punishment and restrictions on that account, were exempted from all further punishment or service restrictions.[5]

These concessions were extended to the staff of institutions and civil administration by virtue of an edict issued on June 8, 1920.[6] Wrangel also wished to improve relations with the non-Russian people, especially with the Don and Kuban Cossacks. He considered

> . . . the policy of the former government conducted under the slogan "indivisible Russia," an irreconcilable struggle against all people who inhabited Russia, . . . wrong, and would try to unite all the anti-Bolshevik forces.[7]

In widening his search for allies against the Bolsheviks, however, Wrangel lost the support of the British government. On April 29, 1920, General Percy, chief of the British Military Mission, announced: "Should General Wrangel prolong the struggle, it can have only one result, and we cannot encourage it by subsidies in money or kind."[8] According to Wrangel the British government insisted that he should enter into direct negotiations with the Bolsheviks:

> They warned me that a continuation of the struggle might have fatal results, and that in any case I could not count on any assistance from them. It was clear that the British Government, which sought closer relations with the Bolshevik Government, wished above all to see hostilities come to an end.[9]

Wrangel rejected British advice and continued his preparation for an offensive; consequently, the British government recalled its representatives and military mission from the Crimea.[10] However, the ensuing war between Soviet Russia and Poland favored Wrangel's cause. On the advice of the head of the French Military Mission, General Mangin, that Wrangel coordinate his activities with the Polish and Ukrainian armies, Prince Trubetskoi, Wrangel's representative in Paris, wrote on May 17, 1920, to Mangin:

> The Commander-in-Chief is ready to accept all the collaboration which offers itself, and will be more than willing to cooperate with the Polish and Ukrainian forces. [However] . . . he does not want to broach the political side of the question, nor to take his stand on the recent news of the political agreement between Poland and Ukraine. The aim of the Armed Forces of South Russia is the essentially practical and military one of fighting the Bolshevists.[11]

Although Wrangel's desire to coordinate his own activities with those of the Polish and Ukrainian forces was thwarted by the latter's rapid retreat into Poland, each army derived some benefit from the other; Wrangel had aided Poland by diverting large Bolshevik forces to South Ukraine and the Kuban, while the Poles later permitted about ten thousand of General Bredov's troops to transfer to the Crimea and join Wrangel.[12] On August 10, 1920, Alexander Millerand, the prime minister of France, in a letter to the Russian Embassy in Paris, declared:

> I have the honour to inform you that the Government of the Republic has decided to accord *de facto* recognition to the Government of South Russia, and will send a diplomatic agent to Sevastopol . . . at the same time notifying the Allied and Associated Governments of its decisions.[13]

This recognition of Wrangel's government and the subsequent support given to him was largely motivated by the French desire to establish an allied Polish state against Germany and to save it from the Bolshevik invasion. According to Wrangel:

> At the time when hostilities began between Poland and the Government of the Soviets, France thought it necessary to support the White Armies, which might attract to their front a portion of the Red forces. Later Millerand . . . made a public acknowledgment that the help which had been lent to the White Armies had no other aim beyond the saving of Poland.[14]

At the end of 1919 the Ukrainian Army was forced by the superior Bolshevik and anti-Bolshevik Russian forces to retreat westward where it encountered the Polish Army. Petliura decided it was impossible under these circumstances to continue orthodox warfare without external aid. He felt, however, that the struggle against the invading

Russian forces should continue in the form of guerrilla warfare. Part of the army, about fourteen thousand men, was reorganized and, on December 7, 1919, under General Mykhailo Omelianovych-Pavlenko, moved far to the rear of the Bolshevik and Denikin forces to fight them and to support the Ukrainian partisans. This "Winter Campaign" continued through the winter of 1919–20.[15]

Petliura realized that Ukraine could not survive in her struggle against the Russian Reds and Whites without assistance from the Entente. Therefore, he tried to come to terms with the Polish government, which, in his judgment, was the bridge to the Entente. At first reluctant, Poland came awake when the erosion of the Ukrainian position threatened to remove the barrier that had protected Poland from the Bolshevik threat since Germany's defeat. Thus, once the Polish Army attained the desired frontiers, the Zbruch River and western Volyn up to the Styr River, at the expense of Ukraine, the Poles agreed to negotiate. The Directory was obliged to issue a declaration on December 2, 1919, without the consent of its Galician members, accepting this line as the Polish-Ukrainian frontier.

After prolonged negotiations the two governments concluded a treaty, consisting of a political agreement and a military convention. Both governments expressed their profound conviction "that each people possesses the natural right to self-determination and to define its relations with neighboring peoples, and is equally desirous of establishing a basis for concordant and friendly coexistence for the welfare and development of both peoples."[16] Although the treaty had many weaknesses and was sharply criticized by many on both sides, and in addition it did not achieve the Directory's hope of winning French or British support, both the Polish and Ukrainian armies, including the participants in the winter campaign, joined in fighting the Red Army. On May 8, 1920, they liberated Kyiv. The Bolshevik counteroffensive, however, forced them to retreat deep into Poland where the Bolsheviks were finally defeated. The Soviet Russian government proposed an armistice and a preliminary peace that the Polish government accepted without consulting the Ukrainian government. When Ukraine asked to participate in the peace negotiations, the Polish minister of foreign affairs, Prince Eustachy Sapieha, referred this question to the Soviet Russian government:

> In our negotiations with the Bolsheviks the problem of Petliura will not be taken into consideration at all; nevertheless, today I sent a message to Chicherin informing him that Petliura's government wishes to negotiate with the Russian delegation at Riga. This proposal, however, should in no way create difficulties for the depar-

ture of our delegation, even if Chicherin rejects negotiation with Petliura, which I think is certain.[17]

Although in the Treaty of Warsaw the Polish government had agreed "not to conclude any international agreements directed against Ukraine," the preliminary peace treaty and armistice between Soviet Russia and Poland were signed on October 12, 1920, and the final peace treaty was signed on March 18, 1921.

In the meantime, however, because the Crimea was too small, either to supply food for such a large army for long and ensure foreign trade or to serve as a base for major operations against the Bolshevik forces, Wrangel's primary task was to capture northern Tavriia, in his words "a matter of life and death for us."[18] The outbreak of the Polish-Bolshevik war at the end of April benefited Wrangel because it diverted the Bolsheviks' attention and relieved the pressure, enabling him to launch an offensive against the Bolsheviks in Tavriia on June 6.[19] In a series of battles Wrangel penetrated north, forcing a general Bolshevik retreat and capturing more than eleven thousand prisoners, sixty big guns, three hundred machine guns, two armored cars, and a huge collection of small arms and bayonets.[20] As Wrangel advanced deeper into the Left Bank, Makhno retreated north to the Kharkiv region, leaving behind small partisan units in the villages and towns to carry on covert destruction of the Bolshevik administrative apparatus and supply bases.[21] According to a Soviet author:

Fighting against the Red units was more and more violent and the Makhno movement, under various guises and pretexts, moved into the deep rear, causing colossal destruction. Railroad lines, the supplies of products, materials, ammunition—everything that was necessary for the struggle against the White guards. What was burned and destroyed, of course, echoed upon the results of the fighting against Wrangel.[22]

Wrangel attempted to reach an agreement with Makhno after receiving this encouraging note that he believed was from him: "The Bolsheviks killed my brother. I am going to avenge him. After my vengeance I will come to assist you."[23] It is not known whether Makhno wanted to mislead Wrangel or whether somebody else sent the letter, but Wrangel took it seriously. According to the war correspondent with the Wrangel troops:

On the whole, at headquarters, special attention is paid to the partisan movement. Especially . . . the Makhno movement. Now Makhno is considered not a bandit, but a representative of peasant aspirations, a kind of uncrowned tsar of peasants.[24]

To gain support from Makhno, Wrangel decided to enter into

contact with him, disregarding warnings from his intelligence staff that Makhno was an agrarian-anarchist and a bandit who could hardly be expected to enter into an agreement with a tsarist general.[25] On July 1, 1920, an envoy, Ivan Mikhailov, left Wrangel's headquarters at Melitopil' with a letter signed by Wrangel's chief of staff, General Pavel N. Shatilov, and General Konovalov:

To the ataman of the partisan forces, Makhno. The Russian army is fighting exclusively against the Communists in order to help the people save themselves from the commune and commissars and to secure for the working peasants the lands of the state, the landlords, and other private properties. The latter we are already putting into effect. Russian soldiers and officers are fighting for the people and for their well-being. Everybody who is fighting for the people should proceed hand in hand with us. Therefore, now intensify fighting against the Communists by attacking their rear, destroying their transport, and helping in every possible way in the final destruction of Trotsky's troops. The Supreme Command will do what it can to help you by supplying arms and ammunition, and also by sending specialists. Send your representative to headquarters with reports on what you particularly need and for an agreement about operational matters.[26]

On July 22, after considering this proposal, Makhno and his staff gave an emphatic reply to Wrangel by executing the envoy. In spite of this rejection both sides spread rumors about Makhno's cooperation with Wrangel: the Bolsheviks, to discredit him; the anti-Bolsheviks, to win the confidence of the peasants. Speaking about military conditions on the southern front, Trotsky said: "this Crimean partisan [Wrangel] who united with the Ukrainian partisan Makhno, is advancing northward."[27] Later, on October 14, 1920, Trotsky retracted this statement:

Wrangel really tried to come into direct contact with Makhno's men and dispatched to Makhno's headquarters two representatives for negotiations. . . . [However] Makhno's men not only did not enter into negotiation with the representatives of Wrangel, but publicly hanged them as soon as they arrived at the headquarters.[28]

Nevertheless, rumors were widely circulated and accepted by both the leaders and the people that a close alliance had been concluded; that Makhno and his staff were subordinate to Wrangel, that Makhno had been given a command in Wrangel's army, and that Makhno had lavishly received Wrangel's delegates and toasted to the honor of the chief commander. Later, the newspapers published reports that "Wrangel's ally Makhno had taken Kharkiv and Katerynoslav and the Makhno detachments would join the left flank of Wrangel's army in advancing along the railroads toward Oleksandrivs'k-Katerynoslav."[29]

As the campaign developed, Wrangel realized that his Crimean-Tavriian base of operation was inadequate and precarious. The Crimea was short of everything and could not feed its own population or the large influx of refugees, let alone the Wrangel forces. Tavriia, however, was threatened by growing Bolshevik presence, partisan activities, and peasant uprisings. Moreover, Wrangel's army was too small to secure any more extensive territory in hostile Ukraine. Wrangel had taken to heart the lessons of Denikin's disastrous drive on Moscow without consolidating his rear. He felt that for larger operations he needed to procure a less hazardous base, to enlarge his army and supplies. The Kuban and the Don basins were the only places where Wrangel could find what he needed. During Denikin's retreat thousands of Cossacks had returned to their homes in those areas, taking with them horses, arms, and ammunition. Moreover, these regions were rich in natural resources. If they could be reconquered, Wrangel planned to retreat to the Crimea and defend it at the Isthmus of Perekop, while making the Kuban his base of operation. Because of these circumstances and the Cossacks' hostility toward the Bolshevik regime, Wrangel was encouraged to direct his offensive against the Don and the Kuban.[30]

On July 22, a detachment headed by Colonel Nazarov, consisting of 1,000 infantry, cavalry, field artillery, armored cars, and two trucks, landed in the area of Novomykolaivka west of Taganrog. Nazarov's aim was to bring about uprisings of the Don Cossacks and prepare for Wrangel's advance into the Don Basin by widening Wrangel's front against the Bolsheviks and obtaining new recruits. Moreover, Nazarov intended to establish contact with General Ulagai, who was to be landed in the Kuban, to secure his position on the lower Don and Manych rivers from the north. Although Nazarov's unit advanced rapidly through the Don, instigating a revolt against the Bolsheviks on the way, and he increased his detachment of 2,500 through mobilization, it failed to accomplish its goal because of its distance from the base and its lack of popular support. It was practically destroyed in a battle at Konstantinovka on July 24–28, though Nazarov himself made his way alone back to the Crimea.[31]

On August 13 a detachment headed by General Ulagai, consisting of 4,500 infantry and cavalry with 130 machine guns, 26 big guns, some armored cars, and 8 airplanes, landed successfully near Primorsko-Akhtiarsk, on the Kuban coast of the Sea of Azov. Ulagai's aim was to advance rapidly on Ekaterinodar, striking at the Bolshevik forces separately and encouraging Cossack uprisings. A separate unit of 500 infantry and 2 guns landed near Anapa, on the Taman Peninsula, as a demonstration. At the outset Ulagai's forces won a few victories and occupied a number of settlements on the road to Ekaterinodar, creating panic in the city and forcing Bolshevik military and civilian institutions to evacuate.[32] However, he vacillated for several days, fearing for his base, thus losing his momentum and allowing the Bolsheviks to concentrate their forces. According to Wrangel:

> Ulagai unfortunately encumbered himself with enormous rearguard impediments. Great reserves of arms, ammunition and provisions had been left at the landing-stage. . . . Thus, even whilst they advanced, our units were compelled to look back all the time. [Meantime] the enemy had begun to collect their forces to attack our advanced detachment. There was no time to be lost; every day we wasted gave the enemy another day in which to bring up fresh troops. Yet General Ulagai did not stir . . . the enemy now enjoyed an overwhelming numerical superiority.[33]

Ulagai's troops were forced to retreat to Achuev on the Sea of Azov coast and on September 7 they sailed to the Crimea. The unit that landed at Anapa was largely wiped out.[34] Wrangel's Kuban invasion failed because of General Ulagai's indecisiveness; the unwillingness of Cossacks to support the invasion, which seemed to them only an adventure; and Bolshevik military superiority. However, in spite of heavy losses, Ulagai brought back more troops than he had taken with him because of Bolshevik deserters and new recruits.

Wrangel's failure to extend his territorial base into the Kuban and the Don was a turning point of his campaign:

> The failure of the Kuban operation had robbed us of our last hope of finding a way of continuing the struggle on neighboring Russian territory. Abandoned to our fate as we now were, we would inevitably perish sooner or later.[35]

Wrangel, nevertheless, decided to make another effort to strike the Bolsheviks from a different direction, primarily to gloss over his failure in the Kuban. He informed the French government that because of Bolshevik defeat on the Polish front, "the centre of our operations will have to be shifted to Ukraine."[36] Subsequently he decided to strike in two directions: across the Dnieper, and north and east from his lines. He wished to secure both banks of the Dnieper preparatory to a deeper northern penetration, and to advance into the central Ukraine to establish contact with the Poles.

Prior to the trans-Dnieper operation, Wrangel began to advance into the Left Bank, threatening the partisans' position. Consequently Makhno was compelled to seek an understanding with the Bolsheviks. The Revolutionary Military Council and Makhno's staff agreed to propose a cessation of hostilities against the Bolsheviks and to join forces with them against Wrangel, but no reply was received.[37] Thus Makhno found himself caught between two forces and had to fight both simultaneously. However, in mid-September Wrangel penetrated north to the vicinity of Katerynoslav, and east toward Taganrog, capturing a number of towns including Melitopil', Oleksandrivs'k, the railroad junction at Synel'nikove, Berdians'k, and Mariupil'. Now Wrangel launched his trans-Dnieper operation near Oleksandrivs'k, forcing the Red troops to retreat all along the front. In several days of fighting he captured over three thousand prisoners, eight guns, six armored cars, and an armored train. Mikhail V. Frunze, the newly appointed commander of the southern front of the Bolsheviks, admitted that "by capturing the railroad station in Synel'nikove an undisturbed northward road was open to Wrangel where we had no troops at all."[38]

Wrangel's success caused the Bolshevik leaders to reconsider Makhno's earlier proposal. Their motives were "to liberate the Red Army's rear from Makhno's detachment [and to achieve] an immediate victory over Wrangel."[39] Lenin explained:

> According to Trotsky, the question of Makhno was very seriously discussed in military circles, and it was concluded that nothing could be expected but gains. . . . elements grouped around Makhno have already experienced Wrangel's regime and what they can expect from him would not satisfy them. [Thus] our agreement with Makhno is secured by guaranty that he would not act against us. This is the same situation as with Denikin and Kolchak: as soon as they touched the interests of "kulaks" and peasants in general, the latter were coming to our side.[40]

Thus the Bolshevik authorities decided to contact Makhno. Rakovskii wired Makhno at his headquarters at Bilovodsk in Starobil's'k district, Kharkiv province, to negotiate directly about a joint campaign against Wrangel. At that time, however, Makhno, being seriously wounded, authorized three members of his staff, Semen Karetnyk, Viktor Bilash, and Viktor Popov, to carry on preliminary negotiations on September 28, with Rakovskii's representatives, Bela Kun, Frunze, and Sergei J. Gusev (IAkov Davidovich Drabkin).[41] The preliminary military and political agreement was sent to Kharkiv for ratification. For this purpose and for maintaining subsequent contact with the staff of the south front in Kharkiv, Makhno's military and political representatives, headed by Vasyl Kurylenko and Popov, were dispatched. On October 15 the agreement, which was both military and political, was accepted by both parties.[42]

The military agreement contained four clauses:

> 1. The Revolutionary Partisan Army of Ukraine (Makhnovites) would join the armed forces of the Republic, as a partisan army, subordinate operationally to the

supreme command of the Red Army; it would retain its own internal organization, and the bases of the Red Army would not be introduced.

2. While moving through Soviet territory, or across the fronts, the Revolutionary Partisan Army of Ukraine (Makhnovites) would accept into its ranks neither detachments nor deserters from the Red Army.[43]

Remarks:

a. The Red Army units and isolated Red soldiers, who have met and joined the Revolutionary Partisan Army behind the Wrangel front, should reenter the ranks of the Red Army when they again make contact with it.

b. Makhno partisans behind the Wrangel front and local people, again joining the ranks of the Partisan Army, would remain in the latter, even if they were previously mobilized by the Red Army.

3. For the purpose of destroying the common enemy, the White Guards, the Revolutionary Partisan Army of Ukraine (Makhnovites) would inform the working masses who supported it of the agreement that has been concluded, it would call upon the people to cease hostile action against the Soviet authorities; for its part, the Soviet authorities should immediately publish the clauses of the agreement.

4. The families of the Revolutionary Partisan Army (Makhnovites) living in Soviet-held territory were to enjoy the same rights as the families of the Red Army and would receive from the Soviet authorities of Ukraine necessary documents.

The political agreement contained three clauses:

1. Immediate release, and an end to the persecution of all Makhno men and anarchists in the territories of the Soviet Republics, except those who carry on armed resistance against the Soviet authorities.

2. Makhno men and anarchists were to have complete freedom of expression for their ideas and principles, by speech and the press, provided that nothing was expressed that tended to a violent overthrow of Soviet government, and on condition that the military censorship be respected. The Soviet authorities would provide Makhno men and anarchists, as revolutionary organizations recognized by the Soviet government, with technical facilities for publications, subject to the technical rules for publications.

3. Makhno men and anarchists were to enjoy full rights of participation in elections to the soviets, including the right to be elected, and free participation in the organization of the forthcoming Fifth All-Ukrainian Congress of Soviets, which should take place next December.

There was a fourth clause in the political agreement that the Bolshevik representatives refused to sign, arguing that it needed a separate discussion and contact with Moscow:

One of the basic principles of the Makhno movement being the struggle for self-administration of the toilers, the Partisan Army brings up a fourth point: in the region of the Makhno movement, the worker and peasant population is to organize and maintain its own free institutions for economic and political self-administration; this region is subsequently to be federated with Soviet republics by means of agreements to be freely negotiated with the appropriate Soviet governmental organ.[44]

Although Makhno demanded that the agreement should be published immediately if he were to act on it, the Bolshevik authorities, under various pretexts, delayed its publication. Finally they published only the military agreement, delaying the political agreement for several days, thus blurring its real meaning. As for the fourth political clause, it never was ratified because it was "absolutely unacceptable to the dictatorship of the proletariat." The agreement, according to a Bolshevik military historian, was justified only by its "strategic importance." However, Trotsky rejoiced "that Makhno men from now on wished to fight not against us, but with us against Wrangel."[45] To assure Makhno's full cooperation, the Bolsheviks released a number of Makhno men and anarchists from prison and the Bolshevik newpaper, the *Proletarian*, and other Kharkiv newspapers published Trotsky's declaration, which he issued on October 14, 1920, under the title *Makhno i Vrangel*:

> Undoubtedly Makhno actually cooperated with Wrangel, and also with the Polish *szlachta*, as he fought with them against the Red Army. However, there was no formal alliance between them. All the documents mentioning a formal alliance were fabricated by Wrangel. . . . All this fabrication was made to deceive the protectors of Makhno, the French, and other imperialists.[46]

After the agreement, Makhno moved to the area of the Forty-Second Division, arriving at the end of October and setting up his headquarters at Petropavlivka. His army of over ten thousand men consisted mainly of cavalry and machine-gun regiments.[47] Subsequently sensational reports began to appear in the foreign press about Makhno's joining the Red Army. These reports had a depressing effect upon Wrangel's troops because, according to the Russian war correspondent,

> Great hopes were building around Wrangel's imaginary alliance with Makhno. . . . [Now] the front and the rear, which were based on belief in the existence of a Wrangel-Makhno alliance, received a serious blow to morale. Now it was revealed how false had been the reports about certain of Makhno's grand successes and about his friendly attitude toward Wrangel.[48]

Wrangel complained, "The bands of the famous 'Father' Makhno who up till now had been 'working' behind the Red lines, suddenly realized the possibility of profits to be made from plundering the Crimea, and joined the Soviet troops."[49] After liberating Huliai-Pole, Makhno pursued Wrangel southward and in a fierce battle in the area of Orikhiv defeated the strong Drozdovskii group, taking four thousand prisoners.[50] He then returned to Huliai-Pole to prepare for further campaigns.

In mid-October he turned against Wrangel with a strong partisan army of about ten thousand men headed by Karetnyk. It included cavalry units under Oleksander Marchenko and machine-gun detachments under Khoma Kozhyn. Because of his wound, Makhno did not accompany his troops but stayed in Huliai-Pole with his staff and about three thousand men.[51] This act initiated the last phase of Wrangel's efforts. His temporary success in the trans-Dnieper operation ended when he was defeated at the armed fortress of Kakhivka and driven back across the Dnieper with heavy losses. Moreover, the Bolsheviks established an important strategic foothold on the left bank of the Dnieper at Kakhivka, from which they could easily strike at the approach to the Crimea, endangering Wrangel's position in northern Tavriia.[52] The collapse of this operation greatly undermined the spirit of the troops.

At about the same time, Wrangel received the news that the Poles had signed an armistice and a preliminary peace treaty with Soviet Russia. Gradually the Red Army command began to transfer troops from the Polish front to the south under a slogan "all against Wrangel."[53] Realizing the seriousness of the situation, Wrangel called a conference of his closest advisors to decide whether to confront the enemy in northern Tavriia or to retreat behind the Isthmus of Perekop. Finally they chose the former alternative because

> A retreat beyond the isthmus into the Crimea peninsula would not only condemn us to hunger and every kind of privation, but would be the confession of our powerlessness to continue an active struggle; this would deprive us of all future help from France. Once we were shut up in the Crimea, we would cease to be a menace to the Soviet government, and therefore to be of any interest to the Western Powers.[54]

The final battles took place toward the end of October. The Red Army command planned to destroy Wrangel in northern Tavriia by cutting him off from the Crimea, but the Wrangel troops fought their way to the Isthmus of Perekop, where fierce fighting developed.[55] To break Wrangel's resistance there, the Red Army commander, Frunze, asked the Makhno army to move in behind Wrangel's troops across the Syvash Lagoon. Karetnyk and his chief of staff, Petro Havrylenko, were, however, very hesitant to advance into the Crimea because they were suspicious of the Bolsheviks' intentions. Frunze confessed:

> It seems that Makhno's men did not quite trust me and were terribly hesitant to take the field fearing, probably, a kind of trap. Several times Karetnyk and his chief of staff would leave and come to me under the pretext of getting this or that information. Only early in the morning about 5 o'clock did I succeed in sending them to the front.[56]

Early on the morning of November 7 the Makhno troops made a

surprise attack across the ice of the Syvash Lagoon, beating and driving back the Kuban Cossacks commanded by General Fostikov, who were guarding the Lithuanian peninsula southeast of Perekop. They broke through the heavy fire, advancing into the rear of the Perekop forces located at the first fortified position, Armiansk Bazar, and attacking Wrangel's rear from the left flank. Wrangel's effort to regain the peninsula by counterattack failed. General Kutepov then retreated from the Perekop position to a second fortified line between Perekop and IUshun. With incredible difficulty, his detachments retreated with heavy losses, leaving their artillery in place. On November 8, the Red troops began a strong frontal attack on the Perekop Isthmus that broke Wrangel's resistance; his troops, fearing to be cut off, retreated to the southern part of the isthmus, where the struggle went on for a few days. The Red troops continued to force their way deeper into the Crimea, threatening Wrangel's headquarters at Dzhankoi; Makhno's troops advanced toward Symferopil', occupying a number of towns, and on November 13–14 they took the city by storm.[57]

According to Berkman, who arrived in Moscow at about this time:

> I was surprised to find the city in festive attire and the people jubilant. The walls were covered with posters announcing the complete rout of Wrangel. Still greater was my astonishment when I glanced at the Bolshevik newspapers. They were full of praise for Nestor Makhno. They called him the Nemesis of the Whites and recited how his cavalry was at that very moment pursuing the remnants of Wrangel's army across the Crimean Peninsula.[58]

Wrangel ordered his troops to retreat to various ports of the Crimea for evacuation. Since the termination of the Polish-Soviet Russian war, Wrangel had foreseen the possibility of a Bolshevik invasion of the Crimea, and he now ordered General Shatilov and Admiral M. A. Kedrov to put into effect the plan of evacuation that had been prepared jointly by the General Staff and the Admiral of the Fleet at the beginning of May when the British asked Wrangel to come to terms with the Bolsheviks. Moreover, Wrangel had written to King Alexander of Serbia begging him to give the Russian troops shelter in case of need.[59] As the troops reached the ports the evacuation began. From November 13 to November 16, 126 ships left the ports of Kerch, Feodosiia, Yalta, Sevastopil', and Evpatoriia carrying 150,000 persons, two-thirds of them officers and soldiers, the other third civilians. Some of the refugees were taken to Turkey and temporarily put in camps. Gradually they were settled in European countries, including Serbia, Bulgaria, Romania, and Greece.[60]

The Wrangel movement was the last Russian attempt to overthrow the Bolshevik regime in Russia. Wrangel had inherited a most unfavorable situation from Denikin, and had less support than he from prominent Russian statesmen wishing to serve in his government. Like Denikin, he attempted to arouse the population against the Bolshevik regime not in Russia but in Ukraine, in the Don, and the Kuban, with Allied support. But Wrangel's army, except for the Don and Kuban armies, consisted primarily of the Russian upper classes, and Wrangel himself was a tsarist officer of aristocratic background. Thus the Wrangel movement respected neither the national aspirations of Ukrainians and other non-Russians, nor the civil liberties of its own people. These circumstances gave the movement the character of a force fighting against the achievements of the Revolution.

Wrangel could not bridge the wide gulf of suspicion and hostility between the movement and the population, which was the basic cause of the defeat of the anti-Bolshevik movement. His army was only a vestige of the former Volunteer Army, both in quantity and quality. It had been so decimated and demoralized that its reorganization in the Crimea had been a futile attempt to resuscitate a dead cause. The defeat of the Kuban landing, the destruction of the trans-Dnieper operation, the Polish-Bolshevik armistice, the dread prospect of spending a winter in the Crimea, the growing indications that the White regime did not have the support of the population—all these factors undermined the morale of the army. Moreover, Wrangel's army contained, besides non-Russians, a large number of Red prisoners, who were inadequately screened and hence unreliable.

Wrangel could not establish secure bases in Ukraine, the Don, or the Kuban, for in the former it was considered a foreign occupation and in the other areas the people had already lost confidence in the leadership of the movement and in the movement itself, prior to the Novorossisk catastrophe. The majority of the Russian people either supported the Bolsheviks or were neutral. Even France supported Wrangel primarily for Poland's sake and after the end of the Polish-Bolshevik war, France abandoned him. Although Makhno fought both the Bolsheviks and Wrangel, his contribution to the final defeat of the latter was essential, as is proved by the efforts of both sides to have him as an ally. Without adequate operational bases and a large army, Wrangel could not have coped with the constantly growing Red forces and the Ukrainian partisans for long, and his defeat was almost a foregone conclusion.

Nestor I. Makhno

Makhno's staff. *Front row from left*: Oleksander Marchenko, Semen Karetnyk, Vasyliv; *back row*: Vasyl' Kurylenko, Viktor Bilash, Petro Petrenko, Roma, Fedir Shchus', Mel'nyk (Makhno's driver)

Nestor Makhno, Paris, 1930–31

20. The Last Phase of the Makhno Struggle

Wrangel had been the last major enemy the Bolsheviks had to deal with. Once that threat had passed, they had sufficiently established their power in South Ukraine to dispense with Makhno's aid. Makhno, for his part, seems to have hoped the Bolsheviks would allow a degree of autonomy for the region of the Makhno movement. According to Victor Serge: "Trotskii was much later (1938, I think) to recount that Lenin and he had thought of recognizing an autonomous region for the anarchist peasants of Ukraine, whose military leader Makhno was."[1] Makhno assumed the coming conflict with the Bolsehviks could be limited to the realm of ideas, feeling that the strong revolutionary ideas and feelings of the peasants, together with their distrust of the foreign invaders, were the best guarantees for the movement's territory. Moreover, Makhno believed that the Bolsheviks would not attack his movement immediately. A respite of some three months would have allowed him to consolidate his power and to win over much of the Bolshevik rank and file. It seems Makhno was not the only one who contemplated the idea of Red troops deserting to the partisans. According to the British war correspondent:

> General Keyes, the chief British political officer in South Russia, went down to Sochi from Novorossisk in a British man-of-war to get into touch with the Greek commanders. He found that the prevailing impression among them was that, once Denikin's forces were disposed of, the Bolshevik armies would crumble, from desertion and mutinies.[2]

According to a Bolshevik officer who fought against Makhno, it was under the impact of repeated Makhno attacks and the hardships of the march that desertions began in the cavalry. Daily the percentage of those who lagged behind or were lost increased. Desertions occurred even among the mounted reconnaissance patrol, usually under the guise of changing a horse in the village. Thus the Makhno partisan movement adversely affected and promoted the demoralization of the cavalry.[3]

The gravity of the problem of desertion from the Red Army to Makhno can be judged from the wording of the military agreement between Makhno and the Bolsheviks on October 15, 1920, against Wrangel. According to the second clause and the "remarks" that followed it:

> While moving through Soviet territory, or across the fronts, the Revolutionary Partisan Army of Ukraine (Makhnovites) would accept into its ranks neither detachments nor deserters from the Red Army. Red Army units and isolated Red soldiers, who have met and joined the Revolutionary Partisan Army behind the Wrangel front, should reenter the ranks of the Red Army when they again make contact with it.[4]

However, events moved too fast for Makhno. On November 23, an order was issued by Frunze at Melitopil':

> With the termination of military action against Wrangel because of his defeat, the Revolutionary Military Soviet of the southern front considers that the task of the Partisan Army is completed and asks the Revolutionary Military Council of the Partisan Army to begin immediately the work of integration of the partisan insurrectionary detachments into regular military units of the Red Army. The existence of the Partisan Army as a separate organization is no longer required by the military circumstances. On the contrary, its existence alongside the Red Army detachments, but with separate organization and purpose, would give rise to a completely inadmissable situation.[5]

Frunze concluded that he would wait till November 26 for the response to his order. This order, however, was not made public till mid-December in the Kharkiv newspaper, *The Communist.*[6]

As soon as Karetnyk took Symferopil' he was ordered to occupy the coast from Saky to Zamruk, south from Evpatoriia, where the Red Army command intended to surround him. On November 26, the plan was ready: one cavalry corps and a division on the north and northeast; one division and three brigades on the west; four brigades on Karetnyk's south; three in the northwestern part of the Crimea—all were to attack and destroy on November 27.[7] However, on the evening of November 26, Karetnyk learned about the plot and promptly advanced to the Symferopil'-Perekop highway, where he soon encountered and defeated the

Seventh Cavalry Division and proceeded toward Dzhuma-Ablam. Although the other divisions pursued him they failed to halt his advance.

On the night of November 27 Karetnyk arrived at Armians'kyi Bazar, where he divided his troops into two groups, sending one across the Syvash Lagoon, and the other to Perekop, which was held by the First Red Sharpshooters Division. The second group learned the enemy password and passed through their lines at night.[8] On the morning of November 28 both groups united at Strohanivka, north of Perekop. In two days Karetnyk had advanced 130 kilometers. On November 30 a cavalry regiment barred his advance, but he passed it by and attacked and captured a regiment at Tymoshivka. However, the other regiments and two brigades of the Fourth Cavalry Division rescued the prisoners and forced Karetnyk to retreat. Meanwhile, large forces had been concentrated in the area of Karetnyk's advance and on December 1 the Red troops attacked Karetnyk near Fedorivka, north of Melitopil', where half of his troops were destroyed. Karetnyk and his staff were captured and executed there. The troop train and all machine guns and rifles were lost. The other half, in loose formations, penetrated the Red lines. Not all, however, managed to get away: some were killed, about 200 were captured, and Marchenko's cavalry detachment escaped with only 250 of 1,500 men.[9]

Simultaneously the Red Army command had decided to destroy Makhno in Huliai-Pole and its environs. This task was assigned to the Melitopil' group that on November 25 completed a double encirclement of Makhno's forces.[10] On November 26, prior to attacking Huliai-Pole, the 126th Brigade, a cavalry regiment, and an armored car unit surrounded Makhno's Third Regiment at Mala Tokmachka, while the Boguchar Brigade seized the Second Regiment at Voskresenka. However, on the evening of November 26–27, a few hours before the Red troops were to attack Huliai-Pole, Makhno learned about the plot and with his bodyguard of about two hundred cavalrymen, attacked the enemy and routed them. From there he moved to Novo-Uspenivka. On his way he encountered a cavalry regiment, which hastily retreated, and an International Cavalry Brigade. He avoided heavy engagement and slipped away at night.

Instead of pursuing Makhno, the brigade proceeded to Huliai-Pole as ordered, but after reaching the town, the commander failed to notify the other units in the vicinity. Consequently on the morning of November 27 a Red unit attacked Huliai-Pole and fighting ensued for the entire day. Meantime the Second Cavalry Corps took up pursuit of

Makhno, forcing him to retreat to Rozivka and the Starodubivka area. During this week of campaigns Makhno not only managed to escape from the enemy's encirclement, but destroyed some Bolshevik units, including a cavalry regiment, and captured two Bolshevik batteries. Moreover, he organized a number of new detachments from independent partisan groups and Red troops who left their units, all of which increased his army to 2,500 including 1,000 cavalry.[11]

After this failure, the Red command decided to surround Makhno with more troops in a larger area between the Dnieper and the Sea of Azov. Moreover, to prevent possible cooperation between the Red troops and the Makhno partisans, they used international units, Russian troops from the trans-Volga region, and Kirghizians.[12] In addition, on December 6, they decided to replace the Melitopil' group with the augmented Fourth Army. This force formed a Melitopil'–Berdians'k–Huliai-Pole western front line. Simultaneously a northern group was established that formed a Pokrovs'ke–Velyka Mykhaihvka–Bahatyr front line. The Second Cavalry Corps operated against Makhno from the east.[13]

As the Red command concentrated its forces against Makhno, his units were in the vicinity of a Greek town, Staryi Kermenchyk, in Mariupil' district. On December 7 Marchenko's cavalry detachment arrived at Kermenchyk. Marchenko reported to Makhno: "I have the honour of announcing the return of the Crimean Army. . . . Yes, brothers . . . now, at last, we know what the Communists are."[14] Some time later Makhno declared in the same vein:

> In this difficult and responsible revolutionary position the Makhno movement made one great mistake: alliance with the Bolsheviks against a common enemy, Wrangel and the Entente. In the period of this alliance that was morally right and of practical value for the revolution, the Makhno movement mistook the Bolshevik revolutionism and failed to secure itself in advance against betrayal. The Bolsheviks and their experts treacherously circumvented it and, although with difficulty, for the time being defeated [us].[15]

Later, Volin, who in the Cheka prison in Moscow told the chief of the operations section of the Cheka that the Bolshevik action against Makhno was treacherous, received this answer:

> Ah, you call it treacherous? That only demonstrates your ineradicable naïvete. As for us Bolsheviks, we see it as a proof that we learned much since the beginning of the Revolution and have now become really skilful statesmen. This time we did not let ourselves be victimized. When we needed Makhno, we took advantage of him, and when we had no further need of his services, and he began to be something of a nuisance, we got rid of him completely.[16]

As the Bolsheviks were closing the circle, Makhno, instead of breaking through the line as the Bolsheviks expected, by a skillful maneuver advanced toward the Sea of Azov. On December 12 Makhno attacked Berdians'k, destroyed its garrison, a cavalry brigade of the Second Don Division, the Cheka, and Communists. Also he captured war material, including three guns.[17] Again the Red Troops surrounded Makhno and scheduled an attack on December 15. However, on the evening of December 14 Makhno advanced north and made a surprise attack on the 126th Brigade in the early morning; after four hours, he defeated it at Andriivka. Simultaneously other Makhno units fought the Kharkiv Brigade of the Elite Troops, units of the 124th Brigade, and the Ninth Cavalry Division. According to Makhno, in the battle at Andriivka he imprisoned the entire Forty-Second Division and half of the Fortieth Division thus capturing over eight thousand prisoners, of whom a large number volunteered to join him. The same night Makhno released his prisoners,[18] divided his troops into small groups, and slipped through the enemy lines. Early the next morning he routed a cavalry regiment and two brigades at Popivka, and several miles away, at Kinski-Rozdory, Makhno captured their supply base.[19]

A Bolshevik author asks:

> How did it happen, how could it happen, when, in order to catch Makhno, an entire army was brought into action? Very simple. At this time our command failed to take into account the speed of Makhno's advance, lost track [of him] for one day, and was very skeptical about the likelihood of Makhno's attack on Berdians'k because it was indeed already enclosed, as if in a sack. However, by his audacity and speed Makhno not only defeated Berdians'k and slipped out of the sack, but also escaped from the circle of our troops before they took up their positions for putting their plan into action.[20]

That night when Makhno left Andriivka, units of the Forty-Second Division and a composite division occupied the town. Later the Second Cavalry Corps attacked the town, creating panic and confusion in both groups. Meanwhile Makhno advanced northwest toward Nikopil', crossing the frozen Dnieper to the Right Bank and bypassing the First Cavalry Army sent from Katerynoslav against him. From there he moved north; having passed Katerynoslav he again crossed the Dnieper and advanced through the Poltava province to Biriuch, Voronezh province. Then he turned west and by way of Kupianka, Lyman, and Bakhmut was by the end of January 1921 back at Huliai-Pole. This long raid was made at such speed that the Red troops pursuing Makhno frequently lost touch with him. Moreover, the presence of other partisan groups on the Left Bank further confused the Bolshevik command

and made the pursuit of Makhno yet more difficult. Thus the Bolsheviks failed to surround and destroy Makhno both at Huliai-Pole and at Staryi Kermenchyk. Later a Bolshevik author regretfully declared that the plan "to finish Makhno at one stroke failed."[21]

After the attack on Huliai-Pole the partisans found undated leaflets on the captured Bolshevik prisoners, issued by the political section of the Fourth Army, entitled *Forward against Makhno!* and *Death to Makhno!* They admitted they had received them on November 15–16. These leaflets accused Makhno of violating the agreement, of having refused to go to the Caucasian front, and of having planned an uprising against the Bolshevik regime. At the same time that Karetnyk was attacked in the Crimea and Makhno at Huliai-Pole, the Bolsheviks, in a concerted series of moves, arrested all the known anarchists in Ukraine under their control. The entire Makhno delegation in Kharkiv was seized and sent to Moscow, where they were executed in 1921. All anarchist organizations and presses were destroyed.[22]

During the 1920–21 winter campaign, to assure a victory over Makhno, the Red Army command employed the device of mass encirclement. This tactic, however, proved ineffective, for they moved aimlessly without close coordination or adequate information, among a hostile population. According to Robert P. Eideman, the commander of the Red troops pursuing Makhno: "The struggle against Makhno at this period was of an extremely unsystematic, almost chaotic, character. Units were advancing, marching as if blind."[23] According to a Bolshevik officer: "After the end of the Crimean campaign our command selected very large forces to destroy Makhno, but the result turned out to be insignificant. Makhno slipped away, kept his army almost intact, made deep raids throughout Ukraine."[24] In contrast to the Red Army, the Makhno troops maneuvered skillfully and swiftly, violently attacking the enemy when and where he was least expected. Eideman admitted:

> After careful study of Makhno's routes of advance, it appeared that his advance was not dominated by such chaotic freedom of action as it seemed to us during the first period of the struggle. The basic advantages of a partisan are his speed of movement combined with a constant change of horses (slogan: each village has a horse depot); familiarity with the countryside and hence advantage in battle; an intelligence system and perfect reconnaisance that was based on the sympathy of the population. [However], all that taken together limits the partisans' freedom of action and binds them to certain areas. [Moreover], Makhno never burdened himself with unnecessary supply trains; the wounded were left to the care of the sympathetic population, and superfluous arms and cartridges were hidden in certain spots and areas.[25]

The support of the population was a significant advantage to

Makhno, for they supplied the partisans with needed material, including horses and food, while the Red troops operated among a foreign and hostile people. Moreover, they not only "met Red Army detachments maliciously, refusing to give anything, [but they also] gave no answers to questions; when there were answers, then [they were] extremely vague and confusing."[26] In contrast to the Bolsheviks, Makhno partisans received detailed, accurate information from the population at all times. A Bolshevik officer complained that Makhno's informers were everywhere and knew about the movement of the Red troops:

All the region of Katerynoslav, Synel'nikove, Hryshyne, Dolia, Volnovakha, Mariupil', Berdians'k, Melitopil' was full of bandit groups of different sizes and different kinds. Spies and informers of the Makhno partisans were in each village, in each grange, roamed all the time and everywhere, appearing as beggars, Red Army men seeking their units, workers from mines exchanging coal for bread, seemingly repentant deserters, or even former Communists, injured women, widows, and orphans looking for "shelter and justice, and others." This is why the staff of Makhno men was always provided with accurate, verified, and timely information.[27]

With great determination Makhno continued to fight the pursuing Red troops. His numerous victories gave him a large supply of arms and ammunition, and his army more than doubled. At the turn of 1920, it consisted of ten to fifteen thousand men.[28] Eideman admitted that:

The problem of this prolonged campaign lies not only in general conditions (political, weakness of the Soviet apparatus in Ukraine, especially the village, and others), but in the army itself, and above all, in its lack of knowledge in fighting an adversary who was using partisan tactics. . . . brought to perfection by Makhno. All of these were new to most of the commanders; it required experience on the battlefield itself, and sometimes there was a high cost for the lesson.[29]

The growing strength of the Makhno army and its successes caused serious concern in the Bolshevik regime, so it was decided to increase the number of troops opposing Makhno. Before long he was being opposed by several divisions of infantry and cavalry, but by skillful maneuvers he succeeded in breaking through the enemy lines and attacking their rear. Still, the situation was growing worse as the number of Red troops was increasing. Makhno learned from captured Red officers that the command was planning to surround his army with four army corps, two cavalry, and two mixed, and that several divisions were coming soon. Similar information was supplied by peasants, and it also agreed with Makhno's own observations and conclusions.[30]

In view of the enormous mass of Red troops assembled in the

region, it became apparent that the defeat of two or three Red divisions was of no importance. Makhno's previous illusions that by winning some victories he would force the Red troops to retreat from his region soon evaporated. The question was no longer one of achieving victory over the Red troops, but of escaping complete annihilation. In addition, the Bolshevik command began to study the areas where people were sympathetic to Makhno, his supply centers, and his moves. Gradually it began to understand that their tactics of fighting Makhno were wrong because, as one Bolshevik officer pointed out,

> this "small war" requires different organization, different training of troops, from the war against Wrangel or, let us say, against the White Poles. Our units maintained a cumbersome, burdensome rear; hence, we acted slowly, heavily, while Makhno, on the other hand, [used] speed and bold maneuver. We have not considered the environment that nourishes the criminal bands. They have their bases, that is, certain segments of the population, a flexible structure, stand behind them.[31]

Consequently the Red command worked out new plans to fight Makhno by stationing whole regiments, primarily cavalry, in the occupied villages to terrorize the peasants and prevent them from supporting Makhno. The movement of multitudes of Red Army troops through the countryside created difficulties and did great damage to the population. Also the Cheka punitive units were constantly trailing the partisans, executing Makhno's sympathizers and the partisans' families.[32] According to Eideman:

> Our punitive policy directed against the bandits among the "kulaks" and the "atamans" themselves, assisted by a general amnesty for common criminals, brought about a decay in Makhno's band [and] undermined the confidence of his own subjects.[33]

To pursue Makhno more effectively, the Red Command improved the communication system and established an intelligence service to watch and inform Red units and local authorities about his movements.

In view of the Bolsheviks' enormous numerical superiority the Revolutionary Military Council agreed there was no prospect of holding the southern region. Consequently Makhno began to expand his territory of movement, covering all Ukraine, and even beyond its borders to the Don, Volga, Kuban, and Kursk-Saratov regions. As a result, the Bolsheviks began to apply new tactics in fighting Makhno, and Frunze was placed in charge of Eideman's operations. The strategy was

> a continuous pursuit of Makhno without respite. Formation of flexible, specially designed mobile units, and armored car detachments. Denial of partisan access to the areas sympathetic to them. Broad propaganda work among the population to

explain the measures taken by the Bolshevik authorities in the village to win all the layers of poor and middle peasants to their side.[34]

Makhno was contantly surrounded by a network of Red troops and pursued by small detachments, especially by cavalry and armored car units.[35] All his movements either along or across railroad lines were watched and harassed by armored trains. Moreover, the partisans were barred from the main roads and they had to move across the fields and roadless steppes. During the winter and most of the spring such routes were covered with snow, ice, and mud. Although Makhno was thus able to avoid encounters with large Red units, the conditions necessitated abandoning all his artillery and certain supplies.[36] Makhno had to divide his army into small detachments to facilitate crossing enemy lines, after which they would reassemble in an agreed place. During these movements the partisans destroyed railroad lines, blew up trains and bridges, and seized military supply stores. In spite of the difficult conditions Makhno was able to attract some Red Army soldiers and even whole units to his side. When the partisans were fighting Budenny's Fourth Cavalry Division, their First Brigade, commanded by Maslak, joined Makhno.[37]

In early spring the partisans were chased back and forth across southern Ukraine. In mid-March a Makhno detachment of 1,500 cavalry and two regiments of infantry was attacked by large Red units, but Makhno counterattacked, capturing many prisoners and war material. Two days later, however, he was attacked again by fresh Bolshevik troops. During a counterattack Makhno was badly wounded and the partisans, assuming he was killed, lost spirit and retreated. He lost much blood and was unconscious for one day, subsequently retiring with a small unit to safety, but on March 16, the Ninth Cavalry Division came upon the unit and pursued it for thirteen hours over 180 versts. Although the next day Makhno eluded his pursuers, changing horses at Slobidka, on the shore of the Azov Sea, soon he was attacked again. Near Starodubky, in the Mariupil' district, the unit undertook delaying action against the Red troops with heavy machine-gun fire.[38]

According to Makhno:

Five of my machine-gun men surrounded me, bidding me farewell and saying: "Bat'ko, you are needed by our peasant organization. This cause is dear to us. We will die now, but by our death we will save you and all who are faithful to you and guard you; do not forget to convey this to our parents." Someone kissed me, and then I saw none of them around me. . . . I heard only the rattle of machine guns and the detonation of grenades; these were the machine-gun men blocking the way of the Bolsheviks.[39]

Although the entire force died, Makhno escaped in a peasant cart. After his recovery Makhno assembled about two thousand men, mostly cavalrymen, in Kobeliaky district, Poltava province, and advanced against the Bolshevik headquarters at Kharkiv. His troops, however, encountered several divisions of cavalry and infantry and over sixty armored cars. During the ensuing weeks of combat in the area, Makhno's troops suffered many losses, including a few commanders.[40] Makhno retreated to the south and ran into Budenny, whose Nineteenth Cavalry Division was advancing from Katerynoslav province toward the Don on May 18 to put down a peasant uprising. Budenny had ordered his sixteen armored cars to advance along the main road toward Novohryhoriivka while he and part of the division moved across the fields. Budenny arrived before the cars, was overtaken by Makhno, and the following battle became a nightmare. Budenny's unit consisted of Russians, including Siberians, who came to Ukraine unfamiliar with the situation and the Makhno movement. They had been assured the Makhno partisans were common bandits and it was a point of honor not to retreat before bandits. Subsequently many of Budenny's soldiers deserted and victorious Makhno formed a combat unit from the Siberians, under the command of Glazunov, that was sent to Siberia to fight the Bolsheviks.[41]

On another occasion Budënny's unit ran into a small detachment of Makhno men. An eyewitness described the reaction of the Makhno men:

> They had evidently not seen us and were taken by surprise. . . . We prepared to pursue them—we were sure they'd turn and flee—we outnumbered them five to one. Well, before we knew it, they had galloped straight into us, slashing right and left with their sabres and shouting "Liberty or death." Their attack was so unexpected, so incredibly reckless, that our men became panicky. We fled.[42]

The unequal fighting continued during the summer. The Bolsheviks began to use smaller, more flexible Red units and armored cars in fighting Makhno.[43] Meanwhile, through combat losses, hardship, and sickness, the number of Makhno partisans was diminishing and they were cut off from their main sources of recruits and supplies. The Ukrainian peasants were tired of the endless terror caused by the successive occupation of village after village by the Red troops and the Cheka. The continuous fighting and requisitions were leaving the peasants with little food and horses for the partisans. They could not live in a state of permanent revolution. Moreover, there was extreme drought and consequently a bad harvest in Ukraine, especially in the region of the

Makhno movement. Some moved to the region of Kuban, Tsaritsyn, and Saratov; others toward Kyiv and Chernihiv; while Makhno moved to the Volga and back across the Don.[44] Finally, the impact of economic and other conditions in Russia and the occupied lands, and the Kronstadt uprising at the beginning of March, forced Lenin to find a way out of the chaotic situation that War Communism brought about. Consequently, on March 8, a compromise economic system, the New Economic Policy (NEP) was inaugurated that annulled the hated requisitions. This measure reconciled or pacified some of the revolution-weary peasants.

In the light of these conditions and of the severity of Makhno's wounds, it was decided that Makhno would go abroad for medical treatment. On August 13, Makhno, accompanied by a cavalry unit consisting of one hundred men and several commanders including Kozhyn, Petrenko, and Zabud'ko, who also were wounded, set out west toward the Dnieper. Three days later they crossed the Dnieper between Kremenchuk and Orlyk.[45] When Makhno turned westward, Vasilii K. Bliukher, who arrived in the Makhno region in the summer of 1921 to study his campaign movements,[46] learned about the direction of Makhno's movement from the peasants. He concluded that Makhno was moving toward Bessarabia and wired Frunze in Kharkiv about his assumption concerning Makhno's plan. Bliukher's aide expressed his optimism: "Now Makhno will not escape from Ukraine; he will not be allowed to slip through into Bessarabia."[47]

On August 19, Makhno came upon the Seventh Cavalry Division camping along the Inhulets River, about 12 versts from Bobrynets. Since he was seen by Red troops, Makhno felt there was no retreat; he attacked the division's machine-gun unit stationed in a nearby village, overwhelming it and capturing sixteen machine guns. Later Makhno attacked the other troops, including the Thirty-Eighth Regiment, cut a passage through and rode 110 versts, pursued by the enemy without respite. In the course of the struggle Makhno lost seventeen brave friends and on August 22 was again severely wounded. Four days later the unit was again attacked and two commanders, Petrenko and Ivaniuk, were killed. Subsequently Makhno changed the course of the advance and on August 28 he and his remaining eighty-three followers crossed the Dniester, near IAmpil into Romania.[48]

21. Epilogue

The Romanian authorities put Makhno, his wife, and his followers into an internment camp in a medieval citadel in Braşov, Transylvania, which had been converted into a military prison.[1] The Bolshevik government sent a series of sharp diplomatic notes demanding Makhno's extradition, which were rejected by the Romanian government,[2] who, nevertheless, to avoid a possible conflict with Soviet Russia, encouraged Makhno to leave the country. After seven and one-half months in Romania, Makhno and his followers crossed the Polish border on April 11, 1922, and gave themselves up to the Polish police.[3] They were interned in a camp at Strzałków, with the troops of the Ukrainian People's Republic.[4]

Polish authorities also considered Makhno's presence in Poland undesirable. Moreover, Moscow demanded his extradition on the ground that he was a criminal and not entitled to political asylum.[5] Although the Polish government rejected this demand, it accused Makhno of organizing an insurrection in East Galicia with the intention of incorporating it into the Ukrainian Soviet Socialist Republic. This alleged organization of an uprising was a provocation of the Polish political police, who were in contact with the Bolshevik mission in Warsaw. Consequently at the end of October 1922, Makhno was arrested and put in the Mokotow prison in Warsaw.[6] He was suffering from tuberculosis and in prison his health deteriorated. When a visitor to the prison offered him a cigarette,

> . . . Makhno inhaled smoke into his lungs again and a strong cough overwhelmed him. Uttering the words with difficulty and coughing, he went on: "I acquired lung

illness at the time of my imprisonment at the Butyrki prison. It seemed that with years, it had passed; however, it is not so. Now the illness is appearing again.[7]

With a certain pride Makhno told the visitor that his wife was with him and that she had given birth to a daughter called Liusia. Although Makhno was brought to trial, he was subsequently acquitted and, on November 27, 1923, after thirteen months in prison, was released. He remained in Poland under police surveillance until late fall of 1924, when he left for Danzig, where he was arrested again.[8] However, because he was suffering from tuberculosis, he was brought to the Danzig city hospital by police who regularly checked transients for communicable diseases. The anarchists in Danzig eventually helped him to escape from the hospital, and for forty days he hid in the city. The anarchists tried to smuggle him to Stettin by ship, but when they failed, Makhno and two others crossed the Polish Corridor to Germany in March 1925. From there he went to Paris, where he had decided to settle. Later he wrote: "[Now] I am in Paris, among foreigners, and among political enemies whom [I had] so much to fight."[9]

For many reasons Makhno's life in Paris was most difficult, and he was unable to improve his material conditions or rise above his psychological misery. He was suffering from consumption and wounds that failed to heal.[10] He never succeeded in learning sufficient French and was not able to adapt himself to the environment that was so different from what he was accustomed to in Ukraine. According to Berkman:

I was shocked at his appearance. The storm and stress of his year-long struggle, physical and mental suffering, had reduced the strong, stockily built *povstantsy* leader to a mere shadow. His face and body were scarred by wounds, his shattered foot made him permanently lame. Yet his spirit remained unbroken and he still dreamed of returning to his native land and taking up again the struggle for liberty and social justice. Life in exile was insupportable to him; he felt torn out by the very roots and he yearned for his beloved Ukraina.[11]

Although occasionally he got work at a plant or in a factory, his illness and inadequate knowledge of French prevented him from holding work for long. French, Spanish, and American anarchists collected money to provide Makhno with a modest income for his life. Makhno's wife and daughter opened a small grocery store in Vincennes, Seine, 18, rue de la Jarry; Makhno, however, lived a largely separate life.[12]

Makhno devoted some of his time to writing and publishing a number of articles in different anarchist periodicals and newspapers and, although he apparently intended to write the history of his struggle, he failed to do so.[13] He managed, however, to write incomplete memoirs dealing with the Ukrainian Revolution. Three volumes appeared, the first in Russian and French, while the author was still alive; the second and third in Russian only, posthumously.

Makhno, physically and psychologically tormented, was further distressed by bitter feuds among the anarchist leaders in Paris. Disagreements developed and divided Arshinov from Alexander Berkman, Emma Goldman, and Volin. Initially Makhno aligned himself with Arshinov; however, when Arshinov advocated an anarchist policy of recognizing the Stalin regime in 1931, he withdrew his support and generally remained aloof from the anarchist leaders' feud.[14]

During his last years Makhno grew weary of life and nostalgia for Ukraine filled his thoughts. His health declined steadily and he spent the last months of his life in Tenon Hospital in Paris. On July 27, 1934, Makhno died, and the next day he was cremated. About four hundred French, Russian, Spanish, Italian, and Jewish anarchists, including only two Ukrainians, his widow and his daughter, paid last tribute to Makhno.[15] Many speakers, including the French anarchist Bonar, and Volin, glorified Makhno as a fighter for liberty. The urn containing Makhno's ashes was placed in Père-Lachaise cemetery.[16] Later it was moved several times and vault 6706 was finally purchased at Père-Lachaise by anarchists from New York as a permanent resting place.[17]

Conclusion

The developments in Ukraine during the Revolution were to a great extent the result of the Ukrainian political, cultural, and socioeconomic heritage. Through the destruction of the Zaporozhian Sich and the autonomous hetman state, Ukraine was deprived of its defensive force and of its political and cultural institutions. Large estates were carved out of the lands of the Zaporozhian Cossacks, mainly as grants to court favorites and later for the foreign elements that were settled there. The Cossack officers in the former hetman state were tied to the interests of the Russian Empire as a result of receiving the privileges of the Russian nobility, whereas the peasantry was reduced to serfdom, widening social differences between the classes and weakening the unity of the Ukrainian people.

The submission of the metropolitan of Kyiv to the jurisdiction of the patriarch of Moscow dealt a severe blow to the Ukrainian Orthodox church. In addition, the Ukrainian schools, because their curricula were subjected to hostile Russian censorship, were forced to become instruments for denationalization. The institutions of higher learning and secondary schools, which were founded by the church and were open to all classes, gradually decayed when the Russians seized church properties.

The combination of resentment at the oppressive measures against Ukrainian national life, the influx of new ideas from the French Revolution, the Napoleonic wars, and the Polish uprising in 1830–31, stimulated the national revival. The Crimean War and Russia's defeat brought about far-reaching reforms. Ukrainian scholars and littérateurs strove for a cultural revival by collecting various documents and studying national history, folklore, and language. Educational and cultural activities were launched among the emancipated peasants to improve their difficult economic condition and to increase their national consciousness. Similarly, in the cities, societies were organized to foster national consciousness among the population. The Russian government, seeing a threat to the unity of the empire in these activities, initiated a period of systematic persecution of the national movement that lasted, except for brief interludes, until 1917.

At the turn of the century, awareness of national identity increased, stimulated by the revolutionary activities in Russia, the growth of industrialization, and the construction of railroads. However, industrial expansion also altered the composition and distribution of the population. The Russian and other non-Ukrainian population increased substantially, the new socioeconomic structure strengthened ties with Russian interests and, to some extent, handicapped the national movement. Its full impact, however, was not evident until the Revolution in 1917. Although the Revolution of 1905 and the October Manifesto awakened great expectations among national leaders, their hopes soon vanished when the brief respite of the Revolution regressed to an even more oppressive policy. The outbreak of the First World War only intensified coercive measures against Ukrainian national life.

At the time that the Russian Revolution broke out in 1917, the establishment and maintenance of the Ukrainian state was proving difficult. The struggle for national revival prior to the Revolution was confined primarily to the cultural sphere and offered its devotees little practical administrative and political experience. Although initially the national-political aspirations of the Ukrainian people were unequivocally manifested in the creation of the Central Rada, which ultimately directed its efforts toward attaining the complete independence of Ukraine, the Rada was unable to translate them into a concrete program of administrative, social, and military reform. The interference of the Russian Provisional Government in Ukrainian affairs, the presence of Russian armies in Ukraine fighting on the Austro-German fronts, and the Rada's inability to train and establish a strong administrative apparatus prevented it from firmly establishing its power. Because of its broad interpretation of democracy, the Rada did little to stop the activities of hostile elements against Ukrainian statehood. Nor did it build a military force that could lend muscle to the national struggle, thinking in terms of a militia rather than a standing army. Moreover, the Ukrainian educated class was divided over the conflicting currents of national independence and socialist internationalism. Thus the national leaders failed to unite the nation under one leadership or to organize one front to defend the state.

Although the patriotic slogans employed by the Rada were appealing to the middle class and to educated peasants and workers, many of the peasants were captivated by the Bolshevik promise of land. The outlook of the Rada was constantly lagging behind the rapid advance of the Revolution, particularly with regard to the agrarian question, for the leaders of the Rada were not yet prepared to face the peasant problem.

The cumulative weight of the internal obstacles to national unity was very serious, and the newly established state was immediately challenged by the Bolshevik invasion. The Austro-German troops invited to help repel the invaders overthrew the Rada, which was supplanted by the hetman government.

From the outset the hetman worked under difficult conditions, being hemmed in between conflicting foreign and national interests. The presence of Austro-German troops limited his sovereignty and at the same time the reactionary members of his cabinet and administration, consisting to a great extent of Russians or Russified elements, tolerated the hetman state only so long as international politics made it necessary. Furthermore, they made efforts to discredit the hetman government and Ukrainian statehood in the eyes of the populace. In contradistinction to German and Russian goals, the Ukrainians hoped the hetman would maintain order, preserve their freedom, and provide security from Austro-German interference and the Bolshevik threat.

Although the hetman intended to give his government a national character and to pursue an independent national policy, he had only partial success. The reactionary nature of the regime's new policies turned the progressive majority, and hence the whole population, against the hetman. Moreover, favoritism toward the upper class, especially the landlords, who collaborated with the Austrian and German troops to organize punitive expeditions against the peasants, made the situation worse. There was passive resistance at first, and subsequently a self-defense force, the partisan movement. After the defeat of the Germans by the Western powers in 1918, the hetman regime was overthrown by the troops of the Directory.

The Directory had to face even more serious domestic and foreign problems than its predecessor. The consolidation of power started by the Rada had been interrupted by the Austro-German and Russian interference. Some of the administrative personnel of the hetman period left the country or went into hiding, leaving the Directory with still fewer trained personnel. Moreover, leaders in distant provinces seeking to establish contact with the Directory were cut off from the center by the lack of communications and by enemy invasions, and the Directory was unable to establish its power in the country. Some of the distant provinces were controlled by various partisan leaders, who worked with the Directory; other partisan leaders were unwilling to subordinate themselves to the Directory, and some even followed independent courses of opposition. The constant change of authority and the interminable warring created apathy among the population. The peasants, in particular, had considered the Austro-German troops and the landlord-police punitive detachments their enemies, and they fought them desperately. When those enemies were gone and the Russian Communists were not yet a threat, most of the partisans who fought under the banner of the Directory left the army, feeling that their war was over.

The country was threatened from all sides. The most serious threat came from the new Soviet Russian invasion and the French intervention assisted by the Denikin troops. One view expressed in the Directory favored an understanding with the Bolsheviks against the French; the opposite, common action with the French against the Bolsheviks. When the latter view prevailed, the Social Democrats and Socialist Revolutionaries withdrew from the Directory, which then sought the active support of the Entente against the Bolshevik invasion. The Entente, however, adhered to the policy of a "united and indivisible Russia." As a result of negotiations with representatives of the Entente, the Directory undermined its own unity and aroused opposition from Ukrainian parties of both the Right and the Left. It also gave the Bolsheviks material for propaganda, for they accused the Directory of inviting a new foreign invasion, and rekindled the fear that Denikin, now associated with the Entente, would restore the rule of the landlords.

The Directory was further weakened when the two main partisan leaders, Hryhor'iv and Makhno, whose objectives appeared to have greater appeal than those of the Directory, joined the Red Army instead of the Directory in its fight against the invaders. Thus the Directory struggled against overwhelming odds, without adequate arms, military equipment, or medical supplies, and with, in the midst of all this, a devastating typhus epidemic. Consequently the superior invasion forces of the Bolsheviks and Denikin compelled the exhausted Ukrainian Army to retreat to the western limits of Right Bank Ukraine and seek the support of the Entente through alliance with Poland.

Meanwhile, the Directory reorganized its forces for guerrilla warfare. Although allied with the Poles, at the sacrifice of Ukrainian territory, and together with them fighting the Bolsheviks, the Directory failed to gain the support of the Entente, and the Polish government, ignoring the Directory, made its own separate peace settlement with the Bolsheviks in the autumn of 1920.

The Ukrainian governments were not able to establish firm authority in the country and to defend it, not only because they and the people were ill-prepared for statehood, but also because Ukraine was an object of foreign invasions, a battleground of the Russian Civil War, and a highway for invading forces. The Russian anti-Bolshevik movement, which was organized outside Russia proper, seriously affected the Ukrainian Revolution, for although Denikin's primary aim was to overthrow the Bolshevik regime in Russia, he first fought to destroy Ukrainian statehood.

As a result of the terror and exploitation of the invasions and the residue of military experience and arms brought from the war, a partisan movement came into existence, particularly in Left Bank Ukraine. These partisans were isolated from one another and were never organized into a single nationwide force. Moreover, some of the partisan troops failed to coordinate their actions with the Ukrainian regular army. The strongest partisan force that led its warfare independently from other partisan groups and the Ukrainian army was that of Nestor Makhno.

Makhno was a product of an environment that had nearly lost its national identity. The absence of Ukrainian schools and cultural and political organizations, as a result of Russian policy, left people, especially the younger generation, without strong national leadership. Political terror perpetrated by the regime, especially during the Revolution of 1905, led Makhno, like other young men, to radical, nonnationalist organizations and to terrorist actions, resulting in imprisonment. Although during his years of imprisonment in Russia Makhno matured intellectually by reading, conversation, and introspection, the environment distracted him from Ukrainian national life and problems. Moreover, the experience in prison increased Makhno's bitterness against prisons and governmental authority. In prison Makhno solidified his anarchist ideology and developed a sense of sociopolitical mission that he manifested later in his activities.

Makhno was freed after the February Revolution and he arrived in his native town as a political hero, subsequently playing a leading role in shaping the sociopolicial life of his town and gradually of the region. He initiated the peasants' movement, confiscating and distributing landlords' land and goods, and encouraging the workers to take over factories and workshops, at first "legally" and later by force. Undoubtedly the terrorist actions were the continuation of Makhno's prearrest period but on a larger scale. To carry on his actions more effectively, Makhno organized armed detachments, making raids upon landlords' estates, depots, freight and passenger trains, expropriating goods and terrorizing the owners. Attempts of the local authorities and patriotic Ukrainians to prevent Makhno from destructive involvement failed, while he was hardly aware that he spread destruction; he believed he was building a new and better world.

The vicissitudes of the Revolution, the Bolshevik invasion, and the arrival of the Austro-German troops halted Makhno's terrorist activities. The overthrow of the Central Rada and the establishment of the hetman regime, however, created conditions that brought Makhno back into action, in what became known as the Makhno movement. The hetman's policies created adverse conditions that were particularly manifested in the Austro-German and landlords' punitive expeditions against the countryside. Such policies brought about spontaneous peasant uprisings that played into Makhno's hands, giving him a cause and new strength.

During this period of his activities, Makhno was no longer a terrorist, but rather a popular leader fighting the enemies of the people, defending their properties and freedom. With the development of the Revolution, Makhno became more conscious of his movement's role and task. New obstacles spurred him to greater efforts in which he displayed unusual cunning, initiative, bravery, will power, and great resourcefulness. Makhno learned to make quick decisions in critical situations. In time, the confidence the partisans had in him bound the movement together and his terrorism and dictatorial inclination were substantially checked by the increasingly constructive and patriotic attitudes of the army, the population upon which Makhno heavily depended, and the cause for which he was fighting.

Makhno was keenly aware of the importance of an effective military force to defend the achievements of the Revolution. In contrast to other partisan leaders and some national leaders, Makhno devoted his ability, energy, and time to this goal and managed not only to unify all the partisan groups in southeastern Ukraine, but to organize and discipline them into a most effective partisan army. Moreover, together with his associates, Makhno invented new tactics for the conditions he faced: swift and maneuverable light carts armed with machine guns, clever ruses in military operations, disguises, and infiltration in enemy ranks—all of which brought terror to the hearts of his adversaries. The population not only supported the partisans, giving them lodging, food, and horses, but also put pursuing enemy troops on a false trail, while the partisans remained in the village, or went in the opposite direction.

As an anarchist Makhno strongly opposed not only the landlords and factory owners, but all governments, native or foreign, because he felt that all forms of government represented the violence of a minority over the majority. Makhno was the veritable incarnation of the peasants' social revolutionary spirit. He fought in the name of what he, and the peasants supporting him, believed was freedom. The peasants should look after the land, the workers after the factories, and if there were any problems they should get together and decide what should be done. Such ideas were appealing to the peasants and made Makhno popular.

In contrast to his unique military ability and success in the field, Makhno lacked the broader worldly orientation he needed to understand political problems and to make correct decisions. In that respect he was not equal to the task brought on him by revolutionary conditions, and his actions were unequal to the gravity of the situation. If two enemies threatened his movement, Makhno would join forces with the less dangerous against the more dangerous in order to prevent strengthening both of them. Although Makhno collaborated with the Bolsheviks, he was critical and suspicious of them from the beginning. His distrust, however, was based not upon knowledge of the Bolsheviks' character, but upon his experience with them; therefore, each time he failed to take the necessary steps to secure the movement against Bolshevik betrayal. Had Makhno possessed more political sophistication, he would have placed less trust in Bolshevik promises and used his numerous victories to secure his movement against the enemy. During the earlier stage of the Revolution, Makhno assumed that the conflict with the Bolsheviks could be limited to the realm of ideas; he thought that the radical revolutionary attitude of the peasants and their resentment of the foreign invaders were the best guarantees for the territory of his movement. Moreover, Makhno naïvely believed that the outstanding contributions of the partisans in defeating both Denikin and Wrangel would protect his movement against Bolshevik provocations, assuming that in case of conflict the Red troops would make common cause with the partisans over the heads of their leaders when they met face to face.

The movement over-all lacked educated partisans to give it political leadership. They depended heavily upon Makhno's judgment. When they were asked: "Why do you fight?" their usual reply was: "Ask Makhno; it is his problem." Paradoxically, although Makhno's struggle against the Bolsheviks may well have prolonged the Russian Civil War, by his vital role in the defeat of the forces of Denikin and Wrangel he contributed to the triumph of bolshevism.

Although Makhno was strongly aware of the social nature of the Revolution whose instrument he was, he failed to comprehend its national aspect because of his inadequate national consciousness. Makhno, like his movement, was the outgrowth of the deplorable state of national conditions that denied him the opportunity to develop according to his ability. Nevertheless, he did retain a strong sense of nationality as a Ukrainian and not as a Russian. As for his own movement, it reflected the state of the ideas at that time of national self-determination that he himself described as "not adequately developed. Among the Ukrainian people there appeared a number of different political groups, each of which interpreted the idea of self-determination in its own way, according to their own party's interests."

This state of affairs, in both its positive and negative aspects, was strongly reflected in Makhno's activities. In most cases Makhno did not fight the Ukrainian Army because he and they had a self-imposed unwritten agreement of neutrality. But he stubbornly fought the enemies of Ukraine, the Austro-German punitive expeditions, and the Bolshevik and anti-Bolshevik Russian forces, either simultaneously or by joining one against the other. Although Makhno was not a Ukrainian nationalist, he was also not a traitor to his country because he never joined the enemy with the aim of assisting them to occupy Ukraine. Thus, while fighting the enemies of Ukraine, Makhno was indirectly an ally of the Ukrainian armed forces and it was not his fault that the Directory failed to take advantage of Denikin's defeat in Ukraine and Makhno's effective struggle against the Red troops.

Makhno's primary failure was his unwillingness to coordinate his activities with other partisan groups and the Ukrainian armed forces in fighting common enemies during a critical period of Ukrainian history. Moreover, Makhno had no positive goal either as a Ukrainian or as an anarchist. Although he led the strongest partisan movement, he was isolated from the national forces that strove to maintain the independence of Ukraine. In addition, Makhno had not worked out a plan for—and under the circumstances it would not have been possible to establish—a stateless society in the region of the movement. Although the Makhno partisan army fought very bravely, shed a great deal of blood, including Ukrainian, and destroyed material goods, it ended in ruin. Makhno was never defeated during three years of uninterrupted campaigns. His army was overwhelmed by the superior power of the Bolshevik armies and overcome by the exhaustion and war weariness of the population. To change the course of events of the Revolution would have required a much greater effort by the people and its leaders. Only the united effort of all national forces under unified leadership and with a single goal could have established and maintained an independent Ukrainian state. Thus the Makhno movement was not a constructive factor in the Ukrainian National Revolution; important as its role was in the final outcome, it reflected all too well the lack of unity, the disparate aims within Ukrainian national development.

Appendix

LEADERS OF THE MAKHNO ARMY

Most of Makhno's associates were selected carefully from among his friends at Huliai-Pole; however, as the movement widened, a number of able partisans from other places joined the leadership. Almost to a man, they were of poor peasant origin, with little formal education. Most of them, however, had good military training. According to a Bolshevik author, Makhno's commanders "completed the school of the [First World] War, acquiring combat experiences. Some of them served in the tsarist army and were promoted to the rank of noncommmissioned officers, sergeant majors and ensigns."[1] Ideologically, they were largely either Anarchists or Socialist-Revolutionaries. Besides Makhno, the most prominent leader of the partisan army was Fedir Shchus', a former sailor on the tsarist mine layer *Ioann Zlatoust* and the son of a respectable peasant of Divrivka (Velyka Mykhailivka). He started his partisan career as an associate of the partisan leader Nykyfor Brova, a former sailor who was killed in the second half of July 1918. Shchus' took his place as a commander of Brova's partisan group. In September, he joined Makhno and became his close associate. Although he occupied various positions in the army, including chief of staff, he was famous as commander of the Makhno cavalry that was composed of peasant Cossacks who spent their lives on horseback.[2] This was the best cavalry in the field during the Revolution, unmatched by either the Bolsheviks or Denikin. For example, at the end of July 1919, at the town of Hlodosy, Kherson province, a cavalry force of 100 men under Shchus' routed an elite Bolshevik cavalry four times its size.[3] In June 1921, Shchus' was killed in a battle against the Bolsheviks in Poltava province.[4]

Another of Makhno's closest and ablest associates was Semen Karetnyk, a peasant from Huliai-Pole who had attended school for only one year before joining the Anarchists in 1907. In 1918 he was co-founder of the partisan army and from that time on he remained in the movement in various capacities including membership on the Revolutionary Military Council and, occasionally, commander of the army. His main job, however, was to command an infantry brigade. Karetnyk was wounded several times during his campaigns. After Makhno made an agreement with the Bolsheviks against Wrangel, Karetnyk was appointed commander and was instrumental in attacking Wrangel across the frozen Syvash Lagoon and in storming Symferopil'. However, on November 26, immediately after Wrangel was defeated, Frunze ordered the Red troops to attack Karetnyk forces. While he was struggling back to his region, Karetnyk and his staff were killed by the Bolsheviks.[5] Only the cavalry unit commanded by Marchenko, who had learned the Red troops' password, escaped.

Marchenko himself, a peasant from Huliai-Pole, was a prominent associate of Makhno. He received elementary education in his home town and in 1907 joined the Anarchist group. He helped to found the partisan army, in which he served at different times, as a member of the Revolutionary Military Council and commander of a cavalry regiment. He was wounded in battle several times and was once a prisoner of Denikin. Marchenko managed to escape from the trap in which Karetnyk was killed, though only 250 of his 1,500 men survived. In January 1921, in a battle against the Bolsheviks in Poltava province, he too was killed.[6]

Borys Veretelnyk, like most of the partisan leaders, was a poor peasant from Huliai-Pole. He worked in a local factory and later went to Petrograd to the Putilov factory. Following the outbreak of the Revolution he became actively involved in it, revealing organizational and oratorical abilities. In mid-February 1918 he returned to Huliai-Pole via Odessa, where he became preoccupied with revolutionary propaganda. In contrast to other leaders, he was a Socialist Revolutionary and joined the Anarchist group, as well as the partisan army, only after he returned to Huliai-Pole. In the army he rose to the position of chief of staff. In early June 1919, while leading a hastily organized detachment in a battle to defend Huliai-Pole against superior Denikin forces, Veretelnyk was surrounded and perished with his detachment near the village of Sviatodukhivka.[7]

Petro Havrylenko, a peasant from Huliai-Pole, and an Anarchist since the 1905 Revolution, was a member of the Makhno staff and commander of the Third Brigade. He played a major role in defeating

Denikin at Perehonivka in September 1919. During most of 1920 he was in the Bolshevik prison in Kharkiv. After Makhno agreed with the Bolsheviks in mid-October to fight Wrangel, Havrylenko was released and appointed chief of staff of the Crimean Army. Following Wrangel's defeat, Havrylenko and his entire staff were executed by the Bolsheviks.[8]

Among the other cofounders of the army were Hryhorii Vasylivs'kyi, Vasyl Danyliv, and Izydor Liutyi. Vasylivs'kyi, a peasant from Huliai-Pole, was a family man who had received an elementary education and joined the Anarchist group before 1917. He was a member of Makhno's staff and occasionally substituted for him as commander of the army. In December 1920 he was killed fighting the Bolsheviks in Kyiv province. Danyliv, a poor peasant blacksmith from Huliai-Pole, served in the artillery during the war and commanded a partisan artillery detachment.[9] Liutyi, a peasant and house painter from Huliai-Pole, who was also a close friend of Makhno, had obtained an elementary education and was an Anarchist. In September 1919, he was killed in the battle against Denikin at Perehonivka.[10]

Also among Makhno's associates were two brothers, Oleksander and Ivan Lepetchenko, peasant Anarchists from Huliai-Pole. They commanded their own partisan detachment against the Austro-German troops and later joined Makhno. In the spring of 1920 Oleksander was seized by the Bolsheviks at Huliai-Pole and, after he refused to join them, he was shot. His brother Ivan, according to a Soviet source, gave himself up to the Bolsheviks in the fall of 1921.[11]

In the ranks of the partisan army were Makhno's two older brothers, Sava and Hryhorii. The former, the oldest, was active in the movement against the Austro-German troops and Denikin, but did not fight the Bolsheviks, preferring to stay home with his large family. Nevertheless, at the end of February 1920, the Bolsheviks captured and executed him. Hryhorii was a large, strongly built, and good-hearted man. He was active in the movement from the very beginning and he served as an associate of the chief of staff. He was killed in September 1919 in the battle against Denikin at Perehonivka.[12]

Viktor Bilash was a railroad engineer from Novospasivka and joined Makhno at the beginning of 1919, serving as commander of the Second Brigade, a member of the staff, and chief of staff. He was Makhno's best strategist. Because of his partisan activities, Austrian troops destroyed his homestead and executed his grandfather, father, and cousin. In 1921 Bilash was seized by the Bolsheviks and put in prison where he wrote his memoirs about the Makhno movement.[13]

Similarly educated, and also from Novospasivka, was the peasant, Vasyl Kurylenko. Kurylenko had been an Anarchist since 1910 and a popular militant propagandist, as well as an able commander of a cavalry regiment, a member of the Revolutionary Military Council, and occasionally Makhno's diplomatic representative. Kurylenko was wounded five times and, on July 8, 1921, he was killed by the Bolsheviks near the village Mariivka.[14]

One of the most dynamic and popular partisan leaders was Vdovychenko, a Novospasivka peasant with an elementary school education. After joining Makhno, he became an infantry brigade commander and played an important role in the defeat of Denikin at Perehonivka. In March 1921 he was wounded and captured by the Bolsheviks, who tried to recruit him to their ranks. He refused and later, when he failed in an attempt to take his own life, he was executed.[15]

One of Makhno's earliest associates was Oleksander Chubenko, a railroad engineer and Socialist Revolutionary. He joined Makhno's movement from the outset, occupying different positions, including that of Makhno's aide and diplomatic representative. At the beginning of 1920 he was seized and imprisoned by the Bolsheviks. He was among those released after Makhno's agreement with the Bolsheviks to fight against Wrangel, and was appointed commander of a special commando demolition unit.[16]

Still another prominent partisan leader, Khoma Kozhyn, a peasant, was a nonparty man who began his career in the partisan group led by Shchus'. After joining Makhno, Kozhyn became a commander of a machine-gun regiment and participated in the defeat of Denikin at Perehonivka. Kozhyn was mortally wounded in August 1921.[17]

In contrast to other partisan leaders, Oleksander Kalashnykiv was a worker who had been a second lieutenant during the war. In 1917 he became secretary of the Anarchist group at Huliai-Pole and was a cofounder of the partisan army in which he was commander of an infantry brigade. In the summer of 1919, he organized the uprising of Makhno troops in the Red Army and headed their subsequent arrival at the Makhno camp with some Red units. In the summer of 1920, Kalashnykiv was killed in a battle against the Bolsheviks.[18]

One of the few educated men in the Makhno movement was Chornoknyzhnyi, a teacher from Novopavlivka, in the Pavlohrad district. He served as chairman of the Second Congress, which was held on February 12, 1919, at Huliai-Pole. He also participated in the campaign against the Bolshevik and anti-Bolshevik Russian forces.[19]

Sereda, a peasant, was commander of a partisan detachment. In the fall of 1920 he was seriously wounded during the fighting against Wrangel and was taken to Kharkiv for an operation. One week later, after Wrangel's defeat, he was transferred to jail and in March 1921 he was shot by the Bolsheviks.[20]

Dermenzhi was a telegrapher from Izmail and a sailor who participated in the uprising on the Russian warship *Potemkin* in the summer of 1905. He commanded an independent partisan group and in the fall of 1918 joined Makhno who appointed him head of the field communication service.[21]

Petro Petrenko, from Huliai-Pole, was a junior officer of the tsarist army. He headed an independent partisan group and in the fall of 1918 joined Makhno and was appointed commander of the Chaplino-Hryshyne front, and later commanded a brigade. He was killed in the fighting.[22]

Although most of the leaders of the Makhno movement were Ukrainians, especially from Huliai-Pole, a number of them, in the later period, were either Russian or Jewish Anarchists who came mainly from Russia in the spring and summer of 1919 after the Bolshevik regime destroyed the Anarchist groups in Soviet Russia.

The most prominent of them was Peter Arshinov (Marin), a smith from Katerynoslav, who started his revolutionary career in 1905 as a Bolshevik. For several months he edited the illicit Bolshevik newspaper *Molot* (Hammer) at Kizyl-Arvat in Turkmenistan. In the summer of 1906 he returned to Amur, outside Katerynoslav, where he worked in the Shoduara factory and soon joined the Anarchist group. At the beginning of March 1907, he was sentenced to death for the assassination of Vasylenko, a chief of a railroad workshop in Oleksandrivs'k, but at the end of April he escaped to Paris via St. Petersburg and Helsinki. At the beginning of 1909 he returned to Russia and in Briansk he was arrested, but escaped and settled in Moscow. In August 1910 he was arrested in Austria for transporting arms to Russia and jailed for nine months in Ternopil, Galicia. In May 1911 he was handed over to the Russian authorities and a Moscow court sentenced him to twenty years imprisonment in Butyrki where he met Makhno.[23] On March 1, 1917, Arshinov was released and remained in Moscow as an editor of Anarchist publications.

After the destruction of Anarchist groups in Russia, Arshinov moved to Ukraine and at the end of April 1919 he became Makhno's secretary. Subsequently Makhno put him in charge of educational and propaganda activities, including the publication of newspapers. In the summer of 1920 Arshinov left the partisan army to write the history of the Makhno movement. In 1922 he went abroad, first to Berlin and in 1925 to France, where he was editor of the Anarchist periodical *Delo truda*. In 1935 he rejoined the Bolsheviks and returned to Soviet Russia where he soon disappeared.[24]

Next to Arshinov, the most prominent Russian in the Makhno movement was Volin (Boris M. Eichenbaum), an educated man who had been a Socialist Revolutionary since 1905. In 1907 he was imprisoned for revolutionary activities, but he escaped to France where he joined the Anarchists in 1911. In August 1916 he was arrested for his antiwar propaganda, but managed to escape to America where he worked in the Anarchist movement. In July 1917, he returned to Russia as coeditor of the Anarchist newspaper *Golos truda*, published in St. Petersburg. After the destruction of the Anarchist groups in Russia, he came to Ukraine as a *Nabat* editor. At the end of August 1919, he joined the Makhno army, where he became Arshinov's assistant in the education and propaganda section and chairman of the Revolutionary Military Council. In November while doing propaganda among the population in the Kryvyi Rih area, Volin apparently deliberately fell into Bolshevik hands and was taken to Moscow, but released on October 1, 1920, after the Makhno agreement with the Bolsheviks against Wrangel. At the end of November, he was again arrested in Kharkiv and put into Butyrki prison in Moscow. Soon after, he was released and authorized to leave Russia. For a while he lived in Berlin where, with Arshinov, he published a monthly, *Anarchicheskii vestnik*. In 1925 he went to France where he died in 1945 at the age of 63.[25]

Another leading member of Nabat was Aaron Baron. The tsarist regime exiled him to Siberia for his revolutionary activities, but he managed to escape to America, where he settled in Chicago as coeditor of the Anarchist paper *Alarm*. In June 1917, he returned to Russia and became active in the Anarchist movement. In the fall of 1918, he was one of the organizers of Nabat. In 1919 Baron joined Makhno's army, occupying prominent political and military positions. He even dreamed of taking over its leadership. In November 1920, while attending the Anarchist conference in Kharkiv, the Bolsheviks arrested him and jailed him at Orel for two years, whence he was transferred to the Solovetsky Islands until January 5, 1925. After returning to Moscow, he was soon arrested again and exiled to Altai, Siberia. His wife, Fania Avrutska, also was arrested.[26]

IAkov Sukhovolskii, known as IAsha Alyi, was exiled by the tsarist regime for his activities during the 1905 Revolution, but he escaped at first to Britain and then to America. In 1917 he returned to Russia where he became active in the Anarchist movement. He, too, actively participated in the organization of Nabat and in 1919 joined the partisan army where he became a close collaborator of Makhno. In September 1920, the Bolsheviks seized and shot him.[27]

Josif Gutman, known as Emigrant, a printer, emigrated to America in his youth and joined an Anarchist group. After the outbreak of the Revolution, he returned to Ukraine where he became active in the Anarchist movement. He was one of the organizers of Nabat and became one of its secretaries. In 1919 he joined the Makhno movement, working in the propaganda section. In September 1920, when Gutman was on his way from Kharkiv to Makhno's headquarters at Starobil'sk', he was seized the Bolsheviks and shot. Gutman's wife, Liia, also a member of Nabat, was arrested in November 1920 and imprisoned in Butyrki.[28]

Ivan Kartashev was an active Anarchist and a member of Nabat. In 1919 he joined the Makhno propaganda section. In November 1920, on the way to Kharkiv, he and his wife were seized by the Bolsheviks and shot.[29]

Aronchik was a worker and from 1917 an active Anarchist in Russia and in Ukraine. He was one of the leading members of the Nabat organization. In 1919 he joined the Makhno movement working as political propagandist at Huliai-Pole and its vicinity. He was seized by the Bolsheviks but after their agreement with Makhno he was released. In November 1920, he was again arrested by the Bolsheviks.[30]

Abram Budanov was a worker from the Donets Basin and an active Anarchist. He was the cofounder of Nabat and one of its leaders. In 1919 he joined the Makhno movement, occupying various positions including commander of a partisan detachment, political propagandist, and a diplomatic agent. In October 1920, he was a member of a delegation that arranged the agreement with the Bolsheviks against General Wrangel. A few months later, he was arrested by the Bolsheviks and sent first to the prison in Moscow and then to Riazan. He escaped from prison twice, the second time in summer 1921.[31]

Besides the members of Nabat, a number of Anarchists from Russia joined the Makhno movement either in groups or individually. In May 1919, a group of thirty-six Anarchists from Ivanovo-Voznesenske, near Moscow, arrived at Huliai-Pole. Some of them joined the combat units, propaganda section, or the village communes. A few of them became prominent partisan leaders.[32]

One was Makeev, a worker from Ivanovo-Voznesenske, and a member of its Anarchist group. He was active during all the phases of the

Revolution in Russia; later, however, he became disillusioned with the Bolshevik regime. After coming to Huliai-Pole in April 1919, he worked as a political propagandist in the area, and later joined the army. Subsequently he became a member of the Makhno staff. At the end of November 1919, during the fighting against General Slashchov near Oleksandrivs'k, Makeev was killed.[33]

Aleksandr Cherniakov, a bookkeeper, spent three years in exile for his revolutionary activity. During the Revolution, he worked as political activist in Petrograd and later in Ivanovo-Voznesenske. In 1918 he was arrested several times by the Bolsheviks and in 1919 along with thirty-six others joined the Makhno army, working in the propaganda section. After the defeat of General Wrangel, Cherniakov was arrested by the Bolsheviks and sent to prison in Russia.[34]

Peter Rybin, called Zonov, was a worker from Orel province. He emigrated to America where he participated in the Anarchist movement, but following the outbreak of the Revolution he returned to Russia. Later he settled in Katerynoslav and joined the local Bolshevik group as a specialist, to organize industry and transport. In the summer of 1920 he became disillusioned with the Bolsheviks and left their ranks. In the fall he joined the Makhno movement in the propaganda section, and later served as secretary of the Revolutionary Military Council. In January 1921, he went to Kharkiv to deliver a protest to Rakovskii against breaking the agreement with Makhno and the arrest of Anarchists. However, he too was arrested and one month later was shot by the Bolsheviks.[35]

Viktor Popov, a former sailor, was a Russian Socialist Revolutionary. In 1919 he organized a partisan detachment to fight Denikin. Subsequently, as he moved into Ukraine, Popov joined Makhno's army and the Anarchists. Besides his combat duties as a commander of a partisan detachment, he worked as diplomatic agent. At the end of September, he became a member of the delegation to negotiate an agreement with the Bolsheviks against General Wrangel. Later, he was appointed Makhno's military and political representative, with Kurylenko and Budanov, to Kharkiv. In November, after the defeat of Wrangel, Popov was arrested in Kharkiv and sent to a prison in Moscow where after one year he was shot.[36]

Mikhalev-Pavlenko was a former engineer officer and a member of the Petrograd Anarchist group. At the beginning of 1919 he joined the Makhno army. He organized and commanded an engineering detachment that operated on the railroad lines. On June 15–16, 1919, while fighting Denikin, he was seized along with Burbyha by the Bolsheviks at the Haichur railroad station, and, on the next day, he was shot in Kharkiv.[37]

One of the most devoted Anarchists in the Makhno army was IAkovlev (Kahan), called IAsha. He joined the partisan army in 1919, soon became a member of Makhno's staff, and at one point was a chairman of the Huliai-Pole council. In September 1919, in the battle at Perehonivka, he was seriously wounded and taken to the hospital at Uman'. When the Denikin troops occupied Uman', IAkovlev was seized and, in spite of protests by the hospital personnel, he was shot.[38]

There were a number of other prominent partisan leaders who played important roles in the Makhno movement whose lives and activities were scarcely known. Among them was Petro Havriushenko, called Havriusha, chief of Makhno's bodyguard; he was killed in 1920 fighting against the Bolsheviks. Koliada was a commander of an independent partisan unit and in the fall of 1918 he joined Makhno who appointed him a member of his staff. Havrylo Troian was one of the cofounders of the Makhno army and the gentlest among Makhno's associates. In 1921 he was killed fighting the Bolsheviks. Tykhonenko was the head of the supply service. Seregin, a peasant and an Anarchist since 1917, was among the first who joined Makhno and for some time was commander of the supply service.[39] Moisei Kalynychenko was a worker from Huliai-Pole and an Anarchist from 1907, who joined the Makhno movement in 1918 and was a member of the Revolutionary Military Council. Lev Holyk was the head of counterintelligence in the Makhno army.[40]

Abbreviations

The following abbreviations are used in the notes and in the bibliography.

AV	*Anarkhicheskii vestnik* [Anarchist news]. Berlin.
ARR	*Arkhiv russkoi revoliutsii* [Archives of the Russian Revolution]. Berlin.
AR	*Armiia i revoliutsiia* [Army and revolution]. Kharkov.
BA	*Belyi arkhiv* [White archive]. Paris.
BY	*Byloe* [The past]. Leningrad.
DT	*Delo truda* [Labor cause]. Paris, Chicago, New York.
DT-P	*Delo truda—Probuzhdenie* [Labor cause—awakening]. New York.
FA	*Fashist*. Putnam, Conn.
IM	*Istorik marksist* [Marxist historian]. Moscow.
IKCK (+year)	*Istorychnyi kaliendar-al'manakh Chervonoi Kalyny* [Historical yearbook of the red guelder rose]. Lvov.
JG (+year)	*Jahrbücher für Geschichte* [History yearbook]. Munich.
KD (+year)	*Kaliendar-al'manakh Dnipro* [Yearbook of the Dnieper]. Lvov
KCK (+year)	*Kaliendar Chervonoi Kalyny* [Yearbook of the red guelder rose]. Lvov.
KA	*Krasnyi arkhiv* [Red archives]. Moscow.
LNV	*Literaturno-naukovyi vistnyk* [Literary and scholastic newsletter]. Lvov.

LHKD	*Literaturnyi i hromads'ko-politychnyi kaliendar-al'manakh Dnipro* [Literary and sociopolitical almanac of the Dnieper]. Lvov.
LCK	*Litopys Chervonoi Kalyny* [Chronicle of the red guelder rose]. Lvov.
LR	*Litopys revoliutsii* [Chronicle of the Revolution]. Kharkov.
NRS	*Novoe russkoe slovo* [New Russian word]. New York.
PER	*Pereklichka* [Roll call]. New York.
PRO	*Probuzhdenie* [Awakening]. Berlin, Detroit.
PR	*Proletarskaia revoliutsiia* [Proletarian revolution]. Moscow.
PS	*Put' k svobode* [Path to freedom]. Huliai-Pole.
RN	*Rozbudova natsii* [Building of the nation]. Prague.
SV	*Svoboda* [Freedom]. Jersey City, N.J.
TR	*Tryzub* [Trident]. New York.
UE	*Ukraine: A Concise Encyclopaedia*. Toronto.
UI	*Ukrains'kyi istoryk* [Ukrainian historian]. New York.
VK	*Visti kombatanta* [Newsletters of the combatants]. Toronto.
VIZ	*Voenno-istoricheskii zhurnal* [Historical-military journal]. Moscow.
VR	*Voina i revoliutsiia* [War and revolution]. Moscow.
VO	*Volna* [Wave]. New York.
VI	*Voprosy istorii* [Problems of history]. Moscow.

Notes

Prelude to Revolution

1. N. D. Polons'ka-Vasylenko, *The Settlement of the Southern Ukraine, 1750–1775* (New York: The Ukrainian Academy of Arts and Sciences in the U.S.A., 1955), p. 181.

2. Zaporozhian Sich was a military-political organization of the Ukrainian Cossacks (free armed men). They appeared on the south Ukrainian steppes at the end of the fifteenth century as hunters, fishermen, and honey collectors, who gradually grouped into bands and became a permanent fighting force. Their free life on the steppes and their campaigns against the Tatars attracted daring peasants, burghers, and some nobles. In the 1540s a number of scattered groups were united and organized as an independent military focre by Prince Dmytro Vyshnevyts'kyi. He founded a Cossack center, the Sich, on the island Khortytsia beyond the Dnieper rapids. This center became known as the Zaporozhian Sich, or an armed camp beyond the rapids. The head of the Cossacks was the hetman, an elected leader. The Cossacks lived in stern simplicity, under military conditions, without wives or families.

At the beginning of the seventeenth century the Polish government, which at the time controlled most of the Ukrainian territory, legalized the Cossacks as a knightly class because it needed their help against its enemies: Muscovy, the Ottoman Empire, and Sweden. However, Polish gentry's misrule brought about an uprising under the leadership of the Cossacks against Poland in 1648, and subsequently an independent Ukraine was proclaimed. A prolonged war against Poland forced Hetman Bohdan Khmel'nyts'kyi into a close alliance with the Muscovite tsar in 1654. After the establishment of the independent hetman state, the Zaporozhians remained an independent republic. Moreover, after the death of Khmel'nyts'kyi in 1657, the Cossacks of the Sich began to follow their own policy and even interfered in the affairs of the hetman state in the name of the popular masses.

The fate of the Zaporozhians radically changed when Hetman Ivan Mazepa made an alliance with King Charles XII of Sweden and the Zaporozhian republic under its head Kost Hordiienko joined Mazepa against Tsar Peter I. After the defeat at Poltava in 1709, the tsar destroyed the Sich, and the Zaporozhians settled on the Tatar's territory. In 1734 the Cossacks acknowledged Russian suzerainty and were allowed to return home because the Russians needed them for war against the Turks. After the war, however, the Russian government began to colonize Zaporozhian land with foreigners and limit the freedom of the Cossacks, who stubbornly resisted until the destruction of the Sich republic in 1775. See N. Polons'ka-Vasylenko, "The Kozaks," in UE, 1:629 ff.; B. Krupnytsky, "The Rebirth of the State," in UE, 1:634 ff.

3. Michael Hrushevsky, *A History of Ukraine*, ed. O. J. Frederiksen (New Haven: Yale University Press, 1949), pp. 455–56.

4. Dmytro Doroshenko, *Narys istorii Ukrainy* (Munich: Dniprova khvylia, 1966), 2:243; Krupnytsky, "Rebirth of the State," p. 663.

5. *Istoriia ukrains'koho viis'ka*, p. 234; E. Borschak, "Ukraine in the Russian Empire in the Nineteenth and Early Twentieth Centuries (1800–1917)," in UE, 1:668.

6. Borschak, "Ukraine in the Russian Empire," 1:668.

7. Hrushevsky, *History of Ukraine*, p. 412.

8. Vasyl' Bidnov, "Ukrains'ka tserkva," in *Ukrains'ka kul'tura: Zbirnyk lektsii*, ed. Dmytra Antonovycha (Podebrady, 1940), pp. 137–38.

9. K. V. Kharlampovich, *Malorossiiskoe vliianie na Velikorusskuiu tserkovnuiu zhizn'* (Kazan': M. A. Golubov, 1914), pp. 665–66; Dmytro Doroshenko, *Pravoslavna tserkva v mynulomu i suchasnomu zhytti ukrains'koho narodu* (Berlin, 1941), p. 41.

10. Hrushevsky, *History of Ukraine*, p. 460.

11. Vasyl' Bidnov, "Shkola i osvita na Ukraini," in *Ukrains'ka kul'tura*, p. 31.

12. V. Kubijovyc, "The Size and Structure of the Population," in UE, 1:176–77.

13. Oleksandr Lotots'kyi, "Ukrains'ke drukovane slovo," in *Ukrains'ka kul'tura*, p. 61.

14. Ibid., pp. 62, 65.

15. Ivan Krypiakevych [Ivan Kholms'kyi], *Istoriia Ukrainy* (Munich: Nakl. Naukovoho t-va im. Shevchenka, 1949), p. 309; Hrushevsky, *History of Ukraine*, p. 475; Borschak, "Ukraine in the Russian Empire," 1:670.

16. Hrushevsky, *History of Ukraine*, p. 476; D. Doroshenko, *Narys istorii Ukrainy*, 2:276.

17. D. Doroshenko, *Narys istorii Ukrainy*, 2:285–87.

18. Dmytro Doroshenko, *A Survey of Ukrainian Historiography*; Olexander Ohloblyn, *Ukrainian Historiography, 1917–1956* (New York: The Ukrainian Academy of Arts and Sciences in the U.S., 1957), pp. 79–80, 99.

19. There were several earlier attempts to establish universities. As early as 1760 Hetman Rozumovskyi had planned to create a university in Baturyn and to convert the Kiev Academy into a university. His deposition prevented him from carrying out his plans. Five years later Piotr Rumiantsev, at the behest of the Ukrainian nobility, attempted to organize universities in Kyiv (Kiev) and Chernihiv (Chernigov), but the Russian government rejected his proposal. In 1786, Grigorii A. Potemkin, the favorite of Catherine II, applied for, and eventually received, permis-

sion to establish a university in Katerynoslav (Dnepropetrovsk), but after his death in 1791 the project was abandoned.

In addition, a university had existed at L'viv (Lemberg in German, Lwów in Polish, Lvov in Russian) in the Austrian-controlled part of Ukraine, since 1784.

20. D. Doroshenko, *Narys istorii Ukrainy*, 2:274.

21. Eduard Winter, *Byzanz und Rome im Kampf um die Ukraine, 955–1939* (Leipzig: O. Harrassowitz, 1949), p. 154; Borschak, "Ukraine in the Russian Empire," 1:673.

22. D. Doroshenko, *Survey of Ukrainian Historiography*, p. 163.

23. Pavlo Zaitsev, *Zhyttia Tarasa Shevchenka* (New York: 1955), pp. 51–53.

24. A. Zaionchkovskii, *Kirillo-Mefodievskoe obshchestvo, 1846–1959* (Moscow: Izd-vo Moskovskogo universiteta, 1959), p. 61.

25. It is of interest to note that Kyiv was favored as a Slavic capital even by M. Czajkowski, a Pole, providing it became part of Poland, and by the Russian Slavophile A. Khomiakov, who believed that its position on the border between two worlds would be advantageous (John P. Sydoruk, *Ideology of Cyrillo-Methodians and Its Origin* [Winnipeg: Ukrainian Free Academy of Sciences, 1954], p. 51).

26. D. Doroshenko, *Narys istorii Ukrainy*, 2:281; Michael T. Florinsky, *Russia: A History and Interpretation*, 2 vols. (New York: Macmillan Co., 1959), 2:811; C. A. Manning, *The Story of the Ukraine* (New York: Philosophical Library, 1947), pp. 169–70.

27. Manning, *Story of the Ukraine*, p. 171.

28. Krypiakevych [Kholms'kyi], *Istoriia Ukrainy*, p. 319.

29. D. D[oroshen]ko, "Ielisaveta Ivanovna z Skoropads'kykh Myloradovych," *Khliborobs'ka Ukraina* 5 (Vienna, 1924–25): 286.

30. D. Doroshenko, *Survey of Ukrainian Historiography*, pp. 177 ff.

31. Hrushevsky, *History of Ukraine*, p. 496; Lotots'kyi, "Ukrains'ke drukovane slovo," p. 62.

32. Winter, *Byzanz und Rome*, p. 168.

33. Lotots'kyi, "Ukrains'ke drukovane slovo," p. 63; Borschak, "Ukraine in the Russian Empire," 1:684.

34. Lotots'kyi, "Ukrains'ke drukovane slovo," p. 63; Herbert Adams Gibbons, "The Ukraine and the Balance of Power," *The Century Magazine* 102, no. 3 (July 1921): 467; Ievhen Chykalenko, *Spohady, 1861–1907* (New York: Ukrainian Academy of Arts and Sciences in the U.S., 1955), p. 380.

35. John S. Reshetar, Jr., *The Ukrainian Revolution, 1917–1920*, p. 33.

36. Krypiakevych [Kholms'kyi], *Istoriia Ukrainy*, p. 330; D. Doroshenko, *Survey of Ukrainian Historiography*, p. 196.

37. Volodymyr Doroshenko, "The Life of Mykhailo Drahomanov," in *Mykhailo Drahomanov: A Symposium and Selected Writings*, ed. Ivan L. Rudnytsky (New York: The Ukrainian Academy of Arts and Sciences in the U. S., 1952), p. 14.

38. Oleksander Hrushevskyi, "Drahomanov i halyts'ka molod' 1870-kh rr.," *Ukraina*, no. 6 (20) (Kiev, 1926), p. 49; Matvii Stakhiv, "Drahomanov's Impact on Ukrainian Politics," in *Mykhailo Drahomanov*, p. 53.

39. D. Doroshenko, *Survey of Ukrainian Historiography*, p. 264.

40. Dmytro Doroshenko, *Z istorii ukrains'koi politychnoi dumky za chasiv svitovoi vinny*, p. 19.

41. *Samostiina Ukraina: R.U.P.* (Wetzlar: Vyd. Soiuza Vyzvolennia Ukrainy,

1917), p. 22; Serhii Shemet, "Mykola Mikhnovs'kyi," *Khliborobs'ka Ukraina*, 5:7.

42. Borschak, "Ukraine in the Russian Empire," 2:687.

43. Nicholas L. Chirovsky, *Old Ukraine: Its Socio-Economic History Prior to 1781* (Madison, N.J.: The Florham Park Press, 1963), p. 365; Margaret Miller, *The Economic Development of Russia, 1905–1914*, 2nd ed. (New York: A. M. Kelly, 1967), p. 59.

44. Borschak, "Ukraine in the Russian Empire," 2:680.

45. Harry Schwartz, *Russia's Soviet Economy* (New York: Prentice-Hall, 1950), p. 63; Miller, *Economic Development of Russia*, p. 259.

46. L. Ivanov, "Revoliutsiia 1905 goda na Ukraine," VI, nos. 5–6 (1945), p. 23; H. R. Weinstein, "Land Hunger and Nationalism in the Ukraine, 1905–1917," *The Journal of Economic History* 2 (1942):32.

47. Otto Hoetzsch, "The Ukrainian Movement in Russia," in *Ukraine's Claim to Freedom: An Appeal for Justice on the Behalf of Thirty-Five Millions* (New York: Ukrainian National Association and the Ruthenian National Union, 1915), p. 95; Krypiakevych [Kholms'kyi], *Istoriia Ukrainy*, p. 334.

48. After the dissolution of the First Duma on July 8, 1906, some two hundred of its members journeyed to nearby Viborg, in Finland, where they issued an appeal to the population urging them to offer "passive resistance" by refusing to pay taxes or comply with army drafts. The appeal, however, brought no popular response, while the signatories were sentenced to three months in prison and were disfranchised, thus terminating their parliamentary careers (Florinsky, *Russia*, 2:1192; Alexander Kerensky, *Russia and History's Turning Point* (New York: Duell, Sloan and Pearce, 1965), p. 73).

49. Vladimir Korostovetz, *Seed and Harvest* (London: Faber and Faber, 1931), p. 285.

50. D. Doroshenko, *Narys istorii Ukrainy*, 2:321.

51. Mykhailo IEremiiv, "Za lashtunkamy Tsentral'noi Rady," UI, nos. 1–4 (17–20) (1968), p. 98; Nicholas Czubatyj, "The Modern Ukrainian Nationalist Movement," *Journal of Central European Affairs* 4, no. 3 (October 1944): 288; E. N. Burdzalov, *Vtoraia russkaia revoliutsiia: Moskva, front, periferiia* (Moscow: "Nauka," 1969), p. 219.

52. Dmytro Doroshenko, *Moi spomyny pro nedavnie mynule, 1914–1920*, p. 23; "The Czar's Rule in Galicia, 1914," in *Ukraine's Claim to Freedom*, p. 114; D. Doroshenko, *Moi spomyny*, pp. 33–35.

Chapter 1, The Ukrainian Revolution

1. Dates are new style except in cases where it was impossible to determine from available sources which dating system was used.

2. Pavlo Khrystiuk, *Zamitkyi i materiialy do istorii Ukrains'koi revoliutsii, 1917–1920 rr.*, 1:16.

3. Victor Chernov, *The Great Russian Revolution*, p. 267; Khrystiuk, *Zamitky i materiialy*, 1:38.

4. V. Kedrovs'kyi, "Ukrainizovani chastyny i reguliarna armiia," VK, no. 2 (33) (1968), p. 37; N. N. Sukhanov, *The Russian Revolution 1917: A Personal Record* (London: Oxford University Press, 1955), pp. 113 ff.; George Vernadsky, *A History of Russia* (New York: New Home Library, 1944), pp. 236–37.

5. Stepan Lazurenko, "Bohdanivtsi na fronti 1917 roku," TR, no. 33 (1965), p. 13.

6. Aleksander Shul'hyn, "The Period of the Central Rada (Council)," in UE, 1:731. According to Kedrovs'kyi the regiment was organized on April 18, 1917 (V. Kedrovs'kyi, "Pochatok ukrainizatsii v rossis'kii armii i Pershyi Ukrains'kyi viis'kovyi z'izd," VK, no. 1 (27) (1968), p. 25.

7. Iakiv Zozulia, *Velyka Ukrains'ka revoliutsiia*, p. 16.

8. Khrystiuk, *Zamitky i materiialy*, 1:102, 65–66; Chernov, *Great Russian Revolution*, p. 276.

9. Robert Paul Browder and Alexander F. Kerensky, eds., *The Russian Provisional Government, 1917*, 1:383.

10. Frank Alfred Golder, ed., *Documents of Russian History, 1914–1917* (New York: The Century Co., 1927), no. 440; Chernov, *Great Russian Revolution*, pp. 280–81.

11. Browder and Kerensky, *Russian Provisional Government*, 1:376, 389, 401; Dmytro Doroshenko, "Voina i revoliutsiia na Ukraine," in *Revoliutsiia na Ukraine po memauram belykh*, ed. S. A. Alekseev, p. 67; Korostovetz, *Seed and Harvest*, p. 290.

12. V. Vynnychenko, *Vidrodzennia natsii*, 2:40.

13. Khrystiuk, *Zamitky i materiialy*, 2:12.

14. Ibid., 2:41.

15. James Bunyan and H. H. Fisher, comps., *The Bolshevik Revolution, 1917–1918*, p. 435.

16. Ibid.

17. Ibid.

18. David Plotkin [D. Kin], *Denikinshchina*, p. 9; I. A. Poliakov, *Donskie kozaki v bor'be s bol'shevikami: Vospominaniia* (Munich, 1962), p. 26; Chernov, *Great Russian Revolution*, p. 416.

19. Mykola Kovalevs'kyi, *Pry dzherelakh borot'by*, pp. 312–13.

20. V. I. Lenin, *Collected Works* (Moscow: Progress Publisher, 1964), p. 22.

21. Kiev. Instytut istorii partii, *Istoriia KP(b)U* (Kiev, 1933), 2:126, as quoted in Richard Pipes, *The Formation of the Soviet Union: Communisim and Nationalism, 1917–1923* (Cambridge: Harvard University Press, 1954), p. 68.

22. Dmytro Doroshenko, *Istoriia Ukrainy* (New York: Bulava, 1954), 1:200–201.

23. Bunyan and Fisher, *Bolshevik Revolution*, p. 440.

24. Khrystiuk, *Zamitkyi materiialy*, 2:69; Bunyan and Fisher, *Bolshevik Revolution*, p. 441.

25. To make Antonov more appealing to the Ukrainian masses Lenin reminded him of the name of his Ukrainian mother "Ovsienko" and asked him to add it to his name. Thus, Antonov became Antonov-Ovseenko. See Kovalevs'kyi, *Pry dzherelakh borot'by*, p. 326.

26. Zozulia, *Velyka Ukrains'ka revoliutsiia*, p. 44; A. A. Gol'denveizer, "Iz Kievskikh vospominanii, 1917–1921 gg.," ARR 6 (1922):204; Zozulia, *Velyka Ukrains'ka revoliutsiia*, pp. 52–53.

27. Vynnychenko, *Vidrodzennia natsii*, 2:246–47.

28. Arnold D. Margolin, *From a Political Diary*, pp. 182–83; Vynnychenko, *Vidrodzennia natsii*, 2:232–43.

29. U.S., Department of State, *Papers Relating to the Foreign Relations of the United States, 1918–1919. Russia*, 2:660.

30. Louis Fischer, *The Soviets in World Affairs*, 1:53.

31. Fritz Fischer, *Germany's Aims in the First World War* (London: Chatto and

Windus, 1967), pp. 497–98; John W. Wheeler-Bennett, *The Forgotten Peace*, p. 220; Gustav Gratz and Richard Schulder, *The Economic Policy of Austria-Hungary during the War in Its External Relations* (New Haven: Yale University Press, 1928), p. 255.

32. Khrystiuk, *Zamitky i materiialy*, 2:138–39; D. Doroshenko, "Voina i revoliutsiia na Ukraine," p. 97.

33. Erich von Ludendorff, *Ludendorff's Own Story, August 1914–November 1918* (New York: Harper & Brothers, 1919), 2:258–59; F. Fischer, *Germany's Aims*, p. 544.

34. Reshetar, *Ukrainian Revolution*, p. 119; U.S., Department of State, *Papers*, 2:675.

35. Vynnychenko, *Vidrodzennia natsii*, 2:321.

36. James Bunyan, ed., *Intervention, Civil War, and Communism in Russia, April–December 1918*, p. 5.

37. Ludendorff, *Own Story*, 2:260.

38. D. Doroshenko, *Istoriia Ukrainy*, 2:18.

39. Ibid., 2:19; Vynnychenko, *Vidrodzennia natsii*, 2:323.

40. Khrystiuk, *Zamitky i materiialy*, 2:135.

41. IAroslav Okunevs'kyi, "Rozmova z arkhykniazem Vil'hel'mom dnia 4. serpnia 1918 roku," *Dilo*, no. 100 (May 8, 1931), p. 2; I. Osipov, *Na prolomie*, p. 39; George Stewart, *The White Armies of Russia*, pp. 51–52; D. Doroshenko, *Istoriia Ukrainy*, 2:24–26.

42. 40,000 dessiatines, or over 200,000 acres (1 dessiatine equals 2.7 acres).

43. Pavlo Skoropadskyi, "Uryvok zi 'Spomyniv,'" *Khliborobs'ka Ukraina* 4 (1924):3; N. M. Mogilianskii, "Tragediia Ukrainy," ARR 11 (1923):91–92; Kovalevs'kyi, *Pry dzherelakh borot'by*, p. 318; Korostovetz, *Seed and Harvest*, p. 290.

44. D. Doroshenko, *Istoriia Ukrainy*, 2:49–50.

45. Max Hoffman, *Die Aufzeichnungen* (Berlin: Verlag für Kulturpolitik, 1929), 1:194; A. I. Denikin, *Ocherki russkoi smuty*, 4:184; V. B. Stankevich, *Vospominaniia, 1914–1919 gg.* (Berlin: I. P. Ladyzhnikov, 1920), p. 322; V. Miakotin, "Iz nedalekogo proshlogo," in *Revoliutsiia na Ukraine*, ed. S. A. Alekseev, p. 223.

46. G. N. Leikhtenbergskii, *Vospominaniia ob "Ukraine," 1917–1918*, p. 27; see also Stankevich, *Vospominaniia*, p. 326.

47. Kovalevs'kyi, *Pry dzherelakh borot'by*, pp. 487–89; Panas Fedenko, *Ukrains'kyi rukh u 20 stolitti*, p. 149; Khrystiuk, *Zamitky i materiialy*, 3:14 ff.; D. Doroshenko, *Istoriia Ukrainy*, 2:43.

48. Dmytro Dontsov, *Rik 1918, Kyiv*, p. 32; Vasyl' Ivanys, *Symon Petliura—Prezydent Ukrainy, 1879–1926*, p. 75; G. N. Leikhtenbergskii, "Kak nachalas' 'IUzhnaia Armiia,'" ARR 8 (1923):166–67.

49. Dmytro Solovei, *Vasylenko, Miliukov i samostiinist' Ukrainy v 1918 r.* (Winnipeg, 1965), p. 37; Mykhailo Hrushevs'kyi, *Vybrani pratsi*, p. 78.

50. D. Doroshenko, *Istoriia Ukrainy*, 2:116–17.

51. Denikin, *Ocherki*, 4:187.

52. Alexander Shul'hyn, "The Period of the Hetmanate," in UE, 1:750; Maksym Slavins'kyi, *Istoriia Ukrainy* (Podebrady, 1934), p. 171; Wheeler-Bennett, *Forgotten Peace*, p. 322.

53. D. Doroshenko, *Istoriia Ukrainy*, 2:215 ff.; Théophil Hornykiewicz, ed.,

Ereignisse in der Ukraine, 1914–1922, 3:482 ff.; Viktor Andriievs'kyi, *Z mynuloho*, 2:68; U.S., Department of State, *Papers*, 2:696; Dontsov, *Rik 1918*, pp. 22–23; Bunyan, *Intervention*, pp. 57–58; D. Doroshenko, *Istoriia Ukrainy*, 2:214.

54. D. Doroshenko, *Istoriia Ukrainy*, 2:191–99; Khrystiuk, *Zamitky i materiialy*, 3:108–110

55. P. N. Krasnov, "Vsevelikoe Voisko Donskoe," ARR 5:237–40; see also Vasyl' Ivanys, *Stezhkamy zhyttia*, 2:300; A. I. Denikin, "Getmanstvo i Direktoriia na Ukraine," in *Revoliutsiia na Ukraine*, ed. Alekseev, p. 147.

56. Reshetar, *Ukrainian Revolution*, pp. 189–92; Wheeler-Bennett, *Forgotten Peace*, p. 324; Shul'hyn, "Period of the Hetmanate," 1:749; Vynnychenko, *Vidrodzennia natsii*, 3:158–59.

57. Shul'hyn, "Period of the Hetmanate," 1:751; Ivan Tsapko, "Partyzany na Skhidnii Ukraini: Starobil's partyzans'kyi zahin," *Visti*, no. 109 (1963), p. 7; Krasnov, "Vsevelikoe Voisko Donskoe," 5:236; IEvhen Konovalets', *Prychynky do istorii ukrains'koi revoliutsii*, p. 16; Denikin, "Getmanstvo i Directoriia na Ukraine," p. 146; Germany, Auswartiges Amt. *Germany and the Revolution in Russia, 1915–1918*, p. 134; D. Doroshenko, *Istoriia Ukrainy*, 2:381 ff.

58. The Sich Riflemen (Sichovi Stril'tsi) was a military formation organized in November 1917 in Kyiv from West Ukrainian prisoners of war in Russia formerly in the Austrian army. Hence some writers call the formation the Kyivan Sich Riflemen. The leading organizers of the unit were colonels IEvhen Konovalets' and Andrii Mel'nyk. As the formation developed from a battalion to a corps many Ukrainians from East Ukraine joined the formation. The Sich Riflemen were the best and most reliable Ukrainian military formation during the Revolution. See Dmytro Herechanivs'kyi, "Pochatky Sichovykh Stril'tsiv," VK, no. 3 (27) (1967), pp. 29 ff.; Dmytro Herechanivs'kyi, "Prykmetni rysy Sichovykh Stril'tsiv (S.S.)," VK, no. 3 (34) (1966), pp. 16 ff.; Hryts' Hladkyi, "Sichovi Stril'tsi (S.S.)," LCK, no. 6 (1935), pp. 4 ff.; *Istoriia ukrains'koho viis'ka*, pp. 428–49; Oleksander Udovychenko, *Ukraina u viini za derzhavnist'* (Winnipeg: D. Mykytiuk, 1954), p. 42; Samovydets [pseud.], *Nedavna het'manshchyna* (Chicago, 1933), p. 55; Ant. Kushchyns'kyi, "Korotka heneza istorii Serdiuts'kykh formatsii," *Visti*, no. 106 (1962), pp. 69–70.

59. A. Lukomskii, "Iz vospominanii," ARR 5 (1922):183; Zenon Stefaniv, *Ukrains'ki zbroini syly, 1917–1921 rr.*, 2nd rev. ed. (n.p., SUV, 1947), 1:109; V. I. Gurko, "Politicheskoe polozhenie na Ukraine pri Getmane," in *Revoliutsiia na Ukraine*, ed. Alekseev, pp. 215–16.

60. D. Doroshenko, *Istoriia Ukrainy*, 2:260; Khrystiuk, *Zamitky i materiialy*, 3:39; I. Mazepa, *Ukraina v ohni i buri revoliutsii, 1917–1921*, 1:54–55; Iwan Majstrenko, *Borot'bism: A Chapter in the History of Ukrainian Communism* (New York: Research Program on the U.S.S.R., 1954), p. 72.

61. Mogilianskii, "Tragediia Ukrainy," 11:97–98; Osyp Nazaruk, *Rik na Velykii Ukraini*, p. 77; Mykola Kapustians'kyi, *Pokhid ukrains'kykh armii na Kyiv-Odesu v 1919 rotsi*, 1:13; Antin Krezub, "Mizh Biloiu Tserkvoiu i Motovylivkoiu," LCK, no. 1 (1930), p. 7; Denikin, "Getmanstvo i Direktoriia na Ukraine," p. 139.

62. Kovalevs'kyi, *Pry dzherelakh borot'by*, p. 514; *Die deutsche Okkupation der Ukraine*, pp. 24, 48 ff., as quoted in Pipes, *Formation of the Soviet Union*, p. 134.

63. *Istoriia ukrains'koho viis'ka*, p. 424; Khrystiuk, *Zamitky i materiialy*, 3:55;

D. Doroshenko, *Istoriia Ukrainy*, 2:269; Vynnychenko, *Vidrodzennia natsii*, 3:71; V. Zadoianyi, "Povstans'ka stykhiia," TR, no. 46 (1968), p. 14; I. Kapulovskii, "Organizatsiia vostaniia protiv getmana," LR, no. 4 (1923), pp. 98–99; S. Paladiichuk, "Spohady pro 'Hrebenkivshchynu,'" VK, no. 1 (27) (1967), p. 35.

64. *Die deutsche Okkupation der Ukraine*, p. 201, as quoted in Xenia Joukoff Eudin, "The German Occupation of the Ukraine in 1918," *The Russian Review* 1 (1941): 100.

65. IA. Shelygin, "Partizanskaia bor'ba s getmanshchinoi i avstrogermanskoi okkupatsiei," LR, no. 6 (33) (1928), p. 64.

66. Zadoianyi, "Povstans'ka stykhiia," no. 49, p. 5; V. Aussem, "K istorii povstanchestva na Ukraine," LR, no. 5 (20) (1926), p. 8; *Istoriia Ukrains'koho viis'ka*, p. 424; Zadoianyi, "Povstans'ka stykhiia," no. 47, p. 14.

67. "Russia's Reign of Terror," *The New York Times Current History*, 9:76; D. Doroshenko, *Istoriia Ukrainy*, 2:119–21; Dontsov, *Rik 1918*, p. 17. Doroshenko gives the figures of 200 killed and 1000 wounded.

68. D. Doroshenko, *Istoriia Ukrainy*, 2:122–23; William Henry Chamberlin, *The Russian Revolution, 1917–1918* (New York: Macmillan, 1947), 2:126.

69. I. K. Kakhovskaia, "Delo Eikhgorna i Denikina," in *Puti revoliutsii*, p. 218; Hornykiewicz, *Ereignisee in der Ukraine*, 3:181–84; D. Doroshenko, *Istoriia Ukrainy*, 2:124–25.

70. Kakhovskaia, "Delo Eikhgorna i Denikina," p. 219.

Chapter 2, The Partisan Movement

1. Field Marshall Ludendorff reported: "Hetman Skoropadsky told me that he never noticed how his corps, which he commanded in the war, dissolved. It simply vanished all at once. This simple story made a tremendous impression on me" (Ludendorff, *Own Story*, 2:125).

2. Chamberlin, *Russian Revolution*, 2:226; Kapulovskii, "Organizatsiia vostaniia protiv getmana," p. 98; Pavlo Shandruk, *Arms of Valor*, p. 75; Kovalevs'kyi, *Pry dzherelakh borot'by*, p. 500; Vynnychenko, *Vidrodzennia natsii* 3:71; N. Kryvoruchko, "Likvidatsiia ob'edinenoi bandy Gryzlo, Tsvetkovskogo i Guliai-Gulenko," in *Vospominaniia o G. I. Kotovskom*, ed. M. P. Belyi, p. 104; N. I. Shtif, *Pogromy na Ukraine*, p. 3; M. A. Rubach, ed., "K istorii grazhdanskoi voiny na Ukraine," LR, no. 3 (8) (1924), p. 177; Vladimir A. Maevskii, *Povstantsy Ukrainy, 1918–1919 gg.* (Novi Sad: S. F. Filonov, 1938), p. 39.

3. Voyageur, "A Bird's Eye View of the Ukraine," *The New Europe* 15 (June 3, 1920): 182; see also A. Valiis'kyi, "Povstanchyi rukh v Ukraini v rokakh 1917–1922," VK, no. 4 (1961), p. 13.

4. Kapustians'kyi, *Pokhid ukrains'kykh armii*, 1:13–14; Udovychenko, *Ukraina u viini za derzhavnist'*, p. 44; Tsapko, "Partyzany na Skhidnii Ukraini," p. 7; Mykhailo Omelianovych-Pavlenko, *Na Ukraini 1917–1918*, pp. 86–87.

5. Omelianovych-Pavlenko, *Zymovyi pokhid*, 2:22–23; Zadoianyi, "Povstans'ka stykhiia," no. 46, p. 15; Roman Gul', "Kievskaia epopeia, noiabr'–dekabr', 1918 g.," ARR 2 (1925): 59; Shelygin, "Partizanskaia bor'ba s getmanshchinoi," p. 65; H. Karpenko, "Selians'kyi rukh na Kyivshchyni za chasiv avstro-hermans'koi okkupatsii ta hat'manshchyny," LR, nos. 1–2 (46–47) (1931), p. 74; M. Vinogradov, "Chermu ia byl svidietelem," p. 12.

6. Valiis'kyi, "Povstanchyi rukh v Ukraini v rokakh," p. 14; Mazepa, *Ukraina*

v ohni, 2:45; Vynnychenko, *Vidrodzennia natsii*, 3:432–33.

7. Dmytro Solovei, *Holhota Ukrainy* (Winnipeg: Nakl. Ukrains'koho holosu, 1953), p. 22; Arthur E. Adams, *Bolsheviks in the Ukraine*, p. 233; Fedenko, *Ukrains'kyi rukh*, p. 185.

8. L. Poltava, "Povstantsi na pivdni Ukrainy v 1920–21 rokakh," VK, no. 3 (28) (1967), pp. 32, 35.

9. Kryvoruchko, "Likvidatsiia ob'edinennoi bandy Gryzlo," p. 104; see also N. P-a, "Protybol'-shevytski povstannia v Ukraini v 1921 r.," VK, no. 6 (43) (1969), pp. 57–58; P. Liutarevych, "Istoriia odnoho povstannia na Poltavshchyni ta ukrain-s'ke pidpillia v rokakh, 1920–1926," *Ukrains'kyi zbirnyk*, no. 4 (1955), p. 136.

10. Fedenko, *Ukrains'kyi rukh*, p. 214.

11. Isaak Mazepa, "Zymovyi pokhid i partyzans'kyi rukh na Ukraini v 1919 r.," KD 1936, p. 92; Oleksander Dotsenko, *Zymovyi pokhid*, pp. CXXVII–CXXVIII; IUrko Tiutiunyk, *Zymovyi pokhid 1919–20 rr.*, 1:72; Zadoianyi, "Povstans'ka stykhiia," no. 46, pp. 14–15.

12. Tiutiunyk, *Zymovyi pokhid*, 1:72.

13. Mazepa, *Ukraina v ohni*, 2:46–47; Tiutiunyk, *Zymovyi pokhid*, 1:73; Dotsenko, *Zymovyi pokhid*, pp. CXXVIII, CXL; Panas Fedenko, "Mynulo pivstolittia," SV, no. 220, November 30, 1971; A. Valiis'kyi, "Povstanchyi rukh v Ukraini i otamaniia," SV, no. 54, March 21, 1957.

14. Dotsenko, *Zymovyi pokhid*, p. CXXXVIII.

15. Tiutiunyk, *Zymovyi pokhid*, 1:72.

16. M. Maiorov, *Iz istorii revoliutsiinoi borot'by na Ukraini, 1914–1919*, p. 86.

17. Denikin, "Getmanstvo i Direktoriia na Ukraine," pp. 149–50.

18. The "Neutral Zone" was established by agreements between the German and Soviet Russian local commanders along the northern boundary of Ukraine. The area varied in width from six to twenty-five miles. In theory it was a no-man's land; in reality, however, both sides constantly trespassed it. This buffer strip was designed to prevent clashes between German and Russian troops. See Aussem, "K istorii povstanchestva na Ukraine," p. 8; Adams, *Bolsheviks in the Ukraine*, pp. 19–20; Denikin, "Getmanstvo i Direktoriia na Ukraine," pp. 149–50; Vasyl' Prokhoda, *Zapysky nepokirlyvoho: Istoriia nastional'noho usvidomlennia, zhyttia i diial'nosty zvychainoho ukraintsia* (Toronto: "Porboiem," 1967), 1:269; A. I. Egorov, *Razgrom Denika 1919*, p. 8.

19. Aussem, "K istorii povstanchestva na Ukraine," p. 8; *Istoriia ukrains'koho viis'ka*, pp. 431–32; Paladiichuk, "Spohady pro 'Hrebenkivshchynu,'" p. 36; Prokhoda, *Zapysky nepokirlyvoho*, 1:269–72.

Chapter 3, The Socioeconomic Background of Peasant Unrest in Makhno's Region

1. M. Kubanin, *Makhnovshchina*, pp. 3–4; IUrii Mahalevs'kyi, "Bat'ko Makhno," KD 1930, p. 60; *Bolshaia Sovetskaia entsyklopediia* (Moscow: "Sovet-skaia entsyklopedia," 1938), 38:500; Akademiia nauk URSR, Kiev. Instytut istorii a arkheolohii, *Narys istorii Ukrainy* (Ufa: vyd-vo Akademiia nauk URSR, 1942), p. 176; V. V. Rudnev, *Makhnovshchina*, p. 3; D. Doroshenko, *Narys istorii Ukrainy*, 2:231.

2. N. D. Polons'ka-Vasylenko, *The Settlement of the Southern Ukraine, 1750–1775* (New York: Ukrainian Academy of Arts and Sciences in the U.S.A.,

1955), pp. 326–27; E. I. Druzhinina, *Severnee Prichernomore'e v 1775–1800 gg.* (Moscow, 1959), p. 260.

3. D. Doroshenko, *Narys istorii Ukrainy*, 2:238–40; *Dnipropetrovs'ka oblast'* (Kiev, 1969), p. 13; Kharytia Kononenko, "Dvi manifestatsii," LHKD 1937, p. 12; Krypiakevych [Kholms'kyi], *Istoriia Ukrainy*, p. 307; *Krest'ianskoe dvizhenie v Rossii v 1796–1825 gg.*, p. 855; *Dnipropetrovs'ka oblast'*, p. 15.

4. *Krest'ianskoe dvizhenie v Rossii v 1796–1825 gg.*, pp. 449, 452.

5. A. A. Romanov, "V Tavriiu za volei: Vospominaniia ochevidtsa," *Istoricheskii vestnik* 84 (1901): 264–65, 273.

6. Borschak, "Ukraine in the Russian Empire," 1:669; Polonska-Vasylenko, *Settlement of the Southern Ukraine*, pp. 201, 241–43; S. D. Bodnar, *Sekta Mennonitov v Rossi* (Petrograd: V. D. Smirnov, 1916), pp. 1–2.

7. A. Bondar, "Kto takoi Grigor'ev?" PS, no. 3, pp. 6–7, 12; C. H. Smith, *The Story of the Mennonites*, pp. 377–78.

8. D. Doroshenko, *Narys istorii Ukrainy*, 2:239.

9. Smith, *Story of Mennonites*, p. 23; Druzhinina, *Severnee Prichernomor'e*, p. 166; W. Ohnesseit, "Die deutschen Bauernkolonien in Südrussland von ihrer Grundung bis zur Gegenwart," *Preusussische Jahrbücher*, no. 206 (1926), p. 169.

10. Harry Schwartz, *Russia's Soviet Economy* (New York: Prentice-Hall, 1950), p. 63.

11. Kononenko, "Dvi manifestatsii ' p. 136.

12. D. Doroshenko, *Narys istorii Ukrainy*, 2:292.

13. N. N. Lashchenko, *Krest'ianskoe dvizhenie na Ukraine v sviazi provedeniem reformy 1861 goda. 60-e gody XIX st.* (Kiev, 1959), p. 520.

14. V. P. Teplysts'kyi, *Reforma 1861 roku i agrarni vidnosyny na Ukraini* (Kiev, 1959), p. 292, as quoted in *Dnipropetroys'ka oblast'*, p. 17; *Krest'ianskoe dvizhenie v Rossi v 1881–1889 gg.*, pp. 780 ff.; *Krest'ianskoe dvizhenie v Rossi v 1890 1900 gg.*, pp. 601 ff.

15. *Krest'ianskoe dvizhenie v Rossii v 1881–1889 gg.*, p. 741.

16. Geroid Tanquary Robinson, *Rural Russia under the Old Regime: A History of the Landlord-Peasant World and a Prologue to the Peasant Revolution in 1917* (London: Longmans, Green, 1932), pp. 138–40; Ivanov, "Revoliutsiia 1905," pp. 28–29.

17. Herbert J. Ellison, *History of Russia* (New York: Holt, Rinehart, and Winston, 1966), pp. 264–66; Kononenko, "Dvi manifestatsii," pp. 97–100; Vasyl' Prokhoda, *Zapysky nepokirlyvoho: Istoriia nastional'noho usvidomlennia, zhyttia i diial'nosty zvychainho ukraintsia* (Toronto: "Proboiem," 1967), p. 122; S. M. Dubrovskii, *Stolypinskaia zemel'naia reforma: Iz istorii sel'skago khoziaistva i krest'ianstva Rossii v nachaie XX veka* (Moscow: 1963), pp. 572, 580.

Chapter 4, The Peasants and the Ukrainian Government

1. Illia Vytanovych, "Agrarna polityka ukrains'kykh uriadiv rokiv revoliutsii i vyzvol'nykh zmahan', 1917–20," UI, nos. 3–4 (15–16) (1967), pp. 19–27.

2. Khrystiuk, *Zamitky i materiialy*, 1:37.

3. Bunyan and Fisher, *Bolshevik Revolution*, pp. 435–36.

4. Shul'hyn, "The Period of the Central Rada (Council)," 1:743.

5. Bunyan and Fisher, *Bolshevik Revolution*, p. 446.

6. Bunyan, *Intervention*, pp. 16–17.

7. Shul'hyn, "The Period of the Hetmanate," 1:747; Vytanovych, "Agrarna polityka ukrains'kykh uriadiv," p. 50.

8. Ibid.; Bunyan, *Intervention*, pp. 30–32; Panas Fedenko, "The Period of the Directory," in UE, 1:756–57.

9. M. Irchan [M. Babiuk], "Makhno i makhnovtsi," IKCK 1936, p. 116. The British war correspondent with the Denikin troops, John E. Hodgson, reports that Makhno "in an endeavour to bind the poorer people to his cause, distributed spurious charters which claimed to grant free tracts of land to all and sundry. I have seen one of the documents. It was elegantly worded and bore Makhno's signature" (John Ernest Hodgson, *With Denikin's Armies*, p. 119); Mazepa, *Ukraina v ohni*, 1:62; Mazepa, "Zymovyi pokhid i partyzans'kyi rukh," p. 92.

10. Nestor Makhno, *Russkaia revoliutsiia na Ukraine*, 1:14.

11. Makhno himself was a replica of a well-known Zaporozhian Cossack leader Ivan Sirko (d. 1680) who was born in Merefa in present Kharkiv province. A very active and brave military leader, Sirko's main aim had been preserving the Orthodox religion and attaining personal fame in the struggle against the Turks and Tatars. He organized over twenty large expeditions and many smaller campaigns against the Turks and Tatars by way of the Dnieper and the steppes, gaining great respect among the Cossacks and fear among his enemies. Sirko, however, like Makhno, was a primitive statesman who contributed greatly to the destruction of Ukrainian political independence. Sirko saw no problems other than his campaigns. He damaged the plan of Hetman Ivan Vyhovs'kyi in his war against Muscovy in 1659, by attacking his allies, the Tatars. He did similar harm to Hetman Petro Doroshenko in his joint struggle with the Turks and Tatars against Poland in 1668 (Krypiakevych [Kholms'kyi], *Istoriia Ukrainy* [Munich: Nakl. Naukovoho-t-va im. Shevchenka, 1949], pp. 265–66; IEvhen Onats'kyi, "Nestor Makhno," *Ukrains'ka mala entsyklopediia* [Buenos Aires: Nakl. Administratury UAPTs v Argentini, 1965], p. 1748).

12. Makhno, *Russkaia revoliutsia*, 1:14.

13. Nestor Makhno, *Ukrainskaia revoliutsiia*, 3:149.

14. Pavlo Dubas, "Z raionu Makhna," LCK, no. 3 (1932), p. 8.

15. Although the Russian peasants had been living under a national government for several centuries, their national and political attitude toward their country was not much different from the attitude of the Ukrainian peasants in the region of the Makhno movement: "The War and the Revolution revealed, indeed, an astonishing absence of civil spirit in even the educated classes of Russia; but the simple peasant soldiers had not even the most elementary notions of patriotism. Denikin quotes a story, often told in Russia during the war, about a group of peasant soldiers who had been listening to talk about the danger of the Germans overrunning Russia. 'We are from Tambov,' they said, 'the Germans will never advance as far as Tambov'" (Michael S. Farbman, *Bolshevism in Retreat* [London: W. Collins, 1923], p. 30).

Chapter 5, The Anarchism of the Peasants and Makhno

1. Margolin, *From a Political Diary*, p. 24.

2. Emma Goldman, *Living My Life*, p. 109.

3. Emma Goldman, *My Disillusionment in Russia*, pp. 96, 104.

4. D. Erde, "Politychna prohrama anarkho-makhnovshchyny," LR, no. 1 (40) (1930), p. 53.

5. Goldman, *Living My Life*, p. 109.

6. Goldman, *My Disillusionment in Russia*, pp. 103, 104.

7. Ibid., p. 105.

8. Volin, "Nestor Makhno," DT, no. 82 (1934), p. 6.

9. Voline, *The Unknown Revolution*, p. 158.

10. P. Str[uve], ed., "Istoricheskie materialy i dokumenty: Ideologiia makhnovshchiny," *Russkaia mysl'*, nos. 1–2 (1921), p. 231.

11. Makhno, *Ukrainskaia revoliutsiia*, 3:7–8.

12. Nestor Makhno, *Makhnovshchina i ee vchorashnie soiuzniki-bol'sheviki*, p. 16.

13. V. Holubnychyi, "Makhno i makhnivshchyna," in *Entsyklopediia ukrainoznavstva*, 4:1494.

14. P. Arshinov, *Istoriia makhnovskogo dvizheniia, 1918–1921 gg.*, p. 49; David Footman, "Nestor Makhno," in *St. Antony's Papers*, no. 6, p. 79; Struve, "Istoricheskie materialy i dokumenty," p. 228; Edward Hallett Carr, *The Bolshevik Revolution, 1917–1923* (New York: Macmillan Co., 1951), 1:320.

15. G. Novopolin, "Makhno i guliai-pol'skaia gruppa anarkhistov," *Katorga i ssylka*, no. 34, p. 71. Valdemar Antoni was a Czech who in his youth lived with his uncle, a saloon owner, in Huliai-Pole where he attended school. After graduation Antoni left the town for Katerynoslav. Upon his return some years later he carried out political activities among his friends, bringing anarchist pamphlets and brochures from Katerynoslav, where he was a member of an anarchist group. Having gained the confidence of his friends, he suggested that they form an anarchist group under the direction of the Katerynoslav group headquarters, and Antoni acted as liaison between the two groups. The irony is that while many of the original members of the group paid with their lives for their activities, Antoni, the organizer of the first anarchist group at Huliai-Pole, emigrated to the United States in 1911 or 1912 (Anatol' Hak, "Pravda pro Huliai-Pole," *Suchasnist'* 12, no. 9 [1972]: 68, 72; Victor Peters, *Nestor Makhno*, pp. 19–24).

16. Makhno, *Russkaia revoliutsiia*, 1:58–59.

17. I. Teper [Gordeev], *Makhno*, pp. 22–23.

18. Makhno, *Russkaia revoliutsiia*, 1:107.

19. G. D. H. Cole, *A History of Socialist Thought* (London: Macmillan & Co., 1958), 4:1, 211; Chamberlin, *The Russian Revolution, 1917–23*, 2:232.

20. Muromets, "Nestor Makhno," *Probuzhdenie*, nos. 52–53 (1934), p. 16.

21. Teper, *Makhno*, p. 27.

22. Paul Avrich, *The Russian Anarchists*, p. 56; George Woodcock, *Anarchism*, p. 20; Iwan Majstrenko, *Borot'bism*, p. 2.

23. D. Novak, "The Place of Anarchism in the History of Political Thought," *The Review of Politics* 20 (1958): 321; Paul Avrich, "The Anarchists in the Russian Revolution," *The Russian Review* 26, no. 4 (1967): 341–42.

24. Novak, "Place of Anarchism," pp. 321–22; Avrich, *Russian Anarchists*, pp. 72–73; Woodcock, *Anarchism*, p. 21; M. Ravich-Cherkas'kyi, *Anarkhisty*, pp. 37 ff.; Erde, "Politychna prohrama anarkho-makhnovshchyny," p. 44.

25. Novak, "Place of Anarchism," pp. 322–23; Avrich, *Russian Anarchists*, p. 56; Woodcock, *Anarchism*, p. 324.

26. V. V. Komin, *Anarkhizm v Rossii*, p. 203.

27. Ibid., pp. 203–4.

28. *Izvestiia*, no. 83 (347), April 26, 1918, as quoted in Komin, *Anarkhizm v Rossii*, p. 204.

29. *Izvestiia*, no. 91 (355), May 10, 1918, as quoted in Komin, *Anarkhizm v Rossii*, p. 205; see also B. I. Gorev, " 'Anarkhizm podpol'ia' i makhnovshchina," in *Anarkhizm v Rossii*, pp. 126–27.

30. Arshinov, *Istoriia makhnovskogo dvizheniia*, pp. 236–37; Romuald Wojna, "Nestor Machno," *Z pola walki* 13, no. 2 (50) (1970):66; P. Rudenko, *Na Ukraine*, p. 21; Teper, *Makhno*, p. 38.

31. *Pervaia konferentsiia anarkhistskikh organizatsii Ukrainy "Nabat,"* pp. 5–7.

32. *Rezoliutsii pervogo s'ezda Konfederatsii anarkhistskikh organizatsii Ukrainy "Nabat,"* pp. 7–19.

33. Teper, *Makhno*, pp. 16–18; Volin, "Primechaniia" in Makhno, *Pod udarami kontr-revoliutsii*, 2:158; Anatolii Gorelik, *Anarkhisty v rossiiskoi revoliutsii*, pp. 19–20; IA. IAkovlev, *Russkii anarkhizm v velikoi russkoi revoliutsii*, p. 16; Wojna, "Nestor Machno," p. 66.

34. Teper, *Makhno*, pp. 38, 111.

35. Goldman, *Living My Life*, p. 813.

36. During its existence over forty issues were published, but only a few numbers are to be found in the libraries of Western countries; some of the thousands of leaflets issued by the Makhno army can likewise be found in the West (I. J. van Rossum, ed., "Proclamations of the Makhno Movement, 1920," *International Review of Social History* 13, pt. 2:249).

37. Voline, *Unknown Revolution*, p. 157; Ravich-Cherkas'kyi, *Anarkhisty*, pp. 58–59; Footman, "Nestor Makhno," pp. 110–11; Anatolii Gorelik, *Goneniia na anarkhizm v Sovetskoi Rossii*, p. 20; G. P. Maximoff, *The Guillotine at Work*, p. 358; Kubanin, *Makhnovshchina*, p. 206.

38. Woodcock, *Anarchism*, p. 424; Volin, "Delo 'Nabata,'" DT, nos. 7–8 (1925–26), p. 4; Rudenko, *Na Ukraine*, pp. 22–24; Kubanin, *Makhnovshchina*, p. 213.

39. Goldman, *Living My Life*, p. 765.

Chapter 6, Nestor Makhno

1. N. Klassen, "Makhno und Lenin," *Der Bote*, March 1, 1966, p. 12; Pietro Quaroni, "Makhno," in *Diplomatic Bags*, p. 11; F. Meleshko, "Nestor Makhno ta ioho anarkhiia," LCK, no. 1 (1935), p. 12; V. Kalyna, "V Umani," SV, January 19, 1953; V. Belash, "Makhnovshchina," LR, no. 3 (1928), p. 212; M. Gutman, "Pod vlast'iu anarkhistov," *Russkoe proshloe*, no. 5 (1923), p. 67; Mahalevs'kyi, "Bat'ko Makhno," p. 61; Mikhail Kiselev, *Agitpoezd*, p. 29.

2. Makhno, "Zapiski Nestor Makhno," AV, no. 1 (1923), p. 16; G. Kuz'menko, "Vidpovid' na stattiu 'Pomer Makhno' v 'Novii pori,'" PRO, nos. 50–51 (1934), p. 17; "N. I. Makhno," *Seiatel'*, no. 6 (1934), p. 20; Mahalevs'kyi, "Bat'ko Makhno," p. 61. There is a discrepancy concerning Makhno's birth. Some authors give 1884, but Makhno and those who knew him personally give the date 1889. Judging from the commutation of the death penalty to life imprisonment in 1910 because he was underage in 1906 when he committed the crime, the second date must be correct.

3. Interview with Vasyl' Luzhnyi (born 1906, near Huliai-Pole) by author, on July 21, 1970, Idaho Springs, Colo.; Woodcock, *Anarchism*, p. 416; V. A. Auerbakh, "Revoliutsionnoe obshchestvo po lichnym vospominaniiam," ARR 16 (1925), p. 98. Huliai-Pole was established in 1785 and subsequently became

an administrative, industrial, and commercial center, with two churches, one synagogue, three schools, a hospital, a post office, two steam mills and a few dozen windmills, two factories of agricultural machinery, many artisan workshops, stores, grain market, and distilleries, as well as great fairs. A few kilometers from the town was a railroad station on the Chapline-Berdians'k line (Hak, "Pravda pro Huliai-Pole," p. 66; Peters, *Nestor Makhno*, pp. 16–17).

4. Voline (V. M. Eichenbaum), "Nestor Makhno," DT, no. 82 (1934), p. 4. In Paris Makhno lived under the name Mikhnenko.

5. Kerner owned an agricultural machinery factory, a mill, a large store, and 500 dessiatines of land near Huliai-Pole that he rented to German colonists. One of his sons, Hryhorii, known as Kernenko, who received higher education in Kharkiv and München, Germany, was a Ukrainian poet and translator (Hak, "Pravda pro Huliai-Pole," p. 67).

6. Makhno, "Zapiski," no. 1, pp. 16–17, and *Russkaia revoliutsiia*, 1:9; Hak, "Pravda pro Huliai-Pole," p. 70; Arshinov, *Istoriia makhnovskogo dvizheniia*, p. 49; Komin, *Anarkhizm v Rossii*, p. 219; Max Nomad, *Apostles of Revolution*, p. 303; Peters, *Nestor Makhno*, p. 15.

7. *The Mennonite Encyclopedia*, 3:431.

8. Hak, "Pravda pro Huliai-Pole," pp. 66–67, 70; Dotsenko, *Zymovyi pokhid*, p. 205; Novopolin, "Makhno i guliai-pol'skaia gruppa anarkhistov," pp. 70–71; Teper, *Makhno*, p. 22; Rudnev, *Makhnovshchina*, p. 16; Kuz'menko, "Vidpovid' na stattiu 'Pomer Makhno' v 'Novii pori,'" p. 17; Anatol' Hak, *Vid Huliai-Polia do N'iu Iorku*, p. 23.

9. Novopolin, "Makhno i guliai-pol'skaia gruppa anarkhistov," pp. 71, 75; Str[uve], "Istoricheskie materialy i dokumenty," p. 228.

10. Novopolin, "Makhno i guliai-pol'skaia gruppa anarkhistov," p. 75.

11. Ibid., pp. 72–74; Hak, "Pravda pro Huliai-Pole," pp. 70–71; Novopolin, "Makhno i guliai-pol'skaia gruppa anarkhistov," p. 74. In the fall of 1909 Semeniuta avenged his brother by killing Karachentsev. In 1911 when he went home, the police surrounded the house and before they could get him, he shot himself (Hak, "Pravda pro Huliai-Pole," pp. 71–72).

12. Makhno, "Zapiski," no. 1, p. 18.

13. Novopolin, "Makhno i guliai-pol'skaia gruppa anarkhistov," p. 75. Makhno was locked in cell no. 8, where he was allowed to have visitors once a month and change of linens and bath every two weeks (Makhno, *Russkaia revoliutsiia*, p. 127).

14. Ihor and Antin Bondarenko, Klym Kyrychenko, IUkhym Orlov, Fylyp Cherniavs'kyi, Ivan Shevchenko, Fylyp and Petro Onyshchenko, Serhii Zablods'kyi, Mariia Martynova, Naum Althauzen, Lev Gorelik, and Kazymyr Lisovs'kyi. According to Makhno's account the group consisted of sixteen. Not all, however, were brought to trial because Antoni escaped abroad. Khshyva was executed on June 17, 1909, and Levadnyi escaped from prison in Oleksandrivs'k in the winter, but on his way to Huliai-Pole he died from cold (Novopolin, "Makhno i guliai-pol'skaia gruppa anarkhistov," pp. 71, 77; Hak, "Pravda pro Huliai-Pole," p. 71; Makhno, "Zapiski," no. 1, p. 18). Hak and Peters maintained that Makhno was not directly associated with the conspirators; however, they do not elaborate on the reason for Makhno's death sentence (Hak, "Pravda pro Huliai-Pole," p. 71; Peters, *Nestor Makhno*, p. 22).

15. Makhno, "Zapiski," no. 1, p. 18; Alexander Berkman, *The Bolshevik Myth*,

pp. 190–91; Rudnev, *Makhnovshchina*, p. 17; "N. I. Makhno," p. 20. According to Arbatov, Makhno was not exiled to hard labor in Siberia because of his illness at the time of his arrival at Butyrki. However, in the same article, the author makes no comment while quoting Makhno, whom he visited in the Warsaw prison in 1922: "The illness in my lungs I acquired at the time of my imprisonment in the Butyrki prison" (Z. Arbatov, "Bat'ko Makhno," *Vozrozhdenie*, 29 [1953] :104, 114).

16. Voline, *Unknown Revolution*, p. 86; Arshinov, *Istoriia makhnovskogo dvizheniia*, p. 50; Makhno, "Zapiski," no. 1, p. 18; Max Nomad, "The Epic of Nestor Makhno," *The Modern Monthly* 9, no. 6:335; Berkman, *Bolshevik Myth*, p. 191; L. Lipotkin, "Nestor Makhno," *Probuzhdenie*, nos. 50–51 (1934), p. 15.

17. Makhno, *Russkaia revoliutsiia*, 1:8; Nikolai N. Golovin, *Rossiiskaia kontr'-revoliutsiia*, 3, pt. 6:37.

18. It is interesting to note that "there were no Bolsheviks at all in the villages at that time" (Makhno, *Russkaia revoliutsiia*, 1:42; Emelian IAroslavskii, *History of Anarchism in Russia*, p. 61). Makhno, *Russkaia revoliutsiia*, 1:13–14, 18–20. At that time the Eighth Regiment of the Serbian Army was stationed in Huliai-Pole; it was joined by a company of the Russian Army. A few officers from these units headed the local administration.

19. Makhno, "Zapiski," no. 1, p. 22; Makhno, *Russkaia revoliutsiia*, 1:27–29; Nomad, *Apostles of Revolution*, p. 304; Mahalevs'kyi, "Bat'ko Makhno," p. 62.

20. Makhno, *Russkaia revoliutsiia*, 1:32, 33, 57.

21. At the end of July, Kornilov was appointed commander in chief of the Russian Army, succeeding General Brussilov, who had failed to restore the army's discipline and capacity to fight. Kerensky hoped that Kornilov, who had a reputation for great energy and iron will, might be more effective. He was also known for his more liberal outlook upon social and political problems than most high officials. Before taking the office, Kornilov demanded: full power for the commander; no governmental interference in his military orders; and the restoration of military discipline. Although these terms were accepted, soon it became obvious that conflict between Kornilov and Kerensky was inevitable because Kornilov was backed by Monarchists, right wing groups, and, above all, officers representing the old order. When Kornilov attempted to restore discipline by reinstating death penalty for military offenses, it brought him into an open opposition to Kerensky. Consequently, Kerensky dismissed Kornilov; however, the latter not only refused to resign, but issued a proclamation to the people asking for support against the government. Moreover, he instructed the cavalry to advance to the capital. After abortive efforts at compromise, Kerensky, with the help of the Mensheviks, Socialist-Revolutionaries, and Bolsheviks, succeeded in neutralizing the conspirators without bloodshed and arrested them, including Kornilov, Lukomskii, and Romanovskii. They were brought to the Bikhov monastery near Mogilev where they were soon joined by Denikin, Markov, and others. After the October counter-revolution, the generals easily escaped from Bikhov to the Don Territory where they subsequently played a prominent role in the organization of the Volunteer Army (Stewart, *White Armies of Russia*, pp. 12–15; Chamberlin, *Russian Revolution*, 1:212 ff.).

22. Makhno, *Russkaia revoliutsiia*, 1:40; Makhno, "Zapiski," no. 1, pp. 22–23; Arshinov, *Istoriia makhnovskogo dvizheniia*, p. 51; Nomad, *Apostles of Revolution*, p. 304; Mahalevs'kyi, "Bat'ko Makhno," p. 65.

23. Makhno, *Russkaia revoliutsiia*, 1:64; see also Nestor Makhno, "Velikii Oktiabr' na Ukraine," DT, no. 29 (October 1927), p. 10.

24. Footman, "Nestor Makhno," p. 81; Makhno, *Russkaia revoliutsiia*, 1:203.

25. Makhno, *Russkaia revoliutsiia*, 1:68–69.

26. Mahalevs'kyi, "Bat'ko Makhno," p. 66.

27. Alexander Berkman, "Nestor Makhno: The Man Who Saved the Bolsheviki," personal recollection, p. 12.

28. Mahalevs'kyi, "Bat'ko Makhno," pp. 63–66; Osyp Dumin, *Istoriia Liegionu Ukrains'kykh Sichovykh Stril'tsiv*, p. 254; Dotsenko, *Zymovyi pokhid*, p. 209; Belash, "Makhnovshchina," p. 194; Kiselev, *Agitpoezd*, pp. 31–32. In the fall of 1919 Nikiforova was captured and hanged by General Slashchov in Symferopil' (Mahalevs'kyi, "Bat'ko Makhno," p. 66). According to Makhno, it was his and Nikiforova's detachments that disarmed a battalion stationed at Orikhiv; it was part of the Forty-Eighth Regiment stationed in Berdians'k (Makhno, *Russkaia revoliutsiia*, 1:152).

Chapter 7, Makhno's National Consciousness

1. Makhno, *Ukrainskaia revoliutsiia*, 3:154.

2. Makhno, *Pod udarami kontr-revoliutsii*, 2:153.

3. Omelianovych-Pavlenko, *Zymovyi pokhid*, 2:29; see also M. Irchan, "Makhno i makhnivtsi," IKCK 1936, p. 120.

4. Makhno, *Russkaia revoliutsia*, 1:6.

5. Makhno, *Pod udarami kontr-revoliutsii*, 2:124, 212.

6. Ibid., p. 132.

7. Makhno, *Russkaia revoliutsiia*, 1:93.

8. Makhno, "Neskol'ko slov o natsional'nom voprose na Ukraine," DT, no. 19 (December 1926), pp. 4–5.

9. Makhno, *Pod udarami kontr-revoliutsii*, 2:39.

10. According to Emma Goldman who met Makhno's wife in 1920, in Kyiv: "She was a woman of twenty-five" (Goldman, *Living My Life*, p. 148).

11. Meleshko, *Nestor Makhno ta ioho anarkhiia*, no. 1, pp. 10–11; Irchan, *Makhno i makhnivtsi*, p. 19.

12. Natal'ia Sukhogorskaia, "Vospominanie o makhnovshchine," *Kandal'nyi zvon*, no. 6 (1927), pp. 54–55.

13. Goldman, *Living My Life*, pp. 147–48. Berkman, *Bolshevik Myth*, pp. 235–36.

14. Meleshko, "Nestor Makhno ta ioho anarkhiia," no. 1, p. 11.

15. Goldman, *Living My Life*, pp. 150–51.

16. Berkman, *Bolshevik Myth*, p. 236.

17. Omelianovych-Pavlenko, *Zymovyi pokhid*, 2:29.

18. Z. Arbatov, "Ekaterinoslav 1917–22 gg.," ARR 12 (1923):95.

19. Tsapko, "Partyzany na Skhidnii Ukraini," p. 8.

20. Gutman, "Pod vlast'iu anarkhistov," p. 64.

21. Omelianovych-Pavlenko, *Zymovyi pokhid*, 2:27; Dotsenko, *Zymovyi pokhid*, p. CXXXIV; Arshinov, *Istoriia makhnovskogo dvizheniia*, p. 95.

22. Omelianovych-Pavlenko, *Zymovyi pokhid*, 2:27.

23. Kubanin, *Makhnovshchina*, p. 165; Holubnychyi, "Makhno i makhnivshchyna," p. 1494; N. P-pa, ed., "Protybol'shevyts'ki povstannia na Ukraini v 1921 r.," LCK, no. 6 (1932), p. 22; "Povstancheskoe dvizhenie na Ukraine," *Revoliutsionnaia Rossiia*, no. 11 (192–), p. 23; "1919 god v Ekaterinoslave i Aleksandrovske," LR, no. 4 (13) (1925), p. 9; V. I. Miroshevskii, "Vol'nyi Ekaterinoslav," PR, no. 9 (1922), p. 199.

24. Teper, *Makhno*, pp. 20, 87; Erde, "Politychna prohrama anarkho-makhnovshchyny," no. 2, p. 39.

25. *Holos makhnovtsia*, no. 1 (November 1, 1920), as quoted in Erde, "Politychna prohrama anarkho-makhnovshchyny," no. 2, p. 39.

26. Kubanin, *Makhnovshchina*, pp. 165–66.

27. Teper, *Makhno*, p. 114.

28. Fedenko, "Mynulo pivstolittia," SV, no. 221 (December 1, 1971), p. 2.

29. Makhno, *Makhnovshchina*, pp. 9–10.

30. Voline, *Unknown Revolution*, p. 124; see also N. Makhno, "Otkrytoe pis'mo t-shchu Maksymovu," DT, no. 15 (1926), p. 11.

Chapter 8, Makhno, the Bolsheviks, and the Central Rada

1. Makhno, "Velikii Oktiabr' na Ukraine," p. 10; see also his *Russkaia revoliutsiia*, 1:99–100.

2. Makhno, *Ukrainskaia revoliutsiia*, 3:7–8; see also his "Put' bor'by protiv gosudarstva," DT, no. 17 (October 1926), pp. 5–6.

3. Makhno, *Russkaia revoliutsiia*, 1:96.

4. Makhno, "Neskol'ko slov o natsional'nom voprose na Ukraine," p. 6.

5. Makhno, *Russkaia revoliutsiia*, 1:14.

6. Ibid., p. 47.

7. Ibid., p. 71.

8. Mahalevs'kyi, "Bat'ko Makhno," p. 67.

9. Makhno, *Russkaia revoliutsiia*, 1:110.

10. Ibid., pp. 114–15.

11. Mahalevs'kyi, "Bat'ko Makhno," p. 67.

12. V. A. Antonov-Ovseenko, *Zapiski o grazhdanskoi voine*, 1:23.

13. Makhno, *Russkaia revoliutsiia*, 1:136.

14. Mahalevs'kyi, "Bat'ko Makhno," p. 67; Belash, "Makhnovshchina," p. 196.

15. Makhno, *Russkaia revoliutsiia*, 1:141.

16. Ibid., p. 164.

17. Ibid., pp. 152, 160–63.

18. Ibid., pp. 189, 192.

19. Ibid., pp. 193–94.

20. *Istoriia ukrains'koho viis'ka*, p. 417.

21. Makhno, *Russkaia revoliutsiia*, 1:181; Mazepa, *Ukraina v ohni*, 1:48.

22. Makhno, "Zapiski," no. 1, p. 24; Rudnev, *Makhnovshchina*, p. 18.

23. To undermine Makhno's effective assistance of the Bolshevik troops, the agriculturist Dmytrenko, a Socialist Revolutionary, who was the chairman of the Huliai-Pole Prosvita association, together with two young men, P. Kovalenko and M. Konoplia, in behalf of the Ukrainian troops cut all the wires leading to Huliai-

Pole. When Makhno after four or five months later discovered this action, his men assassinated Dmytrenko (Makhno, *Russkaia revoliutsiia*, 1:210–11).

24. Ibid., pp. 206–8.

25. Makhno, *Pod udarami kontr-revoliutsii*, 2:11; Arshinov, *Istoriia makhnovskogo dvizheniia*, p. 52; Footman, *Civil War in Russia*, p. 82.

26. Nestor Makhno, "Pechalnye stranitsy russkoi revoliutsii," *Rassvet*, January 29–February 18, 1932, p. 6.

27. Ibid., pp. 6–7.

28. Makhno, *Pod udarami kontr-revoliutsii*, 2:14.

29. Nestor Makhno, "K 10-i godovshchine revoliuts. povstanchestva na Ukraine-makhnovshchiny," DT, nos. 44–45 (1929), p. 4; Makhno, *Pod udarami kontr-revoliutsii*, 2:18–24; Makhno, "Zapiski," no. 1, p. 24; Footman, *Civil War in Russia*, pp. 82–83.

30. Mazepa, *Ukraina v ohni*, 1:24; Mykhailo Omelianovych-Pavlenko, *Na Ukraini 1917–18*, pp. 12–14.

Chapter 9, Makhno's Visits with Kropotkin and Lenin

1. Makhno, *Pod udarami kontr-revoliutsii*, 2:89.
2. Ibid., pp. 32–35.
3. Ibid., pp. 61 ff.
4. Ibid., p. 102.
5. Ibid., p. 107.
6. Ibid. Makhno remembered not only Kropotkin's words but also Kropotkin himself. Makhno supplied him with necessary food in time of need. Kropotkin admitted that "the anarchists of the Ukraine have been trying to make his life easier by supplying him with flour and other products. Makhno, also, when still friendly with the Bolsheviki, had sent him provisions" (Berkman, *Bolshevik Myth*, p. 75).
7. Footman, *Civil War in Russia*, p. 83.
8. Makhno, *Pod udarami kontr-revoliutsii*, 2:122.
9. Ibid., pp. 127–28.
10. Ibid., p. 130.
11. Ibid., p. 131.
12. Ibid.
13. Ibid., p. 132.
14. Zatonskyi was a prominent Ukrainian Communist who later occupied important positions in the Soviet Ukrainian government, including the post of minister of education. In 1937 he and his wife were liquidated by Stalin (*Entsyklopediia ukrainoznovstve: Slovnykova chastyna*, 2:759–60).
15. Makhno, *Pod udarami kontr-revoliutsii*, 2:134–35.
16. Makhno, "K 10-i godovshchine revoliuts.," p. 3.
17. Makhno, *Pod udarami kontr-revoliutsii*, 2:140, 149.
18. One verst equals 3,500 feet.
19. Makhno, *Pod udarami kontr-revolutsii*, 2:154–55.

Chapter 10, The Origin of Makhno's Partisan Movement

1. Makhno "K 10-i godovshchine revoliuts.," p. 3.
2. Makhno, *Ukrainskaia revoliutsiia*, 3:8.

3. Ibid., p. 12.

4. Ibid., pp. 25–27.

5. This was one of the reasons that most of the sources dealing with Makhno portrayed him as a schoolteacher.

6. Makhno, *Ukrainskaia revoliutsiia*, 3:27–30.

7. Ibid., p. 33.

8. Ibid., pp. 35–36.

9. Ibid., pp. 37–38.

10. Ibid., pp. 50 ff.; Makhno, "Zapiski," no. 2, pp. 29–30.

11. Makhno, *Ukrains'kaia revoliutsiia*, 3:62; see also Makhno, "Zapiski," no. 2, pp. 30–31.

12. Makhno, "Zapiski," no. 2, p. 32; Makhno, *Ukrainskaia revoliutsiia*, 3:89–90.

13. Andrii Moskalenko to L. Bykovskyi, New York, July 18, 1971.

14. Makhno, *Ukrainskaia revoliutsiia*, 3:70–71; Omelianovych-Pavlenko, *Zymovyi pokhid*, 2:25; Ivan Hnoiovyi, "Chy 'Bat'ko' Nestor Makhno—Ukr. natsional'nyi heroi?," TR, no. 38 (1966), p. 12; S. Chernomordik (Larionov), *Makhno i makhnovshchina*, p. 13.

15. Makhno, *Ukrainskaia revoliutsiia*, 3:73; see also Makhno, "Zapiski," no. 2, p. 33.

16. Makhno, *Ukrainskaia revoliutsiia*, 3:74–75; Makhno, "Zapiski," no. 2, pp. 34–35; Footman, *Civil War in Russia*, p. 91.

17. Makhno, *Ukrainskaia revoliutsiia*, 3:82–84; Makhno, "Zapiski," no. 2, pp. 36–37.

18. Makhno, *Ukrainskaia revoliutsiia*, 3:84.

19. Ibid.; Belash, "Makhnovshchina," p. 208; Nomad, "Epic of Nestor Makhno," no. 6, p. 337. "Bat'ko" is an affectionate Ukrainian term for "Father" with the additional meaning of supreme military leader. Makhno took this honor seriously and retained it as his title.

20. Makhno, *Ukrainskaia revoliutsiia*, 3:88–91; Makhno, "Zapiski," nos. 3–4, pp. 23–24; Komin, *Anarkhizm v Rossii*, p. 224; Arshinov, *Istoriia makhnovskogo dvizheniia*, pp. 57–58; Rudnev, *Makhnovshchina*, pp. 23–24.

21. Makhno, "Zapiski," nos. 3–4, pp. 24–28; Makhno, *Ukrainskaia revoliutsiia*, 3:118–19; Arshinov, *Istoriia makhnovskogo dvizheniia*, pp. 58–59.

22. Makhno, "Zapiski," nos. 3–4, pp. 27–38; Makhno, *Ukrainskaia revoliutsiia*, 3:96–98, 104–5.

Chapter 11, Organization and Tactics of Makhno's Partisan Army

1. Makhno, *Ukrainskaia revoliutsiia*, 3:123.

2. Goldman, *Living My Life*, p. 149.

3. Makhno, *Ukrainskaia revoliutsiia*, 3:128 ff.; Arshinov, *Istoriia makhnovskogo dvizheniia*, p. 59.

4. Dm. Varetskii, "Marshal V. K. Bliukher," *Novyi zhurnal* 27 (1951):259; Oleksander Udovychenko, *Tretia Zalizna dyviziia*, p. 49.

5. Makhno, *Ukrainskaia revoliutsiia*, 3:142.

6. IA. Slashchov, "Iz opyta voiny: Materialy dlia istorii grazhdanskoi voiny v Rossii: Operatsii belykh, Petliury i Makhno v iuzhnoi Ukraine v poslenei chetverty 1919 goda," *Voennyi vestnik*, nos. 9–10 (1922), pp. 38–39.

7. M. Kapustians'kyi, "Makhno i makhnovshchyna," SV, no. 243 (November 17, 1934), p. 2.

8. Omelianovych-Pavlenko, *Zymovyi pokhid*, 2:25.

9. Slashchov, "Iz opyta voiny," pp. 38–39.

10. Omelianovych-Pavlenko, *Zymovyi pokhid*, 2:26.

11. Kapustians'kyi, "Makhno i makhnovshchyna," p. 2.

12. I. Danilov, "Vospominaniia o moei podnevol'noi sluzhbie u bol'shevikov," ARR 16 (1925): 162.

13. V. M., "Dontsy na makhnovskom frontie," *Kazach'i dumy*, no. 13 (1923), pp. 9–10.

14. Mahalevs'kyi, "Bat'ko Makhno," p. 69; Belash, "Makhnovshchina," p. 213.

15. Kubanin, *Makhnovshchina*, pp. 167–68; V. M., "Dontsy na makhnovskom frontie," no. 13, p. 10; "Makhnovskaia armiia" (manuscript), pp. 9–10; Teper, *Makhno*, pp. 76–77; Vl. Miroshevskii, "Vol'nyi Ekaterinoslav," p. 202; L. Nikulin, "Gibel' makhnovshchiny," *Znamia*, no. 3 (1941), p. 179; Volin, "V dopolnenie k 'otkrytomu pis'mu t-shchu Maksymovu' t-shcha N. Makhno," DT, no. 16 (1926), p. 16; Rudnev, *Makhnovshchina*, p. 73.

16. Antonov-Ovseenko, "V borot'bi za Radians'ku Ukrainu," LR, no. 5 (1932), p. 117; Teper, *Makhno*, p. 76; V. M., "Dontsy na makhnovskom frontie," no. 13, p. 10; Victor Serge, *Memoirs of a Revolutionary, 1901–1941*, p. 121; Igrenev, "Ekaterinoslavskiia vospominaniia," p. 238; Mazepa, *Ukraina v ohni*, 1:62; Vasyl' Dubrovs'kyi, *Bat'ko Nestor Makhno—Ukrains'kyi natsional'nyi heroi*, p. 8; E. IAkymiv, "Hostyna Makhna v Umani," IKCK 1929, p. 79; Miroshevskii, "Vol'nyi Ekaterinoslav," p. 199; Hodgson, *With Denikin's Armies*, p. 117.

17. "Makhnovskaia armiia," p. 3; N. Makhno, "K voprosu o zashchite revoliutsii," DT, no. 25 (1925), p. 14; Kubanin, *Makhnovshchina*, p. 172; Miroshevskii, "Vol'nyi Ekaterinoslav," p. 201.

18. Kubanin, *Makhnovshchina*, pp. 189–90; R. Eideman, "Piataia godovshchina odnogo uroka," VR, no. 12 (1926), p. 37; N. A. Efimov, "Deistviia protiv Makhno s ianvaria, 1920 g. po ianvar 1921 g.," *Sbornik trudov Voenno-nauchnogo obshchestva* 1 (1921):200; Miroshevskii, "Vol'nyi Ekaterinoslav," p. 200.

19. Osyp Tsebrii, "Vospominaniia partizana," DT-P, no. 32 (1950), p. 14.

20. "Makhnovskaia armiia," p. 1; Vinogradov, "Chemu ia byl svidietelem," pp. 10–11; IAkymiv, "Hostyna Makhna v Umani," p. 79.

21. Makhno, *Makhnovshchina*, p. 18.

22. Makhno, *Russkaia revoliutsiia*, 1:198; idem, *Ukrainskaia revoliutsiia*, 3:70–71; Omelianovych-Pavlenko, *Zymovyi pokhid*, 2:25.

23. Belash, "Makhnovshchina," p. 214; Arshinov, *Istoriia makhnovskogo dvizheniia*, p. 56; Rudnev, *Makhnovshchina*, p. 23.

24. Makhno, *Ukrainskaia revoliutsiia*, 3:147–48; Kubanin, *Makhnovshchina*, pp. 40–41; S. G. Semanov, "Makhnovshchina i ee krakh," VI, no. 9 (1966), p.39.

25. Makhno, *Ukrainskaia revoliutsiia*, 3:95.

26. Belash, "Makhnovshchina," p. 221; Mykh. Mykhailyk, "Ukrains'ke selo v chasy natsion. revoliutsii,"LCK, no. 2 (1934), p. 7; Bulavenko, "Kuban' na perelomi," *Rozbudova natsii*, nos. 3–4 (74–75) (1934), pp. 90–91; Antonov-Ovseenko, *Zapiski*, 4:304; idem, "V borot'bi za Radians'ku Ukrainu," no. 5, p. 115.

27. Dubrovs'kyi, *Bat'ko Nestor Makhno*, p. 11; Meleshko, "Nestor Makhno ta ioho anarkhiia," no. 1 (1935), p. 12; "Makhnovskaia armiia," p. 3; Voline, *Uknown*

Revolution, p. 142.

28. D. Kin, "Povstancheskoe dvizhenie protiv denikinshchiny na Ukraine," LR, nos. 3–4 (1926), p. 79; Kubanin, *Makhnovshchina*, p. 174; Miroshevskii, "Vol'nyi Ekaterinovslav," pp. 201, 208; Gutman, "Pod vlast'iu anarkhistov," p. 62; Denikin, *Ocherki russkoi smuty*, 5:234.

29. Arshinov, *Istoriia makhnovskogo dvizheniia*, pp. 157–59; Gutman, "Pod vlast'iu anarkhistov," p. 68; Semanov, "Makhnovshchina i ee krakh," p. 52; Teper, *Makhno*, p. 65; Peters, *Nestor Makhno*, pp. 62–63; Miroshevskii, "Vol'nyi Ekaterinoslav," p. 206.

30. Efimov, "Deistviia protiv Makhno," pp. 203–4.

31. IAkovlev, *Russkii anarkhizm*, p. 34; idem, "Makhnovshchina i anarkhizm," *Krasnaia nov*, no. 2, p. 253; Margushin, "Bat'ko Makhno," NRS, October 13, 1964, p. 2; Arshinov, *Istoriia makhnovskogo dvizheniia*, p. 188; Volodymyr Dubiv, "Ulamok z moho zhyttia," *Vyzvol'nyi shliakh*, no. 6 (219) (1966), p. 191; Kubanin, *Makhnovshchina*, p. 159; D. Lebed', *Itogi i uroki trekh let anarkho-makhnovshchiny*, p. 40; Premysler, "Razgrom banditizma na Ukraine, 1921 g.," *Voenno-istoricheskii zhurnal*, no. 9 (1940), p. 44.

32. Arshinov, *Istoriia makhnovskogo dvizhenniia*, p. 197.

33. Danilov, "Vospominaniia," 16:175; E. Esbakh, "Poslednie dni makhnovshchiny na Ukraine," *Voina i revoliutsiia*, no. 12, pp. 41–42; Kubanin, *Makhnovshchina*, p. 170; Stefan Szpinger, *Z Pierwsza Konna*, p. 178.

34. Szpinger, *Z Pierwsza Konna*, p. 178.

35. Kubanin, *Makhnovshchina*, p. 169; Kapustians'kyi, "Makhno i makhnivshchyna," p. 2; Vl. Vygran, "Vospominaniia o bor'bie s makhnovtsami" (manuscript), p. 6; Eideman, "Piataia godovshchina odnogo uroka," p. 37; P. Sergeev, "Poltavskaia operatsiia protiv Makhno," VR, no. 9 (1927), pp. 122–23; Serge, *Memoirs of a Revolution*, p. 121.

According to a Bolshevik officer, "If we succeed in destroying a detachment, this still does not mean an end to the matter. Indeed, there have been cases in which a commander reports the destruction of a band, and the next day is hit by the same band, often is disarmed, and even lands in prison" (*Komandarm Uborevich: Vospominaniia druzei i soratnikov*, p. 82).

36. Kubanin, *Makhnovshchina*, pp. 169–70; Vl. Maevskii, *Povstantsy Ukrainy, 1918–1919 gg.*, p. 77; Kapustians'kyi, "Makhno i makhnivshchyna," p. 2; Eideman, "Piataia godovshchina odnogo uroka," p. 37.

37. Szpinger, *Z Pierwsza Konna*, pp. 178–79.

38. Danilov, "Vospominaniia," 16:175–76.

39. Mykhailyk, "Ukrains'ke selo v chasy natsion revoliutsii," p. 6.

40. "Makhnovskaia armiia," p. 4; Meleshko, "Nestor Makhno ta ioho anarkhiia," p. 17; Teper, *Makhno*, p. 28; M. Irchan, "Makhno i makhnivtsi," IKCK 1936, p. 120; Volin, "Nestor Makhno," p. 7; Esbakh, "Poslednie dni makhnovshchiny na Ukraine," p. 48.

41. Arbatov, "Ekaterinoslav 1917–22 gg.," 12:98; see also idem, "Bat'ko Makhno," 29:111.

42. Meleshko, "Nestor Makhno ta ioho anarkhiia," no. 4, pp. 16–17; P. A. Pavlov, "Voennye khitrosti," *Voennyi vestnik*, no. 4 (1921), p. 13; C. E. Bechhofer, *In Denikin's Russia and Caucasus, 1919 and 1920*, p. 176; Nikulin, "Gibel' Makhnovshchiny," p. 179.

43. Pavlov, "Voennye khitrosti," p. 13; Esbakh, "Poslednie dni Makhnovshchiny na Ukraine," p. 41.

44. Teper, *Makhno*, pp. 164–65.

Chapter 12, The Overthrow of the Hetman and the Establishment of the Directory

1. Vynnychenko, *Vidrodzennia natsii*, 3:29; see also Doroshenko, *Istoriia Ukrainy*, 2:379.

2. Doroshenko, *Istoriia Ukrainy*, 2:103 ff.; Khrystiuk, *Zamitky i materiialy*, 3:62 ff.

3. Doroshenko, *Istoriia Ukrainy*, 2:107 ff.

4. Ibid., pp. 111–14; Ivanys, *Symon Petliura*, pp. 71, 74, 77; St. Siropolko, "Dva areshtuvannia S. Petliury za het'mana P. Skoropads'koho," KD 1938, pp. 75–77; Reshetar, *Ukrainian Revolution*, pp. 152–53.

5. Doroshenko, *Istoriia Ukrainy*, 2:386 ff.; Khrystiuk, *Zamitky i materiialy*, 3:87 ff.; Fedenko, *Ukrains'kyi rukh*, p. 160; Vynnychenko, *Vidrodzennia natsii*, 3:73 ff.

6. Doroshenko, *Istoriia Ukrainy*, 2:389, 397–98; Khrystiuk, *Zamitky i materiialy*, 3:114; Fedenko, *Ukrains'kyi rukh*, p. 161.

7. Winston S. Churchill, *The Aftermath* (New York: C. Scribner, 1929), p. 168.

8. Serhii Shemet, "Do istorii Ukrains'koi Demokratychno-khliborobs'koi Partii," *Khliborobs'ka Ukraina* 1 (1920): 75; Viktor Andriievs'kyi, *Z mynuloho*, 2, pt. 1:210–11; Doroshenko, *Istoriia Ukrainy*, 2:408; Leikhtenbergskii, "Kak nachalas 'IUzhnaia Armiia,'" 8:38; *Volia* 4, no. 5 (1920): 271; Khrystiuk, *Zamitky i materiialy*, 3:120; Doroshenko, *Istoriia Ukrainy*, 2:114–15.

9. Zenon Stefaniv, *Ukrains'ki zbroini syly 1917–21 rr.*, 1:112; Fedenko, *Ukrains'kyi rukh*, p. 163; Stewart, *White Armies of Russia*, pp. 75–76; Mazepa, *Ukraina v ohni*, 1:59.

10. Khrystiuk, *Zamitky i materiialy*, 3:131–32.

11. Ibid.

12. Nazaruk, *Rik na Velykii Ukraini*, p. 35; Stefaniv, *Ukrains'ki zbroini syly*, 1:113–15; *Istoriia ukrains'koho viss'ka*, pp. 452–54; Vynnychenko, *Vidrodzennia natsii*, 3:130–31; Stefaniv, *Ukrains'kyi zbroini syly*, 1:116–17; V. Stankevich, *Sud'by narodov Rossii* (Berlin: I. P. Ladyzhnikov, 1921), p. 90.

13. Nazaruk, *Rik na Velykii Ukraini*, p. 35; Leikhtenbergskii, "Kak nachalas 'IUzhnaia Armiia,'" p. 42; Vynnychenko, *Vidrodzennia natsii*, 3:157.

14. Nazaruk, *Rik na Velykii Ukraini*, pp. 75–78; Stefaniv, *Ukrains'ki zbroini syly*, 1:118; Udovychenko, *Tretia Zalizna dyviziia*, pp. 46–47; Leikhtenbergskii, "Kak nachalas 'IUzhnaia Armiia,'" p. 45.

15. Sviatoslav Dolenga, *Skoropadshchyna*, p. 140; M. Ivanov, ed., "'Ot vlasti otkazyvaius,'" LR, no. 7 (1924), p. 224.

16. Later, Vynnychenko accused Petliura of knowing the hetman's hiding place in Kyiv but of not denouncing him (Vynnychenko, *Vidrodzennia natsii*, 3:163, 165); Nazaruk, *Rik na Velykii Ukraini*, pp. 77–78; Stewart, *White Armies of Russia*, p. 76; Reshetar, *Ukrainian Revolution*, p. 204; Sergey Markow, *Armee ohne Heimat*, p. 95.

17. For the text of the declaration, see Vynnychenko, *Vidrodzennia natsii*, 3:168 ff.; Khrystiuk, *Zamitky i materiialy*, 4:15 ff.

18. Arnold Margolin, *Ukraina i politika Antanty*, p. 98; Ivanys, *Symon Petliura*, p. 85; Mazepa, *Ukraina v ohni*, 1:75; Vynnychenko, *Vidrodzennia natsii*, 2:184; Fedenko, *Ukrains'kyi rukh*, p. 176; Vynnychenko, *Vidrodzennia natsii*, 3:244–45.

19. Vynnychenko, *Vidrodzennia natsii*, 3:151; Andriievs'kyi, *Z mynuloho*, 2, pt. 2:20–21.

20. Lonlyn Tsehel's'kyi, *Vid Legend do pravdy*, pp. 143–45; 258–60; Kovalevs'kyi, *Pry dzherelakh borot'by*, p. 536; Vynnychenko, *Vidrodzennia natsii*, 3:242–43.

21. Mazepa, *Ukraina v ohni*, 1:88; Khrystiuk, *Zamitky i materiialy*, 4:57–68; Tsehel's'kyi, *Vid legend do pravdy*, pp. 273–83; Mazepa, *Ukraina v ohni*, 1:87–95; Fedenko, *Ukrains'kyi rukh*, pp. 180–81; Moissey G. Rafes, *Dva goda revoliutsii na Ukraine*, pp. 143–52; Reshetar, *Ukrainian Revolution*, pp. 231–32.

22. Mazepa, *Ukraina v ohni*, 1:66–67.

23. Great Britain, Foreign Office, *Documents on British Foreign Policy, 1919–1939*, ed. E. L. Woodward and Rohan Butler (London, first series), 3:361–62.

24. Stewart, *White Armies of Russia*, pp. 154–55; Mazepa, *Ukraina v ohni*, 1:67.

25. Denikin, *Ocherki*, 5:10; Jean Xydias, *L'intervention française en Russie, 1918–1919*, p. 165; Reshetar, *Ukrainian Revolution*, p. 239.

26. Vladimir Margulies, *Ognennye gody*, pp. 6–7.

27. Ibid.; Xydias, *L'intervention française en Russie*, p. 170; Denikin, *Ocherki*, 5:11.

28. Denikin, *Ocherki*, 5:11; Udovychenko, *Tretia zalizna dyviziia*, p. 55.

29. F. Anulov, "Soiuznyi desant na Ukraine," in A. G. Shlichter, ed., *Chernaia kniga*, p. 111; Xydias, *L'intervention française en Russie*, pp. 160, 170–72.

30. Terry L. Smart, "The French Intervention in the Ukraine, 1918–1919," (Ph.D. diss., University of Kansas, 1968), p. 102; Manuil S. Margulies, *God interventsii*, 1:225; A. Gukovskii, "Inostrannaia intervetsiia na Ukraine, 1917–1919 goda," IM 1, no. 71 (1939):93; Chamberlin, *Russian Revolution*, 2:165; Mazepa, *Ukraina v ohni*, 1:68–69; Khrystiuk, *Zamitky i materiialy*, 4:28–29.

31. "Ocherk vzaimootnoshenii vooruzhennykh sil IUga Rossii i predstavitelei frantsuzskago komandovaniia," ARR 16:249–50.

32. Mazepa, *Ukraina v ohni*, 1:69; E. N. Trubetskoi, "Iz putevykh zamietok biezhentsa," ARR 18:194–95; Margulies, *God interventsii*, 1:163 ff.; Kapustians'kyi, *Pokhid ukrains'kykh armii*, 1:31.

33. Denikin, *Ocherki*, 5:34.

34. Trubetskoi, "Iz putevykh zamietok biezhentsa," 18:174; John Bradley, *Allied Intervention in Russia*, p. 148.

35. Nazaruk, *Rik na Velykii Ukraini*, pp. 119–20.

36. Ibid., pp. 126–31; Mazepa, *Ukraina v ohni*, 1:97–98; Vynnychenko, *Vidrodzennia natsii*, 3:259; Khrystiuk, *Zamitky i materiialy*, 4:42; Reshetar, *Ukrainian Revolution*, p. 241.

37. Mazepa, *Ukraina v ohni*, 1:99–100.

38. Margolin, *Ukraina i politika Antanty*, pp. 113–19.

39. Margolin, *From a Political Diary*, pp. 37–38.

40. Ibid., p. 70; Nazaruk, *Rik na Velykii Ukraini*, pp. 124–33.

41. Henry G. Alsberg, "The Situation in the Ukraine," *The Nation* 109 (1919): 570.

42. *Narys istorii Ukrainy*, ed. K. Huslystoho, L. Slavina, and F. Iastrebova (Ufa: Vyd-vo Akavemii nauk URSR, 1942), pp. 172–73.

43. Fedenko, *Ukrains'kyi rukh*, pp. 177–78; *Grazhdanskaia voina na Ekaterinoslavshchine, fevral' 1918–1920 gg.*, pp. 72–73.

44. On November 11 the Council of People's Commissars "decided to direct the Revolutionary Military Council of the [Russian Soviet Federated Socialist] Republic to launch an attack within ten days in support of the workers and peasants of Ukraine who rose against the Hetman" (Antonov-Oseenko, *Zapiski*, 3:11, 14).

45. The fears of the rightist Communist group were expressed by a Communist from Katerynoslav: "Although the workers and many peasants, especially in the Chernihiv province, are on our side, there is no basis to think that a [pro-Bolshevik] revolutionary movement can arise, let alone succeed, in Ukraine without the support of considerable forces of the Red Army" (Antonov-Ovseenko, *Zapiski*, 3:12). See also V. Zatonskii, "K voprosu ob organizatsii Vremennogo Raboche Krest'ianskogo Pravitel'stva Ukrainy noiabr' 1919 g.," LR, no. 1 (10) (1925), pp. 139 ff.

46. Zatonskyi, "K voprosu ob organizatsii," p. 149; M. Rubach, "K istorii grazhdanskoi bor'by na Ukraine," LR, no. 4 (9) (1924), p. 164; Mazepa, *Ukraina v ohni*, 1:72; Vynnychenko, *Vidrodzennia natsii*, 3:209–10.

47. Antonov-Ovseenko, *Zapiski*, 3:13–14.

48. Lev Trotskii, *The Trotsky Papers 1919–1922*, 1:242.

49. Antonov-Ovseenko, *Zapiski*, 3:17.

50. Nazaruk, *Rik na Velykii Ukraini*, pp. 135–36; Adams, *Bolsheviks in the Ukraine*, p. 113.

51. Vynnychenko, *Vidrodzennia natsii*, 3:205–8; Khrystiuk, *Zamitky i materiialy*, 4:35–36.

52. Khrystiuk, *Zamitky i materiialy*, 4:37.

53. Ibid., p. 39; Vynnychenko, *Vidrodzennia natsii*, 3:221–23; Mazepa, *Ukraina v ohni*, 1:72–73.

54. Khrystiuk, *Zamitky i materiialy*, 4:40; Mazepa, *Ukraina v ohni*, 1:73.

55. Zynaida Shepel', "Bat'ko povstantsia," LCK, no. 2 (1932), p. 5; Antin Krezub, "IAk zhynuv otaman Zelenyi," *Literaturno-naukovyi visnyk*, no. 10 (1927), pp. 110–13; Mykhailo Sereda, "Otamanshchyna," LCK, no. 2 (1930), pp. 6–8, no. 9, pp. 14–16; Iv. Kozub, "Povstannia proty het'manshchyny ta petliurovshchyny," LR, no. 5 (44) (1930), p. 284.

56. Mazepa, *Ukraina v ohni*, 1:72, 96; Stepan Lazurenko, "Povstannia proty Het'mana i druha viina z bol'shevykamu, 1918–1919 rr.," TR, no. 41 (1966), p. 8; I. Drabatyi, "Epizod z evakuatsii Kyieva v 1919 r.," TR, no. 30 (1964), pp. 3–5; Khrystiuk, *Zamitky i materiialy*, 4:91; Tsehel's'kyi, *Vid Legend do pravdy*, p. 294; Udovychenko, *Tretia Zalizna dyviziia*, pp. 52–53; Antonov-Ovseenko, *Zapiski*, 3:162; Goldenveizer, "Iz kievskikh vospominami, 1919–1921 gg.," ARR 6:236.

57. Khrystiuk, *Zamitky i materiialy*, 4:94–98; Vynnychenko, *Vidrodzennia natsii*, 3:276–77; Udovychenko, *Tretia Zalizna dyviziia*, p. 56.

58. Vynnychenko, *Vidrodzennia natsii*, 3:289–90; Khrystiuk, *Zamitky i materiialy*, 4:119–20.

59. V. I. Lenin, *Sochineniia*, 24:154.
60. Khrystiuk, *Zamitky i materiialy*, 4:172–73.
61. Lenin, *Sochineniia*, 24:75.
62. Khrystiuk, *Zamitky i materiialy*, 4:130–31.
63. Lenin, *Sochineniia*, 24:47–48.
64. A. Shlikhter, "Bor'ba za khleb na Ukraine v 1919 godu," LR, no. 2 (29) (March–April 1928), p. 135.
65. Fedenko, *Ukrains'kyi rukh*, p. 185.
66. Kapustians'kyi, *Pokhid ukrains'kykh armii*, 1:33–34.
67. Antonov-Ovseenko, *Zapiski*, 3:324.
68. Kapustains'kyi, *Pokhid ukrains'kykh armii*, 1:37; Khrystiuk, *Zamitky i materiialy*, 4:116; Bulavenko, "Kuban u pershii polovyni 1919 r.," *Rozbudova natsii*, nos. 5–6 (1934), pp. 135–36.
69. Kapustians'kyi, *Pokhid ukrains'kykh armii*, 1:35–36; Shandruk, *Arms of Valor*, p. 83.
70. Mykhailo Lozyns'kyi, *Halychyna v rr. 1918–1920*, pp. 747 ff.; Reshetar, *Ukrainian Revolution*, pp. 79–80.
71. Matthew Stachiw and Jaroslaw Sztendera, *Western Ukraine at the Turning Point of Europe's History, 1918–1923*, 2:54; Lozyns'kyi, *Halychyna*, pp. 134 ff.; Marian Kukiel, *Zarys historii wojskowosci w Polsce*, p. 231; Roman Dashkevych, *Artyleriia Sichovykh Stril'tsiv u borot'bi za zoloti kyivs'ki vorota*, p. 181; Liubomyr Savoika, "IAk povstala armiia Halliera," *Visti*, no. 122 (1966), p. 66; Marion Romeyko, *Przed i po Maju* (Warsaw, Wydawn. Ministerstwa Obromy Narodowej, 1967), 1:76.
72. Stachiw and Sztendera, *Western Ukraine at the Turning Point*, 2:247–49; Reshetar, *Ukrainian Revolution*, p. 272.
73. *Istoriia ukrains'koho viis'ka*, pp. 506–14; Fedenko, *Ukrains'kyi rukh*, pp. 188–89; Shandruk, *Arms of Valor*, pp. 86–87; Stachiw and Sztendera, *Western Ukraine at the Turning Point*, 2:245 ff.; Volodymyr Galan, *Bateriia smerty* (New York: "Chervona Kalyna," 1968), pp. 82–84; Zepon Stefaniv, "Dva roky v Ukrains'kii armii," LCK, no. 11, p. 14.
74. Lozyns'kyi, *Halychyna*, p. 143.
75. Ibid.
76. Kapustians'kyi, *Pokhid ukrains'kykh armii*, 2:52–59; Stachiw and Sztendera, *Western Ukraine at the Turning Point*, 2:259; Nazaruk, *Rik na Velykii Ukraini*, pp. 183, 187; Lozyns'kyi, *Halychyna*, p. 168; Osyp Levyts'kyi, *Halyts'ka armiia na Velykii Ukraini*, pp. 9–11; Luka Myshuha, *Pokhid ukrains'kykh viis'k na Kyiv, serpen' 1919*, pp. 6–8; *Istoriia ukrains'koho viis'ka*, p. 515.
77. Nazaruk, *Rik na Velykii Ukraini*, p. 184.
78. IAromir Diakiv, "Strategichne polozhennia UHA po perekhodi cherez Zbruch litom 1919 r.," *Ukrains'kyi skytalets'*, no. 6 (28) (1923); Myshuha, *Pokhid ukrains'kykh*, pp. 6–8; Levytsky, *Halyts'ka armiia*, pp. 10–11; Mazepa, *Ukraina v ohni*, 2:17–23; Reshetar, *Ukrainian Revolution*, pp. 284–86; Oleksander Dotsenko, *Litopys ukrains'koi revoliutsii*, 2, pt. 4: 14; *Pro ukrains'ki povstannia*, pp. 8–9; Andrii Holub, "Zbroina vyzvol'na borot'ba na Khersonshchyni v zapilliu voroha, 1917–1919 roku," *Za derzhavnist'*, 11:183.
79. When the Ukrainian troops approached Kyiv, the command issued a vague order: "It is absolutely essential not to enter into hostile action; ask the Denikin

troops not to occupy those localities which are already in our hands, or which we will soon take; ask them to withdraw from the region of our advance in order not to delay us; apply all efforts to find out details of the organization, condition of the troops, strength, intent, morale, armament, uniform, and ammunition of the Denikin Army. Furthermore, [you] must find out the attitude of the Denikin troops toward the Ukrainian state and toward our troops" (Dotsenko, *Litopys ukrains'koi revoliutsii*, 2, pt. 4: 9–10).

80. Dotsenko, *Litopys ukrains'koi revoliutsii*, 2, pt. 4: 15–16; Shandruk, *Arms of Valor*, p. 104; Levyts'kyi, *Halyts'ka armiia*, pp. 51–53; *Istoriia ukrains'koho viis'ka*, p. 560; Udovychenko, *Tretia zalizna dyviziia*, pp. 112–13, 115–16; Myshuha, *Pokhid ukrains'kykh*, pp. 12–18; Denikin, *Ocherki*, 5:123; *Istoriia ukrains'koho viis'ka*, p. 562.

81. Shandruk, *Arms of Valor*, p. 112; *Istoriia ukrains'koho viis'ka*, pp. 563–64; Omelianovych-Pavlenko, *Zymovyi pokhid*, 1:41–43.

82. Alsberg, "Situation in the Ukraine," pp. 569–70.

83. Tiutiunyk, *Zymovyi pokhid*, 1:9.

84. Myshuha, *Pokhid ukrains'kykh*, p. 23.

85. Levyts'kyi, *Halyts'ka armiia*, pp. 103–9, 122–24.

86. Lozyns'kyi, *Halychyna*, pp. 193–94; Levyts'kyi, *Halyts'ka armiia*, pp. 139–41.

87. For the text of the treaty see Lozyns'kyi, *Halychyna*, pp. 198–99; Tiutiunyk, *Zymovyi pokhid*, 1:12–13; Dmytro Paliiv, "Zymovyi pokhid," LCK, nos. 7–8 (1935), p. 8.

Chapter 13, Makhno and the Directory

1. Makhno, *Ukrains'kaia revoliutsiia*, 3:283.

2. Ibid., pp. 154–55, 283.

3. Ibid., pp. 156–57, 164; M. S., "Makhno ta ioho viis'ko," LCK, no. 6 (1935), p. 17.

4. The two brothers were Ukrainized Russians. Their original name was Vorob'ev. Mykola was a Tsarist artillery officer. As early as summer 1917 they organized the Ukrainian Free Cossacks, consisting of Katerynoslav workers (Panas Fedenko, *Isaak Mazepa*, p. 22).

5. V. I. Gureev, "Ekaterinoslavskii pokhod," (manuscript), pp. 5–7; Mahalevs'kyi, "Bat'ko Makhno," KD 1930, p. 68; Mazepa, *Ukraina v ohni*, 1:60–63.

6. Mazepa, *Ukraina v ohni*, 1:63; Makhno, *Ukrainskaia revoliutsiia*, 3:168–69.

7. Makhno, *Ukrainskaia revoliutsii*, 3:172–73; Voline, *Uknown Revolution*, p. 103. According to Mahalevs'kyi, Otaman Horobets and Makhno's delegates concluded an agreement: (1) The troops of the Directory and Makhno should act together against the Don; (2) Makhno received arms and uniforms from the troops of the Directory, (3) the troops of the Directory would be permitted to carry out mobilization in the area occupied by Makhno (Mahalevs'kyi, "Bat'ko Makhno," p. 69; see also Dubrovs'kyi, *Bat'ko Nestor Makhno*, pp. 7–8; Liubomyr Vynar, "Zv'iazky Nestora Makhno z armiieiu U. N. R., 1918–1920," *Rozbudova derzhavy*, no. 3 (11) (1953), p. 16.

8. Makhno, *Ukrains'kaia revoliutsiia*, 3:173.

9. Ibid., pp. 174–75.

10. Gureev, "Ekaterinoslavskii pokhod," p. 102; G. Al'mendinger, "K pis'mu

v redaktsiiu rotmistra Labinskogo," *Pereklichka*, no. 106 (1960), p. 13; Mazepa, *Ukraina v ohni*, 1:63; Igrenev, "Ekaterinoslavskiia vospominaniia," ARR 3:235–36; Mahalevs'kyi, "Bat'ko Makhno," p. 68; Lebed', *Itogi i uroki trekh*, p. 13; Kubanin, *Makhnovshchina*, p. 40.

11. Omelianovych-Pavlenko, *Zymovyi pokhid*, 2:26; Borys Monkevych, "Oborona Katerynoslava," LCK, no. 9 (1935), p. 6; P. Arshinov, *Dva pobega*, p. 83; Mazepa, *Ukraina v ohni*, 1:64; Belash, "Makhnovshchina," LR, no. 3 (1928), p. 213; Footman, *Civil War in Russia*, p. 94; Igrenev, "Ekaterinoslavskiia vospominaniia," p. 237; Lebed', *Itogi i uroki*, pp. 13–14; Kubanin, *Makhnovshchina*, pp. 42–43; Mahalevs'kyi, "Bat'ko Makhno," p. 69.

12. IA. IAkovlev, *Russkii anarkhizm*, p. 15; Kubanin, *Makhnovshchina*, p. 44; Gutman, "Pod vlast'iu anarkhistov," p. 68; Chernomordik, *Makhno i makhnovshchina*, p. 15; Arshinov, *Dva pobega*, p. 83; Belash, "Makhnovshchina," pp. 214–18; Dubrovs'kyi, *Bat'ko Nestor Makhno*, p. 8; Rudnev, *Makhnovshchina*, p. 23.

13. Lazurenko, "Povstannia proty Het'mana," no. 41, pp. 8–9; no. 42, p. 14.

14. Antonov-Ovseenko, *Zapiski*, 3:193; Stepan Samiilenko, *Dni slavy*, pp. 78–79; *Istoriia ukrains'koho viss'ka*, p. 458; Lazurenko, "Povstannia proty Het'mana," no. 42, pp. 14–15; Monkevych, "Oborona Katerynoslava," p. 8; Mahalevs'kyi, "Bat'ko Makhno," p. 70; Arthur E. Adams, "Bolshevik Administration in the Ukraine, 1918," *The Review of Politics* 20 (1958): 93–94.

Chapter 14, Makhno and the Bolsheviks

1. Kapustians'kyi, *Pokhid ukrains'kykh armii*, 1:30.

2. Belash, "Makhnovshchina," p. 225; Arshinov, *Istoriia makhnovskogo dvizheniia*, p. 94; Voline, *Unknown Revolution*, pp. 114–15; Footman, *Civil War in Russia*, p. 98.

3. Denikin, *Ocherki*, 4:73. According to Denikin: "On January 23 (O. S.) the Ninth Boy Scout Battalion (the Taman) came from Kerch to Perekop to fight against the Bolshevik and Makhno bands who were concentrated in the north Tavriia. It refused to carry out the order, left the front, and moved back to the Kuban. The spokesmen of the battalion declared that this campaign was against Ukraine and until they received orders from the State Rada the boy scouts would not fight against the 'Petliura men'" (*Ocherki*, 4:57; see also Bulavenko, "Kuban' na perelomi," p. 93).

4. Vl. Vygran, "Vospominaniia o bor'be s makhnovtsami," p. 1; A. G. Shkuro, *Zapiski belogo partizana*, p. 204; *Kornilovskii udarnyi polk*, p. 116; Antonov-Ovseenko, *Zapiski*, 3:199.

5. Vygran, "Vospominaniia," pp. 2–4; Arshinov, *Istoriia makhnovskogo dvizheniia*, p. 92; Vinogradov, "Chemu ia byl svidietelem," pp. 9–10; Antonov-Ovseenko, "V borot'bi za Radians'ku Ukrainu," no. 3, pp. 115–16; Shkuro, *Zapiski*, p. 205.

6. Shkuro, *Zapiski*, p. 213; Vinogradov, "Chemu ia byl svidietelem," p. 11; Denikin, *Ocherki*, 5:76–77; Bulavenko, "Kuban' u pershii polovyni," p. 135; Arshinov, *Istoriia makhnovskogo dvizheniia*, p. 92.

7. Shkuro, *Zapiski*, p. 214; Arshinov, *Istoriia makhnovskogo dvizheniia*, p. 91; Vygran, "Vospominaniia," p. 14; Vinogradov, "Chemu ia byl svidietelem," pp. 11–12, 17.

8. Erde, "Politychna prohrama anarkho-makhnovshchymy," pp. 45–46.

9. Serge, *Memoirs of a Revolutionary*, p. 119.

10. Kiselev, *Agitpoezd*, p. 24.

11. Voline, *Unknown Revolution*, p. 158.

12. Rossum, "Proclamations of the Makhno Movement, 1920," pp. 253–54; Kubanin, *Makhnovshchina*, p. 103.

13. Voline, *Unknown Revolution*, pp. 160–61; Gutman, "Pod vlastiu anarkhistov," p. 66; Rossum, "Proclamations of the Makhno movement, 1920," p. 254; Vl. Miroshevskii, "Vol'nyi Ekaterinoslav," pp. 199, 204.

14. Kubanin, *Makhnovshchina*, pp. 99–100; Gutman, "Pod vlastiu anarkhistov," p. 66; Rossum, "Proclamations of the Makhno Movement, 1920," p. 254; p. 71.

15. Arshinov, *Istoriia makhnovskogo dvizheniia*, pp. 176–77; Footman, *Civil War in Russia*, p. 111; James Joll, *The Anarchists*, p. 186; Teper, *Makhno*, pp. 38, 110.

16. Arshinov, *Istoriia makhnovskogo dvizheniia*, pp. 177–79; Wojna, "Nestor Machno," p. 70.

17. Belash, "Makhnovshchina," pp. 218–19; Dubrovs'kyi, *Bat'ko Nestor Makhno*, p. 8.

18. Dubrovs'kyi, *Bat'ko Nestor Makhno*, p. 8; Arshinov, *Istoriia makhnovskogo dvizheniia*, pp. 86–87; Footman, "Nestor Makhno," p. 96; Voline, *Unknown Revolution*, pp. 107–8; Struve, "Istoricheskie materialy i dokumenty," p. 226; Rudnev, *Makhnovshchina*, p. 31.

19. Rudnev, *Makhnovshchina*, pp. 31–32.

20. Struve, "Istoricheskie materialy i dokumenty," p. 227.

21. Ibid., pp. 228–29.

22. Rudnev, *Makhnovshchina*, p. 32; see also Struve, "Istoricheskie materialy i dokumenty," p. 228.

23. Kubanin, *Makhnovshchina*, pp. 46, 53; see also Struve, "Istoricheskie materialy i documenty," p. 230.

24. Arshinov, *Istoriia makhnovskogo dvizheniia*, p. 87.

25. Struve, "Istoricheskie materialy i dokumenty," p. 231; Rudnev, *Makhnovshchina*, pp. 34–35.

26. Arshinov, *Istoriia makhnovskogo dvizheniia*, pp. 88–89; Rudnev, *Makhnovshchina*, p. 35; Footman, "Nestor Makhno," p. 96.

27. Struve, "Istoricheskie materialy i dokumenty," p. 231.

28. Kubanin, *Makhnovshchina*, p. 55; see also Struve, "Istoricheskie materialy i dokumenty," p. 231.

29. Struve, "Istoricheskie materialy i dokumenty," pp. 229–30.

30. Igrenev, "Ekaterinoslavskii vospominaniia," p. 240.

31. Kubanin, *Makhnovshchina*, pp. 54–56.

32. Antonov-Ovseenko, "V borot'bi za Radians'ku Ukrainu," no. 5, p. 113.

33. *Arkhiv Krasnoi armii*, delo no. 30701, shtab Ukrfronta, oper. otdelen., "Banditsk vosst. v Aleksandrovskom U.," as quoted in Kubanin, *Makhnovshchina*, p. 47. Within the Red Army invading Ukraine were a number of units consisting of Chinese, Latvians, Germans, Hungarians, Poles, Jews, and others (Lazurenko, "Povstannia proty Het'mana," no. 41, p. 8).

34. Kubanin, *Makhnovshchina*, pp. 47–48.

35. Ibid., pp. 50–51.

36. According to a Soviet author present at the congresses of peasants, workers, and partisans on January 23 and February 12: "In 1919 when I asked the chairman of the two Congresses (a Jewish farmer) whether the 'kulaks' were allowed to participate in the Congress, he angrily responded: 'When will you finally stop talking about kulaks? Now we have no kulaks among us; everybody is tilling as much land as he wishes and as much as he can' " (Teper, *Makhno*, p. 63).

37. Kubanin, *Makhnovshchina*, p. 61.

38. Arshinov, *Istoriia makhnovskogo dvizheniia*, pp. 96–97.

39. Dubrovs'kyi, *Bat'ko Nestor Makhno*, p. 10; Arshinov, *Istoriia makhnovskogo dvizheniia*, p. 97; Antonov-Ovseenko, "V borot'bi za Radians'ku Ukrainu," no. 5, p. 118; "O dobrovol'noi mobilizatsii," *Put k svobode*, no. 2 (May 24, 1919), p. 1; Kubanin, *Makhnovshchina*, p. 59.

40. Voline, *Unknown Revolution*, pp. 120–22.

41. Antonov-Ovseenko, "V borot'bi za Radians'ku Ukrainu," no. 5, p. 114.

42. Trotskii, *Trotsky Papers*, 1:458.

43. Arshinov, *Istoriia makhnovskogo dvizheniia*, p. 104.

44. V. S., "Ekspeditsiia L. B. Kameneva dlia prodvizheniia prodgruzov k Moskve v 1919 godu," *Proletarskaia revoliutsiia*, no. 6 (41) (1925), pp. 137–38; Arshinov, *Istoriia makhnovskogo dvizheniia*, pp. 104–5.

45. V. S., "Ekspeditsiia L. B. Kameneva," pp. 137–38.

Chapter 15, Nykyfor Hryhor'iv

1. I. Maistrenko, "Ukrains'ka chervona armiia," *Visti* 4, nos. 1–2 (27–28) (1953), p. 11; Antonov-Ovseenko, *Zapiski*, 4:335; Kubanin, *Makhnovshchina*, p. 64; Irchan, "Makhno i makhnivtsi," p. 119; Fedenko, *Mynulo pivstolittia*, p. 35; Volodymyr Kedrovs'kyi, *1917 rik*, p. 279; Mykhailo Sereda, "Kholodnyi Iar," *Dilo*, August 4, 1934; Makhno, "Zapiski," nos. 5–6, p. 24; Kiselev, *Agitpoezd*, p. 38.

2. S. Ryndyk, "Otaman Hryhor'iv," *Prometei*, March 24, 1960. The date of Hryhor'iv's birth is not certain. Some sources give 1888, or even 1884 (*Entsyklopediia ukrainoznavstva: Slovnykova chastyna*, 2:435; Lev Shankovs'kyi, "Hryhorievshchyna: Problemsa i literatura," *Al'manakh: Kaliendar Providinnia*, 1966, p. 83).

3. Ryndyk, "Otaman Hryhor'iv"; interview with Stepan Ryndyk by the author on June 28, 1972, Chicago.

4. Ryndyk, "Otaman Hryhor'iv"; Andrii Holub, "Zbroina vyzvol'na borot'ba," 11:180; Kedrovs'kyi, *1917 rik*, 1:279.

5. Kedrovs'kyi, *1917 rik*, 1:279.

6. *Bol'shaia sovetskaia entsiklopediia*, 19:360; Kubanin, *Makhnovshchina*, p. 65.

7. Antonov-Ovseenko, *Zapiski*, 3:89; Vasyl Zadoianyi, "Otaman Hryhor'iv u svitli nimets'koho admirala Hopmana," TR, no. 33 (1965), p. 12; IA. Riappo, "Revoliutsionnaia bor'ba v Nikolaeve: Vospominaniia," LR, no. 4 (9) (1924), pp. 7–8.

8. Antonov-Ovseenko, *Zapiski*, 3:89–90; see also G. Frants, "Evakuatsiia germanskimi voiskami Ukrainy," *Istorik i sovremennik*, 2 (1922): 262–63;

Kubanin, *Makhnovshchina*, pp. 65–66.

9. Mazepa, *Ukraina v ohni*, 1:75–76; Khrystiuk, *Zamitky i materiialy*, 4:78.

10. As early as the end of 1917, there emerged within the Socialist Revolutionary party a distinct faction of the Left, the so-called Internationalists. They were critical of the Central Rada for overemphasizing the national struggle at the expense of socioeconomic problems (Khrystiuk, *Zamitky i materiialy*, 2:65). At the Fourth Congress of the Socialist Revolutionaries convened illegally near Kyiv on May13–16, 1918, the party split into a left and right wing. One of the delegates of the left complained:

> Those who summoned the Germans were little interested in the revolution. They stifled our revolution and have delayed its outbreak in Germany. They wanted to save the state at any price. Social issues were of secondary importance. Now they are ready immediately to abandon the socialization of the land. We are now divided into two groups—the Internationalists and the Statists (I. Majstrenko, *Borot'bism*, p. 66).

The Internationalists controlled the party's organ, an illegal weekly, *Borot'ba* (The Struggle), and adopted the name *Borot'bists*. While the moderate Socialist parties endeavored to democratize and nationalize the Hetman regime (A. Khvylia, "Borot'bisty," *Bol'shaia sovetskaia entsiklopediia*, vol. 7, col. 193), the Borot'bists attempted to establish contact with revolutionary socialist groups in Europe, especially Germany, believing that the world revolution was at hand. After the fall of the Hetman the Borot'bists refused to recognize the Directory and drifted toward the Bolshevik position. They were disappointed by both the Central Rada and the Directory for their reliance upon the Central Powers and the Entente, which they felt undermined the Ukrainian state. The Borot'bists' ideological move toward the left was reflected in the new party name adopted in March 1919: "Ukrainian Party of Socialist Revolutionaries Communists-Borot'bists" (Khrystiuk, *Zamitky i materiialy* 3:23–24).

However, the Borot'bists stood for an independent Soviet Ukraine. Therefore, in mid-January 1919, they formed their own government, parallel with the Provisional Workers' and Peasants' Government of Ukraine, under the name "Council of Revolutionary Emissaries" (Rafes, *Dva goda revoliutsii na Ukraine*, p. 154). Also, they tried to organize a Ukrainian Red Army as a counterpart to the Russian Red Army to defend the independence of Ukraine (Majstrenko, "Ukrains'ka chervona armiia," p. 191). According to Rafes, "This was not simply a gesture, for the Borot'bists conducted a great operation, collected large partisan detachments (p. 154). The first such military formation was the partisan army of Hryhor'iv, who agreed to go along with Borot'bist plans. The Borot'bists wanted to present the Bolsheviks with an accomplished fact and thus prevent them from interfering in Ukrainian affairs and "helping to liberate" the Ukrainian proletariat.

11. M. Rubach, "K istorii grazhdanskoi voiny na Ukraine," p. 178.

12. Ibid., p. 180.

13. Ibid., p. 184.

14. Ibid., p. 181.

15. Ibid., p. 185.

16. Antonov-Ovseenko, *Zapiski*, 3:247; Vladimir Maiborodov, "S frantsuzami," ARR, 16 (1925): 126.

17. Alexander Lukomskii, *Memoirs of the Russian Revolution*, pp. 135–41;

Antonov-Ovseenko, *Zapiski*, 3:228; "Ocherk vzaimootnoshenii vooruzhennykh," ARR 16 (1925): 246–47; A. Gukovskii, "Inostrannaia interventsiia na Ukraine, 1917–1919 goda," IM, no. 1 (71), p. 95; Adams, *Bolsheviks in the Ukraine*, pp. 167–68; Chamberlin, *Russian Revolution*, 2:166; Kapustians'kyi, *Pokhid ukrainskykh armii*, 1:35.

18. Adams, *Bolsheviks in the Ukraine*, p. 177. Before leaving Kherson, the Greek troops rounded up hostages—men, women, and children—and drove them into a warehouse close to the docks. On the morning of March 9, while the transports were leaving the wharves, naval guns shelled the city and set fire to the warehouse holding the hostages. Then Allied machine guns cut down the frantic people as they tried to claw their way out of the flames. Of approximately two thousand people imprisoned in the warehouse, at least five hundred died.

19. "Ocherk vzaimootnoshenii vooruzhennykh," p. 247.

20. Antonov-Ovseenko, *Zapiski*, 3:225; Gukovskii, "Inostrannaia interventsiia na Ukraine," p. 95; Margulies, *Ognennye gody*, p. 11; Kapustians'kyi, *Pokhid ukrains'kykh armii*, 1:35.

21. U.S., Department of State, *Papers*, p. 753.

22. Antonov-Ovseenko, *Zapiski*, 3:240, 242; Gukovskii, "Inostrannaia interventsiia na Ukraine," p. 96; Maiborodov, "S frantsuzami," pp. 127–35; Ukraine, Arkhivne upravlinnia, *Grazhdanskaia voina na Ukraine, 1918–1920*, 1, pt. 2:231; Margulies, *Ognennye gody*, p. 15; U.S., Department of State, *Papers*, p. 754.

23. "Ocherk vzaimootnoshenii vooruzhennykh," p. 249; see also Antonov-Ovseenko, *Zapiski*, 3:246–47; Fischer, *Soviets in World Affairs*, 1:228; Lukomskii, *Memoirs*, p. 221; R. Eideman and N. Kakurin, *Hromadians'ka viina na Ukraini*, p. 33, "Ocherk vzaimootnoshenii vooruzhennykh," p. 250; U.S., Department of State, *Papers*, p. 752. Judging from Hryhor'iv's statement to the representative of the Odessa underground Bolshevik organizations: "I don't need your blood. . . . Only give me 15,000 pairs of boots," probably he had an army of 15,000 partisans (Adams, *Bolsheviks in the Ukraine*, p. 197). Antonov also states that Hryhor'iv had about 15,000 combat troops at the beginning of May (Antonov-Ovseenko, *Zapiski*, 4:45).

24. Margulies, *Ognennye gody*, pp. 33, 34, 36; Reshetar, *Ukrainian Revolution*, p. 249.

25. Antonov- Ovseenko, *Zapiski*, 3:249.

26. Kubanin, *Makhnovshchina*, pp. 67–68; Margulies, *Ognennye gody*, pp. 47–49.

27. Antonov-Ovseenko, *Zapiski*, 3:249.

28. Ibid., 4:27.

29. Vynnychenko, *Vidrodzennia natsii*, 3:322–23; see also Lozyns'kyi, *Halychyna*, pp. 102–3.

30. Antonov-Ovseenko, *Zapiski*, 4:275.

31. Fischer, *Soviets in World Affairs*, 1:194.

32. Antonov-Ovseenko, *Zapiski*, 3:16.

33. Ibid., 4:84. Count Aleksandr Suvorov was a military commander under Catherine II and Paul I. In 1799, he led the allied armies of anti-French coalition into Italy and Switzerland.

34. Ibid.

35. Lenin, *Sochineniia*, 24:27.

36. B. V. Kozel's'kyi, "Hryhor'ievshchyna: Z nahody shostykh rokovyn likvidatsii Hryhor'ievshchyny," *Chervonyi shliakh*, no. 5 (1925), p. 68.

37. Antonov-Ovseenko, *Zapiski*, 4:83.

38. Ibid., p. 47; Margulies, *Ognennye gody*, pp. 118–21.

39. Mazepa, *Ukraina v ohni*, 3:182; see also V. T. Krut', "Do istorii borot'by proty hryhor'ivshchyny na Ukraini," LR, nos. 5–6 (54–55) (1932), pp. 146–47.

40. Mazepa, *Ukraina*, 3:183.

41. Kozel's'kyi, "Hryhor'ievshchyna," p. 69; Antonov-Ovseenko, "V borot'bi za Radians'ku Ukrainu," no. 5, p. 119; S. Dubrovskii, "Likvidatsiia grigor'evshchiny, 1919 g.," VIZ, no. 2 (1941), p. 32.

42. S. Dubrovskii, "Grigor'evshchina," VR, no. 4 (1928), pp. 22–23; "Grigor'evskaia avantiura, mai 1919 goda," LR, no. 3 (1923), pp. 156–59; Fedenko, "Period of the Directory," p. 758.

43. Lenin, *Sochineniia*, 35:327, 329.

44. Kapustians'kyi, *Pokhid ukrains'kykh armii*, 2:61; *Istoriia ukrains'koho viis'ka*, p. 535; Dubrovskii, "Likvidatsiia grigor'evshchiny, 1919 g.," pp. 40–41; Antonov-Ovseenko, *Zapiski*, 4:309.

45. Mazepa, *Ukraina v ohni*, 2:29.

46. Ibid., p. 112; Antonov-Ovseenko, *Zapiski*, 4:72, 100, 308; Teper, *Makhno*, p. 39; Meleshko, "Nestor Makhno ta ioho anarkhiia," no. 3, p. 14.

47. Antonov-Ovseenko, *Zapiski*, 4:100.

48. Arshinov, *Istoriia makhnovskogo dvizheniia*, p. 107; see also Rudnev, *Makhnovshchina*, p. 38.

49. Arshinov, *Istoriia makhnovskogo dvizheniia*, p. 109.

50. Ibid., p. 110; see also Rudnev, *Makhnovshchina*, pp. 38–39.

51. Lenin, *Sochinennia*, 29:500; S. Chernomordik, *Makhno i Makhnovshchina*, p. 20.

52. Arshinov, *Istoriia makhnovskogo dvizheniia*, pp. 132–33; Mazepa, *Ukraina v ohni*, 2:112; Mahalevs'kyi, "Bat'ko Makhno," p. 70; Denikin, *Ocherki*, 5: 131–32.

53. Arshinov, *Istoriia makhnovskogo dvizheniia*, pp. 133-34; "Ubiistvo Grigor'eva," LR, no. 2, pp. 232-34; Peters, *Nestor Makhno*, p. 70; Makhno, "Makhnovshchina i antisemitizm," DT, nos. 30–31 (1927), p. 18.

54. Meleshko, "Nestor Makhno ta ioho anarkhiia," no. 3, p. 14; Sereda, "Kholodnyi IAr," August 4, 1934.

55. According to one source about 2,000 partisans joined Makhno (M. Mykhailyk, "Ukrains'ke selo v chasy natsion," no. 2, p. 16).

56. Meleshko, "Nestor Makhno ta ioho anarkhiia," p. 14; Louis Fischer, *The Life of Lenin* (New York: Harper & Row, 1964), p. 365.

Chapter 16, The Bolsheviks Break with Makhno

1. "Makhnovshchina," *V puti*, no. 51, June 2, 1919; in L. Trotskii, *Materialy i dokumenty po istorii Krasnoi armii*, 2, pt. 1:190.

2. Goldman, *My Disillusionment in Russia*, pp. 99–100; see also Berkman, *Bolshevik Myth*, p. 189; Voline, *Unknown Revolution*, p. 124; Makhno, *Makhnovshchina*, p. 59; N. Makhno, "Otkrytoe pis'mo t-shchu Maksymovu," p. 11.

3. Lenin, *Sochineniia*, 26:214; see also "Makhnovshchina," in *Bol'shaia sovetskaia entsiklopediia*, cols. 500–501.

4. Arshinov, *Istoriia makhnovskogo dvizheniia*, pp. 117–18; see also Kubanin, *Makhnovshchina*, p. 77; Akademiia nauk URSR, Kiev, Instytut istorii, *Radians'ke budivnytstvo na Ukraini v roky hromadians'koi viiny, lystopad, 1918-Serpen, 1919*, p. 142.

5. Arshinov, *Istoriia makhnovskogo dvizheniia*, pp. 119–20; see also Mazepa, *Ukraina v ohni*, 2:111; Averin, "Do borot'by proty hryhor'ievshchyny ta denikinshchyny za Dnipropetrovs'ke," LR, no. 3 (48) (1931), p. 122; Berkman, "Nestor Makhno," p. 17.

6. Arshinov, *Istoriia makhnovskogo dvizheniia*, pp. 126–27.

7. Kubanin, *Makhnovshchina*, p. 78; Voline, *Unknown Revolution*, pp. 136–37.

8. Arshinov, *Istoriia makhnovskogo dvizheniia*, pp. 127–28; Makhno, *Makhnovshchina*, p. 55; Gorelik, *Goneniia na anarkhizm*, pp. 28, 31; Trotskii, *Materialy i dokumenty po istorii Krasnoi Armii*, 2, pt. 1: 210.

Chapter 17, The Volunteer Army and Makhno

1. Lukomskii, *Memoirs*, pp. 129 ff., 135, 141; Denikin, *Ocherki*, 2:156; Vera Vladimirova, *God sluzhby sotsialistov kapitalistam*, p. 12; L. G. Orlov, "Osnovatel' Dobrovol'cheskoi Armii," *Chasovoi*, no. 329 (1953).

2. Denikin, *Ocherki*, 2:189; Lukomskii, *Memoirs*, p. 140; Orlov, "Osnovatel' Dobrovol'cheskoi Armii," no. 329.

3. Lukomskii, *Memoirs*, p. 141; Denikin, *Ocherki*, 2:157, 189; Markow, *Armee ohne Heimat*, p. 15; V. E. Pavlov, *Markovtsy v boiakh i pokhodakh za Rossiiu v osvoboditel'noi voine 1917–1920 godov*, 1:73; Stewart, *White Armies of Russia*, p. 32; P. N. Miliukov, "Dnevnik," *Novyi zhurnal*, no. 66 (1961), pp. 173, 179; Karol Wedziagolski, *Pamietniki: Wojna i revolucja, kontrrewolucja, Bolszewicki przewrot, Warszawski epilog*, p. 291.

4. P. M. Volkonsky, *The Volunteer Armies of Alexiev and Denikin*, pp. 7–8; Roman Gul', *Ledianoi pokhod*, pp. 17–18; Bechhofer, *In Denikin's Russia and the Caucasus, 1919–1920*, p. 94.

5. Lukomskii, *Memoirs*, p. 147; Volkonsky, *Volunteer Armies*, p. 7; Denikin, *Ocherki*, 2:166; Markow, *Armee ohne Heimat*, p. 21; Pavlov, *Markovtsy v boiakh*, 1:93; I. A. Poliakov, *Donskie kazaki v bor'be s bol'shevikami*, pp. 111–12; Bunyan and Fisher, *Bolshevik Revolution*, pp. 420–21.

6. Gul', *Ledianoi pokhod*, pp. 108–9; Bunyan and Fisher, *Bolshevik Revolution*, p. 428.

7. Gul', *Ledianoi pokhod*, pp. 119–23; Vasyl' Ivanys, *Borot'ba Kubani za nezalezhnist'*, p. 37; Bunyan and Fisher, *Bolshevik Revolution*, p. 428; Orlov, "Osnovatel' Dobrovol'cheskoi Armii."

8. Poliakov, *Donskie kazaki v bor'be*, p. 98.

9. Shkuro, *Zapiski*, p. 209.

10. Denikin, *Ocherki*, 3:86.

11. Poliakov, *Donskie kazaki v bor'be*, pp. 115–17.

12. I. Borisenko, *Sovetskie respubliki na Severnom Kavkaze v 1918 godu*, 1:81.

13. A. V. Turkul, *Drozdovtsy v ogne*, pp. 19–22; Drozdovskii, *Dnevnik*, pp. 133–37; Poliakov, *Donskie kazaki v bor'be*, pp. 196–200; Bunyan, *Intervention*, pp. 33, 35, 131–32; Bunyan and Fisher, *Bolshevik Revolution*, p. 422; Ivanys, *Stezhkamy zhyttia*, 2:106; Volkonsky, *Volunteer Armies*, p. 23.

14. Krasnov, "Vsevelikoe Voisko Donskoe," ARR 5:201; see also Denikin, *Ocherki*, 3:155.

15. At that time there were out of nine thousand men only over two thousand Russians (Ivanys, *Stezhkamy zhyttia*, 2:130; Krasnov, "Vsevelikoe Voisko Donskoe," 5:192, 201; Dmytro Doroshenko, "Deshcho pro zakordonnu polityku Ukrains'koi Derzhavy v 1918 rotsi," *Khliborobs'ka Ukraina*, 2:56–57; Reshetar, *Ukrainian Revolution*, p. 187.

16. A. I. Denikin, *The White Army* (London: J. Cape, 1930), p. 158; Drozdovskii, *Dnevnik*, pp. 139, 150.

17. Volkonsky, *Volunteer Armies*, p. 27; Peter P. Wrangel, *Always with Honour*, p. 52; Denikin, *White Army*, p. 184; Denikin, *Ocherki*, 3:197–98; Pavlov, *Markovtsy v boiakh*, 1:304–5; Chamberlin, *Russian Revolution*, 2:139.

18. Denikin, *Ocherki*, 4:107, 111, 113; Chamberlin, *Russian Revolution*, 2:142; *Bor'ba trudiashchikhsia mass za ustanovlenie i uprochenie Sovetskoi vlasti na Stavropol'e, 1917–apr. 1921 gg.*, pp. 102–3; Borisenko, *Sovetskie respubliki*, 2:175–78; Wrangel, *Always with Honour*, p. 68; Lukomskii, *Memoirs*, pp. 208 ff.; Pavlov, *Markovtsy v boiakh*, 1:338 ff.

19. M. Svechinikov, *Bor'ba Krasnoi Armii na Severnom Katze* (Moscow: Gos. voen. izd-vo, 1926), p. 221, as quoted in Chamberlin, *Russian Revolution*. 2:146.

20. K. N. Sokolov, *Pravlenie generala Denikina*, pp. 43, 91; Lukomskii, *Memoirs*, p. 205; Pavlov, *Markovtsky v boiakh*, 1:317; 2:5; Denikin, *Ocherki*, 3:271–72; Chamberlin, *Russian Revolution*, 2:209; Wrangel, *Always with Honour*, p. 68.

21. Stewart, *White Armies of Russia*, p. 75. At the beginning of May 1919 in Kharkiv the Volunteer Corps was reorganized and renamed the Volunteer Army, consisting of the Alekseev, Markov, Kornilov, Drozdovskii divisions, and some regiments and groups. The Caucasian Volunteer Army was renamed the Caucasian Army (Sokolov, *Pravlenie generala Denikina*, p. 119; Vygran, "Vospominaniia o bor'be s makhnovtsami," p. 4; Kapustians'kyi, *Pokhid ukrains'kykh armii*, 2:154.

22. Chamberlin, *Russian Revolution*, 2:141.

23. Churchill, *Aftermath*, p.165.

24. D. Lloyd George, *The Truth about the Peace Treaties* (London: Gollancz, 1938), p. 317.

25. Churchill, *Aftermath*, p. 165; see also Denikin, *Ocherki*, 4:36; Lukomskii, *Memoirs*, p. 209.

26. Wrangel, *Always with Honour*, p. 75; Denikin, *Ocherki*, 4:86; George von Rauch, *A History of Soviet Russia* (New York: F. A. Praeger, 1967), p. 108.

27. Hodgson, *With Denikin's Armies*, pp. 280, 174.

28. Peter P. Wrangel, *The Memoirs of General Wrangel*, p. 70.

29. B. Simonov, *Razgrom denikinshchiny*, p. 24; see also Bulavenko, "Kuban' i 'moskovs'kyi shliak,'" RN, nos. 7–8 (78–79), p. 193.

30. George A. Brinkley, *The Volunteer Army and Allied Intervention in South Russia, 1917–1921*, p. 187. By midsummer the Denikin army had increased to about 150,000 combat troops: the Volunteer Army of Mai-Maevskii, 40,000; the Don Army, 45,000; the Crimean Volunteer Corps, 15,000; the Caucasian Army, 20,000; and Wrangel's Army, 30,000 (Brinkley, pp. 187, 363).

31. Dotsenko, *Zymovyi pokhid*, p. CXXVIII.

32. Akademiia nauk URSR, Kiev, Instytut istorii, *Radians'ke budivnytstvo na ukraini*, p. 167.

33. Denikin, *Ocherki*, 5:84.

34. Lukomskii, *Memoirs*, pp. 226–29; Vladimir Maevskii, *Gvardeiskie sapery*, p. 1; idem, *Povstanty Ukrainy*, p. 2; Fischer, *Soviets in World Affairs*, p. 209; Averin, "Do borot'by," p. 126; Chamberlin, *Russian Revolution*, 2:244–45.

35. Wrangel, *Memoirs*, pp. 88–89; Bulavenko, "Kuban i 'moskovs'kyi shliakh,'" p. 187. According to the aide of Mai-Maevskii, Makarov: While speaking to Mai-Maevskii in Katerynoslav, Denikin remarked: "Do not advance your valiant units too fast. Kolchak is approaching Viatka; [he] will cross the Volga, occupy Nizhnii Novogorod and then Moscow. We might be left out; let him be checked a little. And we always will have time to take Moscow" (P. V. Makarov, *Ad'iutant generala Mai-Maevskogo*, p. 32).

36. Wrangel, *Memoirs*, p. 89.

37. Sokolov, *Pravlenie generala Denikina*, pp. 195–96.

38. Denikin, *Ocherki*, 5:142.

39. Arbatov, "Ekaterinoslav 1917–22 gg.," p. 94; Shkuro, *Zapiski*, p. 216.

40. Mazepa, *Ukraina v ohni*, 2:33; Kin, *Denikinshchina*, p. 241; Dubiv, "Ulamok z moho zhyttia," no. 6 (219), p. 738; M. Bohun, "Fragmentu zi spomyniv pro 'Narodniu Oboronu Khersons'koi gubernii,'" *Ukrains'kyi skytalets'* 4, no. 2:36.

41. Kin, *Denikinshchina*, pp. 241–42.

42. Levyts'kyi, *Halyts'ka armiia na Velykii Ukraini*, pp. 126–27.

43. Ibid.

44. Kin, *Denikinshchina*, pp. 243–44.

45. Wrangel, *Always with Honour*, p. 185.

46. Denikin, *Ocherki*, 4:218.

47. P. Miliukov, *Rossiia na perelomie*, 2:205.

48. Ibid., 2:162; see also Lukomskii, "Iz vospominanii," 6:132–33.

49. Miliukov, *Rossiia na perelomie*, 2:205.

50. "*Realdop* [realization of booty] became a part of our troops at a time when [it] was still the main . . . source of means for the Volunteer Army. . . . 'gratuitous requisition' also became an 'everyday habit' in the Army. . . . robbery of the population was an unhindered and systematic [phenomenon]" (Sokolov, *Pravlenie generala Denikina*, p. 162; see also *Kornilovskii udarnii polk*, p. 148).

51. G. N. Rakovskii, *Vstanie bielykh*, p. 11; see also Arbatov, "Ekaterinoslav 1917–22 gg.," pp. 93–94; L. L., "V chotyrokutnyku smery," LCK, 2, no. 2 (1930): 14.

52. Denikin, *Ocherki*, 4:95.

53. Wrangel, *Memoirs*, p. 127.

54. Fischer, *Soviets in World Affairs*, 1:232.

55. Kin, *Denikinshchina*, p. 50.

56. Makhno, *Makhnovshchina*, p. 59.

57. S. N. Semanov, "Makhnovshchina i ee krakh," p. 46; Bulavenko, "Kuban' u pershii polovyni," p. 137; G. Gordienko, "Svidetel'stva o Makhno: Glazami iunoshi," NRS, March 16, 1970, p. 7.

58. Kapustians'kyi, *Pokhid ukrains'kykh armii*, 2:155; Udovychenko, *Tretia Zalizna dyviziia*, p. 106; *Kommandarm IAkir*, pp. 62, 78–79; I. E. IAkir, *Vospominaniia o grazhdanskoi voine*, p. 36.

59. Makhno, *Makhnovshchina*, p. 59.

60. S. Uritskii, "Mezhdu Odessoi i Nikolaevom: Boi 1919 goda," in *Grazhdanskaia voina, 1918–1921*, ed. A. S. Bubnova, S. S. Kameneva, and R. P. Eideman

(Moscow: "Voennyi vestnik," 1928), 1:99, 101; Semanov, "Makhnovshchina i ee krakh," pp. 45–46; Nikulin, "Gibel' makhnovshchiny," pp. 176–77; Dubrovs'kyi, *Bat'ko Nestor Makhno*, p. 11; Kapustians'kyi, *Pokhid ukrains'kykh armii*, 2:155–56.

61. Uritskii, "Mezhdu Odessoi i Nikolaevom," 1:98, 100; see also *Kommandarm IAkir*, pp. 86–87; V. Nikolskii, "Novye rukovoditeli Kr. Armii," *Chasovoi*, no. 206 (February 15, 1938), p. 5.

62. E. A. Men'chukov, *Istoricheskii ocherk boev v usloviiakh okruzheniia*, p. 159; *Kommandarm IAkir*, p. 87; Kapustians'kyi, *Pokhid ukrains'kykh armii*, 2:156.

63. Voline, *Unknown Revolution*, p. 141; Miroshevskii, "Vol'nyi Ekaterinoslav," p. 207; Ol. Dotsenko, "Reid otamana Sahaidachnoho," LCK, no. 11 (1932), p. 5.

64. "Makhnovskaia armiia," p. 3; "Zamietki k knigi Arshinova," p. 6; Voline, *Unknown Revolution*, pp. 142, 260–63; Arshinov, *Istoriia makhnovskogo dvizheniia*, p. 135; Makhno, *Makhnovshchina*, p. 49; Footman, "Nestor Makhno," p. 103; Dubrovs'kyi, *Bat'ko Nestor Makhno*, p. 11; Rudnev, *Makhnovshchina*, p. 46; Nikulin, "Gibel' Makhnovshchiny," p. 176; Fischer, *Life of Lenin*, pp. 365–66; Teper, *Makhno*, pp. 76–77; Kapustians'kyi, "Makhno i makhnovshchyna," no. 243.

65. Originally it had a punitive function, but because of improper treatment of prisoners of war, it was deprived of its punitive function, and commanders and partisans were categorically prohibited from shooting prisoners upon their own initiative. A commission was organized in the Revolutionary Military Council to deal with prisoners. The representatives of the anarchists had the right to participate in its decisions (Teper, *Makhno*, pp. 81–82; Rudnev, *Makhnovshchina*, pp. 74–75).

66. Arshinov, *Istoriia makhnovskogo dvizheniia*, p. 95; Voline, *Unknown Revolution*, pp. 110, 140; Udovychenko, *Ukraina u viini*, p. 106; R. L. Suslyk, *Kryvavi storinky z nepysanykh litopysiv*, p. 80; Esbakh, "Poslednie dni makhnovshchiny na Ukraine," pp. 41–42; Semanov, "Makhnovshchina i ee krakh," p. 42; Efimov, "Deistviia protiv Makhno," p. 204; IAkymiv, "Hostyna Makhna v Umani," p. 78.

67. IA. Slashchov, "Materialy dlia istorii grazhdanskoi voiny v Rossii," *Voennyi vestnik*, nos. 9–10, pp. 38, 39; Men'chukov, *Istoricheskii ocherk boev*, p. 176; Arshinov, *Istoriia makhnovskogo dvizheniia*, p. 135; V. Al'mendinger, *Simferopol'skii ofitserskii polk 1918–1920*, p. 18; N. Makhno, "Razgrom Denikintsev," *Put' k svobode*, no. 4 (October 30, 1919), as quoted in Al'mendinger, *Simferopol'skii*, p. 23.

68. Slashchov, "Materialy do istorii," p. 40; Al'mendinger, *Simferopol'skii*, pp. 18–20; "Makhnovskaia armiia," p. 4; "Zamietki k knigi Arshinova," p. 7; Arshinov, *Istoriia makhnovskogo dvizheniia*, pp. 135–36; Nikulin, "Gibel' makhnovshchiny"; Denikin, *Ocherki*, 5:234.

69. Slachshov, "Materialy do istorii," p. 41; Voline, *Unknown Revolution*, pp. 143–44; Al'mendinger, *Simferopol'skii*, p. 20; Arshinov, *Istoriia makhnovskogo dvizheniia*, p. 137; IAkymiv, "Hostyna Makhna v Umani," pp. 79–80; V. Kalyna, "V Umani"; M. Irchan, "Makhno i makhnivtsi," p. 116; Denikin, *Ocherki*, 5:234; Dubrovs'kyi, *Bat'ko Nestor Makhno*, p. 12; Rudnev, *Makhnovshchina*, p. 48; Omelianovych-Pavlenko, *Zymovi pokhid*, 2:26; Dotsenko, *Zymovi pokhid*, p. CXXXIV.

70. Trotskii, *Materialy i dokumenty po istorii Krasnoi Armii*, 2, pt. 1:304.

71. Wrangel, *Always with Honour*, p. 101.

72. Sokolov, *Pravlenie generala Denikina*, p. 119; Vinogradov, "Chemu ia byl svidietelem," p. 15.

73. Wrangel, *Always with Honour*, pp. 98, 101.

74. Slashchov, "Materialy do istorii," p. 39.

75. Meleshko, "Nestor Makhno ta ioho anarkhiia," no. 4, p. 15; Semanov, "Makhnovshchina i ee krakh," p. 48.

76. Mustafin, "Proryv Makhno," *Pereklichka*, no. 21, p. 13; G. Sakovich, "Proryv Makhno," *Pereklichka*, no. 116, p. 14.

77. Arshinov, *Istoriia makhnovskogo dvizheniia*, pp. 139–41; Al'mendinger, *Simferopol'skii*, pp. 21–23; Semanov, "Makhnovshchina i ee krakh," p. 48; Nikulin, "Gibel' makhnovshchiny," p. 177; "Prilozhenie: Svodka o reide Makhno po denikinskim tylam oseniu 1919 g.," PR, no. 9, p. 208; M. Makhnovskii, "Pravda o Makhno," NRS 59, no. 20 (March 2, 1969): 8; Kubanin, *Makhnovshchina*, p. 86; Denikin, *Ocherki*, 5:234; Alain Sergent, *Les anarchistes*, pp. 135–37; Mustafin, "Proryv Makhno," pp. 11–13; Sakovich, "Proryv Makhno," pp. 12–13, 14; Makhno, "Razgrom denikintsev," in Al'mendinger, *Simferopol'skii*, p. 23.

78. Sakovich, "Proryv Makhno," p. 11.

79. Nomad, "Epic of Nestor Makhno," no. 7, p. 410; "Prilozhenie," p. 208; Dubrovs'kyi, *Bat'ko Nestor Makhno*, p. 13; Denikin, *Ocherki*, 5:234; Fedenko, *Mynulo pivstolittia*, p. 14; Rudnev, *Makhnovshchina*, p. 49; Sakovich, "Proryv Makhno," p. 14.

80. Arshinov, *Istoriia makhnovskogo dvizheniia*, pp. 145–46; "1919 god v Ekaterinoslave i Aleksandrovske," pp. 81–82; Miroshevskii, "Vol'nyi Ekaterinoslav," p. 203; Erde, "Politychna prohrama anarkho-makhnivshchyny," no. 2, pp. 36–37; Kubanin, *Makhovshchina*, p. 103.

81. Voline, *Unknown Revolution*, pp. 163–73; Miroshevskii, "Vol'nyi Ekaterinoslav," pp. 201–2; Arshinov, *Istoriia makhnovskogo dvizheniia*, pp. 146–47; "1919 god v Ekaterinoslave i Aleksandrovske," pp. 81–82, 91–92. The Fourth Congress, called for June 15, 1919, did not take place because the Bolsheviks prevented it. According to Kubanin, the congress took place on October 26 and was composed of about 300 delegates (Kubanin, *Makhnovshchina*, pp. 91–92).

82. Rossum, "Proclamations of the Makhno Movement, 1920," p. 263.

83. "1919 god v Ekaterinoslave i Aleksandrovske," p. 92; Voline, *Unknown Revolution*, pp. 171–73.

84. Kubanin, *Makhnovshchina*, p. 115.

85. Kin, "Povstancheskoe," p. 79; "Prilozhenie," no. 9, p. 208; Kubanin, *Makhnovshchina*, p. 174; Panas Fedenko, *Isaak Mazepa*, p. 80; Gutman, "Pod vlast'iu anarkhistov," p. 62; Denikin, *Ocherki*, 5:234.

86. Tsebrii, "Vospominaniia partizana," no. 32, p. 14.

87. Hodgson, *With Denikin's Armies*, pp. 184.

88. Kubanin, *Makhnovshchina*, pp. 86–87; Margushin, "Bat'ko Makhno," p. 2; Denikin, *Ocherki*, 5:234; Arshinov, *Istoriia makhnovskogo dvizheniia*, pp. 142–43; "Prilozhenie," no. 9, p. 208.

89. Sokolov, *Pravlenie generala Denikina*, p. 190.

90. Ibid.

91. A. Lobanov-Rostovsky, *The Grinding Mill*, p. 359.

92. Hodgson, *With Denikin's Armies*, pp. 119–20.

93. Bechhofer, *In Denikin's Russia*, p. 176.

94. Ibid., p. 178; Rudnev, *Makhnovshchina*, p. 53; Arbatov, "Ekaterinoslav 1917–22 gg.," pp. 96–97; Denikin, *Ocherki*, 5:235; Gutman, "Pod vlast'iu anarkhistov," p. 65; P. Teslenko, "K vospominaniiam V. Belasha," LR, no. 3 (1928), p. 230.

95. Gutman, "Pod vlast'iu anarkhistov," p. 63.

96. Ibid., pp. 63–64.

97. Arbatov, "Ekaterinoslav 1917–22 gg.," p. 98.

98. V. Primakov, "Srazhenie pod Orlom, oktiabr'–noiablr' 1919 goda," *Bor'ba klassov*, no. 2 (1931), p. 52; Nikulin, "Gibel' makhnovshchiny," p. 179; "Prilozhenie," no. 9, p. 208; Kin, "Povstancheskoe," nos. 3–4, pp. 78–79; Dubrovs'kyi, *Bat'ko Nestor Makhno*, p. 13; Kubanin, *Makhnovshchina*, p. 90; Teper, *Makhno*, p. 48.

99. Rakovskii, *V stanie bielykh*, pp. 11–12.

100. Wrangel, *Memoirs*, pp. 98–99.

101. Makarov, *Ad'iutant generala Mai-Maevskogo*, p. 62.

102. Marion Aten and Arthur Orrmont, *Last Train over Rostov Bridge*, p. 161.

103. Denikin, *Ocherki*, 5:234.

104. Vygran, "Vospominaniia o bor'be s makhnovtsami," p. 6; V. M., "Dontsy na makhnovskom frontie," *Kazach'i dumy*, no. 13, p. 16; Denikin, *Ocherki*, 5:258; Simonov, *Razgrom denikinshchiny*, p. 27.

105. V. M., "Dontsy na makhnovskom frontie," no. 10, pp. 11–13.

106. Makarov, *Ad'iutant generala Mai-Maevskogo*, p. 29.

107. Levyts'kyi, *Halyts'ka armiia*, pp. 121–22.

108. Simonov, *Razgrom denikinshchiny*, pp. 27–28.

109. Ibid., p. 60.

110. P. N. Shatilov, "Petr Nikolaevich Vrangel," *Obshchestvo Gallipoliitsev*, October 1953, p. 3.

111. Denikin, *Ocherki*, 5:232–33; Lukomskii, *Memoirs*, pp. 230–31.

112. Wrangel, *Memoirs*, p. 106.

113. Bechhofer, *In Denikin's Russia*, p. 117.

114. P. Zaliesskii, "Glavnyia prichiny neudach bielago dvizheniia na IUgie Rossii," BA 2–3:160.

115. Lukomskii, *Memoirs*, p. 231.

116. Churchill, *Aftermath*, p. 266.

117. Denikin, *Ocherki*, 5:235.

118. Ibid., p. 232.

119. Miliukov, *Rossiia na perelomie*, 2:212.

120. Bechhofer, *In Denikin's Russia*, p. 149; Wrangel, *Always with Honour*, p. 112.

121. Brinkley, *Volunteer Army*, p. 224; Rakovskii, *V stanie bielykh*, pp. 223, 236–37, 257–58; Zaliesskii, "Glavnyia prichiny neudach bielago dvizheniia na IUgie Rossii," pp. 161–62; V. Dobrynin, *Bor'ba s bol'shevizmom na iugie Rossii*, p. 109; Stewart, *White Armies of Russia*, pp. 346–47; Lukomskii, *Memoirs*, p. 246; Vinogradov, "Chemu ia byl svidietelem," p. 22; G. N. Rakovskii, *Konets bielykh: Ot Dniepra do Bosfora*, p. 6.

122. Tiutiunyk, *Zymovyi pokhid 1919–20 rr.*, 1:74.

123. Primakov, "Srazhenie pod Orlom," pp. 53, 54.

124. Denikin, *Ocherki*, 5:134.

125. Trotskii, *Materialy i dokumenty po istorii Krasnoi Armii*, 2, pt. 2:28.

126. Bohun, "Fragmenty zi spomyniv pro 'Narodniu Oboronu khersons'koi gubernii,' " pp. 35, 36; Dotsenko, *Zymovyi pokhid*, p. CXLI.

127. F. Shteinman, "Otstuplenie ot Odessy," ARR 2:87.

128. Rakovskii, *V stanie bielykh*, p. 1.

129. Denikin, *Ocherki*, 5:235.

130. Pierre Berland [Georges Luciani], "Makhno," *Le Temps*, August 28, 1934.

Chapter 18, Makhno's Army Outlawed by the Bolsheviks

1. Nikulin, "Gibel' makhnovshchiny," p. 181.

2. Ibid.; N. Makhno, *Po povodu "raz'iasneniia" Volina*, p. 9; IAkovlev, *Russkii anarkhizm*, p. 25; Margushin, "Bat'ko Makhno," p. 2; Arshinov, *Istoriia makhnovskogo dvizheniia*, p. 157; Rudnev, *Makhnovshchina*, p. 64.

3. Semanov, "Makhnovshchina i ee krakh," p. 52.

4. Makhno, *Po povodu "roz'iasneniia" Volina*, p. 9; Teper, *Makhno*, p. 66; *Grazhdanskaia voina na Ekaterinoslavshchine*, pp. 210, 218; IAkir, *Vospominaniia*, p. 38.

5. Arshinov, *Istoriia makhnovskogo dvizheniia*, pp. 157–58; Gutman, "Pod vlast'iu anarkhistov," p. 68; Semanov, "Makhnovshchina i ee krakh," p. 52.

6. N. A. Efimov, "Deistviia protiv Makhno," pp. 199–204; Rudnev, *Makhnovshchina*, p. 67.

7. Men'chukov, *Istoricheskii ocherk boev*, pp. 179–81; Efimov, "Deistviia protiv Makhno," p. 205.

8. Arshinov, *Istoriia makhnovskogo dvizheniia*, p. 158.

9. IU. Romanchenko, "Epizody z borot'by proty makhnovshchyny," LR, no. 4 (49) (1930), p. 128.

10. Sergeev, "Poltavskaia operatsiia protiv Makhno," pp. 122–23; Nikulin, "Gibel' makhnovshchiny," p. 182; Dubrovs'kyi, *Bat'ko Nestor Makhno*, p. 15; Semanov, "Makhnovshchina i ee krakh," pp. 52–53; "Ukraina," *Volia* 4, no. 5 (1920): 263.

11. Arshinov, *Istoriia makhnovskogo dvizheniia*, p. 165; Semanov, "Makhnovshchina i ee krakh," p. 54; Efimov, "Deistviia protiv Makhno," p. 201.

12. Meleshko, "Nestor Makhno ta ioho anarkhiia," no. 4, p. 14.

13. Voline, *Unkown Revolution*, p. 182; Margushin, "Bat'ko Makhno," p. 2; Peters, *Nestor Makhno*, p. 85.

14. Arshinov, *Istoriia makhnovskogo dvizheniia*, p. 160.

15. A. Manuilsky, "The Agrarian Policy in Ukraine," *Soviet Russia* 3, no. 16 (1920): 369; Kubanin, *Makhnovshchina*, pp. 130–31.

16. M. I. Remnev, "Deiatel'nost' Komitetov nezamozhnykh selian na Ukraine v 1920 godu," VI, no. 4 (1954), p. 96; M. V. Tymoshenko, "Komnesamy Ukrainy ta ikh rol' u zmitsneni orhaniv Radians'koi vlady na seli v 1920 rotsi," *Pytannia istorii narodiv SRSR*, no. 7 (1968), p. 33; Kubanin, *Makhnovshchina*, p. 136; B. M. Myhal', "Konfiskatsiia zemel'nykh lyshkiv u kurkul's'kykh hospodarstvakh na Ukraini v 1920–1923 rr.," *Pytannia istorii narodiv SRSR*, no. 6 (1969), p. 111; V. Bronshtein, "Komitety bednoty v RSFSR," IM, no. 5 (60) (1938), pp. 77–78; A. I. Lepeshkin, *Sovety-vlast' trudiashchykhsia, 1917–1936*; Mazepa, *Ukraina v ohni*, 3:26.

17. M. V. Frunze, *Sobraniie sochinenii*, 1:181; Nomad, "Epic of Nestor Makhno," p. 414.

18. Teper, *Makhno*, p. 19; Kubanin, *Makhnovshchina*, pp. 136–44; Max Nomad, *Apostles of Revolution*, p. 332.

19. "The Ukrainian Peasants," *Soviet Russia* 3, no. 22 (New York, November 27, 1920): 529; P. S. Zahors'kyi and P. K. Stoian, *Narysy istorii komitetiv nezamozhnykh selian*, p. 36.

20. IA. A. Slashchev-Krymskii, *Trebuiu suda obshchestva i glasnosti: Oborona i sdacha Kryma: Memuary i documenty* (Constantinople, 1921), p. 6.

21. Efimov, "Deistviia protiv Makhno," p. 208.

Chapter 19, Makhno between Wrangel and the Bolsheviks

1. Peter P. Wrangel, "The White Armies," *The English Review* 47:379; Stewart, *White Armies of Russia*, p. 361; Frunze, *Sobranie sochinenii*, 1:268; *Kornilovskii udarnyi polk*, p. 162. According to Gukovskii the strength of Slashchov's Crimean Corps was from 7,000 to 8,000 men, while Slashchov gives only about 3,000 men [Al. Gukovskii, ed., "Nachalo vrangelevshchiny," KA 2 [21] [1922]: 174; Slashchev-Krymskii, *Trebuiu suda obshchestva i glasnosti*, p. 13).

2. Wrangel, *Always with Honour*, p. 146.

3. Ibid.; see also A. A. Valentinov, "Krymskaia epopeia," ARR 5:5.

4. A. L. Gukovskii, ed., "Agrarnaia politika Vrangelia," KA 1 (26) (1928): 61.

5. Wrangel, *Memoirs*, p. 186.

6. Ibid.

7. Gukovskii, "Nachalo vrangelevshchiny," p. 178.

8. Stewart, *White Armies of Russia*, p. 364.

9. Wrangel, "White Armies," pp. 379–94.

10. Ibid.

11. Wrangel, *Always with Honour*, pp. 208–9.

12. *Grazhdanskaia voina*, 3:503–4; N. P. Lipatov, *1920 god na Chernom more*, p. 251; R., "Bredovskii pokhod," *Chasovoi*, no. 49 (1931), p. 22.

13. Wrangel, *Always with Honour*, p. 254.

14. Wrangel, "White Armies," p. 380.

15. Dotsenko, *Zymovyi pokhid*, pp. VIII ff.; Shandruk, *Arms of Valor*, p. 116; Dmytro Paliiv, "Zymovyi pokhid," LCK, no. 6 (1935), pp. 8–10.

16. Polska Akademia Nauk, Pracownia Historii Stosunków Polsko-Radzieckich, *Dokumenty i materialy do istorii stosunków Polsko-Radzieckich* (Warsaw: Ksiazka i Wiedza, 1964), 3:745-47.

17. Ibid., 3:409–10; see also Polska Akademia Nauk, Instytut Historii, *Materialy archiwalne do historii stosunków Polsko-Radzieckich* (Warsaw: Ksiazka i Wiedza, 1957), 1:288.

18. Wrangel, *Memoirs*, p. 236.

19. Frunze, *Sobranie sochinenii*, 1:269–70; Semanov, "Makhnovshchina i ee krakh," p. 55; Konstantin Anan'ev, *V boiakh za Perekop*, p. 7.

20. Wrangel, *Always with Honour*, p. 231.

21. Trotskii, *Materialy i dokumenty po istorii Krasnoi Armii*, 2, pt. 2:210; *Grazhdanskaia voina*, 3:511; Rudnev, *Makhnovshchina*, pp. 80–81; Efimov, "Deistviia protiv Makhno," p. 208.

22. Teper, *Makhno*, p. 93.

23. V. Obolenskii, "Krym pri Vrangele," in *Denikin-IUdenich-Vrangel'*, comp.

S. A. Alekseev, p. 395. It is true that at the end of February 1920, the Bolsheviks seized Makhno's oldest brother Sava at his home and, although he did not participate in the campaign against the Bolsheviks, he was shot (Gorelik, *Goneniia na anarkhism*, p. 31).

24. Rakovskii, *Konets bielykh*, p. 33.

25. Ibid.

26. Denikin, *Ocherki*, 5:135; see also Arshinov, *Istoriia makhnovskogo dvizheniia*, pp. 168–69; Rudnev, *Makhnovshchina*, p. 83; Rakovskii, *Konets bielykh*, pp. 33–34.

27. Arshinov, *Istoriia makhnovskogo dvizheniia*, p. 169; Kubanin, *Makhnovshchina*, p. 151; Semanov, "Makhnovshchina i ee krakh," p. 55; Nikulin, "Gibel' makhnovshchiny," p. 187; Rudnev, *Makhnovshchina*, p. 83; Rakovskii, *Konets bielykh*, p. 81; Trotskii, *Materialy i dokumenty po istorii Krasnoi Armii*, 2, pt. 2:187.

28. Trotskii, *Materialy i dokumenty po istorii Krasnoi Armii*, 2, pt. 2:214.

29. Rakovskii, *Konets beilykh*, pp. 81–82, 134.

30. Wrangel, *Always with Honour*, pp. 235–36; Rakovskii, *Konets bielykh*, pp. 115 ff.; *Grazhdanskaia voina*, 3:497.

31. Lipatov, *1920 god na Chernom more*, pp. 173–78, 212; Chamberlin, *Russian Revolution*, 2:325–27; Lukomskii, *Memoirs*, p. 251; Rakovskii, *Konets bielykh*, pp. 78–79, 129.

32. Wrangel, *Always with Honour*, p. 249; I. M. Podshivalov, *Desantnaia ekspeditsiia Kovtiukha*, pp. 11–12, 15–16; Rakovskii, *Konets biebykh*, pp. 122–28. According to a Soviet source, Ulagai's detachment, before the end of the offensive, consisted of 4,500 infantry, 4,500 cavalry, 243 machine guns, and 17 guns. The other unit consisted of 4,400 men mostly infantry, 40 machine guns, and 8 guns (*Grazhdanskaia voina*, 3:498).

33. Wrangel, *Always with Honour*, pp. 258, 260.

34. Ibid., p. 262; Stewart, *White Armies of Russia*, p. 373; Podshivalov, *Desantnaia ekspeditsiia Kovtiukha*, pp. 48–49; *Grazhdanskaia voina*, 3:499–500.

35. Wrangel, *Always with Honour*, p. 261.

36. Ibid., p. 262.

37. Voline, *Unknown Revolution*, p. 187; Chernomordik, *Makhno i makhnovshchina*, p. 24.

38. Kubanin, *Makhnovshchina*, p. 134; Chamberlin, *Russian Revolution*, 2:328; Wrangel, *Always with Honour*, p. 290; Frunze, *Sobranie sochinenii*, 1:271; M. V. Frunze, "Vrangel," in *Perekop i Chongar*, p. 20.

39. IAkovlev, *Russkii anarkhizm*, p. 34; see also Efimov, "Deistviia protiv Makhno," p. 208; Rudnev, *Makhnovshchina*, p. 90.

40. *Leninskii sbornik*, 36:151.

41. Nestor Makhno, "Otkrytoe pis'mo partii VKP i ee TS. K.," DT, nos. 37–38 (1928), p. 10; Romanchenko, "Epizody z borot'by proty makhnovshchyny," p. 132; *Grazhdanskaia voina*, 3:512; Serge, *Memoirs of a Revolutionary*, p. 122; IAkovlev, *Russkii anarkhizm*, p. 34. When Bela Kun visited Makhno, on October 20, 1920, at Ulianivka he asked Makhno what he would do if he had been commander of the Bolshevik troops that had been defeated on the Polish front, crossed into East Prussia, and been disarmed. Makhno replied: "I would not remain in Prussian territory a single hour. [I would] divide my troops into separate effective units and move deep into the rear of the Polish armies, destroying all roads and

means of supplies and arms" (Makhno, "Otkrytoe pis'mo partii VKP i ee TS. K.," p. 11).

42. Berkman, "Nestor Makhno," p. 26; Nikulin, "Gibel' makhnovshchiny," pp. 188–89; Lipatov, *1920 god na Chernom more*, p. 306; Semanov, "Makhnovshchina i ee krakh," p. 56; IAkovlev, *Russkii anarkhizm*, p. 34; Margushin, "Bat'ko Makhno," p. 2; Arshinov, *Istoriia makhnovskogo dvizheniia*, p. 171.

43. This point was demanded by the Bolshevik authorities (Arshinov, *Istoriia makhnovskogo dvizheniia*, p. 172).

44. Arshinov, *Istoriia makhnovskogo dvizheniia*, pp. 171–73; see also Lebed', *Itogi i uroki trekh*, pp. 38–39; Kubanin, *Makhnovshchina*, pp. 157–58; *Grazhdranskaia voina*, 3:512; Footman, *Nestor Makhno*, pp. 121–22; IAroslavskii, *History of Anarchism in Russia*, p. 75; IAkovlev, *Russkii anarkhizm*, pp. 33–34.

45. Kubanin, *Makhnovshchina*, pp. 158–59; *Grazhdanskaia voina*, 3:512; Trotskii, *Materialy i dokumenty po istorii Krasnoi Armii*, 2, pt. 2:212; see also Voline, *Unknown Revolution*, p. 190.

46. Trotskii, *Materialy i dokumenty po istorii Krasnoi Armii*, 2, pt. 2:214; see also Voline, *Unknown Revolution*, p. 90.

47. Efimov, "Deistviia proty Makhno," p. 209; A. Buiskii, *Krasnaia Armiia na vnutrennem fronte*, p. 76.

48. Rakovskii, *Konets bielykh*, p. 168.

49. Wrangel, *Always with Honour*, p. 300.

50. Dubiv, "Ulamok z moho zhyttia," no. 7 (220), p. 919; Makhno, *Makhnovshchina*, pp. 51–52; Voline, *Unknown Revolution*, p. 191; Rudnev, *Makhnovshchina*, p. 90.

51. Dubiv, "Ulamok z moho zhyttia," no. 7, p. 919; Margushin, "Bat'ko Makhno," p. 2; Gorelik, *Goneniia na anarkhizm*, p. 30; Semanov, "Makhnovshchina i ee krakh," p. 57; Teper, *Makhno*, p. 109; Kubanin, *Makhnovshchina*, p. 159; Lebed', *Itogi i uroki trekh*, p. 40.

52. *Grazhdanskaia voina*, 3:506–8.

53. P. N. Shatilov, "Petr Nikolaevich Vrangel'," p. 3.

54. Wrangel, *Always with Honour*, p. 294; see also P. N. Shatilov, "Pamiatnaia zapiska o Krymskoi evakuatsii," *Bieloe dielo* 4:93.

55. Frunze, *Sobranie sochinenii*, 1:272; *Grazhdanskaia voina*, 3:513–15, 533–36; Anan'ev, *V boiakh za Perekop*, pp. 36–37; Wrangel, *Always with Honour*, pp. 308–9.

56. M. V. Frunze, *Izbrannye proizvedeniia*, p. 109; see also M. Frunze, "Pamiati Perekopa i Chongara," *Voennyi vestnik*, no. 6 (1928), p. 47.

57. Frunze, *Sobranie sochinenii*, 1:272; *Grazhdanskaia voina*, 3:538; Shatilov, "Pamiatnaia zapiska o Krymskoi evakuatsii," pp. 94–95; Anan'ev, *V boiakh za Perekop*, p. 51; Vygran, "Vospominaniia o bor'bie s makhnovtsami," p. 12; N. Rebikov, "Latyshskie strelki v Rossii," *Chasovoi*, no. 500 (1968), p. 18; V. Grebenshchikov, "K dvenadtsatiletiiu osvobozhdeniia Kryma," VR, nos. 11–12 (1932), pp. 114–16; Arshinov, *Istoriia makhnovskogo dvizheniia*, pp. 174–75; Dubiv, "Ulamok z moho zhyttia," p. 919; Margushin, "Bat'ko Makhno," p. 171; Gorelik, *Goneniia na anarkhizm*, p. 30; Peters, *Nestor Makhno*, p. 87.

58. Berkman, "Nestor Makhno," p. 25.

59. Wrangel, *Memoirs*, p. 310; Shatilov, "Pamiatnaia zapiska o Krymskoi evakuatsii," pp. 95, 98; P. Shatilov, "Ostavlenie Kryma," *Chasovoi*, no. 44 (1930), pp. 14–15; Wrangel, "White Armies," p. 379.

60. Wrangel, "White Armies," pp. 381 ff.; Shatilov, "Pamiatnaia zapiska o Krymskoi evakuatsii," p. 107; Lukomskii, *Memoirs*, p. 253; Vygran, "Vospominaniia o bor'bie s makhnovtsami," p. 12.

Chapter 20, The Last Phase of the Makhno Struggle

1. Serge, *Memoirs of a Revolutionary*, p. 119.
2. Bechhofer, *In Denikin's Russia*, p. 180.
3. M. Rybakov, "Deistviia letuchego korpusa tov. Nestorovicha," in *Sbornik trudov Voenno-nauchnogo obshchestva pri Voennoi akademii*, 4 (1923): 110.
4. Arshinov, *Istoriia makhnovskogo dvizheniia*, p. 172; see also Danilov, "Vospominaniia," 16:163.
5. Frunze, *Sobranie sochinenii*, 1:176.
6. Voline, *Unknown Revolution*, p. 202.
7. Efimov, "Deistviia protiv Makhno," pp. 212–13; Men'chukov, *Istoricheskii ocherk boev*, pp. 182–83.
8. P. A. Pavlov, "Voennye khitrosti," p. 13.
9. Men'chukov, *Istoricheskii ocherk boev*, pp. 182–84; Nikulin, "Gibel' Makhnovshchiny," p. 192; Kubanin, *Makhnovshchina*, p. 159; Lebed', *Itogi i uroki trekh*, p. 40; Arshinov, *Istoriia makhnovskogo dvizheniia*, pp. 221–22, 188–89; Efimov, "Deistviia protiv Makhno," pp. 216–17; Berkman, "Nestor Makhno," p. 26; Semanov, "Makhnovshchina i ee krakh," p. 58; Omelianovych-Pavlenko, *Zymovyi pokhid*, 2:28.
10. The first circle consisted of the Forty-Second Division's 125th Brigade, the 126th Brigade, the 124th Brigade, the Boguchar Separate Sharpshooter's Brigade, the International Separate Cavalry Brigade, and the Third Reserve Cavalry Brigade. The reserve circle included the Trans-Volga Cavalry Brigade, two sharpshooter regiments of the internal security troops, the Second Cavalry Corps, the First Cavalry Army, the Fourth Cavalry Division, and the Composite Division of Elite troops (Efimov, "Deistviia protiv Makhno," p. 213; Men'chukov, *Istoricheskii ocherk boev*, p. 184).
11. Men'chukov, *Istoricheskii ocherk boev*, pp. 184–86; Efimov, "Deistviia protiv Makhno," pp. 215, 217; Arshinov, *Istoriia makhnovskogo dvizheniia*, p. 189; Voline, *Unknown Revolution*, p. 206.
12. Dubrovs'kyi, *Bat'ko Nestor Makhno*, p. 18.
13. Men'chukov, *Istoricheskii ocherk boev*, p. 186; Efimov, "Deistviia protiv Makhno," p. 217.
14. Arshinov, *Istoriia makhnovskogo dvizheniia*, p. 189; see also Voline, *Unknown Revolution*, p. 204; Omelianovych-Pavlenko, *Zymovyi pokhid*, 2:28.
15. Makhno, "K 10-oi godovshchine," p. 7. Some twenty years later one of the best of European diplomats and statesmen, Eduard Beneš, president of the Czechoslovak Republic, echoed Makhno's disappointment. In 1947, while writing his memoirs, Beneš asked himself about his treaty with the Bolsheviks of December 1943: Was I right or wrong?" At the end of August 1948, a few days before he died, he answered the question himself: "My greatest mistake was that I refused to believe to the very last that even Stalin lied to me cynically, both in 1935 and later, and that his assurances to me and to Masaryk were an intentional deceit" (E. Taborsky, "Beneš and Stalin, Moscow, 1943 and 1945," *Journal of Central European Affairs* 13, no. 2 [1953]: 162n).

16. Voline, *Unknown Revolution*, pp. 204–5.

17. Esaulov, "Nalet Makhno na Berdians'k," LR, no. 3 (1921), pp. 84 ff.; Men'chukov, *Istoricheskii ocherk boev*, pp. 186–87; Efimov, "Deistviia protiv Makhno," p. 218; Danilov, "Vospominaniia," 16:176.

18. Efimov, "Deistviia protiv Makhno," pp. 218–19; Danilov, "Vospominaniia," 16:176; Men'chukov, *Istoricheskii ocherk boev*, p. 187; Makhno, *Makhnovshchina*, p. 37; Arshinov, *Istoriia makhnovskogo dvizheniia*, pp. 189–90; Voline, *Unknown Revolution*, p. 206. According to a Bolshevik source Makhno released 1,200 prisoners (Men'chukov, *Istoricheskii ocherk boev*, p. 187).

19. Makhno, *Makhnovshchina*, p. 37; Efimov, "Deistviia protiv Makhno," p. 219; Men'chukov, *Istoricheskii ocherk boev*, p. 187.

20. Esaulov, "Nalet Makhno na Berdians'k," p. 83.

21. Danilov, "Vospominaniia," 16:176; Men'chukov, *Istoricheskii ocherk boev*, p. 187; Efimov, "Deistviia protiv Makhno," pp. 219–20; Nikulin, "Gibel' makhnovshchiny," p. 192.

22. Voline, *Unknown Revolution*, p. 199; Nomad, "Epic of Nestor Makhno," no. 7, p. 416; Kubanin, *Makhnovshchina*, p. 213; Semanov, "Makhnovshchina i ee krakh," p. 58; Voline, *Nineteen-seventeen*, pp. 157–58; Gorelik, *Goneniia na anarkhizm*, p. 32; IAkovlev, "Makhnovshchina i anarkhizm," *Krasnia nov*, no. 2 (1921), p. 255; G. Maksimov, "Vsevolod Mikhailovich Eikhenbaum (Volin)," DT-P, no. 16 (1946), p. 17; Emma Goldman, *My Further Disillusionment in Russia*, p. 80.

23. Eideman, "Piataia godovshchina odnogo uroka," p. 36; see also Esbakh, "Poslednie dni makhnovshchiny na Ukraine," no. 12, p. 41.

24. *Komandarm Uborevich*, p. 82.

25. Eideman, "Piataia godovshchina odnogo uroka," p. 37.

26. Rybakov, "Deistviia letuchego korpusa tov," p. 111.

27. M. Rybakov, "Makhnoskie operatsii v 1920 g.," KA, no. 12 (March 1922), pp. 12–13, as quoted in Dubrovs'kyi, *Bat'ko Nestor Makhno*, p. 18; Kapustians'kyi, "Makhno i makhnovshchyna," p. 2; see also Esbakh, "Poslednie dni makhnovshchiny na Ukraine," pp. 41–42.

28. Premysler, "Razgrom banditizma na Ukraine, 1921 g.," pp. 44; N. P-pa, "Protybol'shevyts'ki povstannia na Ukraini v 1921 r.," no. 6, p. 22. According to Esbakh, at the beginning of 1921 the Makhno army consisted of 5,000 to 6,000 men (Esbakh, "Poslednie dni makhnovshchiny na Ukraine," p. 40).

29. Eideman, "Piataia godovshchina odnogo uroka," pp. 36–37.

30. Arshinov, *Istoriia makhnovskogo dvizheniia*, pp. 190–91; Semanov, "Makhnovshchina i ee krakh," p. 58.

31. *Komandarm Uborevich*, p. 82.

32. Esbakh, "Poslednie dni makhnovshchiny na Ukraine," p. 42; Men'chukov, *Istoricheskii ocherk boev*, p. 189; Varetskii, "Marshal V. K. Bliukher," p. 258; Makhno, *Makhnovshchina*, pp. 37–39.

33. Eideman, "Piataia godovshchina odnogo uroka," p. 38.

34. Esbakh, "Poslednie dni makhnovshchiny na Ukraine," p. 42; see also Sergeev, "Poltavaskaia operatsiia protiv Makhno," pp. 124–25; Szpinger, *Z pierwsza konna*, p. 178.

35. Eideman, "Piataia godovshchina odnogo uroka," p. 35.

36. Footman, "Nestor Makhno," p. 125; M. P. Belyi, R. A. Kuznetsova, and K. F. Chumak, comps., *Vospominaniia o G. I. Kotovskom*, p. 32.

37. Premysler, "Razgrom banditizma na Ukraine, 1921 g.," p. 44; Danilov, "Vospominaniia," 16:175; Arshinov, *Istoriia makhnovskogo dvizheniia*, p. 194.

38. Arshinov, *Istoriia makhnovskogo dvizheniia*, pp. 196–97. This and subsequent information referring to Arshinov's book *Istoriia makhnovskogo dvizheniia* is taken from a letter that Makhno wrote to Arshinov from abroad and that was later incorporated into the latter's book.

39. Ibid., p. 197.

40. Premysler, "Razgrom banditizma na Ukraine, 1921 g.," p. 44; Arshinov, *Istoriia makhnovskogo dvizheniia*, pp. 197–98.

41. Arshinov, *Istoriia makhnovskogo dvizheniia*, pp. 198–99.

42. Berkman, "Nestor Makhno," pp. 5–6.

43. Eideman, "Piataia godovshchina odnogo uroka," p. 35; Esbakh, "Poslednie dni makhnovshchiny na Ukraine," pp. 44–45.

44. Omelianovych-Pavlenko, *Zymovyi pokhid*, 2:27; Arshinov, *Istoriia makhnovskogo dvizheniia*, p. 199; Semanov, "Makhnovshchina i ee krakh," p. 196.

45. Arshinov, *Istoriia makhnovskogo dvizheniia*, pp. 199–200; Nikulin, "Gibel' makhnoshchiny," p. 196.

46. Varetskii, "Marshall V. K. Bliukher," p. 254.

47. Ibid., p. 259.

48. Arshinov, *Istoriia makhnovskogo dvizheniia*, p. 200; Semanov, "Makhnovshchina i ee krakh," p. 60; Nikulin, "Gibel' makhnovshchiny," p. 197; Rudnev, *Makhnovshchina*, p. 95; Premysler, "Razgrom banditizma na Ukraine, 1921 g.," p. 44; Woodcock, *Anarkhism*, p. 424; Footman, "Nestor Makhno," p. 126; Esbakh, "Poslednie dni makhnovshchiny n Ukraine," p. 48; R. S., "Platone Makhno, il liberatore dell'ukraina, assassinato?," *L'Avvenire Anarchico* (Pisa), September 23, 1921.

Chapter 21, Epilogue

1. Interviews by the author with Dr. Cyrille Radeff on September 15, 1973, Paris, and with Dr. Serhii S. Yermolenko on August 18, 1975, Minneapolis, Minn.

2. Berkman, "Nestor Makhno," pp. 28–29; Frunze, *Sobranie sochinenii*, 1:385.

3. Gorelik, *Goneniia na anarkhizm*, p. 56; Peters, *Nestor Makhno*, p. 89; Nomad, *Apostles of Revolution*, p. 338.

4. Omelianovych-Pavlenko, *Zymovyi pokhid*, 2:28–29.

5. Arbatov, "Bat'ko Makhno," p. 112.

6. Peter Arshinov, "Opravdanie Nestora Makhno," AV, nos. 5–6 (1923), p. 25; Nomad, *Apostles of Revolution*, p. 338; Edward Ligocki, *Dialog z przeszloscia*, pp. 259–61; "Protiv gotoviashchegosia prestupleniia russkogo i pol'skogo pravitel'stv," VO, no. 2 (1922), p. 9.

7. Arbatov, "Bat'ko Makhno," p. 114.

8. Ibid.; Volin, "Nestor Makhno," p. 27; Arshinov, "Oprovdanie Nestora Makhno," p. 25; Voline, *Unknown Revolution*, p. 216; Footman, "Nestor Makhno," p. 126; Denikin, *Ocherki*, 5:134.

9. N. Makhno, *Po povodu "raz'iasneniia,"* pp. 12–14; Aleksei Nikolaev, *Zhizn' Nestora Makhno*, p. 156.

10. Makhno was wounded about twelve times, including twice seriously (Volin, "Nestor Makhno," p. 7).

11. Berkman, "Nestor Makhno," p. 29.

12. Makhno to [Lev] Chykalenko; Peters, *Nestor Makhno*, p. 91; Avrich, *Russian Anarchists*, p. 24.

13. Makhno, *Makhnovshchina*, p. 34.

14. Peters, *Nestor Makhno*, p. 96.

15. At present the fate of Makhno's wife and daughter is unkown. According to Ida Mett, who knew them and Makhno from their arrival in Paris, the Germans sent Makhno's wife and daughter to Berlin during the German occupation, where his wife was presumably killed during an air raid. What happened to Makhno's daughter is unknown. In September 1973, the author visited Paris and talked with people who knew them to find a trace of their whereabouts, but in vain. However, the prevailing opinion reinforced that described by Mett (Ida Mett, "Souvenirs sur Nestor Makhno," p. 4).

16. Berland, "Makhno"; Volin, "Nestor Makhno," p. 7; Arbatov, "Bat'ko Makhno," p. 115; Meleshko, "Nestor Makhno ta ioho anarkhiia," no. 1, p. 10; Muromets, "Nestor Makhno," p. 16; "Smert' N. I. Makhno," PRO, nos. 47–49 (1934), p. 1; "N. I. Makhno," p. 20; Peters, *Nestor Makhno*, pp. 96–97; Berkman, "Nestor Makhno," p. 30.

17. Interview with Cyrille Radeff.

Appendix

1. Nikulin, "Gibel' Makhnovshchiny," p. 173; see also Efimov, "Deistviia protiv Makhno," pp. 206–7.

2. Andrii Moskalenko to L. Bykovskyi; Makhno, *Ukrainskaia revoliutsiia*, 3:70–73; Vasyl' Dubrovs'kyi to author; Omelianovych-Pavlenko, *Zymovyi pokhid*, 2:25; Chernomordik, *Machno i makhnovshchina*, pp. 225–26.

3. "Makhnovskaia armiia," pp. 2–3; Dubrovs'kyi to author.

4. "Makhnovskaia armiia," p. 2; "Zamietki k knigi Arshinova," p. 7.

5. Arshinov, *Istoriia makhnovskogo dvizheniia*, pp. 180, 221; Voline, *Unknown Revolution*, p. 260; Gorelik, *Goneniia na anarkhizm*, p. 30; Footman, "Nestor Makhno," p. 124; Omelianovych-Pavlenko, *Zymovyi pokhid*, 2:28; Kubanin, *Makhnovshchina*, p. 159; "Makhnovskaia armiia," p. 6; Dubiv, "Ulamok z moho zhyttia," no. 7, p. 919; "Zamietki k knigi Arshinova," p. 6; Serge, *Memoirs of a Revolutionary*, p. 122.

6. Arshinov, *Istoriia makhnovskogo dvizheniia*, p. 221; Voline, *Unknown Revolution*, p. 260; Footman, "Nestor Makhno," p. 124; Omelianovych-Pavlenko, *Zymovyi pokhid*, 2:28; Kubanin, *Makhnovshchina*, p. 159; Semanov, "Makhnovshchina i ee krakh," p. 58.

7. Voline, *Unknown Revolution*, pp. 260–61; Arshinov, *Istoriia makhnovskogo dvizheniia*, pp. 125, 221–22; Makhno, *Russkaia revolutsiia*, 1:170–71.

8. Voline, *Unknown Revolution*, p. 261; Arshinov, *Istoriia makhnovskogo dvizheniia*, p. 222; Gorelik, *Goneniia na anarkhizm*, p. 29; "Zamietki k knigi Arshinova," p. 6; Serge, *Memoirs of a Revolutionary*, p. 122.

9. Voline, *Unknown Revolution*, p. 260; Arshinov, *Istoriia makhnovskogo dvizheniia*, pp. 221, 225; "Zamietki k knigi Arshinova," p. 6.

10. Arshinov, *Istoriia makhnovskogo dvizheniia*, p. 226; Voline, *Unknown Revolution*, p. 263; "Zamietki k knigi Arshinova," p. 6.

11. Semanov, "Makhnovshchina i ee krakh," p. 60; Gorelik, *Goneniia na anarkhizm*, p. 31; Voline, *Unknown Revolution*, p. 263; Arshinov, *Istoriia makhnovskogo dvizheniia*, p. 226.

12. Meleshko, "Nestor Makhno ta ioho anarkhiia," no. 2, p. 10; Gorelik, *Goneniia na anarkhizm*, p. 31; Arshinov, *Istoriia makhnovskogo dvizheniia*, p. 227; Voline, *Unknown Revolution*, p. 263; "Zamietki k knigi Arshinova," p. 6; Sakovich, "Proryv Makhno," p. 12; Peters, *Nestor Makhno*, p. 15.

13. Makhno, *Makhnovshchina*, p. 49; Arshinov, *Istoriia makhnovskogo dvizheniia*, p. 223; Belash, "Makhnovshchina," pp. 199–200.

14. Esbakh, "Poslednie dni makhnovshchiny na Ukraine," p. 44; Arshinov, *Istoriia makhnovskogo dvizheniia*, p. 222; Voline, *Unknown Revolution*, p. 261; "Zamietki k knigi Arshinova," p. 6; Semanov, "Makhnovshchina i ee krakh," p. 60; Antonov-Ovseenko, "V borot'bi za Radians'ku Ukrainu," no. 5, p. 117.

15. Arshinov, *Istoriia makhnovskogo dvizheniia*, pp. 194, 223; Voline, *Unknown Revolution*, pp. 210–11, 261; "Zamietki k knigi Arshinova," p. 6; Nikulin, "Gibel' makhnovshchiny," p. 196.

16. Makhno, *Makhnovshchina*, p. 49; Mazepa, *Ukraina v ohni*, 1:63; Kubanin, *Makhnovshchina*, pp. 26, 176; Arshinov, *Istoriia makhnovskogo dvizheniia*, p. 227; Semanov, "Makhnovshchina i ee krakh," p. 49.

17. "Makhnovskaia armiia," p. 6; "Zamietki k knigi Arshinova," p. 6; Arshinov, *Istoriia makhnovskogo dvizheniia*, p. 226; Voline, *Unknown Revolution*, p. 263; Semanov, "Makhnovshchina i ee krakh," p. 60.

18. Arshinov, *Istoriia makhnovskogo dvizheniia*, pp. 224–25; Voline, *Unknown Revolution*, p. 262.

19. Arshinov, *Istoriia makhnovskogo dvizheniia*, p. 225; Voline, *Unknown Revolution*, p. 263.

20. Gorelik, *Goneniia na anarkhizm*, p. 33; Voline, *Unknown Revolution*, p. 263.

21. Belash, "Makhnovshchina," p. 217; Makhno, *Makhnovshchina*, p. 24; Makhno, *Ukrainskaia revoliutsiia*, 3:142.

22. Voline, *Unknown Revolution*, p. 263; Arshinov, *Istoriia makhnovskogo dvizheniia*, p. 227; Kubanin, *Makhnovshchina*, p. 175.

23. P. Arshinov, *Dva probega*, pp. 21–26, 58–59, 71–73.

24. Gorelik, *Goneniia na anarkhizm*, p. 48; Makhno, *Makhnovshchina*, p. 48; Semanov, "Makhnovshchina i ee krakh," pp. 40, 43; E. Z. Dolin (Moravskii), *V vikhri revoliutsii*, p. 442; Nomad, *Apostles of Revolution*, p. 340; L. Lipotkin, "Vsevolod Mikhailovich Eikhenbaum (Volin)," DT-P, no. 17, pp. 16–19; Arshinov, *Istoriia makhnovskogo dvizheniia*, pp. 12–16; "K voprosu ob anarkho-bol'shevizme i ego roli v revoliutsii," AV, no. 1 (July 1923), p. 64; Peters, *Nestor Makhno*, pp. 27, 96; Avrich, *Russian Anarchists*, pp. 241–43.

25. Lipotkin, "V. Eikhenbaum (Volin)," pp. 18–19; Maksimov, "V. Eikhenbaum (Volin)," pp. 13–19; Gorelik, *Goneniia na anarkhizm*, pp. 50–51; Makhno, "Otkrytoe pis'mo t-shchu Maksymovu," p. 11; Makhno, *Po povodu "raz'iasneniia" Volina*, pp. 5–10; Goldman, *Living My Life*, pp. 786–87; Woodcock, *Anarchism*, p. 416; Serge, *Memoirs of a Revolutionary*, pp. 110, 153; Arshinov, *Istoriia makhnovskogo dvizheniia*, p. 237; Teper, *Makhno*, p. 54.

26. Gorelik, *Goneniia na anarkhizm*, pp. 36–37; Maximoff, *Guillotine at Work*, pp. 510–12, 540, 542–43; Teper, *Makhno*, p. 32; Serge, *Memoirs of a Revolu-*

tionary, p. 153; Semanov, "Makhnovshchina i ee krakh," p. 55; "Goneniia na anarkhizm," AV, no. 1 (July 1923), pp. 74–75; Avrich, *Russian Anarchists*, p. 215.

27. Gorelik, *Goneniia na anarkhizm*, p. 34; Teper, *Makhno*, p. 85.

28. Gorelik, *Goneniia na anarkhizm*, pp. 29, 38; Belash, "Makhnovshchina," p. 226.

29. Gorelik, *Goneniia na anarkhizm*, p. 30.

30. Ibid., pp. 27–28.

31. Ibid., p. 49; Voline, *Unknown Revolution*, p. 263.

32. Arshinov, *Istoriia makhnovskogo dvizheniia*, pp. 236–37; Wojna, "Nestor Makhno 'Anarchism czynu,' " p. 66.

33. Arshinov, *Istoriia makhnovskogo dvizheniia*, p. 225; Voline, *Unknown Revolution*, p. 262; Gorelik, *Goneniia na anarkhizm*, p. 57; "Zamietki k knigi Arshinova," p. 6.

34. Gorelik, *Goneniia na anarkhizm*, p. 61; Makhno, *Makhnovshchina*, p. 48.

35. Gorelik, *Goneniia na anarkhizm*, pp. 32–33; Arshinov, *Istoriia makhnovskogo dvizheniia*, pp. 223–24; Voline, *Unknown Revolution*, pp. 261–62; Maximoff, *Guillotine at Work*, p. 348.

36. Gorelik, *Goneniia na anarkhizm*, p. 32; Maximoff, *Guillotine at Work*, p. 128.

37. Voline, *Unknown Revolution*, p. 262; Arshinov, *Istoriia makhnovskogo dvizheniia*, p. 225; Gorelik, *Goneniia na anarkhizm*, p. 31.

38. "Makhnovskaia armiia," p. 6; Semanov, "Makhnovshchina i ee krakh," p. 40.

39. Voline, *Unknown Revolution*, pp. 263–64; Arshinov, *Istoriia makhnovskogo dvizheniia*, pp. 226–27; Kubanin, *Makhnovshchina*, p. 175; "Zamietki k knigi Arshinova," p. 6.

40. Makhno, *Russkaia revoliutsiia*, 1:159, 163; Makhno, *Makhnovshchina*, p. 50.

Bibliography

Primary Sources

Akademiia nauk URSR, Kiev. Instytut istorii. *Moriaki v bor'be za vlast' Sovetov na Ukraine, noiabr' 1917–1920 gg.: Sbornik dokumentov* [Sailors in the struggle for Soviet power in Ukraine, November 1917–1920: collection of documents]. Compiled by V. I. Aleksandrova and T. S. Fedorova; edited by N. I. Suprunenko. Kiev: Izd-vo Akademii nauk Ukr. SSR, 1963. The Bolshevik sailors' struggle for Bolshevik power in Ukraine October 1917–December 1920; 509 items from Russian and Ukrainian state and regional archives.

———. *Radians'ke budivnytstvo na Ukraini v roky hromadiankoi viiny, lystopad 1918–serpen' 1919: Zbirnyk dokumentiv i materialiv* [Soviet build-up in Ukraine during the Civil War years, November 1918–August 1919: collection of documents and materials]. Edited by M. A. Rubach. Kiev: Vyd-vo Akademii nauk Ukr. RSR, 1962. Materials, including Lenin's articles and speeches, on the Bolshevik struggle for power in Ukraine, and the organization of authorities from central to local, including the committees of the poor; 468 documents from Russian and Ukrainian state and regional archives.

Aleksandrov, comp. "Boevaia deiatel'nost' S. K. Timoshenko na frontakh grazhdanskoi voiny: Iz dokumentov proshlogo" [Military activity of S. K. Timoshenko on the fronts of the Civil War: from documents of the past]. VIZ, no. 2 (February 1941), pp. 76–95.

Orders (23) of Marshal S. K. Timoshenko to divisions of the First Cavalry Army dealing with the struggle mainly against Denikin and Wrangel from November 1919 to November 1920.

Alekseev, S. A., comp. *Denikin, IUdenich, Vrangel.* Moscow: Gos. izd-vo, 1927. Selected memoirs of the three generals as well as from Lukomskii, Rakovskii, Voronovich, Skobtsov, Obolenskii, Valentinov, Gori, and others, dealing with the Russian Civil War and the intervention.

———. *Revoliutsiia na Ukraine po memuaram belykh* [Revolution in Ukraine according to memoirs of the Whites]. Edited by N. N. Popova. Moscow: Gos. izd-vo, 1930. Memoirs of Russian and Ukrainian military and political personages on the Ukrainian Revolution.

Aleksieev, I. *Iz vospominanii levogo esera* [From the memoirs of a Leftist Socialist Revolutionary]. Moscow: Gos. izd-vo, 1922. The underground movement in Ukraine during 1917 and 1918, sympathetic to the Bolsheviks.

Andriievs'kyi, Viktor. *Z mynuloho* [From the past]. 2 vols. Berlin: Ukrains'ke slovo, 1921. Revolutionary events from May 1917 to summer 1919, primarily in Poltava province, where the author was a prominent politician.

Antonov-Ovseenko, Vladimir. "V borot'bi proty Denikina i soiuznyts'koi okupatsii" [In the struggle against Denikin and the Allied occupation]. LR, no. 1 (45) (1931), pp. 111–54.

———. "V borot'bi proty Dyrektorii" [In the struggle against the Directory]. LR, no. 1 (40) (1930), pp. 103–32; no. 2 (41), pp. 104–51; nos. 3–4 (42–43), pp. 78–107; no. 5 (44), pp. 173–93. A personal account of the Directory's social policy in 1919, the Bolshevik intervention of 1919, the French intervention in South Ukraine, and Makhno's campaigns against Denikin.

———. "V borot'bi za Radians'ku Ukrainu" [In the struggle for Soviet Ukraine]. LR, no. 2 (46) (1931), pp. 85–114; no. 3 (47); no. 4 (48), pp. 78–107; no. 5 (49) (1932), pp. 112–52. A detailed account of Makhno's campaigns against Denikin in the spring of 1919, the conflict with the Bolsheviks, Makhno's alleged cooperation with Hryhor'iv and Hryhor'iv's uprising against the Bolsheviks.

———. *Zapiski o grazhdanskoi voine* [Notes about the Civil War]. 4 vols. Moscow: Izd. Vysshii voen. red. sovet, 1924–33. These fairly objective, well-documented memoirs, by a Red Army commander, include orders, telegrams, letters, and recorded conversations on the campaigns on the Volga and Ukrainian fronts as well as on the organization, tactics, and strategy of the Red troops.

Arbatov, Z. "Bat'ko Makhno" [Father Makhno]. *Vozrozhdenie* (Paris) 29 (1953): 102–15. A personal account of Makhno's life and activities through his release from Polish prison.

———. "Ekaterinoslav 1917–1922 gg." ARR 12 (1923): 83–148. Valuable memoirs of the Revolution, including Makhno's activities in Katerynoslav, stressing the terror of the Denikin and Bolshevik troops.

Astrov, N. "IAsskoe sovieshchanie: Iz dokumentov" [Reports of the Jassy Conference: from documents]. *Golos minuvshago na chuzhoi storonie* [Voice of the past in a foreign land], 16, no. 3 (Paris, 1926): 39–76.

Ataman Grigor'ev. *Memoirs*. 12 pp. Copy in author's possession.

Aten, Marion, and Arthur Orrmont. *Last Train over Rostov Bridge*. New York: J. Messner, 1961. Combat experiences during the Russian Civil War, 1918–20, by an American pilot who joined the anti-Bolshevik Russian forces.

Auerbakh, V. A. "Revoliutsionnoe obshchestvo po lichnym vospominaniiam" [Revolutionary society according to personal memoirs]. ARR 14 (1924): 5–38; 16 (1925): 49–99. Memoirs of the Revolution, largely in Ukraine, including Katerynoslav province.

Aussem, V. "K istorii povstanchestva na Ukraine: O dvukh partizanskikh diviziakh" [To the history of the partisan movement in Ukraine: about two partisan divisions]. LR, no. 5 (20) (1921), pp. 7–21. Five documents as well as an article by a Bolshevik partisan leader on the organization of the Bolshevik partisans in the Neutral Zone in the second half of 1918.

Averdukh, K. K. [Averius]. *Odesskaia "Chrezvychaika": Bol'shevitskii zastienok: Fakty i nabliudaniia* [The Odessa "Chrezvychaika": Bolshevik torture-chamber: facts and observations]. Vol. 1. Kishinov, 1920.

Bachyns'kyi, Vasyl'. "Povstanchyi viddil bratslavs'koho povitu" [A partisan unit of Bratslav district]. LCK, no. 3 (1930), pp. 5–6. Campaigns of a partisan group, primarily Ukrainian Galician troops, against the Bolsheviks in Bratslav district during the spring of 1920.

Balkovskii, A. "Begstvo na Don k generalam Alekseevu i Kornilovu v 1917-m godu: Vospominaniia komandira baterii" [Escape to the Don to Generals Alekseev and Kornilov in 1917: memoirs of a battery commander]. *Voennyi sbornik* (Paris), no. 6 (January 1965), pp. 39–45.

Bechhofer, C. E. *In Denikin's Russia and the Caucasus, 1919–1920:*

Being the Record of a Journey to South Russia, the Crimea, Armenia, Georgia, and Baku in 1919 and 1920. London: W. Collins, 1921. Account by a British war correspondent of the Denikin campaigns, emphasizing the internal conditions within the Volunteer Army, from October 1918 to March 1920.

Bekesevych, P. "Moi spomyny z ostannikh dniv okupatsii Ukrainy avstro-nimets'kymy viis'kamy" [Memoirs from the last days of the occupation of Ukraine by the Austro-German troops]. LCK, no. 3 (1931), pp. 4–6. Political and military conditions in the Right Bank Ukraine during the second half of 1918.

Belash, V. "Makhnovshchina: Otryvki iz vospominanii" [The Makhno movement: excerpts from memoirs]. LR, no. 3 (30) (May–June 1928), pp. 191–231. The Makhno movement by one of its commanders, later its chief of staff. Written in Bolshevik captivity.

Beliaevskii, V. A. *Kto vinovat: Vospominaniia o belom dvizhenii, 1918–1920* [Who is guilty: memoirs about the White movement, 1918–1920]. Buenos Aires, 1960.

Belyi arkhiv [BA] [White archive]. Edited by IA. M. Lisovoi. 3 vols. Paris, 1926–28. Documents, memoirs, articles, transcripts of conferences, correspondence, and reports, concerning Bolshevik history and anti-Bolshevik Russian movements.

Belyi, M. P., R. A. Kuznetsova, and K. F. Chumak, comps. *Vospominaniia o G. I. Kotovskom* [Memoirs about G. I. Kotovskii]. Kishinev: Kartia moldoveniaske, 1961.

Berkman, Alexander. *The Bolshevik Myth: Diary 1920–1922.* New York: Boni and Liveright, 1925. A 2-year diary of observations of political life in Soviet Russia and Ukraine by a Russian-American Anarchist.

———. "Nestor Makhno: The Man Who Saved the Bolsheviki." Personal recollections. Nice. 30 pp. Copy in author's possession. Firsthand account of Makhno and his movement with additional information from other eyewitnesses.

Bieloe dielo: Lietopis bieloi borby [The White affair: chronicle of the White struggle]. 7 vols. Berlin: "Miednii vsadnik," 1926–33. The Russian anti-Bolshevik movement from 1917 through 1920. Accounts by Generals P. Shatilov, P. N. Wrangel, and the Kuban Ataman A. P. Filimonov.

Bobriv, Vasyl'. "Do zustrichiv ta portretiv" [About meetings and portraits]. SV, no. 229 (October 3, 1927).

———. "Zustrichi ta portrety: Otaman Zelenyi" [Meetings and portraits: Otaman Zelenyi]. SV, no. 172 (July 27, 1927). Memoirs about Otaman Zelenyi's conflict with the Directory, January 1919.

"Boevye dokumenty N. A. Shchorsa" [Military documents of N. A. Shchorsa]. VIZ, no. 1 (1939), pp. 122–25. War operations, military reports, and other documents dealing with the military campaigns in Ukraine by the Bolshevik partisan units, organized in the Neutral Zone, December 1918–August 1919.

Bohun, M. "Fragmenty zi spomyniv pro 'Narodniu Oboronu Khersons'koi gubernii': Na peredodni kintsia denikinshchyny na Khersonshchyni" [Fragments from memoirs about the people's defense of Kherson province: on the eve of the end of the Denikin movement in Kherson province]. *Ukrains'kyi skytalets*, no. 2 (24) (1923), pp. 32–37. Attitudes of different groups within the Volunteer Army toward Ukrainian statehood, its policy in Ukraine, and the disintegration of the army during the second half of 1919.

Bor'ba trudiashchikhsia mass za ustanovlenie i uprochenie Sovetskoi vlasti na Stavropol'e, 1917–apr. 1921 gg.: Sbornik dokumentov i materialov [The struggle of the workers for the establishment and consolidation of Soviet power in the Stavropol' region, 1917–April 1921: collection of documents and materials]. Stavropol: Kn. Izd-vo, 1967. A one-sided selection dealing with Red troops against the Kuban and Terek Cossacks and the Volunteer Army in the North Caucasus from the end of 1917 to 1921.

Bozhyk, Stepan. "Deshcho pro ukrains'kykh partisan v 1919 rotsi: Uryvok z dennyka" [Something about Ukrainian partisans in 1919: excerpts from a diary]. KCK 1924, pp. 140–44. Activities of Makhno, Hryhor'iv, and other partisan leaders in 1919.

Browder, R. P., and A. F. Kerensky, eds. *The Russian Provisional Government 1917*. Documents. 3 vols. Stanford, Calif.: Stanford University Press, 1961. Documents issued by the Provisional Government, military communications, memoirs, and other items from the collection of the Hoover Institution.

Brylyns'kyi, Maksym. "Z denikintsiamy: Opovidannia-spomyn" [With Denikin's men: story-memoirs]. LCK, no. 2 (1929), pp. 8–10.

Budak. "Borot'ba z nimtsiamy ta hetmantsiamy; Istymivs'kyi raion na Zynovyivshchyni: Spohady komandira Pershoho Khersons'koho chervono-gvardiishoho, partyzans'koho, armii Muraviova, zahonu t. Tsymbaliuka" [Struggle against the Germans and the Hetman's men; Istymiv district in the Zynoviiv region: recollections of the commander of the First Kherson Red-Guard, Partisan Army of Muraviov, a unit of comrade Tsymbaliuk]. *Visti*, no. 265 (1927).

Bunyan, J., comp. *Intervention, Civil War, and Communism in Russia,*

April–December, 1918: Documents and Materials. Baltimore, Md.: The John Hopkins Press, 1936. Domestic and international affairs of Russia from April to December, 1918.

Bunyan, J., and H. H. Fisher, comps. *The Bolshevik Revolution, 1917–1918: Documents and Materials.* Stanford, Calif.: Stanford University Press, 1934. Public documents, reports of the contemporary press, participants, and observers, with summaries of events described in the documents.

Ch., M. "Desiat' dniv u Kyivi v sichni 1919 r.: Spomyny z Trudovoho Kongresu" [Ten days in Kiev, January 1919: memoirs from the Labor Congress]. LCK, no. 5 (1931), pp. 5–8; no. 6, pp. 3–6. The Labor Congress in Kyiv in January 1919 and the unification of eastern and western Ukraine.

Cheriachukin, A. "Donskiia delegatsii na Ukrainu i Berline v 1918–1919 gg." [The Don delegations in Ukraine and Berlin in 1918–1919]. *Donskaia lietopis* (Belgrad) 3 (1924): 163–231. Memoirs of the Don Cossacks' envoy to the hetman about his negotiations over the Ukrainian–Don Cossack border, political conditions in Ukraine, the anti-hetman activities of Denikin's followers, and the uprising against the hetman.

Cherkasov. "Pravda o huliaipol'skikh sobytiiakh" [The truth about the Huliai-Pole events]. *Nabat* (Kharkov), no. 21 (June 30, 1919), p. 2.

Chubinskii, M. " 'Na Donu': Iz vospominanii Ober-Prokurora" [In the Don: from memoirs of public procurator]. *Donskaia lietopis'* (Belgrad), no. 1 (1923), pp. 131–68; no. 3 (1924), pp. 268–309.

Chykalenko, IEvhen. *Spohady, 1861–1907* [Memoirs, 1861–1907]. New York: Ukr. Vil'na Akademiia Nauk u SSh. A., 1955. A prominent patron of learning and politician deals with national life and aspirations.

———. *Uryvok z moikh spomyniv za 1917 r.* [An excerpt from my memoirs for 1917]. Prague: Vyd. Fondu im. IE. Chykalenka pry Ukrains'komu akademichnomu komiteti, 1932.

D., O. "Mestnyky: Spomyny iz partyzanky na Velykii Ukraini" [Avengers: memoirs from the partisan movement in Ukraine]. KCK 1923, pp. 158–66. Partisan activities against the Bolsheviks and the local authority in Poltava province, July 1921.

Danilov, I. "Vospominaniia o moei podnevol'noi sluzhbie u bol'shevikov" [Memoirs about my forced service with the Bolsheviks]. ARR 14 (1924): 39–131; 16 (1925): 162–230. A Bolshevik officer who later defected to the West describes the Bolshevik campaigns against Makhno from the end of 1920 to the spring of 1921.

Daushkov, S. "Skarbynyk otamana Makhna" [Treasurer for Otaman Makhno]. *Kaliendar dlia ukrains'kykh pratsiuiuchykh liudei pry-iatel' narodu na rik 1938*, pp. 45–48. Lvov: Nakl. "Hrumads'koho holosu," 1937.

Davatts, V. *Gody: Ocherki piatilietnei bor'by* [Years: essays of five years of struggle]. Belgrade: Russkaia tip., 1926.

———. *Na Moskvu* [On Moscow]. Paris: I. Rirakhovskii, 1921.

Davnyi, R. *Pro Sichovykh Stril'tisiv* [About the Sich Riflemen]. Vienna: Nakl. "Chornohory," 1921. The campaign of the Sich Riflemen against the Bolsheviks and Denikin from late 1917 through 1919. Includes an article by D. Doroshenko about the victims of the Red troops at Kruty.

Degras, F., ed. *Soviet Documents on Foreign Policy*. Vol. 1. London: Oxford University Press, 1951. Diplomatic statements, communiques, reports, interviews, and speeches. Vol. 1 includes 1917 to 1924.

Denikin, A. I. "Bor'ba generala Kornilova" [Struggle of General Kornilov]. FA, no. 37 (1937), pp. 12–13. The formation of the Volunteer units by General Alekseev in the Don at the end of 1917.

———. "Getmanstvo i Direktoriia na Ukraine" [The hetman government and the Directory in Ukraine]. In *Revoliutsiia na Ukraine po memuaram belykh*, pp. 136–85. Compiled by S. A. Alekseev. Moscow, 1930. A selection from vols. 3–5 of *Ocherki russkoi smuty*; deals with the hetman government, stressing the German, Bolshevik, and anti-Bolshevik Russian policies in Ukraine in 1918, the establishment of the Directory, and French intervention.

———."Kubanskii pokhod" [The Kuban march]. FA, no. 41 (1938), pp. 13–17; no. 42, pp. 2–15. The fighting between the Volunteer troops and Bolsheviks in the Kuban during winter and spring, 1918, the death of General Kornilov and the treatment of his corpse by the Bolsheviks, the formation of a volunteer unit in Jassy, Romania, by Colonel Drozdovskii, and its march to the Don.

———. *La décomposition de l'armée et du pouvoir Fevrier–Septembre 1917*. Paris: J. Povolozky, 1922.

———. *Ocherki russkoi smuty* [Sketches of the Russian turmoil]. 5 vols. Paris: J. Povolozky, 1921–26. Detailed memoirs of World War I and the anti-Bolshevik movement, from 1914 to April 1920. Includes numerous documents.

"Denikintsy o sostoianii svoego tyla: Soobshch. Kandidov" [Denikin's men (commenting) about the conditions in the rear: Kandidov's report]. KA 5 (72) (1935): 191–99. A report to General Wrangel at the end of March 1920 by a member of a military court about the causes of evacuation of Odessa by the troops of the Volunteer Army and their demoralization.

Derevenskii, Iv. [pseud.]. "Bandity: Ocherki perioda grazhdanskoi voiny" [Bandits: essays of the Civil War period]. BY, no. 24 (1924), pp. 252–73. Partisan activities of Orlyk, Struk, and others in the district of Kyiv and of the peasants' attitude from August 1920 to May 1922, by a Soviet Russian agent.

Die deutsche Okkupation der Ukraine: Geheimdokumente. Strasbourg: Editions Promethée, 1937. Confidential diplomatic papars, military reports, and other materials that passed between the German and Austro-Hungarian representatives in Ukraine and the Ministries of Foreign Affairs in Berlin and Vienna from February to November 1918. They depict the German colonial policy of oppressions and punitive expeditions, and the disintegration of their troops.

"Dnevnik i vospominaniia kievskoi studentki" [Diary and memoirs of a Kiev student girl]. ARR 15 (1924): 209–53. Political events in Kyiv from February 1919 through March 1920, stressing the terror of the Bolsheviks and Denikin troops.

Dobranitskii, M. "Zelenye partizany, 1918–1920 gg." [Green partisans, 1918–1920]. PR, nos. 8–9 (31–32) (1924), pp. 72–98.

"Doklad nachal'nyku operatsionnago Otdeleniia germanskago vostochnago fronta o polozhenii del' na Ukraine v marte 1918 goda" [Report to the chief of the operational division of the German Eastern Front about conditions in Ukraine in March 1918]. ARR 1 (1921): 288–94. Conditions in Ukraine in March 1928 by Collin Ross, a German publicist, who accompanied German troops in Ukraine and served with the military section of the Ministry of Foreign Affairs after autumn 1917.

"Doklad o dieiatel'nosti Kievskago tsentra Dobrovol'cheskoi armii" [Report about the activities of the Kiev center of the Volunteer Army]. BA, nos. 2–3 (1928), pp. 119–32. A report of the Volunteer Army section in Kyiv during 1919.

Dontsov, Dmytro. *Rik 1918, Kyiv* [The year 1918, Kiev]. Toronto: Homin Ukrainy, 1954. Diary of political events in Kyiv from May 1918 to February 1919.

Doroshenko, Dmytro. *IAk bulo proholosheno het'manstvo u Kyivi 29 kvitnia, 1918 roku* [How the hetman regime was proclaimed in

Kiev April 29, 1918]. Winnipeg: Vyd. Tsentralia "Sichei," 1927.

———. *Istoriia Ukrainy 1917–1923 rr.* 2 vols. 2nd ed. New York: Bulava, 1954. An authoritative study by a prominent Ukrainian historian and minister of foreign affairs of the hetman government of the first two years of the Ukrainian Revolution, including the Central Rada and the hetman state.

———. *Moi spomyny pro nedavnie mynule, 1914–1920* [My memoirs about the recent past, 1914–1920]. 2nd ed. Munich: Ukrains'ke vyd-vo, 1969. Objective view of sociopolitical conditions in Ukraine and the Revolution, based on the author's recollections and on documents. Emphasizes Russian efforts to destroy Ukrainian national life in occupied Galicia.

———. "Pis'ma" [Writings]. *Vozrozhdenie* (Paris), no. 17 (1951), pp. 152–57. Letter to S. Melgunov in 1926 in response to his article about Russo-Ukrainian relations. Doroshenko maintained that neither he nor the Ukrainian people hated Russia, but were striving for the independence of both the Ukrainian and Russian states.

———. "Voina i revoliutsiia na Ukraine" [War and revolution in Ukraine]. In *Revoliutsiia na Ukraine po memuaram belykh*, pp. 64–98. Compiled by S. A. Alekseev. Moscow, 1930.

———. "Voina i revoliutsiia na Ukraine: Iz vospominanii" [War and the Revolution in Ukraine, from memoirs]. *Istorik i sovremennik* (Berlin) 1 (1922): 207–45; 2:180–205; 4 (1923): 178–209; 5 (1924): 73–125. Russian occupation of East Galicia during World War I, and the effort to eliminate Ukrainian national life; the Central Rada's conflict with the Provisional Government, the first Bolshevik invasion, and the assistance of Austro-German troops in expelling the enemies.

Doroshenko, Natalia. "Poltavs'ki spomyny, 1917–20: Fragmenty" [Poltava memoirs, 1917–20: fragments]. KD 1933, pp. 56–92.

Dorożyńska, Elzbieta [Zaleska]. *Na ostatniej placowce: Dziennik z zycia wsi podolskiej w latach 1917–1921* [In the last stronghold: diary from the life in a village in Podillia province]. Warsaw: Gebethner i Wolff, 1925. A Polish landowner and physician describes life in Podillia province during the Ukrainian Revolution.

Dotsenko, Oleksander. *Litopys ukrains'koi revoliutsii: Materiialy i dokumenty do istorii ukrains'koi revoliutsii, 1917–1923* [Chronicle of the Ukrainian Revolution: materials and documents about the history of the Ukrainian Revolution]. Vol. 2, pts. 4–5. Kiev, 1923–24. By the aide of S. Petliura based on official documents and the author's archives, diaries, recollections, captured secret documents, and interviews with political and military leaders as well as on contemporary publications, Ukrainian and foreign; a substantial portion consists of letters, memoranda, telegrams, appeals to the population, and other documents pertaining to the Ukrainian government and its relations with foreign countries. A number of documents in Polish deal with Petliura-Piłsudski relations.

———. *Zymovyi pokhid: 6.XII, 1919–6.V, 1920* [The winter campaign: December 6, 1919–May 6, 1920]. 2nd ed. New York (?), 1966 (?). Guerrilla warfare in the rear of the Denikin and Bolshevik forces: an account of the prelude to the campaign, the campaign, partisan activities, Bolshevik policy in Ukraine, and related documents. Published in Warsaw in 1932 as vol. 2, pt. 6, of the author's *Litopys ukrains'koi revoliutsii*.

Drabatyi, L. "Epizod z evakuatsii Kyieva v 1919 r." [An episode during the evacuation of Kiev in 1919]. TR, no. 30 (1964), pp. 3–6. Evacuation of the Directory from Kyiv at the beginning of February 1919, as a result of the Bolshevik attack.

Drozdovskii, M. G. *Dnevnik* [A diary]. Berlin: O. Kirkhner, 1923. A Russian officer describes the advance of his troops through South Ukraine from Jassy to the Don, February to April, 1918: conditions there, the attitude of the populace toward the Russians and Germans, and the conflict in the Volunteer Army.

Dubas, Pavlo. "'Nestor Makhno ta ioho anarkhiia'—F. Meleshka" ["Nestor Makhno and his anarchy"—F. Meleshka]. *Novyi shliakh* (Winnipeg), January 18, 1960. An account similar to the author's "Z raionu Makhna," below.

———. "Z raionu Makhna" [From the region of Makhno]. LCK, no. 3 (1932), pp. 7–8. A Galician Ukrainian officer in the Austrian army describes an Austrian punitive expedition.

Dubiv, Volodymyr. "Ulamok z moho zhyttia: Spomyn " [Fragment from my life: memoirs]. *Vyzvol'nyi shliakh* (London), no. 6 (219) (1966), pp. 737–44; no. 7 (220), pp. 916–23. Bolshevik persecution of Ukrainians, including Makhno men, in a prison in Kharkov at the end of 1920.

Dubreuil, Charles. *Deux années en Ukraine, 1917–1919*. Paris: H. Paulin, 1919. Ukraine, its land, people, and history, based on observations of a traveler during the Revolution.

Dubrovs'kyi, Vasyl'. Letter to author. Richmond, Va., July 25, 1964.

Dubynets', Ivan. *Horyt' Medvedyn: Istorychno-memuarnyi narys* [The burning of Medvedyn: historic and memoir sketch]. New York:

1952. Uprisings of a village in Kaniv district against the Bolshevik regime at the end of 1920, and its subsequent destruction by Bolshevik troops.

Dunin-Kozicka, Marja. *Burza od wschodu: Wspomnienia z Kijowszczyzny, 1918–1920* [Storm from the east: memoirs from the Kiev province, 1918–1920]. Warsaw: Dom Ksiażki, 1929. A Polish landowner describes her vicissitudes in Kyiv province during the Ukrainian Revolution and the Bolshevik and Denikin invasions.

Eideman, R. "Makhno." AR, nos. 1–2 (1923), pp. 27–28. Memoirs of the commander of the Bolshevik forces fighting against Makhno in 1920.

———. "Piataia godovshchina odnogo uroka: Zamechaniia k state'e tov. Esbakha" [Fifth anniversary of a lesson: remarks about the article of Comrade Esbakh]. VR, no. 12 (1926), pp. 32–39. Campaign of the Red troops against Makhno during the first half of 1921, stressing Makhno's military tactics. The author, formerly an officer in the tsarist army, commanded Red troops against Denikin and against Makhno. Arrested in the late 1930s, he died in the Cold Hill prison in Kharkov in 1937.

"The Fastov Pogrom." *The Nation* 111 (December 8, 1920): 646–47.

Fedenko, Panas. *Isaak Mazepa, borets' za voliu Ukrainy* [Isaak Mazepa, fighter for the freedom of Ukaraine]. London: Nashe slovo, 1954.

———. *Istoriia revoliutsii, 1917–1921* [History of the Revolution]. I. Tsentral'na Rada. N.p., n.d.

———. "Mynulo pivstolittia: Zymovyi pokhid Armii Ukrains'koi Narodnoi Republiky 1919–1920 rr." [A half-century later: the winter campaign of the Army of the Ukrainian People's Republic, 1919–1920]. SV, no. 218 (November 26, 1971), p. 2; no. 219 (November 27), p. 2; no. 220 (November 30), p. 2; no. 221 (December 1), p. 2; no. 222 (December 2), p. 2; no. 223 (December 3), p. 2; no. 224 (December 4), p. 2; no. 225 (December 5), p. 2. Reprinted in book form. New York: Svoboda, 1972. The winter campaign in the rear of the Russian Bolshevik and anti-Bolshevik forces from December 1919 to May 1920, set against the political and military background.

———. *Ukrains'kyi rukh u 20 stolitti* [The Ukrainian movement during the twentieth century]. London: Nashe slovo, 1959. Competent survey of the Ukrainian national movement in the twentieth century.

———. *Vlada Pavla Skoropads'koho: Piat'desiati rokovyny perevorotu v Ukraini* [The government of Pavlo Skoropads'kyi: the fiftieth anniversary of a coup d'état in Ukraine]. London: Nashe slovo, 1968.

Filippov, N. *Ukrainskaia kontrrevoliutsiia na sluzhbie u Anglii, Frantsii i Pol'shi* [The Ukrainian counterrevolution at the service of England, France, and Poland]. Moscow: Moskovskii rabochii, 1927. The Directory's foreign relations, supplemented by a number of documents, including the Ukrainian-Polish political and military conventions of April 21 and 24, 1920.

Frunze, M. V. *Izbrannye proizvedeniia* [Selected works]. Moscow: Voen. izd-vo, 1965. Articles and speeches dealing with the organization of the Red Army, its struggle during the Civil War, its military and political education, and the role of the rear in the war.

———. "Pamiati Perekopa i Chongara: Stranichka iz vospominanii" [In memory of Perekop and Chongar: a page from memoirs]. *Voennyi vestnik* (Moscow), no. 6 (1928), pp. 40–48.

———. *Sobranie sochinenii* [Collected works]. 3 vols. Moscow: Gos. izd-vo, 1926–29. Volume 1 includes documents about Frunze's military operations in Turkestan, and subsequently in Ukraine against Wrangel and Makhno, from January 1919 through 1920.

———. "Telegrammy i prikazy" [Telegrams and orders]. *Borba klassov* (Moscow), no. 12 (1935), pp. 50–61. Telegrams to Lenin and orders to the Bolshevik troops of the south from September to November 1920.

———. "Vrangel." In *Perekop i Chongar: Sbornik statei i materialov* [Perekop and Chongar: a collection of articles and materials]. Moscow: Gos. voen. izd-vo, 1933.

Genkin, E. B., comp. *Razgrom nemetskikh zakhvatchikov v 1918 godu: Sbornik materialov i dokumentov* [Defeat of the German invaders in 1918: a collection of materials and documents]. Edited by M. B. Mitina and I. I. Mintsa. Moscow: Gos. Polit. izd-vo, 1943. German policy in East Europe, largely in Ukraine, and the struggle of the populace against the Germans from February 1918 to February 1919.

Gerasimenko, K. V. *Bat'ko Makhno: Iz vospominanii belogvardeitsa* [Father Makhno: from memoirs of a White guard]. Edited by P. E. Shchegolova. Moscow: Giz, 1928. A Soviet revision of the author's original article "Makhno."

———. "Makhno." *Istorik i sovremennik* (Berlin) 3 (1922): 151–201. A biased, personal account containing factual errors about Makhno and his movement by a Denikin follower and later a Bolshevik agent acting in West Europe, particularly in Czechoslovakia.

Gerasimov, E., and M. Erlikh. *Nikolai Aleksandrovich Shchors: Boevoi put'* [Nikolai Aleksandrovich Shchors: road of struggle]. Moscow: Gos. voen. izd-vo NKO SSR, n.d. The biography of a Red Army commander, with emphasis on his campaign against the Ukrainian forces during the Revolution.

Germany. Auswartiges Amt. *Germany and the Revolution in Russia, 1915–1918: Documents from the Archives of the German Foreign Ministry*. Edited by Z. A. B. Zeman. London: Oxford University Press, 1958. Documents (136) related to German policy toward the Revolution in Russia from January 1915 to March 1918.

Gol'denweizer, A. A. "Biegstvo: Iiul'–oktiabr' 1921 g." [Escape: July–October 1921]. ARR 6 (1922): 161–303. Comprehensive, subjective, personal account of a jurist about political events in Kyiv, emphasizing Russian life there, from February 1917 to July 1921.

Golder, Frank Alfred, ed. *Documents of Russian History, 1914–1917*. Translated by Emannel Aronsberg. New York: The Century Co., 1927. Materials taken largely from two newspapers, *Rech'* and *Izvestiia*, which contained most of the official documents of the period.

Goldman, Emma. *Anarkhizm*. Petrograd: Knigoizd-vo "Golos truda," 1921.

———. *Living My Life*. Garden City, N.Y.: Garden City Publishing Co., 1931. Autobiography of a Russian-American anarchist, containing a description of her visit to Soviet Russia that revealed the greatly disappointing conditions of life under the Bolshevik dictatorship.

———. *My Disillusionment in Russia*. Garden City, N.Y.: Doubleday, 1923. Detailed account of the author's trip to Soviet Russia where she met many revolutionary and anarchist leaders.

———. *My Further Disillusionment in Russia: Being a Continuation of Miss Goldman's "My Disillusionment in Russia."* Garden City, N.Y.: Doubleday, 1924. An indictment of the Bolshevik regime by an eyewitness.

Gordienko, G. "Svidetel'stva o Makhno: Glazami iunoshi" [Evidences about Makhno: in the eyes of a youth]. NRS, March 16, 1970, p. 7. A personal account describing the behavior of Makhno partisans in Oleksandrivs'k in August 1919.

Grazhdanskaia voina na Ekaterinoslavshchine, fevral' 1918–1920 gg.: Dokumenty i materialy [The Civil War in Ekaterinoslav province, February 1918–1920: documents and materials]. Edited by

A. IA. Pashchenko. Dnepropetrovsk: "Promin'," 1968. Partisan activities and the Bolshevik struggle "for Soviet power" in Katerynoslav province. It contains, in chronological order, 292 documents, most of which are published for the first time.

Grazhdanskaia voina na Ukraine, 1918–1920: Sbornik dokumentov i materialov [The Civil War in Ukraine, 1918–1920: collection of documents and materials]. Edited by S. M. Korolivskii, N. K. Kolesnik, and I. K. Rybalka. 3 vols. in 4. Kiev, 1967. The struggle of the Bolshevik and anti-Bolshevik Russian forces for power in Ukraine, the policy of Austro-German troops, and Allied intervention in South Ukraine. It contains 2,682 items from Russian and Ukrainian state and regional archives, including Bolshevik party and military organizations and institutions. Dates and sources are provided.

Grebenshchikov, V. "K dvenadtsatiletiiu osvobozhdeniia Kryma: Dokumenty grazhdanskoi voiny" [To the twelfth anniversary of the liberation of the Crimea: documents of the Civil War]. VR, nos. 11–12 (1932), pp. 113–17. Orders of M. V. Frunze to the Bolshevik troops at the southern front, November 5 to 17, 1920.

"Grigor'ievskaia avantura (mai 1919)" [The Hryhor'iv adventure (May 1919)]. LR, no. 3 (1923), pp. 152–59. The struggle of the Red Army against Otaman Hryhor'iv.

Grunfel, Judith. *Iz vospominanii o bor'be za svobodu i narodovlastie v Odesse, 1918–1920 gg.* [From memoirs about a struggle for freedom and people's authority in Odessa, 1918–1920]. New York, 1962.

Gukovskii, A. I., ed. "Agrarnaia politika Vrangelia" [The agricultural policy of Wrangel]. KA 1 (26) (1928): 51–96. Application of White Army law from May 25, 1920, and reports about the situation in the villages, compiled for the Allies by Wrangel's Department of Agriculture.

———. "Iz istorii vneshnei politiki pravitel'stva Vrangelia: Economicheskiie otnosheniia s Frantsiei" [From the history of the Wrangel government's domestic policy: economic relations with France]. KA 1 (32) (1929): 125–57. Reports from Paris by a commercial agent of Wrangel's government from May to July, 1920; includes documents about the foundation of a Russo-French commercial society for trade, industry, and transportation.

———. "Krym v 1918–1919 gg.: Materialy osvedomitel'nykh organow Dobrovol'cheskoi armii i diplomatichekogo predstavitelia Vsevelikogo voiska donskogo" [Crimea in 1918–1919: materials of the intelligence of the Volunteer Army and the diplomatic representative of the Great Don Army]. KA 2 (27) (1928): 142–81; 3 (28): 55–85. Documents of the Volunteer Army concerning the attitude of the populace toward it, the labor movement, and the underground activities of the Bolsheviks and their partisans.

———. "Nachalo vrangelevshchiny" [Origin of the Wrangel movement]. KA 2 (21) (1927): 174–81. Minutes of the first conference of the Council of the Commander in Chief of the Armed Forces of South Russia on April 9, 1920, dealing with the political and economic situation in Crimea.

———. "V tylu 'Vooruzhennykh sil IUga Rossii' " [In the rear of the 'Armed Forces of South Russia']. KA 3 (34) (1929): 224–28. Political and economic conditions in the Crimea during the occupation by Wrangel in April 1920.

Gul', Roman. "Kievskaia epokheia, noiabr'–dekabr' 1918 g." [Kievan epic, November–December, 1918]. ARR 2 (1922): 59–86. The Ukrainian struggle against the German and Russian forces, largely in Kyiv.

———. *Ledianoi pokhod: S Kornilovym* [Ice march: with Kornilov]. Berlin: S. Efron, 1921. A Russian officer's account of the Kornilov campaigns against the Bolsheviks in the Don and Kuban basins in the winter of 1917–18.

Gulevich, K., and R. Gassanova. "Iz istorii borby prodovolstvennykh otriadov rabochikh za khleb i ukreplenie sovetskoi vlasti, 1918–1920 gg." [From the history of the struggle of the workers' food collecting detachments for bread and the consolidation of Soviet power, 1918–1920]. KA 4–5 (89–90) (1938): 103–53.

Gurev, V. I. "Ekaterinoslavskii pokhod: Vospominaniia" [Katerynoslav march: memoirs]. Manuscript, 1939. Copy in author's possession. Unpublished memoirs of a Russian officer about the Eighth Corps, in late 1918, organized under the hetman and stationed in Katerynoslav.

Gurko, V. I. "Iz Petrograda cherez Moskvu, Parizh i London v Odessu, 1917–1918 gg." [From Petrograd via Moscow, Paris, and London to Odessa, 1917–1918]. ARR 15 (1924): 5–84. Firsthand account of the early formation of the anti-Bolshevik Russian organizations, their conflicts, records of the Jassy Conference, activities of the delegations to Paris and London, and the French intervention in South Ukraine.

———. "Politicheskoe polozhenie na Ukraine pri getmane" [Political conditions in Ukraine during the hetman regime]. *Revoliutsiia na Ukraine po memuaram belykh*, pp. 212–21. Compiled by S. A.

Alekseev. Moscow, 1930.

Hak, Anatol'. "Pravda pro Huliai-Pole: Spohad" [The truth about Huliai-Pole: recollection]. *Suchasnist'* (Munich) 12, no. 9 (141) (1972): 65–73.

———. *Vid Huliai-Polia do N'iu Iorku: Spohady* [From Huliai-Pole to New York: memoirs]. Neu Ulm, W. Germany, 1973.

Halahan, Mykola. *Z moikh spomyniv* [From my memoirs]. 4 vols. Lvov: "Chervona Kalyna," 1930. A Ukrainian Social Democrat and diplomat deals with the underground activities in the Russian Empire prior to 1905, the disintegration of the tsarist regime, and the vicissitudes of World War I and the Ukrainian Revolution; stresses the activities of the political parties, the spontaneous organization of Ukrainian military formations, the conflict with the Russian regime, and his diplomatic missions in the Kuban, Romania, and Hungary.

Hal'chevskyi-Voinarovs'kyi, IAkiv. "Proty chervonykh okupantiv" [Against the Red invaders]. *Krakivs'ki visti* (Krakow), nos. 139–289 (294–444) (June 29–December 27, 1941). Detailed account of a former partisan leader about the partisans' campaigns against the Bolsheviks during the Revolution.

Hirniak, Nykofor, ed. "Avstriis'ki ta nimets'ki generaly i dyplomaty proty Vasylia Vyshyvanoho" [Austrian and German generals and diplomats against Vasyl' Vyshyvanyi]. *Visti* [The news] (Munich), no. 102 (1961), pp. 51–53; no. 103, pp. 79–84; no. 104, pp. 124–26; no. 105 (1962), pp. 18–21; no. 106, pp. 64–66; no. 107, pp. 80–90. Correspondence between Austrian and German diplomats and generals about the activities of Archduke Wilhelm F. Hapsburg (Vasyl' Vyshyvanyi) and the Ukrainian Sichovi Stril'tsi in Katerynoslav and Kherson provinces from May to October, 1918.

Hodgson, John E. *With Denikin's Armies: Being a Description of the Cossack Counterrevolution in South Russia, 1918–1920.* London: L. Williams, 1932. A British war correspondent for the *Daily Express* deals with the military operations and policies of the Denikin forces and the Don Cossacks, mainly in the Don Basin and Ukraine.

Hoffman, Max. *Der Krieg der versaumten Gelegenheiten.* Munich: G. Pehl, 1924. Chief of staff of the German eastern front deals with German policy in Eastern Europe, including the Brest-Litovsk Treaty and the German evacuation of the eastern front after November 1918.

Holub, Andrii. "Zbroina vyzvol'na borot'ba na Khersonshchyni v zapilliu voroha, 1917–1919 roky" [Armed liberation struggle in Kherson province in the rear of the enemy, 1917–1919]. *Za derzhavnist'* (Toronto), no. 11 (1966), pp. 175– 89.

Holyns'kyi, Petro. "Ostanni dni UHA: Uryvok zi spomyniv" [The last days of the UHA: excerpt from memoirs].IKCK 1930, pp. 142–60.

Horbenko, Kh. "Spohady pro denikinshchynu" [Memoirs about the Denikin movement]. *Strilets'ka dumka Starokonstantyniv*, nos. 48–49 (1919).

Hornykiewicz, Théophil, ed. *Ereignisse in der Ukraine 1914–1922, deren Bedeutungen und historishche Hintergrunde*. 4 vols. Philadelphia: W. K. Lypynsky East European Research Institute, 1966–70. Austrian State Archives documents about the Ukrainian question under the Habsburgs, the events of the Ukrainian Revolution, and East European problems in general.

Hryhor'iv, N., ed. *The War and Ukrainian Democracy: A Compilation of Documents from the Past and Present*. Toronto: Industrial and Educational Publishing Co., 1945. Source material concerning the democratic spirit and tradition of the Ukrainian people, with the emphasis on the nineteenth and twentieth centuries.

Hryshko, H. "1917 rik v Odesi: Spomyny z chasiv vyzvol'nykh zmahan'" [The year 1917 in Odessa; memoirs from the period of the liberation struggle]. RN, nos. 5–6 (29–30) (1930), pp. 128–35; nos. 7–8 (31–32), pp. 178–87; nos. 9–10 (33–34), pp. 237–45; nos. 11–12 (35–36), pp. 281–92. Memoirs about the political and military movement headed by Dr. Ivan M. Lutsenko in Odessa in 1917 and after.

Hrytsyk, Ustia. "Deshcho z toho, shcho perezhyla" [Something from what (I) experienced]. IKCK 1929. pp. 89–97. A young woman's account of the events in Poltava province during the war and the Revolution.

IAkir, I. E. *Vospominaniia o grazhdanskoi voine* [Memoirs from the Civil War]. Moscow: Voen. izd-vo, 1957. A Red Army commander's account of the campaign of the Red troops against the Ukrainian troops, Makhno, and Denikin.

IAkymiv, E. "Hostyna Makhna v Umani: Zi spomyniv ochevydtsia" [Makhno's visit to Uman': from memoirs of an eyewitness]. IKCK 1930, pp. 78–80. Makhno and his partisans during their visit to the Ukrainian Galician military unit at Uman' at the end of August 1919.

IEremiiv, Mykhailo. "Za lashtunkamy Tsentral'noi Rady: Storinky zi spohadiv" [Behind the scenes of the Central Rada: pages from memoirs]. UI, nos. 1–4 (17–20) (1968), pp. 94–104. The secretary of the Central Rada reveals its inner workings.

IEroshevych, P. "Spohady z chasiv het'mana Pavla Skoropadskoho na Ukraini i povstannia narodu Ukrains'koho proty vlady het'mana ta nimtsiv-okupantiv" [Memoirs from the period of the Hetman Pavlo Skoropads'kyi in Ukraine and the uprising of the Ukrainian people against the hetman and the German invaders]. *Tabor: Voenno literaturnyi zhurnal* (Kalisz), no. 9 (1929), pp. 57–80; no. 10, pp. 75–83.

Igrenev, G. "Ekaterinoslavskiia vospominaniia, avgust, 1918 g.–iiun', 1919 g." [Katerynoslav memoirs, August 1918–June 1919]. ARR 3 (1922): 234–43. A teacher of law deals with political and military developments in Katerynoslav from August 1918 to June 1919, particularly the struggle for control of the city between the Ukrainian and the Makhno-Bolshevik forces.

"Instruktsiia Trots'koho ahitatoram-komunistam na Ukraini" [The instructions of Trotsky to the propagandist-Communists in Ukraine]. *Syn Ukrainy*, no. 1 (August 7, 1920), pp. 9–10.

Irchan, M. [Babiuk, M.]. *Makhno i makhnivtsi: Vrazhinnia ochevydtsia* [Makhno and his men: observations of an eyewitness]. Kamenets Podolski: Strilets', 1919.

———. "Makhno i makhnivtsi:Vrazhinnia ochevydtsia" [Makhno and his men: observations of an eyewitness]. IKCK 1936, pp. 115–22. An account by a Ukrainian officer, based on a meeting with them at their headquarters on September 24, 1919.

———. *Pro ukrains'ki povstannia: Sokolovs'kyi i susidni hrupy* [About the Ukrainian partisans: Sokolovs'kyi and neighboring groups]. Kamenets Podolski: Strilets', 1919.

IUrtyk, H. [Tiutiunyk, IUrii]. "Stykhiia: Zi spomyniv" [Spontaneity: from memoirs]. LNV, no. 3 (1921), pp. 233–38.

———. "Zvenyhorods'kyi Kish vil'noho kozatstva" [Zvenyhorod camp of Free Cossacks]. LNV, no. 2 (1921), pp. 125–33.

Ivanov, M., ed. "'Ot vlasti otkazyvaius': Dokumenty o getmanshchine iz arkhiva Khar'kovskogo gubernskogo starosty" [(I) 'abdicate my authority': documents about the hetman government from the Kharkiv province Starosta]. LR, no. 2 (7) (1924), pp. 224–31. Telegrams and dispatches of the district Starostas and declarations of landlords indicating dissatisfactions and uprisings of the peasants against the hetman government from June to December 1918.

Ivanys, Vasyl'. *Borot'ba Kubani za nezalezhnist* [The struggle in Kuban for independence]. Munich, 1968.

———. *Stezhkamy zhyttia: Spohady* [Roads of life: memoirs]. 5 vols. Toronto: Peremoha, 1958–62. Comprehensive, objective memoirs, including documentary material and interviews, by a member of the Kuban Rada (1918–20), minister of commerce and industry (1919), and the head of the government (1920), from the end of the nineteenth century to the 1950s. Vols. 2, 3, and 4 deal with the Revolution and Civil War in the territories of the Kuban and Don Cossacks.

"Iz deiatel'nosti M. V. Frunze na frontach grazhdanskoi voiny" [From the activities of M. V. Frunze on the fronts of the Civil War]. VIZ, no. 10 (1940), pp. 143–49. Telegrams, orders, and reports of M. V. Frunze from February 1919 to November 1920.

"Iz istorii grazhdanskoi voiny na Ukraine v 1918 g." [From the history of the Civil War in Ukraine in 1918]. KA, no. 4 (95) (1939), pp. 180–82.

"Iz istorii Sovvlasti na Ukraine: O Pervom Vseukrainskom S'ezde Sovetov i Pervom Sovetskom Pravitel'stve Ukrainy" [From the history of Soviet authority in Ukraine: about the First All-Ukrainian Congress of Soviets and the First Soviet Government of Ukraine]. LR, no. 4 (9) (1924), pp. 166–85. Memoirs and documentary material about the attempt to establish the first Soviet government in Ukraine.

"Iz materialov kievskoi chrezvychaiki" [From the materials of the Kiev secret police]. BA, nos. 2–3 (1928), pp. 113–16. A brief description of people executed by the Bolshevik secret police in Kyiv for their alleged anti-Bolshevik activities.

"Iz materialov Zafrontbiuro: Deiatel'nost Kompartii v Kharkove i Khar'kovskom okruge" [From materials of the bureau at the rear: activities of the Communist party in Kharkiv and the Kharkiv region]. LR, no. 1 (10) (1925), pp. 25–36. A report to the Central Committee of KP(b)U from the secretary of the Kharkiv underground district committee and other reports about Communist underground activities during the occupation of Ukraine by Denikin's army from November to December 1919.

Kak nemetskie okkupanty ugnetali i grabili nash narod v 1918 g.: Istoricheskie dokumenty [How the German invaders suppressed and robbed our people in 1918: historic documents]. 2nd ed. Moscow: Voenizdat., 1941. The German policy of repression in Ukraine in 1918, documents selected for propaganda value.

Kakhovskaia, I. K. "Delo Eikhgorna i Denikina:Iz vospominanii" [Affair of Eichhorn and Denikin: from memoirs]. In *Puti revo-*

liutsii: Stat'i, materialy, vospominaniia, pp. 191–260. Berlin: Skify, 1923. A Russian Left Socialist Revolutionary's memoirs dealing with the assassination of Field Marshal von Eichhorn in Kyiv in late July 1918, the attempt on the life of the hetman, and Denikin's occupation of Kyiv in August 1919.

Kalyna, V. "Na Odesu" [To Odessa]. SV, no. 255 (September 26, 1952), p. 3. An account by an officer of a Ukrainian Sich Riflemen unit of its campaign against the Bolshevik troops in the Uman' region at the end of summer 1919, its meeting with Makhno, and its subsequent agreement against Denikin.

———. "V Umani" [In Uman']. SV, January 19, 1953. An account of Makhno during his visit to the Ukrainian Galician military unit at Uman' at the end of August 1919.

Kandiskaliv, P. *Dolyna troiand i smerty: Spohady: Materiialy dlia istorii tak zvanoho "Beloho Dvizheniia"* [The valley of roses and death: memoirs: materials for the history of the "White movement"]. Manuscript. 1964.

Kantorovich, Vl. "Frantsuzy v Odesse" [The French in Odessa]. BY, no. 19 (1922), pp. 198–210.

Kapulovskii, I. "Organizatsiia vostaniia protiv Getmana" [Organization of the uprising against the hetman]. LR, no. 4 (1923), pp. 95–102. Deals with organization of partisan groups and uprising against the hetman police and the German troops in the Zvenyhorodka district in the spring and summer of 1918.

Karinskii, N. "Epizod iz evakuatsii Novorossiiska" [Episode from the evacuation of Novorossisk]. ARR 12 (1923): 149–66.

Kedrovs'kyi, V. *1917 rik: Spohady chlena Ukrains'koho Viis'kovoho Heneral'noho Komitetu i tovarysha sekretaria viis'kovykh sprav u chasi Ukrains'koi Tsentral'noi Rady* [The year 1917: memoirs of a member of the Ukrainian Military Central Committee and deputy of the secretary of military affairs during the Ukrainian Central Rada]. Winnipeg: Tryzub, 1967. Authoritative memoirs written in 1923 describing the Ukrainian Revolution from March to October 1917, stressing the organization of military forces.

———. "Pochatok ukrainizatsii v rossiis'kii armii i Pershyi ukrains'kyi viis'kovyi z'izd" [The beginning of Ukrainization in the Russian Army and the First Ukrainian Military Convention]. VK, no. 1 (27) (1967), pp. 24–31.

———. "Ukrainizatsiia v rossiis'kii armii" [Ukrainization in the Russian Army]. UI, nos. 2–3 (15–16) (1967), pp. 61–77. Deals with the formation of separate Ukrainian military units in the

Russian Army during the first half of 1917.

———. "Ukrainizovani chastyny i reguliarna armiia" [Ukrainized units and the regular army]. VK, no. 2 (33) (1968), pp. 37–39.

Kedryn, I., ed. *Beresteis'kyi myr—z nahody 10-tykh rokovyn 9-11-1918–9-11-1928: Spomyny ta materialy* [The Brest-Litovsk peace conference—on the occasion of its tenth anniversary, November 9, 1918–November 9, 1928: memoirs and materials]. Lvov, 1928. Memoirs and other materials by German, Austrian, and Ukrainian participants in the Brest-Litovsk peace conference, including Ludendorff, Hoffman, Czernin, Liubyns'kyi, and Serviuk.

Kharakternyk. "Zhadky z mynuloho" [Recollection of the past]. LNV 106, no. 6 (1931): 503–10. Activities of the Russians in Ukraine during the second half of 1918, and the coup against the hetman regime.

Kiev. Instytut istorii partii. *Bolshevistskie organizatsii Ukrainy v period ustanovleniia i ukrepleniia sovetskoi vlasti (noiabr' 1917–aprel' 1918 gg.): Sbornik dokumentov i materialov* [Bolshevik organizations of Ukraine during the time of the establishment and consolidation of Soviet power (November 1917–April 1918): collection of documents and materials]. Kiev: Gos. izd-vo polit. lit-ry USSR, 1962. The Bolshevik struggle for establishing and maintaining power in Ukraine; contains 652 items from the Russian and Ukrainian state, central, and regional party archives from November 1917 to April 1918.

Kievshchina v gody grazhdanskoi voiny i inostrannoi voennoi interventsii, 1918–1920 gg.: Sbornik dokumentov i materialov [Kiev province during the Civil War and foreign military intervention, 1918–1920: collection of documents and materials]. Compiled by I. U. F. Borshch and edited by P. T. Tron'ko. Kiev: Gos. Izd-vo polit. Lit-ry USSR, 1962. Documents (510) from Russian and Ukrainian state and regional party archives; the Bolshevik struggle for power against the Ukrainian government; and the German and Austrian forces in Kyiv province from March 1918 to December 1920.

Kin, D., ed. "K istorii frantsuzskoi interventsii na iuge Rossii, dekabr' 1918–aprel' 1919 gg." [History of French intervention in South Russia, December 1918–April 1919]. KA 6 (19) (1926): 3–38. Reports from an associate of the "South Russian National Center" and V. V. Shulgin to Admiral Kolchak about French intervention and conditions in South Ukraine.

Kiselev, Mikhail. *Agitpoezd: Vospominaniia o bor'be s kontrrevoliutsiei na Ukraine, 1918–1919 gg.* [The agitation train: memoirs about the struggle against the counterrevolution in Ukraine]. Moscow: Molodaia gvardiia, 1933. An officer of the Red Army describes Bolshevik propaganda in Ukraine and the campaigns against Hryhor'iv, Makhno, and Denikin, especially the Bolshevik retreat from Ukraine.

Kochehar, Mykhailo. "Tretii viis'kovyi zizd u Kyivi" [The Third Military Convention in Kiev]. IKCK 1934, pp. 128–29. Reminiscences of the Ukrainian congress in November 1917, its impact on the actions of the Central Rada, and the formation of the First Ukrainian Revolutionary Regiment.

Kokh, S. E. "Vstriecha s Makhnovtsami: Materialy po grazhdanskoi voinie" [Meeting with the Makhno men: materials about the Civil War]. *Chasovoi* (Paris), nos. 35–36 (192–). Description of an attack by one of Denikin's regiments on a Makhno detachment in October 1919 near Katerynoslav and Oleksandrivs'k.

Kokovs'kyi, Frants. "Z rosiis'koi invasii" [From the Russian invasion]. IKCK 1931, pp. 35–36.

Kolomiets. "Vospominaniia o revoliutsionnoi bor'be v Elizavetgrade v 1917–1919 gg." [Memoirs about the revolutionary struggle in Yelysavethrad in 1917–1919]. LR, no. 1 (1922), pp. 194–201.

Komandarm IAkir: Vospominaniia druzei i soratnikov [Commander IAkir: recollections of friends and companions-in-arms]. Moscow: Voen. izd-vo, 1963.

Komandarm Uborevich: Vospominaniia druzei i soratnikov [Commander Uborevich: recollections of friends and companions-in-arms]. Compiled by P. N. Aleksandrov and edited by V. I. Savost'ianova]. Moscow: Voen. izd-vo, 1964.

Komitety nezamozhnykh selian. [Committee of the poor peasants]. Odessa: Inform. instrukt. p/otd. Otd. upr. gubrevkoma, 1920. Laws, regulations, and supporting documents governing the peasant committees, and land and grain allotments.

Kononenko, Kharytia. "Dvi manifestatsii: Spohady z pershykh dniv revoliutsii 1917 r." [Two manifestations: memoirs from the first days of the Revolution, 1917]. LHKD 1936, pp. 80–85.

Konovalets', IEvhen. *Prychynky do istorii ukrains'koi revoliutsii* [Supplements to the history of the Ukrainian Revolution]. 2nd ed. N. p. Nakl. Provodu Ukrains'kykh Natsionalistiv, 1948. The Ukrainian Revolution, stressing the role of the Corps of the Sich Riflemen, by its commander.

Korduba, Myron. "V posol'stvi do Het'mana" [With a diplomatic mission to the hetman]. LCK, no. 10 (1930), pp. 12–14; no. 11, pp. 5–10; no. 12, pp. 11–15.

Koroliv, V. "Kinets' het'manatu: Fragment spohadiv" [The end of the hetman regime: fragments of memoirs]. KD 1927, pp. 79–95. The coup against the hetman regime, the negotiations that led to the capitulation of the hetman, and the arrival of the Directory in Kyiv.

Kosgov, I. *Uchastie konnitsy v partizanskoi voine: Opyt issledovaniia* [Cavalry participation in a partisan war: experience of research]. Edited by N. Kozmin. Moscow: Gos. izd-vo, otdel voen. lit-ry, 1928.

Kostomarov, G., ed. "Iz istorii organizatsii komitetov nezamozhnych selian Ukrainy" [From the organizational history of poor peasant committees in Ukraine]. IM 6 (58) (1936): 164–75. Report on the progress of the organization and work of Ukraine's poor peasant committees from July 1 to September 10, 1920.

Kovalevs'kyi, Mykola. *Pry dzerelakh borot'by: Spomyny, vrazhennia, refleksii* [At the source of struggle: memoirs]. Innsbruck, 1960. A former Ukrainian minister of agriculture deals with various aspects of Ukrainian national life from 1905 to 1939, particularly political parties, groups, and leaders in the period of the Revolution.

Koval'-Stepovyi, P. "Shliakhamy zrady: Spomyn pro Liubars'ku tragediiu 1919 roku" [On the roads of betrayal: memoirs about the Liubar tragedy, 1919]. KD 1933, pp. 45–49. Political and military conditions on the Right Bank in the fall of 1919, with emphasis on the betrayal of Otaman Volokh in November 1919.

Kovtiuk, E. *Ot Kubani do Volgi i obratno: Iz vospominanii o pokhodakh i boiakh krasnykh tamanskikh chastei* [From the Kuban to the Volga and back: from memoirs about campaigns and battles of the Red Taman detachments]. Moscow, Gos. izd-vo, otdel voen. lit-ry, 1928(?).

Kozub, Iv. "Povstannia p'roty het'manshchyny ta petliurovshchyny: Notatky z istorii povstans'koho rukhu v Pereiaslavs'komu, Pyriatyns'komu, ta Zolotonos'komu povitakh: Kinets' 1918–pochatok 1919 rr." [Uprisings against the hetman and Petliura: notes from the history of the partisan movement in Pereiaslav, Pyriatyn, and Zolotonosha districts: the end of 1918–beginning of 1919]. LR, no. 5 (44) (1930), pp. 274–88. Bolshevik partisan activities against the hetman regime and the Directory on the Left Bank at the turn of 1918–19.

Krat, Mykhailo. "Svitloi pam'iati polkovnyka Bohdanivtsiv" [To the glorious memory of the colonel of the Bohdan men]. SV, no. 149 (August 16, 1969), pp. 2-3.

Kravs, Antin. *Za ukrains'ku spravu: Spomyny pro III. korpus U.H.A. pislia perekhodu za Zbruch* [For the Ukrainian cause: recollections about the Third Corps of the U.H.A. after crossing the Zbruch].

Krest'ianskoe dvizhenia v Rossii v xix-nachale xx veka: Sbornik dokumentov [The peasant movement in Russia in the 19th–beginning of the 20th century: collection of documents]. 9 vols. Moscow: Izd-vo sotsial'no-ekon. Lit-ry, 1961. Documents selected from the "Marxist-Leninist concept" on the peasants' struggle against feudalists, capitalists, and the regime, ranging from requests to armed uprisings, from 1796 to 1917. Consists of reports from local to central authorities, documents from peasants, and illegal publications; most published for the first time from the Central Historical Archives, State Archives, Military-Historical Archives, and archives of the republics and provinces.

Krezub, Antin [Dumin, Osyp]. "IAk zhynuv otaman Zelenyi" [How Otaman Zelenyi died]. LNV, no. 10 (1927), pp. 109–13. Otaman Zelenyi's relations with the Ukrainian Army and his subsequent assassination.

———. "Mizh Biloiu Tserkvoiu i Motovylivkoiu" [Between Bila Tserkva and Motovylivka]. LCK, no. 1 (2) (1930), pp. 5–8; no. 2 (3), pp. 9–13.

———. *Partyzany: Spomyny* [Partisans: memoirs]. 2 vols. Lvov: Chervona Kalyna, 1930.

———. "Partyzany: Zbirka spomyniv iz partyzanky na Naddniprianskii Ukraini" [Partisans: collection of memoirs from the partisan movement in Ukraine]. LNV 87 (1925): 246–61.

———. "Za khlibom" [After the bread]. *Litopys* (Berlin), nos. 19–20 (1924), pp. 292–98.

Kritskii, M. "Istoki dobrovol'chestva i ego sushchnost' "[The sources of the Volunteer movement and its nature]. *Vozrozhdenie* (Paris), no. 193 (1968), pp. 33–52; no. 194, pp. 42–59; no. 195, pp. 53–66; no. 196, pp. 64–79; no. 197, pp. 56–68; no. 200, pp. 67–86; no. 201, pp. 79–89; no. 202, pp. 92–103; no. 203, pp. 74–89; no. 204, pp. 99–110; no. 206 (1969), pp. 57–68.

———. "Krasnaia armia na IUzhnom fronte v 1918–1920 gg.: Po dokumentam i sekretnym prikazom, zakhvachennym v boiakh 1-ym Korpusom Dobrovol'cheskoi armii" [The Red Army on the southern front in 1918–1920: according to documents and secret orders taken in the fighting by the 1st Corps of the Volunteer

Army]. ARR 18 (1926): 254–300. Documents of the Red Army seized by the First Corps of the Volunteer Army about their struggle from May 1919 to early 1920.

"Krym v 1918–1919 gg." [The Crimea in 1918–1919]. KA 3 (28) (1928): 142–81; 4 (29): 55–85. Telegrams from Denikin's chief of staff in Symferopil to the representative of the Volunteer Army with the Entente Command in Crimea about the intervention and conditions in South Ukraine, the Bolshevik propaganda activities among the French troops, and the Tatar movement in Crimea.

Kurovs'kyi, Vol. "Na okupovanykh nimtsiamy zemliakh Kholmshchyny, Pidliashshia i Polissia: Iz spomyniv Syn'ozhupannyka" [On the Kholmshchyna, Pidliashshia, and Polissia territories occupied by the Germans: from memoirs of Syn'ozhupannyka]. KD 1931, pp. 81–85.

Kushchyns'kyi, Ant. "Kil'ka dokumentiv pro 'ukrains'ke pytannia' u Vrangelia" [A few documents concerning the "Ukrainian question" with Wrangel]. TR, nos. 26–27 (1926), pp. 23–27.

Kustelian, M. "Denikinskoe podpol'e" [Denikin's underground activities]. LR, no. 2 (17) (1926), pp. 7–12. Bolshevik underground agents' activities in the area of Kyiv during the Denikin occupation in 1919.

Kuz'menko, G. "Vidpovid' na stattiu 'Pomer Makhno' v 'Novii pori' vid 9-ho serpnia 1934 roku, hor. Detroita, Mich." [Answer to the article "Makhno died" in *Nova Pora*, August 9, 1934, in Detroit, Mich.]. PR, nos. 50–51 (1934), pp. 17–18. An intimate biography of Makhno by his wife.

Lantukh, I. "Iz istorii grazhdanskoi voiny na Ekaterinoslavshchine, 1919 g." [From the history of the Civil War in Katerynoslav province]. LR, no. 2 (17) (1926), pp. 51–59. Organization and activities of the Bolshevik partisans; destruction of military stores and headquarters, communications, and propaganda, in the rear of the Volunteer Army in the Katerynoslav area.

Lazurenko, Stepan. "Povstannia proty het'mana i druha viina z bol'shevykamy, 1918–1919 rr.: Spohad bohdanivtsia" [Uprising against the hetman and the second war against the Bolsheviks, 1918–1919: memoirs of a Bohdan man]. TR, no. 39 (1966), pp. 17–18; no. 40, pp. 3–5; no. 41 (1967), pp. 6–9; no. 42, pp. 13–15.

Leikhtenbergskii, G. "Kak nachalas 'IUzhnaia Armiia'" [How the South Army originated]. ARR 8 (1923): 166–82. The organization of the Volunteer Army as seen from Ukraine from July through December 1918.

———. *Vospominaniia ob 'Ukraine' 1917–1918 gg.* [Memoirs about Ukraine, 1917–1918]. Berlin: Izd. Dietinets, 1921. Experiences and anti-Ukrainian activities of a Russian nobleman in Ukraine from 1917 to the end of 1918.

Lenin, Stalin, Frunze, Voroshilov o razgrome Vrangelia: Stat'i, rechi, dokumenty [Lenin, Stalin, Frunze, Voroshilov on Wrangel's defeat: articles, speeches, documents]. Edited by R. M. Vul'. Simferopol: Gos. izd-vo Krymskoi ASSR, 1940. Documents, articles, and speeches on Bolshevik military operations in Ukraine against the Polish-Ukrainian and Wrangel forces from June through November 1920.

Leninskii sbornik [Lenin's collection]. Moscow: Gos. izd-vo polit. lit-ry, 1959.

Leontovych, Volodymyr. "Uryvok spohadiv iz revoliutsiinykh chasiv" [Excerpt of memoirs from the revolutionary period]. KD 1935, pp. 67–76.

Levyts'kyi, Kost'. *Velykyi zryv: Do istorii ukrains'koi derzhavnosty vid bereznia do lystopada 1918 r. na pidstavi spomyniv ta dokumentiv* [A great upheaval: about the history of Ukrainian statehood from March to November 1918, based on memoirs and documents]. New York: Vyd-vo Chartoryis'kykh, 1968. The events of the first two years (1917–18) of the Ukrainian Revolution and establishment of the West Ukrainian Republic in November 1918.

Levyts'kyi, Osyp. *Halyts'ka armiia na Velykii Ukraini: Spomyny z chasu vid lypnia do hrudnia 1919* [The Galician Army in eastern Ukraine: memoirs from July to December 1919]. Vienna, 1921. The campaign of the Ukrainian Galician Army in eastern Ukraine from July to December 1919.

Liutarevych, P. "Istoriia odnoho povstannia na Poltavshchyni ta ukrains'ke pidpillia v rokakh 1920–1926" [History of an uprising in Polta province and Ukrainian underground activity in 1920–1926]. *Ukrains'kyi zbirnyk* (Munich), no. 4 (1955), pp. 131–51.

———. "A Resistance Group of the Ukrainian Underground 1920–1926." *Ukrainian Review* (Munich), no. 2 (1956), pp. 84–91.

Lobanov-Rostovsky, A. *The Grinding Mill: Reminiscences of War and Revolution in Russia, 1913–1920.* New York: Macmillan Co., 1935. World War I, the Russian Revolution, and the Civil War, based on the diary of a Russian prince during service in the Russian Army, 1913–20.

L-oi, L. "Ocherki zhizni v Kievie v 1919–20 gg." [Sketches of life in Kiev in 1919–20]. ARR 3 (1921): 210–33.

Lotots'kyi, Oleksandr. *Storinky mynuloho* [Pages from the past]. 4 vols. Bound Brook, N.J.: Vyd-vo Ukr. pravoslavnoi tserkvy v SSh A, 1966. Prominent scholar and statesman on different aspects of national life, stressing the profiles of the Ukrainian contemporary leaders from the end of the nineteenth century to 1919.

Lukomskii, A. "Iz vospominanii" [From memoirs]. ARR 2 (1921): 14–44; 5:101–89; 6 (1922): 81–160. A leading Russian general, using some documents, deals with different aspects of the Russian Revolution and the Civil War, including organization of the Volunteer Army, its operations, policies, and relations with the British and French during the interventions in South Ukraine.

———. *Memoirs of the Russian Revolution*. London: T. F. Unwin, 1922.

———. "Protivosovetskie organizatssi na Ukraine" [Anti-Soviet organizations in Ukraine]. In *Revoliutsiia na Ukraine po memuaram belykh*, pp. 196–211. Compiled by S. A. Alekseev. Moscow, 1930. From memoirs, "Iz vospominanii." ARR, vol. 5, 1922.

———. *Vospominaniia* [Memoirs]. 2 vols. Berlin: O. Kirchner, 1922.

Lulu, L. "Desiatylittia perekhodu Zbrucha, 1919, 16, VII–1929: Spomyn" [Decade of crossing the Zbruch, July 16, 1919–1920: memoirs]. IKCK 1929, pp. 76–81. The joint campaign of the Galician Army and the Ukrainian Army of the Directory against the Bolsheviks in the summer of 1919.

Lymarenko, Danylo. "45 rokiv tomu" [45 years before]. TR, no. 28 (1964), pp. 18–21; no. 29, pp. 14–20; no. 30, pp. 14–17; no. 31, pp. 13–18.

M., V. "Dontsy na makhnovskom frontie" [The Don Cossacks on the Makhno front]. *Kazach'i dumy* (Sofia), no. 10 (1923), pp. 9–13; no. 13, pp. 9–16. The campaign of the Don Cossacks against Makhno in the fall of 1919 and the organization of Makhno's army.

———. *Frunze na frontakh grazhdanskoi voiny: Sbornik dokumentov* [M. V. Frunze on the fronts of the Civil War: collection of documents]. Moscow: Voen. izd-vo, 1941. Frunze's activities on several fronts, including the Ukrainian against Makhno, from January 1919 to December 1920.

Maevskii, Vladimir A. *Gvardeiskie sapery* [Field engineer guards]. Novi Sad: S. F. Filonov, 1938(?). The Austro-German punitive expeditions in Ukraine in 1918 and Denikin's campaigns of 1919, mainly on the Left Bank, against the Bolsheviks, the Ukrainian forces, and the partisans.

———. *Povstantsy Ukrainy* [Partisans of Ukraine]. Novi Sad, 192–.

Sketchy memoirs by a Denikin officer about the Ukrainian partisan movement against the Austro-German troops, the Bolsheviks, and the Volunteer Army from 1918 through early 1920. Emphasizes the partisan leader Kotsur, who operated in the region of Kremenchuk, Chyhryryn, Znamianka, and Oleksandriia.

Mahalevs'kyi, IUrii. "Bat'ko Makhno" [Father Makhno]. KD 1929, pp. 60–70. A sketchy account about Makhno and his movement from the spring of 1917 to the winter of 1919, stressing Makhno's terrorist activities and political conditions in Katerynoslav province.

———. "Oleksandrivs'k-Kyiv: Spomyn 1917–1918" [Oleksandrivs'k-Kyiv: memoirs, 1917–1918]. KD 1931, pp. 61–72. Political conditions in Ukraine and the fighting of the Ukrainian forces in Kyiv and Oleksandrivs'k against the Bolshevik invasion at the end of 1917.

———. "Uryvok iz spomyniv" [Fragments of memoirs]. IKCK 1929, pp. 155–61. Political conditions in Ukraine and the Ukrainian fighting against the Bolshevik uprising in Kyiv during the winter of 1918.

Maiborodov, Vladimir. "S frantsuzami" [With the Frenchmen]. ARR 16 (1925): 100–161. A Russian monarchist deals with the French intervention in South Ukraine and the relations between Denikin's representative and the French command in Odessa.

Maiorov, M. *Z istorii revoliutsiinoi borot'by na Ukraini, 1914–1919* [From the history of revolutionary struggle in Ukraine, 1914–1919]. Kharkov: Derzh. vyd-vo Ukrainy, 1928. A member of a Bolshevik underground organization recounts Bolshevik activities, mostly in Kyiv during the war, and the subsequent struggle for power in Ukraine in 1917–19; includes a survey of the activities of the Communist party (b) of Ukraine.

Makarov, P. V. *Ad'iutant generala Mai-Maevskogo: Iz vospominanii nachal'nika otriada krasnykh partizan v Krymu* [General Mai-Maevskii's aide: from memoirs of a Red partisan unit commander in the Crimea]. Leningrad: "Priboi," 1921. General Mai-Maevskii's aide, a Bolshevik agent, deals with the Volunteers' campaign, the internal conditions at headquarters, in 1919, emphasizing their negative aspects, and describing the author's subsequent arrest, escape, and partisan activities in the Crimea in 1920 against Wrangel.

Makarushka, Liubomyr. "Fragmenty z chortkivs'koi ofenzyvy" [Fragments from the Chortkiv offensive]. IKCK 1934, pp. 68–80. Personal account by an officer of the Polish invasion of West Ukraine and the "Chortkiv offensive" in June 1919.

Makhno, Nestor. *Au Congrès des camarades francais.* Paris(?), 1930.

———. "Chego dobivaiutsia povstantsy-maknovtsy" [What the partisans-Makhnomen strive for]. PS, no. 1 (May 17, 1919), pp. 2–3; no. 2 (May 24,), pp. 2–3.

———. "K 10-i godovshchine revoliuts. povstanchestva na Ukraine-makhnovshchiny" [On the tenth anniversary of the revolutionary partisan movement in Ukraine of the Makhno movement]. DT, nos. 44–45 (1929), pp. 3–7. The author's activities, mainly in 1918, including his trip to Soviet Russia.

———. Letter to Fuks. Paris (?), June 15, 1926.

———. Letter to Fuks and Piza. Vincennes, October 21, 1926.

———. Letter to [Lev] Chykalenko. [Paris], May 20, 1927.

———. "Mon autobiographie." *Le libertaire* (Paris), nos. 50–75 (1926), with the exception of nos. 60, 63, 67, 69, 72.

———. "Otkrytoe pis'mo partii VKP i ee TsK" [Open letter to the party VKP and its TsK]. DT, nos. 37–38 (1928), pp. 10–12. Makhno's agreement with the Bolsheviks against Wrangel in September–October 1920 and Makhno's meeting with Bela Kun.

———. "Pechal'nye stranitsy russkoi revoliutsii: Vospominaniia" [Sad pages of the Russian Revolution: memoirs]. *Rassvet* (Chicago), January 29–February 18, 1932 (according to Hoover Institution). Largely first half of the author's second volume: *Pod udarami kontr-revoliutsii.*

———. *Pod udarami kontr-revoliutsii: Aprel'–iiun' 1918 g.* [Under the blows of counterrevolution: April–June 1918]. Vol. 2. Edited by Volin. Paris: Izd-vo Komiteta N. Makhno, 1936.

———. *La révolution russe en Ukraine: Mars 1917–avril 1918.* Paris: La Brochure mensuelle, 1927. The first volume of the author's memoirs in French.

———. *Russkaia revoliutsiia na Ukraine: Ot marta 1917 g. po aprel' 1918 g.* [Russian Revolution in Ukraine: from March 1917 to April 1918]. Vol. 1. Paris: Izd-vo Biblioteka makhnovtsev, 1929. Three volumes of very useful memoirs dealing with the author's life and his partisan movement through the end of 1918. Its value is enhanced by the author's reliable memory and ability to recount his experiences.

———. *Ukrainskaia revoliutsiia: Iiul'–dekabr' 1918 g.* [Ukrainian Revolution: July–December 1918]. Vol. 3. Edited by Volin. Paris: Izd-vo Komiteta N. Makhno, 1937.

———. "Zapiski Nestora Makhno" [The writings of Nestor Makhno]. AV, no. 1 (1923), pp.16–29; no. 2, pp. 27–37; nos. 3–4, pp. 23–

29; nos. 5–6, pp. 17–25. A valuable account of the author's life and his movement through the second half of 1918, supplementing rather than duplicating his memoirs. The last article deals with the attitude of the Makhno movement toward Jews, including the assassination of Hryhor'iv.

"Makhnovskaia armiia" [The army of Makhno]. Manuscript. 16 pp. Copy in author's possession.

Makhnovskii, M. "Pravda o Makhno" [The truth about Makhno]. NRS 59, no. 20 (March 2, 1969), pp. 446–48.

Maksymenko, IA. "Do istorii borot'by z denikintsiamy i petliurivshchynoiu 1919 roku" [About the history of the struggle against Denikin and Petliura in 1919]. LR, no. 1 (40) (1930), pp. 161–73. The activities of both the Bolsheviks and the Makhno partisans behind the Denikin and Ukrainian armies in the summer of 1919.

Maliarevskii, A. [Sumskoi, A.]. "Na pereekzaminovkie: P. P. Skoropadskii i ego vremia" [Verification: P. P. Skoropads'kyi and his time]. *Arkhiv grazhdanskoi voiny* (Berlin) 2 (1922): 105–42. An interesting, critical account by a Russian journalist about the administration of the hetman government, whose mission he saw was to reestablish the old regime in Russia with Ukraine as a base for the struggle against the Bolsheviks.

Manilov, V., ed. *Iz istorii Oktiabr'skoi revoliutsii v Kieve: Vospominaniia uchastnilkov* [From the history of the October Revolution in Kiev: memoirs of participants]. Kiev: Gos. izd-vo Ukrainy, 1927.

———. ed. *Pid hnitom nimets'koho imperializmu, 1918 r. na Kyivshchyni: Statti, spohady, dokumenty, kronika* [Under the oppression of German imperialism, 1918, in Kiev province: articles, memoirs, documents, chronicles]. Kiev: Derzh. vyd-vo Ukrainy, 1927. Partisan activities and Bolshevik tactics during the Austro-German occupation in 1918, in Kyiv province.

Margolin, Arnold D. *From a Political Diary: Russia, the Ukraine, and America, 1905–1945.* New York: Columbia University Press, 1946. A former deputy foreign minister in the Directory deals with his political activities in Russia and in the Ukrainian liberation movement and his observations of American life; includes a number of valuable documents pertaining to his activities.

———. *Ukraina i politika Antanty: Zapiski evreia i grazhdanina* [Ukraine and the Entente's policy: notes of a Jew and a citizen]. Berlin: S. Efron, 1922. Ukrainian relations with the Entente, 1918–20, by a Ukrainian jurist, member of the Socialist-Federalist party and of the Directory mission in Paris, and an envoy to London.

Margulies, Manuil S. *God interventsii* [The year of intervention]. 3 vols. Berlin: Izd-vo Z. I. Grzhebina, 1923. A left-wing liberal criticizes the policy of the Entente in dealing with the anti-Bolshevik Russian groups' seeking the Entente's aid; also covers the Jassy conference, Russian organizations in Odessa, their relations with the French and the Volunteer Army, and the author's work in Paris and London. Vol. 1, September 1918–April 1919; vol. 2, April–September 1919; vol. 3, September 1919–December 1920. First published in LR, no. 11.

Margulies, Vladimir. *Ognennye gody: Materialy i dokumenty po istorii voiny na iuge Rossii* [Stormy years: materials and documents on the history of war in South Russia]. Berlin: "Manfred," 1923. Historically valuable, deals with the revolutionary events in South Ukraine, including the Hryhor'iv and Makhno movements, from mid-March 1917, to the author's departure from Odessa in mid-August 1919.

Markov, S., ed. "Iz istorii grazhdanskoi voiny na Ukraine v 1918 g." [From the history of the civil war in Ukraine in 1918]. KA 4 (95) (1939): 73–102. Uprisings against the German troops in the Zvenyhorodka and Tarashcha districts, and the organization of Bolshevik partisans in the Neutral Zone, from March 1918 to March 1919.

Martynov, A. *Moi ukrainskie vpechatleniia i razmyshleniia* [My Ukrainian impressions and reflections]. Moscow: Gos. izd-vo, 1923.

"Materialy po izucheniiu revoliutsionnogo dvizheniia v Rossii" [Materials for the study of the revolutionary movement in Russia]. VO, no. 58 (1924), pp. 37–42.

Maximoff, G. P. *The Guillotine at Work: Twenty Years of Terror in Russia: Data and Documents*. Chicago: The Chicago Section of the Alexander Berkman Fund, 1940. An indictment of the Soviet regimes in Russia and Ukraine for their suppression of Anarchists: documents, chronicles of persecution and arrests, letters from concentration camps and prisons, from 1918 to 1939.

Mazepa, I. *Ohneva proba: Ukrains'ka polityka i strategiia v dobi Zymovoho pokhodu 1919–20* [Fire test: Ukrainian policy and strategy during the winter campaign, 1919–20]. Prague: "Proboiem," 1941.

———. *Ukraina v ohni i buri revoliutsii, 1917–1921* [Ukraine in the fire and storm of the Revolution, 1917–1921]. 3 vols. Munich: Vyd-vo "Prometei," 1950–51. One of the best documented and most objective memoirs on the Ukrainian Revolution by a prime minister during the Directory; valuable especially for its wealth of information on all political parties.

Mazlakh, Serhii. "Oktiabr'skaia revoliutsiia na Poltavshchine" [October

Revolution in Poltava province]. LR, no. 1 (1922), pp. 126–42. Bolshevik activities in Poltava province in the fall of 1917, and its occupation by Red troops in the winter of 1918.

Mechov, Leontii. "Zapiski dobrovol'tsa, 1919–1920 gg." [Notes of a volunteer, 1919–1920]. *Bielo dielo* (Berlin) 7 (1933): 7–198.

Meleshko, F. "Hlodosy v chasi natsional'noi revoliutsii" [Hlodosy during the national revolution]. LCK, nos. 7–8 (1934), pp. 20–24. A response to Mykhailyk's article, "Ukrains'ke selo v chasy natsion. revoliutsii," with his interpretation of the events at the town of Hlodosy.

———. "Nestor Makhno ta ioho anarkhia" [Nestor Makhno and his anarchy] LCK, no. 1 (1935), pp. 10–14; no. 2, pp. 12–14; no. 3, pp. 9–11; no. 4, pp. 14–17. Also in *Novyi Shliakh* (Winnipeg), January–February 1960. One of the best personal accounts about Makhno and his movement by a Ukrainian officer who, with his wife and two others, was invited by Makhno to do educational work with the partisans in the second half of 1919.

Mett, Ida. "Souvenirs sur Nestor Makhno." Paris, February 1948. Manuscript. Copy in author's possession.

Meyer, Henry Cord. "Germans in the Ukraine, 1918: Excerpts from Unpublished Letters." *American Slavic and East European Review* 9 (1950): 105–15. A record of German policy in Ukraine.

Miakotin, V. "Iz nedalekogo proshlogo: Otryvki vospominanii" [From the recent past: fragments of memoirs]. In *Revoliutsiia na Ukraine po memuaram belykh,* compiled by S. A. Alekseev, pp. 222–38. Moscow, 1930. Political and socioeconomic life in Kyiv and Odessa under the hetman government, with emphasis upon the activities of the organizations of refugees from Soviet Russia.

Miliukov, P. N. "Dnevnik" [Diary]. *Novyi zhurnal* (New York), no. 66 (1961), pp. 173–203; no. 67 (1962), pp. 180–218. Miliukov's negotiations with the Germans in Kyiv, his activities against the hetman state and his work in the Volunteer Army.

———. *Rossiia na perelomi: Bol'shevistskii period russkoi revoliutsii* [Russia at a turning point: the Bolshevik period of the Russian Revolution]. Paris, 1927.

Mints, I. I., and E.N. Gorodetski, eds. *Dokumenty o razgrome germanskikh okkupantov na Ukraine v 1918 godu* [Documents on the defeat of the German invaders in Ukraine in 1918]. Moscow: Goz. izd-vo polit. lit-ry, 1942.

———. "Vrangelevshchina: Iz materialov Parizhskogo 'posol'stva' Vremenogo pravitelstva [The Wrangel movement: from the materials of the Provisional Government's Paris embassy]. KA 2 (39) (1930): 3–46; 3 (40): 3–40. Correspondence of the embassy in Paris with other Volunteer Army representatives abroad, and the Wrangel government, revealing political conditions under its control in South Ukraine and foreign policy, from June to November 1920.

Miroshevskii, Vl. "Vol'nyi Ekaterinoslav" [Free Katerynoslav]. PR, no. 9 (1922), pp. 197–208. A Communist's account of the Bolshevik-Makhno relations in Katerynoslav and Makhno's activities in Denikin's rear in the fall of 1919.

Mogilianskii, N. M. "Tragediia Ukrainy: Iz perezhitogo v Kievie v 1918 godu" [The tragedy of Ukraine: from experience in Kiev in 1918]. ARR 11 (1923): 74–105. Primarily events in Kyiv in 1918, with emphasis on the sociopolitical conflict between the population and the Austro-German troops, including the upper class.

Monkevych, Borys. *Chorni Zaporozhtsi: Zymovyi pokhid i ostannia kampaniia Chornykh Zaporozhtsiv* [The Black Zaporozhians: the winter campaign and the last campaign of the Black Zaporozhians]. Lvov, 1929.

———. "Oborona Katerynoslava: Uryvok zi spomyniv" [Defense of Katerynoslav: excerpt from memoirs]. LCK, no. 9 (1935), pp. 5–8. One officer's version of the defense of Katerynoslav against both the Bolshevik and Makhno troops in January 1919.

———. *Slidamy novitnikh zaporozhtsiv* [In the footsteps of the modern Zaporozhian]. Lvov: "Dobra knyzhka," 1928.

———. *Spomyny z 1918 r.* [Memoirs from 1918]. Lvov: "Dobra knyzhka," 1928.

Mstislavskii, S. D. "Medovyi mesiats: Iz vospominanii o denikinshchine na Ukraine" [Honeymoon: from memoirs about the Denikin regime in Ukraine]. BY, no. 25 (1924), pp. 221–46; no. 26, pp. 159–76; nos. 27–28, pp. 301–33; no. 1 (29) (1925), pp. 180–98; no. 2 (30), pp. 176–94. Detailed account of Denikin's rule in Kyiv in 1919, including documentary material, by a member of the Central Committee of the Socialist party who carried on illegal activities in Kyiv province.

Mustafin. "Proryv Makhno" [Makhno's breakthrough]. PER, no. 121 (1961), pp. 10–14. An eyewitness account of the campaign of the Simferopil' Officers' Regiment against Makhno in September 1919.

Mykhailyk, Mykh. "Den' 16 sichnia 1918 r. (st. st.)" [The days of January 16, 1918 (old st.)]. LCK, no. 2 (1932), pp. 11–13.

———. "Ukrains'ke selo v chasy natsion. revoliutsii: Spomyn z chasiv borot'by za vyzvolennia odnoho sela" [Ukrainian village during the national revolution: memoirs of the struggle for the liberation of a village]. LCK, no. 1 (1934), pp. 10–14; no. 2, pp. 5–9. The populace of the town of Hlodosy, Kherson province, resist deserters from the Russian Army, the Bolsheviks, the Austro-German troops, and Denikin during the Revolution.

———. "Ukrains'kyi natsional'nyi rukh v Krymu v 1917 r." [Ukrainian national movement in the Crimea in 1917]. LCK, nos. 7–8 (1932), pp. 22–26. Vicissitudes of the Revolution in the Crimea in 1917 and the organization of Ukrainian national life there.

———. "Vystup Pershoi ukrains'koi viis'kovoi shkoly" [Stepping forward by the first Ukrainian military school]. LCK, no. 3 (1932), pp. 18–22.

———. *Za strilets'ku slavu: spomyny z rr. 1919–20* [For the riflemen's glory: memoirs from 1919–20]. Lvov: I. Tyktor, 1936.

Myronov, IE. "Z pidpillia za Tsentral'noi Rady i het'manshchyny: Spohady pro pidpil'nu robotu na Katerynoslavshchyni 1918 r." [From the underground during the Central Rada and the hetman state: memoirs about the underground activities in Katerynoslav province, 1918]. LR, nos. 3–4 (42–43) (1930), pp. 138–47. Memoirs of a Communist agent and underground activities in Katerynoslav province in 1918.

Myshuha, Luka. *Pokhid ukrains'kykh viis'k na Kyiv, serpen', 1919* [March of the Ukrainian troops on Kiev, August 1919]. Vienna: Vyd. Ukrains'kyi praporu, 1920. The struggle of the Galician Army against the Bolshevik and Denikin forces in the second half of 1919, with emphasis on the circumstances of the liberation of Kyiv.

Mytsiuk, O. *Doba Dyrektorii UNR: Spomyny i rozdumy* [The period of the Directory UNR: memoirs and reflections]. Lvov: Vyd-vo "Hromads'koho Holosu," 1939.

Naumenko, IUrii. "Moia sluzhba v 5 Khersons'kii Strilets'kii Divizii" [My service in the Fifth Kherson Riflemen Division]. *Za derzhavnist'* (Kalisz) 7 (1937): 165–80.

Nazaruk, Osyp. *Rik na Velykii Ukraini; Konspekt spomyniv z ukrains'koi revoliutsii: Ukrains'ki memuary* [One year in East Ukraine; abridged memoirs from the Ukrainian Revolution: Ukrainian memoirs]. Vienna: Vyd. Ukrains'kyi prapor, 1920. Political events in Ukraine from November 1918 to November 1919, as seen from the decision-making centers.

———. "Ukrains'ka armiia v chasi katastrofy" [Ukrainian Army during the catastrophe]. *Ukrains'kyi prapor* (Vienna), no. 3, January 13, 1920. The struggle of the Galician Army against the Bolshevik and

Denikin forces and its physical condition in the fall of 1919.

Nefterev, ed. "Iz boevoi deiatel'nosti tov. Timoshenko v gody grazhdanskoi voiny v SSSR" [From military activities of comrade Timoshenko during the civil war in SSSR]. KA 1 (104) (1941): 54–102. Orders of Marshal Timoshenko to the Sixth and Fourth divisions of the First Cavalry Army fighting Makhno, partisans, Denikin, and Wrangel armies, as well as reports to his superiors from April 1919 to December 1920.

Nemirovich-Danchenko, V. *V Krymu pri Vrangele: Fakty i itogi* [In the Crimea with Wrangel: facts and results]. Berlin, 1922. The author's recollections of General Wrangel's campaign in 1920, stressing his socioeconomic policy in the Crimea and conditions there.

Notes presentées par la delegation de la Republique Ukrainienna à la Conference de la Paix à Paris. 2 vols. Paris: Robinet-Houtain, 1919. Official communications of the Ukrainian delegation to the Peace Conference in Paris, arranged chronologically from February to July 15, 1919.

Oberuchev, K. M. *Vospominaniia* [Memoirs]. New York: Izd. Gruppy pochitatelei pamiati K. M. Oberucheva, 1930. From the last quarter of the nineteenth century through November 1917, with the emphasis on his service as Military Commissar of the Kyiv region, 1917.

Obolenskii, V. "Krym pri Vrangele" [The Crimea under Wrangel]. In *Denikin-IUdenich-Vrangel'*, edited by S. A. Alekseev, pp. 385–417. Moscow: Gos. izd-vo, 1927. General Wrangel's plan of land reform, domestic policy in the Crimea, and his attempt to reach agreement with Makhno against the Bolsheviks.

"Ocherk vzaimootnoshenii vooruzhennykh sil IUga Rossii i predstavitelei frantsuzskago komandovaniia" [Essay on the relations between the forces of South Russia and the representatives of French Command]. ARR 16 (1925): 232–62. The main source of information on the Entente's intervention in South Ukraine, its strength, and the relations between the representatives of the Entente and the Volunteer Army, from November 1918 to April 1919. Prepared by General Denikin's staff as a top secret document, and published in Katerynodar in 1919, in a limited number.

Oktiabr'skaia revoliutsiia: Pervoe piatiletie 1917–1922 [The October Revolution: the first five years 1917–1922]. Kharkov: Gos. izd-vo Ukrainy, 1922. A valuable collection of articles by participants about different aspects of the Ukrainian Revolution, including military campaigns, the economy, and foreign trade.

Okunevs'kyi, IAroslav. "Rozmova z arkhykniazem Vil'helmom dnia 4, serpnia 1918 roku" [Conversation with Archduke Wilhelm on August 4, 1918]. *Dilo* (Lvov), no. 102 (May 10, 1931), p. 2. A conversation between the author, an admiral of the Austrian Navy, and Archduke Wilhelm F. Habsburg, on August 4, 1918, concerning the Ukrainian question and the archduke's ties with Ukrainian circles.

Omelianovych-Pavlenko, Mykhailo. "Na choli Zaporozhtsiv v 1919 r. u borot'bi z denikintsiamy" [At the head of the Zaporozhians in 1919 in the struggle against the Denikin men]. KD 1929, pp. 46–60. Valuable reminiscences by the commander of the Zaporozhian corps on its campaigns against Denikin on the Right Bank in the fall of 1919.

———. *Na Ukraini 1919; perehovory i viina z rossis'koiu Dobrovol'choiu armiieiu: Spomyny holovy delegatsii ta komandyra Zaporiz'koi hrupy* [In Ukraine 1919; negotiations and war against the Russian Volunteer Army: memoirs of the head of the delegation and commanders of the Zaporozhian group]. Prague: Stilus, 1940.

———. *Na Ukraini 1917–1918* [In Ukraine 1917–1918]. Prague: Stilus, 1935. A high-ranking Ukrainian officer on the revolution in Ukraine, with emphasis on Katerynoslav province.

———. *Perehovory z Dobrarmiieiu* [Negotiations with the Volunteer Army]. Lvov: Nakl. T-va dopomohy emihrantam z Velykoi Ukrainy, 1930. Ukrainian preparations for negotiations with Denikin and the negotiations themselves in mid-September 1919, for a joint operation against the Bolsheviks, set against a background of partisan fighting by Makhno, especially in the rear of the Bolsheviks and of Denikin.

———. " Perehovory z Dobrarmiieiu" [Negotiations with the Volunteer Army]. KD 1931, pp. 47–60.

———. "Spomyny" [Memoirs]. LNV, no. 10 (1929), pp. 888–97; no. 11, pp. 963–74; no. 12, pp. 1068–77; no. 1 (1930), pp. 26–35; no. 2, pp. 128–34; no. 4, pp. 321–31.

———. *Spomyny* [Memoirs]. Lvov: Nakl. Ukrains'koi vydavnychoi spilky, 1930. The Ukrainian campaigns against Poland, the Bolsheviks, and the Volunteer Army, set against the political and military background of the Revolution, 1917–21.

———. *Ukrains'ko-pol's'ka viina 1918–1919* [Ukrainian-Polish war in 1918–1919]. Prague: Nakl. Merkur-fil'mu, 1929.

———. *Zymovyi pokhid: 6, XII, 1919–6, V, 1920* [Winter Campaign: December 6, 1919–May 6, 1920]. Kalisz: Ukr. voenno-istorychne t-vo, 1929–34. Authoritative and objective memoirs concerning guerrilla warfare in the rear of the Denikin and Bolshevik forces from December 1919 to May 1920; based on the author's diaries and experience as well as on diaries of other eyewitnesses.

"Organitzatsiia vlasti na iuge Rossi v period Grazhdanskoi voiny, 1918–1920 gg." [Organization of authority in South Russia during the period of the civil war, 1918–1920]. ARR 4 (1922): 241–51. Relating to the territory controlled by the Volunteer Army from September 1918 to November 1920.

Osipov, I. *Na prolomie: Ocherki 1914–1920 gg.* [At the turning point: sketches of 1914–1920]. Przemysl: Sovremennaia biblioteka, 1922. Memoirs of a Ukrainian Russophile in the Russian service, describing Russian policy in Galicia and Denikin's attitude toward Ukrainian refugees from Galicia in the Don Basin.

Otechestvennaia voina protiv germanskikh okkupantov v 1918 g.: Dokumenty [Patriotic war against German invaders in 1918: documents]. Moscow: Gos. polit. izd-vo, 1941. Documents, including appeals, orders, letters, telegrams, and reports, on the struggle of the people against the German troops in Ukraine and Belorussia from February 1918 to March 1919.

Otmarshtein, IUrii Vas. "Do istorii povstanchoho reidu gen. khor. IU. Tiutiunyka v lystopadi 1921 r.: Doklad" [About the history of the partisan raid of General IU. Tiutiunyk in November 1921: report]. LCK, no. 6 (1930), pp. 12–13; nos. 7–8, pp. 17–20.

Paladiichuk, S. "Spohady pro' Hrebenkivshchynu' " [Memoirs about the Hrebenko movement]. VK, no. 1 (27) (1967), pp. 35–36. A personal account of the uprising against the Germans and the hetman administration in the summer of 1918 in Kyiv province.

Palii-Sydorians'kyi. " 'Na reidi': Zi spohadiv" [On the raid: from memoirs]. *Tabor* (Warsaw), no. 5 (1930), pp. 9–13.

Paliiv, Dmytro. "Zhmut spomyniv: Za generalamy" [Handful of memoirs: with generals]. KCK 1935, pp. 40–46.

Pasmanik, D. S. *Revoliutsionnye gody v Krymu* [Revolutionary years in the Crimea]. Paris: Impr. de Navarre, 1926. Personal account, by a member of the Constitutional Democratic party, of the Revolution in the Crimea from February 1917 to April 1919, set in the sociopolitical and military scene.

Pavlovich, V. "Novorossiiskaia tragediia: 1920 god" [The Novorossisk tragedy: the year 1920]. PER, no. 59 (1956), pp. 9–11.

Pekarchuk, Stepan. "Povstannia na Bratislavshchyni" [Uprisings in Bratslav province]. LCK, no. 4 (1930), pp. 9–10. A personal account of an uprising against the Bolsheviks in the Bratslav district in April 1919.

Pervaia konferentsiia anarkhistskikh organizatsii Ukrainy "Nabat": Dekliaratsiia i rezoliutsii [First conference of the Anarchist organizations in Ukraine "Nabat": declarations and resolutions]. Buenos Aires: Izd-vo Rab. gruppa Resp. Argentine, 1922.

Petliura, Symon. *Statti, lysty, dokumenty* [Articles, letters, documents]. New York: Vyd. Ukr. vilnoi akademmi u SSHA, 1956. Selections from the writings and official transactions of the onetime head of the government of the Ukrainian People's Republic and commander in chief of the armed forces.

Petriv, Vsevolod. "Do istorii formuvannia viis'ka na Ukraini pidchas revoliutsii" [About the formation of the army in Ukraine during the Revolution]. LNV 104, no. 11 (1930): 981–87.

———. *Spomyny z chasiv ukrains'koi revoliutsii, 1917–1921* [Memoirs from the period of the Ukrainian Revolution, 1917–1921]. 4 vols. Lvov: Vyd. Chervona Kalyna, 1927–31. Valuable memoirs of a high-ranking officer; special references to the formation of the armed forces and description of some of its leaders, including Petliura, Bolbachan, and the Archduke Wilhelm F. Habsburg.

Piontkovskii, S. A., ed. *Grazhdanskaia voina v Rossii, 1918–1921 gg.: Khrestomatiia* [The civil war in Russia, 1918–1921: a reader]. Moscow: Izd-vo Kommunisticheskogo universiteta, 1925. Documents, correspondence, excerpts from memoirs, and other materials dealing with the Russian Civil War and intervention in South Ukraine.

Poliakov, I. A. *Donskie kazaki v bor'be s bol'shevikami: Vospominiia* [Don Cossacks in the struggle with the Bolsheviks: memoirs]. Munich, 1962.

Polovoi-Polianskii, K. "Vooruzhennaia bor'ba s denikintsami na Verkhnedneprovshchine i Kremenchugshchine: Iz vospominanii" [Armed struggle against Denikin men in Verkhniedniprovsk and Kremenchuk regions: from memoirs]. LR, no. 6 (21) (1926), pp. 86–97. A personal account of partisan activities in the rear of the Denikin forces in Ukraine in 1919.

Polska Akademia Nauk. Instytut Historii. *Materialy archiwalne do historii stosunków polsko-rad-zieckich* [Archival materials about the history of Polish-Soviet relations]. Edited by Natalia Gąsiorowska. Warsaw: Książka i Wiedza, 1957–.

———. Pracownia Historii Stosunków Polsko-Radzieckich. *Dokumenty i materialy do historii stosunków polsko-radzieckich* [Documents and materials about the history of Polish-Soviet relations].

Edited by Natalia Gąsiorowska-Grabowska et al. Vol. 1. Warsaw: Książka i Wiedza, 1961–.

Popov, P. "Doklad v Zafrontbiuro TSK KP(b)U o poezdke v Ukrainskuiu narodnuiu respubliku" [Report to the bureau of the rear TSK KP(b)U about the mission to the Ukrainian People's Republic]. LR, no. 2 (17) (1926), pp. 43–50. October 1919 report concerning conditions in Ukraine, and the attitudes of the workers, peasants, educated class, and political groups.

Porokhivs'kyi, Hnat. "Persha ukrains'ka dyviziia: Spomyn" [The First Ukrainian division: memoirs]. KD 1935, pp. 50–67.

P-pa, N., ed. "Protybol'shevyts'ki povstannia na Ukraini v 1921 r.: Na osnovi offitsiial'nykh bol'shevyts'kykh zvidomlen' i inshykh nepublikovanykh materiialiv" [Anti-Bolshevik uprisings in Ukraine in 1921: based on official Bolshevik reports and other unpublished materials]. LCK, no. 6 (1932), pp. 19–22; no. 9, pp. 6–7. Ukrainian partisan activities in 1921, largely from Bolshevik reports.

Prikaz Glavnokomanduiushchago Vooruzhennymi silami na iuge Rossi o zemlie ot 20 maia, 1920 goda: So vsieme dopolneniiami [Order of the commander in chief of the armed forces of South Russia about the land [question] of May 20, 1920: with all supplements]. Istanbul: Izd. Biuro russkoi pechati, 1920(?).

Pro ukrains'ki povstannia: Sokolovs'kyi i susidni hrupy [About the Ukrainian uprisings: the Sokolovs'kyi and neighboring groups]. Kamenets-Podolski: Vydannia "Striltsia," 1919.

Proekt-deklaratsiia na revoliutsionno-vzhztanicheskata armiia v Ukraina (Makhnovtsi) [Project-declaration of the revolutionary-partisan army ın Ukraine (Makhnovites)]. Sofia: Edison, 1921.

Prokhoda, Vasyl'. "Siri abo sirozhupannyky" [The Grays or Graycoats]. VK, no. 4 (28) (1967), pp. 35–42; no. 2 (33) (1968), pp. 40–44; no 3 (34), pp. 37–41. Memoirs about the campaigns of the Ukrainian division, composed of Ukrainian prisoners of war in Austria against the Bolshevik invasion in 1919.

———. *Zapysky nepokirlyvoho: Istoriia natsional'noho usvidomlennia, zhyttia i diial'nosty zvychainoho ukraintsia* [Notes of an indocile: a history of national consciousness, the life and activities of a simple Ukrainian]. Toronto: "Proboiem," 1967.

Ptashynskyi, P., ed. "Dokumenty do istorii borot'by KP(b)U proty het'mana ta interventiv, 1918r." [Documents about the history of the struggle of the KP(b)U against the hetman and invaders, 1918]. LR, nos. 1–2 (56–57) (1933), pp. 225–81. Forty-eight hitherto unpublished documents, some in full text, dealing with the partisan movement in Ukraine during the hetman period. Chronologically arranged, with an editor's introduction sympathetic to the Bolsheviks.

———. "Do istorii nimetskoi-avstriis'koi interventsii na Ukraini" [About the history of the German-Austrian intervention in Ukraine]. *Arkhiv Radians'koi Ukrainy* (Kiev), nos. 1–2, pp. 64–106. A selection of twenty-four formerly unpublished documents on the policy of the Austro-German troops in Ukraine.

Puzyts'kyi, A. "Borot'ba za dostupy do Kyiva" [Struggle for the approach to Kiev]. *Za derzhavnist'* (Kalisz) 5 (1935): 9–61; 6 (1936): 13–64; 7 (1937): 9–56.

Quaroni, Pietro. *Diplomatic Bags: An Ambassador's Memoirs*. Translated and edited by Anthony Rhodes. New York: D. White Co., 1966.

Rafes, Moissey G. "Moi vospominaniia" [My memoirs]. *Byloe*, no. 19 (1922), pp. 177–97.

"Raport gen. sht. podpolkovnika N. predstaviteliu Dobrovol'cheskoi armii v. g. Kievie" [Report of the General Staff Lt. Colonel N. to a representative of the Volunteer Army in Kiev]. BA, nos. 2–3 (1928), pp. 138–44. A secret report of a high-ranking officer about his activities in the Red Army in Ukraine from July 10 to August 15, 1919.

"Raport sostoiashchago v shtabie predstavitelia verkhovnago komandovaniia Dobrarmii gen. sht. podpolkovnika S-go predstaviteliu Verkhovnago komandovaniia v Kievie" [Report made at headquarters by a representative of the high command of the Volunteer Army, General Staff Lt. Colonel S., to the representative of the high command in Kiev]. BA, nos. 2–3 (1928), pp. 145–50. A secret report of a high-ranking officer regarding his activities in the Red Army in Ukraine; prepared for the Volunteer Army during the summer of 1919.

Ravich-Cherkas'kyi, M. [Rabinovich], ed. *Revoliutsiia i KP(b)U v materialakh i dokumentakh: Khrestomatiia* [Revolution and the KP(b)U in materials and documents: a reader]. Kharkov: "Proletarii," 1926.

Reiks, O. "Z bil'shovyts'koho pidpilla v Odesi, 1918–1919 rr." [From the Bolshevik underground in Odessa, 1918–1919]. LR, nos. 1–2 (46–47) (1931), pp. 169–86.

Rezoliutsii pervogo s'ezda Konfederatsii anarkhistskikh organizatsii Ukrainy "Nabat" no. 7 sostoiavshegosia v g. Elisavetgrade 2–7 aprelia 1919 g. [Resolutions of the First Conference of the Confederation of Anarchist Organizations in Ukraine "Nabat" no. 7, which took place in IElysavethrad April 2–7, 1919]. Buenos Aires(?): Izd. Rabochei izd. gruppy v Resp. Argentine, 1923.

Riappo, IA. "Revoliutsionnaia bor'ba v Nikolaeve: Vospominaniia" [Revolutionary struggle in Mykolaiv: memoirs]. LR, no. 4 (9) (1924), pp. 5–43. A Bolshevik agent deals with the relations between the authorities in Mykolaiv and the German and Entente troops during the first half of 1919, and with the Hryhor'iv and Makhno uprisings against the Red troops.

———. "Vosstanie nikolaevskogo proletariata protiv nemtsev" [The uprising of Mykolaiv proletarians against the Germans]. LR, no. 1 (1922), pp. 107–23. Further memoirs of a Bolshevik agent about Mykolaiv.

Rohatyns'kyi, I. "Viina mizh dvoma selamy: Epizod z revoliutsiinykh dniv na Velykii Ukraini" [War between two villages: episode from revolutionary days in Great Ukraine]. IKCK 1933, pp. 25–30.

Romanchenko, IU. "Epizody z borot'by proty makhnovshchyny, cherven'–hruden' 1920 r." [Episodes from the struggle against the Makhno movement, June–December 1920]. LR, no. 4 (49) (1931), pp. 124–32. A personal narrative dealing with the campaign of the Internal Security Troops of the Republic (VOKhR) against Makhno during the second half of 1920.

Romanov, A. A. "V Tavriu za volei: Vospominaniia ochevydtsa," [To Tavriia for freedom: memoirs of an eyewitness]. *Istoricheskii viestnik* (St. Petersburg) 84 (1901): 264–73. Recollections of the peasants' escape from their landlords in Katerynoslav and Kherson provinces to Tavriia province on the eve of the emancipation of 1861.

Rossum, I. J. Van, ed., "Proclamations of the Makhno Movement, 1920: Documents." *International Review of Social History* (Amsterdam) 13 (1968), pt. 2: 246–68. Eleven documents issued by the Makhnoists in the first half of 1920 with valuable information on some aspects of the movement.

Rostov, B. *Pochemu i kak sozdalas' Dobrovol'cheskaia armiia i za chto ona boretsia* [Why and how the Volunteer Army was established and what it fights for]. Rostov-on-Don: Osvag, 1919.

Rubach, M. "K istorii grazhdanskoi bor'by na Ukraine: K voprosu ob organizatsii Vremennogo Raboche-Krest'ianskogo Pravite'stva Ukrainy" [About the history of civil struggle in Ukraine: to the question about organization of Provisional Workers-Peasants Government of Ukraine]. LR, no. 4 (9) (1924), pp. 151–65. A valuable account of political conditions in Ukraine, including a number of documents.

———. "K istorii grazhdanskoi voiny na Ukraine: Perekhod Grigor'eva k Sovetskoi vlasti" [About the history of the civil war in Ukraine: Hryhor'iv joins the Soviets]. LR, no. 3 (8) (1924), pp. 175–88; no. 4, pp. 151–65. Telegrams and conversations between Hryhor'iv and the Soviet military command in early 1919.

———, ed. "Do istorii ukrains'koi revoliutsii: Zamitky i dokumenty, hruden' 1917–sichen' 1918 r." [About the history of the Ukrianian Revolution: notes and documents, December 1917–January 1918]. LR, no. 1 (16) (January–February 1926), pp. 41–84.

Russia (1932–USSR) Glavnoe arkhivnoe upravlenie. *Direktivy glavnogo komandovaniia Krasnoi armii, 1917–1920: Sbornik dokumentov* [Directions from the general headquarters of the Red Army, 1917–1920: collection of documents]. Moscow: Voennoe izd-vo, 1969.

Ryndyk, S. "Otaman Hryhor'iv: Spohad" [Otaman Hryhor'iv: memoirs]. *Prometei* (New York), March 24, 1960. A schoolmate's valuable and objective biographical account of Otaman Hryhor'iv's youth.

S., M. "Makhno ta ioho viis'ko: Materialy to istorii ukrains'koi vyzvol'noi borot'by" [Makhno and his troops: materials about the history of the Ukrainian liberation struggle]. LCK, no. 6 (June 1935), pp. 16–17. Contemporary but largely inaccurate reports about Makhno and his movement collected by the Ukrainian military command.

S., R. "Osin' 1918 r. na Kharkivshchyni" [Autumn 1918 in Kharkiv province]. LCK, no. 3 (1930), pp. 7–9. Also in IKCK 1934, pp. 136–41. An account of political and military conditions in Kharkiv and its province during the second half of 1918, and the coup against the hetman regime and the Germans.

———. "Platone Makhno, il liberatore dell' Ukrainia, assassinato?" *L'Avvenire Anarchicio* (Pisa), September 23, 1921.

S., V. "Ekspeditsiia L. B. Kameneva dlia prodvizheniia prodgruzov k Moskve v 1919 godu" [Expedition of L. B. Kamenev for good transportation to Moscow in 1919]. PR, no. 6 (41) (1925), pp. 116–54. Description of Kamenev's trip to the Volga Valley and to Ukraine to solve a conflict about food transportation to Russia and Hryhor'iv's anti-Bolshevik uprising.

Sadovs'kyi, Mykhailo. Letter to author. Toronto, January 1, 1961.

Sakovich, G. "Proryv Makhno" [Makhno's break-through]. PER, no. 116 (1961), pp. 11–14. A description by a Russian officer of the campaign of the Simferopol Officers' Regiment against Makhno in September 1919.

Sal's'kyi, Volodymyr and Pavlo Shandruk, eds. *Ukrains'ko-Moskovs'ka viina 1920 roku v dokumentakh* [The Ukrainian-Moscowian war of 1920 in documents]. Warsaw, 1933. Nearly 800 documents of the general staff of the Ukrainian Army covering May to November 1920.

Samiilenko, Stepan. *Dni slavy: Spohady polkovnyka ukrains'koi armii* [Days of glory: memoirs of a colonel of the Ukrainian Army]. New York: Ukr. vil'na akademiia nauk u SShA, 1958.

Savchenko, V. "Narys borot'by viiska U. N. R. na Livoberezhzhi naprykintsi 1918 ta pochatku 1919 rr." [A sketch of the struggle of the U. N. R. troops on the Left Bank at the end of 1918 and the beginning of 1919]. *Za derzhavnist'* (Kalisz) 5 (1935): 158–85; 6 (1936): 119–54.

———. "Spomyny viis'kovyka z 1918 r." [Memoirs of a military man from 1918]. KD 1937, pp. 60–74.

Savinkov, B. "General Kornilov: Iz vospominanii" [General Kornilov: from memoirs]. BY, no. 3 (31) (1925), pp. 182–97.

Serge, Victor. *Memoirs of a Revolutionary, 1901–1941*. London: Oxford University Press, 1963. Memoirs of a Russian Communist born in Belgium describing Russian revolutionary leaders, including Makhno, most of whom were later liquidated by Stalin, set against the political conditions current in Russia.

Sergeev, A. *Denikinskaia armiia sama o sebe: Po dokumentam sobrannym na boyevykh liniiakh voennym korrespondentom "Rosta"* [The Denikin army (speaks) about itself: according to documents collected on the front lines by a military correspondent of *Rosta*]. Moscow: Gos. izd-vo, 1920.

Shandruk, Pavlo. *Arms of Valor*. New York: R. Speller, 1959. Memoirs dealing with the political and military aspects of the Ukrainian Revolution.

———. "Ukrains'ka armiia v borot'bi z Moskovshchynoiu" [The Ukrainian Army in struggle against Muscovy]. *Za Derzhavnist'* (Kalisz) 4 (1934): 201–36.

Shatilov, General P. N. "Ostavlenie Kryma" [Evacuation of Crimea]. *Chasovoi* (Brussels), no. 44 (1930), pp. 14–15.

———. "Pamiatnaia zapiska o Krymoskoi evakuatsii: Dokumenty; iz arkhiva Russkoi armii" [Memorable notes about the Crimean evacuation: documents; from the archives of the Russian Army]. *Bieloe dielo* (Paris) 4 (1928): 93–107. Problems of the evacuation of the Volunteer Army under General Wrangel from Crimea in the fall of 1920, prefaced by General Shatilov.

———. "Petr Nikolaevich Vrangel." *Obshchestvo gallipoliitsev* (Sofia), October 1935.

Shchegolev, P. E., ed. *Frantsuzy v Odesse: Iz belykh memuarov gen. A. I. Denikin, M. S. Margulies, M. V. Braikevich* [Frenchmen in Odessa: from the White Guard memoirs of Gen. A. I. Denikin, M. S. Margulies, M. V. Braikevich]. Leningrad: Izd. "Krasnaia gazeta," 1928.

Shchekun, O., ed. *Perekop: Sbornik vospominanii* [Perekop: collection of memoirs]. Moscow: Gos. sotsial'no-ekon. izd-vo, 1941.

———. "Razgrom Vrangelia" [Defeat of Wrangel]. KR 5 (72) (1935): 3–44; 6 (73): 9–73. Frunze's orders, telegrams, and wires to and from headquarters of the Fourth, Sixth, Thirteenth, First Cavalry, and Second Cavalry armies, from September through November 1920.

Shemet, Serhii. "Do istorii Ukrains'koi Demokratychno-khliborobskoi partii" [About the history of the Ukrainian Democratic-Agrarian party]. *Khliborobs'ka Ukrainia* (Vienna) 1 (1920): 63–79.

———. "Mykola Mikhnovs'kyi: Posmertna z hadka" [Mykola Mikhnovs'kyi: posthumous recollection]. *Khliborobs'ka Ukraina* 5 (1924–25): 3–30.

Shepel, Zynaida. "Bat'ko povstantsia: Spohad" [Father of a partisan: recollection]. LCK, no. 2 (1932), p. 5. An account of the partisan leader IAkiv Shepel and the execution of his father by the Bolsheviks, written by Shepel's sister.

Shkuro, A. G. *Zapiski belogo partizana* [Notes of a White partisan]. Buenos Aires: Seiatel', 1961. Memoirs of one of Denikin's generals, written in 1920–21, about his campaigns during World War I and against the Bolsheviks and Makhno during the civil war.

Shlikhter, A. G. "Bor'ba za khleb na Ukraine, v 1919 godu" [The struggle for bread in Ukraine in 1919]. LR, no. 2 (29) (1928), pp. 96–135.

———, ed. *Chernaia kniga: Sbornik statei i materialov ob interventsii Antanty na Ukraine v 1918–1919 gg.* [Black book: collection of articles and materials about Allied intervention in Ukraine in 1918–1919]. Kharkov: Derzh. vyd-vo Ukrainy, 1925. A valuable collection, including captured material, of documents and articles by Soviet Russian and Ukrainian eyewitnesses, including F. Anulov, S. Ostapenko, and IU. Tiutiunyk, dealing with the Allied intervention and its economic background in South Ukraine.

Shteinman, F. "Otstuplenie ot Odessy: IAnvar 1920 g." [Retreat from

Odessa: January 1920]. ARR 2 (1921): 87–97. A participant's account of German colonists in the Volunteer Army's campaigns against the Bolsheviks and Hryhor'iv and their subsequent retreat to Romania.

Shtern, Sergei. *V ognie grazhdanskoi voiny: Vospominaniia, vpechatlieniia, mysli* [In the fire of the civil war: recollections, impressions, reflections]. Paris, 1922.

Shukhevych, Stepan. *Spomyny z Ukrains'koi Halytskoi Armii, 1918–1920* [Memoirs from the Ukrainian Galician Army, 1918–1920]. 5 vols. Lvov: "Chervona Kalyna," 1929. A high-ranking officer in the Galician Army describes the war against Poland, the Bolsheviks, and Denikin, severe physical conditions and epidemics, and the disagreements with the Directory over the policy of agreements with Denikin and Poland.

———. "Za hetmans'kykh chasiv v Odessi" [During the hetman period in Odessa]. IKCK 1930, pp. 47–52. An eyewitness account of the formation of Ukrainian units from Galician soldiers in the Austrian army in Odessa at the end of 1918.

Shulgin, V. V. *"1920 g.": Ocherki* ["1920": sketches]. Sofia: Rossisko-bolgarskoe knigoizd-vo, 1921. The Russian Civil War, from the author's first-hand observations.

Shul'hyn, Oleksander. *L'Ukraine contre Moscow 1917*. Paris: F. Alcan, 1935. Memoirs of the revolutionary events of 1917, with emphasis on the diplomatic relations of Ukraine with the Entente and Soviet Russia.

Sidorov, A. H. "Z istorii borot'by proty vrangelivshchyny i bandytyzmu na Mykolaivshchyni 1920 r." [About the history of the struggle against the Wrangel movement and banditry in the Mykolaiv region in 1920]. LR, no. 1 (46) (1931), pp. 187–202. The struggle between Ukrainian partisans, including IU. Tiutiunyk and Red troops in Mykolaiv province in 1920.

Sikar, Stepan Matviienko. "Try spomyny: Delegaty Sovnarkomu do Uriadu UNR v 1919 r.; 'Bat'ko Makhno'; Basarabs'ka Dyviziia 1919 r." [Three memoirs: delegates of the Sovnarkom to the Government of UNR in 1919; "Father Makhno"; Bessarabian Division in 1919]. In *Nashe slovo, zbirnyk no. 3. Isaakovi Mazepi na vichnu pamiat'*, pp. 89–108. Munich, 1973.

Skoropads'kyi, Pavlo. "Uryvok zi 'Spomyniv'" [Fragments from "Memoirs"]. *Khliborobs'ka Ukraina* 4 (1924): 3–40; 5 (1924–25): 31–92. Valuable and informative reminiscences by the hetman about his military and political activities, including the Ukrainization of his Thirty-Fourth Corps, from March 1917 to April 1918.

Slashchov, IA. A. *Krym v 1920 g: Otryvki iz vospominanii* [Crimea in 1920: fragments from memoirs]. Moscow: Gos. izd-vo, 1924.

———. "Materialy do istorii grazhdanskoi voiny v Rossii: Operatsii belykh, Petliury i Makhno na Ukraine" [Materials for the civil war in Russia: operations of the Whites, Petliura, and Makhno in Ukraine]. An authoritative personal account about the campaign of the Third Corps of the Volunteer Army against Makhno and the Ukrainian troops on the Right Bank in the second half of 1919.

Sokil, Ivan. "Vid Zbrucha do Kyiva: Slidamy III. kurenia 5-oi sokal's'koi brygady: Spomyn uchasnyka pokhodu" [From Zbruch to Kyiv: in the footsteps of the Third Company of the Fifth Sokal' Brigade: memoirs of a participant in the campaign]. LCK, no. 5 (1938), pp. 3–5.

Sokolov, K. N. *Pravlenie generala Denikina: Iz vospominanii* [The government of General Denikin: from memoirs]. Sofia: Rossiisko-Bolgarskoe knigoizd-vo, 1921. Memoirs of a legal advisor to Denikin's Special Council: internal history of the Volunteer Army, with emphasis upon the political and administrative regime in the occupied territories during the civil war.

Sokolovs'kyi i susidni hrupy [Sokolovs'kyi and the neighboring groups]. Kaminets Podolski: Vyd. Stril'tsia, 1919. A description of four partisan groups, including the group led by brothers Oleh and Dmytro Sokolovskyi, against the Bolshevik and anti-Bolshevik Russian forces in Kiev province, mainly in 1919.

Stanomir, Osyp. *Moia uchast' u vyzvol'nykh zmahaniakh, 1917–1920* [My participation in the liberation struggle, 1917–1920]. Toronto, 1966. A personal narrative about the Ukrainian Galician Army in the revolution in eastern Ukraine.

Stechyshyn, Stepan. "Zi spomyniv polonenoho" [From the memoirs of a prisoner]. LCK, nos. 7–8 (1938), pp. 17–21. Memoirs of a Ukrainian Galician prisoner of war in eastern Ukraine about the disintegration of the tsarist regime and Bolshevik propaganda from 1916 to 1918.

Stefaniv, Zenon. "Dva roky v Ukrains'kii Armii: Spomyny 17-litnoho pidkhorunzhoho" [Two years in the Ukrainian Army: memoirs of a 17-year-old subensign]. LCK, no. 9 (1932), pp. 8–10; no. 10, pp. 9–13; no. 11, pp. 13–16; no. 12, pp. 6–8. A young officer describes the uprising against Hetman Skoropads'kyi and the campaigns against the Bolsheviks, Poles, and Denikin during the Ukrainian Revolution.

Steifon, M. B. *Krizis dobrovol'chestva* [Crisis of the Volunteer movement]. Belgrade: Russkaia tip., 1928. A survey by a regimental commander about Denikin's campaigns against the Bolsheviks in Ukraine from April to October 1919, praising the Volunteers and criticizing the behavior of General Mai-Maevskii and his aide Makarov. The author deals at some length with the life of the troops in Kharkiv.

Struts', Volodymyr. "Try misiatsi u povstantsiv" [Three months with the partisans]. IKCK 1933.

Struve, Petr, ed. "Istoricheskie materialy i dokumenty: Ideologiia makhnovshchiny" [Historic materials and documents: ideology of the Makhno movement]. *Russkaia mysl'* (Sofia), nos. 1–2 (1921), pp. 226–31. Minutes of the second Huliai-Pole area conference of the Makhno movement, held on February 12, 1920.

Sukhogorskaia, Natal'ia. "Vospominanie o makhnovshchine" [Memoirs about the Makhno movement]. *Kandal'nyi zvon* (Odessa), no. 6 (1927), pp. 37–63. An eyewitness acount, partially unreliable hearsay, of the Revolution at Huliai-Pole from 1918 to 1920, stressing the terror and suffering of the populace under the occupation forces: Austro-Hungarians, Bolsheviks, Denikin, and Makhno.

Sumskii, S. "Odinnadtstat' perevorotov: Grazhdanskaia voina v Kievie" [Eleven coups: the civil war in Kyiv]. In *Revoliutsiia na Ukraine po memuaram belykh*, pp. 99–114. Edited by S. A. Alekseev. Moscow, 1930. Memoirs of a Bolshevik journalist about conditions in Kyiv during the Bolshevik invasion in January 1918 and German policies in Ukraine through April 1918.

Suslyk, R. L. *Kryvavi storinky z nepysanyk litopysiv: Kozats'ko-khutorians'ka Poltavshchyna v borot'bi proty moskovs'koho kommunizmu* [Bloody pages of unpublished chronicles: a cossack-farmstead, Poltava province, in the struggle against Muscovite communism]. Derby, Conn., 1956. Memoirs dealing with the partisan movement in Poltava province during the Revolution and the author's experiences in Russian concentration camps thereafter.

Suvorin, Bor. *Za rodinoi: Geroicheskaia epokha Dobrovol'cheskoi Armii, 1917–1918 gg.: Vpechatleniia zhurnalista* [For the motherland: heroic epoch of the Volunteer Army, 1917–1918: impressions of a journalist]. Paris, 1922. A survey, based on the author's diaries and other eyewitness accounts, of the formation of the Volunteer Army and its campaigns against the Red forces in the Don and Kuban basins from November 1917 to November 1918.

T. V. "Iz dalekogo proshlogo: Vospominaniia o N. I. Makhno" [From the distant past: memoirs about N. I. Makhno]. DT-P, no. 41 (1925), pp. 25–27.

Tintrup, Hans. *Kreig in der Ukraine: Aufzeichnungen eines deutschen Offiziers*. Essen: Essener Verlagsanstalt, 1938. Memoirs of a German infantry officer about his experiences and observations during the campaigns in Ukraine from Kovel to Rostov from the beginning of 1918 to January 1919.

Trotskii, Lev. *Materialy i dokumenty po istorii Krasnoi Armii: Kak vooruzhalas' revoliutsiia; na voennoi robote* [Materials and documents about the history of the Red Army: how the Revolution was armed; on the military work]. 3 vols. in 5. Moscow: Vysshyi voen. red. sovet, 1923–25. The formation of the Red Army and its struggle against its adversaries, including the Makhno partisan army.

———. *The Trotsky Papers, 1917–1922*. Vol. 1. Edited and annotated by Jan Meyer. The Hague: Mouton, 1964. Correspondence, primarily with Lenin, in Russian with English translations. Contains, in chronological order, 435 documents from 1917 to 1919, including several photocopies.

Trubetskoi, E. N. "Iz putevykh zamietok biezhentsa" [From itinerary notes of an escapee]. ARR 18 (1928): 137–207. The author's experiences in Ukraine and in the Kuban , the French intervention in South Ukraine, and Denikin's policies in Ukraine. It covers the period from September 1918 to June 1919.

Tsebrii, Osyp. "Vospominaniia partizana" [Memoirs of a partisan]. DT-P, no. 31 (1949), pp. 17–19; no. 32 (1950), pp. 13–14; no. 33, pp. 41–42; no. 34, pp. 20–22. How a peasant partisan detachment was organized against the Austro-German punitive expeditions in 1918 on the Right Bank, its efforts to coordinate its activities with the Makhno Army, and the leader's subsequent escape to Yugoslavia and his experiences there.

Tsehel'skyi, Lonlyn. *Vid legend do pravdy: Spomyny pro podii v Ukraini zviazani z Pershym Lystopadom 1918 r.* [From legends to the truth: memoirs about the events in Ukraine associated with the First November of 1918]. New York: Bulava, 1960. Authoritative but controversial memoirs by a former deputy minister of foreign affairs of the Directory; deals with the struggle for preservation of political independence from November 1918 to February 1919.

Ts'okan, Il. *Vid Denikina do bil'shevykiv: Fragment spomyniv z Radians'koi Ukrainy* [From Denikin to the Bolsheviks: fragment of memoirs from Soviet Ukraine]. Vienna: Vyd-vo Ukrains'koho praporu, 1921. A description of the campaign of the Ukrainian Galician Army against the Denikin and Bolshevik forces at the turn of 1920.

U. S. Dept. of State. *Papers Relating to the Foreign Relations of the United States, 1918–1919. Russia.* 3 vols. Washington, D.C.: U.S. Government Printing Office, 1931–37.

Ukraine, Arkhivne upravlinnia. *Grazhdanskaia voina na Ukraine, 1918–1920: Sbornik dokumentov i materialov* [The civil war in Ukraine, 1918–1920: collection of documents and materials]. 3 vols. in 4. Edited by S. M. Korolivskii. Kiev: Naukova dumka, 1967. A collection of 2,682 documents and articles from Russian and Ukrainian archives concerning events from 1918 to 1920.

L'Ukraine sovietiste: Quatre années de guerre et blocus. Berlin, 1922. Acrimonious exchanges between the Soviet Russian and Soviet Ukrainian governments on the one hand and the Romanian government on the other concerning Makhno's extradition from Romania.

Ukraine. Tsentral'nyi derzhavnyi arkhiv Zhovtenvoi revoliutsii i sotsialistychnoho budivnytstva. *Vseukrains'kyi tsentral'nyi komitet nezamozhnykh selian: Opys dokumental'nykh materialiv fondu P-257* [The All-Ukrainian Central Committee of Poor Peasants: description of documental materials in the fund P-257]. Sklarenko O. I. E. Kryvosheievoiu. Edited by I. K. Rybalka. Kharkov: Kharkivske obl. vyd-vo, 1957.

Ukrains'ka Halyts'ka Armiia u 40-richchia ii uchasty u vyzvol'nykh zmahanniakh: Materiialy do istorii [The Ukrainian Galician Army on the 40th anniversary of its participation in the struggle for liberation (of Ukraine): materials on the history]. Edited by Myron Dol'nyts'kyi. Winnipeg: D. Mykytiuk, 1958–. The Ukrainian Galician Army and its struggle against Poles and the Bolshevik and anti-Bolshevik Russian forces from 1917 to 1923.

"Ukraintsi u rossiis'koho voiennoho gubernatora L'vova—Sheremetieva: Iz zapysok ochevydtsia" [Ukrainians at the Russian military governor of L'viv—Sheremetiev: notes of an eyewitness].

V., A. "Dnevnik obyvatelia" [A diary of a citizen]. ARR 4 (1922): 252–88. A Soviet Russian escapee's diary of the Revolution in Crimea (mainly Yalta) from July 26, 1918, to April 4, 1919.

V., Dmytro. "Lystopad v 1918 r. na Ukraini: Vyrvanyi lystok iz voiennykh spomyniv" [November 1918 in Ukraine: a leaf torn from war memoirs]. *Ukrains'kyi skytalets',* no. 9 (1921), pp. 5–13; no. 10, pp. 2–3; no. 11 (1922), pp. 11–12; no. 12, pp. 4–6; no. 13, pp. 13–14.

———. "Osin' 1918 roku na Ukraini: Vyrvanyi lystok iz voiennykh spomyniv" [The fall of 1918 in Ukraine: a leaf torn from war memoirs]. IKCK 1925, pp. 62-82.

V., S. "Povstanchi otamany i otamanshchyna" [The partisan otamans and the otaman movement]. *Kaliendar-al'manakh Ukrains'koho holosu na rik 1968*, pp. 105–6. Winnipeg, Man., Canada,1968.

Valentinov, A. A. "Krymskaia epokeia: Po dnevnikam uchastnikov i po dokumentam" [The Crimean epic: according to diaries of participants and documents]. ARR 5 (1922): 5–100. A lengthy account about the struggle of the Volunteer Army in South Ukraine from May to November 1920, based upon the author's diary and documents.

Varetskii, Dm. "Marshall V. K. Bliukher." *Novyi zhurnal* (New York), no. 27 (1951), pp. 250–65. Memoirs of a Bolshevik officer describing the conditions and struggle of V. K. Bliukher against Makhno's partisans in the summer of 1921.

Velikaia Oktiabr'skaia sotsialisticheskaia revoliutsiia na Ukraine, fevral' 1917–April 1918: Sbornik dokumentov i materialov [The Great October Socialist Revolution in Ukraine, February 1917–April 1918: a collection of documents and materials]. 3 vols. Edited by S. M. Korolivskii. Kiev: Gos., izd-vo polit. lit-ry USSR. 1957. More than two thousand documents issued by the Soviet organizations and trade unions on the Ukrainian Revolution from February 1917 to April 1918.

Venhrynovych, Stepan. "Vesna 1920 r. na Ukraini" [Spring of 1920 in Ukraine]. LCK, no. 5 (1932), pp. 6–8.

Vinaver, M. *Nashe pravitel'stvo: Krymskiia vospominaniia 1918–1919 gg.* [Our government: Crimean memoirs, 1918–1919]. Paris, 1928.

Vinogradov, M. "Chemu ia byl svidietelem" [To that which I have witnessed]. Manuscript. November 25, 1954. 24 pp. Copy in author's possession. An authoritative unpublished personal account by a Denikin officer about the campaigns against Makhno and the Bolsheviks on the Left Bank in 1919 and at the beginning of 1920.

Volin, S. [Eichenbaum]. "V dopolnenie k 'Otkrytom pis'mu t-shchu Maksymovu' t-shcha N. Makhno" [Supplement to an open letter to Comrade Maksimov by Comrade N. Makhno]. DT, no. 16 (1926), pp. 15–16.

Volyts'kyi, Vasyl. *Na L'viv i Kyiv: Voenni spohady, 1918–1920* [On to L'viv and Kyiv: recollection of the war, 1918–1920]. Toronto: Homin Ukrainy, 1963. Memoirs of a military man of his combat experiences during the Ukrainian Revolution from the end of 1918 through the spring of 1920.

"Vosstanovlenie Sovvlasti na Ukraine: Materialy k piatiletiiu vziatiia Kharkova 12 dekabria 1919 g." [Establishment of Soviet authority in Ukraine: materials about the fifth anniversary of the occupation of Kharkiv, December 12, 1919]. LR, no. 1 (10) (1925), pp. 56–58. Order of the Kharkiv Military-Revolutionary Committee, appeals of the All-Ukrainian Revolutionary Committee to all the party organizations of the KP(b)U, and other documents of December 1919.

Vygran, Vl. "Vospominaniia o bor'bie s makhnovtsami" [Memoirs about the struggle against the Makhno men]. Manuscript. San Francisco, March 15, 1954. Copy in author's possession. Unpublished memoirs of a Denikin officer, based on his diaries and recollections, dealing with military operations against Makhno on the Left Bank from the fall of 1918 to the end of 1919.

Vynnychenko, V. *Vidrodzennia natsii* [The rebirth of the nation]. 3 vols. Kiev-Vienna: Vyd. Dzvin, 1920. Biased but valuable memoirs of the former prime minister of the Central Rada, president of the Directory, and leftist Social Democrat, dealing with the Revolution; contains authentic records of the period.

Wedziagolski, Karol. *Pamietniki: Wojna i rewolucja, Kontrrewolucja, Bolszewicki przewrót, Warszawski epilog* [Memoirs: war and revolution, counterrevolution, Bolshevik coup, Warsaw epilogue]. London: Nakl. Polskiej Fundacji Kulturalnej, 1972.

Wertheimer, Fritz. *Durch Ukraine und Krim*. Stuttgart: Franckh'sche Verlagshandlung, 1918. A personal account of a German military man traveling through Ukraine and Crimea from March to May 1918.

Wrangel, Peter N. *Always with Honour*. New York: R. Speller, 1957.

———. *The Memoirs of General Wrangel, the Last Commander-in-Chief of the Russian National Army*. London: Williams & Norgate, 1929. Translation of the author's *Zapiski: Noiabr' 1916–1920*, originally published as vols. 5 and 6 of *Bieloe dielo*. Berlin, 1928. The first chapter deals with the events of 1917; the others are devoted to the struggle of Denikin and Wrangel against the Bolsheviks and other adversaries through 1920. It contains documents on the Allied policy and aid.

———. *Vospominaniia: Materialy sobrannye i razrabotannye P. N. Vrangelem, G. N. Leikhtenbergskim i A. P. Livenom* [Memoirs: materials collected and arranged by P. N. Wrangel, G. N. Leikhtenbergskii, and A. P. Liven]. Edited by A. A. von-Lampe. Frankurt a.

M.: "Posev," 1969. Memoirs dealing with World War I and the Russian Civil War from November 1916 to November 1920. The author criticized Volunteer Army operations under Denikin and Allied policy and aid.

———. "The White Armies: In Russia and Later." *The English Review* 47 (October 1927): 375–94. A sketchy personal account of British and French attitudes toward Wrangel, his defeat, and the escape of his forces from the Crimea in the fall of 1920.

Xydias, Jean. *L'intervention francaise en Russie, 1918–1919: Souvenirs d'un, têmoin*. Paris: Les Editions de France, 1927. Memoirs of a Russified Greek financier in Odessa about the Allied intervention in South Ukraine, and French policies and French relations with the Ukrainian government and the Volunteer Army, stressing the leading personalities in its ranks.

Za derzhavnist': Materiialy do istorii viis'ka ukrains'koho [For independence: historical materials of the Ukrainian Army]. 11 vols. Kalisz: Vyd-vo Ukrains'ke voiennoistorychne to-vo, 1926–66. The organization and operations of the Ukrainian forces during World War I and the Revolution.

Zadoianyi, Vasyl'. "General IUrko Tiutiunyk: U 50-tu richnytsiu Pershoho zymovoho pokhodu armii UNR v zapillia voroha" [General IUrko Tiutiunyk: to the 50th anniversary of the first winter campaign of the UNR army at the enemy's rear]. TR, no. 59 (1970), pp. 13–18; no. 60, pp. 10–16; no. 61, pp. 11–19; no. 62 (1971), pp. 6–16; no. 63, pp. 10–20; no. 64, pp. 9–16; no. 65, pp. 11–17; no. 66 (1972), pp. 9–15; no. 67, pp. 15–21. Memoirs about Tiutiunyk during the Revolution, and the policy of the Volunteer Army in Ukraine.

———. "Khronika ukrains'koi vyzvol'noi borot'by doby 1917–21 rokiv" [Chronicle of the Ukrainian liberation struggle during the period of 1917–21]. TR, no. 33 (1965), pp. 10–13; no. 34, pp. 20–22; no. 35, pp. 13–16.

———. "Povstanska stykhiia" [Partisan spontaneity]. TR, no. 46 (1967), pp. 11–15; no. 47 (1968), pp. 8–14; no. 48, pp. 14–18; no. 49, pp. 4–8. Memoirs about partisan uprisings against landlord and German punitive expeditions in the Tarashcha and Zvenyhorodka districts in the summer of 1918, their suppression, and the partisans' retreat to the Neutral Zone.

Zaklyns'kyi, Myron. "Karni ekspedytsii U. S. S.–iv u Kherzonshchyni" [Punitive expeditions of U. S. S. in Kherson province]. KCK 1932, pp. 67–77. A valuable account of the Sich Riflemen's activities and the Austrian troops' policy in Kherson province from June to October 1918.

———. "Nastup USS-iv na Oleksandrivs'k 1918 r." [Attack of USS on Oleksandrivs'k in 1918]. KCK 1931, pp. 46–51. A personal account of the struggle of the Sich Riflemen against the Bolsheviks to relieve the city of Oleksandrivs'k in the spring of 1918.

———. "Pershyi raz na Velykii Ukraini" [The first time in Great Ukraine]. KCK 1930, pp. 19–29. Personal experiences of a Ukrainian Galician officer in eastern Ukraine in the spring of 1918.

———. "Sichovi Stril'tsi na Kherzonshchyni" [Sich Riflemen in Kherson province]. KCK 1932, pp. 54–67. A valuable narrative about the hetman and Austrian troops' policies and about the cooperation between the Sich Riflemen and the local populace in Kherson province in the summer of 1918.

———. "Tyf u Halyts'kii Armii: Spohad" [Typhus in the Galician Army: memoirs]. *Vistnyk* (Lvov) 4, no. 12 (1935): 873–83.

"Zamietki k knigi Arshinova" [Notes about Arshinov's book]. Manuscript. 1953. Copy in author's possession. A critical review of Arshinov's work about the Makhno movement, stressing the lack of Anarchist ideology in the movement.

Zarits'kyi, Vas. "Vypad povstanchoho zahonu: Vid Husiatyna pid Kyiv, 1921 r." [Attack of a partisan detachment: from Husiatyn to Kiev, 1921]. IKCK 1931, pp. 87–97.

Zatonskii, V. "K voprosu ob organizatsii Vremennogo Raboche-Krestianskogo Pravitel'stva Ukrainy noiabr' 1918 g." [About the question of the organization of the Provisional Workers'-Peasants' Government of Ukraine, November 1918]. LR, no. 1 (10) (1925), pp. 139–49.

Zbirnyk pamiaty Symona Petliury, 1879–1926 [Collection in the memory of Symon Petliura, 1879–1926]. Prague: Nakl. Mizhorhanizatsiinoho komitetu dlia vshanuvannia pamiaty Symona Petliury v Prazi, 1930.

Zelins'kyi, Viktor. *Syn'ozhupannyky* [Gray coats]. Berlin: Nakl. "Ukrains'koho natsional'noho obiednannia," 1938. Memoirs about the organization and activities of two Ukrainian divisions in 1917–18, by a general and commander of these units.

Zhuk, Andrii. "Verbna nedilia u Kyivi 1918 roku: Uryvok iz spomyniv" [Palm Sunday in Kiev 1918: fragment from memoirs]. KD 1937, pp. 22–40.

Secondary Sources

Adams, Arthur E. "Bolshevik Administration in the Ukraine, 1918," *The Review of Politics* 20 (1958): 289–306.

———. "The Bolsheviks and the Ukrainian Front in 1918–1919," *Slavonic and East European Review* 36 (1958): 396–417.

———. *Bolsheviks in the Ukraine: The Second Campaign, 1918–1919.* New Haven: Yale University Press, 1963. A well-documented study of the Bolsheviks' effort to occupy Ukraine following the fall of the hetman regime, with emphasis upon the Otaman Hryhor'iv.

Agureev, K. V. *Razgrom belogvardeiskikh voisk Denikina: Oktiabr', 1919–mart, 1920* [Defeat of White troops of Denikin: October 1919–March 1920]. Moscow: Voen. izd-vo, 1961. A survey of the struggle of the Red Army against the Denikin forces, stressing the role of the Communist party.

Aleksashenko, A. P. *Krakh denikinshchiny* [Failure of the Denikin movement]. Moscow: Izd-vo moskovskogo universiteta, 1966. Survey of the Red troops' campaigns against Denikin, set against the sociopolitical background and stressing the role of Ukrainian partisans.

———, comp. *Protiv Denikina: Sbornik vospominanii* [Against Denikin: collection of memoirs]. Moscow: Voen. izd-vo, 1969. The Bolsheviks and partisans against the Denikin forces in South Russia and in Ukraine.

Alekseev, V. N., ed. *Boguchartsy: K istorii 40-i Bogucharskoi divizii v obrabotke M. Borisova* [Boguchartsy: about the history of the 40th Boguchar Division prepared by M. Borisov]. Voronezh: Istpartotdel Voronezhskogo Obkoma VKP (b), 1935.

Al'mendingen, G. "K pis'mu v redaktsiiu rotmistra Labinskago" [About a letter to the editor captain Labinskii]. PER, no. 106 (1960), pp. 13–15.

Al'mendinger, V. *Simferopol'skii Ofitserskii polk, 1918–1920: Stranitsa k istorii Belogo Dvizheniia na Iuge Rossii* [Simferopol Officers' Regiment, 1918–1920: a page about the history of the White movement in South Russia]. Los Angeles, California, 1962. A valuable survey of the history of the Simferopol Officers' Regiment, its campaigns against the Ukrainian troops and Makhno in the second half of 1919, and its vicissitudes until August 1920; based on K. A. Stol'nikov's and the author's work.

Alsberg, Henry G. "The Situation in the Ukraine." *The Nation* 109 (1919): 569–70.

Anan'ev, Konstantin. *V boiakh za Perekop* [In the fight for Perekop]. Moscow: Gos. voen. izd-vo, 1938.

Antanta i Vrangel: Sbornik statei [Entente and Wrangel: collection of articles]. Moscow: Gos. izd-vo, 1923. Relations between Wrangel and the Entente, Wrangel's economic policies, the underground movement and the Tatar question in 1920, from the Bolshevik point of view.

"Armiia Zelenoho i Sichovi Stril'tsi" [The army of Zelenyi and the Sich Riflemen]. *Strilets'ka dumka*, no. 54 (Staronkonstantyniv, October 1919).

Arshinov, P. "Anarkhizm i makhnovshchina: Otvet na voprosy i vozrazheniia" [Anarchism and the Makhno movement: answer to questions and objections]. AV, no. 2 (1923), pp. 27–37. An Anarchist leader associated with Makhno describes the Makhno movement and its relation to the Anarchists. Also in VO, nos. 28–34 (192–).

———. "Anarkhizm i sindikalizm" [Anarchism and syndicalism]. DT, no. 9 (1926), pp. 6–9.

———. "Chego dobivaiutsia povstantsy-Makhnovtsy" [What the partisans-Makhnomen want to achieve]. PS, no. 1 (May 17, 1919), pp. 1–2; no. 2 (May 24, 1919), pp. 2–4. A response to the Bolshevik denunciation of the Makhno movement.

———. *Dva pobega: Iz vospominanii anarkhista 1906–9 gg.* [Two escapes: from memoirs of an anarchist 1906–9]. DT, 1929. Reminiscences of a Russian Anarchist's early years in the movement.

———. *Geschichte der Machno-Bewegung, 1918–1921.* Berlin: "Der freie Arbeiter" (R. Oestreich), 1923.

———. *Geschiedenis der Machno-beweging, 1918–1921.* Amsterdam: De Boemerang, 1935.

———. *History of the Makhnovist Movement, 1918–1921.* Detroit: Black & Red, 1974.

———. *Istoriia makhnovskogo dvizheniia, 1918–1921 gg.* [A history of the Makhno movement, 1918–1921]. Berlin: Izd. "Gruppy russkikh anarkhistov v Germanii," 1923. A noncomprehensive, semiofficial history of the Makhno movement, with emphasis on the military aspect, by a Russian Anarchist who was in charge of propaganda and editor of publications for Makhno. It provides a counterbalance to the Bolshevik author M. Kubanin (*Makhnovshchina.* Leningrad, 1927).

———. "Makhnovshchina i ee vchorashnie soiuzniki—Bol'sheviki: N. Makhno Otvet na knigu M. Kubanina 'Makhnovshchina'" [The

Makhno movement and its previous allies—the Bolsheviks: Makhno's answer to the book of M. Kubanin *Makhnovshchina*]. DT, nos. 41–42 (1928), pp. 20–22. Author's criticism of Kubanin's work and Makhno's booklet *Makhnovshchina i ee vchorashnie soiuzniki*. It supplements Makhno's booklet by stressing the role of foreign anarchists in the Makhno movement.

———. "Na zlobu dnia: Eshche o Grigor'eve, Bolshevizm, Anarchizm, Pis'mo Shkuro" [On the evil of the day: more about Hryhor'iv, bolshevism, anarchism, a letter from Shkuro]. PS, no. 3 (May 31, 1919), pp. 2–3. A response to Bolshevik speculations about Makhno-Hryhor'iiv relations and a letter of appeal from General Shkuro to Makhno to join the Volunteer Army.

———. "Opravdanie Nestora Makhno" [Acquittal of Nestor Makhno]. AV, nos. 5–6 (November–December, 1923), p. 25. Makhno's release from the prison in Warsaw.

———. "Povstanchestvo i Krasnaia armii" [The partisan movement and the Red Army]. *Ekaterinoslavskii Nabat*, no. 1 (January 7, 1920), pp. 1–2.

———. "Spory vogrug krest'ianstva" [Disputes about the peasantry]. DT, no. 17 (October 1926), pp. 1–3.

———. *Storia del movimento machnovista, 1918–1921*. Naples, 1954.

Avenarius, M. "Povorot v obshchestvennom mnenii k Makhno" [Change of society's opinion about Makhno]. VO, no. – (19–), pp. 19–20.

Averin. "Do borot'by proty hryhor'ievshchyny ta denikinshchyny za Dnipropetrovs'ke" [About the struggle against the Hryhor'iv and Denikin movements for Dnipropetrovs'ke]. LR, no. 3 (48) (1931), pp. 115–29. Political conditions in Katerynoslav and the Bolshevik struggle against Hryhor'iv, Makhno, and Denikin during May–June, 1919.

Avrich, Paul. "The Anarchists in the Russian Revolution." *The Russian Review* 26, no. 4 (October 1967): 341–60.

———. *The Russian Anarchists*. Princeton, N.J.: Princeton University Press, 1967. A well-documented, sympathetic survey of the Russian Anarchist movement from its origins through the Revolution including a survey of Makhno movement (pp. 209–22).

Bachyns'kyi, IUllian. *Bol'shevyts'ka revoliutsiia i Ukraintsi: Krytychni zamitky* [The Bolshevik Revolution and Ukrainians: critical works]. Berlin, 1928.

Baier, Mykola. *Prychyny agrarnoi revoliutsii na Ukraini i shliakhy do rozviazky agrarnoi spravy* [The causes of agrarian revolution in

Ukraine and the ways to the solution of the agrarian problem]. Kiev: Vyd-vo UNR Svoboda i pravo, 1920.

Baron, A. "Pravda o Makhno" [The truth about Makhno]. *Odesskii Nabat*, no. 7 (June 16, 1919). A general account of the Makhno movement by an Anarchist.

Baumgart, Winfried. "Ludendorff and das Auswartige Amt zum Bezetzung der Krim 1918." *Jahrbücher für Geschichte Osteuropas* (Munich) 14, no. 4 (1966): 429–538.

Belash, V. "Makhnovets o rabochem stroitel'stve" [Makhnoman about the workers' construction]. PS, no. 43 (June 5, 1920), pp. 2–3. An account claiming that the peasants were supporting Makhno's partisans.

Belopolski, IU. "Epizod iz epokhi Grigor'evshchiny" [An episode from the Hryhor'iv movement]. *Kandal-nyi zvon* (Odessa), no. 8 (1927), pp. 84–91.

Berland, Pierre [Luciani, Georges]. "Makhno." *Le Temps*, Paris, August 28, 1934. An objective account about Makhno movement by the Moscow correspondent of *Le Temps* who maintains that it was Makhno who defeated Denikin.

Bezruchko. "Grupa S. S. v boiakh na pidstupakh do Kamiantsia-Podil'skoho: Bii pid Smotrychem 22 lypnia 1919 roku" [A group of S. S. in battles on the approach to Kamianets'-Podil'skyi: fighting at Smotrych on July 22, 1919]. KCK 1927, pp. 114–24.

Bilan, IU. IA. *Heroichna borot'ba trudiashchykh Ukrainy proty vnutrishn'ioi kontrrevoliutsii ta inozemnykh interventiv u 1918–1920 robakh* [Heroic struggle of the workers of Ukraine against domestic counterrevolution and foreign intervention in 1918–1920]. Kiev, 1957.

Bitenbinder, A. "Ekivoki voennoi strategii" [Equivoque about military strategy]. NRS, December 18, 1968, pp. 2–3.

Bjorkman, Edwin, ed. *Ukraine's Claim to Freedom: An Appeal for Justice on Behalf of Thirty-five Millions*. New York: The Ukrainian National Association and the Ruthenian National Union, 1915. Twelve articles by prominent historians and politicians, including Hrushevs'kyi, on the Ukrainian question in the Austria-Hungarian and Russian Empires.

Boi. "Ukrains'ki Sichovi Stril'tsi (U.S.S.) i Sichovi Stril'tsi (S.S.)" [Ukrainian Sich Riflemen (U.S.S.) and Sich Riflemen (S.S.)]. KCK 1923, pp. 68–78.

Boldyr, A. V. "V Krymu vo vremia gen. Slashcheva i Vrangelia 1920 g.: Zapiski" [In the Crimea during the period of General Slashchev and

General Wrangel: memoirs]. BY, no. 2 (30) (1925), pp. 195–229.

Bol'shaia sovetskaia entsiklopediia. 1st ed. 65 vols. Moscow, 1926–49.

Bondar, A. "Kto takoi Grigor'ev?" [Who is Hryhor'iv?]. PS, no. 3 (1919), pp. 3–4. A biographical account of Hryhor'iv, his role during the Revolution, and of his assassination.

Borisenko, I. *Sovetskie respubliki na Severnom Kavkaze v 1918 godu: Kratkaia istoriia respublik* [Soviet republics in the North Caucasus in 1918: a short history of the republic]. Edited by N. Likhnitskii. Rostov: Severnyi Kavkaz, 1930. An informative study of the Bolshevik struggle for power in the North Caucasus, set against the socioeconomic, political, and military background.

Borman, Arkadii. "Moi otvet A. Karmazinu" [My answer to A. Karmazin]. NRS, February 22, 1969.

———. "Strannaia sud'ba Makhno" [The strange fate of Makhno]. NRS, February 2, 1969, p. 4.

Borowsky, Peter. *Deutsche Ukrainepolitik 1918: Unter besonderer Berücks. d. Wirtschaftsfragen*. Lübeck: Matthiesen, 1970.

Borys, Jurij. *The Russian Communist Party and the Sovietization of Ukraine: A Study of the Communist Doctrine of the Self-Determination of Nations*. Stockholm, 1960. A competent, well-documented analysis of Bolshevik policies in Ukraine, with emphasis on the doctrine of self-determination of nations as applied in Ukraine up to its Russification.

Bosh, Evgeniia. *God bor'by: Bor'ba za vlast na Ukraine s aprelia 1917 g. do nemetskoi okkupatsii* [The year of struggle: the struggle for power in Ukraine from April 1917 to German occupation]. Moscow: Gos. izd-vo, 1925. A detailed account of Bolshevik activities in Ukraine prior to German occupation, including the struggle of the Ukrainian elements within the RSDRP(b) for an independent Ukraine.

———. *National'noe pravitel'stvo i sovetskaia vlast' na Ukraine* [National government and Soviet power in Ukraine]. Moscow: Izd-vo Kommunist, 1919. An account by a Russian Communist of the Bolshevik invasion and underground activities in Ukraine during the Ukrainian Revolution from 1917 to the first half of 1918.

Bradley, John. *Allied Intervention in Russia*. New York: Basic Books, 1968.

Brazhnev, E. "Partizanshchina" [The partisan movement]. *Novyi mir* (Moscow), no. 7 (1925), pp. 61–84.

Bredis, IE. "Partiine pidpillia v Odesi za denikinshchyny: Narys" [Party underground in Odessa during the Denikin movement: a sketch].

LR, nos. 3–4 (42–43) (1930), pp. 110–37.

Brinkley, George A. *The Volunteer Army and the Allied Intervention in South Russia, 1917–1921: A Study in the Politics and Diplomacy of the Russian Civil War.* Notre Dame, Ind.: University of Notre Dame Press, 1966. A well-documented analysis of the Volunteer Army, the Allied intervention in South Ukraine, and their interrelations.

Bronshtein, V. "Komitety bednoty v RSFS" [The Committee of the Poor in RSFS]. IM 5 (69) (1938): 71–96.

Buguraev, Maksim. "Denikin o Makhno" [Denikin on Makhno]. NRS, February 21, 1969. Excerpts from Denikin's *Ocherki russkoi smuty*.

Buiski, A. *Bor'ba za Krym i rargrom Vrangelia* [The struggle for Crimea and defeat of Wrangel]. Moscow: Gos. izd-vo, 1928.

———. *Krasnaia Armiia na vnutrennem fronte: Bor'ba s belogvardeiskimi vostanniami, povstanchestvom i banditizmom* [The Red Army in the domestic front: the struggle against the White insurrections, partisans, and banditry]. Moscow: Gos. izd-vo, 1929.

Bulavenko. "Borot'ba na Kubani v druhii polovyni 1918 r." [Struggle in the Kuban during the second half of 1918]. RN, nos. 1–2 (72–73) (1934).

———. "Kuban' i 'moskovs'kyi shliakh'" [The Kuban and the Moscow road]. RN, nos. 7–8 (78–79) (1934), pp. 187–97.

———. "Kuban' na perelomi" [The Kuban at the turning point]. RN, nos. 3–4 (74–75) (1934), pp. 86–95.

———. "Kuban' u pershii polovyni 1919 r." [The Kuban during the first half of 1919]. RN, nos. 5–6 (76–77) (1934), pp. 133–42.

———. "Vyzvolennia Kubani z pid bol'shevyts'koi vlady v 1918 r." [Liberation of the Kuban from Bolshevik authority in 1918]. RN, nos. 11–12 (70–71) (1933), pp. 265–75.

Burdzhalov, E. N. *Vtoraia russkaia revoliutsiia: Moskva, front, periferiia* [The second Russian Revolution: Moscow, front, periphery]. Moscow: "Nauka," 1971.

Butyrets. "Makhno i bol'sheviki" [Makhno and the Bolsheviks]. *Nabat* (Kharkov), no. 21 (June 30, 1919), pp. 2–3.

Bzhes'kyi, Roman. *Narysy z istorii ukrains'kykh vyzvol'nykh zmahan', 1917–1922 rr.: "Pro shcho istoriia movchyt"* [Sketches from the history of Ukrainian liberation struggle, 1917–1922]. 2 vols. Detroit, 1961. A detailed survey dealing with the Ukrainian Revolution.

Chabanivs'kyi, V. "Vstup ukrains'kykh viis'k do Kyiva 31 serpnia 1919 roku" [Entry of the Ukrainian troops to Kiev on August 31, 1919]. *Za Derzhavnist'* (Warsaw) 8 (1938): 152–54.

Chamberlin, William Henry. *The Russian Revolution, 1917–1921.* 2 vols. New York: The Universal Library, 1965. A well-documented, useful study of the Russian Civil War with emphasis upon the political and military aspects, by an American correspondent who visited Russia and Ukraine in the 1920s and 1930s.

Chaplenko, Vasyl'. *"Ukraintsi": Povist'* [Ukrainians: a novel]. A novel on the Makhno movement based on documentary material.

Chernomordik, S. [Larionov, P.]. *Makhno i makhnovshchina: Anarkhisty za "rabotoi"* [Makhno and the Makhno movement: the anarchists at work]. Moscow: Izd-vo Politkat., 1933. A survey of the Makhno movement, seen as counterrevolutionary.

Chernov, Victor. *The Great Russian Revolution.* New Haven, Conn.: Yale University Press, 1936. An authoritative history of the Russian Revolution by a Socialist Revolutionary and the minister of agriculture in the Kerensky government; the English version of the first part of a projected four-volume work.

Chernova, R. [Roza Shcherbataia]. "Podgotovka vooruzhennogo vostaniia na Ukraine v 1918–1919 godu" [Preparation of armed uprising in Ukraine in 1918–1919]. *Voennyi vestnik* (Moscow), no. 7 (1928), pp. 40–43.

Chetyrkin, A. "Krest'ianstvo IUga Rossii pod vlastiiu Denikina: Agrarnaia politika denikinshchyny" [Peasantry of South Russia under the Denikin regime: agrarian policy of the Denikin movement]. IM 5 (93) (1941): 61–73.

Chornohor, Bohdan. "Dukh stepiv—chy otamanshchyna" [The spirit of the steppes—or 'otamanshchyna']. LCK, no. 1 (1937), pp. 16–18.

Chornota. "Ostanni zakhidn'o-ukrains'kyi chastyny na Velykii Ukraini" [The last West Ukrainian units in Great Ukraine]. LCK, no. 9 (1932), pp. 14–16.

———. "Reid otamana Zalizniaka: Khyriv, Horodyshche, Svynarka, Zhashkiv, Volodarka–z tsykliu: Chotyry povstans'ki reidy i ikh likvidatsiia" [The raid of Otaman Zalizniak: Khyriv, Horodyshche, Svynarka, Zhashkiv, Volodarka—from the series: four partisan raids and their liquidation]. LCK, no. 12 (1932), pp. 2–3. An account of the partisans' campaign against the Red troops in 1919, stressing their tactics and contemporary political conditions.

Chykalenko, Levko. "Pomylka Tsentral'noi Rady" [A mistake of the Central Rada]. LHKD 1936, pp. 96–100.

Chyz, Yaroslav J. "The Ukrainian Peasant in Revolt." *Ukrainian Life* (Scranton, Pa.) 2, no. 10 (October 1941): 8–10, 15.

Crisp, Olga. "Some Problems of French Investment in Russian Joint-Stock Companies, 1894–1914." *Slavonic and East European Review* 35 (1956–57): 223–40.

Czubatyi, Nicholas. "The Modern Ukrainian Nationalist Movement." *Journal of Central European Affairs* 4 (1944): 281–305.

———. "The national revolution in Ukraine, 1917–1919." *The Ukrainian Quarterly*, vol. 1 (October 1944).

Dashkevych, Roman. *Artyleriia Sichovykh Stril'tsiv u borot'bi za zoloti kyivs'ki vorota* [Artillery of the Sich Riflemen in the struggle for the golden gate of Kyiv]. New York: "Chervona Kalyna," 1965.

Degot', V. "Menshevizm i belogvardeishchina vo vremia grazhdanskoi voiny v Odesse" [Menshevism and the White Guard movement during the period of the Civil War in Odessa]. *Katorga i ssyslka* (Moscow), no. 7 (80) (1931), pp. 26–39. Attempt by Denikin troops jointly with the German colonists to control Odessa in the summer of 1918.

Denikin, A. I. "Okrainnyi vopros" [The Ukrainian question]. *Posliedniia novosti.* Paris, n.d.

Diakiv, IAromir. "Strategichne polozhennia UHA po perekhodi cherez Zbruch litom 1919 r." [Strategic conditions of the UHA after crossing the Zbruch in the summer of 1919]. *Skytalets'*, no. 6 (18) (October 15, 1923), pp. 13–16. A valuable description of the Ukrainian Galician Army in the summer of 1919.

Dobrotvors'kyi, Osyp. "Lystopad 1921 roku na Velykii Ukraini: Korotkyi narys pov.-partizans'koho rukhu pid komandoiu hen. IUrka Tiutiunyka" [November 1921 in Great Ukraine: a brief sketch of partisan movement under the command of General IUrii Tiutiunyk]. KCK 1923, pp. 142–50.

Dobrynin, V. *Bor'ba s bol'shevizmom na iugie Rossii: Uchastie v bor'bie donskogo kazadhestva, fevral' 1917–mar't 1920: Ocherk* [The struggle against bolshevism in South Russia: participation in the struggle of the Don Cossacks, February 1917–March 1920: essay]. Prague: Slavianskoe izd-vo, 1921. A survey of the campaign of the Don Cossacks against the Red forces, by the chief of the intelligence service and operational department of the Don Army.

Dolenga, Sviatoslav. *Skoropadshchyna* [The Skoropads'kyi movement]. Warsaw: M. Kunyts'kyi, 1934. An indictment of Hetman Skoropads'kyi's regime consisting largely of quotations from other sources to prove the author's point.

Dolin, E. Z. [Moravskii]. *V vikhri revoliutsii* [In the vortex of the Revolution]. Detroit: "Drug," 1954.

Doroshenko, Dmytro. "Mykhailo Dragomanov and the Ukrainian National Movement." *The Slavonic and East European Review* 16, no. 48 (1938): 654–66. A valuable account of Drahomanov's scholarly and political activities, set against the background of the contemporary sociopolitical conditions.

———. *Z istorii ukrains'koi politychnoi dumky za chasiv svitovoi viiny* [From the history of Ukrainian political thought during the World War]. Prague, 1936.

Doroshenko, Volodymyr. "Politychnyi rozvytok Naddniprians'koi Ukrainy" [Political development in the Dnieper Ukraine]. KD 1935, pp. 50–66.

Dotsenko, Oleksander. "Reid otamana Sahaidachnoho: Kholodyni IAr-Kherson–z tsykliu: Chotyry povstanski reidy i ikh likvidatsiia" [The raid of Otaman Sahaidachnyi: Kholodnyi IAr-Kherson–from the series: four partisan raids and their liquidation]. LCK, no. 11 (1932), pp. 4–5. Valuable account of the partisans' struggle against the Bolsheviks in 1919, stressing their tactics and contemporary political conditions.

Dubinin. "Meshchanskaia trusost'" [Petty bourgeois cowardice]. DT, no. 28 (1927), pp. 19–20. The author's defense of Makhno against Bolshevik criticism.

Dubrovskii, S. "Grigor'evshchina" [The Hryhor'iv movement]. VR 4 (1928): 86–98; 5:90–100.

———. "Likvidatsiia grigor'evshchiny, 1919 g." [The liquidation of the Hryhor'iv movement in 1919]. VIZ, no. 2 (1941), pp. 28–41. A regimental political commissar's account of the Red Army's struggle against Hryhor'iv's uprising in May 1919 from the Bolsheviks' point of view.

Dubrovs'kyi, Vasyl'. *Bat'ko Nestor Makhno—ukrains'kyi natsional'nyi heroi* [Father Nestor Makhno—Ukrainian national hero]. A well-documented account, mainly from Soviet sources, of the Makhno movement, praising the partisans for their excellent tactics and bravery in fighting Russian Bolshevik and anti-Bolshevik forces. It is part of the author's unpublished work "Peoples of the URSR" written in 1943.

Dumin, Osyp. *Istoriia Liegionu Ukrains'kykh Sichovykh Striltsiv, 1914–1918* [History of the Legion of Sich Riflemen, 1914–1918]. Lvov: "Chervona kalyna," 1936. An authoritative history of the Ukrainian Sich Riflemen, 1914–18, by one of its officers.

———. *Narys istorii ukrains'ko-pols'koi viiny, 1918–1919* [Sketch of the history of the Ukrainian-Polish war, 1918–1919]. New York: Oko, 1966. A survey, covering as well the Entente policy in the conflict.

Dushnyk, Walter. "The Kerensky Provisional Government and the Ukrainian Central Rada." *The Ukrainian Quarterly* 23, no. 2 (1967): 109–29.

———. "Russia and the Ukrainian National Revolution." *The Ukrainian Quarterly* 2 (1946): 363–75.

Dziabenko. "Pershyi ukrains'kyi viis'kovyi z'izd" [The First Ukrainian Military Congress]. *Ukrains'kyi kombatant* (Munich), no. 2 (1954), pp. 9–13.

E., M. "Nestor Makhno, 1889–1934." *Kaliendar-al'manakh Ukrains'koho holosu na rik 1968*, p. 107.

Efimov, N. A. "Deistviia protiv Makhno s ianvaria 1920 g. po ianvar' 1921 g." [Activities against Makhno from January 1920 to January 1921]. *Sbornik trudov Voenno-nauchnogo obshchestva* (Moscow) 1 (192–): 192–222. A detailed account of the Bolshevik campaign against Makhno from early 1920 to early 1921, stressing the attempt of the Red troops to destroy the Makhno detachments in the Crimea and the Huliai-Pole region in late 1920.

———. *Deistviia 2-oi Konnoi armii v 1920 godu* [Activities of the 2nd Cavalry Army in 1920]. Moscow: Gos. izd-vo, otdel voen. lit-ry, 1928(?).

Egorov, A. I. *Razgrom Denikina 1919* [Defeat of Denikin, 1919]. Moscow: Gos. voen. izd-vo, 1931. A valuable detailed study, based on the author's personal accounts, archival material, and secondary sources, by the commander of the Red forces of the Southern Front; the strategic plans and the Bolshevik campaign of 1919 against Denikin are set against the socioeconomic, political, and military background of the two adversaries.

Eideman, R. *Borba s kulatskim povstanchestvom i banditizmom* [The struggle against the kulak partisans and banditry]. Kharkov, 1921.

———. *Ochagi atamanshchiny i banditizma* [Center of the otaman movement and banditry]. Kharkov, 1921.

Eideman, R., and N. Kakurin. *Hromadians'ka viina na Ukraini* [The Civil War in Ukraine]. Kharkov: Derzh. Vyd-vo Ukrainy, 1928. A general survey, from the Bolshevik point of view, of the Soviet Russian struggle for power in Ukraine, emphasizing the campaigns against Makhno and other partisan groups.

Erde, D. [Raikhshtein]. "Politychna prohrama anarkho-makhnovshchiny" [Political program of the Anarchist-Makhno movement]. LR, no. 1 (40) (1930), pp. 41–63; no. 2 (41), pp. 28–49. A Soviet view of the political program of the Makhno movement and Makhno's relations with the Russian Anarchists, the Bolsheviks, and other partisan groups.

———. *Revoliutsiia na Ukraine: Ot Kerenshchiny do nemetskoi okkupatsii* [The Revolution in Ukraine: from the Kerensky movement to the German occupation]. Kharkov: Izd. Proletarii, 1927. A Bolshevik writer's account of the Ukrainian Revolution from February 1917 to April 1918, stressing the growth of the Bolshevik influence in Ukraine.

Esaulov. "Nalet Makhno na Berdiansk" [Makhno's raid on Berdiansk]. LR, no. 3 (1924), pp. 82–86.

Esbakh, E. "Poslednie dni makhnovshchiny na Ukraine" [The last days of the Makhno movement in Ukraine]. VR 12 (1926): 40–50. A detailed account based on documentary material about the Bolsheviks' struggle against Makhno from January to August, 1921.

Eudin, Xenia Joukoff. "The German Occupation of the Ukraine in 1918: A Documentary Account." *Russian Review* 1 (1941): 90–105. German policy in Ukraine during the summer of 1918, consisting largely of documentary quotations.

———. "Soviet National Minority Policies, 1918-1921." *The Slavonic and East European Review* 21, no. 2 (1943): 31–55.

Fedenko, Panas. "1917 rik v istorii Ukrainy" [The year 1917 in Ukrainian history]. LHKD 1937, pp. 52–62.

Filonenko, IE. "Volyns'ki povstantsi v krivavykh dniakh 1920–24 rokiv" [Volynian partisans in the bloody days of 1920–1924]. *Za Derzhavnist'* (Warsaw) 8 (1938): 215–35.

Fischer, Louis. *The Life of Lenin*. New York: Harper & Row, 1964.

———. *The Soviets in the World Affairs: A History of the Relations between the Soviet Union and the Rest of the World, 1917–1929*. 2 vols. Princeton, N.J.: Princeton University Press, 1951. A survey of Soviet foreign policy by an American journalist who gained access to confidential information and private official documents owing to his friendly relations with Soviet officials.

Footman, David. *Civil War in Russia*. London: Faber and Faber, 1961. A brief essay by a former British diplomat on the six most important developments of the Civil War, including the Makhno movement.

———. "Nestor Makhno." *St. Antony's Papers*, no. 6; *Soviet Affairs*, no. 2, pp. 77–127. A valuable and objective survey of the Makhno movement based on limited sources. It also appears in the author's *Civil War in Russia* (pp. 245–302).

———. "Nestor Makhno and the Russian Civil War." *History Today* 6 (1956): 811–20.

Frants, G. "Evakuatsiia germanskimi voiskami Ukrainy: Zima 1918–1919 gg." [Evacuation of the German troops from Ukraine: winter 1918–1919]. *Istorik i sovremennik* (Berlin) 2 (1922): 262–69. German-Ukrainian negotiations concerning the German evacuation, including Hryhor'iv's ultimatum to the German garrison in Mykolaiv.

Furer, Veniamin. *Borot'ba za zhovten'na seli* [The struggle in October for the village]. Kharkov, 1928.

G., D. "Dve knigi o Makhno" [Two books about Makhno]. PRO, nos. 76–77 (1936), p. 28.

———. "Novaia kniga N. Makhno" [A new book about N. Makhno]. PRO, nos. 76–77 (1936), pp. 28–29.

Gibbons, Herbert Adams. "The Ukraine and the Balance of Power." *The Century Magazine* 102, no. 3 (1921): 463–71.

Goldelman, Saloman. *Jewish National Autonomy in Ukraine, 1917–1920.* Chicago: Ukrainian Research and Information Institute, 1968. An objective study based on the author's personal accounts, documents, and secondary sources by a prominent scholar and Ukrainian Jewish politician.

Gol'del'man, Solomon I. *Zhydivs'ka natsional'na avtonomiia v Ukraini, 1917–1920* [Jewish national autonomy in Ukraine, 1917–1920]. Munich: "Dniprova khvylia," 1967.

Golovin, Nikolai Nikolaevich. *Rossiskaia kontr'-revoliutsiia v 1917–1918 gg.* [Russian counterrevolution of 1917–1918]. 5 vols. Tallin: "Libris," 1937.

Golubev, A. *Grazhdanskaia voina, 1918–1920 gg.* [The Civil War, 1918–1920]. Moscow: Molodaia gvardiia, 1932. Survey of the Russian Civil War, including the Bolshevik-Ukrainian and Bolshevik-Polish wars, emphasizing the military aspect.

———, ed. *Perekop i Chongar: Sbornik statei i materialov* [Perekop and Chongar: collection of articles and materials]. Moscow: Gos. voen. izd-vo, 1933.

"Goneniia na anarkhizm" [Persecutions of anarchism]. AV, no. 1 (July 1923).

Gonta, Dmytro. "Na pantsyrnyku 'Khortytsia'" [On the armored train 'Khortytisa']. IKCK 1932, pp. 71–86.

———. "Otamanshchyna." *Kyiv* (Philadelphia), no. 1 (1957),

pp. 107–15; no. 3, pp. 159–62; no. 4, pp. 197–200; no. 5, pp. 262–67.

Gorelik, Anatolii. *Anarkhisty v rossiiskoi reoliutsii.* [The anarchists in the Russian Revolution]. Buenos Aires: Rabochaia izd-ia gruppa v Resp. Argentine, 1922.

———. *Goneniia na anarkhizm v Sovetskoi Rossii* [Persecution of anarchism in Soviet Russia]. Berlin: Izd-vo Gruppy russkikh anarkhistov v Germanii, 1922. Brief accounts by various authors of Anarchist groups in Russia and Ukraine, their persecution by the Bolshevik regime in 1918–22, and biographical sketches of leading Anarchists and Makhno followers.

Gorev, B. I. [Goldman, B. I.]. "'Anarkhizm podpol'ia' i makhnovshchina" [The "anarchism of the underground" and the Makhno movement]. In *Anarkhizm v Rossii: Ot Bakunina do Makhno*, pp. 126–39. Moscow: Molodaia gvardiia, 1930. A one-sided survey of the Makhno movement, stressing its relations with the Bolsheviks and Anarchists; includes numerous quotations to prove the author's point. The work is based largely on Kubanin's *Makhnovshchina.*

Gorlov, V. P. *Geroicheskii pokhod: Voenno-istoricheskii ocherk o geroicheskom boevom puti Tamanskoi armii* [Heroic march: military-historical description about the heroic military way of the Taman army]. Moscow: Voen. izd-vo, 1967. The Red troops' campaign against Denikin in the Kuban and Caucasus from August 1918 to February 1919.

Gorodestkii, E. *Otechestvennaia voina protiv germanskikh okkupantov na Ukraine v 1918 g.* [Patriotic war against the German invaders in Ukraine in 1918]. Moscow, 1941.

Gospodyn, Andrii. "Z povstanchoi borot'by" [From the partisans' struggle]. *Ukrains'ka strilets'ka hromada v Kanadi 1928–1938*, pp. 146–47. Saskatoon: Nakl. Ukrains'koi strilets'koi hromady v Kanadi, 1938.

Grazhdanskaia voina, 1918–1921 [The Civil War, 1918–1921]. Edited by A. S. Bubnov, S. S. Kamenev, and R. P. Eideman. 3 vols. Moscow: "Voennyi vestnik," 1928–30. A valuable work by prominent Bolshevik military leaders, later purged; includes Bolshevik and German interventions in Ukraine and the Polish-Soviet war in 1920. Much space is devoted to organizational, strategic, political, and economic aspects of the Red Army, presenting views and data omitted from later Soviet accounts.

Guerin, Daniel. *Anarchism: From Theory to Practice.* Introduction by

Noam Chomsky. Translated by Mary Klopper. New York: Monthly Review Press, 1970. A summary of basic anarchist beliefs, taken mainly from Proudhon and Bakunin, and a survey of anarchist participation in the workers' movement from the First International to the Spanish Civil War, with some discussion of the Makhno movement.

Gukovskii, A. I. *Frantsuskaia interventsiia na iuge Rossii, 1918–1919 gg.* [The French intervention in the south of Russia, 1918–1919]. Moscow: Gos. izd-vo, 1928. A well-documented Soviet study of the French intervention in South Ukraine, the interrelation of French and anti-Bolshevik groups and Bolshevik underground activities in Odessa.

———. "Innostrannaia interventsiia na Ukraine v 1917–1919 godakh" [The foreign intervention in Ukraine]. IM 1 (71) (1939): 76–100.

Gusev, S. I. *Grazhdanskaia voina i Krasnaia Armiia: Sbornik statei* [The Civil War and the Red Army: collection of articles]. Moscow: Voen. izd-vo, 1958. A collection of articles written between 1918 and 1925 about the Civil War, with emphasis upon the organization and development of the Red Army and army politics.

Gutman, M. "Pod vlast'iu anarkhistov: Ekaterinoslav v 1919 godu" [Under the regime of the anarchists: Katerynoslav in 1919]. *Russkoe proshloe* (Petrograd), no. 5 (1923), pp. 61–68. The struggle between the Ukrainian troops, the Bolsheviks, Makhno, and Denikin for the control of Katerynoslav in 1919.

Halahan, Mykola. "Bohdanivs'kyi polk" [The Bohdan regiment]. LCK, no. 6 (1937), pp. 3–5.

Hermaize, O. *Narysy z istorii revoliutsiinoho rukhu na Ukraini* [Sketches from the history of the revolutionary movement in Ukraine]. 2 vols. Kiev, 1926. A well-documented, scholarly work, written from the Marxist point of view, dealing with the revolutionary movement in Ukraine at the turn of the twentieth century, stressing the socioeconomic aspects.

Hirniak, Nykofor. *Polk. Vasyl' Vyshyvanyi* [Colonel Vasyl' Vyshyvanyi]. Winnipeg: M. Mykytiuk, 1956. Biographical survey of Archduke W. F. Hapsburg-Lotharingen and his relations with Ukraine during World War I.

Hnoiovyi, Ivan. "Chy 'Bat'ko' Nestor Makhno—ukr. natsional'nyi heroi?" [Was "Father" Nestor Makhno a Ukrainian national hero?]. TR, no. 38 (1966), pp. 9–14. A sketchy, critical account about the Makhno movement based partly on the author's experience.

Holubnychyi, V. "Makhno i makhnivshchyna" [Makhno and the

Makhno movement]. *Entsyklopediia ukrainoznavstva: Slovnykova chastyna*, 4: 1493–94. Munich: "Molode zhyttia," 1962.

Hrushevs'kyi, Mykhailo. "V ohni i buri" [In the fire and storm]. LHKD 1936, pp. 78–80.

———. *Vybrani pratsi: Vydano z nahody 25-richchia z dnia ioho smerty 1934–1959* [Selected works: published on the occasion of the twenty-fifth anniversary of his death, 1934–1959]. New York: Nakl. Holovnoi upravy OURDP v SSh A, 1960. A selection of the author's political writings, mainly from the years 1917–1924, reflecting basic ideas and principles of Ukrainian internal and foreign policies.

Hurwicz, Elias. *Staatsmanner und Abenteurer: Russische Portraits von Witte bis Trotzki, 1891–1925*. Leipzig: C. L. Hirschfeld, 1925.

IAkovlev, E. *Kak i dlia chego organizuiutsia komitety nezamozhnikh selian, ikh prava i obiazannosti* [How and why the Committee of Peasants is organized, their rights and obligations]. Kharkov: IUridichesk. izd-vo Narkom'iusta USSR, 1925.

IAkovlev, IA. [Epstein]. "Makhnovshchina i anarkhizm: K itogam makhnovshchiny" [The Makhno movement and anarchism: about the results of the Makhno movement]. *Krasnaia nov* (Moscow), no. 2 (1921), pp. 243–57. A Communist's account of the collaboration between the "Nabat" Anarchists and Makhno and their struggle against the Bolsheviks and Denikin.

———. "Nasha politika na Ukraine i ukrainskii seredniak" [Our policy in Ukraine and the Ukrainian middle (peasant)]. *Ezhenedel'nik pravdy*, no. 12 (1919), pp. 13–19. The Bolshevik agricultural policy in Ukraine in 1920.

———. "Perspektivy krestian'skogo dvizheniia na denikinskoi Ukraine" [Perspectives of the peasant movement in Ukraine under the Denikin occupation]. *Ezhenedel'nik pravdy*, no. 11 (1919), pp. 16–18.

———. *Russkii anarkhizm v velikoi russkoi revoliutsii* [Russian anarchism in the great Russian Revolution]. Moscow: Gos. izd-vo, 1921. One-sided survey of Russian anarchism, including the Makhno movement, from spring 1918 through 1921.

IAkovliv, Andrii. "Beresteis'kii dohovir i sprava avtonomii Skhidnoi Halychyny: Uryvok spomyniv z r. 1918" [The Brest-Litovsk Treaty and the question of autonomy in East Galicia: excerpt from memoirs of 1918]. KD 1937, pp. 14–21.

IAkushkin, E. E. *Angliiskaia interventsiia v 1918–1920 gg.* [English intervention in 1918–1920]. Moscow: Gos. izd-vo, 1928.

———. *Frantsuzsakaia interventsiia na iuge, 1918–1919 gg.* [French intervention in the South, 1918–1919]. Moscow: Gos. izd-vo, 1929. A one-sided survey of the French intervention in South Ukraine.

IAroslavskii, Emelian. *History of Anarchism in Russia.* New York: International Publishers, 1937. A survey of anarchism in Russia, including the Makhno movement, written from the Bolshevik point of view.

IAvors'kyi, M. *Narysy z istorii revoliutsiinoi borot'by na Ukraini* [Sketches from the history of revolutionary struggle in Ukraine]. Kharkov: Derzh. Vyd-vo Ukrainy, 1927.

Ignat, S. *Pod prikrytiem "klassovosti"—Anarkho-sindikalistskii uklon v ukrains'kom komsomole, 1920–1921: Istoriia iunosheskogo dvizheniia* [Under the cover of "class character"—Anarcho-Syndicalist deviation in Ukrainian Komsomol, 1920–1921: a history of the youth movement]. Moscow: Izd-vo Molodaia gvardiia, 1931.

Ihnatov, N. "Chervonoarmiis'kyi zahin u borot'bi za khlib" [A Red Guard unit in the struggle for bread]. LR, nos. 1–2 (1933), pp. 175–87.

Istoriia grazhdanskoi voiny v SSSR [The history of the Civil War in SSSR]. 5 vols. Edited by M. Gorkii. Moscow, 1935–60. Official Bolshevik history of the Civil War.

Istoriia ukrains'koho viis'ka [The history of Ukrainian forces]. 2nd ed. Winnipeg: Kliub pryiateliv ukr. knyzkhy, 1953. A comprehensive collective history of the Ukrainian armed forces from their origins through 1952.

Ivanys, Vasyl'. *Symon Petliura–Prezydent Ukrainy, 1879–1926.* Toronto: Nakl. 5. stanytsi Suiuzu buvshykh ukr. voiakiv, 1952. A valuable biography of the president of the Ukrainian National Republic, set against the background of East European history from 1905 to 1925.

Jabłoński, Henryk. "Ministerium Spraw Polskich Ukrainskiej Republiki Ludowej, 1917–1918" [The Ministry of Polish Affairs in the Ukrainian People's Republic]. *Niepodleglość* (Warsaw) 20, no. 1 (1939): 65–88.

———. *Polska autonomia narodowa na Ukrainie, 1917–1918* [Polish national autonomy in Ukraine, 1917–1918]. Warsaw: Nakł. Towarzystwa Milosników Historii, 1948.

Joll, James. *The Anarchists.* Boston: Little, Brown, 1965. A survey of Anarchists and the development of anarchism's doctrine.

Jurylko, Stefan. "Niemcy na Ukraine" [The Germans in Ukraine].

Problemy Europy Wschodniej (Warsaw), no. 4 (1939).

Juzwenko, Adolf. *Polska a "Biala" Rosja od listopada 1918 do kwietnia 1920 r.* [Poland and "White" Russia from November 1918 to April 1920]. Wrocław: Zakł. Narodowy im. Ossolinskich, 1973.

"K istorii makhnovskogo dvizheniia v Rossii" [About the history of the Makhno movement in Russia]. VO, no. – (192–), pp. 15–17.

K., V. "Ukrains'ki povstans'ki otamany" [Ukrainian partisan otamans]. SV, October 2, 1934. A valuable characterization of a number of partisan leaders and their negative role during the Ukrainian Revolution.

"K voprosu ob anarkho-bol'shevizme i ego roli v revoliutsii" [The question about anarchism-bolshevism and its role in the Revolution]. AV, no. 1 (July 1923).

Kachyns'kyi, B. "Ahrarnyi rukh za chasiv het'manshchyny" [Agrarian movement during the hetman regime]. LR, no. 1 (28) (1928), pp. 52–64; no. 2 (29), pp. 76–95.

Kachyns'kyi, V. *Selianskii rukh na Ukraini v roky 1905–1907* [Peasant movement in Ukraine 1905–1907]. 2 vols. Kharkov, 1927. A well-documented work about the peasant uprisings and their socioeconomic and political causes.

Kagan, S. *Agrarnaia revoliutsiia na Kievshchine: K voprosu o sotsial'nykh i politicheskikh protsesakh na sele: Iz materialov obrannykh i izuchennykh gubernskim Komitetom KP(b)U na Kievshchine* [Agrarian revolution in Kiev province: on the question of social and political processes in the village: from materials collected and studied by the province committee of KP(b)U in Kiev province]. Kiev: Goz. izd-vo Ukrainy, 1923.

Kakurin, Nikolai. *Kak srazhalas revoliutsiia* [How the Revolution was fought]. 2 vols. Moscow, 1925–26. An account of the fighting during the Civil War and the Allies intervention, by a Bolshevik military expert.

Kamenets'kyi, Ihor. "Nimetska polityka suproty Ukrainy v 1918—mu rotsi ta ii istorychna geneza" [The German policy toward Ukraine in 1918 and the history of its genesis]. UI, nos. 1–4 (17–20) (1968), pp. 5–18; nos. 1–3 (21–23) (1969), pp. 74–85.

Kamins'kyi, "Borot'ba z kontrrevoliutsieiu v 1920 i 1921 rotsi Hub. Ch. K. na Chernyhivshchyni" [The struggle against counterrevolution in 1920–1921 Provincial Ch. K. in the Chernihiv province]. *Visty* (Kharkov), no. 298 (1927).

Kapustians'kyi, M. *Pokhid ukrains'kykh armii na Kyiv-Odesu v 1919 rotsi: Korotkyi voienno-istorychnyi ohliad* [The march of the Ukrainian armies on Kyiv and Odessa in 1919: a short military-historical survey]. 2 vols. Munich, 1946. The military campaign in Ukraine in 1919, including partisan activities and the mood of the populace, by a member of the General Staff of the Ukrainian Army.

———. "Slavetna diia pid Chornym Ostrovom: Spomyn." [Famous action at Chornyi Ostriv: memoirs]. In *Ukrains'ka strilets'ka hromada v Kanadi 1928–1938*, pp. 107–10. Saskatoon: Nakl. Ukrains'koi strilets'koi hromady v Kanadi, 1938.

Kapustians'kyi, Mykola. *Ukrains'ka zbroina syla i ukrains'ka natsional'na revoliutsiia* [Ukrainian armed forces and the Ukrainian national revolution]. Saskatoon: Novyi shliakh, 1936.

Kapustyns'kyi [sic], Mykola. "Makhno i makhnovshchyna" [Makhno and the Makhno movement]. SV, no. 243 (November 17, 1934). A critical description of the Makhno movement and a characterization of Makhno's personality.

Karelin, A. *Gosudarstvo i anarkhisty* [The state and the Anarchists]. Moscow: Izd-vo L. Fedorova, 1918.

———. *Vol'naia zhizn'* [Free life]. Detroit: Profsoiuz g. Detroita, 1955.

Karmazin, A. "Makhno i ego strategiia" [Makhno and his strategy]. NRS, January 23, 1969.

———. "O Makhno" [About Makhno]. NRS, February 16, 1969.

Karpenko, H. "Selians'ki rukhy na Kyivshchyni za chasiv het'manshchyny" [The peasant movement in Kyiv province during the hetman regime]. LR, no. 3 (30) (1928), pp. 55–73.

———. "Selians'kyi rukh na Kyivshchyni za chasiv austro-hermans'koi okupatsii ta het'manshchyny" [The peasant movement in Kyiv province during the Austro-German occupation and the hetman regime]. LR, nos. 1–2 (46–47) (1931), pp. 67–91. The Central Rada's agricultural policy in 1918, and the beginning of peasant uprisings against the Germans and the hetman regime.

Karpenko, O. IU. *Imperialistychna interventsiia na Ukraini, 1918–1920* [Imperialistic intervention in Ukraine, 1918–1920]. Lvov: Vyd-vo L'vivs'koho univ-tu, 1964. A one-sided, well-documented analysis dealing with the intervention of the Central Powers, the Entente, and Poland in Ukraine.

Kartashev, Ivan. "Pesnia makhnovtsev" [A song of Makhnomen]. PRO, nos. 56–57 (1935), p. 32.

Kenz, Peter. "A. I. Denikin." *The Russian Review* 3, no. 2 (1973): 139–52.

Kessel, J. "Buccaneers of the Steppes." *The Living Age*, vol. 315 (December 9, 1922).

———. "Deux grands aventuriers russes: L'Ataman Semenof, 'Batka' Makhno." *La Revue de France* 5 (1922): 340–56.

Khrystiuk, Pavlo. *1905 rik na Ukraini* [Ukraine in 1905]. Kharkov, 1925.

———. "Provyna pered ukrains'koiu revoliutsiieiu" [The issue of guilt and the Ukrainian Revolution]. *Boritesia-Poborete* (Vienna), no. 5 (1920), pp. 36–66.

———. *Zamitky i materiialy do istorii ukrains'koi revoliutsii, 1917–1920 rr.* [Notes and materials for the history of the Ukrainian Revolution, 1917–1920]. 4 vols. in 1. New York: Vyd-vo Chartoryis'kykh, 1969. An authoritative history of the Ukrainian Revolution based on documents and the author's experiences as state secretary and secretary of internal affairs. It contains numerous documentary materials integrated into the text.

Khudolei, V. " 'Istoriia makhnovskogo dvizheniia' P. Arshinova" ["The history of the Makhno movement" by P. Arshinov]. VO, no. 51 (1924), pp. 15–20.

Kin, D. [Plotkin, David]. *Denikinshchina* [The Denikin movement]. Leningrad: Izd-vo "Priboi," 1927. A well-documented work that includes the Allied intervention in South Ukraine, and the Makhno movement, from spring 1918 to April 1920.

———. "Povstancheskoe dvizhenie protiv denikinshchiny na Ukraine: Prichiny i tipy dvizheniia" [The partisan movement against the Denikin movement in Ukraine: causes and types]. LR, nos. 3–4 (18–19) (1926), pp. 70–90.

Klassen, N. "Makhno und Lenin." *Der Bote* (Saskatoon, Canada), March 1, 1966.

Klepikov, S. "Neurozhai 1921 g." [Bad harvest in 1921]. *Krasnaia nov'* (Moscow), no. 2 (1921), pp. 223–36.

Kohan, S., and N. Mezhberh. "Druhyi period Radvlady na Odeshchyni" [The second period of the Soviet regime in the Odessa region]. LR, no. 1 (40) (1930), pp. 5–40.

Kokh, H. *Dohovir z Denikinom vid 1 do 17 lystopada, 1919 r.* [Agreement with Denikin from November 1 to 17, 1919]. Lvov: "Chervona Kalyna," 1930. A justification of the Galician Army's agreement with Denikin in November 1919, employing the military and political conditions in Ukraine during the second half of 1919 and the physical condition of the Army.

Komin, V. V. *Anarkhizm v Rossii: Spets. kurs lektsii, prochit. na ist. fak. ped. in-ta.* [Anarchism in Russia: special course of lectures read in the Department of History of the Pedagogical Institute]. Kalinin, 1969. A well-documented, one-sided survey of Russian anarchism, including the Makhno movement.

Kononenko, Konstantyn. *Ukraine and Russia: A History of the Economic Relations between Ukraine and Russia, 1654–1917.* Milwaukee: Marquette University Press, 1958. The development of commerce, agriculture, and industry in Ukraine and Russian economic policies toward Ukraine; emphasis is on the nineteenth century.

———. *Ukraina i Rosiia: Sotsiial'no-ekonomichni pidstavy ukrains'koi natsional'noi idei, 1917–1960* [Ukraine and Russia: socioeconomic bases of the Ukrainian national idea]. Munich, 1965.

Korn, M. [Goldschmidt, M.]. *Revoliutsionnyi sindikalizm: Bor'ba s kapitalizmom i vlastiu* [Revolutionary syndicalism: the struggle against capitalism and authority]. Petrograd: "Golos truda," 1920.

Kornilovskii udarnyi polk [Kornilov's assault regiment]. Paris, 1936. Articles based on documents and material from the archives of the General Kornilov Regiment as well as memoirs and diaries of its officers, describing the activities and campaigns of the General Kornilov Regiment from the middle of 1917 to November 1920, mostly against the Bolsheviks.

Korolivs'kyi, S. M., and M. A. Rubach. *Peremola Velykoi Zhovtnevoi sotsialistychnoi revoliutsii na Ukraini* [The victory of the great October socialist revolution in Ukraine]. 2 vols. Kiev: "Naukova dumka," 1967.

Korotkov, I. S. *Razgrom Vrangelia* [Wrangel's defeat]. Moscow: Voen. izd-vo, 1955. A study based largely on archival material dealing with the Bolshevik campaigns against Wrangel during the second half of 1920.

Korsak, V. "U bielykh" [With the Whites]. *Golos minuvshago na chuzhoi storonie* (Berlin) 15, no. 2 (1926): 195–243.

Kovalenko, A. "Grigor'evshchina" [The Hryhor'iv movement]. *Odesskii Nabat*, no. 4 (May 26, 1919), pp. 1–2. A denunciation of Hryhor'iv's activities.

———. "Povest s pechal'nym kontsom: Eshcho o Makhno" [A story about a sad end: more about Makhno]. *Odesskii Nabat*, no. 7 (June 16, 1919), pp. 2–3.

Kovalevs'kyi, Mykola. *Opozytsiini rukhy v Ukraini i natsional'na polityka SSSR, 1920–1954* [Oppositional movements in Ukraine and the national policy of SSSR]. Munich, 1955. Bolshevik oppression in Ukraine and resultant insurrections.

Koval'-Medzviedska, K. "Kyivs'ki perezhyvannia v 1919 r." [The Kyivan experience in 1919]. *Za Derzhavnist'* (Warsaw) 8 (1938): 142–51.

Kozel'skyi, V. V. "Hryhor'ievshchyna: Z nahody shostykh rokovyn likvidatsii Hryhor'ievshchyny" [The Hryhor'iv movement: on the occasion of the sixth anniversary of the liquidation of the Hryhor'iv movement]. *Chervonyi shliakh* (Kharkov), no. 5 (1925), pp. 67–71. A subjective account of the uprising of Otaman Hryhor'iv against the Bolsheviks in May 1919, which is shown as thwarting Bolshevik plans for sending military aid to Soviet Hungary.

Kozlov, E. "Krovavoe podpol'e: K 5-i godovshchine osvobozhdeniia Khar'kova ot belykh" [A bloody underground: on the 5th anniversary of Kharkiv liberation from the Whites]. LR, no. 4 (9) (1924), pp. 44–52.

Kratkaia zapiska istorii vzaimootnoshenii Dobrovol'cheskoi Armii s Ukrainoi [A short note on the history of relations between the Volunteer Army and Ukraine]. Rostov-on-Don: Tip. Donskogo akts. o-va pech. i Izd-vo Diela, 1919. A survey of the Volunteer Army's relations with the hetman government.

Krezub, Antin. "Partyzans'kyi zahin imeny otamana Zelenoho" [A partisan detachment in the name of Otaman Zelenyi]. KCK 1924, pp. 110–16.

———. "Persha umova Dyrektorii UNR z Nimtsiamy z dnia 17. XI. 1918 r." [The first agreement of the Directory of UNR with the Germans on November 17, 1918]. LNV 99, no. 5 (1929): 458–64.

———. "Povstannia proty het'mana Skoropads'koho i Sichovi Stril'tsi: Kil'ka zavvah do ioho istorii" [Uprising against Hetman Skoropads'kyi and the Sich Riflemen: a few observations on its history]. LNV 11 (1928): 219–25; 12:309–18.

———. "Povstannia Zelenoho proty Dyrektorii v sichni 1919 r." [Uprising of Zelenyi against the Directory in January 1919]. LNV 5 (1927): 26–41.

———. "Tsily nimets'koi viis'kovoi polityky na Ukraini 1918 r." [The aims of the German military policy in Ukraine in 1918]. LCK, no. 1 (1929), pp. 14–17; no. 2, pp. 4–8.

Krut', V. T. "Do istorii borot'by proty hryhor'ivshchyny na Ukraini" [The history of the struggle against the Hryhor'iv movement in Ukraine]. LR, nos. 5–6 (54–55) (1932), pp. 119–47. A subjective account of Hryhor'iv uprising against the Bolsheviks in May 1919, set against the background of the contemporary conditions in

Ukraine.

Kubanin, M. "K istorii kulatskoi kontr-revoliutsii" [History of the "kulak" counterrevolution]. *Na agrarnom fronte* (Moscow), nos. 7–8 (1925), pp. 98–129; no. 9, pp. 83–96.

———. *Makhnovshchina: Krest'ianskoe dvizhenie v stepnoi Ukraine v gode grazhdanskoi voiny* [The Makhno movement: the peasant movement in the steppes of Ukraine during the civil war]. Leningrad: Izd-vo "Priboi," 1927. A well-documented, subjective work on the Makhno movement and Soviet Russian agrarian and national policy in Ukraine during the Revolution. The work was written upon the recommendation of the Party to elicit an anti-Makhno reaction.

Kucher, Mykhailo. "Manifest Otamana Hryhor'iva" [Manifesto of Otaman Hryhor'iv]. TR, no. 27 (1964), pp. 10–13. An account of the Hryhor'iv manifesto that initiated the uprisings against the Bolsheviks in May 1919 and the conditions that brought about the uprising.

Kukiel, Marjan. *Zarys historii wojskowosci w Polsce* [Outline of the military history of Poland]. 5th ed. London: Nakł. Orbisu, 1949.

Kulish, G. *Bor'ba Kommunisticheskoi partii za reshenie natsional'nogo voprosa v 1918–1920 godakh* [The struggle of the Communist Party for determination of the national question in 1918–1920]. Kharkov: Izd-vo Khar'kovskogo un-ta, 1963. A one-sided analysis of the role of the Bolsheviks—and their subversive activities—in establishing Russian regimes in Ukraine and Belorussia.

———. "Pervyi dessant na beregakh Kryma, 1920" [The first disembarkation on the shores of Crimea, 1920]. LR, no. 4 (1923), pp. 131–52.

Kulychenko, M. I. *Bolsheviki khar'kivshchiny v bor'be za vlast' sovetov, 1918–1920 gg.* [The Bolsheviks of Kharkiv province in struggle for power of the soviets]. Kharkov: Izd-vo Kharkovskogo un-ta, 1966. A survey of the development and struggle for power of Bolshevik organizations in Kharkiv province.

Kulyk, I. "Ekonomichni chynnyky frantsuzs'koi interventsii" [Economic factors of the French intervention]. *Chervonyi shliakh* (Kharkov), no. 3 (1923), pp. 122–28.

Kupchyns'kyi, Roman. *Persha ukrains'ka selians'ka armiia im. Bat'ka Makhna* [The first Ukrainian partisan army of Father Makhno]. N.p., n.d.

Kurash, P. S. "Povstannia sela Parafiievky na Chernyhivshchyni" [Uprising of the village Parafiivka in the Chernihiv region]. LR, no. 3 (30) (1928), pp. 174–90.

Kurgan, R. *Stranitsa grazhdanskoi voiny* [A page from the Civil War]. Kharkov: Gos. izd-vo Ukrainy, 1959.

Kurmanovych, Viktor. "Do spravy vidvorotu U.H.A. za Zbruch" [Concerning the retreat of U.H.A. across the Zbruch]. RN, nos. 3–4 (74–75) (1934), pp. 82–86. The Ukrainian-Polish campaign in East Galicia in the summer of 1919 and plans for the defensive retreat of the Ukrainian Galician Army either southward beyond the Dniester into the Carpathian Mountains or eastward beyond the River Zbruch.

Kuryllo, Stefan. "Niemcy na Ukrainie" [The Germans in Ukraine]. *Problemy Europy Wschodniej* (Warsaw) 1, no. 4 (1939): 224–34.

Kushchyns'kyi, Ant. "Korotka geneza istorii Serdiuts'kykh formatsii" [A brief historical genesis of the Serdiuk formations]. *Visti* (Munich), no. 106 (1961), pp. 69–70.

Kushnir, M. *Zemel'na sprava na Ukraini* [The land question in Ukraine]. Kiev: Vyd-vo Ts. K. U. P. S. F., 1917. A valuable brief account of the land question in Ukraine on the eve of the Revolution.

Kutrzeba, Tadeusz. *Wyprawa kijowska 1920 roku* [Kyiv campaign in 1920]. Warsaw: Nakl. Gebethnera i Wolffa, 1937. An objective, scholarly work by a Polish general and historian on the Polish-Ukrainian alliance of 1920 and their common struggle against the Bolsheviks.

Kuzelia, Zenon. *Rik 1918 na Ukraini* [The year 1918 in Ukraine]. Salzwedel: Souiz vyzvolennia Ukrainy, 1918.

Kuz'min, G. V. *Grazhdanskaia voina i voennaia interventsiia v SSSR: Voenno-politicheskii ocherk* [The Civil War and the military intervention in SSSR: military-political sketch]. Moscow: Voen. izd-vo, 1958.

Kuz'min, N. F. "K istorii razgroma belogvardeiskikh voisk Denikina" [History of the defeat of the White Guard forces of Denikin]. VI, no. 7 (1956), pp. 18–32.

———. *Kommunisticheskaia partiia-organizator razgroma belogvardeiskikh voisk Denikina* [The Communist Party—organizer of the defeat of the White forces of Denikin]. Moscow: Znanie, 1956.

———. *Krushenie poslednego pokhoda Antanty* [The defeat of the last expedition of the Entente]. Moscow: Gos. izd-vo polit. lit-ry, 1958.

Kuznetsov, IA. "Rabota Ekaterinoslavskogo gubkoma v 1918 g." [Activity of the Katerynoslav gubkom in 1918]. In *Bor'ba za Sovety na Ekaterinoslavshchine*. Dnepropetrovsk, 1927.

Kuznetsova, N. V. "Bor'ba frantsuzskogo naroda protiv otkrytoi antisovetskoi interventsii antanty vesnoi 1919 goda" [The struggle of the French people against an open anti-Soviet intervention of the Entente in spring 1919]. VI, no. 11 (1957), pp. 109–26.

Kviring, E. "Ekaterinoslav, dekabr' 14 g.–iiun' 15 g." [Katerynoslav, December 1914–June 1915]. LR, no. 2 (1923), pp. 125–35.

———. "Nekotoree popravki k vospominaniiam o Ekaterinoslave" [Some corrections concerning recollections about Katerynoslav]. LR, no. 2 (1928), pp. 136–43.

Lampe, A. A. *Puti vernykh: Sbornik statei* [The ways of the faithful: a collection of articles]. Paris, 1960. A Russian general discusses his anti-Bolshevik activities during the Civil War and later abroad.

Lazors'kyi, V. "Z povstants'koho rukhu na Poltavshchyni 1918 roku" [From the partisan movement in the Poltava region in 1918]. LR, no. 2 (1930), pp. 211–25.

Lebed', D. *Itogi i uroki trekh let anarkho-makhnovshchiny* [Results and lessons of three years of the Anarcho-Makhno movement]. Kharkov: Vseukr. gos. izd-vo, 1921. A survey of the Makhno movement, viewing it as peasant banditry brought about by socioeconomic circumstances, and the struggle of the Russian Communists against it. Numerous quotations included to prove the author's point.

Legler. "Bela Kun—Makhno." *Vechornaia Moskva*, June 1928.

———. "Makhno i Bela Kun." *Posliedniia novosti* (Paris), July 1928.

Lehovich, Dymitry V. "Denikin's Offensive." *The Russian Review* 32, no. 2 (1973): 173–86.

———. *White against Red: The Life of General Anton Denikin*. New York: Norton, 1974. Biography of Denikin and his associates, based mainly on the Denikin family's documents and the author's reminiscences.

Lenin, V. I. *Lenin i natsional'nii vopros* [Lenin and the national question]. Kharkov: Izd-vo "Put' prosveshchennia," 1924.

———. *Sochineniia* [Works]. 2nd ed. 30 vols. Moscow, 1926–32. 3rd ed. Moscow: Partizdat, 1935–37. 4th ed. 35 vols. Moscow: Gos. izd-vo polit. lit-ry, 1941–52. (Preference given to second edition when available.)

———. *Stat'i i rechi ob Ukraine: Sbornik* [Articles and speeches about Ukraine: collection]. Edited by N. N. Popov. Kiev: Partizdat TSK KP(b)N, 1936. Selections from Lenin's articles and speeches dealing with the Ukrainian problem.

Lepeshkin, A. I. *Sovety—vlast' trudiashchykhsia, 1917–1936* [Soviets—authority of workers]. Moscow, 1966.

Levyns'kyi, V. *Sotsialistychna revoliutsiia i Ukraina* [Socialist revolution in Ukraine]. Edited by Orhan Zakordon. Vienna: Komitetu Ukr. kom. partii, 1920.

Ligocki, Edward. *Dialog z przeszlością* [Dialogue with the past]. Warsaw: Czytelnik, 1970.

Likharevskii. "Andreevski konfuz: Boi s Makhno 14, XII, 1920, v Andreevke" [Embarrassment at Andriivka: fighting against Makhno, December 14, 1920, in Andriivka]. AR, nos. 4–5 (1921), pp. 114–20. Defeat of the Red troops by Makhno at Andriivka, near Mariupil' in mid-December, 1920.

Linster, B. "Iz istorii revoliutsionnogo dvizhenniia v Elisavetgrade" [From the history of the revolutionary movement in IElesavethrad]. LR, no. 5 (1928), pp. 100–115.

Lipatov, N. P. "Nekotorie voprosy istorii razgroma vrangelevshchiny" [Some questions of the history of defeat of the Wrangel movement]. VI, no. 12 (1957), pp. 35–48.

———. *1920 god na Chernom more: Voenno-morskie sily v razgrome Vrangelia* [The year 1920 at the Black Sea: military-naval power in defeating Wrangel]. Moscow: Voen. izd-vo, 1958.

Lipotkin, L. "Nestor Makhno." PRO, nos. 50–51 (1934), pp. 15–16. A general account of Makhno's life and activities.

———. "Nestor Makhno i evreiskii vopros" [Nestor Makhno and the Jewish question]. DT-P, no. 58 (1959), pp. 17–19.

———. "Vsevelod Eikhenbaum (Volin)." DT-P, no. 17 (1946), pp. 18–19.

Lohrenz, Gerhard. "Nonresistance Tested." *Mennonite Life* (Newton, Kansas) 17, no. 2 (1962): 66–68.

Lozyns'kyi, Mykhalio. *Halychyna v rr. 1918–1920* [Galicia in the years 1918–1920]. New York: "Chervona Kalyna," 1970. An authoritative political history based on documents and reminiscences; contains numerous documents integrated into the text.

Lukomskaia, I. "Proletariat Donbasa i realizatsiia stalinskogo plana razgroma Denikina" [Proletarians of the Donbas and the realization of Stalin's plan for Denikin's defeat]. IM 1 (77) (1940): 98–119.

L'vov, N. "Bieloe dvizhenie: K 20-tilietiiu ego zarozhdeniia" [The White movement: 20th anniversary of its origin]. FA, no. 37 (1937), pp. 5–11. A general survey of the fall of the Russian monarchy and the establishment of the "White" movement in the Don and in Siberia in the fall of 1917.

Lykholat, A. V. *Razgrom natsionalisticheskoi kontrrevoliutsii na Ukraine, 1917–1922 gg.* [The destruction of the nationalistic counterrevolution in Ukraine, 1917–1922]. Moscow: Gos. izd-vo polit. lit-ry, 1954. An official Stalinist interpretation of the Ukrainian Revolution in which Stalin is credited with various accomplishments.

———. *Zdiisnennia lenins'koi natsional'noi polityky na Ukraini, 1917–1920* [Realization of Lenin's national policy in Ukraine, 1917–1920]. Kiev: Naukova dumka, 1967. A one-sided survey dealing with Lenin's nationality policy and its application in Ukraine by the Russian Communist party.

M., I. "Godovshchina *Delo truda*" [Anniversary of *Delo Truda*]. DT, nos. 13–14 (1926), pp. 23–24.

M., S. "Makhnovshchina" [The Makhno movement]. *Revoliutsionnaia Rossiia* (Dorpat), no. 7 (192–), pp. 23–25.

Maistrenko, I. "Ukrains'ka chervona armiia: Sproby ukrains'kykh komunistiv tvoryty vlasnu armii" [The Ukrainian Red Army: attempts of the Ukrainian Communists to create their own army]. *Visti* (New York) 4, nos. 1–2 (27–28) (1953): 10–11. Attempt by the Borot'bists to organize a Ukrainian Red Army using the partisans of Otaman Hryhor'iv as the nucleus.

Majstrenko, Iwan. *Borot'bism: A Chapter in the History of Ukrainian Communism*. New York: Research Program on the U.S.S.R., 1954. A well-documented, objective study dealing with the activities of the Borot'bists, a Ukrainian leftist group, during the Revolution, stressing biographical sketches of the members.

Makeev, P. V. *Na Denikina: Rol latyshskikh strelkov v razgrome denikinskikh polchishch* [On Denikin: the role of the Latvian riflemen in the defeat of Denikin's hordes]. Riga: Latviiskse gos. izd-vo, 1960. Bolshevik campaign against Denikin, with the emphasis on the Latvian units in the Red Army.

"Makhno i Bol'sheviki" [Makhno and the Bolsheviks]. *Nabat* (Huliai-Pole), no. 21 (1919).

"Makhno i tekushchie sobytiia" [Makhno and current events]. *Nabat* (Huliai-Pole), June 2, 1919. The Makhno-Hryhor'iv relationship.

Makhno, Nestor. "Anarkhisty i zashchita revoliutsii: Nasha pozitsiia" [Anarchists and the defense of the Revolution: our position]. *Nabat* (Kharkov), no. 21 (June 30, 1919), pp. 1–2.

———. "Anarkhizm i nashe vremia" [Anarchism and our time]. DT, no. 4 (1925), pp. 7–8.

———. "Ideia ravenstva i bol'sheviki" [The idea of equality and the Bolsheviks]. DT, no. 9 (1926), pp. 9–10.

———. "K evreiam vsekh stran" [To the Jews in all countries]. DT, nos. 23–24 (1927), pp. 8–10. The author's rebuttal of his enemies' accusation of anti-Jewish pogroms during the Revolution.

———. "K voprosu o zashchite revoliutsii" [The question of defense of the Revolution]. DT, no. 25 (1927), pp. 13–14. An account of organization of the partisan army and its struggle against its enemies in defense of the social achievements of the Revolution.

———. "Kak lgut' bol'sheviki: Pravada ob anarkhiste Zhelezniakove" [How the Bolsheviks are lying: the truth about the anarchist Zhelezniak]. DT, no. 22 (1927), p. 12.

———. "Krest'ianstvo i bolsheviki" [The peasantry and the Bolsheviks]. DT, nos. 33–34 (1928), pp. 7–9.

———. "Makhnovshchina i antisemitizm" [The Makhno movement and anti-Semitism]. DT, nos. 30–31 (1927), pp. 15–18. The attitude of the Makhno movement toward Jews, stressing the large number of Jews participating in the movement.

———. *Makhnovshchina i ee vchorashnie soiuzniki—bol'sheviki: Otvet na knigu M. Kubanina "Makhnovshchina"* [The Makhno movement and its yesterday's allies—Bolsheviks: answer to Kubanin's book "Makhno movement"]. Paris: Izd-vo "Biblioteki makhnovtsev," 1928.

———. "Mirovaia politika Anglii i mirovye zadachi revoliutsionnego truda" [England's world policy and the world aims of the revolutionary workers]. DT, nos. 26–27 (1927), pp. 10–12. Britain's conflict with Germany, her colonial policy, and the opposition of the working classes to that policy.

———. "Na putiakh proletarskoi vlasti: Ocherk" [On the road to proletarian power: a sketch]. PRO, no. – (19–), pp. 45–48.

———. "Nad svezhoi mogiloi T. N. Rogdaeva" [At the fresh grave of T. N. Rogdaev]. PRO, nos. 52–53 (1934), pp. 21–31.

———. "Neskol'ko slov o natsional'nom voprose na Ukraine" [A few words about the national question in Ukraine]. DT, no. 19 (1926), pp. 4–7.

———. "O revoliutsionnoi distsipline" [About the revolutionary discipline]. DT, nos. 7–8 (1925–26), p. 6. Criticism of the Russian anarchists for lack of organization, resulting in their defeat by the Bolsheviks during the Revolution.

———. "O XIII-m s'ezde Federatsii argentinskogo 'Golosa truda'" [About the 13th congress of the Argentinian "Voice of Labor"]. DT, nos. 48–49 (1929), pp. 7–8.

———. "1-oe maia—symvol novoi ery v zhizni i bor'by trudiashchikhsia" [May 1—a symbol of a new era in the life and struggle of toilers]. DT, no. 36 (1928), pp. 2–3.

———. "Otkrytoe pis'mo t-shchu Maksymovu" [An open letter to friend Maksymov]. DT, no. 15 (1926), pp. 10–12. The author's negotiations and agreement with the Bolsheviks in October 1920 to fight General Wrangel.

———. "Otvet na otkrytoe pis'mo t. Angartsa" [An open letter to friend Angarts]. *Guliaipol'skii Nabat*, no. 5 (February 22, 1919), p. 4. Makhno's assurance to Angarts that in the region of the movement there is no manifestation of anti-Semitism.

———. "Pamiati kronshtadskogo vosstanniia" [In commemoration of the Kronstadt uprising]. DT, no. 10 (1926), pp. 3–4. Glorification of the Kronstadt uprising against the Bolshevik regime in March 1921.

———. *Po povodu "raz'iasneniia" Volina* [In connection with Volin's "explanations"]. Paris, 1929.

———. "Po povodu sobytii v muzee imeni P. A. Kropotkina" [On the occasion of events at the museum in the name of A. Kropotkin]. DT, nos. 46–47 (1929), pp. 20–21.

———. "Polozhenie revoliutsionnoi Rossii" [The position of revolutionary Russia]. PS, no. 1 (1919), pp. 1–2.

———. "Put' bor'by protiv gosudarstva" [A road of struggle against the state]. DT, no. 17 (1926), pp. 5–6.

———. "Rossiia." DT, no. 12 (1926), pp. 14–15. Description of the persecution of anarchists in the Soviet Union by the Bolshevik regime.

———. "Sovetskaia vlast', ee nastoiashchee i budushchee" [The Soviet regime, its present and future]. *Bor'ba*, nos. 19–20 (19–), pp. 2–3.

———. "Velikii Oktiabr' na Ukraine" [The great October in Ukraine]. DT, no. 29 (1927), pp. 9–11. An account describing the socioeconomic changes in the Makhno movement area prior to the October Revolution of 1917.

Maksimov, G. "Nestor Makhno i pogromy" [Nestor Makhno and the pogroms]. DT, no. 84 (1935), pp. 13–14.

———. "Otvet Klevetnikam: O N. Makhno i makhnovshchine" [An answer to the cheaters: about N. Makhno and the Makhno movement]. DT-P, no. 51 (1946), pp. 23–28.

———. "Vsevolod Mikhailovich Eikhenbaum (Volin)." DT-P, no. 16 (1946), pp. 13–19.

———. *Za chto i kak bol'sheviki izgnali anarkhistov iz Rossi?: K osveshcheniiu polozheniia anarkhistov v Rossii* [Why and how did the Bolsheviks banish the Anarchists from Russia?: towards an interpretation of the anarchists' position in Russia]. Berlin(?):

Izd. Anarkho-kommun. gruppy, 1922.

Makushenko, N. "Operatsii protiv band Makhno s 9 po 16 iiunia 1921 g." [Operations against the bands of Makhno June 9–16, 1921]. AR, nos. 3–4 (1922).

Malinovskii, P. "I Konnaia v Severnoi Tavrii" [1st Cavalry in North Tavriia]. *Voennyi vestnik* (Moscow), no. 44 (1924), pp. 15–19.

Malishev, V. I. "Pro dopomohu RRFSR u stvoreni zbroinykh syl Radians'koi Ukrainy v 1918 r." [Concerning the assistance of RRFSR in the organization of the armed forces of Soviet Ukraine in 1918]. *Ukrains'kyi istorychnyi zhurnal* (Kiev), no. 5 (1964), pp. 105–7.

Mal't, M. "Denikinshchina i krest'ianstvo" [The Denikin movement and the peasantry]. PR, no. 1 (24) (1924): 140–57. Denikin's agricultural policy and the resulting peasant uprisings against the Volunteer Army.

Manilov, V., ed. *1917 god na Kievshchine* [The year 1917 in Kiev province]. Kiev: Gos. izd-vo Ukrainy, 1928. Revolutionary developments in Kyiv province in 1917, based on archival materials.

Manuilsky, A. "The Agrarian Policy in Ukraine." *Soviet Russia* 3, no. 16 (1920), pp. 369–71.

Margushin, P. "Bat'ko Makhno" [Father Makhno]. NRS, October 13, 1964, p. 2. A survey of the Makhno movement from summer 1918 to the end of the movement.

Markow, Sergey. *Armee ohne Heimat*. Leipzig: R. A. Höger, 1935.

Martenko, Ihor R. "Denikin and Ukraine." *Ukrains'ka tribuna* (Munich), August 24, 1947, p. 3.

Martos, Borys. "Zavoiuvannia Ukrainy bol'shevykamy" [Conquest of Ukraine by the Bolsheviks]. *Ukrains'kyi zbirnyk* (Munich) 1(December 1954): 3–38.

Marushchenko–Bohdanivs'kyi, A. "Ukrainizatsiia chastyn v rosiis'kii armii" [Ukrainization of detachments in the Russian Army]. IKCK 1934, pp. 1930–34.

Mazepa, I. *Bol'shevyzm i okupatsiia Ukrainy: Sotsiial'no-ekonomichni prychyny nedozrilosty syl ukrains'koi revoliutsii* [Bolshevism and the occupation of Ukraine: socioeconomic reasons for immature strength of the Ukrainian Revolution]. Lvov: M. Hankevych, 1922.

———. "Ukrainia under Bolshevist Rule." *Slavonic and East European Review* 12 (1934): 323–46.

———. "Zymovyi pokhid i partyzans'kyi rukh na Ukraini v 1919 r." [The winter campaign and the partisan movement in Ukraine in 1919]. KD 1935, pp. 89–96. An authoritative account of the winter campaign, 1919–20, of the Ukrainian Army and the activities of the partisans, including those led by Makhno and Hryhor'iv, against the Bolshevik and anti-Bolshevik Russian forces, set against the background of sociopolitical and military conditions in Ukraine.

Mazlakh, Serhii, and Vasyl' Shakhrai. *Do khvyli: Shcho diietsia na Ukraini i z Ukrainoiu* [To the moment: what is happening in Ukraine and with Ukraine]. New York: Proloh, 1967.

Men'chukov, E. A. *Istoricheskii ocherk boev v usloviiakh okruzhenii* [Historical sketch of battles while surrounded]. Moscow: Gos. izd-vo, 1930. A well-documented work about twenty selected military operations involving encirclement, mostly battles of World War I and the Civil War; it includes accounts of the fighting against Makhno.

The Mennonite Encyclopedia: A Comprehensive Reference Work on the Anabaptist-Mennonite Movement. 4 vols. Hillsboro, Kansas: Mennonite Brethren Publishing House, 1955–59.

Meyer, Henry Cord. "Rohrbach and His Osteuropa." *The Russian Review* 2 (1942): 60–69.

"Miatezh Griogor'ieva" [The revolt of Hryhor'iv]. In *Piataia godovshchina Oktiabr'skoi revoliutsii,* pp. 199–206. Ekaterinoslav, 1922.

Mirchuk, Petro. *Mykola Mikhovs'kyi: Apostol ukrains'koi derzhavnosty* [Mykola Mikhnovs'kyi: apostle of Ukrainian statehood]. Philadelphia: T-vo ukr. studiiuiuchoi molodi im. M. Mikhovs'koho, 1960. A biography of a proponent of Ukrainian statehood, set against the background of political conditions in Ukraine prior to and during the Revolution.

Morei de Moran, I. L. "Partyzans'kyi otriad 30 kvitnia" [Partisan detachment of April 30]. In *Ukrains'ka strilets'ka hromada v Kanadi 1928–1938,* pp. 117–20. Saskatoon: Nakl. Ukrains'koi strilets'koi hromady v Kanadi, 1938.

Moskalenko, Andrew. "The Hetmanate in 1918 and Bolshevik Aggression in Ukraine." *Ukrainian Review* (London) 11, no. 2 (195?): 81–84.

Mrachnyi, M. "Makhnovshchina: V poiskakh 'bat'kivshchiny' " [The Makhno movement: in search of the fatherland]. *Rabochii put'* (Berlin), no. 5 (1923), pp. 1–3.

M-t, P. "Ukrains'ka viis'kova deliegatsiia u Vrangelia, 10, 9, 1920" [Ukrainian military delegation with Wrangel on September 10, 1920]. LCK, nos. 7–8 (1933), pp. 5–7.

Muromets, "Nestor Makhno," PRO, nos. 52–53 (1934), pp. 16–19. Makhno's anarchism and his struggle against both Denikin and the

Bolsheviks.
Myhal', B. K. "Konfiskatsiia zemel'nykh lyshkiv u kurkul's'kykh hospodarstvakh na Ukraini v 1920–1923 rr." [Confiscation of land remnants of the 'kurkuls' farms in Ukraine, 1920–1923]. *Pytannia istorii narodiv SRSR* (Kharkov) 6 (1969): 109–19.
"N. I. Makhno: Nekrolog" [N. I. Makhno: necrology]. *Seiatel'* (Buenos Aires), no. 6 (August 1934), p. 20.
"Na Ukraine: I-yi S'ezd Konfederatsii anarkhicheskikh organizatsii Ukrainy 'Nabat' (Rezoliutsiia)" [In Ukraine: the first congress of the confederations of Anarchist organizations of Ukraine 'Nabat' (resolution)]. *Trud i volia* (Moscow), no. 6 (May 20, 1919), p. 3.
Nahornyi, I. "Do desiatyrichchia zvil'nennia Donbasu vid denikinshchyny" [To the 10th anniversary of the liberation of the Donbas from the Denikin movement]. LR, no. 1 (40) (1930), pp. 194–97.
Naida, S. F., and D. A. Kovalenko, eds. *Reshaiushchie pobedy sovetskago naroda nad interventamy i belogvardeitsiami v 1919 g.: Sbornik statei* [Decisive victories of the Soviet people over the invaders and the Red Guards in 1919: collections of articles]. Moscow: Gos izd-vo polit lit-ry, 1960.
Nettlan, Max. *Ocherki po istorii anarkhicheskikh idei: Stat'i po raznym sotsial'nym voprosam.* [Sketches on the history of anarchist ideas: articles on different social questions]. Detroit: Profsouiz, 1951.
Nikolaenko, I. "Grazhdanskaia voina v Luganske: Bor'ba s belogvardiitsami" [Civil war in Luhans'k: struggle against the White Guards]. LR, no. 1 (28) (1928), pp. 202–12.
Nikolaev, Aleksei. *Bat'ko Makhno: Rasskazy* [Father Makhno: stories]. Riga: Laikmets, 193–. Stories about Makhno and his movement.
———. "Kratkaia pamiatka o Nestore Makhno" [A brief recollection about Nestor Makhno]. PRO, nos. 76–77 (1936), p. 31. Glorification of Makhno and his achievement.
———. *Pervyi sredi ravnykh: Roman* [First among equals: a novel]. Detroit: Profsoiuz, 1947. A novel about the Makhno movement.
———. *Zhizn' Nestora Makhno* [The life of Nestor Makhno]. Riga: "Obshchedostupnia biblioteka," 1936.
V. Nikolskii, "Novye rukovoditeli Kr. Armii" [The new leaders of the Red Army]. *Chasovoi*, no. 206 (February 15, 1938), p. 5.
Nikulin, L. "Gibel' makhnovshchiny" [The downfall of the Makhno movement]. *Znamia* (Moscow), no. 3 (1941), pp. 169–97. A survey of the Makhno movement by a Bolshevik intelligence agent who acted mainly in France.
"1919 god v Ekaterinoslave i Aleksandrovske" [The year of 1919 in

Katerynoslav and Oleksandrivs'k]. LR, no. 4 (13) (1925), pp. 74–103. A report of the provincial committee of the Katerynoslav Zafront biuro TSK KP(b) about conditions in Makhno's army, relations between the Bolsheviks and Makhno, and Bolshevik underground work.

Nomad, Max. *Apostles of Revolution.* Boston: Little, Brown, 1939. Brief biographies of seven radical leaders, including Makhno.

———. "The Epic of Nestor Makhno: The 'Bandit' Who Saved Red Moscow." *Modern Monthly* 9, no. 6 (1935): 334–46; no. 7 (1936): 409–16; no. 8 (1936): 490–92.

Novak, D. "The Place of Anarchism in the History of Political Thought." *The Review of Politics* (Notre Dame, Ind.) 20 (1958): 307–29.

Novikov, S. *Ekonomicheskoe znachenie iuzhnogo fronta* [Economic importance of the southern front]. Moscow: Izd-vo Politotdela X armii, 192–.

Novopolin, G. "Makhno i guliai-pol'skaia gruppa anarkhistov: Po ofitsial'nym dannym" [Makhno and the Huliai-Pole group of anarchists: according to the official data]. *Katorga i ssylka* (Moscow), no. 34 (1927), pp. 70–77. A valuable account about the activities of the Huliai-Pole Anarchist group from 1906 to 1910, and the trial of some, based upon official records.

"O dobrovol'noi mobilizatsii" [About the voluntary mobilization]. PS, no. 2 (May 24, 1919), p. 1.

Obertas, I. L. *Komandarm Fed'ko* [Commander Fed'ko]. Moscow: Voen. izd-vo, 1973.

Obolenskii, V. "Krym v 1917–1920 gg." [The Crimea in 1917–1920]. *Na chuzhoi storonie* (Berlin), nos. 5–6 (1923), pp. 5–40.

———. "V period Krymskago pravitel'stva" [During the Crimean government]. *Na chuzhoi storonie,* no. 7 (1924), pp. 81–110.

Obshchestvo sodeistviia zhertvam interventsii: K desiatiletiiu interventsii, sbornik statei [Society for assistance to the victims of the intervention: to the tenth anniversary of the intervention, a collection of articles]. Moscow: Gos. izd-vo, 1929. Articles sympathetic to the Bolsheviks dealing with the French intervention in South Ukraine and English support for the anti-Bolshevik elements in Transcaspia.

Ohnesseit, Wilhelm. "Die deutschen Bauernkolonien in Südrussland von ihrer Gründung bis zur Gegenwart." *Preussische Jahrbücher,* no. 206 (October–December 1926), pp. 169–79.

Oiticica, José. *A doutrina anarquista ao alcance de todos.* N.p., n.d.

Ol', P. V. *Inostrannye kapitaly v Rossi* [Foreign capital in Russia]. Petrograd: 4-ia Gos. tip., 1922.

Onats'kyi, IEvehn. "Nestor Makhno." In *Ukrains'ka mala entsyklopediia*, pp. 937–38. Buenos Aires, 1960. A valuable critical survey of the Makhno movement.

Ordon, W. "Polska ofenzywa na Ukrainie" [Polish offensive in Ukraine]. *Rzad i Wojsko* (Warsaw), no. 19 (May 9, 1920), pp. 7–8; no. 20 (May 16, 1920), pp. 6–8.

Orlinski. "Banditizm i bor'ba s nim" [Banditry and the struggle against it]. AR, nos. 2–3 (1921), pp. 3–16.

Orlov, L. G. "Osnovatel' Dobrovol'cheskoi armii" [Organizer of the Volunteer Army]. *Chasovoi* (Brussels), no. 329 (1953).

Ozerov, M. *Po sledam geroev revoliutsii* [In the footsteps of the heroes of the Revolution]. Simferopol: "Krym," 1967. An account of the participation of foreign Communists in the Bolshevik Revolution in the Crimea, 1917–20.

P. "Sytuacja strategiczna na Ukrainie" [Strategic situation in Ukraine]. *Rzad i Wojsko* (Wąrsaw), no. 2 (1920), pp. 9–10.

Paliiv, Dmytro. "Na chystu vodu" [On the clear water]. LCK, no. 6 (1930); nos. 7–8, pp. 12–13.

———. "Zymovyi pokhid" [Winter campaign]. LCK, no. 6 (1935), pp. 8–9; nos. 7–8, pp. 7–10.

Panchenko, Petro. *Ukrains'ki partyzany u vitchyznianii viini 1918 roku* [The Ukrainian partisans in the patriotic war 1918]. Saratov, 1942.

Pavlov, P. A. "Voennye khitrosti" [Military ruses]. *Voennyi vestnik* (Moscow), no. 4 (1921), pp. 12–14. A brief account of Makhno's military tactics.

———. "Vyvody iz opyta bor'by s Makhno svodnoi divizhii kursantov 6 noiabria i dekabre 1920 g. i ianvare 1921 g." [Conclusions from the experiences of struggle against Makhno by the elite troops, November 6 and December 1920 and January 1921]. AR, nos. 2–3 (1921), pp. 97–111.

Pavlov, V. E. *Markovtsy v boiakh i pokhodakh za Rossiiu v osvoboditel'noi voine, 1917–1920 godov* [Markov's men in the campaigns and marches for Russia in the liberation war]. 2 vols. Paris, 1962.

Pavlovich, Michael. "Ukraine." *Soviet Russia* 3, no. 23 (December 4, 1920): 545–48.

Peake, Thomas R. "Jacques Sadoul and the Russian intervention, 1919." *The Russian Review* 32, no. 1 (1973): 54–63.

Pelletier, Lucile. "Nestor Makhno est mort." *R. P.*, no. 181 (August 25, 1934), pp. 11–12.

Perfets'kyi, A. "Smert' chety kinnykh Chornomortsiv: Pamiaty poliahlykh" [The death of a cavalry unit of the 'Chornomortsi': in memory of the fallen]. KCK 1924, pp. 116–19.

Peters, Victor. *Nestor Makhno: The Life of an Anarchist.* Winnipeg: Echo Books, 1970. An objective and well-documented study of the Makhno movement and of Makhno's exile in Paris.

Petrovs'kyi, H. I. *Rady za periodu hromadians'koi viiny i za myrnoho budivnytstva* [The councils during the civil war and peaceful construction]. Kharkov: Derzh. vyd-vo Ukrainy, 1927.

Petrovych, A. "Huliaipil'skyi bat'ko i ukrains'ka entsyklopediia." *Vil'nyi svit* (Winnipeg), August 8, 1966.

Pevnyi, P. *Za voliu ta derzhavnist'* [For freedom and statehood]. Stanislav, 1920. Personal observations and documents about the winter campaign against the Bolshevik and Denikin forces from December 1919 through May 1920.

Pidmohyl'nyi, V. *Tretia revoliutsiia* [The Third Revolution]. Lvov, 1922.

Pipes, Richard. *The Formation of the Soviet Union, Communism and Nationalism, 1917–1923.* Rev. ed. Cambridge, Mass.: Harvard University Press, 1964. A thorough and well-documented scholarly work dealing with the disintegration of the Russian Empire, the establishment of national states, and the subsequent formation of the Soviet Union. The emphasis is on the political aspects of the national movements by new states that later became part of the Soviet Union.

Podshivalov, I. M. *Desantnaia ekspeditsiia Kovtiukha: Likvidatsiia vrangelevskogo desanta na Kubani v avguste 1920 g., takticheskii ocherk* [The landing expedition of Kovtiuk: liquidation of Wrangel's landing in the Kuban in August 1920, a tactical sketch]. Moscow: Gos. izd-vo, 1927.

Pois, Robert A. "Friedrich Meinecke and Eastern Europe: A Study of the World War I Period." *East European Quarterly* 1, no. 3 (1967): 249–60.

Pokrovski, Georgii. *Denikinshchina: God politiki i ekonomiki na Kubani, 1918–1919 gg.* [The Denikin movement: a year of politics and economics in the Kuban]. Berlin: Z. I. Grzhebina, 1923. Relations between the government of the Kuban Cossacks and the Volunteer Army from 1918 through 1920.

Pokrovskii, M. N. *Ob Ukraine: Sbornik statei i materialov* [About Ukraine: collection of articles and materials]. Kiev: Sotsekgiz. Ukrainy, 1935.

Polevoi. "Anarkhizm i makhnovshchina" [Anarchism and the Makhno movement]. PS, no. 43 (June 5, 1920), pp. 1–3. Author's opinion is that although the Makhno movement was not an Anarchist movement, it was deeply revolutionary and was being led by a group of Anarchists.

Polishchuk, Klym. *Huliaipil'skyi "bat'ko"* [The "father" from Huliai-Pole]. 2 vols. Kolomyya: Vyd-vo Oka, 1925–26. A novel about the Makhno movement.

Ponomarenko, P. M. "O politeke partii v ukrainskoi derevne v 1919–1920 gg" [About the policy of the party in a Ukrainian village in 1919–1920]. *Voprosy istorii* (Moscow), no. 8 (1956), pp. 105–7.

Popov, I. "Vziatie Perekopa" [The capture of Perekop]. AR, nos. 2–3 (1921), pp. 93–99.

Popov, N. A. "Uchastie kitaiskikh internatsional'nykh chastei v zashchite Sovetskoi Respubliki v period Grazhdanskoi voiny, 1918–1920 gody" [Participation of the Chinese international detachments in defense of the Soviet Republic during the civil war, 1918–1920]. *Voprosy istorii* (Moscow), no. 10 (1957), pp. 109–23.

"Povstancheskoe dvizhenie na Ukraine" [The partisan movement in Ukraine]. *Revoliutsionnaia Rossiia* (Berlin, Prague), no. 11 (192–), pp. 22–25.

"Povstannia na Khersonshchyni proty Skoropads'koho" [Uprisings in the Kherson province against Skoropads'kyi]. *Strilets'ka dumka* (Starokonstantyniv), no. 61 (1919).

Premysler, I. "Razgom banditizma na Ukraine, 1921 g." [Defeat of banditry in Ukraine, 1921]. VIZ, no. 9 (1940), pp. 34–44. An account of partisan groups, including Makhno, against the Bolshevik regime and the Red troops in Ukraine in 1921.

Preobrazhenskii, E. "Evgeniia Bogdanova Bosh." PR, no. 2 (37) (1925), pp. 5–16. A detailed biography.

Primakov, V. "Bor'ba za sovetskuiu vlast' na Ukraine" [The struggle for Soviet power in Ukraine]; In *Piat'let Krasnoi Armii: Sbornik statei, 1918–1923,* pp. 171–95. Moscow, 1923.

Primakov, V. M. "Konnyi boi u Perekopa" [Cavalry battle at Perekop]. *Vennyi vestnik* (Moscow), no. 5 (1923), pp. 41–43.

———. "Srazhenie pod Orlom: Oktaibr' 1919–noibr' 1919 goda" [Battle at Orel: October 1919–November 1919]. *Bor'ba klassov* (Moscow), no. 2 (1931), pp. 50–60. Denikin's campaign against the Red Army in the region of Orel and Kursk in the second half of 1919; includes an account of Latvian and Estonian troops fighting Denikin and of Makhno's activities at his rear.

Prokhoda, V. "Sirozhupannyky v povstani proty uriadu het'mana Skoropads'koho" [Graycoats in the uprising against the government of Hetman Skoropadsky]. *Tabor* (Warsaw), no. 9 (1928), pp. 90–95.

"Protiv gotoviashchegosia prestupleniia russkogo i pol'skogo pravitel'stv" [Against the preparation of the treason of the Russian and Polish regimes]. VO, no. 2 (1922), pp. 9–12.

Putsenko, V. "Povstanchyi zahin iampil'shchyny" [A partisan detachment of the IAmpil region]. *Ukrains'ka strilets'ka hromada v Kanadi 1928–1938,* pp. 157–59. Saskatoon: Nakl. Ukrains'koi strilets'koi hromady v Kanadi, 1938.

R. "Bredovskii pokhod" [Bredov's campaign]. *Chasovoi* (Brussels), no. 49 (February 15, 1931), p. 22.

R., J. G. "Machno, Nestor." *The Mennonite Encyclopedia,* pp. 430–31. Scottdale, Pa., 1957.

Radziejowski, Janusz. "Ruch narodowy i rewolucyjny na Ukrainie w okresie dzialalnosci Centralnej Rady (Marzec 1917–Kwiecień 1918 r." [National and revolutionary movement in Ukraine during the period of the Central Rada, March 1917–April 1918]. *Studia z dziejów ZSRR i Europy Srodkowej* (Warsaw) 9 (1973): 53–84.

Rafes, Moissey G. *Dva goda revoliutsii na Ukraine: Evoliutsiia i raskol "Bunda"* [Two years of revolution in Ukraine: evolution and the split of the "Bund"]. Moscow: Gos. izd-vo, 1920. A valuable account of the Ukrainian Revolution and the development and attitude of the Jewish organization "Bund" toward Ukrainian statehood; written by one of its leaders, who was a member of the Central Rada and later a member of the Russian Communist Party.

Rakovskii, G. N. *Konets bielykh; ot Dniepra do Bosfora: Vyrozhdenie, agoniia i likvidatsiia* [The end of the Whites; from the Dnieper to Bosporus: degeneration, agony and liquidation]. Prague: Izd-vo "Volia Rossii," 1921. A sequel to the author's *V stanie bieklykh*, dealing with the final phase of the Russian Civil War in 1920.

———. *V stanie bielykh: Ot Orla do Novorossiiska* [In the camp of the Whites: from Orel to Novorossiisk]. Istanbul: Izd G. N. Rakovskago, 1920. A competent, critical analysis of the Russian Civil War from 1918 to 1919 and the cause of its failure, by a Russian journalist associated with the information agency of the Volunteer Army.

Rakovskii, Kh. G. *Bor'ba za osvobozhdenie derevni* [The struggle of liberation of a village]. Kharkov: Izd. Politotdela Ukrsovtrudaarma, 1920. A unique account of the struggle of Bolshevik authorities and the Red Army against Ukrainian uprisings and peasant revolts during the Bolshevik invasion of Ukraine in 1919, based upon the records of the Red Army, the Cheka, and the Commissariat of Internal Affairs.

———."Il'ich i Ukraina," LR, no. 2 (11) (1925), pp. 5–10. Lenin's Ukrainian policy from the summer of 1918 to the summer of 1919.

———. *Otchet Raboche-Krest'ianskogo Pravitel'stva Ukrainy IV-mu Vseukrainskomu S'ezdu Sovetov Rabochikh, Krest'ianskikh i Krasnoarmeishkikh deputatov 16–20 maia 1920 gg.* [A report of Workers-Peasants Government of Ukraine to the 4th All-Ukrainian Congress of the Soviets of Workers, Peasants, and Red Army deputies on May 16–20, 1920]. Kharkov: Vseukrainskoe izd., 1920.

Ravich-Cherkas'kyi, M. [Rabinovich]. *Anarkhisty.* Kharkov: "Proletarii," 1929.

———. "Fevral'–dekabr' 1917 g. v Ekaterinoslave: Ocherki" [February–December in Katerynoslav: sketches]. LR, no. 1 (1922), pp. 74–80. The activities of the Bolshevik activists among the workers and soldiers in Katerynoslav in 1917.

———. *Makhno i makhnovshchyna* [Makhno and the Makhno movement]. Ekaterinoslav: Vseukr. izd-vo, 1920.

———, ed. *Zhovtnevyi zbirnyk: Revoliutsii roku VII, 1917–1924* [October collection: revolutions of the seventh year, 1917–1924]. Kiev: Derzh. vyd-vo Ukrainy, 1924.

Rebikov, N. "Latyshskie strelki v Rossii" [Latvian sharpshooters in Russia]. *Chasovoi* (Brussels), no. 500 (1968), pp. 17–18.

Reik. "Povest o pechal'nym kontsom (Eshche o Makhno)" [A story about the sad end (more about Makhno)]. *Odesskii Nabat,* no. 7 (June 16, 1919), pp. 2–3.

Remnev, M. I. "Deiatel'nost' Komitetov nezamozhnykh selian na Ukraine v 1920 godu" [Activities of the Committees of Poor Peasants in Ukraine in 1920]. VI, no. 4 (1954), pp. 93–103.

Rêpression de l'anarchisme en Russie sovietique. Paris, 1923. An account of the Russian Anarchists, of their persecution by the Soviet regime, and of Makhno's associates.

Reshetar, John S., Jr. *The Ukrainian Revolution, 1917–1920: A Study in Nationalism.* Princeton, N.J.: Princeton University Press, 1952. A thorough and well-documented scholarly work on the development of the Ukrainian Revolution and its origins in the mid-nineteenth century, stressing the relations with Central Powers, Entente, Volunteer Army, and Poland.

Richyts'kyi, And. *Tsentral'na Rada, vid liutoho do zhovtnia: Narys z istorii ukrains'koi revoliutsii* [The Central Rada, from February to October: a sketch of the history of the Ukrainian Revolution]. Kharkov: Derzh. vyd-vo Ukrainy, 1930.

Ripets'kyi, S. "Povstans'kyi rukh na Ukraini 1918–22" [The partisan movement in Ukraine 1918–22]. In *Entsyklopediia ukrainoznavstva: Slovnykova chastyna,* 6: 2117–22. Munich: "Molode zhyttia," 1970.

Romeyko, Marian. *Przed i po Maju* [Before and after the May (coup)]. 2 vols. Warsaw: Wydawn. Ministerstwa Obrony Narodowej, 1967.

Rosenberg, William G. *A. I. Denikin and the Anti-Bolshevik Movement in South Russia.* Amherst: Amherst College Press, 1961.

Roshchin. "Kto takoi Grigor'ev?" [Who was Hryhor'iv?]. PKS, no. 1 (May 17, 1919), p. 3. A denunciation of Otaman Hryhor'iv as an agent of Denikin and a supporter of the "kulaks."

Rudenko, P. *Na Ukraine: Povstanchestvo i anarchicheskoe dvizhenie* [In Ukraine: partisan and anarchist movements]. Buenos Aires: Izd. Rabochei gruppy v Resp. Argentine, 1922. A general survey of the Makhno movement and the Anarchist organization Nabat.

Rudnev, V. V. *Anarkhicheskii kommunizm i marksizm* [Anarchist communism and Marxism]. St. Petersburg: "Narodnaia polza," 1906.

———. *Makhnovshchina* [Makhno movement]. Kharkov: Knyhospilka, 1928. A general survey of the Makhno movement from the spring of 1918 to the summer of 1921, by a Bolshevik, formerly a Socialist Revolutionary, who occupied various official positions, including prosecutor of the Cheka-GPU. Although the author had access to the archival material, he lists no sources.

———. *Makhnovshchyna: Populiarnyi narys* [Makhno movement: a popular sketch]. Kharkov: Knyhospilka, 1928.

Runkle, Gerald. *Anarchism, Old and New.* New York: Delacorte Press, 1972.

Rybakov, M. "Deistviia letuchego korpusa tov. Nestorovicha" [Operations of a flying corps of comrade Nestorovich]. *Sbornik trudov Voenno-nauchnogo obshchestva pri Voennoi akademii* (Moscow), no. 4 (1923), pp. 104–34. A detailed account by a Bolshevik official describing the campaigns of the Red troops against Makhno during the winter of 1921 in Poltava province.

———. "Makhnovskie operatsii v 1920 g." [Makhno operations in 1920]. *Krasnaia armiia* (Moscow), no. 12 (1922), pp. 11–27. A detailed account dealing with the struggle of the Red troops against Makhno in 1920.

Rybalka, I. K. *Rozhrom burzhnazno-natsionalistychnoi Direktorii na Ukraini* [The destruction of the bourgeois-nationalistic directory in Ukraine]. Kharkov: Vyd-vo Kharkivs'koho universytetu, 1962.

Sadovs'kyi, V. "Shliakhy ukrains'koi revoliutsii" [The developments of the Ukrainian Revolution]. KD 1927, pp. 13–26.

Sakhno, V. "Delegatom vid povstantsiv, lystopad–hruden' 1919 r." [A delegate from the partisans, November–December 1919]. *Tabor* (Warsaw), no. 7 (1928), pp. 70–83.

Santil'ian, D. "Bakunizm i makhnovshchina" [Bakunism and the Makhno movement]. AV, nos. 3–4 (1923), pp. 23–25.

Savoika, Liubomyr. "IAk povstala armiia Halliera" [The origin of the Haller army]. *Visti* (New York), no. 122 (1966).

Semanov, S. G. "Makhnovshchina i ee krakh" [The Makhno movement and its collapse]. *Voprosy istorii* (Moscow), no. 9 (1966), pp. 37–60. A well-documented and useful survey of the Makhno movement by a Soviet Russian historian.

Sereda, Mykhailo. "Kholodnyi IAr" [Cold Ravine]. LCK, no. 12 (1931), pp. 11–14.

———. "Kholodnyi IAr" [Cold Ravine]. *Dilo* (Lvov), August 4, 1934. An account of the meeting and subsequent assassination of Otaman Hryhor'iv by Makhno.

———. "Ostanni dni zbroinoi borot'by, 21, XI, 1920 r.–21, XI, 1921 r." [The last days of armed struggle, November 21, 1920–November 21, 1921]. LCK, no. 12 (1930), pp. 2–5.

———. "Otamanshchyna" [The otaman movement]. LCK, no. 3 (1929), pp. 22–24; no. 1 (1930), pp. 10–12; no. 2, pp. 6–8; no. 3, pp. 15–17; no. 4, pp. 12–14; no. 5, pp. 12–14; no. 6, pp. 17–20; nos. 7–8, pp. 21–25; no. 9, pp. 14–16; no. 10, pp. 15–17; no. 11, pp. 11–13; no. 12, pp. 18–20. Biographical sketches by a Ukrainian officer about a number of partisan leaders, including Palienko, Anhel, Bozhko, Volokh, Volynets', Shepel', Liakhovych, and Tiutiunyk, which describes their campaigns against the Bolshevik and anti-Bolshevik Russian forces during the Revolution. The work is based mainly on the author's memoirs and on secondary sources.

———. "Storinka z istorii vyzvol'noi borot'by" [A page from the history of the struggle for liberation]. LCK, no. 11 (1931), pp. 15–17. An account of the Ukrainization of the 34th Army Corps under General Pavlo Skoropads'kyi in the summer of 1917 and the Corps' fight against the Bolshevik forces under Evgeniia Bosh, which threatened the Central Rada.

———. "Viis'kova narada v kabineti general'noho sekretaria Porsha dnia 18 (5 st. st.) sichnia 1918 r." [A military conference in the office of Secretary-General Porsh on January 18 (5 O. S.) 1918]. LCK, no. 5 (1937), pp. 2–3.

Sergeev, P. "Poltavskaia operatsiia protiv Makhno" [The Poltava operation against Makhno]. VR, no. 9 (1927), pp. 122–34. A detailed account of the Red Army operation in Poltava province during the first half of 1921, stressing Makhno's military tactics.

Sergent, Alain. *Les anarchistes: Scènes et portraits presentes et commentes*. Paris: F. Chambriand, 1951.

——— and Claude Harmel. *Histoire de l'anarchie*. Paris: Le Portulan, 1949.

Shakhrai, Vasyl M. *Revoliutsiia na Ukraini* [The Revolution in Ukraine]. Saratov: Borba, 1919.

Shankovs'kyi, Lev. "Hryhorievshchyna—problema i literatura" [The Hryhor'iv movement—the problem and the literature]. *Al'manakh kaliendar Providinnia*, 1966.

———. *Ukrains'ka armiia v borot'bi za derzhavnist'* [The Ukrainian Army in the struggle for statehood]. Munich: Dniprova khvylia, 1958. A well-documented survey of the organization and activities of the Ukrainian armed forces, including the partisans, 1917–21.

———. "Za Ukrainu–proty Moskvy: Ukrains'kyi narodnii povstans'kyi rukh proty Moskvy pid chas vyzvol'noi viiny 1917–1920 rr. i pislia zakinchennia viiny v 1921–1924 rr." [For Ukraine–against Muscovy: Ukrainian national partisan movement against Muscovy during the liberation war 1917–1920 and after the end of the war 1921–1924]. *Al'manakh-kalendar Soiuzu Ukraintsiv Katolykiv Ameryky "Provydinnia" na rik 1971*, pp. 111–26. Philadelphia, Pa.: Vyd-vo "Ameryka," 1970.

Shapoval, Mykyta. *Velyka revoliutsiia i ukrains'ka vyzvol'na programa* [The great revolution and the Ukrainian liberation program]. Prague: "Vil'na spilka," 1927. A valuable history of the Ukrainian Revolution based mainly upon the author's reminiscences, seen against the political and socioeconomic background.

———. *Zanepad U. N. R.* [The decline of the U. N. R.]. Prague: "Vil'na spilka," 1928.

——— and O. Slobodych. *Velykyi zryv: Narys istorii ukrainskoi revoliutsii, 1917–1920* [The great upheaval: a sketch of the history of the Ukrainian Revolution, 1917–1920]. Lvov: Vyd. Samoosvita, 1930.

Shatz, Marshall S., ed. *The Essential Works of Anarchism*. New York: Quadrangle Books, 1972.

Shchadenko, E. A. *Grigor'evshchina: Bor'ba Krasnoi armii protiv Grigor'eva* [The Hryhor'iv movement: the Red Army against

———. "Grigor'evshchina" [The Hryhor'iv movement]. In *Grazhdanskaia voina, 1918–1921*, 1: 68–95. Edited by A. S. Budnov. Moscow, 1928–30.

Shekhtman, I. B. *Pogromy Dobrovol'cheskoi armii na Ukraine: K istorii antisemitizma na Ukraine v 1919–1920 gg.* [Pogroms of the Volunteer Army in Ukraine: about the history of anti-Semitism in Ukraine in 1919–1920]. Berlin, Ostjudisches historisches Archiv, 1932.

Shelygin, IA. *Krasnaia armiia na Ukraine: Kratkii ocherk* [The Red Army in Ukraine: a short sketch]. Kharkov: Izd-vo Knyhospilka, n.d.

———. "Partizanskaia bor'ba s getmanshchinoi i avstro-germanskoi okkupatsiei" [The partisan struggle against the hetman regime and the Austro-German invaders]. LR, no. 6 (33) (1928), pp. 61–101. A valuable, detailed survey, consisting largely of documentary quotations.

Shevchuk, H. M. *Borot'ba trudiashchykh Radians'koi Ukrainy proty kontr-revoliutsii na Pivdni v 1920 r.* [The struggle of the toilers of Soviet Ukraine against counterrevolution in the south in 1920]. Kiev: Vyd-vo Akademii nauk Ukr. RSR, 1956.

Shrag, N. "Ekonomicheskie predposylki interventsii Antanty na Ukraine" [Economic conditions before the intervention of the Entente in Ukraine]. In *Chernaia kniga: Sbornik statei i materialov ob interventsii Antanty na Ukraine v 1918–1919 gg.*, pp. 13–27. Ekaterinoslav: Gos. izd-vo Ukrainy, 1925.

Shtein, B. "Iz istorii pervonachal'nogo perioda grazhdanskoi voiny" [From the history of the initial period of the civil war]. IM, no. 4 (80–81) (1940), pp. 12–35.

Shtif, N. I. *Pogromy na Ukraine: Period dobrobol'cheskoi armii* [The pogroms in Ukraine: the period of the Volunteer Army]. Berlin: "Vostok," 1922.

Shul'hyn, Olexander. "Ukraine and Its Political Aspirations." *The Slavonic Review* 13 (1935): 350–62.

Siedlecki, Krzysztof. "'Brześć Litewski'—rokowania pokojowe i traktaty" ["Brest-Litovsk"—negotiations of peace and treaties]. *Bellona* (Warsaw) 15, no. 2 (1924): 113–36; 15, no. 3: 239–58; 16, no. 1: 16–29.

Simonov, B. *Razgrom denikinshchiny: Pochemu my pobedili v oktiabre 1919 g.* [Destruction of the Denikin movement: why we triumphed in October of 1919]. Moscow: Gos. izd-vo, Otd-nie Voen. lit-ry, 1928. The Bolshevik campaign against Denikin in September and October 1919 and the causes of the latter's defeat.

Siropolko, St. "Dva areshtuvannia S. Petliury za het'mana P. Skoropads'koho" [Two arrests of S. Petliura during the time of Hetman P. Skoropads'kyi]. KD 1937.

Sivtsov, A. *Kievskaia krasnaia gvardiia v bor'be za vlast' sovetov* [The Kiev Red Guard in the struggle for Soviet power]. A well-documented work about the partisan struggle against the hetman and the Austro-German troops in 1918, stressing the Communists' role.

Skirda, Alexandre. *Les Anarchistes dans la rêvolution Russe*. Paris: Ed. Tete de Feuilles, 1973.

Skliarenko, IE. M. *Borot'ba trudiashchykh Ukrainy proty nimets'ko-avstriis'kykh okupantiv i het'manshchyny v 1918 rotsi* [The struggle of the workers of Ukraine against the German-Austrian invaders and the hetman regime in 1918]. Kiev: Vyd-vo Akademii nauk Ukr. RSR, 1960.

Skorovstans'kyi, V. [pseud.]. *Revoliutsiia na Ukraine* [The Revolution in Ukraine]. Saratov: Izd-vo Borba, 1919.

Slashchov, IA. *Trebuiu suda obshchestva i glasnosti: Oborona i sdacha Kryma* [(I) demand a court of society and the public: defense and surrender of the Crimea]. Constantinople, 1920.

Slobodych, O. *Borot'ba svitiv na Ukraini: Narys istorii Ukrains'koi revoliutsii, 1918–1920 r.* [The struggle of the worlds in Ukraine: a sketch of the history of the Ukrainian Revolution, 1918–1920]. Lvov: Vyd-vo Samoos' vita, 1930.

"Smert' N. I. Makhno" [The death of N. I. Makhno]. PRO, nos. 47–49 (1934), pp. 1–2.

Smetanich, S. "1917–1918 gody na Poltavshchine" [1917–1918 in Poltava province]. In *Oktiabr'-skaia revoliutsiia: Pervoe piatiletie, 1917–1922*, pp. 259–75. Kharkov, 1922.

Smith, C. Henry. *The Story of the Mennonites*. Newton, Kans.: Mennonite Publications Office, 1950.

Smolenskii, S. *Krymskaia katastrofa: Zapiski stroevoho ofitsera* [The Crimean catastrophe: notes of a combatant officer]. Sofia: Rossiisko-Bolgarskoe knigoizd-vo, 1921. A survey of Wrangel's fighting against the Bolsheviks and his subsequent defeat in the Crimea.

Smolinchuk, P. I. *Bol'sheviki Ukrainy v bor'be za Sovety, mart 1917–ianvar 1918 gg.* [The Bolsheviks of Ukraine in the struggle for the Soviets, March 1917–January 1918]. Lvov: Izd-vo L'vovskogo un-ta, 1969.

Sokolov, A. "Povstanchestvo i bol'shevizm: Prichiny razgroma bol'shevikami revoliutsionnogo povstanchestva" [The partisan movement and bolshevism: reasons for the defeat by the Bolsheviks of the revolutionary partisan movement]. *Nabat* (Kharkov), no. 22 (July 7, 1919), p. 2.

Solovei, Dmytro. *Vasylenko, Miliukov i samostiinist' Ukrainy v 1918 r.: Sproba kharakterystyky z nahody 45-richchia vid chasu proholoshennia tret'oho i chetvertoho universaliv Tsentral'noi Rady* [Vasylenko, Miliukov, and the independence of Ukraine in 1918: an attempt at characterization on the 45th anniversary of the proclamation of the Third and Fourth Universals of the Central Rada.

"Souiz Makhno-Vrangel'" [The Makhno-Wrangel alliance]. *Volia Rossii* (Prague), September 25, 1920.

Spiridonov, P. I. *Bol'sheviki v tylu belogvardeishchiny* [The Bolsheviks in the rear of the White Guards]. Kerch: "Kerchenskii rabochii," 1940.

Stachiw, Matthew [Matvii Stakhiv]. *Ukraina v dobi Dyrektorii UNR* [Ukraine in the period of the Directory of UNR]. Scranton, Pa.: Ukr. naukovo-istorychna biblioteka, 1962–66. A multi-volume work on the Ukrainian Revolution from November 1918 to November 1920, stressing the directory's endeavor to gain international recognition and military support from the Entente.

——— and Jaroslaw Sztendera. *Western Ukraine at the Turning Point of Europe's History*. New York: The Shevchenko Scientific Society, 1971.

Stebnyts'kyi, Petro [P. Smutok, pseud.]. *Pomizh dvokh revoliutsii: Narysy politichnoho zhyttia za rr. 1907–1918* [Between two revolutions: sketches of political life for the years of 1907–1918]. Kiev: "Chas," 1918.

———. *Ukraina v ekonomike Rossii* [Ukraine in the Russian economy]. Petrograd, 1918.

Stefaniv, Zenon. *Ukrains'ki zbroini syly 1917–21 rr.* [Ukrainian armed forces, 1917–21]. 2nd ed. Vol. 1. Munich: SUV, 1947.

Stewart, George, *The White Armies of Russia: A Chronicle of Counter-revolution and Allied Intervention*. New York: Macmillan, 1933. The Russian anti-Bolshevik movement from 1918 to 1922 and Allied intervention; based mainly on secondary sources, it contains a number of factual errors.

Stolnikov, K. A. *Pamiatnaia zapiska k istorii Simferopol'skogo offitserskogo polka* [A memorable note about the history of the Simferopol

Officers' Regiment]. Sofia (?), 1921–22. A study based on documents, diaries, and memoirs of eyewitnesses of the organization and campaigns of the Simferopol Officers' Regiment against Makhno and the Ukrainian troops on the Right Bank during the second half of 1919.

"Strategiczna Sytuacja na Ukrainie w r. 1919" [The strategic situation in Ukraine in 1919]. *Rzad i Wojsko* (Warsaw), no. 9 (February 29, 1920), pp. 7–9; no. 10 (March 7), pp. 9–10; no. 11 (March 14), pp. 9–10.

Struve, Petr. *Razmyshleniia o russkoi revoliutsii* [Reflections on the Russian Revolution]. Sofia: Rossiisko-bolgarskoe knigoizd-vo, 1921.

Sukhov, A. A. *Inostrannaia interventsiia na Odeshchine v 1918–1919 gg.* [Foreign intervention in the Odessa region]. Odessa: Izd. Istpart. Otdel Odesskogo Obkoma KP(b)U, 1927.

Sukiennicki, Wiktor. "Moskwa a Ukraina po klesce Niemiec w 1918 r." [Moscow and Ukraine after the defeat of Germany in 1918]. *Zeszyty historyczne* (Paris), no. 5 (1964), pp. 133–43.

Sullivant, Robert S. *Soviet Politics and the Ukraine, 1917–1957.* New York: Columbia University Press, 1962. A study of the Russian Communist Party's nationality policy in Ukraine, stressing the relationship of industrial-agrarian and the nationality questions.

Suprunenko, N. I. "Bor'ba ukrainskikh partizan protiv denikinshchiny" [The struggle of the Ukrainian partisans against the Denikin movement]. *Istoricheskii zhurnal* (Moscow), no. 5 (1942), pp. 27–37.

———. *Ocherki istorii grazhdanskoi voiny i inostrannoi voennoi interventsii na Ukraine, 1918–1920* [Sketches of the history of the civil war and foreign military intervention in Ukraine]. Moscow: Nauka, 1966. A well-documented but subjective study of the Ukrainian Revolution and foreign intervention in Ukraine.

———. "Ustanovlenie sovetskoi vlasti na Ukraine" [The establishment of the Soviet regime in Ukraine]. *Voprosy istorii* (Moscow), no. 10 (1957), pp. 49–70.

Szpinger, Stefan. *Z Pierwsza Konną* [With the First Cavalry]. Lódź: Wydawn. Lódskie, 1967.

Tavricheskii, A. "U Makhno ne bylo programy" [Makhno had no program]. NRS, April 8, 1969.

Teper, I. [Gordeev, I.]. *Makhno: Ot "edinogo anarkhizma" k stopam rumynskogo korolia* [Makhno: from a "united anarchism" to the feet of the Romanian king]. Kharkov: Molodoi rabochii, 1924. An interesting account by a former Anarchist and follower of Makhno of the internal policies of the Makhno movement; includes biographies of its leaders.

Teslar, Kazimir Valerian. "Gulai-Pole." *La revue anarchiste* (Paris), no. 15 (1923), pp. 19–20.

Teslenko, P. "K vospominaniiam V. Belasha" [To the memory of V. Belash]. LR, no. 3 (30) (1928), pp. 228–30.

Tiutiunyk, IUrko. *Zymovyi pokhid 1919–20 rr.* [The winter campaigns of 1919–20]. New York: Vyd-vo Chartoryis'kykh, 1966. An authoritative, subjective account of the Ukrainian Army's guerrilla warfare in the rear of the Denikin and Bolshevik forces from December 1919 to May 1920, stressing the political aspects of the campaign, by a high-ranking officer.

Tolokol'nikov, Grigorii Abramovich. *Aleksandr Parkhomenko*. Moscow: Znanie, 1962.

Tragediia kozachestva: Ocherk na temu, Kozachestvo i Rossiia [Tragedy of the Cossacks: a sketch on the subject, the Cossacks and Russia]. Vol. 3. Paris, 1936.

Trifonov, I. IA. *Klassy i klassovaia bor'ba v SSSR v nachale NEPa, 1921–1923 gg.* [Classes and class struggle in SSSR at the beginning of NEP, 1921–1923]. Vol. 1. Leningrad, 1964.

Trypils'kyi, Ol. "Na pivdennykh stepakh" [On the southern steppes]. *Chervonyi shliakh* (Kharkov), no. 6 (1924), pp. 97–107.

Tsapko, Ivan. "Partyzany na Skhidnii Ukraini: Starobil'skyi partyzans'kyi zahin" [Partisans in East Ukraine: Starobil'sk partisan detachment]. *Visti* (New York), no. 109 (1963), pp. 6–8; no. 111, pp. 85–89.

Turkul, A. V. *Drozdovtsy v ogne: Kartiny grazhdanskoi voiny 1918–20 gg.* [Drozdov men in battle: pages from the civil war of 1918–20]. Munich: "IAv i byl," 1948.

Tychyna, V. IE. "Kolonial'ne pohrabuvannia Ukrainy nimets'kymy okupantamy u 1918 rotsi" [Colonial pillage of Ukraine by the German invaders in 1918]. *Pytannia istorii narodiv SRSR* (Kharkov), no. 7 (1968), pp. 12–22.

Tymoshenko, M. V. "Diialnist' sil'skykh orhaniv Radians'koi vlady na Ukraini po rozviazanniu zemel'noho i prodovol'choho pytan, 1920 r." [Activities of the village organs of the Soviet regime in Ukraine after the dissolution of land and provision problems, 1920]. *Pytannia istorii narodiv SRSR* (Kharkov), no. 6 (1969), pp. 46–56.

———. "Komnezamy Ukrainy ta ikh rol' u zmitsneni orhaniv Radians'koi vlady na seli v 1920 rotsi" [Committees of Poor Peasants of Ukraine and their role in strengthening the organs of the Soviet regime in the village in 1920]. *Pytannia istorii narodiv SRSR* (Kharkov), no. 7 (1968), pp. 32–41.

"Ubiistvo Grigor'eva" [Assassination of Hryhor'iv]. LR, no. 2 (1924), pp. 232–34.

Udovychenko, Oleksander. *Tretia Zalizna dyviziia: Materiialy od istorii viis'ka Ukrains'koi Narodn'oi Respubliky, rik 1919* [The Third Iron Division: materials on the history of the forces of the Ukrainian People's Republic, 1919]. Vol. 1. New York: Chervona Kalyna, 1971. A history, based on archival material and the author's own recollections, of the Third Iron Division and its campaigns against the Bolsheviks and Denikin from April to December 1919. The last chapters were written by General O. Vyshnivs'kyi.

———. "Vid Dnistra do linii peremyrria i vidvorot za Zbruch: Boiovi chyny pravoi grupy armii UNR" [From the Dniester to the line of armistice and retreat to the Zbruch: military actions of the right wing of the UNR army]. *Za Derzhavnist'* (Kalisz) 5 (1935): 76–123; 6 (1936): 77–109; 7 (1937): 152–64.

"Ukraina." *Volia* (Vienna), vol. 4, no. 5 (1920).

Ukraine: A Concise Encyclopaedia [UE]. Prepared by Shevchenko Scientific Society. Edited by Volodymyr Kubijovyc. Toronto: University of Toronto Press, 1963.

"The Ukrainian Peasants." *Soviet Russia* 3, no. 22 (November 27, 1920): 529.

Ukrains'ka RSR v period hromadians'koi viiny, 1917–1920 rr. [Soviet Ukraine during the period of the civil war]. Kiev: Vyd-vo polit. lit-ry Ukrainy, 1967. A one-sided collective work dealing largely with the struggle of the Bolshevik and anti-Bolshevik Russian forces for power in Ukraine from March 1917 to November 1920.

Ukrainskii vopros [The Ukrainian question]. By the editors of the journal *Ukrainskaia zhizn'*. St. Petersburg: Elektro-tip. N. IA. Stoikovoi, 1914.

Umnov, A. S. *Grazhdanskaia voina i srednee krest'ianstvo, 1918–1920 gg.* [The civil war and the middle peasantry]. Moscow: Voen. izd-vo, 1959.

Val', E. G. F. *K istorii bielago dvizheniia: Deiatel'nost' general-ad'iutanta Shcherbacheva* [About the history of the White movement: the activity of General Shcherbachev]. Tallin, 1935.

———. *Kak Pilsudskii pogubil Denikina* [How Piłsudskii defeated Denikin]. Tallin, 1938.

———. *Znachenie i rol' Ukrainy v voprosie osvobozhdeniia Rossii ot bol'shevikov na osnovanii opyta 1918–1920 gg.* [The significance and role of Ukraine in the question of Russia's liberation from the Bolsheviks on the basis of experiences of 1918–1920]. Tallin, 1937.

Valiis'kyi, A. "Povstanchyi rukh v Ukraini i otamaniia" [The partisan movement and the otamans' movement]. SV, no. 54, March 21, 1957. A lecture by a high-ranking officer about the partisan movement in Ukraine, including Makhno, from 1917 to 1922, reported by Ivan Kedryn.

———. "Povstans'kyi rukh v Ukraini v rokakh 1917–1922" [The partisan movement in Ukraine during the years 1917–1922]. VK, no. 4 (1961), pp. 12–16.

Villiam, Georgii. *Raspad "dobrovol'tsev"; "pobezhdenye": Iz materialov belogvardeiskoi pechati* [Disintegration of the "volunteers"; "defeated": from materials of the White Guards publications]. Moscow: Gos. izd-vo, 1923. A critical account of the disintegration of the Denikin regime and the army. Published also in vol. 6 of *Arkhiv russkoi revoliutsii* (1922).

Vladimirova, Vera. *God sluzhby 'sotsialistov' kapitalistam: Ocherki po istorii kontr-revoliutsii v 1918 godu* [A year of service of 'socialists' for the capitalists: sketches on the history of the counter-revolution in 1918]. Moscow: Gos. izd-vo, 1927.

Vol'fson, B. "Izgnanie anglo-frantsuzskikh interventov iz Kryma i pervye shagi Sovetskoi vlasti" [The expulsion of the Anglo-French interventionists from Crimea and the first steps of the Soviet regime]. IM, nos. 4–5 (80–81) (1940), pp. 36–52.

———. *Konets avantiury barona Vrangelia* [The end of Baron Wrangel's adventure]. Simferopol: Krymgiz., 1940. A survey of Wrangel's domestic and foreign policies and the struggle of the partisans in the rear of Wrangel's forces.

Volin, S. [Eichenbaum, V. M.; Voline]. "Delo 'Nabata': K voprosu ob organizatsii nashikh sil" [The affair of "Nabat": to the question about the organization of our strength]. DT, nos. 7–8 (1925–26), pp. 4–6.

———. *Don i Dobrovol'cheskaia armiia: Ocherki nedavnaigo proshlago* [The Don and the Volunteer Army; sketches of the recent past]. Rostov-on-Don: B. A. Suvorin, 1919.

———. "Eshche neskol'ko slov po povodu ob organizatsii nashikh sil" [A few more words in connection with the organization of our strength]. DT, no. 9 (1926), pp. 10–11.

———. *Men'sheveki na Ukraine, 1917–1921* [Mensheviks in Ukraine]. New York, 1962. A valuable and well-documented survey about

Menshevik political activity in Ukraine, set against the background of the Ukrainian Revolution. Numerous quotations are integrated into the text.

———. "Nasha positsiia" [Our position]. *Kharkovskii Nabat*, no. 6 (1919).

———. "Nestor Makhno." DT, no. 82 (1934), pp. 4–8.

———. *Nineteen-Seventeen: The Russian Revolution Betrayed.* London: Freedom Press, 1954. A translation, mainly of the second part of the author's *La Rēvolution inconnue*, that deals with the events and failures of the February Revolution and makes indictments of the October counterrevolution.

———. "O 'partizanshchine'" [About the partisan movement]. *Nabat* (Kharkov), no. 17 (June 2, 1919), pp. 2–3.

———. *La Rēvolution inconnue, 1917–1921: Documentation in ēdite sur la rēvolution russe*. Paris: Amis de Voline, 1947. An interesting work by a Russian anarchist about the Russian revolutionary movement from the Decembrist uprising in 1825 to the end of the civil war in 1921, including the Makhno movement.

———. *The Unknown Revolution (Kronstadt, 1921, Ukraine, 1918–1921)*. London: Freedom Press, 1955. Translation of the third part of *La Rēvolution inconnue*. Most of the work deals with the Makhno movement; however, it is largely quotations from Arshinov.

Volkonsky, P. M. *The Volunteer Army of Alexeiev and Denikin: A Short Historical Sketch of the Army from its Origin to November 1/4, 1918*. London: Russian Liberation Committee, 1919.

Voloshyn, Rostyslav. "Polityka bol'shevykiv na Ukraini za Tsentral'noi Rady" [Bolshevik policy on Ukraine during the Central Rada]. *Vistnyk* (Lvov) 1, no. 3 (1937): 192–201.

Vorob'ev, A. "Ocherki iz istorii Belogo dvizheniia" [Sketches from the history of the White movement]. *Russkaia mysl'* (Paris), no. 2978 (December 20, 1973), p. 7.

Vynar, Liubomyr. "Prychynky do rann'oi diialnosty Nestora Makhna v Ukraini, 1917–18" [Materials pertaining to the early activities of Nestor Makhno in Ukraine, 1917–18]. *Rozbudova derzhavy* (Montreal), no. 2 (10) (1953), pp. 14–20. Makhno's activities and his attitudes toward the Central Rada.

———. "Zv'iazky Nestora Makhna z armieiu U. N. R., 1918–1920" [Relations of Nestor Makhno with the U. N. R. army, 1918–1920]. *Rozbudova derzhavy* (Montreal), no. 3 (11) (1953), pp. 15–18. An attempt to trace the relationship between Makhno and the Ukrainian Army.

Vyshnivs'kyi, Oleksander. "Otaman i otamaniia" [The otaman and the otamans' movement]. SV, no. 6 (1951), pp. 113–17. A valuable account by a high-ranking officer about the role of the Ukrainian partisans during the Revolution.

———. *Povstans'kyi rukh i otamaniia: Zbirnyk* [The partisan movement and the otaman movement: collection]. Detroit: Kapitula vidznaky khresta zaliznoho stril'tsia, 1973.

———. "Rozhrom Vseukrains'koho povstans'koho komitetu i samohubchyi reid" [The destruction of the All-Ukrainian Partisan Committee and the suicidal raid]. *Visti* (New York), no. 106 (1961), pp. 51–52.

Vyslots'kyi, Ivan, ed. *Het'man Skoropads'kyi v osvitlenni ochevydtsiv* [Hetman Skoropads'kyi as interpreted by contemporaries]. Toronto: Vyd-vo "Ukrains'koho robitnyka," 1940.

Vytanovych, Illia. *Agrarna polityka ukrains'kykh uriadiv, 1917–1920* [The agrarian policy of the Ukrainian governments]. Munich, 1968.

———. "Agrarna polityka ukrains'kykh uriadiv rokiv revoliutsii i vyzvol'nykh zmahan', 1917–20" [The agrarian policy of the Ukrainian governments during the Revolution and the struggle for liberation, 1917–20]. UI, nos. 3–4 (15–16) (1967), pp. 5–60.

Weinstein, H. R. "Land Hunger and Nationalism in the Ukraine, 1905–1917." *Journal of Economic History* 2 (1942): 24–35.

Wheeler-Bennett, John W. *The Forgotten Peace: Brest-Litovsk*. New York: W. Morrow & Co., 1939.

Wojna, Romuald. "Nestor Makhno: 'Anarchizm czynu'" [Nestor Makhno: "anarchism of action"]. *Z pola walki* (Warsaw) 13, no. 2 (50) (1970): 45–76. A well-documented general survey of the Makhno movement, its relations with the peasants and with the Anarchist organization "Nabat."

———. "Z trzeciego okresu wojny domowej w Rosji: Problemy polityczne i spoleczne (Grudzień 1918 r.–Grudzień 1920 r.)" [From the third period of the civil war in Russia: political and social problems (December 1918–December 1920)]. *Studia z dziejów ZSRR i Europy Srodkowej* (Wroclaw), vol. 3 (1967); vol. 6 (1971); vol. 9 (1973).

Wolfdieter, Bihl. "Beitrage zur Ukraine-Politik Osterreich-Ungarns 1918." *Jahrbücher für Geschichte Osteuropas* (Munich), n.s., 14, no. 1 (1966): 51–62.

———. "Einige Aspekte der osterreichisch-ungarischen Ruthenenpolitik, 1914–1918." *Jahrbücher für Geschichte Osteuropas* (Munich), n.s., 14, no. 3 (1966): 539–50.

———. "Die Tätigkeit des Ukrainishchen Revolutionärs Mykola Zaliznjak in 'Osterreich-Ungarn.'" *Jahrbücher für Geschichte Osteuropas* (Munich), n.s., 13, no. 2 (1965): 226–30.

Woodcock, George. *Anarchism: A History of Libertarian Ideas and Movements*. Cleveland: The World Publishing Co., 1962. A valuable general history of anarchism, including the Makhno movement.

"Z armiieiu generala Pavlenka" [With the army of General Pavlenka]. In *Kaliendar kanadiis'koho ukraintsia na zvychainyi rik 1921*, pp. 86–98. Winnipeg, 1921.

Zadoianyi, Vasyl'. *Natsiia v borot'bi za Ukrainu* [The nation in a struggle for Ukraine]. 2 vols. New York, 1968.

———. "Stanovyshche v Ukraini do i pislia prykhodu Austro-Nimets'kykh viis'k, berezen'–kviten' 1918 r." [Conditions in Ukraine before and after the arrival of the Austro-German troops, March–April 1918]. TR, no. 69 (1972), pp. 14–21. An objective account of sociopolitical and military conditions in Ukraine in spring 1918.

Zahora, Feliks. "Pomoc niemiecka Ukrainie w 1918 r.: Na tle żródel niemieckich" [The German assistance for Ukraine: on the basis of German sources]. *Problemy Europy Wschodniej* (Warsaw) 1, no. 4 (1939): 235–41.

Zahors'kyi, P. S. and P. K. Stoian. *Narysy istorii komitetiv nezamoznykh selian* [Sketches of the history of the Committee of Poor Peasants]. Kiev: Vyd-vo Akademii nauk Ukrains'koi RSR, 1960.

Zaitsov, Arsenii A. *1918 g.: Ocherki po istorii russkoi grazhdanskoi voiny* [1918: sketches on the history of the Russian Civil War]. Paris, 1934. A well-documented account by a former Russian officer.

Zalezhskii, V. *Anarkhisty v Rossii* [Anarchists in Russia]. Moscow: "Molodaia gvardiia," 1930.

Zaliesskii, P. I. "Glavnyia prichiny neudach Bielago dvizheniia na IUgie Rossii" [The main reasons for the failure of the White movement in South Russia]. BA, nos. 2–3 (1928), pp. 151–69. An account of the causes of the defeat of the anti-Bolshevik Russian movement in the south, set against the background of the past, by General Zaliesskii, the governor of Kharkiv province during the hetman period.

———. *Prichiny russkoi katastrofy* [The causes of the Russian disaster]. Berlin, 1925. A critical account by a Russian general, governor of Kharkiv province during the hetman period, of the causes of the defeat of the Russian anti-Bolshevik movement during the civil war.

Zastavenko, G. *Krakh nimetskoi interventsii na Ukraini v 1918 r.* [The defeat of the German intervention in Ukraine in 1918]. Kiev: Derzh. Vyd-vo polit. lit-ry, URSR, 1959. A one-sided account of the Austro-German policy in Ukraine in 1918.

Zavads'kyi, V. "Znadibky do istorii 1-ho Ukrains'koho polku im. het'mana Bohdana Khmel'nyts'koho" [Materials concerning the history of the 1st Ukrainian regiment in the name of Hetman Bohdan Khmel'nyts'kyi]. KD 1927, pp. 113–16. An account of the formation of a regiment out of Ukrainian soldiers serving in the Russian Army, set against a background of political conditions in Ukraine.

Zhyvotko, Arkadii. *IAk sovits'ka Moskva zvoiuvala Ukrainu* [How Soviet Muscovy conquered Ukraine]. Lvov: Nak. Soimovohu Kliubu U. S. R. P., 1933.

Zolotarev, A. *Iz istorii Tsentral'noi Ukrains'koi Rady* [From the history of the Ukrainian Central Rada]. Kharkov: Gos. izd-vo Ukrainy, 1922.

Zozulia, IAkiv. "Vseukrains'ki viis'kovi z'izdy v 1917 r." [The All-Ukrainian Military Congress in 1917]. VK, no. 4 (28) (1967), pp. 29–34.

———, comp. *Velyka Ukrains'ka revoliutsiia: Materiialy do istorii vidnovlennia ukrains'koi derzhavnosty; kalendar istorychnykh podii za liut. 1917 r.–ber. 1918 r.* [The Great Ukrainian Revolution: materials on the history of the restoration of Ukrainian statehood; calendar of historical events for February 1917–March 1918]. 2nd ed. New York, 1967. An authoritative, well-documented chronology of the Ukrainian Revolution from February 1917 to March 1918, listing correct dates, both New and Old Styles, its participants, and documentary material.

Index

INSTITUTE FOR COMPARATIVE AND FOREIGN AREA STUDIES PUBLICATIONS ON RUSSIA AND EASTERN EUROPE

1. Sugar, Peter F., and Ivo J. Lederer, eds. *Nationalism in Eastern Europe*. 1969. 487 pp., index.
2. Jackson, W. A. Douglas, ed. *Agrarian Policies and Problems in Communist and Non-Communist Countries*. 1971. 485 pp., maps, figures, tables, index.
3. Muller, Alexander V., trans. and ed. *The* Spiritual Regulation *of Peter the Great*. 1972. 150 pp., index.
4. Pinchuck, Ben-Cion. *The Octobrists in the Third Duma, 1907–1912*. 1974. 232 pp., bibliog., index.
5. Stokes, Gale. *Legitimacy through Liberalism: Vladimir Jovanović and the Transformation of Serbian Politics*. 1975. 280 pp., maps, bibliog., index.
6. Smith, Canfield F. *Vladivostok under Red and White Rule: Revolution and Counterrevolution in the Russian Far East, 1920–1922*. 1975. 304 pp., maps, illus., bibliog., index.
7. Palij, Michael. *The Anarchism of Nestor Makhno, 1918–1921: An Aspect of the Ukrainian Revolution*. 1976. 428 pp., map, illus., bibliog., index.

Institute for Comparative and Foreign Area Studies Publications on Russia and Eastern Europe was formerly Far Eastern and Russian Institute Publications on Russia and Eastern Europe.